Looking-Glass Wars

Spies on British Screens since 1960

Alan Burton
University of Leicester, UK

Series in Cinema and Culture

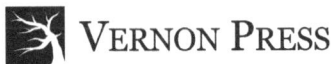
VERNON PRESS

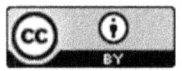
www.vernonpress.com

In the Americas:
Vernon Press
1000 N West Street,
Suite 1200, Wilmington,
Delaware 19801
United States

In the rest of the world:
Vernon Press
C/Sancti Espiritu 17,
Malaga, 29006
Spain

Series in Cinema and Culture

Library of Congress Control Number: 2018930164

ISBN: 978-1-62273-465-8

This publication has been made possible following the award of a research grant from the Austrian Science Fund (FWF): P 26295-G23

Table of Contents

Acknowledgements

Looking-Glass Wars: Spies on British Screens since 1960 was made possible through a grant provided by the FWF Der Wissenschaftsfonds (Austrian Science Fund). The 3-year research project 'British Spy Fiction: Genre, History and Popular Culture' (Project P. 26295-G23) realised a major reference work treating the literary, cinematic and televisual treatment of spies and secret agents in Britain since the late Victorian period, *The Historical Dictionary of British Spy Fiction* (2016, Winner, Outstanding Reference Source, RUSA Committee, American Library Association, 2017), and the ground-breaking essay 'Uncommon Dangers: Alfred Hitchcock and the Literary Contexts of the British Spy Thriller ' published in Wieland Schwanebeck (ed.), *Reassessing the Hitchcock Touch: Industry, Collaboration, and Filmmaking* (2017); and with further plans for a journal article in a ' special issue ' of the *Journal of British Cinema and Television* devoted to ' Spies on British Screens ' (2018). *Looking-Glass Wars: Spies on British Screens since 1960*, while building on these works, is distinctive in being a comprehensive treatment of spies on screen in Britain in the important, but restricted period since 1960, organised thematically as a monograph.

I would like to take the opportunity to thank the FWF for its generous funding of my research into British Spy Fiction.

Appropriately enough, the bulk of this study was written under the shadow of The Cedar Tree public house in Evington, Leicester, UK, the ancestral home of E. Phillips Oppenheim, the great writer of 'blood and thunder' spy thrillers of the first half of the twentieth century. There, I was able to enjoy many a convivial drink while contemplating the finer points of British spy fiction.

Introduction:
Spy Fiction, History and
Popular Literary Culture

The English fascination with spies is gloriously reflected in our litera-
ture, from Kim to A Question of Attribution, and while their Egyptian
and Israeli counterparts remain untranslated, and the Americans un-
readable, English spy novelists rule.
(Lewis Jones, *The Spectator*, 5 February 2011)

The spy is one of the most potent images of our age.
(Phillip Knightley, *Marxism Today*, November 1987: 41)

"*The spy novel came into being in England and has largely remained a British*
preserve". The judgement of the American historian and political commentator Walter Lacquer stands as a useful epithet and prompt for a study of British
spy fiction (1983: 62). The modern spy story appeared early in the twentieth
century in the same historical era that Britain established its first permanent
security and intelligence agency. Widespread concerns regarding imperial
defence, continental military rivalries, armaments races and foreign espionage acted as substantial spurs to writers seeking to warn against the country's lack of military preparedness. These often alarmist voices, which found
popular acceptance with the reading public as well as some influential military figures, put pressure on the authorities to counter the supposed threat to
national defence. The extent of the panic has been termed a 'Spy Fever', and
as a direct consequence, there hastily emerged a framework for dealing with
the alleged peril. A more robust Official Secrets Act was passed in 1911, which
provided the police with greater powers against spies, and an official counter-
intelligence section, the Secret Service Bureau, was established in 1909, and
both were in place by the time of the outbreak of European war in August
1914 (French 1978; Andrew 1985: 34-85).

It was the professed success of British intelligence and propaganda during
World War I which fed the myth of Britain's innate superiority in the art of
clandestine activity and intrigue. It was a view that would survive well into the
middle-century, until some humiliating exposures of Soviet penetration of the
British political and scientific establishments and secret services began to

cast a shadow on the reputation of almost unnatural insight and infallibility previously enjoyed by the security and intelligence organisations in Britain.[1] The first significant and lasting spy stories also appeared in the period leading up to and during the First World War, establishing the singular reputation of British writers for this particular type of thriller fiction. And it is this close inter-relationship of espionage reality and fiction, of historical developments and literary practice, which underpins any proper appreciation of spying and intelligence in 20th century British culture.

The British have never been toppled from the top of the tree as far as spy literature goes. Typical is the view of the American political scientist Thomas J. Price, who comments: "*While the spy story is one of the most popular genres of fiction, it is in England that the grand masters of the genre exist. The likes of Ambler, Buchan, Fleming, Forsyth, Greene and le Carré are found nowhere else in such numbers*" (1994: 55). The American popular historian Wesley Britton agrees, stating that, "*Without question, the best spy literature was British, including the novels of Somerset Maugham, Frederick Forsyth, Graham Greene, Len Deighton, John le Carré and Ian Fleming*" (2004: 94). Revealingly, the two American literary critics John G. Cawelti and Bruce A. Rosenberg, in their influential study *The Spy Story*, provide a list of the 25 'greatest spy stories'. It is headed by Graham Greene's *The Human Factor* (1978), British titles monopolise the first 11 places, and British writers claim a full 18 out of the 25 titles (1987: 231). The general assumption behind this ranking is maintained by the Canadian genre specialist David Skene Melvin, who has claimed, at the height of success for the spy novel, that, "*though the U.S. has produced many novels of espionage, it has not produced an outstanding one. The British have had a corner on the espionage thriller genre right from the beginning*" (1978: 15). It is a view further emphasised by the American cultural critic Michael Denning, who has claimed that, "*The spy thriller has been, for most of its history, a British genre, indeed a major cultural export*" (1987: 6).[2] American literary scholars Matthew Bruccoli and Judith Baughman are brief and to the point: "*The spy Novel is a British genre. If they didn't invent it, they perfected it*" (2004: xi). Eminent American film critic Richard Schickel has adopted a similar attitude for the screen, claiming the spy picture to be the "*greatest of English movie genres*" (Review of *The Whistle Blower*, *Time Magazine*, 7 September 1987). In a different sense, Scandinavian scholar Lars Olé Sauerberg has claimed that spy stories were more popular in Britain than anywhere else in the world (1984: 5). It is evident from this that the spy story has served an important role in British culture.

The literary tradition

In short, espionage fiction intrigues us because it is a parable for our times, a morality play which raises questions about loyalty, honour and innocence.
(Phillip Knightley, *Marxism Today*, November 1987: 41)

It has been estimated that at least 300 British spy novels were published between 1901 and 1914, and that their appearance constituted a *"cultural phenomenon"* (Moran and Johnson 2010: 1). Accordingly, Nicholas Hiley can report that between 1908 and 1918 Britain was invaded by an army of fictional spies:

They landed in their thousands on bookstalls and in bookshops. They used the short story to establish themselves in hundreds of newspapers and magazines, successfully infiltrated dozens of popular stage plays, and were even spotted in cinemas and on the pages of children's comics.
(1990: 55)

The spy story emerged in this period out of the established literary traditions of imperial adventure, sensation writing, especially the novel of terrorism, the late 19th century trend for writing about invasion scares, and, it has been intriguingly suggested, with their secret amorality and locked rooms, Victorian pornography.[3] Spy fiction absorbed many of the characteristics and archetypes of each of these forms and its development paralleled the popular genre of the detective story, with which espionage narratives considerably overlapped.[4] The formative period of the spy story, emerging as it did within the historical context of the industrialisation of warfare and military expansion, relied heavily on the theft or copying of secret plans, documents and blueprints, and therefore placed it alongside the popular form of the crime story.[5] From an early stage, distinctions emerged regarding the literary quality of the spy novel. Prolific and sensational authors like William Le Queux and E. Phillips Oppenheim bashed out stories which were incredibly popular, but usually failed to impress the critics. In contrast, some writers attracted critical notice and the espionage literature of Erskine Childers, John Buchan and W. Somerset Maugham from this early period established the reputation on which later British spy fiction rests.

A structural feature of the British spy story was its adoption and re-presentation of dominant class and national attitudes of the time. As David Stafford points out, *"It quickly became established as a convention of the genre that there was a clear distinction between spies, who were foreign, and secret agents, who were British"*. As he continues, *"The fictional British agent, in direct contrast with his foreign opponent, was and remained, despite his activi-*

ties, quintessentially a gentleman" (1981: 491). The English gentleman, forged in a culture of 'Muscular Christianity', had the natural class attributes and breeding to equip him, without hesitancy or doubt, to confront the enemies of Empire abroad and to resist the subversive foreign ideas and influences that were beginning to circulate among the domestic working-classes. In this sense, the elite heroes of early spy fiction served as guardians of the social hierarchy, and in the stories:

> *Foreign danger and internal revolt thus coalesced in the conservative mind into a peril to the very fabric of society. The gentleman secret agent promised safety not just from foreigners but from basic threats to the social order.*
> (Stafford 1988: 46)

The figure of the 'gentleman adventurer' was recognisable from an earlier imperial fiction, and indeed the two forms overlapped in Kipling's classic *Kim* (1901), which dealt with the adventures of a boy spy on the frontiers of the far flung Empire. Importantly, this novel romanticised the concept of the 'Great Game', the imperial rivalry fought out between the British and Russian Empires in central Asia, and helped translate this idea into spy fiction wherein espionage and intrigue are formulated as a 'great game' enacted by gentlemen players.

While Le Queux, Oppenheim and their imitators gave us a long line of gentlemen spies and agents embroiled in adventures mixing romance, secret diplomacy and high life, of greater substance were the two gentlemen yachting enthusiasts of Erskine Childers' *The Riddle of the Sands* (1903), the first true classic of espionage literature, and Richard Hannay, the archetype of the 'accidental agent', the colonial gentleman cast unexpectedly into danger and rising magnificently to the challenge, who first appeared in Buchan's *The Thirty-Nine Steps* (1915). The essentially amateur status of these heroes, unearthing German invasion plans in the former and thwarting an attempt by German agents to spirit secret naval plans out of the country in the latter, was a central component of the class and imperial myths rooted in the public-school ethos and the ideal of the English gentleman: an archetypal figure, 'trained for nothing, but ready for anything'; a man sure in his duty to King, Country and Empire. The activity of spying was generally believed to be something that a gentleman shouldn't do, and therefore writers had to construct a case for their heroes to act. The two gentlemen sailors of *The Riddle of the Sands* debate their right to serve England in any way necessary, and Julian Symons has revealed how the tricky moral dilemma was generally resolved: "They *are viewed as spies pursuing evil ends, while* We *are agents countering their wicked designs with good ones of our own"* (1972: 234, emphasis in the original).[6] The action of the English secret agent in these fictions is defensive; he is simply called upon to protect English prestige and sovereignty from the aggression and machinations of rival nations.

The archetype of the amateur-gentleman remained dominant in spy fiction for a generation, exemplified by Hannay in further adventures such as *Greenmantle* (1916) and *Mr Steadfast* (1919), writing which has been appreciated as bringing "*new qualities to the thriller, qualities which may be thought to have raised it to a new excellence*" (Howarth 1973: 142). The characterisation was more boorish and brutish in the guise of 'Bulldog' Drummond, a "*convincing combination of athlete and philistine*" as Patrick Howarth has described him (ibid: 153). Drummond appeared in a series of yarns penned by 'Sapper', a "*producer of blood and thunder*" in the words of Julian Symons (1972: 236), and similar figures populated the stories of novelists like Valentine Williams, Francis Beeding and Sydney Horler.[7] Such patriotic gentlemen were the ideal type to stifle the ambitions of the sinister foreigner, whether 'Swinish Hun', various shades of 'Oily Dago', or 'Fiendish Chink', and a far from concealed xenophobia and anti-Semitism was stock in trade for many of the writers whose style remained popular into the 1930s.[8] The novelist Colin Watson has admitted: "*There was something boyishly exuberant about these novels*" (1971: 113). It has been noted, though, that the emerging spy story marked a transition "*from the assertive, confident and expansionist themes of adventure fiction to the increasingly insular, even paranoid, espionage genre that stressed vigilance and protection from invasion*"; a tendency towards darker conspiratorial themes which would become more prominent among subsequent writers in the field (Woods 2008: 26).

An alternative if at the moment minor practice in espionage fiction emerged in the hands of the respected writers Joseph Conrad, G. K. Chesterton and W. Somerset Maugham. The two Conrad novels *The Secret Agent: A Simple Tale* (1907) and *Under Western Eyes* (1911), and the Chesterton story *The Man Who Was Thursday: A Nightmare* (1908), developed out of the tradition of the novel of terror which began to appear in consequence of anarchist and nihilist outrages across Europe in the late-19th century.[9] Revolutionary violence, radical nationalism and subversive organisations dedicated to assassination were the subject of such novels as George Griffith's *Angel of the Revolution. A Tale of the Coming Terror* (1893), Robert Cromie's *The Crack of Doom* (1895), Edgar Wallace's *The Four Just Men* (1905), and the American Jack London's *The Assassination Bureau* (an unfinished novel of 1910).[10] Such themes in the hands of Conrad and Chesterton became literary achievements and as such the novels have attracted critical enquiry and respect well beyond that devoted to the routine spy novel of the period, with the possible exception of John Buchan. The same is true of Somerset Maugham's *Ashenden; or* the British Secret Agent (1928), a composite novel of short tales featuring the eponymous secret agent and his wartime service in Switzerland and Russia. The despairing moral tone of these stories and their treatment of espionage as often routine, dull and ineffective, were in stark contrast to the adventurous romanticism of the mainstream. "After the easy, absurd assumptions made by Buchan, Sapper, and Oppenheim", Symons observes, "the Ashenden stories have the reality of a cold bath" (1972: 237). While offbeat if significant at their time of publication, these novels and stories would eventually have a profound influence on spy fiction in Britain. The Secret Agent and The Man Who Was Thursday would assume a renewed relevance and attract fresh critical inquiry in the 21ˢᵗ century amid the widespread concerns regarding global terror[11]; and the Ashenden stories with their moral and cool realism would serve as a crucial influence on later writers like John le Carré who wished to jettison the romantic patriotism of the former tradition to explore themes of disillusionment and betrayal.[12]

A significant new departure in the writing of spy fiction appeared in the 1930s. Following in the wake of the Great Depression and the rise of totalitarianism there was a leftward political lurch in the spy novel in the hands of Eric Ambler and Graham Greene, bringing a progressive realism and a new seriousness to the writing, which "sought to transform the genre from the verbal banality and minimal characterizations of Le Queux and Oppenheim to a more morally ambiguous world of deception and danger" (Woods 2008: 61). Ambler established himself as a genre specialist with such novels as Epitaph of a Spy (1938) and Journey into Fear (1940); while Greene developed as a more considerable literary figure and produced occasional 'entertainments' like The Confidential Agent (1939) and Ministry of Fear (1943) which ranked highly in terms of espionage literature and excellently served the author's characteristic theme of moral ambivalence. The revisionism of Ambler involved a shift in the protagonist hero to that of an ordinary guy, perhaps an engineer or photographer, who gets caught up in skulduggery and intrigue, and away from what Ambler himself called the "early cloak-and-dagger stereotypes – the black-velveted seductress, the British Secret Service numbskull hero, the omnipotent spymaster" (quoted in Stafford 1988: 43; see also Snyder 2011). Rausch and Rausch refer to Ambler's approach as the "innocent victim school of espionage": essentially unheroic, "the main characters are decent chaps who behave with intelligence while gripped by terror" (1993: 99). The literary scholar Eric Homberger notes the "change in paradigm" with regard the spy thriller following the emergence of Ambler and Greene, in consequence of which the "politics of Buchan and 'Sapper' have been turned on their head: the baddies now are right-wingers, enemies of democracy" (1991: 88)[13]; and Woods writes of Ambler who took the "spy story by its patrician neck, plucked the monocle from its eye, and pulled it down into the world of *the common man, far away from the world of diplomatic aristocrats"* (2008: 61). Both authors continued to write influential spy fiction into the 1970s and have been appreciated as heirs to the more 'naturalistic' approach pioneered by Somerset Maugham in the *Ashenden* stories, and in turn served as influences on that generation of espionage novelists which came to prominence in the 1960s, writers like le Carré and Len Deighton who explored a darker morality and further intensified the sense of 'realism' in the spy story.

More conventional spy fiction in the 1930s was penned by writers such as Bernard Newman (who also published under the name of Don Betteridge), a thriller writer who entered the espionage field in 1935 with *Spy*, and followed with *German Spy* (1936) and *Death under Gibraltar* (1938). Newman and his contemporaries barely had to shift ground following the outbreak of war in 1939, with that author contributing *Secret Weapon* and *Death to the Fifth Column* (both 1941) and *Second Front – First Spy* (1944). A thriller writer like Dennis Wheatley sent his established series character the gentleman adventurer Gregory Sallust on missions to continental Europe during the war in *Faked Passports* (1940) and *'V' for Vengeance* (1942); and new genre specialists emerged such as Helen MacInnes who concocted dangerous missions behind enemy lines in *Above Suspicion* (1941) and *Assignment in Brittany* (1942), and Manning Coles who did something comparable in *Drink to Yesterday* (1940) and *They Tell No Tales* (1942). Some writers established in other fields found the spy novel convenient for expressing their emergent social views in wartime, as was the case with J. B. Priestley and his *Black-Out in Gretley* (1942), or for re-examining the recent experience of the Second World War, as in Elizabeth Bowen's *The Heat of the Day* (1948).

Ambler and Greene remained important writers of espionage fiction in the 1950s, with novels such as *Judgement on Deltchev* (1951) and *Our Man in Havana* (1958). They were joined by new writers who had much material in the experience of the recent World War with its secret missions, double agents and resistance movements (Gilbert Hackforth-Jones, Hammond Innes, Alistair MacLean), and in the development of the Cold War which intensified the sense of ideological struggle and commitment in the realm of espionage (William Haggard, Maurice Edelman, Sarah Gainham). The decade belonged, though, to Ian Fleming and his creation of the secret agent James Bond, described by Maurice Richardson as the "*most compulsive character in popular fiction since the war*" (1964: 18). The series character first appeared in *Casino Royale* (1953) and then regularly until *The Man with the Golden Gun*, which was published posthumously in 1965.[14] Fleming's secret agent stories, often criticised for their poor writing and their perverse violence and sexuality,[15] were a potent mix of traditional elements of the adventure-romance blended with characteristics of post-war modernity; a fertilisation of John Buchan with *Playboy*. Michael Denning has referred to their "*highly successful fusion of traditional themes of Empire and England with the images and spectacles of the consumer society*" (1987: 5-6), and Toby Miller has similarly appreciated the series as embodying the "*end of empire and the start of commercial globalization*" (2003: 129). Bond himself was something of a throwback to the 'Bulldog' Drummond type of un-reconstructured masculinity and class snobbery, an emphatically heroic stature bound to a nationalistic self-assurance, and was often pitted against the type of master criminal bent on world domination who would not have been out of place in a Sax Rohmer novel of two generations earlier.[16] In these terms, the Bond stories were a return to what Colin Watson has labelled the "*thriller of unreason*", wherein "*credible motives were entirely lacking*", the style prevalent in the period around the First World War (1971: 116).

At the same time, "*Bond seemed to have been most cunningly and industriously synthesised to combine all the qualities essential for a new-style, up-to-the-minute, hyper-sexed, ready-made daydream secret-service hero*" (Richardson 1964: 18). With his hand-made cigarettes and taste for vintage wines, Bond was in the vanguard of a conspicuous consumption being made possible by an upsurge in affluence in the 1950s; and according to one analysis, the novels served as "guidebooks *to modern consumerism*" (Sandbrook 2006: 620, emphasis in original). Secret agent 007 enjoyed a liberated *Playboy*-style sexuality without commitment, which was largely fresh to the genre and would prove immensely influential[17]; while the series observed a fetishistic regard to advanced technology with its ingenious devices and gadgets put to the aid of the agent. The approach was also distinct in that 007 was a professional, he was an organisation man within the limits that the rugged individualism demanded by the role allowed. He was loyal to his chief M and to the wider Service, which at this stage hardly suffered from the self-doubts and betrayals which would be a feature of a later 'cynical' school of espionage writing.[18] The oxymoronic quality of the Fleming stories as both nostalgic and hip has been captured by Wesley Wark, who has argued that, "*Bond and his readers escaped from history back into the adventures of an earlier day and forward into a titillating world of consumerism, sexual liberation (of sorts), and global travel*" (1990: 6).

While the Fleming novels sold only moderately before appearing as paperbacks in the late 1950s, their translation to the screen, beginning with *Dr No* in 1962, resulted in a cultural phenomenon and a considerable upsurge in sales of the books. The writing of espionage fiction in Britain, and elsewhere, underwent considerable change in the face of James Bond and led to even greater popularity of the spy novel; although admirers of Fleming, on his death in 1964, thought that, "*The prospect of a Bondless future is bleak*" (Richardson 1964: 18). Of course, many imitators of varying quality entered the market with their omni-competent espionage heroes, as in the case of James Leasor and his agent Dr Jason Love who first appeared in *Passport to Oblivion* (1964), James Mayo and his agent Charles Hood who first appeared in *Hammerhead* (1964),[19] and of James Munro and his agent James Craig who made his début in *The Man Who Sold Death* (1964).[20] Few critics could take James Bond seriously, and this approach was reflected in the writing of some comic spy stories which parodied the style and characters of the Fleming originals, evident in Peter O'Donnell's re-gendering of the super agent in *Modesty Blaise* (1965), John Gardner's anti-heroic Boysie Oakes novels which commenced with *The Liquidator* in 1964, and in the hip reformulations of Adam Diment's *The Dolly Dolly Spy* (1967) and *The Bang Bang Birds* (1968). The most significant response though to Fleming and his secret agent was in the reaction within espionage literature which has been termed 'anti-Bond'. This was a conscious effort to dispense with the fantasy elements, exotic locales and conservative postures of novels such as *Moonraker* (1955) and *Thunderball* (1961), and to introduce a more despairing and critical tone to the stories. Writing in 1969 in response to the emergence of two schools, film critic Raymond Durgnat proposed the bifurcation of the spy cycle into that of "*cool*" and that of "*alienated*" (5).[21] The Fleming originals have been understood as narratives of reassurance in a context of retreat from empire and national decline, while the anti-Bond dynamic was a more realistic response to Britain's imperial and economic predicament in the post-Suez period, as well as a more complex moral treatment of the business of espionage in the face of a series of humiliating spy scandals which cast the social and political elite in a damaging light. As such they represent a critique of the certainties of the Fleming approach, being radical and critical of an authority which is presented now as far from benevolent or progressive, a world of fumbling uncertainty, fluid allegiances and only vague distinctions between the combatants straddling the ideological divide.

In 1991, a piece in the *Mail on Sunday* asked its readers, "*How do you like your spies? Fact or fiction?*" By that time, the bifurcation of the spy story was seen to have delivered up two choices. Did readers prefer (a): "*dreary old pen-pushing civil servants hanging about for days on end, watching, waiting, and dourly playing it by the book on the off-chance that something will come of it?*" Or did they prefer (b): "*exotic wild-eyed loonies with hilarious accents, preposterous aliases, invisible ink, transmitters under the floorboards, and a larderful of false-bottomed pickle jars containing secret codes?*" (24 November).

Choice (a), the new 'realistic school' of espionage writing, had emerged in the hands of Len Deighton and John le Carré and their novels *The Ipcress File* (1962) and *The Spy Who Came in from the Cold* (1963). Such writers published in the shadow of the Suez debacle and the exposure of the Cambridge Spies, and the theme of decline and betrayal occupied a central place in their fiction. The novels had a considerable commercial and critical impact and their tales of treachery, manipulation and perfidy owed something to the anti-romanticism of Somerset Maugham's *Ashenden* stories of the late 1920s with their despondent and bleak atmosphere, as well as to the class antagonism of the literary Angry Young Men of the late 1950s. Indeed, the historian Dominic Sandbrook has referred to *The Ipcress File* as the "Lucky Jim *of spy fiction: the story of a bright, disrespectful, impecunious provincial upstart who dislikes his elegant, well-bred superiors and keenly feels his social exclusion*" (2006: 625). In the face of this writing, the gentleman adventurer, outside of 'fantasy' narratives, could only be appreciated as an anachronism and a fitting figure for critique or satire. The emphasis in the new stories has been seen, instead, as focusing on "*adventures of bureaucratic work in the secret states of 'post-industrial' capitalism*" (Denning 1987: 6), and the secret agent consolidated as "*spy as organizational man*" (Price 1996: 88). Accordingly, in a process in tune with the democratising mood of the 1960s, the traditional archetype began to be replaced, first by the post-World War II generation of grammar school-educated boys, as with the nameless spy in the Deighton series of novels, and later by protagonists with genuinely working-class backgrounds, such as James Mitchell's David Callan and Brian Freemantle's Charlie Muffin, characters often in conflict with their higher-class superiors and colleagues.[22] The Deighton stories *Funeral in Berlin* (1964) and *Billion Dollar Brain* (1966), and the le Carré stories *The Looking-Glass War* (1965) and *A Small Town in Germany* (1968) remained at the forefront of this progressive style of espionage literature in the decade, works which were felt to "*mirror the soul of the state*" in the decades of the 1950s and 1960s (Wark 1990: 7). The literate le Carré, in particular, was seen to offer a substantial critique of British society, stating in a 1976 interview that, the "*figure of the spy does seem to me to be almost infinitely capable of exploitation for purposes of articulating all sorts of submerged things in our society*" (quoted in Sauerberg 1984: 13). Other important new writing included *The Berlin Memorandum*, in which Adam Hall introduced his popular series agent Quiller, and *The Naked Runner* (both 1965) by Francis Clifford, which developed the trend for more complex, reflective and sophisticated spy stories. Occasionally, a major writer would explore the possibilities of the spy genre, as did Anthony Burgess in his brilliant and entertaining *Tremor of Intent* in 1966, and such contributions added credibility to the notion of the 'literary spy thriller'.[23]

Writing in 1972, the novelist and critic Julian Symons felt that the spy story was likely to decline as a consequence of apparent exhaustion, of both writers and readers, following the efforts of Fleming, Deighton, le Carré and many others (246). In fact, British spy fiction proved resilient and many new spy authors joined the fray. Notable newcomers were Ted Allbeury and Anthony Price, and these were complemented by an upsurge in thrillers more generally, influenced by the extraordinary success of writers like Alistair MacLean and Frederick Forsyth, especially the latter's *The Day of the Jackal* (1971), the first in a new-style of 'documentary thriller', which, along with the writing of Ken Follett in the 1970s, have posed *"elaborate secret histories"* (Denning 1987: 6). There have been further claims for the death or decline of the spy novel. Rausch and Rausch, writing in the late 1970s, echoed Symons and complained of an *"overworked genre"* and the expectation of a *"falling off in the number and quality of espionage novels in the years immediately ahead"* (1993: 102). However, the predictions have proved false and the spy novel has resolutely refused to disappear. Perhaps, as one journal has claimed, *"The spy novel is an essential literary genre of our present imagination"* and as such is unlikely to go away (*Spectator*, 27 December 2003).

The period of *Perestroika* and *Glasnost* in the 1980s, and shortly thereafter the end of the Cold War in 1989-91, seemed to remove a fundamental rationale of the modern spy story, and in a wider sense the need for expensive large-scale intelligence organisations, which in America and Britain had attracted damning criticism in the period since the 1970s. However, the threat of terrorism that emerged in a more extensive form following the attack on New York and Washington in 2001 has provided the context for a new spate of Anglo-American thrillers in which security services counter global terrorist organisations. There has also been a notable nostalgia in the writing of contemporary spy fiction, a rejection of the *"chaotic present"* as one reviewer has put it, with many authors exploring the recent history of World War II and the Cold War in their espionage stories (Brooke 2004: 19). In Britain, leading writers of this school are Charles Cumming (*Trinity Six*, 2011), David Downing (*Silesian Station*, 2008) and John Lawton (*Blackout*, 1995); while the foremost American practitioner is Alan Furst (*The Polish Officer*, 1995), who has spent much time in Europe and writes about the intrigues leading up to the Second World War and during the early wartime period. The lasting relevance of spy fiction is also evidenced in the fact that front rank authors continue to turn their hand to espionage literature, often with a historical theme, as with William Boyd and *Restless* (2006) and *Waiting for Sunrise* (2012), Sebastian Faulks and *Charlotte Gray* (1999) John Banville and *The Untouchable* (1997) and Ian McEwan with *The Innocent* (1990) and *Sweet Tooth* (2012).

The spy story and its sister genres of conspiracy and terrorist thrillers remain relevant in the contemporary period. It is instructive to appreciate the shift in focus of the most established and acclaimed of all living espionage novelists, John le Carré, who responded to *Glasnost* in *The Russia House* (1989), and has since begun to examine the worlds of the secret arms trade in

The Night Manager (1993), modern corporate corruption and conspiracy in *The Constant Gardener* (2000) and the new terrorism in *A Most Wanted Man* (2008).[24] There is now a considerable overlap in the fields of the modern thriller, in which espionage constitutes a greater or lesser element, and in which the complex moral issues and political intangibles of the contemporary world can be explored.[25]

Spy history, espionage and popular culture

The one thing to rival the British love of a bit of weather is a decent bit of spying.
(Alan Rusbridger, *Observer*, 18 January 1987)

For most of the twentieth century, representations of intelligence in popular culture were far and away the most influential factors shaping public attitudes and perceptions.
(Len Scott and Peter Jackson 2004: 19)

Perhaps as a result of the many charges against MI5 and the impact of spy cases and spy novels, many people seem prepared to believe any-thing about the secret services.
(Pincher 1991: 298)

There has been an uncommon amount of concern, considering it is a genre of popular literature, regarding the relationship of spy stories with historical reality. While some literary scholars are at pains to deny the mimetic qualities of espionage fiction (Snyder 2011), this view rather ignores the widespread cultural assumption that spy fiction observes a discernible association with spy reality. As a historian of British Intelligence and secrecy has observed, "*Rightly or wrongly, spy fiction has to a large extent shaped public perceptions of intelligence*"; and accordingly popular culture has established the domi-nant frame of reference regarding the secret organisations and their opera-tions (Moran 2011a: 48; Willmetts and Moran 2013: 52). It is a viewpoint ech-oed by a journalist who, appreciative that actual espionage is disconnected from common experience and confused by myth, has commented: "*Much of what the public knows about the UK's Secret Service, or MI6, comes from the world of fiction – whether Ian Fleming's James Bond or John le Carré's George Smiley*".[26] This is a significant point in a society in which details and infor-mation about the security and intelligence services have been actively sup-pressed, a situation more widely appreciated since the notorious '*Spycatcher* Affair' of the mid-1980s when the authorities feared that the floodgates would be opened and former officers would "*blow the gaff on all the national secrets*" (Rimington 2002: 188).[27] As such, rumours abound, and, appropriately some might feel given the context, disinformation freely circulates. In such an uncertain environment, famously described as a *"wilderness of mirrors"* by the legendary American spy chief James Jesus Angleton, the framework for public knowledge and awareness regarding the secret services and clandestine activities will be shaped by the discourses of journalism (never to be entirely trusted), the published memoir (which has to be officially sanctioned), and the popular fictions of espionage, which, as far as a wary public might be concerned, carry an equal validity in a shadowy world of legal gagging, half-truths, lies and deceptions.[28]

Cultural critic Toby Miller has written of *"slippage"* between reality and fantasy, between history and fiction, in the long and ongoing relationship of espionage and society (2003: 38). Chapman Pincher, perhaps uniquely qualified as a journalist specialising in security, a writer on espionage and a spy novelist, has concluded: *"Since anything is possible, it is easy for people to delude themselves. Conditioned by spy fiction, as well as by fact, they are prepared to believe anything about the intelligence services"* (1991: 9). After all, as Robin Winks reminds us: *"what is most important in the study of history is what people believe to be true"*; and it is his contention that spy fiction is capable of being real in *"tone and fact and question and approach"* (1993: 223, 231).[29] In such a context, espionage fiction can be argued to matter.

Historians, especially in dealing with the period of the early 20th century, have acknowledged the impact of spy stories on historical developments. Christopher Andrew emphasises the *"literary war"* promulgated by William Le Queux and Erskine Childers and the impact of *"spy mania"* on policymakers (1985: 36, 43, 58). He recounts how pioneer intelligence officers, sadly lacking in knowledge and experience, consulted some of the more successful spy novels for insights and guidance (51); how patriotic young gentlemen officers, inspired by the example of Carruthers and Davies in *The Riddle of the Sands*, set off on spying expeditions to the Continent, often getting themselves into hot water (80-81; see also Seed 1992: 70-73 and Moran and Johnson 2010: 7-12); and how even some senior members of the emerging secret services delighted in such cloak and dagger affectations of espionage as elaborate disguises and enjoyed the whole activity as *"capital sport"*, an image which originated in the more fanciful of the tales perpetrated by the spy novelists (76). The interplay between reality and fantasy in espionage stories has continued to interest historians and intelligence specialists. The political scientist Adam Svendsen defends spy fiction as a legitimate source, capable of providing valuable insights into intelligence topics. He reminds us that, as with espionage literature, there is a *"close ... blending of fact, fiction and fantasy in the real world of intelligence"*, that *"serious"* spy fiction observes a *"close relationship"* to *"actual-reality"*, thus creating for itself a sense of plausibility and authority (2009: 15). This is surely a more reasoned engagement with the complex issues involved than the blanket rejection of spy fiction by some intelligence 'insiders' who baulk at the confusion some writers show regarding actual intelligence organisations, the fanciful technical gadgets at the disposal of some agents, and the impossible claims made for modern technologies like spy satellites.[30]

There is plenty of anecdotal evidence to suggest a meaningful connection between the imaginary and the real in the realm of espionage. Various spy novelists, including Ian Fleming, Len Deighton and John le Carré, have been attributed with the accolade of being eagerly consulted and read by secret service organisations. The anthologist Hugh Greene, brother of the celebrated novelist Graham Greene, has recounted his personal experience of visiting a favourite bookshop to scout for espionage titles, only to discover that everything in the field had been acquired by a *"foreign government"* (2007: 235). The romanticism bestowed on spying in some of the literature led to individuals seeking employment in the secret world. Tod Hoffman has volunteered that his decision to become an intelligence officer with the Canadian Secret Service in the late 1980s, *"was very much a result of being exposed to spies in pop culture"* (2001: xii). This was also the case with Daphne Park, who joined MI6 in the 1940s and rose to the position of a controller. She has gone on record as saying: *"I suppose it did start with reading Kim, reading John Buchan and reading Sapper and Bulldog Drummond; and I think from a quite early age I did want to go into intelligence. I don't know what kind or how it would be. But I always wanted it"*.[31] Former chief of MI6 Sir Colin McColl has stated how the positive impression that spy fiction has bestowed on the British, at least the impression that British Intelligence counts, has been beneficial in establishing contacts and recruiting agents overseas, as such sources from their reading, *"felt we knew more than anybody else"*.[32] Even the legendary East German spy boss Markus Wolf was capable of confusing fact with fiction, such as when he cast a complimentary eye on the British secret services and claimed: *"Maybe the English were the best, these James Bonds, because they were the ones I knew least about"* (quoted in Kamm 1996: 72).

A crucial element in the sense that British spy fiction can be taken seriously, that it has some meaningful claim to verisimilitude, is that a considerable proportion of the writers of the stories had or claimed some actual experience of intelligence work (Masters 1987). Unfailingly stated in dust jacket blurbs and in author biographies, this seemingly afforded the writers some legitimacy and counted for a public which had a suspicion of other providers of information and perspective on the secret world. As novelist John le Carré has noted of his own experience, *"It has always been my concern not to be authentic but to be credible, to use the deep background I have from the years I spent*

*in intelligence work to present premises that were useful to my stories and that
I knew were rooted in experience"* (quoted in Sanoff 1989: 106). The penetration of these authors into the structures of national security and intelligence
varied greatly. Men like Somerset Maugham, Graham Greene, Ian Fleming,
John le Carré and Alan Judd had actual experience of operations within the
Secret Intelligence Service (SIS) or Naval Intelligence, while others such as
John Buchan fulfilled more general intelligence and propaganda roles during
wartime.[33] Some, like William Le Queux, Erskine Childers and Dennis Wheatley, existed on the fringes of military and foreign office activity, but by dint of
social class and political connections were privilege to insights unavailable to
the general population. Then there are the special cases of Maxwell Knight,
Stella Rimington and Douglas Hurd. Knight and Rimington were both senior
figures in MI5, the former the author of two thrillers, *Crime Cargo* (1934) and
Gunmen's Holiday (1935), which Eric Homberger has declared as *"certainly of
interest to students of popular culture, and of the mentality of the British intelligence community"* (1988: 312), and the latter a popular current practitioner
having retired as Director-General of the Security Service. Hurd was a senior
Conservative politician who spent time at the United Nations, and later
served as both Home Secretary and as Secretary of State for Foreign Affairs,
and who published a series of political thrillers from the early 1970s onwards.
The myth of the secret agent-author was such that it was invoked even when
the writer had only a distant claim on secret service experience, as in the case
of Bryan Forbes whose lowly experience in Field Security early in World War
Two could hardly have had much bearing on his contemporary espionage
novels written four decades later.[34]

   While lacking direct involvement in clandestine service, another substantial
group of spy authors could claim special insight through experience in journalism, very often in the political columns which had given them access to
the corridors of power. To this group belong Lionel Davidson, Francis Clifford,
Gavin Lyle, Hugh McLeave, Anthony Price and Brian Freemantle. An exceptional case is that of Chapman Pincher, author of several spy novels in the
1970s, who achieved some prominence at the *Daily Express* as a correspondent specialising in defence and intelligence matters, as a journalistic mole-
hunter, and later as author of several non-fiction accounts of the secret world
of security and espionage such as *Their Trade is Treachery* (1981), *Traitors: The
Labyrinths of Treason* (1987) and *A Web of Deception: The Spycatcher Affair*
(1987). Such a display of expertise is likely to count when the reading public
engage with the writer's fictions of espionage; and the fact that spy authors
like Bernard Newman (the atom spies), Brian Freemantle (the KGB and the
CIA), Jeremy Duns (the Soviet double-agent Oleg Penkovsky) and Alan Judd
(Mansfield Cumming, first chief of the SIS) have turned their hand to factual

accounts of spy scandals, intelligence organisations and legendary spymasters further lends authenticity to their imaginative writing.

Spy stories deal with ostensible historical reality, their plots, themes and
conspiratorial frameworks being shaped by some discernible geopolitical
context. The historian Brett F. Woods thus treats them as "*hybrid texts*"; ones
that, "*blend fictional premise with certain non-fiction elements*" and which
ultimately "*assume complete historical authority*" (2008: 2). The established
expression for this process and outcome is 'faction', and it has been common
for critics and scholars to relate this term to spy fiction. Nigel West has argued, contrary to what is commonly assumed, that there has been much
written about the British intelligence community from within, and he includes classic spy fiction alongside such factual forms as memoirs (2004: 122).
Some writers of spy fiction have structured their novels in ways suggestive of
reality, using literary devices normally associated with non-fiction to create
what the historian Wesley Wark has called, the "*artifice of apparent realism*"
(1990: 1). Important in this respect have been *The Riddle of the Sands*, in
which Erskine Childers partly structures the narrative through the use of a
diary and appends nautical maps which position the reader in relation to a
discernible actuality, and the novels of Len Deighton, with their celebrated
'scholarly apparatus', typically a series of appendices which ostensibly provide detailed insight into various aspects of the clandestine world of the secret agent. Wark also invokes the notion of 'faction' in his discussion of espionage literature, claiming spy stories as a "*variety of popular history in disguise*" (3).

A fundamental critical concern regarding spy fiction has been the apparent
contrast between the 'romantic' and the 'realistic' schools, and the genre in its
development has oscillated between the two poles. In the beginning, there
was Le Queux to place alongside Childers; the heroic school of the First World
War period eventually gave way to the verisimilitude and commitment of
Ambler and Greene; and swung back again towards fantasy fulfilment and the
simpler formula under the influence of Ian Fleming and his popular creation
James Bond. There was a palpable relief when the spy story re-assumed a
literary direction in the hands of John le Carré and attention focused on the
new realism of the spy story. This cycle of adjustment, reaction and rejection
has characterised the writing and consumption of espionage fiction in Britain
and continues to shape the production and appreciation of thrillers of terrorism and the meticulously researched historical spy novel of the present times.
The history of the spy genre thus reveals a "*typology of alternating modes*", as
Wesley Wark puts it, in which the "*thrill of the adventurous romance vies for
command with the politically charged narrative of societal danger*", and a

sense of realism, through narrative construction, authorial biography and reader strategies, occupies a crucial critical importance (7).

The spy story in Britain is strongly implicated in ideas about nation, class and gender. Literary historian Sam Goodman has recently claimed "*spy fiction's central place within the British cultural imaginary*", noting that the "*figure of the spy has always been bound up with nationhood and what it means to be British*", and commenting on how an iconic character such as the super-agent James Bond can serve as a "*key component*" of national cultural identity (2016: 1). The figure of the spy was swiftly extended to the screen, initially in the cinema, and later on television. There, the secret agent proved a popular and enduring character, winning even more supporters to the fictions of espionage.

Espionage on film and television before 1960

Outside of wartime, the spy drama on film and television in Britain was not prolific before 1960, but was statistically significant. The majority of these productions were routine thrillers and only occasionally was a major filmmaker attracted to the material. The early period of cinema threw up a few spy pictures dealing with intrigue keyed to the actual conflicts of the day; such as the very first example, Robert Paul's *Shooting a Boer Spy* of 1899, and his subsequent *Execution as Spies of Two Japanese Officers* (1904, Russo-Japanese War). Overall, the silent period produced little that was substantial, although there was a predictable vogue for invasion, spy and terrorist dramas in the period leading up to and including the early stages of the First World War. This readily chimed with 'Spy Menace' alarms which were being heralded in the popular press. Pre-war examples included the London Film Company's *The Peril of the Fleet* and Hepworth's *The Spy* both released in July 1909, London's *England's Menace* released to great success in June 1914, and British and Colonial's *The Great Anarchist Mystery* released in January 1912 (Gifford 1966: 6-7). A cycle of spy dramas was unleashed on the opening of hostilities and film historian Rachel Low has epitomised the flavour and characterisations of these pictures. "*German spies were represented as cads, with an habitual tendency to assault English girls*". Sly but fortunately extremely clumsy, "*they were kept busy tracking down numerous secret inventions and deadly explosives upon which the outcome of the war depended*". Meanwhile, "*their honourable British Secret Service antagonists toiled to outwit them, thereby saving such items of national importance as troop trains, London's water supply and even the Houses of Parliament*" (1950: 178).

The quickly-produced films had such titles as *The German Spy Peril, Guarding Britain's Secrets, Britain's Secret Treaty* and *The Kaiser's Spies* (all 1914). One particularly interesting example was *The Raid of 1915* (1914), which derived from William Le Queux's famous novel *The Invasion of 1910* published in 1906 and demonstrated the connection between the popular literature of the period and the production of spy dramas in the cinema. The trade paper *Bioscope* dismissed such pictures as the "*usual orgy of ridiculous and impossible sensationalism*" (quoted in Low 1950: 179), and the cycle clearly drew inspiration from the many spy yarns which featured in the newspapers and magazines at the time. Following the first flush of panic and patriotism, the spy film settled down to calmer and more considered drama, as in the case of Cecil Hepworth's *The Man Who Stayed at Home* (1915), an adaptation from the stage, and Broadwest's *A Munition Girl's Romance* (1916), in which espionage only played a part in a broader drama.

British producers in the 1920s turned regularly to writers of popular thrillers such as E. Phillips Oppenheim, Edgar Wallace, 'Sapper' and Sax Rohmer for stories and characters to film, and some of these touched on the themes of international intrigue and threats to national security. During 1923-4, the Stoll Company released a series of short dramas featuring Rohmer's master criminal Dr Fu-Manchu, starring H. Agar Lyons and Fred Paul as Nayland Smith the government agent who opposes the evil genius. Two films were released featuring the popular character of 'Bulldog' Drummond, an eponymously-titled Anglo-Dutch co-production of 1922 featuring Carlyle Blackwell as the hero, and the more substantial *Bulldog Drummond's Third Round* (1925) starring Jack Buchanan. The first film version of Edgar Wallace's hugely popular *The Four Just Men* appeared in 1921, produced at Stoll, and later in the decade a new company was founded, British Lion, which held the rights to Wallace's works and produced such mystery thrillers as *The Ringer* and *The Man Who Changed his Name* (both 1928), and *The Clue of the New Pin* (1929).[35] Surprisingly, John Buchan was little filmed in the period, although there was a modest version of *Huntingtower* produced at Welsh-Pearson in 1928. An altogether more serious production was Herbert Wilcox's *Dawn*, filmed towards the end of the silent period in 1928, the true story of Nurse Edith Cavell who was shot by the Germans in Belgium in 1915 for spying. The film was graced by a much-admired performance from Sybil Thorndike and encountered serious censorship difficulties, there being some resentment that such a noble theme should be turned to profit, as well as anxiety that the picture might upset the Germans at a time when rapprochement was the political requirement of the day (Robertson 1984). Gainsborough's *The Crooked Billet* (1929) had the distinction of being the last silent and the first sound British spy film, it being released in both versions. A small group of films were produced in response to the Bolshevik assumption of power in Russia in 1917 and the declaration of worldwide communist revolution. *The Flight Commander* (1928) was a silent picture which dealt with the Soviet threat to British interests in China, while the sound productions *Forbidden*

Territory (1934), from the novel by Dennis Wheatley, and *Knight Without Armour* (1937), from the novel by James Hilton, were conservative responses to the international situation and featured British heroes dealing with injustice deep inside Russia.

The return of European tensions in the 1930s once again provided a rationale for out and out espionage dramas and the appearance of several memorable pictures, capitalising, as Marcia Landy has expressed it, on an "*atmosphere of uncertainty, paranoia, and physical and verbal belligerence*" (1991:124).[36] Influential on the cycle of spy thrillers was *Rome Express* (1932), a crime picture produced at Gaumont-British, which starred the great German actor Conrad Veidt and featured a thrilling Continental train-bound drama that would be imitated by such later pictures as *Night Train to Munich* (1940) and *Sleeping Car to Trieste* (1948). Veidt found regular employment in spy pictures in the British cinema of the decade, playing honourable First World War German agents who are outwitted by able British counterparts in *Dark Victory* (1937) and *The Spy in Black* (1939), and of necessity switching to Danish nationality in the wartime *Contraband* (1940) so that he can be opposed to Nazi machinations. Another significant production set during the Great War was Victor Saville's *I Was a Spy* (1933), based on the true exploits of Marthe Cnockaert, a Belgian who spied for the British before her arrest and imprisonment by the Germans.[37] Historical settings were occasionally provided for spy dramas as in the classic *The Scarlet Pimpernel* (1934) and *The Spy of Napoleon* (1935). While espionage never became a regular feature of the costume film, the former, revisited in 1937 and 1950, was updated as a successful wartime propaganda picture in *Pimpernel Smith* (1941), in which the 'Pimpernel' worked secretly in Germany to save victims of Nazi oppression. The character was an important embodiment of the consummate English gentleman, witty, tough and resourceful, able and prepared to confront European tyranny and defend decency and civilisation, whether it is French revolutionaries or National Socialist gangsters (Richards 1986b).

By far the most important contribution to the spy film in the cinema came from Alfred Hitchcock. His famous series of six thrillers produced at Gaumont-British in the mid-late 1930s established the gold standard for this type of sophisticated action film and attracted favourable critical attention which had previously ignored the genre. As Alan Booth has observed regarding Hitchcock:

> *No film director has ever produced more first-quality spy films, many of which have become classics; none has consistently filmed better quality screenplays or introduced more plot devices to draw the viewer into his films and to heighten and sustain audience tension.* (1991: 140)

Of the six thrillers, five were espionage dramas and each of these was derived from a well-known literary source. *The Man Who Knew Too Much* (1934) was loosely drawn from 'Sapper', *The 39 Steps* (1935) from the John Buchan novel, *Secret Agent* (1936) from Maugham's *Ashenden* stories, *Sabotage* (1936) was based on the Conrad novel *The Secret Agent*, and *The Lady Vanishes* (1938) was from the popular mystery story *The Wheel Spins* by Ethel Lina White. There would remain a close relationship between spy screen and spy literature in the British experience, especially in regard of the leading film and television productions, which, with few exceptions, have been adaptations of the more commercially promising writing or the most critically acclaimed novels. This is not to say that Hitchcock did not achieve something entirely cinematic with his pictures, which in their turn have been greatly influential on the spy drama in Britain and elsewhere, as, indeed, have his later espionage thrillers made in Hollywood, pictures such as *Foreign Correspondent* (US, 1940), *Notorious* (US, 1946) and *North by Northwest* (US, 1959), but to make the necessary acknowledgement that the filmmaker absorbed and re-articulated qualities established in popular literature and consciously observed a tradition while translating well-known stories to the screen. As the film historian Tom Ryall has pointed out, some of the most successful elements that we associate with the Hitchcock thriller were already stock in trade for John Buchan writing a generation earlier:

> *The general quality of adventure, the themes of fear and guilt, the narrative patterns of flight and pursuit, the climatic combat, the theme of the 'thin protection of civilisation' to quote Buchan's own words from his novel The Power House, the secret assassination gang working against established governments ...* (1986: 126)

Hitchcock's brilliance was to give these fundamentals visual form and imbue them with his own characteristic concerns with gender and sexuality. *The Man Who Knew Too Much, The 39 Steps* and *The Lady Vanishes* were generally the most successful, offering as they did quick-paced narratives featuring heroes by accident, while *The Secret Agent* and *Sabotage* were centred on a different literary tradition, dealing with the world of professional agents, and the films reflect some of the moral ambiguity and bleakness of the originals. Hitchcock's transformation of the Buchan spy thriller should also be understood in relation to the revisionism of the espionage novel in the 1930s in the hands of Eric Ambler and Graham Greene, a set of influences and counter-influences which have not been sufficiently acknowledged in the literature (Burton 2017).

As British society geared up for war in 1938-9, a spate of spy films was released into cinemas reflecting the contemporary anxiety regarding national security. Titles included *The Last Barricade* and *Anything to Declare?* (both 1938), and *Q Planes, Secret Journey, Spies of the Air* and *An Englishman's Home* (all 1939). *Strange Boarders* (1938), in which intelligence man Tommy Blythe interrupts his honeymoon to investigate the discovery of vital Air Ministry blueprints on a woman killed in a road accident, was taken from a novel by the veteran writer of spy fiction E. Phillips Oppenheim. The wartime period inevitably saw the production of a variety of pictures which dealt with war-time missions, the activities of resistance groups, counter-espionage measures and other aspects of the secret war. Representative examples would be *Cottage to Let* (1941), *The Day Will Dawn* (1942), *Squadron Leader X* (1942), *The Yellow Canary* (1943), *Hotel Reserve* (1944) and *The Man from Morocco* (1945).[38] The films dealing with the secret war demonstrated national vigi-lance, ingenuity and preparedness at a time of acute anxiety regarding the safety of the realm. They therefore served as a welcome reassurance for audi-ences and began to decline in number in the later period of the war when victory was becoming more certain.[39] An exceptional production was Ealing Studio's *The Next of Kin* (1942), which dramatised the propaganda theme of 'Careless Talk Costs Lives' and the need for constant vigilance. A controversial picture, the film illustrated how loose talk can aid the enemy, and potential blame is evenly distributed throughout society. While thought defeatist in some quarters, the film was a critical and popular success (Richards 1986a).

The post-war years were witness to a number of pictures which revealed and celebrated aspects of the secret war. The activities of the Special Opera-tions Executive were featured in *Against the Wind* (1948), *Odette* (1950) and *Carve Her Name with Pride* (1958), the latter films commemorating the re-markable heroism of female agents who served behind enemy lines. Out-standingly successful deception operations against the Germans were drama-tised in *The Man Who Never Was* (1956) and *I Was Monty's Double* (1958). Generally popular and successful pictures, these productions were part of a broader cycle of war films in the 1950s which has been appreciated as a nos-talgic return to the wartime years (Chapman 1996). While such films served as a form of reassurance, a more anxious response to the decade was evident in contemporary spy thrillers which were framed by the Cold War, the threat of subversion and the possibility of nuclear annihilation.

There was a variety of responses within the British film industry to the con-vulsions of the Cold War. Most visible was the adaptation of the classic litera-ture of the ideological conflict, in the form of George Orwell's *Animal Farm* (1954), made with CIA support, and *1984* (1954, television as *Nineteen Eighty-Four*, 1956, film).[40] While a film such as *Seven Days to Noon* (1950) dealt with the moral issues and widespread fears centring on atomic science (Guy 2000), a more overt treatment of espionage was evident in another group of films.

The shrillest response to fears of a fifth column of communist agents working in Britain to undermine democracy was *High Treason* (1951), which featured a gallery of malcontents and debased types from all stations in British society engaged in sabotage. Generally, though, British cinema did not produce a cycle of paranoid films as had appeared in Hollywood under the sway of McCarthyism, although *Conspirator* (1949), made by MGM in Britain and dealing with a Guards Officer trading secrets with an unidentified enemy, can be appreciated in this light and starred the arch anti-communist Robert Taylor.

More typical were films which featured intrepid Britons tackling injustice or securing secrets behind the Iron Curtain. Among the first of these was *State Secret* (1950), which had an American surgeon (Douglas Fairbanks Jnr.) lured to a totalitarian state to operate on an ailing dictator. When the leader dies, the innocent doctor is forced to flee to save his own life. *Highly Dangerous* (1950) was unusual in that it had a female protagonist played by Margaret Lockwood, a scientist, who is persuaded to go behind the Iron Curtain to investigate reports concerning biological warfare experiments. The film is now chiefly important for its script by the master spy writer Eric Ambler who adapted it from his first novel *The Dark Frontier* (1936). These two films served to construct for audiences the image of oppression, distrust and secrecy which characterised societies in Eastern Europe. Occasionally, a leading filmmaker turned his hand to the espionage drama or political thriller and films of quality emerged in the form of Carol Reed's *The Man Between* (1953) and *Our Man in Havana* (1959, from the satirical novel by Graham Greene), Thorold Dickinson's *Secret People* (1952) and Peter Glenville's *The Prisoner* (1955). More common, though, were the rash of spy thrillers produced as second features, with titles such as *Deadly Nightshade* (1953), *Little Red Monkey* and *They Can't Hang Me* (both 1955), *Cloak Without Dagger* (1956), *The Secret Man* (1958) and *Sentenced for Life* (1960). Most of these were dully routine and aimed at undemanding audiences who still enjoyed a whole evening's entertainment at the cinema. A more interesting example of this type of picture was *Suspect* (1960), produced and directed by John and Roy Boulting as a conscious effort to raise the quality of the B-film. The picture, from a post-war novel by Nigel Balchin, dealt with a plot to publish secret research into germ warfare and was more literate than the average low-budget thriller (O'Sullivan 2000). The competition for scientific supremacy between East and West, especially as it affected military capability and threat, was a standard theme in the fictions of the Cold War, and the figure of the traitorous, defecting or duped scientist was a common character.

The early period of the television drama in Britain in the 1950s also came to some accommodation with the spy thriller, although espionage was nowhere as popular in the production schedules as the contemporary police drama and series such as *Fabian of Scotland Yard* (BBC, 1954-56), *Colonel March of Scotland Yard* (ITV, 1955), *Dixon of Dock Green* (BBC, 1955-76), *Mark Saber* (ITV, 1957-62) and *Dial 999* (ITV, 1958). Although it is difficult to assess programmes from this period as the majority are lost, the fledgeling service mounted a handful of prestige espionage drama series as with the six-part adaptations of *Epitaph for a Spy* (BBC, 1953) and *The Schirmer Inheritance* (ITV, 1957), both from Eric Ambler. Classics such as *The Scarlet Pimpernel* (BBC, 1950 and 1955, and ITV, 1955-56) were also obvious choices for television producers.

Recent history was treated in several drama series which centred on the experience of espionage in the Second World War. *Man Trap* and *Secret Mission* (both ITV, 1956) dramatised true stories of wartime espionage, while the Anglo-American series *O.S.S.* (ITV, 1957), dealt with the wartime American Office of Strategic Services and various cloak and dagger escapades on the Continent. *Spy Catcher* (BBC, 1959-61), comprising of four seasons and 24 episodes, was based on the exploits of Lt.-Col. Oreste Pinto of counterintelligence whose job had been to prevent the infiltration of Britain by enemy spies as recounted in the published *Spycatcher* (1952) and *Friend or Foe?* (1953).[41] At the very end of the decade there appeared an updated adaptation of Edgar Wallace's warhorse *The Four Just Men*, which commenced its broadcast early in 1960 and which featured a quartet of wartime buddies, a Briton (Jack Hawkins), two Americans (Richard Conte and Dan Dailey) and an Italian (Vittorio De Sica), banding together to combat injustice and international intrigue in various picturesque locales around Europe. The series of 39 episodes was possibly the first multi-national lead show designed to sell to an international market, a strategy that would be greatly extended in the 1960s.[42] From a modest beginning in the 1950s, the treatment of espionage on British television would progress considerably in the following decade, given the expansion of the broadcasting service, more generous budgets, and significant cultural developments in literature and film which began to position the fictional secret agent as an iconic figure of the 1960s.

Methodology

There have been various historical, literary and critical accounts of espionage and spy stories in Britain.[43] The following is a cultural and historical examination of British spy dramas in the cinema and on television since 1960. As already set out in this introduction, the spy screen is here situated generally in the two dominant contexts of secret agent literature and espionage history. Literary espionage established the significant themes, styles and pleasures for the imaginative treatment of spying, and the majority of films and those television dramas that have been taken more seriously were derived from pre-existing novels, plays and stories. Similarly, public awareness and perceptions of espionage and national security established a framework of audience understanding and expectation to which producers of the spy screen responded.

Like jazz, the spy story comes in 'hot' and 'cool' styles. The first chapter deals with the 'spy thriller' in the cinema, the 'hot' style which developed as a significant cycle under the influence of the James Bond pictures that began to appear from 1962. Such films prioritised excitement and featured action-oriented secret agents most often sent on missions to exotic locales. Such stories belonged to the tradition of 'sensation' or 'romantic' spy fiction, a form colourfully labelled "*Great Bad Writing*". The second chapter treats what I have called 'espionage drama' in the cinema, the alternative 'cold' style of the spy story. Such films, fewer in number, tended to be adaptations of the new-style spy fiction of John le Carré, Len Deighton and their adherents which began to appear in the early 1960s, characterised by more serious themes and sometimes literary ambition, and in contrast labelled "*Great Good Writing*" (*Time*, 3 October 1977). The third and fourth chapters examine spy dramas on television, first the thriller and then the literary type. This gives attention to many drama series and serials previously unconsidered, as well as works in the espionage genre by leading playwrights such as Dennis Potter, Alan Bennett and Stephen Poliakoff. The fifth and sixth chapters take as their focus historical spy dramas, first imaginative treatments of the past which have in many cases cast a nostalgic net around the classics of spy and thriller fiction, and then the often controversial dramatic accounts of agents, spies and operations from history, most obviously and notably the infamous Cambridge Spies who have bewitched and enthralled generations of the British public. The seventh chapter takes a look at the 'secret state' thriller, a largely unconsidered cycle of films and television dramas of the 1980s which adopted a conspiratorial view towards the intelligence services, their actions on behalf of reactionaries and political elites, and their malevolent deeds against innocent radicals and liberals who were demonised as subversives. The final chapter provides an overview of the spy drama since the end of the Cold War. In a slightly more tentative manner, it examines the variety of responses to espionage on the screen after what many felt was the loss of the main rationale for the modern spy story.

The study is the first attempt to bring a broad view to the British spy screen in the period. The separation of spy thrillers and espionage dramas into different lineages, attention on both film and television, a discussion of both costume and historical dramas, and treatment of the 'secret state' thriller, represent a critical engagement with the spy story on screen; a first attempt to delineate the genre according to its dominant themes and styles. The study also brings the spy screen up-to-date, with a consideration of the spy drama since the collapse of the Soviet Union in the early 1990s and on to the most recent dramas and dramatisations such as *London Spy* (2015) and *The Night Manager* (2016).

Spies and spying were a popular, durable and significant topic for British film- and television-makers. Following recent work on crime, horror, comedy, historical and heritage films, espionage is, James Bond apart, arguably the last of the significant British screen genres to receive detailed attention.[44] The following study is also original in that it considers both cinema and television in their engagement with secret agents and espionage. This has been desirable as the screen arts have been increasingly merging in their industrial and representative practices since the 1960s. The approach has set out to be inclusive, dealing with the broad sweep of spy dramas produced for cinema and television in an effort to map out the diverse contours of the spy screen in Britain. This means that many films and drama series are treated for the first time. Such an approach distinguishes the study from previous work on the spy screen in Britain which has been more selective and piecemeal, treating a particularly influential secret agent character such as James Bond, a prominent filmmaker such as Alfred Hitchcock and his spy thrillers in the 1930s, a popular cycle on television such as the adventure series of the 1960s, or have 'cherry picked' from such as these to construct a 'composite' account made-up of 'highlights' in the genre.[45]

It is worthwhile taking a few moments to consider the relative merits of the two approaches. In a recent study of espionage and conspiracy dramas on British television, Joseph Oldham has defended the selective method. He argues for the "*generic case study*", incorporating the "*close analysis of a number of key case study texts*". He suggests that in contrast, the comprehensive approach is unable to provide a "*satisfying depth of analysis*". Of course, this argument can be turned around, and the selective approach can be accused of failing to be adequately representative, and clearly does not lend itself to works of synthesis and synopsis. Oldham's answer to this is to base selection on innovative dramas, those representative of "*moments of intervention*" and marking "*crucial historical turning points*" in the genre (2017: 6-8).[46]

Elsewhere, there has emerged a view that existing approaches to the study of genre have been partial, selective and ultimately misleading. As Steve Neale has argued, "*conventional definitions of genre are often narrow and restrictive*", and that, "*traditional accounts of a number of genres are inaccurate or incomplete*" (2000: 1). Such thinking, of course, runs counter to the type of methodology practised by Oldham. Through an effort to be comprehensive, this study has attempted to avoid the obvious pitfalls, and, as Neale has advocated, it has demonstrated a "*commitment to detailed empirical analysis and thorough industrial and historical research*" (ibid.). Such an approach offers precision and detail, and while at times producing lengthy treatment, it avoids the deracination of a genre into canonical highlights which often merely serve to illustrate exception rather than the norm. Wishing to be generous, it is possible to accept Oldham's proposition that the selective approach is capable of tracing a *"coherent generic strand"* (2017: 196); however, it does not necessarily follow that it provides a better or preferable treatment of a genre. A genre is an extensive and complex cultural entity, and the study of genre will undoubtedly benefit from the prosecution of both approaches: there is room for the selective and the comprehensive, each with their particular merits; and an open-minded attitude will ensure that scholarship will be the ultimate beneficiary. Here is pursued a study of the spy genre on British screens since 1960. Accordingly, it treats the literary underpinning of many spy dramas, social perspectives on espionage and government secrecy, changing narrative styles and imperatives, altering production contexts and market conditions, varying critical responses to the dramas and their narrative styles, and complex and shifting ideological and historical contexts for the productions. Necessarily, this requires some detail. Individual chapters deal with a particular narrative style, such as the spy thriller and the historical spy drama, with a particular theme, such as the 'secret state' thriller, or with a chronological period, as with the final chapter and its examination of the spyscreen since the end of the Cold War. Chapters and sub-chapters are largely organised chronologically, as this seems the best way to appreciate the development of a genre. Where appropriate, the literary source is briefly introduced, and a plot synopsis provided to familiarise readers with what are often unfamiliar texts and to allow for comparisons across texts regarding characterisations and storylines. Production details provide something of the intention of film- and television-makers, and reviews reveal critical and cultural assumptions about spy stories. The following reveals a considerable amount of new perspective and information about the spy story on British screens. The kind of detail that is not possible in a case-study type approach to genre.

Oldham's useful and insightful account of the espionage and conspiracy thriller on British television since the late 1960s, sets out an account of television drama's changing representation of intelligence institutions. In particular, he uses the generic case-study, selecting six representative examples, to provide a *"fresh perspective on the institutional and aesthetic development of the medium over a period of five decades"* (2017: 6). Its attention to the institution of television, its production styles and aesthetic concerns, distinguishes it from the approach taken here. Literary antecedents, espionage history, and critical reception play a far lesser role in Oldham, and the present author argues for their inclusion in a fuller generic treatment of secret agentry on screen. Oldham's focus on 'dramas of national security' means he provides no attention to historical spy dramas, a major sub-genre of the spy screen. This is especially surprising in terms of the omission of screen dramas treating historical treachery, and especially the dramas dealing with the notorious Cambridge Spies. Oldham's approach also fails to find room for the television dramas authored by leading playwrights, Alan Bennett, Dennis Potter and Stephen Poliakoff, who greatly enriched the spyscreen in the period of the 1970s-90s.

The work presented here incorporates an element of the case-study approach, in that each chapter features one or more 'case files', providing greater focus where it is appropriate, and allowing for a more detailed consideration of a significant author, theme, film or television drama as appropriate. However, each case-file is situated in a larger thematic chapter, ensuring that the fuller generic picture is not lost sight of. The general method adopted is that of cultural-historical analysis, of situating the narratives in their historical and literary contexts, and of considering their critical and popular receptions. The commodity nature of the film cycle, the imitative and exploitative drive of its producers, the timeliness of the stories, and the blatant repetition of its films, has generally consigned its products to 'low culture' and tested the patience of critics. The lack of artistry attached to the spy thriller on British screens since 1960 is arguably a contributory factor in the limited scholarly attention accorded the genre. However, Amanda Klein has argued for an increased attention on film cycles and proposed that a proper focus should incorporate filmmakers, audiences, reviewers, marketing and wider cultural discourses, which in turn offers a more pragmatic, localised approach to genre studies (2011: 5). A cycle develops, she argues, out of an "*originary*" text, a commercially successful template with easily reproducible elements which producers can replicate with the prospect of turning a profit (11). Within a relatively short period of time, exhaustion and frustration sets in, probably first with reviewers who become annoyed, and eventually with the target audience which becomes bored, at which point the cycle is likely to run out of steam (15-16). Klein contends that a focus on the film cycle, through the "*revisitation*" of sites of "*release, promotion, and reception*", reinserts history into the study of genre which has traditionally been lacking or absent (20). Such strictures have been borne in mind and the empirically grounded criticism presented here draws on production histories and trends, evolving narrative patterns and character types, and cultural and critical assumptions regarding the imaginative treatment of espionage. As well as the films and television dramas, primary sources include production documents, press reports, publicity materials, trade papers and newspaper and magazine reviews. What is attempted here is genre history grounded in the specific evidence of films and their related documents of production and circulation. The method has been termed 'contextual film history', or alternatively 'contextual cinematic history', where the emphasis is on locating the "*primary sources to document the processes and external contextual factors that shaped the content of the films*" (Chapman 2013: 95). In its evolutionary phase, the approach tended to rely on the case-study (O'Connor and Jackson 1979), but subsequently the method has been successfully adopted to deal with a national cinema in a historical period (Richards 1984), a prominent series of films (Chapman 1999/2007), and filmmakers (Burton and O'Sullivan 2009).

'Contextual film history' has sometimes been criticised for failing to bring an analytic focus to its object of enquiry, for being insensitive to the aesthetics of the screen, the place of technique and style for example, as well as to the viewer's immediate relationship to the visual experience. In the reverse case, though, an over-indulgence towards the *text* and the theoretical moment of spectatorship fails to take adequate notice of the *context*, how the text came into being for example, in the form that it eventually appeared, or the meaning of the text for contemporary viewers as recorded in reviews and criticism. As I will show, these elements are significant in a consideration of the spy screen in Britain after 1960. A close examination of the press response to the films and television dramas, for example, allows for a diachronic assessment of a cycle as it builds and declines. The press response also provides insights into public attitudes and discussion of controversial themes and figures as they were depicted on screen, a noteworthy characteristic of espionage drama with its spies, traitors, class elements and narratives of betrayal. As Colin MacArthur once observed, journalism, criticism and the critical reception of popular culture embody an "*agenda setting power*", laying out and organising the terms around which texts will be appreciated and understood (1985: 79). As will be shown, important and popular spy dramas such as *Tinker Tailor Soldier Spy* (1979), *A Very British Coup* (1988), *Cambridge Spies* (2003) and *Spooks* (2002-11) attracted much comment and generated a critical life beyond the moment of screening.

Where appropriate, the account considers the important ideological aspects of the spy screen, the dominant representational strategies pertaining to class, race, gender, sexuality and empire. However, this has not been the main focus of the study and it is hoped that the detailed survey presented here will tempt and aid future scholars to investigate such significant issues from a much more secure and considered basis. While many of the screen dramas examined here were derived from literary originals, the approach adopted has not specifically considered the process of adaptation, and this is another important area for future research and scholarship. Cultural critic Toby Miller has assessed the spyscreen as an "*under-researched but over-popular genre*" (2003: 170). The following study of the British spyscreen since 1960 aims to bring greater equilibrium to that unbalanced arrangement.

1.
The Spy Thriller in the Cinema

All British spy dramas, you see, must locate themselves on the 'Le Carré-Fleming Scale'. At one end are grim, unglamorous, but intellectually sophisticated worlds, where depressed uglies negotiate the smoke-and-mirrors. At the other, are the all-action, gizmo-enhanced fantasies full of hunky guys and gals with big guns and tight buns.
(*The Times*, 31 May 2003)

We have always had spies, but only recently have we made them our heroes.
(John G. Cawelti and Bruce A. Rosenberg 1987: 78)

The thriller is generally appreciated as a modern style, whose development coincided with urban industrialisation, mass society and those contextual factors and literary traditions which were also responsible for the emergence of the tales of espionage. The two forms of thriller and spy story have remained closely related, bound together in an amalgam of adventure, excitement, menace, mystery and suspense. The thriller offers the pleasure of sensation, often in excess, working primarily to evoke such feelings as "*suspense, fright, mystery, exhilaration, excitement, speed, movement*" (Rubin 1999: 5). Thrillers deal in the transformation of everyday lives into chaos, with individuals and groups coping with crisis, and with the hero's ultimate achievement of triumph (Harper 1969; Palmer 1978). Spy fiction, with its emphasis on intrigue, conspiracy, betrayal and external menace, occupies a significant place in the world of the thriller. Here, the role of adventure and the sense of the exotic are fore-grounded elements, and it is a style which requires the movement away from the domestic environment into the realm of the daring and the alien. The spy thriller is concerned with a double world, of the ordinary contrasted with the extraordinary, of the adventurous contrasted with the timid, and of the exotic contrasted with the familiar. Plots are deliberately complex and mysterious, motivations uncertain, and character loyalties vague and suspicious. Critics have invoked the metaphor of the labyrinth to suggest the complexity of the spy story, its disorientating twists and turns, of the hero's meandering journey of false trails, stumbles, pitfalls and retreats, and of the audience's willing submission to a mysterious trap. What is at stake is a process of anxiety and suspense, and yet with the ultimate promise of release and relief.

While precise figures are hard to come by, there is a general consensus that thrillers became especially popular with readers from the 1960s onwards. By some estimates, this kind of reading accounted for as much as a quarter of novels sold. Predominantly in paperback, they regularly appeared in lists of best sellers, and thriller writers were among the most translated of authors and were mainly read by men (Hugo 1972: 284). One contemporary survey put stress on the popularity of the spy thriller, such that in the 1960s "*espionage became the most popular theme in the suspense field*" (Sauerberg 1983: 99). John le Carré's *The Spy Who Came in from the Cold* sold more than two million copies and "*paperback editions and movies made from James Bond stories made 007 the most highly publicized spy-detective ever*" (ibid.). It has been claimed that in the three decades following the Second World War, the "*appeal of the secret agent story has been second to no other mass-appeal genre*" (Sauerberg 1984: 7); and the intelligence historian Christopher Moran has written of the "*unquenchable public thirst for sensational tales of espionage*" (2011a: 37). Literary historian Sam Goodman has claimed how the popularity of the spy genre "*expanded exponentially*" in the decades following the Second World War, how the character of the spy associated itself more readily with the Cold War than any other period, and how the figure of the secret agent correspondingly rooted itself in the cultural imagination (2016: 2).

Literary scholarship in its engagement with popular fiction's express intention to entertain has drawn on the notion of formula, of highly conventionalised narrative patterns and the dominance of recurring themes and character types. In such terms the reader (or viewer) seeks the reassurance of the familiar, and uses genres such as mystery, romance and the thriller to satisfy personal psychological needs. With regard to the thriller, Cawelti identifies the intense excitement offered the audience, the opportunity to escape routine organised lives, the momentary chance to evade "*our consciousness of the ultimate insecurities and ambiguities that afflict even the most secure sort of life*" (quoted in Sauerberg 1985: 359). In discussing the appeal of recent British spy fiction, Lars Sauerberg, sensitive to historical context, has argued its value as a "*compensatory mechanism*" for the reader experiencing all the uncertainties of the twentieth century. In contrast to the "*triumphant experience*" of the preceding century, the genre has more recently offered a "*compensation both for the reader's sense of frustrated nationalism and for his sense of having been firmly and irrevocably placed along with everyone else in a system of uniform standards*" (1984: 7). The notions of escape, identification and compensation with regard to historical experience readily explained the general appeal of the spy thriller, whose formal design, character archetypes and thematic patterns served to dispense vicarious thrills, suspense, heroic individuality, sensual experience and exoticism.

There have been various attempts to identify the basic formula of thriller and spy fiction. While revealing in some respects, the endeavour is doomed to failure from the outset as popular literature and cinema is produced for a commercial market and must take regard of some degree of innovation. Popular fiction tends to be consumed in cycles, with different styles coming in and out of favour, and with an understandable tendency towards variation. In short, all genres have to balance the conflicting demands of convention and novelty if they are to retain a lasting appeal. For such a reason, rigid, structural appraisals of thriller and spy fiction have limited value as general accounts of genres. Over-time, spy thrillers necessarily demonstrate considerable diversity, and continue to do so after the critic has proposed a definitive account. Is an over-arching approach likely to be able to account for such distinct authors as Ian Fleming *and* John le Carré, or to be relevant to spy stories produced in the Edwardian period as well as modern spy thrillers published since 1960? However, a restricted view, taking account of a limited timeframe in the lifetime of the spy thriller, is likely to have greater precision and value. An assessment of the emergence of a particular cycle of popularity in a genre, the 1960s and 1970s for the spy thriller for instance, is more likely to lend itself to a historical analysis of the formula that came to prominence in that defined period. The translation of the James Bond novels to the cinema in the early 1960s was the catalyst for a new cycle of spy films, or a cycle of new-style spy films, in the British cinema and on television, and it is possible and desirable to chart with some accuracy the progress and achievements of this screen treatment of espionage through a handful of decades.[47] The character of James Bond is fundamental in the appreciation of the spy film cycle as it emerged in the mid-1960s, the hero becoming, as Jeremy Black has pointed out, the *"central figure in the fictional world of British intelligence"* (2004: 135).

Case file: nobody does it better, James Bond – 007

> *He is a handsome, elegant womanizer in a world of sex, snobbery and sudden death – the friskiest, most ruthless and definitely the most bedridden, best-loved spy in the world. There are many imitations, but Bond stands alone.*
> (Sheldon Lane 1965, sleeve notes)

> *I can't think of a folk hero in human history with fewer redeeming qualities than James Bond. He's not even a human being, but just a depart-*

ment store dummy going bang-bang. And he is beyond criticism or spoofing.
(Andrew Sarris, *Village Voice*, 15 June 1967)

The cinema of James Bond as it emerged through the 1960s was exemplary as formula fiction. The successive reviews which appeared in the *Monthly Film Bulletin* clearly reflected the critics' understanding of the nature of this cinema as a highly commercial set of stock techniques and character traits. Thus, *Dr No* (1962) was recognised as "*obviously destined to be the first of a James Bond series*" and that the producers "*could well be onto a good thing*" (October 1962: 135). The following year, *From Russia, With Love* (1963) was seen to be "*made by people who clearly know that they now have a gilt-edged formula to play with*", and it is with justified confidence that the "*film ends with an announcement of the next Bond adventure:* Goldfinger" (November 1963: 155). With an obvious pun to hand, the producers had hit upon a "*gold-plated formula*" by the time of *Goldfinger* (1964), a "*dazzling object lesson in the principle that nothing succeeds like excess*" (November 1964: 161). The basic elements of the Bond formula were seen to be outsize action, extravagant sets, exotic locations, outrageous violence, callous fun, fiendish gadgets, gorgeously amorous girls and a self-mocking tone. In terms of sex and violence, there was a reference to a "*cult of amorality*" (*The Guardian*, 16 March 1964). These qualities, as well as other more specifically cinematic techniques, became the fundamentals of the spy thriller in the 1960s and early 1970s, to be imitated, parodied or consciously subverted as the film-maker desired, but the constant reference point for a genre which entered into an unprecedented phase of popularity and prosperity. The figure of 007 was so pervasive and persuasive that, as Jeremy Packer has observed, it is "*impossible to think of the secret agent as cinematic archetype, pop-cultural icon, or cultural agent without in part thinking of and through the specific figure of James Bond*" (2009b: 13).

Many of the key artists and technicians who would make a crucial contribution to the cinema of James Bond were assembled by producers Albert 'Cubby' Broccoli and Harry Saltzman for the inaugural picture *Dr No*: star Sean Connery, director Terence Young, editor Peter Hunt, cinematographer Ted Moore, musical arranger and composer John Barry, art director Ken Adam, and title designer Maurice Binder.[48] The exotic location of Jamaica and the extravagant villain of Dr No came courtesy of Ian Fleming, as, of course, did the "*brand-name hero*" (Houston 1964/1965: 15); but how the story was visualised on screen was the considerable achievement of the film-makers who worked with the very modest budget of only $1 million.[49] It is the recollection of the participants that much credit should go to the film's director Terence Young, an elegant Englishman who imparted his sense of style onto the character of the secret agent and effectively tutored the relatively inexperienced Connery in the ways of refined living, smart dress and how to speak and move.[50] The casting of the Scottish Connery did much to minimalise the traditional, imperialistic character of the novels and the 'Tory imagination' of Ian Fleming, and situate the secret agent as a representative of modernisation and modernity, achieving in Dominic Sandbrook's words, a *"sophisticated, classless hero of the scientific age and the Cold War"* (2006: 612). Much of what would conventionalise as a Bond film was present in the inaugural production, with *Dr No* sporting a stylised title sequence, the rudiments of the signature James Bond score, the secret agent's interaction with important series characters such as his querulous superior M and the flirtatious secretary Miss Moneypenny, the impressive sets, especially the master criminal's lair which serves as the location for the final elaborate action sequence,[51] and the nonchalant quips with which Bond despatches a henchman. Enhancements to this basic structure were brought to *From Russia, With Love*, made even more effective with a doubling of the budget, in particular an exciting and tantalising 'teaser' sequence preceding the main titles and the addition of a theme song, played here over the final credits, but in later films a hallmark of the title sequence. The reviewer at *Monthly Film Bulletin* was impressed by both of these additions, finding the pre-credits sequence *"brilliantly conceived and shot with enough precision to promise something really out of the way in thrillers"* (November 1963:155).[52] Scriptwriter Richard Maibaum later credited *From Russia, With Love* as the *"one in which we set the style"* of the emerging series (quoted in Field and Chowdhury 2015: 82). By the time of the fifth Bond movie, *You Only Live Twice* (1967), familiarity was breeding contempt in the critic at *Monthly Film Bulletin* who complained that:

> *...the formula has become so mechanical (and Bond himself so predictably indestructible) without any compensation in other directions. Gorgeously amorous girls, fiendish devices and expendable opponents duly make their appearance at carefully regulated intervals; all are handled by the same expressionless competence by Bond; and one couldn't really care less.*
> (August 1967: 122)[53]

What at one time had seemed fresh was quickly turning stale to film critics who were not naturally disposed towards what some considered a *"vicious fiction tradition"*, or an *"adolescent fantasy"* which promoted *"gross wishful-thinking"* and *"snob sex"* (Johnson 1965: 6, 7).[54]

Albert 'Cubby' Broccoli and Harry Saltzman came together to produce the James Bond films and set up the company Eon for the purpose.[55] Both were North Americans who had experience of film-making in Britain, Broccoli at

Warwick Films and Saltzman at Woodfall Films.[56] There had been muted interest throughout the 1950s in adapting the James Bond stories for the screen, with enquiries from the Associated British Picture Corporation, the British film producer Alexander Korda, the Rank Organisation, the American filmmaker Gregory Ratoff, the American television producer Henry Morgenthau III, the Columbia Broadcasting network and independent filmmaker Kevin McClory (Field and Chowdhury 2015: 22-28).[57] Saltzman had optioned the Bond novels from Ian Fleming late in 1960 and Broccoli had let it be known that he was interested in taking on the productions. The proposal for a series of Bond pictures was brought to George Ornstein in 1961 at the recently opened production office of United Artists (UA) in London, and from there referred on to the company's head office in New York. After some initial wrangling over which book to film first and who to cast as the secret agent, the decision was taken to film *Dr No* with the physically impressive Sean Connery as James Bond. The plot of *Dr No* could be accommodated within a limited budget of $1 million, the exotic location of Jamaica was an appealing mid-Atlantic setting for Anglo-American audiences and in addition complied with British quota requirements thus making the picture eligible for subsidy, and a rising star could be signed up for a series, should the initial picture be a success.[58] A great boost to the undertaking was the announcement in *Life* magazine on 17 March 1961 that President Kennedy was a fan of the James Bond novels, citing *From Russia, With Love* as one of his ten favourite books for bedside reading. *Dr No* as the choice for the first James Bond picture, with its Caribbean setting and story involving sinister interference with the American rocket programme, also offered some topicality considering the recent Cuban Missile Crisis and continuing problems for the Americans with their launches from nearby Cape Canaveral. A shift towards a more democratic characterisation in the figure of James Bond was an important element in transferring the stories successfully to the screen. As a reviewer in the *Guardian* noted, the "*Bond of the books is like Ian Fleming himself: he is an upper-class Maverick: he is an extraordinary human type. The Bond of the movies is merely a glamorous version of an ordinary man*" (11 February 1970).[59]

Dr No was premiered at the Pavilion Theatre, London in October 1962, and shortly after was simultaneously released into 198 theatres throughout the British Isles where it grossed a remarkable $840,000 in only two weeks. The picture turned out to be the second most successful film at the British box office in 1962 (Chapman 2014: 63). Special effort was put into marketing the film in the States by United Artists, where it grossed a respectable $2 million, to go alongside the $4 million the picture earned in the overseas market (Balio 1987: 260). This was sufficient to trigger the production of a second Bond movie, and given JFK's choice of bedside reading and the public's familiarity with the title, *From Russia, With Love* was put into production with a budget of $2 million. The picture earned an impressive $12.5 million worldwide. *Goldfinger* was produced on a budget of $3m and grossed a phenomenal $40 million in the world market, the publicity declaring it the "*biggest Bondbuster yet!*" (quoted in Field and Chowdhury 2015: 100). In Britain, *Goldfinger* earned over $400,000 in its first two weeks and the Bond pictures in the 1960s, untypical of British productions, broke even in their home market. It has been estimated that by the time of *Thunderball* (1965), the Bond movies had been seen by some 100 million people (Richler 1971: 341). As the historian of United Artists has commented: "*For each picture, the producers introduced a new exotic locale, a new James Bond woman, and fantastic gadgets to enliven the formula*", and these clearly marked a distinctive pleasure for audiences of the series (Balio 1987: 261).[60] It was a case, as Alexander Walker has described it, where the "*mechanics of money worked hand in glove with the metaphysics of sensation to provide the British cinema of the early 1960s with an image it could impose world-wide for the remainder of the decade*", and, of course, beyond (1986: 198).

The unprecedented success of the films fed back into increased paperback sales of the novels. By the time of *From Russia, With Love*, UA was claiming overall sales of the books at 30 million copies (Balio 1987: 262), and another source was reporting sales in excess of 45 million copies by 1966, the novels being translated into 26 different languages (Richler 1971: 341). James Bond titles accounted for nearly a third of all Pan paperback sales, and of the first 18 books to sell a million copies in Britain, 10 were Bond novels (Bennett and Woollacott 1987: 12; Sandbrook 2006: 608). By the time of *Goldfinger*, the press were proclaiming 'Bondmania', and the iconic secret agent was represented to an eager public through a variety of cultural and commercial forms. The Fleming stories were serialised in *Playboy*, and the magazine also featured a number of spreads of Bond and his women. The character was used to endorse a plethora of merchandise, more than 200 products, encompassing such things as children's toys, men's shoes, toiletries, luggage, sleepwear and vodka, the latter presumably allowing its users the comforting fantasy of being able to mix a Bond-style vodka martini.[61] As one film journalist quipped in 1965:

> *The best dressed Parisian today slips into 007 underpants, draws on a James Bond shirt (with Ian Fleming links), tucks goldfingered kerchief into top pocket, grabs snazzy black briefcase and trench-coat, and considers himself dressed to kill. Or perhaps licensed to kill.*
> (Johnson: 5)

'The James Bond Phenomenon' was widely debated in cultural and social circles, and even attracted the interest of clinical psychologists, one practitioner recognising 007 as a "*psychological phenomenon of widespread signifi-cance*" and claiming the character of Bond as an identification figure for those with masochistic, paranoid trends and homosexual conflicts, a worrying thought considering the extensive popularity of the secret agent (Birner 1968: 13, 15).[62] As an ideological cipher, James Bond was a powerful symbol of Western male privilege during the period of the Cold War, such that the Soviet Bloc found it necessary to counter his influence through the promotion of a literary counter-hero, one who served in a "*truly communist way*" (13). It has been claimed that the KGB had recognised James Bond as a major propagan-da success and sought its own hero to glorify the deeds of Soviet espionage. The Bulgarian writer Andrei Gulyashki came up with *Zakhov Mission* in 1966, the story also being serialised in a Soviet youth paper under the title of *Ava-kum Zakhov versus 07*. Donald McCormick describes the Soviet counterpart in the following terms: "*Avakum Zakhov was, understandably, a much more proletarian figure than Bond; instead of the fastidious culinary tastes of Bond, the Soviet hero gulped down large quantities of cabbage and noodles*" (1979: 115).

For film critic Alexander Walker, Bond was the "*Man of the Decade*", (1986: 178); while the figure of the secret agent was, according to the journalist Mark Feeney, the "*Cold War protagonist par excellence, a complex moral agent in the blunt geopolitical struggle between capitalism and communism*" (quoted in Packer 2009b: 4). As a commercial proposition James Bond was unrivalled, and ambitious film producers, like their literary counterparts, readily turned to the spy thriller in the hope of getting their films made and onto a promis-ing market. Stories and characters were available courtesy of the many imita-tors who wrote in the wake of Ian Fleming, or failing that, scriptwriters turned hopefully to the formula which had been so successfully refined by Albert 'Cubby' Broccoli and Harry Saltzman from the original novels. Writing at the time of the film's release, Penelope Houston claimed in *Sight and Sound*: "*It is* Goldfinger ... *which perfects the formula*" (Winter 1964/1965: 16); and it was the year of *Goldfinger*, 1964, which saw the first attempts of rivals at cashing in on the public interest in new-style secret agents of the screen.

"*Jumping on the Bondwagon*"[63]

Following James Bond's box-office success of last year, everybody's trying to cash in on the spy racket. Nineteen-sixty-four is in danger of going down in screen history as The Year of the Secret Agent. (*Daily Worker*, 23 March 1964)

From Bond straight to Bond parodied to Bond made infantile has been
a really rather remarkable show business progression.
(*Spectator*, 24 April 1967)

In the 1960s, imitation proved that nothing is as successful as someone
else's success.
(Wesley Britton 2004: 179)

Len Deighton has recounted that, "*one must remember that spy stories were*
neither fashionable nor particularly popular in those early days of the 60s"
(Deighton 1994: 20). Film historian Robert Murphy, commenting on the British scene, has noted that before the 1960s, "*spies and secret agents seemed to*
weave in and out of thrillers, melodramas, war films, even comedies, without
having a defined genre of their own", and that by the late 1950s the spy and
secret agent "*seemed to be a spent force*" in the cinema (1992: 218). Typical
Cold War thrillers of the early 1960s were *Shoot to Kill* (1961), and *The Traitors*
and *The Man Who Finally Died* (both 1962): black and white, modestly-
budgeted, routine and uninspiring. All that was about to change as James
Bond, the "ur-*figure of popular spies*", was set to transform the secret agent of
the screen for all time (Miller 2003: 2).

Dr No and *From Russia, With Love* changed everything, demonstrating that
secret agent thrillers with verve, in colour and ambitious could set the box-
office afire. The impact and influence of the films were astonishing; "*absolute-*
ly marinating the movie culture of the mid-1960s in Bondage" was how the
Guardian colourfully expressed it (20 July 2002). By April 1965, the monthly
cinema periodical *Films and Filming* was declaring a state of "*Spy Mania*" in
the British film industry, reporting on the proposed productions of an adaptation of John le Carré's latest novel *The Looking-Glass War* and of Ian Fleming's
Casino Royale, the latter by producer Charles K. Feldman (37). A French observer on the film scene prophesied that, "*We can look forward in 1965 to an*
avalanche of spy stories" and that under the influence of James Bond, these
pictures should "*not be taken too seriously*" (quoted in *Kine Weekly*, 18 February 1965). Steve Neale has suggested that in cinema the term "*cycle*" refers to
"*groups of films made within a specific and limited time span*" and "*founded,*
for the most part, on the characteristics of individual commercial successes"
(2000: 9). The recent history of British cinema had seen cycles of war films,
horror films and 'kitchen sink' dramas, and the film cycle was a conventional
production practice of commercial cinema. Rick Altman has pinpointed the
quality of "*imitation*" inherent to film cycles. "*New cycles*", he has suggested,
"*are usually produced by associating a new type of material or approach with*
already existing genres". A cycle can emerge, he has argued, when elements

(plot, characterisation, settings) can be easily adopted by other producers (1999: 60).

The period since the release of *From Russia, With Love* had indeed witnessed an accelerating series of spy films, and it was evident that the success of the third Bond picture, *Goldfinger,* had "*sent the majors to the drawing boards in search of successful imitations*" (Balio 1987: 267). United Artists put far greater effort in marketing the new Bond film in North America where *Variety* in its inimitable parlance reported that it did "*whammo biz*", and it was around the time of *Goldfinger* that critics began to take note of 'Bondmania' (Field and Chowdhury 2015: 118-20). It is apparent that the early James Bond pictures served as the "*originary*" texts for a cycle of spy thrillers in the cinema of the 1960s (Klein 2011). Some of these pictures were blatant analogues of the Bond style, others were more overtly comic in approach, yet others unsophisticated parodies of the 007 formula, and a final group which referenced the more realistic writing of John le Carré and Len Deighton. Critic Ian Johnson, in exasperation, had "*given up hope of cataloguing them all*" (1965: 5).

In 1965, *Sight and Sound* reported that the immense success of the James Bond films "*meant that no other spy film could be made without reference to the Bond image*" (Summer 1965: 150) The Bond imitations were the most blatant adopters of the 007 archetype and tended to feature a professional agent who is put to some mission for the sake of Queen and Country. In its most reductive form, the emphasis was on action, the seeming indestructibility of the agent, and his effortless conquest of a string of desirable women. The latter quality was tied to the new permissiveness that was sweeping the country in the mid-1960s, and Bond's casual seductions have been rated as a "*canonical motif*" of the secret agent story in the decade, converting "*passing sexual interest into an enshrined feature of the subsequent spy thriller*" (Merry 1976: 13). A far from retiring genre, it became necessary for the pictures to outdo each other as the secret agent cycle got into swing. As a production report in 1967 recorded: "*During the current spy rage, there is constant subterfuge among the films, each trying to find out what the others are doing, to steal something or to make sure that what they're doing hasn't already been stolen or accidently duplicated*" (quoted in Duncan 2012: 142).

The race was on to establish a 'popular hero' as successful as James Bond, and one of the earliest of the imitations onto the market was *Licensed to Kill* (1965), which, as the title indicates, lacked any sense of shame in its attempt to cash in on the Bond mystique. Just in case the point of reference was missed, the film's release title for the North American market was the even more explicit *The 2nd Best Secret Agent in the Whole Wide World*.[64] The film, from an original screenplay, was made for the distributor Golden Era and

directed and co-written by the visiting Canadian Lindsay Shonteff.[65] Golden
Era specialised in distributing European spectaculars like *Goliath and the Sins
of Babylon* (1963) and the prospects of the spy film seemed to make it worthwhile for the company to venture into the genre. As with Albert 'Cubby'Broccoli and Harry Saltzman before them, the main problem facing the
producers was filling the central role of the secret agent. After examining
hundreds of photographs and interviewing many actors, Tom Adams was
spotted on television appearing in *Emergency–Ward Ten* and cast as Charles
Vine (Greenspan 1965: 88). The actor looked the part of the handsome and
suave secret agent and would be kept busy in such roles through the remainder of the 1960s. The improbable plot concerns the British trying to acquire a
revolutionary anti-gravity device and Vine is assigned to protect the Swedish
inventor while the politicians manoeuvre to confirm the deal.

Released in America by Joseph E. Levine's Embassy Pictures with the tagline
"*Charles Vine is only No. 2 ... That's why he tries harder ... and loves more dangerously!*", the picture represented a classic exercise in exploitation, the producers seeking to entice audiences with the promise of James Bond-style
excitement. The American prints re-edited the material to provide, *à la From
Russia, With Love*, an arresting pre-credits sequence in which a brolly-
carrying city-type is dropped off by a chauffeur and strolls onto Hampstead
Heath. There, he is machine-gunned down by a young woman pushing a
pram carrying twin babies. The American distributor also added a ballsy title
song sung by Sammy Davis Jnr., in which the audience is informed that
Charles Vine is "*every bit as good as what'shisname*". The picture is shot
through with allusions to James Bond, and elements of the plot and some
characterisations are derived from *From Russia, With Love*; the Russian agent
Sadistikov – we are informed that he loves killing – being a poor man's stand-
in for the far more impressive and brutal Red Grant in Ian Fleming's original.
When the representative of the Foreign Office requests the best agent for the
mission, perhaps the one who recently settled a "*gold conspiracy*", he is told
he must make do with the second best and Charles Vine is assigned. Vine, like
Bond, is omni-competent, having taken a First in Maths at Oxford, and placed
best in class while training in unarmed combat and weaponry. He is also a
serial lover, always ready with a double-entendre should the moment require
one. Lounging in bed with a beautiful girl, and contacted on the telephone by
his chief who asks if he is engaged at present, he volunteers that he has "*nothing on at the moment*". When he meets a beautiful computer programmer, he
readily admits he has an "*aptitude for figures*". In short, Vine fits the template
of the "*new-style, up-to-the-minute, hyper-sexed, ready-made daydream secret-service hero*" (Richardson 1964). The low-budget denied any prospect of
exotic locations, so the picture was filmed in and around London, and finances only allowed for a single wholly unimpressive gadget, a tiny gun, with one

shot, capable of killing at 10 yards, and somewhat symbolic of the picture's emasculated embodiment of the Bondian. The film suffers from many crudenesses of construction, especially an over-fondness for the zoom into a close-up, and some poor plotting. One faintly interesting aspect of the picture is the aptly-named Asian transvestite assassin Sheehee, who lures an aroused Vine to a hotel room and only just in time reveals his true intention to kill the agent. A relieved Vine declares: "*Three more minutes and this could have been embarrassing for both of us*". Denied a session of kinky sex, the audience is alternatively treated to a bout of martial arts. The finale, in which Vine also has to contend with an exact double planted by the Soviets, is a seemingly endless revelation of double-crosses and surprise turns, and served as an effective parody on what was becoming conventionalised in the spy film by this time.

Unsurprisingly, the critics were not generous towards *Licensed to Kill.* Unprepared to devote more than 10 words to its review, *The Guardian* economically passed-over the film as "*Small-beer spy palaver in which Tom Adams plays the neo-Bond*" (24 January 1966). *Monthly Film Bulletin* was slightly more favourably disposed, accepting the film for what it was, a "*slick burlesque*" which manages a "*relish that is infectiously absurd*", and which served as an "*effective skit on the current licensed-to-kill vogue*" (September 1965: 137). The picture was surprisingly successful in the North American and European markets and Golden Era financed a sequel, with the picture once again distributed in North America by Embassy Pictures. *Where the Bullets Fly*, directed by the more experienced John Gilling from an original script by Michael Pittock, was released in October 1966 and offered a similar mix of sub-Bondian thrills, flirtatious encounters and humorous asides. In this adventure, secret agent Charles Vine is required to thwart the attempts of the villainous Angel (Michael Ripper), described on the film's posters as "*Diabolical Overlord of Vice and Violence*", who seeks to steal a revolutionary device for powering aircraft. The finale, blatantly stolen from the recently released *The Liquidator* (1966), involves Vine scrambling aboard a hi-jacked RAF flight, despatching the villains and having to land the pilotless plane. The *Sun* dismissed *Where the Bullets Fly* as "*tired*", "*jaded*" and "*shoddy*", and while *Licensed to Kill* had had "*verve*" and "*pace*", the sequel was "*stupid in the extreme*" (3 November 1966). The reviewer at *The Times* was already hoping that this might be the "*last gasp of the current run of spy thrillers*", believing that the script "*made little sense*", and the general effect "*rather as though the whole thing had been concocted by a group of rather backward fourth-formers impregnably convinced of their own sophistication and worldly wisdom*" (3 November 1966). It was a sentiment shared at the *Financial Times* where it was hoped that this sort of film "*should serve to bring the James Bond cycle to a quick end*" (4 November 1966). *Monthly Film Bulletin* felt that the film had shifted too far towards comedy, the whole carried out *"with more zest than finesse"* and *"too much of the fun failing to score"* (December 1966: 188). There was one more outing for secret agent Charles Vine played by Tom Adams, in a Spanish production known as *O.K. Yevtushenko* (1968), which demonstrated the equal popularity of the spy film on the continent.

The mainstream spy thriller in British cinema in the 1960s was more likely to be derived from a popular novel and bear a level of production values above that of a mere exploitation film. This was the case with *The Double Man* released in April 1967 and adapted from Henry Maxfield's American secret agent story *Legacy of a Spy* (1958). The book had already gone through a number of printings, notched up impressive sales and been considered for filming by Victor Saville for production at British Lion by the time the property was acquired by the UK-based American producer Hal Chester for production by Warner Bros. in Britain in the mid-1960s (Erwin 1985: 209-10; *Kine Weekly*, 14 and 21 April 1966). Yul Brynner was cast as the unyielding senior CIA officer, Dan Slater, who journey's to snowy Austria to investigate the death of his teenage son in a skiing accident. The boy had been in the care of Frank Wheatley (Clive Reville), a former British Secret Intelligence Service (SIS) agent, who now runs a school in St. Anton in the Tyrol.[66] Dan is suspicious and his enquiries lead him to suspect murder, aimed to lure him into a trap. Soviet and East German agents manage to entice Slater to a remote farmhouse, where he is captured and replaced by an exact double, Kalmar, who will return to the United States and resume Slater's position in the CIA, but serving the communists. Slater is able to escape while he is being driven away for removal, eludes his pursuers during the confusion offered by a night-time ski race, and hides in a deserted cable car station. Killing the pursuing agents, he is finally trapped by Kalmar. Wheatley takes command of the situation, only to be confronted by two identical men. Reacting to Slater's bloody-mindedness – the CIA man insists that Frank shoot both of them as the only way to be sure to eliminate the enemy agent – Wheatley kills Kalmar. Slater boards the train to return to America and there is joined by Gina (Britt Ekland), the young woman who had helped him with information, but whom Slater had abused in his single-mindedness to find the truth.

The Double Man was an Anglo-American production typical of the 'Hollywood UK' period of the middle-1960s. It was made with American finance and in this case there was a minimum of technical contribution from the British. The film was directed by the American Franklin J. Schaffner, featured an American protagonist, but was made by British technicians at Elstree Studios.[67] The main concession to British sensibilities was the character of Frank Wheatley. The former partner of Dan Slater, whose nerves have been wrecked through his experiences as an agent, he serves a symbolic function in his representation of a British Secret Service past its former glories, weak, uncertain and a liability. The confident and strident Slater stands in stark contrast, the epitome of the American individualist, distant from his son and seemingly unable to commit to emotional relationships. There are several scenes in the film which emphasise the resemblance between the CIA officer and his communist counter-part, Col. Berthold (Anton Diffring). This was becoming a common device in the more serious espionage films wherein professional similarity was being marked above ideological difference. The connection between Slater and Berthold in *The Double Man* is most effectively caught in a late scene at the train station as the CIA officer is preparing to return to the States. The disgraced Berthold looks secretly on at his opposite number, a hint of professional admiration, before he is obscured by a passing train, and then has disappeared from the image, whisked away to an unpleasant fate as the price of failure. Producer Hal Chester, while eager to suggest that the picture was an "*action thriller*" and not a "*preachment*", confirmed that the film was interested in the position of the professional spy, claiming in an interview that:

> *It's an examination of the contention that all spies are made by the same process, that they're all interchangeable parts of the same machine, no matter what side they're on. They all think alike and they destroy everything they come into contact with.*
> (Quoted in *Kine Weekly*, 25 August 1966)

Critics generally missed this more serious dimension and tended to be disappointed with the film, in the sense that Schaffner had shown much promise with *The Best Man* (US, 1964) and *The War Lord* (US, 1965), but had only contrived an "*anonymous film*" with *The Double Man* from a "*comparatively ingenious script*" (*Monthly Film Bulletin*, May 1967: 70). The *New Statesman* dismissed the picture as a "*wretched spy-thriller*" which disclosed the plot twist far too early and threw away any hope of suspense (14 April 1967). Some critics carped at a basic plot idea which had already served its time in *The Spy with My Face* (US, 1965) and *Licensed to Kill*, and what was felt to be too obvious process work in the ski scenes, despite the fact that the production had spent four weeks on location in the West Tyrol in the spring of 1966 (*The Times*, 13 April 1967; *Kine Weekly*, 5 May 1966).[68] The cinema trade paper *Kine Weekly* sensed the commercial potential of the film, especially as it fitted with the current popularity of "*special agent stuff*" (8 April 1967); but in contrast *Films and Filming* wondered, "*where did the pulse-pounding excitement go?*" (June 1967: 22).[69] The fundamental premise of *The Double Man* would have allowed a serious investigation of the theme of duplicity which is central to the spy film, but the opportunity was not taken by the film-makers who opted instead for the standard fare of tough-guy posturing and excitement played out in an exotic setting. The one unusual quality of the film was the thorough-going unattractiveness of the protagonist, embodying an *"unflinching ferocity that defies sympathy"* as *Kine Weekly* expressed it (8 April 1967). As we have seen, this is taken to the extreme when the Soviet replacement is exposed through his inability to match the American's ruthlessness. The effect, howev-er, is undermined at the end of the film when Slater and Gina are united in an improbable romantic coupling, the CIA man seemingly and unconvincingly humanised by his recent experiences.

The Austrian Tyrol was also the setting of a British spy thriller released the following year in 1968.[70] The production unit spent a gruelling wintertime shoot in the glamorous ski resort of Kitzbühel and in Munich, before return-ing to London to complete the all-location picture (*Kine Weekly*, 8 April 1967). *Assignment K* was directed by Val Guest and released by Columbia in February 1968.[71] The story concerns Philip Scott (Stephen Boyd) who heads an inde-pendent network of agents which is contracted by the government's mysteri-ous Department K and its officer Harris (Michael Redgrave). While on a mis-sion in Germany and Austria, Scott falls for a beautiful Swedish girl, Antonia Peters (Camilla Sparv), and convinces her to return to London with him. There, she is taken hostage by communist agents headed by Smith (Leo McKern), and Scott is forced to betray his network of agents in Germany. While in Munich, he is able to turn the tables on the captors and only sacrific-es a worthless lowlife who operated on the fringes of espionage. Back in Lon-don, Scott turns to the attack and is able to bomb Smith's hideout and break-up the cell. However, Toni Peters is revealed as having been an enemy agent all along. Scott returns to Department K, states his disillusionment with the business of espionage, desire to quit, and exposes Harris as a traitor. The lat-ter shoots himself, and in a final scene Scott and Peters go their separate ways.

The adaptation of the story from the novel *Department K* (1964) by Hartley Howard reveals much about the ambitions of the spy thriller in the cinema at this time. The original book is a tightly-structured adventure which unfolds across a few days, and is more centred on London. It is a grimmer affair, reads like a contemporary crime novel and ventures only sporadically into the ter-rain of espionage. The Berlin location briefly present in the book is replaced by Munich and Kitzbühel in the film, where the opportunity for the visually splendid is more apparent, and an exotic Swede is substituted for a perfidious English girlfriend. The response of the critics to the film depended on wheth-er a routine spy thriller was acceptable entertainment (*Kine Weekly*, 27 Janu-ary 1968; *The Observer*, 28 January 1968), or a bore (*Films and Filming*, June 1968: 30, 35; *The Times*, 25 January 1968). *Monthly Film Bulletin* took a strong dislike to a picture in which the *"plot meanders from dull beginning to dull end with nothing of interest in between"* (March 1968: 39). Val Guest was at pains to downplay the spy story and to promote the love angle, and a report in *Kine Weekly* explained the director's intention for a *"thriller with a strong element of romance and sophisticated comedy"* (8 April, 1967). In the outcome, the weakest part of the film is the rather gushy relationship between Scott and Peters. There is a belated attempt to examine the consequences of having the archetypal male individualist compromised by a romantic relationship, as when Scott quits with the observation that *"This is a job for loners. People with no sense of responsibility for anyone"*. However, the sentiment rings hollow in the knowledge that the agent has been ruthlessly betrayed by Peters and is victim to the harsh logic of the business of espionage. The two characters going their separate ways at the end of the film is a reference to the climax of the classic *The Third Man* (1949) and would be repeated in the British spy cinema in this period. *Assignment K* also wastes the considerable talents of Michael Redgrave. The scene in which Harris is revealed as a traitor is hardly complex or searching, the characters simply allude to the *"ludicrously childish business we're in"*, and little is asked of the great actor.[72] The strengths of the film lie in the admirable Techniscope cinematography by Ken Hodges and the exciting jazz score by the under-rated Basil Kirchin. A modestly-budgeted picture, *Assignment K* only managed a release as half of a double-bill in the UK.

The new secret agent cycle was also prepared to resurrect and re-polish heroes from the classic age of spy fiction. *Deadlier than the Male* (1966) and *Some Girls Do* (1969) were two up-dated 'Bulldog' Drummond swinging spy comedies produced in the wake of the great success of James Bond on screen. Captain Hugh 'Bulldog' Drummond DSO, MC, had first appeared in an eponymous novel subtitled *The Adventures of a Demobilised Officer Who Found Peace Dull*, written by 'Sapper' and published in 1920. Drummond was an instant success and ultimately an archetype of a new, tougher kind of thriller which appeared in the post-World War I period. The story appealed to a generation of men who had fought in the war, and in adjusting to the drab realities of peace missed the action and companionship of the conflict. Bored, Drummond had advertised his services for adventure with *"Excitement essential"*; and this is what the typical reader craved from the breathless novel. Throughout, the deadly contest with the arch-villain Carl Petersen is referred to as a 'game' and the hero is clearly having an immense amount of fun. In an obvious contrast to the intelligence and ratiocination of Sherlock Holmes, *Bulldog Drummond* displayed an overt anti-intellectualism, with Drummond simple, direct and straight-punching, sometimes to the point of unconscious parody. Drummond featured in a series of novels and the stories are romantic and melodramatic, befitting the period in which they were published, and incorporate characterisations and characteristics carried over from the Victorian period. Chief among these is an exotic villain, a master of disguise, devil-ishly cunning and epic in his criminal intent. 'Bulldog' Drummond was influ-ential on writers in the clubland hero tradition, Valentine Williams, Sydney Horler, Dornford Yates, and even Ian Fleming, who created a modernised, trans-Atlantic hero in James Bond in the 1950s, who was the British 'Sapper' from the waist up, but the American 'Mickey Spillane' from the waist down.[73]

'Bulldog' Drummond was appropriated for theatre, radio (in America) and screen on numerous occasions. The clubland hero was reconfigured for a different generation as the "*Bond-tinged*" form of Richard Johnson in *Deadli-er than the Male* and *Some Girls Do* (*Evening News*, 29 December 1966), in which the film plots "*bore no resemblance to any of the outdated books*" (Box 2000: 255) . As the titles suggest, the two pictures feature an array of lethal ladies who are pitted against Drummond at the direction of master criminal Petersen. In *Deadlier than the Male*, from an original story by Jimmy Sangster, the hero must put a stop to Petersen's (Nigel Green) plans to assassinate the King of Akmata and thereby acquire control of valuable oil concessions. In his way are the "*pin-up killers*" Irma Eckman (Elke Sommer) and Penelope (Sylva Koscina) (*Daily Mail*, 29 December 1966).[74] In *Some Girls Do* Petersen (James Villiers) conspires to prevent the British authorities from successfully testing a new supersonic airliner, the Concorde-like SST1, using revolutionary subson-ic technology, and is aided by a team of seductive android females led by Baroness Helga Hagen (Daliah Lavi). The pictures were produced for Rank by Betty Box and directed by Ralph Thomas, who had been behind the earlier spy comedy *Hot Enough for June!* (1964, also with Koscina).[75] As part of the modernisation of the character, the 'Bulldog' tag was dropped from the film (but retained in the advertising) in favour of his Christian name Hugh; his loyal 'breed' of helpers of the novels was dispensed with and he now found himself "*lumbered*" with his American nephew Robert (Steve Carlson) in the first picture, and the cloying secret agent wannabe Flicky (Sydne Rome) and the hapless man from the Embassy Peregrine Caruthers (Ronnie Stevens) in the latter (*Daily Express*, 30 December 1966); and Drummond is no longer a gifted amateur pugilist, but rather an expert in the more up-to-date martial art of Karate. The amalgamation of traditional traits of heroism and modern permissive attitudes in the character resulted apparently in a "*clean-limbed, dirty-minded hero*" (*The Times*, 29 December 1966). Most reviewers noted the formal similarities with 007, big title songs by the Walker Brothers and Lee Vanderbilt, a thrilling pre-title sequence for the initial picture, continental beauties cast as gorgeous villainesses, lethal gadgetry, classic sports cars, witty put downs, an oriental henchman, a colourful arch-villain occupying an impressive secret lair, and exotic locations in Lerici on the Italian Riviera and Cap Sa Sal and S'Agaró on the Spanish Costa Brava. The approach was suc-cessfully reconfigured to a 'sensational' style of spy thriller fiction, which, as identified by David Buxton, generally condensed into the narrative of "*play-boys who carried out vague missions in tourist playgrounds against secret in-ternational organisations*" (1990: 92); and, as the *Daily Mail* recognised, here was "*another Bond in all but name*" (29 December 1966).

Deadlier than the Male attracted concern regarding what some felt was ex-cessive violence, the comedy thriller surprisingly attracting an adults-only X-certificate. Rated as "*tough to sadistic*", and "*as good as Bond at his most ruth-less*" at the *Evening Standard*, the *Sun* worried that "*this business of portraying violent death as if it were all a bit of a giggle is getting right out of hand*", and the *Evening News* complained of some "*unnecessarily nasty killings and tor-ture*"(all 29 December 1966). Nina Hibbin at the *Morning Star* was particularly revolted by the violence in the film and its casual depiction of the "*favourite topic of the silver screen – sudden death*". Observing the usual point of refer-ence, she noted that, "*Here is Bondism stripped of its panache and expertism, its true nature laid bare. You don't have to be a doctor to pronounce it very sick indeed*". Part of the problem seemed to be that the excessive violence was perpetrated by the female characters who "*flap their seductive eyelids as they torture and kill their male victims and then wriggling their pretty bottoms, murmur pert little death-jokes over the lifeless bodies*" (31 December 1966). This was confirmed by the censor John Trevelyan who confided to Gerald Fairlie that the problem lay with the two villainesses, "*lovely girls beautifully but sexily dressed enjoying sadism*" (quoted in the *News of the World*, 18 De-cember 1966).[76] The pictures were clearly influenced by the emergence of the strong, sexy, athletic femininity of the Bond girls, also apparent in such secret agent dramas as *The Avengers* (TV, 1961-69) and *Modesty Blaise* (1966), and paralleled the female assassins of Dr Noah in the spoof *Casino Royale* (1967).[77]

The trade paper *Kine Weekly*, which served as a guide to exhibitors on the commercial prospects of a picture, pronounced *Deadlier than the Male*, "*Fun with murder*", and judged it a "*Certain winner*" (24 December 1966). Else-where, the picture attracted only lukewarm reviews. The *Guardian* thought *Deadlier than the Male* "*derivative*", and a "*film of a now familiar kind*". "*In-ternational spies, supermen with super gimmicks, passed the point of burlesque several films ago*" it claimed, "*and it's slightly surprising to see so straight a version at this late a date*" (30 December 1966). The *Financial Times* felt the spy lark had run out of steam and found the picture, "*Fetching up a long way behind the post-Bond trend*" (30 December 1966); and *Monthly Film Bulletin* believed that 'Bulldog' Drummond "*resurrected for the screen in a form to meet the demands of contemporary folklore ... comes off rather the worse for it*" and served as only a "*poor imitation*" (March 1967: 44).[78]

Following the commercial success of *Deadlier than the Male*, Box and Thomas acknowledged that it would be *"foolhardy to ignore the worldwide demand for an encore"*, and *Some Girls Do* arrived in the New Year of 1969 (*Some Girls Do*, press book). The film, scripted by David Osbora and Liz Charles-Williams, was a fairly identikit production centring on thrills, girls and megalomaniacal villainy, and effectively used the modernist Hotel Cap Sa Sal for the villain's lair. Here, Richard Johnson reprised his Drummond as the same *"milky James-Bond type"* (*Sunday Times*, 26 January 1969); the action doubly cartoonish and the comedy laid on even more thickly, thus distancing the violence and enabling the picture to be granted a family-friendly 'A'-certificate.

Cheaper and more simplistic, the film at times looked like it had been shot on sets left-over from Rank's earlier *Carry-On* pictures.[79] The *Guardian*, armed with puns referencing the sonic devices in the story, denounced the film as more *"subnormal"* than *"subsonic"*, believing the whole thing should have been kept *"sub rosa"* (24 January 1969). The *Daily Sketch* dismissed the picture as a *"bulldog with no bite"*; the *Sun* warned that the *"acting is worse than the action, which is a kind of achievement in itself, and the result is dismal in the extreme"*; the *Daily Express* found it *"outrageously absurd"* (all 24 January 1969); and the *Evening News*, for once lost for words, declared it *"unspeakable"* (23 January 1969). *Monthly Film Bulletin* speculated that 'Bulldog' Drummond would be turning in his grave (March 1969: 61). While acknowledging the films as *"bad"*, Robert Murphy sees at least the prospect in *Deadlier than the Male* and *Some Girls Do* of a *"feminist inversion of male chauvinist myths"*, with murderous females tearing through the films *"wreaking vengeance on men with sadistic glee"* (1992: 231).

In between the two Drummond pictures, Richard Johnson had appeared in the interesting spy picture *Danger Route* (1967). This had been adapted from *The Eliminator* (1966), Andrew York's first spy thriller to feature the series character Jonas Wilde, an experienced assassin for 'The Route': a small covert team acting for the British government based on the island of Jersey. Wilde returns from a successful operation in Barbados, and intending to retire, he confronts Canning, the civil servant responsible for the outfit, but unhappily accepts a further job: the killing of the defector Salnitz, a valued prize of the Central Intelligence Agency (CIA), but who he is informed is a Soviet plant. This he achieves, but is captured by the CIA, the American intelligence organisation allowing him to leave under close surveillance in the hope Wilde will lead them to a suspected British traitor. The agent returns to Jersey where he is taken captive by his treacherous colleague Stern. Taken out to sea to be killed, Wilde is able to turn the tables during a tremendous storm and makes it back to land alive. Canning orders Wilde to disappear while he clears up the mess.

Wilde is seemingly irresistible to females and there are two principal women in the story. Jocelyn is the steady girlfriend who loves and asks no questions. She is revealed as an enemy plant keeping watch on Jonas, and in the end he adroitly avoids her attempt to poison him and coolly shoots her dead. Meanwhile, the beautiful Marita suddenly appears on the fringes of 'The Route', although Wilde does not trust her and suspects she has been planted by Canning. In fact she is a CIA agent, part of the operation to flush out a British traitor. She survives at sea with Wilde and in the dénouement the British agent takes her with him into his temporary exile.[80]

The Eliminator made it to the big screen as *Danger Route*, a faithful adaptation directed by Seth Holt, starring Richard Johnson and with the able supporting cast of Carol Lynley, Sylvia Syms, Gordon Jackson and Harry Andrews. The film was released with the aggressive tagline, "*He is a weapon! Government-issue! He killed 39 men, each with a single-blow! 6 were mistakes!*" The picture accentuates the jaded feelings of Wilde who wants out of the game; the agent musing at one point, "*I think people in our job ought to be very young and very cool. I'm beginning to think I'm neither*". The *Evening News* only found the picture a "*medium-powered thriller*" (16 November 1967); however, the *Daily Mail* was more energised and felt Richard Johnson showed "*all the requisites for the next James Bond – saturnine good looks, dark brown voice and a virile zest for loving and fighting*" (17 November 1967).

The perceptive review at the *Morning Star* marked *Danger Route* down as a different sort of espionage film, "*world-weary, brutal and grim*"; it was a "*spy thriller with anti-spy pretentions*" (18 November 1967). As such, the picture fell between the two schools of stylish espionage drama, recent examples being *The Ipcress File* (1965) and *The Naked Runner* (1967), and the James Bond thriller extravaganzas. For the 'high-brow' *Monthly Film Bulletin*, the result was a "*tired, and tiring, muddle of a film*" (January 1968: 8); while for the populist *Kine Weekly*, the picture was a "*slick and exciting piece of educated skulduggery*" (18 November 1967). Looking back on *Danger Route*, film historian Robert Murphy has judged it an intriguing failure, a film of complex ambition, "*full of class tensions and cruel surprises*", seemingly lost to a "*stingy budget*" (1992: 229). *Danger Route* is perhaps unjustly forgotten, a picture of some style and ambition and more than merely routine.

1968 saw the release of four modestly-budgeted spy thrillers which sported American leading men: *Hammerhead* starred Vince Edwards, *The Limbo Line* offered Craig Stevens, *The Man Outside* plumped for Van Heflin, and *Subterfuge* featured Gene Barry. *Hammerhead* was produced by Irwin Allen for release by Columbia, the producer's second attempt at the spy thriller genre following his production of the Matt Helm series in Hollywood. *Hammerhead* was arguably Allen's response to missing out on the James Bond bonanza, having been the business partner of Albert 'Cubby' Broccoli before the latter embarked on the wildly successful cycle of 007 films.[81] The picture was adapted from the novel by James Mayo published in 1964, which introduced the secret agent Charles Hood, and planned as a series character from the outset. This was one of the most blatant attempts to ape the literary Bond with its daring mix of sex, snobbery and sadism. The film loses some of this quality, partly through casting an American, partly through up-dating the story to chime with the hip youth scene of the late-1960s, and partly through having to dispense with some extremely graphic scenes of violence and torture which would have been unfilmable at the time. The Americanisation of Charles Hood results in a one dimensional hard-boiled type who requires no gadgets, only his fists. That such a character could be presented as an art expert is unlikely in the extreme. The action is shifted from the South of France of the original story to the coast around Lisbon in Portugal. The master criminal Hammerhead (Peter Vaughan) is a suitably exotic creature, a connoisseur of erotica who sees 'truth' in perversion and pornography. His plot is to kidnap the British ambassador to NATO and substitute a lookalike for a crucial military conference, steal the plans and sell them to the East. The picture was effectively encapsulated in its tagline which exclaimed, "*Fearless fighter Vince Edwards and his innocent Chick from Chelsea Judy Geeson smash arch-villain Hammerhead!*" While the film offered much local colour, action and go-go dancing chicks, it caused few ripples and was poorly reviewed. The left-wing *Morning Star* predictably found the thick-ear adventure "*stupid nonsense*" and "*abysmal*" (19 October 1968), and the *Guardian* commented: "*If it wasn't all so po-faced, you'd think it a parody*" (18 October 1968). *Monthly Film Bulletin* could find little to say about this "*Bond-style farrago*" (November 1968: 179) and Allen did not film any of the subsequent Hood stories such as *Let Sleeping Girls Lie* (1965), *Shamelady* (1966) or *Once in a Lifetime* (1968).

The Limbo Line, produced by London Independent Producers, was adapted from the 1963 novel by the successful thriller writer Victor Canning. The story concerns the agent Manston (Craig Stevens) who is investigating the 'Limbo Line', the method by which Soviet agents locate defecting Russians and return them to Moscow. Manston discovers that Irina (Kate O'Mara), a ballerina, is the next victim, allows her to be kidnapped, and follows the trail through Amsterdam and onto Lübeck, northern Germany. There, Manston is able to destroy the Limbo Line, but not before Irina is whisked away to Moscow. The picture attracted universally bad reviews, critics finding it an unwelcome reminder of the "*absurd anti-Communist films of 15 or so years ago*". Finding it terribly old-fashioned and cliché-ridden, the reviewer at *The Times* continued his attack, drily commenting that it possibly served for "*connoisseurs of something, though I would hesitate to say what*" (12 December 1968: 17). The left-wing *Morning Star* found *The Limbo Line* "*disastrously incompetent*", and towing the party line speculated that "*cold-war spy films have to be crudely made because they are based on crude ideas*" (14 December 1968); and similarly for the *Guardian*, the film was a "*grotesquely inept cold-war spy thriller*" (13 December 1968). *Monthly Film Bulletin* dismissed the picture as a "*Naïvely propagandist espionage thriller*", the reviewer bemoaning the "*Hackneyed dialogue*", the "*feeble direction*", and "*ludicrous histrionics*" of the cast. Echoing other reviewers and reflecting the new sense of political détente, the film gave the "*impression of something left over from the worst days of the Cold War*" (February 1969: 34).

The Man Outside was a further production of London Independent Producers and based on the American pulp thriller *Double Agent* (1959) by Gene Stackelberg. The story concerned the disgraced CIA agent Bill Maclean (Van Heflin) and his efforts to track down a valuable Russian defector and sell him to the Americans.[82] Murders and double-crosses complicate his task, but he is able to deliver the Russian secret policeman, expose a traitor and clear his own name into the bargain. The modest picture was released on a double-bill with the thriller *The Amsterdam Affair* (1968). Reviewers were surprisingly kind to this old-fashioned, thick-ear entertainment. *The Times* found the ingredients "*agreeably familiar*", enjoying the "*car chases through darkened London streets, nocturnal meetings down by the riverside, multiple killings in derelict warehouses and above trendy boutiques*" (6 June 1968). *Monthly Film Bulletin*, like many, admired the old-school professionalism of Van Heflin and his "*rather attractive line in tired charm that underlines his disenchantment with international intrigue*" (June 1968: 92). *Kine Weekly* endorsed it as a "*reliable action attraction*", serving as "*good entertainment without any pretence of artistic frills*" (4 May 1968), but the *Sun* dismissed it as "*very much in the tried and tested and by now tedious espionage formula*", noting its appeal to contemporary tastes in the "*obligatory close-up violence*" (7 June 1968).

Subterfuge, from an original script by David Whitaker, was something of an experimental production by Intertel (VTR Services). The company serviced the television industry and commencing in January 1968 began a series of feature films, one a month and budgeted at £200,000 each, for the Television Enterprise Corporation of America. *Subterfuge* was the first production and was completed in four weeks according to schedule. Speed was maintained through the innovative application of video assist, precluding the need to shoot extensive takes or coverage (*The Observer*, 14 January 1968). The story concerns Donovan (Gene Barry), a special agent of the Pentagon, who has been lured to London to meet a contact. Captured and tortured by enemy agents, he escapes with the help of Peter Langley (Tom Adams), a British Secret Service man. Donovan is subsequently used by Colonel Redmayne (Richard Todd), head of the Service, to track down a traitor in the British ranks and eventually he descends on Langley, who is preparing to leave the country with his young son. The American had become attached to Mrs Langley (Joan Collins), but she wearies of the subterfuge of counter-intelligence and the two go their separate ways. The film didn't make it onto cinema screens in Britain until 1971, where it was quickly passed over. *Monthly Film Bulletin* thought the picture had been manufactured by a "*computer fed on earlier spy thrillers*", and the film makes too obvious references to better films like *The Manchurian Candidate* (US, 1962) and *The Quiller Memorandum* (1966) (October 1971: 82). The parting of the potential romantic couple in the finale is yet another nod to *The Third Man*. As in *Hammerhead*, there were some trendy asides featuring mod sixties creatures and events, in this case the pop group Marmalade and a kinky London gentlemen's club.

These four films, by dint of their low budgets and modest ambitions, failed to rise above the ordinary and in most cases resembled typical 1950s B-films with their imported American leads and routine genre pre-fabrication. This was most obvious with *The Man Outside* which lacked any attempt to move the story to an exotic location and relied on simple strong-arm action. *Hammerhead* and *Subterfuge* take pains to offer a tourist view of London for international audiences who at that moment had a taste for spy films, and made ready reference to the cultural and sexual ramifications of the swinging scene. *Hammerhead* stands in closest relation to the James Bond model, but the picture squanders the opportunity offered by the novel and the character of secret agent Charles Hood and settles instead for a modest if colourful romp in a distinctly sub-Bondian fashion.

Sebastian, released in 1967, was a far better production and more creatively integrated the modish scene of the middle-1960s into its spy narrative. Like many of its contemporaries it was financed by a Hollywood studio, in this case Paramount Pictures, and co-produced by the American Herb Brodkin and Michael Powell, both of whom had been associated with the recent television drama series *Espionage* (1964).[83] The film had originally been a personal project of Powell with the working title of *Mr Sebastian* and intended for Rex Harrison; however, the machinations of Hollywood eventually left Powell with only a producer credit and direction passed over to David Greene, also a veteran of *Espionage*.[84] The picture starred Dirk Bogarde as the titular cryptologist who serves as head of the decoding centre of British Intelligence. The centre is staffed by brilliant young women with agile minds and the latest recruit is Becky Howard (Susannah York) who commences a love-hate affair with the fascinating Sebastian. Meanwhile, the centre's senior decoder, Elsa Shan (Lilli Palmer) a peace-monger, is caught betraying secrets to a left-wing politician and dismissed. The increasingly jaded Sebastian quits, drops Miss

Howard from his affections and returns to the tranquillity of academia at Oxford University. Sebastian returns temporarily to the centre as he is needed to decipher a series of confounding communications signals transmitted from a new Soviet satellite and the anxious communists lay a trap for him. Fed LSD and led to the edge of a high building, Sebastian is saved at the last minute by British security. He belatedly visits Becky, and discovers she has borne him a son. It is while playing with the infant's rattle and listening to its particular beat that the solution to the Soviet code comes to him. Becky is both infuriated and delighted at the mathematician's idiosyncratic behaviour and return.

The film was based on an idea by Leo Marks who had been a wartime cryptographer, heading the codes section of the secretive Special Operations Executive (SOE) supporting resistance agents in occupied Europe. In this role, he had observed the labours of numerous women in the task of dealing with large quantities of agent code. The experience stuck with him and re-emerged two decades later in the idea for *Sebastian*.[85] The film was released with the teasing, very sixties tagline, "*Nobody knows what he does... just that he has 100 girls to do it with!*", and part of the fascination of the film is its blend of modern and traditional.[86] The US Army jeep-driving, discotheque-dancing, fashionable Becky represents youth, fun and progressiveness; while dark suit and old school tie-wearing, umbrella-carrying Sebastian stands for maturity and respectability.[87] The contrasts are maintained through distinctions in music styles. Becky is associated with the twangy and fuzzy sounds of contemporary pop, while Sebastian listens to the elegant and structured compositions of the classical baroque. Similarly, architecture is configured to heighten modernity through depicting a London of skyscrapers, concrete and glass: a world of fashionable youth and computer-age intelligence. Alternatively, Sebastian is coupled with the dreamy spires of Oxford and lives in a faded Edwardian villa. The union of these two poles, the modern and the traditional, was a problem that Great Britain worked through in the 1960s, a decade which sought to embrace 'The White Heat of Technology'; and *Sebastian* with its trendy young women, computers, modern electronic sounds, stuffy British Intelligence, ancient university and venerable gentleman's club proposed an imaginative integration of the seemingly irreconcilable. As Rosie White has noted in a more general sense, spy series of the 1960s offered "*new accounts of the modern man and woman*", and that such representations "*engaged with fantasies and anxieties regarding individual agency, sexual liberation and class mobility*" (2007: 61). The "*mod exterior*" of the film, associated with Becky, tended to divide critics (*Films and Filming*, June 1968: 30). The *Spectator* thought *Sebastian* showed "*some real feeling for the slovenly, bleary, half-smart context of contemporary London*" (22 March 1968); while conversely the reviewer at the *Observer* complained that, "*If I have to see one more heroine taking one more reluctant hero shopping for Carnaby Street gear I shall protest with a sharp scream"* (17 March 1968). A mark of the film's up-to-dateness was the reference to the recent break out from prison by the traitor George Blake, the Soviet signals traffic relating to the escape being the first task we see the decoders take on.

Critics were inclined to find the picture undecided. "*Not quite a comedy, not exactly a human drama, not a spoof or a send-up*" reported a perplexed reviewer in *The Times* (14 March 1968). *Monthly Film Bulletin*, more certain, found the film visually interesting; but felt that the original promise was lost to a "*string of anti-heroic platitudes and a scrappily engineered conclusion*". The reviewer continued in a critical vein, disappointed that, "*ideas which begin to look interestingly enigmatic soon resolve themselves into spy thriller conventions*" (April 1968: 55). A number of critics argued for the film's seriousness. *Kine Weekly* judged *Sebastian* an "*intelligent thriller*", produced with a "*sophisticated gloss and a scientific verisimilitude*" that was most convincing (16 March 1968). The *New Statesman* saw *Sebastian* as an "*offshoot of the spy genre*"; it contended that there was a movie about "*privacy and how speedily we are destroyed when it is taken away*", as well as a witty play on the two meanings of code in the story: code in the sense of digits and morse; and code in the sense of social or moral behaviour. The question posed by the film, it maintained, is: "*can you crack the former code and still keep faith with the latter?*" (21 March 1968). Film historian Robert Murphy has also argued the seriousness of the picture, suggesting that *Sebastian*, despite the 1960s trappings, shares "*thematic concerns with the films of the le Carré school*". As he argues, "*Sebastian himself is patriotic but weary and disillusioned*"; just like John le Carré's Leamas, Avery and Dobbs [Smiley], he is "*acutely conscious of the emotional damage caused by a lifetime's devotion to espionage*" (1992: 232). These opposing views simply confirm that *Sebastian* is a film of two styles, the hip and the traditional, and therefore intriguingly straddled the two dominant schools of spy fiction in the period, that of the spy thriller and the espionage story.

The quality end of the spy thriller was maintained in *A Dandy in Aspic*, adapted from the début novel of Derek Marlowe first published in 1966. Two years later the book was filmed by Columbia Pictures in Europe from a screenplay by Marlowe and released with the teasing tagline, "*A Double Agent Ordered to Kill... Himself!*" In the story, Alexander Eberlin is the KGB mole Krasnevin working in British Intelligence who serves his masters as an assassin, having recently eliminated three British agents. Eberlin, tired of the imposture, is refused permission to return home, and is shocked to be given a new assignment by the British: to identify the Russian assassin Krasnevin and kill him! The action swings from London to Berlin, and Eberlin's frustration is turned to anxiety when he is suspected by Gatiss, a ruthless British counter-espionage officer. Eberlin and the Soviets are finally dismayed when it is re-vealed that British Intelligence knew he was the assassin all along: that Eber-lin had been used so that the British could identify and break up important KGB networks in London and Berlin. Eberlin is returned to Great Britain where he is killed in a car crash, an outcome prefigured in the story.[88]

The début novel, allegedly written in only four weeks while Marlowe worked as a clerk with National Benzole, was critically well-received and especially popular in America (*Guardian*, 23 January 1976). *The Listener* thought *A Dandy in Aspic* a "*highly meritorious spy-thriller*", and in general admired the novelist's style, "*the atrabilious wit and the poetic melancholy*" of his writing (22 June 1972). Many reviewers found the idea of a secret assassin being as-signed to eliminate himself "*intriguing*" and "*arresting*", although some found the central character "*superficial*" (*Book Week*, 30 October 1966). Eber-lin is, indeed, rather unlikable as a protagonist, although considering his fate, the novel could have been too downbeat for popular taste if he had been more agreeable. There is a rather perfunctory romance in the story and the character of the ingénue Christine is mainly there as a symbol of innocence in a world of cynicism and ruthlessness. The novel makes an interesting play on the psychology of the double-agent, the toll exacted by the ceaseless act of imposture and the manipulation of individuals by ruthless intelligence organ-isations. Marlowe assumed a classical definition of the 'dandy' for his story, explaining that it is not simply about dress, but really about self-discipline, a discipline that denies friends, sex and ostentation and therefore references the alienation of the secret agent . His character of Eberlin, he explains, "*re-tires into his own entity, a dandy in aspic, untarnished*" (*Observer*, 8 May 1966).[89]

Hollywood's Anthony Mann bought the movie rights and gambled on the unpublished novel by a complete unknown hoping for a "*new slant on the spy kick*" (*Showguide*, May 1968; Columbia press sheet, 1968). The film version of *A Dandy in Aspic*, if it is remembered at all today, is for the tragic death of the legendary filmmaker during location-shooting in Berlin. The last 10 days of filming were completed by the leading man Laurence Harvey, who, it is com-monly felt, rather ruined the potential of an interesting production. Some years later, Marlowe complained of a "*badly cast Eberlin*", of Harvey directing his own "*mis-talent*" and arrogantly changing the script, "*rather like Mona Lisa touching up the portrait while Leonardo is out of the room*".[90] Perhaps reflecting the unusual production circumstances, some found the film unde-cided, unsure "*whether it is to be the larger-than life, more or less sent-up spy thriller its gaudy style and desperately sophisticated dialogue suggest, or the downbeat, beat-up, gloomy view of secret service squalor which the story seems basically to require*" (*The Times*, 4 April 1968). The *Financial Times* complained of an "*odd fragmented quality*" (5 April 1968), and the *Spectator* of a "*corkscrew plot attached to some inertly flashy filming*" (12 April 1968). *Monthly Film Bulletin* thought that the odd, existential quality of the novel had failed to translate to the screen, the picture turning out a "*routine spy thriller*", and wondered what a filmmaker like Robert Bresson would have made of the promising material. "*All in all*", it concluded, "*a sad end to Anthony Mann's career*" (May 1968: 71).[91]

Film historian Robert Murphy dismisses *A Dandy in Aspic* as "*derivative*" and "*disappointing*", lumping it with other run-of-the-mill spy films of the latter part of the 1960s (1992: 227). *Films and Filming* complained of a "*cheerless 'entertainment'*" (July 1968: 35); Jeanine Basinger found it "*almost tragic to see the purity of Mann's style totally cheapened*" (2007: 13); although a retrospective screening of the movie claimed Mann's hand in the "*excessive use of low angles*" and the "*fondness for baroque dramatics*" in the picture (*National Film Theatre Programme Notes*, 1978: n.p.). Critics were of the view that Harvey was "*more dour than dandy*" (*Sunday Express*, 7 April 1968) and gave another of his trademark "*somnambulistic*" performances (*Observer*, 7 April 1968).

Overall, these views seem a harsh indictment of a stylised spy thriller with a gloomier quality than the norm, imaginatively photographed and designed by Christopher Challis and Carmen Dillon. The "*all-location*" movie paints an unglamorous picture of London and Berlin, where the tourist spots are merely glimpsed and sprinkled with the obligatory characters of the contemporary mod scene. Appropriately, considering that Mann was a master of Hollywood's dark cinema, the film is photographed largely as a *film noir*, and this underpins the paranoid quality of the story. In a rare good notice, the *Daily Mail* felt the picture a "*worthy technical memorial to Anthony Mann*" (5 April 1968). The film can now be enjoyed as a highly mannered spy picture of the genre's baroque period. The film opts for an ending more like the British edition of the novel, and has Gatiss confront Eberlin at the airport in Berlin, the film ending on a freeze frame as the crazed Gatiss hurls his car at Eberlin and the Russian empties his gun into the vehicle carrying his nemesis.[92] *A Dandy in Aspic*, both book and film, typical of the spy thriller in the period, make self-conscious generic allusions to other espionage narratives. The novel quips at the character of Harry Palmer in the recent film version of *The Ipcress File* (1965); while the movie has a sinister Russian dress in the manner of Harry Lime, use the cover-name of Harry, and conduct a meeting with Eberlin high above the city of Berlin in a lift, all references to the classic thriller *The Third Man*. At one point in the novel, Eberlin watches a film version of *The*

Scarlet Pimpernel, envious of the double-agent who can return home after his mission.

The spy cycle in British cinema began to wane as the 1960s drew to a close and American financing began to withdraw. *The Executioner* was an independent film production, made in Great Britain from an original story and released by Columbia Pictures in 1970. The plot concerns the British-born, American-educated secret agent John Shay (George Peppard), who, following the rolling up of his networks in Czechoslovakia, must, with grim determination, confront treachery at the heart of British Intelligence. There follows a near bewildering series of convoluted twists involving duplicitous colleagues, double-agents, marital deceits, threats, a capture by the KGB and bloody killings. It eventually transpires that Shay has stumbled into a long-term British deception operation against the Soviets. The tourist and action codes of the narrative are effectively captured in the tagline, "*From London... to Athens... to the island of Corfu... Everyday he lives, somebody else dies*".

The Executioner is stylishly directed by Sam Wanamaker, with teasing flashbacks, slow motion, and *noir*-like compositions.[93] The action ranges across England, Vienna, Istanbul and Athens. The film is at pains to make the contrast between the brash American, individualist outsider, as "*English as a Hamburger*" is the way he describes himself, with the closed ranks of the clubby English establishment. There is much play with the English gentlemen's notion of espionage as a game, with overt references to such definingly English activities as cricket and snooker, as well as the more universal symbol of chess as intrigue. In exasperation to all this, Shay bursts out: "*It's all a game – it doesn't matter which side wins, as long as it's fun to watch. Well it matters to some*". The snooty Intelligence hierarchy was played by the resoundingly English quartet of actors Keith Michell, Nigel Patrick, Charles Gray and George Baker.

More than one reviewer found the picture "*bewildering*" (*Daily Mail*, 26 June 1970; *Daily Express*, 30 June 1970). The *Evening News* judged it "*fairly tame cloak-and-dagger stuff*" and the *Sun* complained that, "*The suspense is like soggy plastic*" (both 25 June 1970); the *Morning Star* dismissed the film as "*dreary, cold-war, double-double agent routine*" (27 June 1970) and the *Observer* pronounced the script and direction as "*pretentious*" (28 June 1970). There was some comment on the violence in *The Executioner*, the film starting and finishing with a "*staccato blood bath*" (*Daily Mirror*, 26 June 1970). Initially, released with an 'A'-certificate, the picture was re-classified the following month with the new category of an 'AA'-certificate, and restricted to audiences of 14 and over.

The Executioner, though, is perhaps unjustly forgotten, a spy film of perceptible style, wit and tension. In a more favourable review in the *Daily Mail*, it was promoted to readers as one of those *"thickly plotted, fast moving melo-dramas, oozing menace"* (26 June 1970). *Monthly Film Bulletin* discerned some effort to cast a satirical eye over the 'old school tie' world of the British secret services and to test the ethical complexities of modern espionage; however, for the reviewer, the film ultimately *"does not escape from the well-worn shallow groove in which the contemporary spy thriller is in danger of becoming stuck"* (August 1970: 155).

The view that the spy film was becoming stale was increasingly being voiced by critics and the production of spy thrillers in the British cinema began to slow from the turn of the 1970s onwards. This was evident when two pictures which aimed to create popular series characters failed to find much enthusiasm with audiences. In the autumn of 1969, it was announced that *When Eight Bells Toll*, then on a six-week location on the Isle of Mull, would be the first in a continuing series featuring the Treasury agent Philip Calvert (*Kine Weekly*, 20 September and 1 November).[94] The film appeared in April 1971, adapted by the hugely successful thriller writer Alistair MacLean from his own novel, and produced by Jerry Gershwin and Elliot Kastner who had previously enjoyed great success with an adaptation of MacLean's wartime spy romp *Where Eagles Dare* (1969). *When Eight Bells Toll* is an adventure story dealing with skulduggery on the high seas. A number of ships carrying bullion have been hi-jacked in the Irish Sea and Calvert (Anthony Hopkins untypically cast in an action thriller and described in one review as a *"desexed, ungadgeted Bond"*, *Guardian*, 11 March 1971), working undercover as a marine biologist, is on the trail of the criminal gang in the area of the Western Isles of Scotland. There is plenty of action as the agent closes in on the modern day pirates, including a thrilling underwater fight, a machine gun attack on a helicopter, and a final gun battle in the subterranean boathouse of a Scottish castle. In the manner of Len Deighton, the story attends to the class antagonism between the *"north of England grammar school boy"* Calvert and his superior Sir Arthur Arnford-Jason, K.C.B. (Robert Morley). The latter complains of the former as a *"hopeless fellow, comes of not going to a proper school"*, and is appalled when the agent tries to implicate the eminent Sir Anthony Skouras (Jack Hawkins) in the conspiracy, a member of Sir Arthur's own gentlemen's club: *"on the wine committee"* no less. The conflict eventually softens, though, once the two men find themselves on a mission together, the man of action in tow with the Whitehall bureaucrat, where the differences can be played for fun.

Accepting the picture as a *"Bond-derived piece of hokum"*, the critic at the *Observer* correctly judged the boy's own quality of the production, absent-mindedly finding himself feeling in his pocket *"to see if my best conker was still there"* (7 March 1971). Reviewers were divided over the charms of such an old-fashioned, swashbuckling action picture. The *Daily Mirror* warmed to the "*punch-a-minute adventure mystery*" (5 March 1971) and *Kine Weekly* judged it a "*useful toughie for wide exhibition*" (6 March 1971); while conversely the *Daily Express* considered it "*desperately short of other essential elements like surprise, ingenuity, characterisation and interesting dialogue*" (8 March 1971). *Films and Filming* predictably passed over the picture as a "*time-passing jape*" (May 1971: 94), while *Monthly Film Bulletin* felt the "*tested clichés look quite fleshy in a setting and climate that manage to be both appropriately inhospitable and recognisably human*" (October 1971: 85).

In the finale of the film, and a change from the original novel, Calvert exposes the newly installed Mrs Skouras (Nathalie Delon in her first English-speaking film) as a plant of the criminals. However, the two have formed an attraction and he allows the mercenary villainess to escape with a single bar of gold, confirming the agent's attractive insubordination and leaving him unentangled for further adventures in a tentatively planned series. However, Gershwin and Kastner failed to repeat their success with MacLean on this occasion and no further Philip Calvert adventures materialised.[95]

Another series of secret agent adventures was planned by Sagittarius Productions around John Craig, hero of four espionage thrillers written by James Munro, with the author providing the screenplays (*Kine Weekly*, 2 January 1971).[96] Craig made his single film appearance in *Innocent Bystanders* (1972) as a seemingly washed up agent played by Stanley Baker. He is required to locate and apprehend Kaplan, a Soviet scientist in hiding: a man also wanted by the Soviets and the Americans. Craig also has to contend with two younger British agents who have been pitted against him by the devious intelligence chief Loomis (Donald Pleasance). The search takes Craig from London to New York to Turkey and it slowly dawns on the veteran agent that he is considered dispensable. He eventually locates Kaplan and delightedly sells him to Loomis for £100,000 on the condition that the agent returns to London. The chief vengefully attempts to have Craig arrested for theft, but the skilful agent, in an ending changed from the original novel, has taken an alternative flight to Beirut and disappears. The film was directed by the maverick talent of Peter Collinson and was slick, stylish and violent.[97] The picture gets off to an exciting start as the titles unfold over an exciting night-time breakout from a Soviet labour camp. The emphasis is on the eccentric in the opening scene of the British and American intelligence chiefs discussing the possibility of acquiring Kaplan, set over a bizarre dinner in Loomis's club and a brisk walk around a modernist London, shot using dramatic compositions and a fish-eye lens. This is punctuated with jolting snatches of Craig and fellow female agent Benson (Sue Lloyd) energetically blasting away at targets. Collinson maintains visual and dramatic interest in the scenes set in London and New

York, using metropolitan architecture, steel and glass, long echoing corridors, and low camera angles to build a sense of corporate menace, not unlike the contemporary conspiracy thrillers coming to prominence in the New Hollywood such as *The Anderson Tapes* (US, 1971) and *The Parallax View* (US, 1974). Unfortunately, Collinson seems to lose interest with the switch of location to Turkey and the picture flattens to become a routine adventure drama. *Monthly Film Bulletin*, while seemingly pleased that Collinson had abandoned his *"stylistic excesses"*, considered the picture merely a *"late afterthought to the Bond cycle"* (November 1972: 235), while other critics commented on the dark tone of this spy thriller and baulked at what was thought to be excessive violence. *The Guardian* was not impressed by the *"gratuitous nastiness"* and asked, *"if we have a censor, what the hell is he doing passing it?"* (12 October 1972).[98] *The Observer* was struck by the picture's resemblance to the early James Bond formula of the Ian Fleming novels, and as such *"good heartless stuff"*. Preparing to recommend the film as *"perfectly acceptable escapist rubbish"*, the reviewer was ultimately put off by a *"couple of extremely nasty and totally gratuitous sadistic sequences"* (15 October 1972).[99] There were no further cinematic adventures of agent John Craig.

In a now admittedly thinning market, one of the most accomplished of the spy thrillers in the 1970s was John Huston's *The Mackintosh Man* (1973), adapted from the popular thriller *The Freedom Trap* (1971) by Desmond Bagley and released by Warner Bros. The picture was put together by star Paul Newman, director John Huston and producer John Foreman who had previously collaborated on *The Life and Times of Judge Roy Bean* (US, 1971).The story involved the mission to penetrate a secret organisation, the Scarperers, which arranges prison escapes for a price. Joseph Rearden (Newman) is provided with a conviction and committed to Chelmsford Gaol. There he is contacted by a representative of the Scarperers and plans are made to break him out along with a notorious spy, Slade (Ian Bannen).[100] The scheme is the brainchild of Angus Mackintosh (Harry Andrews), a government security officer, and his aide Mrs Smith (Dominique Sanda). Mackintosh is ultimately after Sir George Wheeler (James Mason), a pillar of the Establishment, who he believes is behind the escapes. While Rearden is holed up in a safe house in Ireland, Mackintosh provocatively lets Wheeler know he has a man on the inside. Rearden is now compromised and narrowly escapes with his life. Meanwhile, Wheeler arranges the killing of Mackintosh by a hit a run incident. There follows a series of adventures as Rearden eludes the enemy agents and fixes on the trail of Wheeler. The finale comes in Malta, where Wheeler has taken Slade to pass over to Soviet agents. Rearden confronts the two men in a church and Wheeler is informed that Mackintosh had arranged for the facts to be laid before the prime minister in the event of his death. The three men, in an act of professional solidarity, agree to go their separate ways,

Rearden back to freedom, and Wheeler and Slade onto Soviet Russia. However, Mrs Smith, recently revealed as Mackintosh's daughter, intervenes and shoots dead Wheeler and Slade. She walks away from Rearden in the manner of *The Third Man* and what had seemed a promising relationship.

The film was made with considerable expertise and thoughtfulness.[101] The presentation is downbeat, the colour palette deliberately muted in the expert cinematography of Oswald Morris, the dominant colours being browns and greys, the mise-en-scene is kept ordinary, even unattractive, and offered a *"perfect visual equivalent to the world of subterraneous half-tones in which Huston's characters move"* (*Financial Times*, 9 November 1973). The picture's studied approach and engagement with the ethics of intrigue and the reasons that can lead intelligent men like Slade and Wheeler to treason could make it fit for consideration as a more serious espionage drama. However, the story is ultimately characterised by adventure as Rearden is rapidly taken through the stages of violent robbery, arrest, incarceration in prison, and exciting breakout, before it settles, essentially, into a thrilling man on the run drama. At this point, *The Mackintosh Man* owes a debt to John Buchan and Alfred Hitchcock and the traditions of the classic spy story, involving as it does a 'double-chase', wherein the fugitive is wanted by both the police and the enemy agents, and consequently has only his own resources to pull himself out of the mess and confront the conspiracy.[102] The film only departs substantially from the novel in its ending. The book is more conventional, and has Rearden, now revealed as the agent Owen Stannard, unswerving in his pursuit of Wheeler and Slade, killing both by ramming a launch into Wheeler's yacht moored in harbour in Malta. In an ending more in keeping with *Casablanca* (US, 1943) than *The Third Man*, Stannard and Mrs Smith head off to Morocco and the possibility of a romantic relationship. The film, thus, shifts the finale, with its rhetoric of professional camaraderie and anti-romance, towards the ground usually occupied by the serious espionage drama.

The general critical view was that this was not vintage Huston, and that the picture, like the director's earlier spy thriller *The Kremlin Letter* (US, 1971), failed to *"achieve that cold-hearted relish which gives even lesser Hitchcock its compulsive hold on an audience"* (*Observer*, 11 November 1973). The *Sunday Times* rhetorically pondered: *"who on earth directed this enigmatic series of bashings and chases?"* (11 November 1973); *Time Magazine* found it *"terribly redundant"*, claiming that: *"It seems to have been prematurely disinterred from a time capsule devoted to the cultural artifacts of the 1960s when spies were coming in out of the cold war's shadows to warm themselves in the world's moviehouses"* (27 August 1973); the *Guardian* dismissed it as *"bloodless"* (8 November 1973); and the *Village Voice* believed the picture failed to *"commit itself either to the thrills and chills or to the moral puzzles and paradoxes im-*

plicit in his material" (4 October 1973). Other critics were more loyal to the director of such classic thrillers as *The Maltese Falcon* (US, 1941), *The Times* alluding to *"a quality, not assertive but unmistakable, which sets it apart from the rest because John Huston made it"* (9 November 1973). *New Society* applauded a *"neat, quick, mild spy movie"* (29 November 1973), and *Monthly Film Bulletin* made a flattering comparison with Graham Greene, claiming the film continued the director's *"exploration of the ethics of international espionage"*, praising it as an *"intriguing, enjoyable 'entertainment'"*, and finding the picture a *"highly professional"* production, from a *"film-maker obsessed by the quirks and hazards of an enclosed, underground world where everyone seems to be playing a double game"* (December 1973: 252).

Other veteran Hollywood professionals who tried to revive the ailing British spy thriller were Don Siegel and Blake Edwards. Siegel's *The Black Windmill* (1974) was a major American production, produced in Britain by the Zanuck-Brown company for release by Universal. The film was adapted from the British spy novel *Seven Days to a Killing* by Clive Egleton published in 1973, was set in Britain and France, and dealt with a British intelligence operation. The story concerns spycatcher Major John Tarrant (Michael Caine), an agent of the Department of Subversive Warfare, a sub-section of MI6, who steals a large quantity of diamonds intended for use against an arms ring supported by the KGB to pay the ransom on his kidnapped son. He is outsmarted by the criminals, relieved of the jewels and arrested for the theft. The gang, headed by a character called Drabble (John Vernon), engineers his escape while he is being transported back to Britain, with the intention of silencing him for good. However, Tarrant eludes the killers during a night-time chase through Paris and tracks down the gang to a deserted windmill in the south of England, where he is able to rescue his son and expose the traitor at the top, Sir Edward Julyan (Joseph O'Conor). The action stuff is bounced against a family melodrama in which Tarrant deals with a disintegrating marriage.

The picture was a problematic shoot for Siegel. Preparations were wrecked by a scriptwriters strike in America, he found the British special effects technicians and stuntmen lacking in expertise, and the filmmaker believed he only ever received lukewarm support from the Hollywood studio. He felt lumbered, for example, with the release title of *The Black Windmill*, which he found meaningless as the dénouement of the picture unfolds at distinctive 'twin' windmills, neither of which is black. The film received little 'push' from the distributor and Siegel ended his relationship with Universal.[103]

The common critical response was to suggest that Siegel, a director with a minor reputation as an auteur, had failed, in his handling of the lone-wolf secret service agent, to match the usual flair with which he had recently treated maverick cops and criminals in his American-made *Madigan* (US, 1968),

Dirty Harry (US, 1971) and *Charley Varrick* (US, 1972). A consequence, it was believed, of the director working in an alien environment and captured in the review in the *Observer* which claimed that, "*Away from home Siegel has goofed*" (21 July 1974). The *Sunday Times* found the picture "*not smart enough, fast enough, ingenious enough*", and as a result "*the film sinks into the slightly-above-routine class*". The review concluded that: "*Perhaps Don Siegel, ferociously effective in the vast labyrinth of American crime, hasn't got the measure of our home-grown, tight-lipped, small-scale horrors*" (21 July 1974). The resulting film according to *The Times* was an alarming demonstration of what can happen to an artist in an alien atmosphere, both "*turgid and undistinguished*" and a "*rambling, inconsequential, predictable tall story of corruption in British intelligence*" (19 July 1974). A "*distressingly somnolent thriller*" was how the *Financial Times* viewed it (19 July 1974); while *Monthly Film Bulletin* which had hoped that Siegel might be able to turn a "*revitalising trick*" with the espionage thriller found it all in a too "*familiar groove*" (August 1974: 168). The *Daily Mirror* was intrigued by the emotional aspect of the drama, wherein the estranged Tarrant is brought back into the bosom of the family where he must console his agonising wife (Janet Suzman). This interestingly contrasted with the self-contained individualist archetype of James Bond and the paper observed that, "*Today spies have a wife in the suburbs, and worry about their mortgages and pension schemes*" (19 July 1974).[104]

Blake Edward's *The Tamarind Seed* was a glossy Anglo-American production of 1974 adapted from the recent novel by Evelyn Anthony. The story, which shuttles between London, Paris and Barbados, dealt with Soviet Intelligence officer Sverdlov (Omar Sharif) and his wooing of English secretary Farrow (Julie Andrews) who happens to have access to state secrets. British counter-espionage is quickly onto the affair and aims to nip in the bud a damaging security scandal. It soon turns out that the romance is genuine and Sverdlov offers to defect as his own situation at the Paris Embassy is precarious. A brilliant operation by British Intelligence nets the Russian and exposes a top level Soviet agent in the British Embassy in Paris ‑ a former Cambridge man, and, true to form, queer. Sverdlov and Farrow retreat to happy exile in Canada.

The Tamarind Seed was very much a romance masquerading as a spy thriller. A title sequence of silhouetted bodies paraded against a background of primary colours designed by Maurice Binder and theme music by John Barry signalled the appropriate generic territory, before the picture settled back to languish in its formula romance and off-the-peg exotic locations. *The Times* felt that the "*nice possibilities for intrigue and adventure*" were "*handicapped by a heavily over-written script*" and by the "*difficulties of believing in either an aging, mannered Omar Sharif as an irresistible charmer, or cucumber-cool Mary Poppins (alias Julie Andrews) with her Jessie Matthews diction*" (23 August 1974). Other reviews, in fact, preferred to pontificate on the enigma of Julie Andrews, for which this was a comeback picture and a conscious effort to position her in a more mature role (*Guardian*, 22 August 1974; *Observer*, 25 August 1974). The espionage story in such a context was largely perceived as routine and superfluous. In this sense, *Monthly Film Bulletin* felt that *The Tamarind Seed* was akin to Alfred Hitchcock's failed espionage picture *Topaz* (US, 1969), with both directors unable to prevent the conventions of the international spy saga, with its predictable subterfuges and double-crosses, "*from trivialising their respective approaches to the general theme of people not being quite what they seem*" (1 January 1974: 41).

The *Black Windmill* and *The Tamarind Seed* signalled a partial shift in direction for the spy thriller. As has been argued, the prerequisites of spy fiction required the movement away from the domestic environment into the realm of the daring and the alien. Here, however, there was greater emphasis on the agent's domestic arrangements, obligations and stresses. These were also the subject of the short *The Spy's Wife* (1971), something more original and idiosyncratic than many of the secret agent features coming into circulation at the time. A featurette released as support to the private eye pastiche *Gumshoe* (1971), the film was co-scripted and directed by Gerry O'Hara and produced in only a week at the cost of £11,000. The brief story plays with and overturns conventions of the spy thriller. The husband's (Tom Bell) profession of spying is accepted in a matter of fact fashion by his wife (Dorthy Tutin). When he leaves for a mission a mysterious stranger (Vladek Sheybal) arrives at their flat and at the urging of the wife he searches for bugs. Meanwhile, the husband bypasses the airport and heads on to the apartment of a beautiful woman (Ann Lynn). Before too long, each couple is in bed together, the two men being shown discretely turning face down the photograph of the other man. *Monthly Film Bulletin* found *The Spy's Wife* a "*formal and rather disappointing exercise*", and that the enigma of whether or not the husband is or is not a spy "*quickly loses its appeal*" (January 1972: 39). More recently, Vic Pratt has been kinder, finding the film a "*surprisingly elaborate and complex piece*", with an "*ambitious range of ideas and characters ... crammed into its half hour running time*" (2009: 17).

Three further quirky spy thrillers appeared in 1973, but quickly disappeared and are now long-forgotten. Peter Crane's *Assassin* (1973), from an original script by Michael Sloan, was released by Columbia-Warner and starred Ian Hendry as a freelance hitman hired by MI5 to liquidate a traitor in the Air Ministry. The film is concerned with the assassin's disillusionment and the story spends time with the character's brooding over a previous assignment which went tragically wrong and the brief time he spends with an equally lonely girl he meets in a pub. Late in the day it transpires that British Intelligence has made a mistake and fingered the wrong official. It is therefore necessary to remove the assassin (he is only known as such in the film), but before he can be eliminated by regular officers of MI5, he is killed in a hit and run accident. Too late, it is discovered that the assassin works with a back-up operative and the original contract is completed. The bleak story was filmed in a highly mannered fashion of extreme angles and distorted images, which failed to impress at the *Monthly Film Bulletin* as anything more than "*nudging obviousness*". Overall, it found the picture "*depressingly like an episode from one of those spy and secret agent series which seem to pour non-stop off the assembly line on to the television screen*" (January 1974: 3). *Yellow Dog* was produced and directed by the eminent stills photographer Terence Donovan. He claimed a fascination with Japanese culture and cinema, and commissioned a screenplay from Shinobu Hashimoto, the writer who had previously scripted the classics *Rashomon* (Japan, 1950) and *The Seven Samurai* (Japan, 1954). The film featured the eccentric adventures of a Japanese agent (Jirô Tamiya) in London who is under orders to protect a scientist who will shortly be visiting Japan. Donovan claimed new methods of presentation and style for his picture, drawn from Japanese culture, and the production seemingly had some art cinema ambitions. However, critics were largely confounded. *The Telegraph* complained of "*total incomprehensibility*" (9 November 1973), and the *Spectator* that the "*coincidences and absurdities multiply, and the plot thickens to the consistency of wet concrete*" (17 November 1973). Reviewers predictably judged *Yellow Dog* "*inscrutable*" and deplored the slow-motion violence. The *Monthly Film Bulletin* summed the whole up as "*glossy, camp, violent and needlessly incoherent*", acknowledged the picture as a curiosity and wondered if something had been lost in translation (October 1973, 215).[105] *Who?* was adapted from a celebrated American science-fiction novel of 1958 by Algis Budrys. Although stripping back the more extreme futuristic elements of the setting, the film version of *Who?* still comes across as a spy-fi story, dealing with a key American scientist Lucas Martino (Joseph Bova) who has been reconstructed by the Soviets after a car crash and returned to the West where FBI agent Sean Rogers (Elliot Gould) must find out who is behind the iron mask before the scientist can be returned to the top secret Neptune project. The picture was filmed entirely on location in Germany and Miami, USA, and directed by Jack Gold. Although a British production, the film with its characters, casting and setting feels American. Produced at British Lion at the time the company was going through convulsions in the board room, *Who?* was one of a small group of pictures "*undertaken with the hope of a profit due to pre-production tax arrangements or else simply to keep facilities ticking over*", and had to wait for its airing on television in 1976 and only made a belated showing in British cinemas in 1979 before disappearing to video and such exploitation titles as *Robo Man* and *The Man with the Steel*

Mask (Walker 1986a: 125-6). Gold claimed a philosophical meaning for his drama, a story *"about a search for identity in an East-West spy framework"*, and a broader humanitarian theme about *"two nutcrackers squeezing the individual in the middle"* (Madden and Wilson 1974: 137). The review in *Monthly Film Bulletin* judged the film a *"not inconsiderable epilogue"* to the company if one made allowances for haste, penny-pinching and lapses in continuity. However, the critic disagreed with Gold, believing the adaptation promoted the detective aspects of the story, throwing in a car chase for excitement, and concluded that like Martino, the film *"survives as a patchwork of disparate material for which nobody, sadly, could find much use"* (January 1979: 13).[106]

The dwindling market for secret agent films was partly filled by exploitation film-maker Lindsay Shonteff who returned to the fray of the low budget spy picture in the 1970s. Super agent Charles Bind featured in *No. 1 of the Secret Service* (1977, sometimes known as *Her Majesty's Top Gun*) starring Nicky Henson, *Licensed to Love and Kill* (1979, sometimes known as *The Man from S.E.X.*) starring Gareth Hunt, and *Number One Gun* (1990) starring Michael Howe. These were in the debt of the more playful Roger Moore James Bond films, and provided plenty of thrills, violence and sexual suggestiveness. While acknowledging the *"breathless verve"* of the first of these pictures, *Monthly Film Bulletin* still drew back from an *"over-exploited"* genre (June 1978: 117). The films were popular with less-discerning audiences, and in the markets of the Far East.

The series of spy thrillers which came in the wake of the tremendous success of James Bond eventually began to bore reviewers. Cheap and cheerful imitations like *Licensed to Kill* were tolerated for a while, but it was not an approach to film-making that was likely to impress the critics. Some better films were made in the tradition of the professional secret agent, a leading example being John Huston's *The Mackintosh Man*; however, as is the way with cinema genres, the style began to wane in popularity and such films began to appear only irregularly from the mid-1970s onwards. By 1980, the *Evening News* was lamenting the genre. *"Pity the poor celluloid spy!"* it exclaimed: *"Diluted by overkill at the box office, cheapened by poor imitations, he is fast becoming a shadow of his former intriguing, entertaining self"* (31 January 1980). In contrast, the Bond series was able to continually reinvent itself, mainly through recasting the iconic role of the master secret agent, with Roger Moore in 1973, less successfully with Timothy Dalton in 1987, and more robustly again with Pierce Brosnan in 1995.

In his obituary of Ian Fleming, Maurice Richardson had found the prospect of a Bondless future as *"bleak"*. He feared the rush of imitations, *"most of which are certain to be as intolerably inferior as old rope to finest Persian hash-*

ish" (1964). In the view of many British film critics, the pessimistic prediction was largely borne out and thankfully for them the life cycle of the spy thriller began to draw to a close in the 1980s.

In the wake of the popularity of James Bond there had developed a cycle of 'Eurospy' films, often comic-book in approach and usually financed by some combination of French, Italian, West German and Spanish funding.[107] The popular appetite for spy thrillers was such that the trade paper *Variety* reported early in 1965 that the European film capitals were overrun with American television distributors, *"all of them riding what they think is going to be the James Bond cycle"*. The stampede was on for inexpensive product, with Hollywood screen executives hitting *"the international intrigue trail that's festooned with sport cars, deadly weapons of the future, sexy broads and the focal heroes with a sense of humor, a tuxedo, a tender talent for love making and a lethal talent in Karate"* (27 January). Such films as *Agent 077: Mission Bloody Mary* (Italy/Spain/France, 1965), *Kiss Kiss ... Bang Bang* (Italy/Spain1966) and *OSS 117 - Double Agent* (Italy/France, 1968) were popular on the Continent for a while, and available for cheap distribution in the United States, but failed to endear themselves to the critics.[108] The influence of this Continental production trend was felt in the British cinema mainly in the importation of 'European' starlets like Elke Sommer, Daliah Lavi, Sylva Koscina, Camilla Sparv and Marisa Mell to provide glamour for home-grown spy thrillers. The co-productions *The Serpent* (France/Italy/West Germany, 1973) and *Permission to Kill* (Austria/US, 1975) were more serious in intent with espionage plots centred on defectors and treachery, and featured respected English-speaking actors such as Henry Fonda, Yul Bryner and Dirk Bogarde in the former, and Dirk Bogarde and Ava Gardner in the latter. *Permission to Kill* was directed by Cyril Frankel, scripted by Robin Estridge, photographed by Freddie Young and with music by Richard Rodney Bennett, and so could claim a degree of Britishness by dint of creative input. However, as with the general run of European co-productions, the effort to appeal to disparate markets tended to result in pictures that largely failed to impress anyone. *Permission to Kill*, which dealt with a defector who decides to return to his own country to assassinate the communist dictator, a ruthless Western intelligence's attempts to stop him, and filmed largely in Austria, was dismissed as a *"pretentious political mishmash"* at *Monthly Film Bulletin* (December 1975: 266).

Catch Me a Spy (1972) from the novel by George Marton and Tibor Meray, was an Anglo-American-French co-production and wasted the talents of stars Kirk Douglas, Trevor Howard and Tom Courtney.[109] The picture, filmed on location in Scotland and London, was a light-hearted treatment of East-West spy exchanges which had been in the news since the previous decade, and the convoluted story involved couriers, microfilm, deception and double-agents.

Purportedly a "*sophisticated comedy-thriller*" (*Kine Weekly*, 10 April 1970), the picture failed to impress most critics with its intelligence, wit or excitement. The *Evening News* complained of an "*unbelievably inept story*" (27 October 1971); the *Birmingham Post* of a "*horrendous attempt at a comedy spy film*"; while the *Observer*, wondered: "*How this wooden, cliché-ridden Dick Clement film ever reached the screen*" (both 27 February 1972). Tom Courtney, playing a dim filing clerk pressed into secret service, reprised his role of the 'reluctant spy', which he had essayed to far greater effect in Clement's earlier *Otley* (1969).[110]

Enigma (1983) was a British-French co-production, directed by Jeannot Szwarc and with the cosmopolitan cast of American Martin Sheen, the French Brigitte Fossey and Michael Lonsdale, New Zealander Sam Neill and the English Derek Jacobi and Frank Finlay. The story dealt with an East German defector (Sheen) who is reluctantly recruited to the CIA to return to the DDR to foil a KGB plot to murder five prominent Soviet dissidents in the West. On arrival in East Berlin he discovers that the mission is already compromised and he is ruthlessly hunted by a top KGB agent (Neill) as he tries to fulfil the operation helped by his former girlfriend (Fossey). *Monthly Film Bulletin* suggested that the "*true puzzle of* Enigma *was how so many talented people got mixed up in it*", and squirmed as "*every cliché of the spy cycle*" was served up (March 1983: 68). Actors Sam Neill, Derek Jacobi and Frank Finlay made more substantial contributions to the British spy drama elsewhere, and with its American and French stars, and complete lack of home characters, the film had little discernible connection to Britain and British national identity.

The wholly British *The Jigsaw Man* was a sad and troubled spy picture based on a novel by Dorothea Bennett first published in 1977. A prologue introduces Philip Kimberly, a dissolute British traitor-spy who has outworn the patience of his Russian hosts. His obituary is printed in Moscow, he is forcibly subjected to plastic surgery and instructed to return to England under guard where he will retrieve the secret portfolio he hid a decade before which gives the names of Western agents in the pay of the Soviets. Aware that it is only the insurance provided by the sensitive documents that has kept him alive, he breaks free in London and arranges, under the cover of a Russian diplomat, to sell the portfolio to British Intelligence and passage to safety. In the ensuing days, Kimberly is wounded, contacts his daughter who helps him, and is pursued by both Russian and British Intelligence. The final exchange at Woburn Abbey Park, a centre of wartime intelligence, between Kimberly and Commander Scaith the Head of the SIS, is disrupted by a British traitor, Sir James Chorley, the deputy head of the Service and the long-term mole code-name Earthworm, who must not allow the incendiary documents to fall into Western hands. Chorley is killed and Kimberly hospitalised. In an epilogue, Kimberly and Scaith, the latter now retired with honours, enjoy a leisurely debriefing in a castle in Scotland, fantasising about secret operations they could enact.

The Jigsaw Man was a routine spy thriller, made interesting by its obvious allusions to the traitor-spy Kim Philby. With what is presumably irony, the novel is dedicated to a list of traitors including H. A. R. Philby, Guy Burgess, Donald Maclean, George Blake, John Vassall, *"all those not yet surfaced"*, and to *"My dear friends in the KGB"*. A number of biographical details are given for Kimberly that readily suggests the parallel with Philby, a defection in 1963, a specialist in Soviet affairs and intelligence, and a magnetic and charismatic personality. Historical individuals such as Guy Burgess and Maurice Buckmaster of the wartime SOE are referenced as part of the Kimberly legend to enhance the supposed realism of the story.

Dorothea Bennett was the wife of film director Terence Young, and it was Young who directed the film version released in 1984, scripted by Jo Eisinger, starring Michael Caine as Kimberley and shot on locations in Helsinki and around London. It was an ill-fated production which commenced in March 1982, ran out of money some-way through shooting, was abandoned by its principal actors, only rescued when international businessman Mahmud Sipra stepped in early in 1983 with $5 million, and did not make it to screens until 1984 (*Daily Mail*, 20 May 1982; *Evening Standard*, 11 June and 8 October 1982; *Variety*, 16 June 1982; *Daily Express*, 5 January 1983). The movie made even more references to the long tradition of treachery in Great Britain, somewhat undermines the book's careful allusions to Philby through mentioning the notorious double-agent in a list of other traitor-spies, and elevates Kimberley to a former Director-General of the British Secret Intelligence Service who defected in 1974. *The Jigsaw Man* has to be counted a disappointment considering the proven talent in its production. Terence Young and second unit director Peter Hunt were veterans of the James Bond films, Michael Caine an old hand at spy movies, Freddie Francis a leading cinematographer, and the supporting cast of Laurence Olivier, Robert Powell and Susan George was strong. However, the film was poorly reviewed. Harlan Kennedy wrote in *Film Comment* that the film *"reminds us how incredibly innocent and insular Britain can be when addressing the topic of spies and traitors"* and dismissed it as a *"loony throwback to the old 'DropgunorIkeelyou' days of spy movies"* (1984: 12). *The Voice* in America wrote of a *"senile, John le Carré-style espionage thriller"* with *"more flabby exposition than a month in the House of Lords"*, and dismissed the picture as *"probably the most garrulous and doddering spy movie ever made"* (28 August 1984).[111]

The last substantial entry to the cycle of spy thrillers in the British cinema in the period of the Cold War came in 1987 with *The Fourth Protocol*. The original best-selling novel by Frederick Forsyth had been published in 1984, had sold seven million copies, and was criticised for its right-wing posturing and failure to rise above the *"excitements of a boys' yarn"* (*Guardian*, 20 September 1984). Unhappy with recent screen adaptations of his stories, Forsyth formed a production company with film star and *"old mate"* Michael Caine to produce a movie version of his novel (*Evening Standard*, 12 December 1984; *Daily Mail*, 13 March 1985). Unable to get the Hollywood majors interested in a story which involved terrorism, financing was secured from the Arab businessman Wafic Said.[112] Forsyth said of his story: *"It is about raw power, cynicism in high places, loyalty and betrayal, the ever-shifting game plans of espionage, deception and deliberate disinformation, tacit deals and the expendability of underlings"* (*The Fourth Protocol* press sheet). Claiming that spying was changing on screen, Caine described *The Fourth Protocol* as dealing with the *"reality of treason and espionage"*: *"First of all it was mysterious, then dangerous. With the Bonds it became a game. And now it is so insidious, it is almost like radiation. It is happening, but you don't know: the treachery is ingrown"* (quoted in the *Daily Mail*, 22 July 1986). Forsyth, celebrated for his meticulous research, claimed that he got inside information from a serving MI5 officer and from a former KGB colonel who had defected (*Daily Mail*, 27 July 1986). Hollywood's George Axelrod and John Frankenheimer had originally been approached to write and direct the film; but in the event the screenplay was completed by Forsyth (with additional material by Richard Burridge) and the picture was directed with considerable technical polish by John Mackenzie (*Evening Standard*, 12 December 1984; *Daily Mail*, 13 March 1985). The film was shot on locations in northern Finland, Milton Keynes and around London.

The movie version reduced the book's explicit political angle, which had a Soviet plot, partly engineered by defector Kim Philby, aimed at the replacement of the Thatcher government by a Labour Party led by Neil Kinnock, which in turn would be quickly discredited and superseded by a hard left regime.[113] The story here concentrated instead on the action that was supposed to achieve the political coup, the explosion of a small nuclear device on an American airbase in Britain, which would lead to a forced withdrawal of the American military from Europe and deliver a death blow to the Western military alliance. Forsyth pithily described the resulting film thriller as a *"story about two men and a bomb"* (quoted in *Films and Filming*, December 1986: 18).[114] The secret plot was the brainchild of the reactionary Chairman of the KGB and designed to put an end to the disturbing trend of *glasnost*. The conspiracy is slowly pieced together by the maverick counter-espionage officer John Preston (Caine), who must identify and locate the ace KGB agent Major Petrofsky (Pierce Brosnan) before he can assemble and detonate the bomb. Preston is hampered in his quest by a disbelieving and hostile Internal Security Chief, Brian Harcourt-Smith (Julian Glover). The two loyal agents, Preston and Petrofsky, in the manner of the more serious espionage literature, are identified not only as equally top agents on different sides, and as lonely men, but as dispensable tools in the higher game of departmental power struggles and supra-national personal alliances.

The liberal critics found the picture dated and naive, "*like spending two hours in a time-warp*", according to the *Guardian* (19 March 1987); while credibility remained "*just this side of preposterous*" for *Monthly Film Bulletin* (April 1987: 113). The *Observer* criticised a lack of "*psychological depth, political insight, and historical perspective*", believing the outcome closer to the recent James Bond extravaganza *Octopussy* (1983) than the thought-provoking John le Carré (22 March 1987) [115]; similarly, the *Evening Standard* complained of "*all plot and next to no story*" (19 March 1987); and the *Spectator* found the picture "*prefabricated*" (28 March 1987). With puns ready-to-hand, critics referred to yet another "*Forsyth Saga*" (*Daily Mail*, 20 March 1987; *Western Mail*, 4 April 1987), dismissed *The Fourth Protocol* as "*tenth-rate Third Man stuff*" (*Sunday Today*, 22 March 1987), and as "*fourth-rate spy stuff*" (*Hampstead & Highgate Express*, 3 April 1987). The picture fared no better in the United States, where the *Village Voice* dismissed it as an "*exceptionally dull rehash of espionage clichés*" (15 September 1987). Commenting on the film in his memoirs, Caine confessed that the producers had made the mistake of producing a "*talking picture*" rather than a "*moving picture*" (1992: 441).

While a tense spy thriller, *The Fourth Protocol* represents at least a response to the changing international climate. In the finale, it is revealed that the successful counter-espionage operation led by Preston was aided by crucial information supplied by General Karpov (Ray McAnally), the Deputy Chairman of the KGB, who alone had been able to piece together the conspiracy. The film ends with Karpov in alliance with Britain's chief of MI6, Sir Nigel Irvine (Ian Richardson), and the sense of a new day dawning; although Preston, forever the cynical individualist, sees no fundamental change in 'the game', just a rearrangement of pieces with the elite still occupying the important positions.[116] However, the hint at *glasnost* had little impact on the critical response to the film. Many still found it old-fashioned, both in style and in its political view. The *Independent* pointed out that *The Fourth Protocol* "*depends for its chills entirely on the temperature of the Cold War*" (19 March 1987) and with *The Daily Telegraph* reminding future filmmakers that "*Movies had come in from the cold war now*" (20 March 1987). The left-wing *Morning Star* bemoaned an obvious "*Anti-Soviet exercise*" and dismissed the picture as "*very contrived cold-war stuff and about as subtle as a kick in the crutch*" (27 March 1987). The *Hampstead & Highgate Express* was also uncomfortable with a simplistic *"paranoid Cold War thriller"*, claiming the film's *"gung-ho material about twenty years out of date: as though Maugham, Ambler, Greene or le Carré had never written a word about the business of espionage"* (30 April 1987). The *Mail on Sunday* headlined a *"Cold War chiller that runs out of ice"*, arguing that *"the story's assumptions about spies, in these revelatory days of Peter Wright and others, seem outdated and naïve"* (22 March 1987). Also noting how the exposures of the '*Spycatcher* Affair' were altering perceptions of espionage and the 'secret state', *The Times* identified the conundrum for makers of traditional spy stories: *"The problem these days is that the real thing, like the Wright affair, is usually funnier than fiction"* (20 March 1987). For many reviewers, the spy picture was a *"format that has long since stopped offering anything new"* (*The New York Times*, 28 August 1987). The life-cycle of the genre was drawing to a close and in a great surprise to everybody the animosities of the Cold War were too.

Reluctant spies

A likely thesis for the film addict of two or three years hence might be 'the effect of James Bond on the comedy thriller'.
(*Sunday Telegraph*, 8 March 1964)

A group of spy thrillers that commenced in 1964 took as their central character a 'reluctant spy'; unlike James Bond, a non-professional who is co-opted into the world of espionage by accident or for pragmatic reasons, and mostly the recruitment is supposed to be only a temporary expediency. Such an arrangement, of course, draws on the long-standing tradition in British spy fiction of the amateur spy, the able do-gooder who will risk all for monarch and country. The Bond formula centred on the professional agent and the 'reluctant spy' cycle gained much of its fun and excitement from the clash of ethos between the amateur and the expert, the ingénue and the specialist, qualities intensified in those stories in which the innocent is coupled, or in contest with, a professional female spy. Many of these films were framed as secret agent comedy-thrillers, and a main influence and model for this group of films was Alfred Hitchcock's *North by Northwest* (US, 1959) and its lead character of Roger Thornhill (Cary Grant), an unsuspecting advertising executive who is unwillingly drawn into a web of intrigue and espionage. Several of the British reluctant spy thrillers of the 1960s directly referenced this hugely successful picture, and such iconic scenes as the aerial attack in an open landscape, the character purposely getting himself arrested at a public event in order to evade his antagonists, and the hero forcibly intoxicated and left to drive a precipitous road.

The critic at the *Observer* claimed that since first seeing *Dr No* she had won-dered "*how long it would be before Rank had a bash at doing a hip spy story*" (15 March 1964). The time lag turned out to be 15 months and the leading British film company's *Hot Enough for June!* was released in March 1964, adapted from the prize-winning début novel *The Night of Wenceslas* by Lionel Davidson.[117] The rights to the book had originally been bought by the Holly-wood producer Hal Wallis, but a falling out with the proposed star Laurence Harvey led to the acquisition of the story by the British producer Betty Box (Box 2000: 227). The film "*makes amiable fun of James Bond*" through a pre-credit sequence in which an official is filing away the effects of 007, tragically lost on his latest mission (*The Times*, 5 March 1964); and it was commented at the time of the film's release in America that, "*To make a contemporary spy thriller without sneaking in a nod to James Bond would apparently be an un-thinkable breach of custom*" (*Time*, 20 August 1965).[118] With the loss of 007, the Secret Intelligence Service is short of experienced agents and Nicholas Whistler (Dirk Bogarde), a young, unsuspecting, Czech-speaking, work-shy writer, is recruited, through the Labour Exchange, for a mission in Prague. Whistler believes he is involved in some minor industrial espionage, but it is brought home to him while on his mission that it is considerably more seri-ous than that. Sought by the secret police, he spends some days evading cap-ture before he reaches sanctuary at the British Embassy. Glamour was provid-ed in the guise of Yugoslavian actress Sylva Koscina.

Some reviewers enjoyed the gentle humour of the picture and the expert playing of the supporting actors John Le Mesurier and Robert Morley as bumbling, old-school Secret Service officials. However, others dismissed the picture as "*Not So Hot*" (*Evening Standard*, 5 March 1964), in fact only "*luke-warm*" (*Films and Filming*, April 1964: 27), as a "*piece of spy nonsense*" (*Daily Mail*, 4 March 1964), and as "*unwarrantably languid*" (*New Statesman*, 20 March 1964). The *Guardian* stressed that a "*good situation, funny dialogue and a talented cast are not enough to make a good film*", and that *Hot Enough for June!* "*fails miserably in its attempt to cash in on the James Bond vogue*" (6 March 1964). *Monthly Film Bulletin* argued the widely expressed view that the film fell headfirst into the first trap for the comedy-thriller, that, "*its adven-tures are neither funny enough for parody, nor exciting enough to stand on their own feet*" (April 1964: 57). In this respect, *Hot Enough for June!* was felt to have failed to come up to the standard of the recent American comedy-thrillers *Charade* and *The Prize* (both US, 1963) (*The Telegraph*, 6 March 1964). Many agreed that the location shooting in Padua, Italy, utterly failed to convince as Prague, and that Bogarde, who would later feature in several spy films, was too old for the feckless adventurer.[119]

The more thoughtful critic felt that the film's comedy was aimless and lacking any sense of the poignancy of the times. It was claimed at *The Telegraph* that, "*The recent affairs of Blake, Vassall and Philby should surely have provided any amount of inspiration for a satirist with an eye to the absurdities and hypocrisies involved in operating a peacetime spying system*" (6 March 1964). The reviewer at the *Evening News* was equally considerate of contemporary events, noting the "*grim irony*" of a story about "*a British businessman who unwittingly finds himself working for British Intelligence behind the Iron Curtain*" at the very time that, "*Mrs. Sheila Wynne is in Russia to visit her husband in a prison near Moscow*" and was therefore unlikely to find the picture "*very funny*" (6 March 1964).[120] Betty Box later reported that the picture was popular in Britain, France, Italy and, surprisingly, New York, where it opened on 90 screens (2000: 235).

Basil Dearden and Michael Relph's *Masquerade* appeared in April 1965, part of a production deal the film-makers had with United Artists and which had already realised the psychological drama *Woman of Straw* (1964). The film was based on *Castle Minerva* by the leading thriller writer Victor Canning, a novel Dearden and Relph had initially considered filming in their days at the famous Ealing Studios in the mid-1950s (Burton and O'Sullivan 2009: 294). The original story was a fairly straight adventure yarn typical of the decade and screenwriters Relph and William Goldman updated this to offer a more ironic treatment of the theme of patriotism suitable to a mid-1960s setting, as well as to take account of the re-casting of the lead to an American.[121] The central plot of the comedy-thriller concerned British attempts to retain valuable oil concessions in the Middle-Eastern state of Ramaut. Intelligence officer Colonel Drexel (Jack Hawkins) is detailed to protect the pro-British Prince Jamil (Christopher Witty) in a safe house in Spain for two weeks, until the boy assumes the throne. Opposed to him is the pro-Soviet Regent Ben Fa'id (Roger Delgado). The 'reluctant spy' is the American David Frazer (Cliff Robertson), a wartime comrade of Drexel's, now down on his luck, and recruited for the mission with the promise of £500. The actual conspiracy, though, has Drexel, a disillusioned officer seeking monetary reward for all the years of hardship and danger, arranging for the kidnapping and ransom of Jamil, while fixing the blame on the unsuspecting Frazer. A complex plot has Frazer abducted twice by a troupe of French circus folk paid by Drexel, the intervention of Dunwoody (Bill Fraser) an agent of Ben Fa'id who wants the prince dead, and a thrilling finale on a collapsed rope bridge hundreds of feet above a reservoir. The hapless Frazer at one point declares, "*I'm an internationally-known traitor, I've been in a car wreck, dunked in a wine tanker, hit on the head three times and locked up in a cage with a vulture*". Staring directly at the camera, the exasperated character proclaims, "*Someone up there hates me*". The reviewer at the *Sunday Times* felt Robertson had exactly and agreeably found the "*unheroic bearing of the hero*" (18 April 1965).

In a heavily ironic conclusion, the intelligence chiefs hopelessly misinter-
pret the recent events, place the blame on the now deceased Dunwoody, and
congratulate Drexel and Frazer on an "*entirely successful mission*". The senior
man is rewarded with a lucrative post with a grateful oil company, while the
American has to make do with the promise of a dinner at the chief's club and
a cheque for £11 9s. 2d – the balance left from the £500 after the deduction of
back taxes.

Masquerade included the customary nods to both James Bond and Alfred
Hitchcock. In one scene, Jamil is passing time reading *Goldfinger* and idly
complains that it is too "*far-fetched*"[122]; while a later scene, which has Frazer
abducted in a circus by four clowns in full view of the audience, is a typically
Hitchcockian moment emphasising that danger lurks where least expected. A
catchy theme song sung by Danny Williams, an animated title sequence,
picturesque locations around Alicante on Spain's Mediterranean coast, and
the glamorous continental actress Marisa Mell provided the love interest and
completed the formula attractions of the picture. The general critical assessment was that *Masquerade* offered a pleasurable blend of action and light
comedy, and had a few worthwhile satirical comments to make regarding
espionage narratives and the concomitant fictions of Britain's world standing.
The reviewer at *The Times* felt that Dearden had managed the "*right tongue in
cheek verve*" (15 April 1965); a sentiment echoed at the *Saturday Review*,
which acknowledged the director's "*wink*", "*his tacit admission that he knows
it's nonsense, but isn't it lots of fun*" (May 1965). The view at *Monthly Film
Bulletin*, rarely a friend to Dearden and Relph, was more jaundiced, finding
the picture a "*sluggish thriller*", and dismissive of its "*modish cynicism*" (May
1965: 76).

The popular stage and television comedy double-act Eric Morecambe and
Ernie Wise made three feature films in the 1960s. The first of these was *The
Intelligence Men* (1965), a burlesque of the now commercially viable secret
agent drama and subtitled "*MI5 plus 2 equals 0*". Eric serves in an espresso
coffee bar and Ernie is a glorified tea-boy at Military Intelligence. Accidentally
stumbling on a plot by the criminal organisation Schlecht to do away with a
Soviet trade delegation and prima ballerina Madame Petrovna (April Olrich),
the inept Eric and Ernie are tasked by MI5 to protect the visiting dignitaries.[123] A series of blundering adventures and feeble disguises follows, with
Eric masquerading as a Schlecht assassin and the hapless pair encountering
deadly Mata Hari's, disrupting a cultural reception, and escaping murderous
agents. In the *grand finale*, the mock Secret Service agents take to the stage at
Covent Garden and save Petrovna during a performance of *Swan Lake*.

The film is a succession of infantile jokes, crude slapstick, and weak allusions to the James Bond secret agent archetype interspersed with the odd

song and dance number. The filming is frontal and flat, providing the boys effectively with a proscenium space to perform their characteristic and popular routines. The film was directed by Robert Asher who had previously worked with Britain's most successful screen comedian Norman Wisdom. *Kine Weekly* felt that Morecambe and Wise had been "*brightly translated to the cinema screen*" and that box-office prospects were good (25 March 1965). *Monthly Film Bulletin,* however, marked the picture as an "*exceptionally un-funny comedy*" and wondered, on this evidence, what could possibly have contributed to the popularity of the Morecambe and Wise? (May 1965: 75).

Val Guest's *Where the Spies Are* was released in March 1966 and derived from James Leasor's popular novel *Passport to Oblivion* which had appeared in 1964. The picture had an unusual genesis. Within 10 weeks of reading the novel in proof, Guest had put together a deal with MGM, completed a script with Wolf Mankowitz, and had begun shooting the picture, then known as *One Spy Too Many,* on location in Lebanon.[124] The publisher Heinemann was enthusiastic about the commercial prospects of the novel and its protagonist Dr Jason Love, and commissioned five further titles from Leasor, and Guest immediately optioned these. The hunt was clearly on for a series character to rival James Bond (*Kine Weekly,* 4 February 1965).

The story concerns the recruitment by a hard-pressed MI6 of an English country doctor, Jason Love (David Niven), to investigate a missing agent in Beirut (Teheran in the novel).[125] Reluctant at first, Love, an enthusiast for classic American cars, is persuaded on the promise of a particularly rare au-tomobile. He visits Lebanon on the pretext of a medical conference, and there is embroiled in a Soviet plot to assassinate the president, once again imperil-ling Britain's valuable oil concessions. An expert in judo and equipped with a variety of lethal gadgets, Love is able to disrupt the murder attempt, but is captured by the assassins and spirited aboard a Russian airliner which is presently engaged in a worldwide goodwill tour. There, he is surprised to find Vikki (Françoise Dorléac), a British agent and the film's romantic interest who has been doubled and reveals she is essentially out for herself. Love is able to bring down the liner in northern Canada with one of his devices and escapes with the help of Vikki, but she does the decent thing and dies in the shootout.[126]

Guest claimed that the picture was made "*absolutely factually*", guaranteed by a technical adviser "*who not so very long ago was one of the head men at MI6*" (quoted in *Kine Weekly,* 4 February 1965). This, of course, was nonsense, and *Kine Weekly* was nearer the truth in marking the picture as a "*compelling, exciting adventure*" with some witty dialogue and comic asides. The trade paper found the picture a "*cracking good adventure carrying a great deal more plausibility than we have lately been taught to expect from secret agents*" (3

March 1966). *Monthly Film Bulletin* noted the most recent addition to the *"current tidal wave of post-Bondian spy spoofs"*, and was surprised by the film's *"streak of viciousness"* (April 1966: 64).[127] Many reviews in fact made reference to the torture of Love on-board the Aeroflot plane, ironically situated under a sign reading *"Good Will to all Men"*, and film historian Robert Murphy has shown surprise at a spy thriller that started out as a comedy and which turned *"increasingly black as the death toll mounts"* (1992: 230).[128] While subsequent Jason Love adventures did appear in print, there was no additional attempt to feature the character on screen.

American distributor-producer Joseph E. Levine seemingly enjoyed sufficient success with the two Charles Vine pictures *Licensed to Kill* and *Where the Bullets Fly* to tempt him to bankroll the comedy spy thriller *The Spy with a Cold Nose*, made in Britain and released in 1966. A broad farce filmed around London and at Castle Howard, Yorkshire, the film starred comic actor Lionel Jeffries as inept counter-intelligence agent Stanley Farquhar who dreams up the master plan of bugging the bulldog to be presented to the Soviet prime minister as a gift from the British people. The reluctant spy is the fashionable veterinary surgeon Francis Trevellyan (Laurence Harvey), tasked with the job of inserting the miniature radio device. The bonanza of intelligence is jeopardised when Disraeli the bulldog becomes ill and Farquhar and Trevellyan set off for Moscow, armed with a bitch bulldog as bait, where they attempt to retrieve the bug before the Russians discover the subterfuge.[129] Amidst much confusion, Trevellyan is able to remove the device at the British Embassy; however, Farquhar is injured and treated by Soviet doctors. Back in Britain, the newly elevated Farquhar now advises the prime minister on security, unsuspecting of the bug he is now carrying inside him. Interspersed throughout the action are the glamorous double-agent Princess Natasha Romanova (Daliah Lavi) and the nitwit sidekick Wrigley (Eric Sykes).

There was general praise for the expert comedy timing of Jeffries, and for the zany script from Ray Galton and Alan Simpson, best known for their work on television with Tony Hancock.[130] As was customary, there were several nods to James Bond in the film. While hatching his plan to win one over on the Soviets, Farquhar bones up on Fleming's *From Russia, With Love*. Forever complaining that he never finds a beautiful naked woman waiting for him in his bed as 007 often does, he is startled in his long johns on encountering the voluptuous Romanova in his hotel room. Much of the subversion of the archetype secret agent image is managed through Farquhar's banal domestic life, his unruly children, and a wife who claims he *"shouldn't have become a spy in the first place"* and rues the fact that James Bond is able to gamble away more in one night than Stanley gets in a year. In a crowded market, *Kine Weekly* felt the picture offered a *"new approach to the utterly absurd treatment*

of the well-known thrills and mysteries of special-agents and spy adventures"
(25 March 1967); while a more sober *Observer* judged the picture "*mild and
tiny stuff*", which at least appreciated its own modest scale (16 April 1967).

Following on from *Where the Spies Are*, MGM further tried its hand at an espionage thriller with *The Liquidator*. The film began production in April 1965
but was not released until August 1966 due to legal problems between the
producer and the studio, with the picture passing for a time into the hands of
the Official Receiver (*Kine Weekly* 25 March 1965; *Evening News*, 11 November
1966; Cardiff 1996: 242). *The Liquidator* was based on the new-style spy adventure created by John Gardner and published as a novel in 1964, described
in *Kine Weekly* as "*simultaneously a gripping spy story and a preposterous
joke*" (31 December 1964). In the misadventures of the anti-hero Boysie Oakes, Gardner created a series character who served as a "*reaction to those who
tried to imitate Ian Fleming*" (Godat 1997), and served-up the "*chap-next-
door version of James Bond*" (*Daily Mail*, 23 August 1966). A secret agent by
mistake, a 007 who turns out to be a zero, Oakes is "*stupid, lecherous, a blun-
derer and a coward, who only made it to the end of each adventure by the skin
of his teeth*" (Adrian 1996). The film, directed by Jack Cardiff, was a fairly close
adaptation of the novel, and with its lively, hip, animated title sequence and
big Shirley Bassey theme song, it immediately established its point of reference with the James Bond template. The back-story, set during the liberation
of Paris and established in a pre-credits sequence, has a blundering Sergeant
Oakes (Rod Taylor) stumble across a man being attacked by two Gestapo
thugs. Boysie, actually in a complete panic, drops the assailants with two
seemingly expert shots from his service automatic, and Major Mostyn (Trevor
Howard) of British Intelligence promises to remember the steel-nerved Oakes.

Fast forward 20 years, and Colonel Mostyn, now heading up a special security section, faces a crisis of escalating leaks and scandals in the Secret Service. A drastic plan is proposed, to "*liquidate any suspects*", thus replacing
"*scandals*" with "*accidents*". Offering effectively a "*licence to kill*", Mostyn
remembers the cold-eyed killer of wartime Paris, searches him out, and
tempts him with a secret agent life-style of penthouse apartment,[131] E-Type
Jaguar (number plate BO1), and the prospect of plenty of gorgeous women.
The beefy, sex-mad killer-manqué enjoys the perks of his new found role.
However, it is a considerable shock when he learns that he is to be 'The Liquidator' (code letter L), and that he will be required to kill people suspected of
treachery. After all, "*Life is not all sex and sunlamps*" as Mostyn drily informs
him. With no stomach for nationalised assassination, the squeamish executioner sub-contracts the work to the private enterprise killer Griffen (Eric

Sykes), and Boysie settles back to enjoy the fringe benefits of a 1960s-style secret agent.

Despite the departmental rule that, "*Spies are not allowed to meet with office birds after hours*", Oakes arranges for a dirty weekend in Monte Carlo with Iris (Jill St. John), Mostyn's attractive secretary. Afraid of flying, the flight to Nice is hell for Boysie; and things go from bad to worse when he is kidnapped, threatened with torture, and shot at while escaping his mysterious assailants. Back at his hotel, he is contacted by Quadrant (David Tomlinson), a British agent, and provided with new orders. Oakes is to return to Britain to participate in an exercise testing the security surrounding the Duke of Edinburgh. In fact, this is a Soviet plot to steal Britain's latest bomber which the Duke will be inspecting, and Iris and Quadrant are double-agents. Mostyn is able to piece together the conspiracy and intercedes at the airfield moments before Oakes can unwittingly shoot the V.I.P. dead. A mere diversionary tactic, Quadrant and Iris take control of the RAF's new Vulture jet with a flight plan to Soviet Russia. A panicky Oakes is able to board the taxiing plane and overpower the intruders. Sick with apprehension, he is able to bring the aircraft down with instructions from the control tower. Mostyn is impressed and a reluctant Boysie, with one eye on his superior's new sexy secretary, is welcomed back into the Service.

Although a variation on the 007 blueprint, most critics judged *The Liquidator* as the "*Latest from the Bond belt*" (*Evening Standard*, 25 August 1966) and yet "*another spy film of an all-too-familiar aspect: striking credits backed by pulsating song; one expensive location; an easy-living Bond-type and his Moll; and an embarrassing tendency toward jokey burlesque which has now become traditional to spy films*" (*Guardian*, 26 August 1966). Although sent on the standard crash course in Bondmanship and emerging a professional secret agent, Boysie's disposition means he remains a 'reluctant spy' and shares the essential qualities with other characters in this tradition.

Critics tended to prefer the first half of the film, with its gentle debunking of the English sense of fair-play and witty comments on well-worn conventions of the spy film. *Films and Filming* saw potential in a story which verged on a "*Graham Greene bitterness about materialism, moral seediness and the establishment ethos*", but whose impact was lost after the filmmakers "*scuttled back*" to the tried and tested formula of an exotic location and action stuff (October 1966: 18). The reviewer at *Monthly Film Bulletin* also felt let down after a "*promising beginning*", the film descending into a "*pastiche of the spy film formula*". It was eventually written off as a "*further sortie into sub-Bondian territory*" (October 1966: 154). Similarly, the *Morning Star* found the picture too "*dull-witted*" to work as effective satire (27 August 1966). Meanwhile, the *Daily Mail* was beginning to tire of the "*overplayed secret service*" *game*" (23 August 1966); and *Time Magazine* pointed out that the "*fun is less noticeable than the formula*" (21 October 1966). It is possible that some of the novelty of the film was lost due to its delayed release. The casual and amoral violence of the spy thriller continued to trouble some observers. The *Observer* commented on *The Liquidator*'s "*shifty tone that makes it rather disagreeable*", worrying over the "*comic torture scenes, comic pushing under trains, comic bullets in the guts and a comic attack of fear in a nose-diving aeroplane*", believing "*none of them at all funny because the note of the picture is too craven to be farcical*" (28 August 1966). Once again, there was no further attempt to put a series character enjoying an extended life in print onto the movie screen.[132]

Our Man in Marrakesh (1966) was yet another comedy-spy picture. It was a production of Harry Alan Towers who had featured on the fringes of the Profumo spy scandal of a few years earlier (Summers and Dorrill 1987: 64-6, 67, 70, 191). An innocent American businessman Andrew Jessel (Alan Randall) is caught up in intrigue in Morocco involving a 'money for votes' scandal concerning the United Nations. On the run with the beautiful Kyra (Senta Berger) from both the police and the local gang, Jessel eventually deals with the evil Casimir (Herbert Lom) and clears his name. Reviewers tended to judge the picture fine within its own limited ambitions. *Kine Weekly* informed exhibitors that *Our Man in Marrakesh* represented a "*jolly, entertaining, light, burlesque of spying*" and as such offered itself as a "*Very useful attraction*" (5 May 1966); while at the opposite end of the critical spectrum, *Monthly Film Bulletin* found Randall a "*pleasantly reluctant hero*" and enjoyed the supporting cast of British stalwarts doing their usual stuff with "*reliability and competence*" (1 January 1966: 33).

Arabesque is another light spy thriller with an American character at its centre and a narrative referencing the Middle-East. It was derived from *The Cipher*, a modest spy story by Alex Gordon (real name Gordon Cotler) first published in 1961, set in New York and involving Philip Hoag, a lowly instructor of ancient history who is drawn into a conspiracy of political assassination when he is invited to decode a cipher by an Arab businessman. The action takes place over two days in New York and centres on a state visit by the prime minister of an unnamed Middle-Eastern country. Hoag is the unlikely hero who thwarts the plot of disenchanted nationals and in the process rediscovers some self-respect. The novel was adapted into the stylised thriller *Arabesque* in 1966, filmed in Great Britain as a Stanley Donen Production for Universal Pictures. The movie is a glamorous romantic-comedy thriller starring Gregory Peck and Sophia Loren, and is a quite different proposition to the low-key novel with the action transplanted to a colourful, 'Swinging London' and released with the tagline "*Ultra-Mod! Ultra-Mad! Ultra-Mystery!*" David Pollock (Peck), a mild, unworldly American professor of Egyptology at Oxford who is commissioned to decipher an ancient manuscript, is drawn into a conspiracy which aims to assassinate a visiting prime minister of a Middle-Eastern state. The beautiful Yasmin (Loren) wanders in and out of the threats, attacks and drugging endured by Pollock, who can't decide if she is friend or foe until it is finally revealed she is a government agent.[133]

Critics saw *Arabesque* as an attempt by Donen to recapture the spirit and success of his earlier *Charade* (US, 1963), in which case it was a bit of a disappointment, and further noted obvious borrowings from such thrillers as *The Lady from Shanghai* (US, 1947, substitute an aquarium for a hall of mirrors) and *North by Northwest* (US, 1959, substitute a helicopter for a crop duster). Some felt that *The Ipcress File* (1965) may have been an influence in terms of an eccentric visual style which Donen apparently hoped would mask the inadequacies of the script. He instructed his cameraman, "*See what you can come up with. I want every shot to be different*". Cinematographer Christopher Challis later reported on the novel approach: "*It seemed at times that the whole picture was to be seen in the backs of teaspoons, car mirrors or through tanks of fish*" (1995: 176). The idiosyncratic visual approach was achieved through the novel use of a suspended mounting for an Arriflex camera, enabling the equipment to be "*moved with the lightest touch either up, down, backwards, forwards*", and accomplishing a "*360 degree turn in a flash*" (*Observer*, 11 July 1965).[134]

Visual design was prioritised in other ways in the picture. Maurice Binder, famous for his striking title designs on the James Bond pictures *Dr No* and *Thunderball*, was engaged for the main titles, star Sophia Loren was expensively robed by Christian Dior, and, most unusually, John Rawson, Professor of Psychology at Sheffield University and Britain's foremost authority on colour psychology, was engaged to advise the producers on "*colour design for the picture, as for one of the few times in the history of motion pictures, colour will be scientifically used to heighten the moods of the picture and to induce the appropriate reactions of excitement, fear and suspense in the audience*" (*Arabesque* press release).[135] The lively visual element was further enhanced in the prominent 'Swinging London' quality of the film. With only minimal studio work, the 16-week location schedule took in such "*historic and photogenic*" sites as Trafalgar Square, the British Museum, Regent's Park, the London Zoo including the first public views of the new aviary designed by Lord Snowdon, London Airport, the traditionally sacrosanct Royal Enclosure at Ascot during Ascot Week, St. John's College, Oxford and Waterloo Station (ibid.).

The self-conscious, even weird, camera positions and framing attracted some comments in the reviews. The reviewer writing in the *Evening Standard*, alluding to the opening scene in which a character is dispatched by lethal eye drops from a bogus oculist, observed that the weary spectator of the exhilarating movie, "*may feel his own eyes have been under the same kind of attack*" (*Evening Standard*, 28 July 1966). Many were tested by the "*optical banalities*" of the picture, "*which recur so motivelessly that they attain the dimension of an affliction*" (*Sunday Telegraph*, 31 July 1966). *The Times* complained that, "*Mr. Donen's taste for outré decoration seems to have gone quite mad*", resulting in an "*overwrought style*", which would likely give "*bad aesthetic indigestion*" (28 July 1966); the *Morning Star* was irritated by the "*grotesque camera angles and flash cutting techniques*" (30 July 1966); while the *Sunday Observer* believed that as a comedy-thriller the film "*wrecks itself with blandishments*" (31 July 1966).

Reviewers also tended to find the film predictable. The *Evening News* tired of the "*unfailing formula of the innocent hero caught up in a world of international intrigue*", which Donen had here spiced up with a "*dazzling photographic style ... of swimming colours and reeling images*" (28 July 1966). The *Daily Mail* dismissed such "*fantasticated comic-strip nonsense*" (27 May 1966), the *People* warned of the "*usual spy chase after the usual cipher with the usual foreign power lurking in the background*" (31 July 1966), and the *Morning Star* unenthusiastically promised "*all the kidnappings, chases, murders, false trails and hairs-breadth escapes that belong to the fantasy world of the spy-thriller-mystery-comedy-send-up romance*" (30 July 1966). The American *Saturday Review* reported a "*flimsy yarn of intrigue in London*" (21 June 1966), and *Time* of "*familiar knavery about the assassination of a Middle Eastern Prime Minister*" (20 May 1966). In a more supportive review, *Films and Filming* found the picture "*painstakingly elaborate and stylish, positively luxurious in décor and photography*", but wished Donen would return to making musicals at which he was a true master (September 1966: 12).

Reviewer fatigue with the spy picture was becoming noticeable in 1966. In that year, *Time Magazine* reported that, "*Overproduction is the No.1 problem of the James Bondustry*" (21 October); the *Evening News*, commenting on the spy film cycle, complained of an "*over-cluttered cul-de-sac, a cinema dead-end*" (5 May 1966); while *The Telegraph* wrote of a genre "*which now appears to be at death's door*" (6 May 1966). There was a hint of desperation in a feature which appeared in the *Guardian* newspaper in the summer of 1966, which wondered: "*How long will the spies last? Is the spy bubble about to burst?*" (12 July). The attitude was restated in regard of *Arabesque*, the same paper stating that:

> *With the present state of the market, spy films have got to break new ground or bust. Basically most of them are repetitious and they come to rely more and more on flamboyant set pieces, accepting the fact that they must be copies and covering themselves by self-mockery.*
> (*Guardian*, 24 July 1966)

The *Financial Times* declared, albeit prematurely, that *Arabesque* had the misfortune of appearing at the "*wit's end of the cycle*" (29 July 1966).

Gregory Peck had another stab at a university professor reluctantly drawn into a perilous mission of intrigue in *The Most Dangerous Man in the World*. The story began as a speculative script by Jay Richard Kennedy with plans to star Frank Sinatra together with Yul Brynner and Spencer Tracy. This fell through and he turned it into the novel *The Chairman* published in 1969. The manuscript was picked up by movie producer Arthur P. Jacobs who invited Ben Maddow to write a script and J. Lee Thompson to direct for release by 20th Century Fox in 1969.[136] The Nobel Prize-winning scientist Dr John Hathaway (Peck) is convinced by an unlikely alliance of Western and Soviet intelligence[137] to visit his former teacher in China, Professor Soong Li (Keye Luke), to obtain the formula for a new enzyme which enables crops to grow almost anywhere and promises to solve the world's food problem. Hathaway believes his undertaking is for humanitarian reasons and is invited by Chairman Mao (Conrad Yama) to help perfect the enzyme, but his intelligence masters in London know that whoever monopolises the enzyme controls the developing world. Hathaway is sent into China with a miniature transmitter in his head (à la *The Spy with a Cold Nose*), which allows his spymasters to listen in on his conversations; unknown to the scientist it is accompanied by an explosive device which has been added as a precaution. The radio device is detected by Chinese security and Hathaway flees to the frontier with a copy of the *Little Red Book* in which Soong Li has secreted the formula. Hathaway is saved by a Soviet Red Army patrol moments before London activates the explosive device. On learning that the authorities intend to suppress the discovery, the disillusioned Hathaway decides to fight the decision in the interests of humanity.

The Most Dangerous Man in the World was a troubled production. The crew was met with demonstrations and threats when attempting to shoot locations in Hong Kong, and it was necessary to relocate to Taiwan and finally to mock-up the pursuit along the Sino-Soviet border in north Wales; while the studio scenes shot at Pinewood suffered from a shortage of Chinese extras. Editing and postproduction were bedevilled by interference from 20th Century Fox, something Lee Thompson recalled as a "*nightmare*" (Chibnall 2000: 314-17).

The Most Dangerous Man in the World was neither well-received by the critics nor particularly popular with the public. The *Guardian* warned that Lee Thompson was "*no Frankenheimer*" (4 July 1969) and more than one reviewer commented on the "*dogged*" and "*weary*" direction of J. Lee Thompson (*The Times*, 3 July 1969; *Monthly Film Bulletin*, August 1969: 175; *Observer*, 6 July).[138] The *Evening Standard* thought the film managed about as much suspense as a "*tired skipping rope*" (3 July 1969). *Monthly Film Bulletin* claimed that despite the updated ideology and sci-fi trimmings the tale was surprisingly old-fashioned, more the world of Richard Hannay than James Bond, and putting us "*right back in the golden age of the spy story*". The reviewer pointed to the surprising similarities between *The Most Dangerous Man in the World* and John Buchan's *Greenmantle* (1916), with the hero doing battle in far places for Western civilisation, "*fooling the mighty Chairman as easily as he did the All-Highest himself*", and where he is "*saved by the grandsons of those Cossack cavalry who rode to his rescue over fifty years before*" (August 1969: 175).

The film, though, is memorable for dealing with intelligence and security in the setting of Mao's China. With its East Asian location and possibility of assassination of a national dictator (the Americans push to use the explosive device in Hathaway's head to kill Mao during their meeting), *The Most Dangerous Man in the World* was a forerunner of *The Interview* (US, 2014), the recent controversial picture about an assassination attempt on President Kim Jong-un of North Korea. And as *Monthly Film Bulletin* commented at the time, it was at least novel "*to see the Red Army in the role usually reserved for the 7th Cavalry or the Green Berets in Hollywood-inspired films*" (August 1969: 175).

It was unusual for a female to be recruited/exploited as a 'reluctant spy'. *A Girl Called Fathom* was a contemporary spy thriller written by Larry Forrester and first published in 1967. Fathom, a young athletic British woman, Amazonian in stature and "*unusually sensual*", arrives at a mansion and casually shoots dead a Hollywood film director in his swimming pool. It transpires that he had corrupted her into a sordid life of sex and drugs. The woman is offered an escape from a long prison sentence through recruitment into CELTS (Counter-Espionage [Long Term Security]), an Anglo-American special operations unit whose operatives all have a background in crime and perversion. Fathom undertakes demanding training, during which she is required to execute a captive in cold blood, and is sent on a dangerous mission to Europe to confront the conspiratorial organisation WAR (World of Asia Revolution), a subversive group of Sinophiles within the Soviet hierarchy, which is seemingly plotting to wreck proposals for world peace. Fathom's nemesis is the impressive Black lesbian agent Jo Soon and at the conclusion the two enact a fight to the death on a small boat on the Seine.

Fathom is one of several spy heroines who followed in the wake of the influential Modesty Blaise, a popular comic-strip, novel and movie character who first appeared in the early 1960s.[139] The action, presented in a hard-boiled style, courses through the West Coast of the United States, Arizona, Malaga in Spain, and the Côte d'Azur and Paris in France, and the heroine is supplied with a variety of neat gadgets and surprising chemicals to aid her in her mission. An unusual occurrence is when Fathom experiences her period while on mission and an opportunity for 'sexpionage' is lost!

A comedy movie adaptation of the novel immediately appeared as *Fathom* in 1967 starring Raquel Welch and produced by 20th Century Fox in Europe. The film was directed by Leslie Martinson, who had been responsible for the movie version of *Batman* (US, 1966) in America. The picture was released with the tagline, "*She's A Sky Diving Darling Built for Action!*", referencing a greatly altered story in which Fathom is now an American sky diver touring in Spain who is reluctantly recruited into a North Atlantic Treaty Organisation operation to retrieve the 'Fire Dragon', a nuclear trigger device mechanism lost in a crash in the Mediterranean and for which various enemy agents are searching. Some adventures later, Fathom discovers that the 'Fire Dragon' is in fact a priceless Chinese vase stolen from a Peking museum by a deserter from the Korean War and that she has been working for criminals against other assorted villains. Fathom has to face various escapades, including being chased by a bull in an arena, being pursued by helicopter, evading an underwater assault by harpoon, and at least two knife attacks. In a thrilling finale in a light aircraft, Fathom retrieves the 'Fire Dragon', the crooks are finally dispatched, and she flies off to a likely dinner liaison with the attractive American adventurer Peter Merriweather (Tony Franciosa).

Some critics found the picture undemanding fun, managing, according to *Monthly Film Bulletin*, "*to impart a charm and freshness to all the best worn clichés of the spy film send-up*" (September 1967: 140). Reviewers were predictably drawn to the singular assets of the statuesque lead actress, with the *Guardian* noting the "*ample opportunity to reveal Miss Welch's ample physique in an assortment of less than ample bikinis and parachute outfits with poor zips*" (25 August 1967). The film's poster screamed "Fathom... *The World's Most Uncovered Undercover Agent!*", and appropriately the picture commences with an extraordinarily eye-popping Freudian title sequence, designed by Maurice Binder, in which a skimpily-clad Raquel Welch lovingly unfurls, caresses, straddles and then re-sheaths a huge, red, phallic parachute.[140]

A trio of belated 'Swinging London' films brought the reluctant spy subgenre to a conclusion towards the end of the decade. An original comedy thriller *Salt and Pepper* (1968) was a vehicle for 'Rat Packers' Peter Lawford and Sammy Davis Jnr. Made with Hollywood money, American stars and by American director Richard Donner, it was set in Soho and never missed an opportunity to show minis, car and skirt, a double-decker bus, go-go dancing chicks, or petting couples on the uninhibited streets.[141] Charles Salt (Davis) and Christopher Pepper (Lawford), operators of a groovy night club, are caught in the middle when a sexy British agent Mai Ling (Jeanne Roland) is liquidated in their nightspot. Both British Intelligence and the conspirators want to know what Ling divulged before she died, when in fact all she left was a little notebook containing the names and addresses of military figures who are being bumped off one by one. Salt and Pepper's antics are further complicated by an officious policeman (Michael Bates) who wants to close the club down. The plot centres on a right-wing coup involving the theft of a Polaris submarine and the forced replacement of the legitimate government. While British Intelligence and the police are defeated, the hapless duo wins the day, infiltrating the enemy headquarters and with the help of a medieval cannon bringing the scoundrels to bay.

A prototype 'buddy movie' with a few self-reflexive gestures, *Salt and Pepper* was slaughtered by the press. The *Guardian* complained of a "*would-be hilarious lark as flat as a wet Sunday*" (3 November 1968), and *Monthly Film Bulletin* that the "*pseudo-Bond action*" and the slapstick comedy were "*excruciatingly ill-timed*", that any "*even tolerably witty joke*" was repeated *ad nauseum*, and that the studio-built Soho looked "*studio-built*" (January 1968: 202). The most obvious nod to the 007 formula came in what was dubbed an "*anti-Bond*" car, an amphibious Mini Moke equipped with bullet-proof screen, nail ejector and smoke machine, which goes bonkers in the major slapstick sequence in the picture (*Guardian*, 30 October 1967). As well as James Bond, *Salt and Pepper* owed a debt to the mod trappings of *The Avengers*, a show which also featured stories of die-hard reactionaries attempting to take over the country.

Alvin Rakoff's *Crossplot* (1969) was an original screenplay and an obvious sortie into Hitchcock country. Advertising executive Gary Fenn (Roger Moore) searches for model Marla Kogash (Claudie Lange) who he needs for a new campaign. Following the murder of her photographer boyfriend, she has gone underground taking the uncompleted crossword puzzle he mysteriously handed to her. Tracking Marla down to a Thames-side houseboat, the pair is subjected to murderous attacks. Clues lead them to the pacifist group Marchers of Peace and the stately home of Lord Etherley (Alexis Kanner), who becomes an ally. Fenn is able to decipher the message contained in the crossword revealing a plot to assassinate a visiting African statesman. Fenn and Kogash frustrate the villains at a gun-firing salute in Hyde Park, exposing a cosmetics tycoon and television producer as the conspirators who had been using the Marchers of Peace for their own sinister ends. *Crossplot* was the first of a proposed three-picture deal between Roger Moore and Robert S. Baker, star and producer respectively of the popular television adventure series *The Saint* (1962-69), and United Artists (UA). The film commenced shooting soon after the end of the run of *The Saint* and used creative personnel and some of the crew who had recently worked on the series (Moore 2008: 140, 150). However, the film was not popular, UA did not take up the option on the remaining two films, and Moore and Baker's energies reverted back to television and the successful action series *The Persuaders!* (1971-72). *Monthly Film Bulletin* found *Crossplot* a *"feeble attempt to refurbish the familiar story of the innocent booby frustrating the assassination of a V.I.P at a state ceremony"*. Complaining of *"uninspired direction, a hero singularly devoid of charm, and a plot nearly incomprehensible in its perfunctoriness"*, the bored reviewer noted the picture's *"determined mediocrity and a bedroom ending of almost incredible archness"* (December 1969: 265). The picture, with its advertising executive reluctant hero, was unsparing in its lifting from Alfred Hitchcock's *North by Northwest*.

One of the most reluctant of the new breed of spies was Gerald Arthur Otley who appeared in an eponymous comedy spy thriller published in 1966 by Martin Waddell.[142] Gerald Arthur Otley doesn't like violence, paying taxes, working hard or the general responsibilities of modern life endured by most people. He likes liquor, smoking, girls and odd little antique nick-nacks that people leave lying about the house which he can easily pinch and sell to fund his lifestyle of modest leisure. It is following his pilfering of a small antique at a party that Otley is catapulted into a mad, baffling conspiracy, in which he is knocked out, gagged, framed, pursued by unknown agents and the police, and abducted. Dead bodies begin to pile up around him, he can no longer trust his friends, and he is lured into a fiendishly complex scenario involving national security and a sinister organisation called the International Communications Syndicate (ICS). Throughout all of this madcap action, a beautiful spy known as Grace serves as Otley's protector and fairy godmother. It eventually transpires that senior men in British security, Hendrikson and Hadrian, have gone bad, are in league with ICS and intend to serve up Otley as a scapegoat. Grace despatches the villains and in the process pockets a substantial sum of money. The opportunist Otley, believed to have foiled the plot, emerges an unlikely hero. *Otley* was a story that chimed with the emerging youth trend of the 1960s that wanted to distance itself from the parent culture and in the process offered a mild critique of officialdom and the Secret Service. In *Otley*, the situation is played for comedy and the anti-heroic status of the character is emphasised.[143]

A movie version of *Otley* was filmed in England by Dick Clement for release by Columbia Pictures in 1969. It starred Tom Courtney as the downtrodden anti-hero and closely followed the outline of the novel. The picture was a late submission to the cycle of 'Swinging London' films which had been popular in the middle of the decade and referred to by one critic as belonging to the *"mod-spy genre"* (*Time Magazine*, 18 April 1969).[144] Reviews were generally good, with praise for the perky script, acting, originality of the story and characterisation, and some surprisingly funny scenes. Otley, a light-fingered layabout, was thought to be an original character-type for the overworked spy drama, someone who "*owes Bond nothing*" (*Sun*, 22 May 1969), and the film was felt to have taken a "*hackneyed situation*" and provided it with a "*surprising twist*" (*Daily Express*, 22 May 1969). The picture was judged a "*brilliant début*" by director Dick Clement at the *Daily Sketch* and was reported as drumming up good business in the United States (22 May 1969). The *Morning Star*, not usually favourably disposed towards the secret agent film, judged *Otley*, "*the best spy send-up that has come my way*" (24 May 1969). Most reviewers praised an inventive car chase of "Bullit *ferocity*" in the picture (*Sunday Telegraph*, 25 May 1969); this occurs while Otley, taking his driving test, is suddenly pursued by some heavies and the examination progresses to manic proportions. *The Listener* found this a "*gem of a scene*" (29 May 1969). The *Financial Times* advised its readers that *Otley* was "*Not to be missed, on any account*" (23 May 1969).

While *Films and Filming* thought *Otley* tried too hard to be "*with it*", and that the "*few genuine comedy touches*" became "*swamped in trendy cliché*" (July 1969: 39-40), film historian Robert Murphy has judged it the only British spy picture to succeed "*both as a comedy and a thriller*", managing a "*mundane reality*" and introducing us to a fringe London, "*which has stopped swinging and settled down to become a shambling, easy-going, bohemian backwater*" (1992: 231). The character of Gerald Otley can be compared to Harry Palmer, the rather smoother secret agent of the contemporary films *The Ipcress File* (1965), *Funeral in Berlin* (1967) and *Billion Dollar Brain* (1967). Both are lower-middle-class grammar school boys: Palmer an insubordinate individualist who works painfully within, but is superior to, the system; whereas Otley tells us he has "*dropped out*" and therefore represents the kind of listless rebellion characteristic of the later 1960s. The film, which has some pleasingly idiosyncratic characters and witty lines of dialogue, was scripted by the comedy writers Dick Clement and Ian La Frenais best known for their hit television sitcom *The Likely Lads* (1964-66), and who would later script the espionage dramas *Catch Me a Spy* (film 1971) and *Spies of Warsaw* (TV, 2013).

By the 1970s, the 'reluctant spy' story had pretty much drained all the comic potential there was to be mined from the parent genre of the spy thriller. While the straight spy thriller limped on, the 'reluctant spy' variant disappeared. Some of these comedies had been incorrectly labelled 'spoofs', and it is to the handful, but significant, examples of genuine spy spoofs that attention now turns.

Spy spoofs

After the spy films came the spoof spy films.
(*The Times*, 22 May 1969)

How do you send up a send-up? Since the screen's original 007, Sean Connery, had already burlesqued himself up to the hilt with all his girls, gadgets and lethal genius, he could hardly be burlesqued any further.
(*Daily Mail*, 14 April 1967)

The spy film cycle of the 1960s was in considerable measure fuelled by the commercial prospects of the genre following the enormous popularity of the James Bond stories for the screen. As we have seen, the secret agent film in the decade was in various ways highly imitative of the James Bond template. Imitation and allusion were also at the heart of the spy spoof, of which there were a handful of notable examples in the years following 007's translation to the big screen. Cultural historians have noted the turn to parody in the 1960s, indicative of increasing levels of cultural irony, which by the end of decade would, it has been claimed, reach the level of "*ironic supersaturation*" (Harries 2000: 3). The usual explanation for this departure into self-consciousness was the state of 'genre exhaustion' into which the media literate audience had apparently lapsed, and which had in turn developed a new relationship with the traditional cinema and its formal and thematic paradigms (Ray 1985: 256-268). Popular cinema and television of the 1960s threw up an increasing number of parodies, such as the movie *Cat Ballou* (US, 1965, western), and television series such as *Batman* (US, 1966-68). The spoofing of generic archetypes was especially prominent in the field of spy fiction, in particular in the wake of the James Bond phenomenon, and reviewers made reference to satirical, ironic or camp qualities in many of the spy films of the period. The American television spy spoof *Get Smart* (US, 1965-70) was especially popular and influential. The British series *The Avengers* which ran through most of the 1960s illustrates the kind of influence James Bond had on parody. The early seasons of 1961-63 were more realistic and shot in black and white; however, from 1965 the episodes began to be filmed in colour and now, as the publicity made explicit, "*the whole thriller formula*" was "*sent up even more openly and deliberately than in those early AVENGER days before the Bond films*" (*The Avengers* press sheet 1965). The reviewer in the *Guardian* sensed this, calling the show a "*sweet send-up of James Bond*" (29 September 1965). As has been widely noted, the referential relationship between Bond and his many parodies is complicated by the self-mockery, hip knowingness and humorous self-awareness of the original. However, Hagopian has argued how the existence of a separate parodic Bond-like cinema in fact secured the Bond films as ultimately a conservator of the consumerist modernism out of which they emerged. As he has observed, "*One of the most powerful ways the self-deprecating Bond could be taken seriously as a cultural oracle was to have a rich literature of parody shadow the character, framing him and his series of films as a monolithic and stable voice in culture*". "*The presence of the Bond parody*", he argues, "*helped to ensure that the Bond films would function as a serious engagement with culture without disturbing their protagonist's coolly ironic distance from that culture*" (2009: 23).

As early as 1965, the critic Ian Johnson was already claiming that, "*Some critics have been far too quick to point out that as the Bond films themselves are parodies, it is impossible to make fun of them*". He went on to make an important distinction, "*between a parody taking itself seriously, as in the Bond films, and a parody playing for laughs*" (6). While many of the spy films already mentioned in this survey include parodic moments at the expense of James Bond, few were out and out parodies. Hagopian includes *Hot Enough for June!*, *Licensed to Kill*, *Where the Bullets Fly* and *The Liquidator* in his survey of Bond parodies in the 1960s, but these are best understood as imitators, exhibiting the same sort of self-consciousness as the Bond original (2009).[145] Importantly, the emphasis in these pictures remains on thrills, with some comic elements, and they can best be understood as pastiche, mere imitation, the approach lacking the transformation and critical distance of parody, and creating more similarity than divergence. Yet, we can find in another group of films Johnson's criteria of mainly playing for laughs, films subversive and flippant in their relationship to the prototext, and better fitting the description of parody.

Harries has identified six methods that constitute the construction of the parodic and ironic metatext: reiteration, inversion, misdirection, literalisation, extraneous inclusion and exaggeration; and these qualities are readily observable in the small group of British spy spoofs which emerged from the middle of the 1960s. The first of these was *Carry On Spying*, released in June 1964. This was the ninth entry in a long-running series of comedy films, which had initially poked fun at British institutions like the army (*Carry On Sergeant*, 1958), hospitals (*Carry On Nurse*, 1959) and the police (*Carry On Constable*, 1960), but was just beginning to switch focus towards spoofing films and genres, as with *Carry On Cleo* (1964), *Carry On Cowboy* (1965) and *Carry on Screaming!* (1966). The *Carry On* franchise was the most prolific series in film history, and running through to *Carry On Columbus* in 1992, it embraced 30 feature films, one compilation film, and a host of television specials and stage shows. The film series was produced at Pinewood Studios by Peter Rogers and directed by Gerald Thomas. The low-budget comedies, drawing on the established working-class humour of the music-hall and saucy seaside postcards, and squarely in the tradition of old corn, innocent innuendo, and good natured irreverence, were largely derided by the critics, but popular with audiences. The *Carry On* imprint eventually established itself as a national institution; an undemanding cinema of "*irresistible badness*" (*Observer*, 9 August 1964).

As the *Carry On* formula switched to historical subjects and parodies of established film genres, *Carry On Spying* (1964) targeted the James Bond movies, which had begun to appear two years earlier, and Rogers had registered the title soon after the appearance of *Dr No* in 1962, realising the commercial potential of the idea. In *Spying* a group of raw recruits serving at British Operational Security Headquarters (BOSH) are assigned to recover a secret formula stolen from a research establishment, a situation described in the *Daily Mail* as a "*case of the moron chasing the cretin*" (28 July 1964). The team includes their pompous leader Simkins (Kenneth Williams), Charles Bind (Charles Hawtry, the Bond producers had threatened legal action if Rogers had gone ahead with the planned character name of James Bind), and the glamorous Daphne Honeybutt (Barbara Windsor, agent number 38-22-35). The film has much fun at the expense of the incompetent agents and the camp demeanour of the men. When Bind is asked his agent number, he replies "*Double O, O*". When asked to clarify, he reveals that the officer who assigned the number had simply said "*Double O, oh?*" A pistol with a drooping barrel is an apt symbol of the men's questionable masculinity. James Bond-like, the group is up against a master villain, the cross-gender Dr Crow ('Dr No'!, Judith Furse), first of a new super-race of Men-Women endowed with the physical and mental attributes of both sexes, and head of the evil organisation STENCH: The Society for the Total Extinction for Non-Conforming Humans. A trick attaché case, wristwatch garrotte and Orient Express setting reference the recently successful *From Russia, With Love*, while a radio transmitter concealed in a bra is a typical invention of the *Carry On* brand.

The other main intertextual reference is the classic British crime film *The Third Man*. Accordingly, Vienna is stereotypically constructed in terms of rain-soaked streets, sewers, black cats, balloon-sellers and zither music. When the party of inept spies arrives at the Café Mozart and is shown to a table "*Reserved for Party of British Agents*", there comes the inevitable response: "*Do you think they're onto us?*" The action shifts swiftly to Algiers to allow the film to make its nod to *Casablanca*, and finally to the underground lair of Dr Crow where the team are held captive and where the brainless Honeybutt is subjected to a bout of brainwashing, aimed to make her reveal the secret formula she has memorised ("*take one tablespoon of nitro-glycol ...*"). In a last minute rescue, the group is saved by an agent of The Society for the

Neutralization of Germs (SNOG), and taking an elevator from the secret underground base, emerge directly in the office of the Chief of BOSH – with Dr Crow's secret headquarters set to blow-up imminently.

While it has been customary for critics to pass over the *Carry Ons* as a cinema that "*defied criticism*" (*Daily Herald*, 31 July 1964), the responses to *Carry On Spying* sometimes verged on favourable and this could be because it was too early yet for critics to have become disenchanted with the spy film generally.[146] *The Times* judged the picture a "*return to form*" for the series, and begrudgingly admitted that, when all is said and done, the picture was "*very funny*" (30 July 1964). The reviewer at the *Spectator* enjoyed the burlesque and judged the latest *Carry On* as "*thoroughly outrageous*" and "*probably the funniest and certainly the crudest to date*" (7 August 1964). The *Guardian* found it "*pretty funny if you're in a really undemanding mood*" (31 July 1964). Film historian Robert Murphy has trumpeted *Carry on Spying* as "*the first and best attempt to parody the new spy film*" (1992: 220).

The *Carry On* films delighted in cocking-a-snook at the sort of British authority figures revered in the James Bond tradition, and instead celebrated aspects of national identity such as feyness, gullibility and muddling through which were the exact opposite of the traits demanded of the iconic super agent. In their opposing ways, both James Bond and the *Carry On*'s portrayed something essential about the British and their perception of themselves.

Of a quite different order was the spoof film *Modesty Blaise*. The 'capers' of Modesty Blaise written by Peter O'Donnell initially appeared as comic-strips in the London *Evening Standard* commencing on 13 May 1963 and were syndicated in newspapers around the world. O'Donnell was invited to write a screenplay for a film, and although this was later revised out of recognition by others, he turned the story into a popular novel published as *Modesty Blaise* in 1965. Modesty and her right hand man and friend Willie Garvin crave adventure and agree to serve Tarrant of British Intelligence in an operation to ship £10 million in diamonds to the Sheikdom of Malaurak, a small Middle-Eastern state which will grant Great Britain important oil concessions. The master villain is Gabriel, and Blaise and Garvin enter his camp on the pretext that the skilled Willie will serve on the diving operation that will release the diamonds from the freighter. The robbery takes place, Blaise and Garvin are exposed as agents of the British Secret Service and are kept prisoner with the diamonds on a small island in the eastern Mediterranean. The concluding action of the story is the meticulous escape of the two heroes, the retrieval of the diamonds and the bloody elimination of Gabriel's gang.

Modesty Blaise was an action-packed spy thriller for the 1960s, the adventure unfolding across London, the south of France, Egypt and the eastern Mediterranean. As the reviewer in the *Evening Standard* predictably stated,

"*Comparisons of Modesty with James Bond are irresistible*"; after all, the similarities were marked: "*the restless changing scenes, the ingenuity of both sides,
the violence, the surging confidence in the telling*".[147] Literary historian Rosie
White has indeed referred to Modesty as a "*masculine agent in a feminine
body*" (2007: 76). *Modesty Blaise* deployed the sex, sadism and snobbery associated with Bond, and added to this a stronger sense of camp, as in Gabriel's
predilection for watching Tom and Jerry cartoons. Blaise is accomplished in
dress sense, interior decor, etiquette, cooking, yoga, and armed and unarmed
combat, and as Rosie White has observed, is "*at ease with the burgeoning
global consumer culture*", "*marking her as a product of the new freedoms of
liberated sexuality and consumerism*" (73, 76). The cruder Garvin is a killing
machine, expert in exotic forms of weaponry, and designs gadgets such as an
exploding tie pin which decapitates. However, the story and its characters
also differed from the James Bond template: Blaise and Garvin were not
agents of the state, and embodied a totally different class background, she an
immigrant and he a wayward reform school adventurer. Self-educated and
self-made, the pair were symbols of the era's ideal of meritocracy, posing "*fantasies of freedom and agency in an era when the power of multinational capital was becoming increasingly evident*" (ibid.: 75). The novel was a popular
success, the crime critic in the *Observer* judging it "*Crude, violent, quite exciting, and not totally unreadable*" (11 July 1965).[148]

The rights to the novel were acquired by producer Joseph Janni as a star vehicle for the Italian actress Monica Vitti. He initially gave the assignment to
the veteran filmmaker Sidney Gilliat to write and direct; however, Gilliat withdrew when he discovered that the demanding actress had script approval
(Brown 1977: 153).[149] *Modesty Blaise* was passed on to the American exile
Joseph Losey who turned it into a pop art spoof of the spy film trend of the
middle-1960s, expensively filmed in Amsterdam, Sicily, Naples and London.
As well as Vitti as Blaise, its star cast included Terence Stamp as Garvin and
Dirk Bogarde as Gabriel, the arch-fiend, played, according to *Time Magazine*,
as a "*faggoty Edwardian fop*" (13 July 1966).[150] The picture, released by 20th
Century Fox in 1966, retained only the bare bones of the original story, the
script substantially the work of Evan Jones a regular collaborator with Losey.
The eye-catching design was by Richard Macdonald, another regular associate of the director, and in this respect the *Observer* likened the picture to a
"*travel brochure animated by a surrealist with a sharp eye for witty* bric-à-brac
... *a triumph of inventive obsolescence, with instant rust built into its modish
glitter*" (8 May 1966). Vitti's intransigence and constant deferring to her mentor, Italian director Michelangelo Antonioni, made life difficult for Losey, who
later defensively explained that in a situation of intrigue and hostility he
didn't function well (Ciment 1985: 254).[151]

With its celebrated cast and auteur film director, *Modesty Blaise* was closer to the European art film than popular cinema. Some theorists have argued that through the comic refunctioning of parody, there lies the possibility of critique, achieved through deliberate mockery, ridicule and destabilisation (Palmer 2005: 80). Losey maintained a serious intent for the film, presenting it as a comment on the indiscriminate violence of popular cinema and society, and claiming that he deployed a *"highly satirical approach to violence in order to infiltrate the principles of anti-violence without in any way detracting from the purely entertainment aspect of the film"* (*Modesty Blaise* press sheet). Losey loathed commercial spy thrillers, calling them *"filthy pictures ... abominably made and styleless"*, and he offered instead a stylised critique of the genre (quoted in Leahy 1967: 149). Some critics appreciated the picture on this elevated level, the *Sunday Times* sensing *"Losey's brilliant satire on our modern dream world"* (8 May 1966) and *The Times* acknowledging a picture revelling *"in its own preposterousness"* and managing *"to work inside the conventions of the secret-agent genre and keep us on the edge of our seats even though we giggle"* (5 May 1966). The *Evening Standard* was invigorated by a *"way-out thriller"*, claiming *Modesty Blaise* as a film that *"sums up the mood of the times"*: *"an Advertising Age fantasy, a moral-free fairy-tale for the Novelty Generation, a parody thriller born out of the Pop Art of the comic strips, an outrageously frivolous bit of High Camp, an Op Art extravaganza"* (8 May 1966). Although *Modesty Blaise* has been appreciated as only a minor picture by Losey, his supporters have found things of value in the film. Colin Gardner argues a synthesis of subversive intent between screenwriter and director, a script that manages a postcolonial critique of Western ideological discourse and a film offering a critical mimicry of establishment representations. *Modesty Blaise*, Gardner concludes, stands for a *"well pointed ideological critique of the macho and amoral cliché's of the espionage genre"* (2006: 181). A conscious celebration of instability, he asserts, evident in Modesty's shifting hair colour and clothes *within* a scene (something which annoyed many reviewers), constructed a critical distance and transformed a neutrally playful parody into a more undermining wilful mockery of the spy genre (185). Toby Miller is in broad agreement, suggesting the picture *"exemplifies female identity as a masquerade – shifting, sensual, often expendable"*, judging this a *"breakthrough in representations that borrowed from traditional representations and stereotypes and either hyperbolized or subverted their meaning to create a world of pop espionage"*. And for this critic, the radical approach was not *"at the expense of pleasure"* (2003: 169).

However, the movie adaptation was not generally appreciated in its own time, some reviewers having to dig deep into the picture to find something worth salvaging. The *Sun* warmed to the film as *"the most stylish, the most elegant, the most high camp example so far of high-fashion spy parody"*, a film of "*cold laughter*" and "*calculated sadism*" (4 May 1966). A longer piece in the *New Society* described the picture as "*elite pop*", and declared it a "*fundamentally serious film (short on good jokes) that uses a socially current visual platform as a jumping-off point for a personal and original game with images and symbols*". He saw significance in the film's theme of "*sexual reversal and interchange*", claimed Modesty as a rival to James Bond, yet unlike the women characters in *The Avengers* she was not a sidekick to a superior male protagonist (5 May 1966). The *Spectator* found *Modesty Blaise* "*funny*" and "*exquisitely accomplished*", a welcome riposte to the "*lumpy*" James Bond films, although this didn't raise the picture above "*screen nonsense*" (13 May 1966). Paraphrasing Pablo Picasso, the *Daily Express* ominously warned: "*Before you make satires on spy films you should first know how to make them*" (4 May 1966).

Modesty Blaise, however, substantially failed to please either the art film crowd, which found it cartoonish and insubstantial, nor the popular audience, which found it lacked suspense and was not particularly funny, and the picture was not a success. While the *Guardian* reassured its readers that "Modesty Blaise *is not just another spy spoof*", it couldn't escape the conclusion that it was a "*frivolous work*" (6 May 1966). Other reviewers were confused, uncertain what type of picture Losey had intended. "*Is it*", the *Financial Times* pondered, "*an attempt to interpret in film terms the pop art idioms of the comic strip to which, in origin,* Modesty Blaise? ... *Or is its intention to send up the secret agent film which is already in itself a send-up? Is it surrealist comedy or satirical farce or decorator's piece? Or all three?*" (6 May 1966). The *Daily Mail* complained of a film "*so incomprehensible that the scenes seem to have been shuffled and replaced in the wrong order*" (4 May 1966) and the *Evening News* that the picture added up to little more than a "*beautiful mess*" (5 May 1966). *Time Magazine* believed the "*parroty parody*" added up to a "*near disaster*", the damage done to the chosen target of the James Bond school "*negligible*", and the picture "*less a spoof than a limp-wristed kind of fairy tale, witlessly cluttered up with homosexual malice, artsy gift-shop decor, and the same old gaggy gadgetry on which the Bondsmen have patents pending*" (13 July 1966). It was felt by many that with *Modesty Blaise*, the director had lost himself to self-indulgence, a criticism that would adhere to the filmmaker and future pictures like *Boom!* and *Secret Ceremony* (both 1968).[152] It was also widely thought that Losey was "*slumming*" with *Modesty Blaise* and "*female Bondery*", it being pointedly expressed that, "*this isn't Losey's country. He can't make spy films*" (*Evening News*, 5 May 1966; *Daily Express*, 4 May 1966). In a longer critique, the respected critic Penelope Houston wrote of the film's thrall to the modern, the lure of impermanence and the ephemeral as evident in such contemporary commercial arts as fashion photographs, posters, comic strips, colour supplements and James Bond. While sensing that freewheeling young filmmakers like Richard Lester and Jean-Luc

Godard could engage credibly with the idioms of the moment, she considered Losey a director of an older generation, lacking involvement and unequipped to take disposable civilisation for granted, unable to work from inside its values and sort them out on his own terms. Dedicated to a "*blinding chic*", the film unfortunately drowned in its own decor without making a discernible point (1966).

Film historian Robert Murphy complains of "*smirky, indulgent performances*" and that "*Losey seems to have little understanding of the genre he attempts to subvert*" (1992: 230-1); literary critic Rosie White of a "*bizarre film adaptation*" (2007: 69). It was commonplace to assert that Losey had little natural inclination for comedy and that unfortunately many comic scenes had been "*sacrificed*" through an "*unfunny presentation*". The *Financial Times* continued, judging that if the picture was just a "*smart comic-strip joke*", then it seemed a "*rather long one*" (6 May 1966). The *Morning Star*, hoping against hope for the "*spy film to end all spy films*" and the final bursting of the "*James Bond myth*", was disillusioned to discover that, "*exposing nonsense by ridicule only leads to double nonsense*" (7 May 1966). It could be that *Modesty Blaise* in 'sending up the send up' had gone one contortion too far. The picture now enjoys a reputation as a camp, cult classic, a film of remarkable visual invention and iconic of the playfulness of the high-1960s; while some Losey die-hards discern in the film an old-leftist's critique of conspicuous consumption and an international politics enslaved to oil and power: barren moralities which unthinkingly underpin the routine spy caper ideologically invested in a Cold War economy of limitless greed, violence and amoral cynicism. *Modesty Blaise* was the unsuccessful British entry at the Cannes Film Festival.[153]

Even more wild, confusing and iconoclastic was the first 'unofficial' James Bond picture to hit the screens. Producer Charles K. Feldman had acquired the rights to *Casino Royale*, the only Fleming book not under the control of movie producers Albert 'Cubby' Broccoli and Harry Saltzman, and originally intended his film to be a straight thriller. The celebrated Hollywood screenwriter Ben Hecht had several attempts at a script, and, reportedly, Billy Wilder, George Mandel, Mickey Rose, Frank Buxton, Joseph Heller, Terry Southern, Wolf Mankowitz, Michael Sayers and John Law all took a turn at the alleged 15 versions of the screenplay. The project, which from the outset was impelled to "*out-Bond all the other Bond movies*" increasingly shifted towards an outrageous spoof; a "*far out irreverent comedy*" aimed at young adults much along the lines of Feldman's earlier success *What's New Pussycat?* (US, 1965) (Duncan 2012: 132; *Telegram*, 5 November 1966). During shooting, improvisation from star Peter Sellers, and material from co-star Woody Allen (contracted for 10 weeks he stayed for nine months) and director John Huston for their own scenes, added to the spirit of comedy. The madcap story retains but the bare bones of the original novel. A reclusive Sir James Bond (David Niven) is tempted out of retirement to deal with an unprecedented threat in which agents of the British, American, Russian and French services are being eliminated. Various attempts are made on the life of Bond, all by female operatives in the service of the evil Dr Noah. To confuse the enemy, all Western agents are henceforth to be known as James Bond, which explains the tagline for the movie: "Casino Royale *is too much for one James Bond!*"[154] The mission, about all that is retained from the book, gradually centres on Le Chiffre (Orson Welles), the banker of SMERSH, who urgently needs funds to pay off debts. Evelyn Tremble (Peter Sellers), who has devised an infallible method for baccarat, is despatched by Vesper Lynd (Ursula Andress) to play and defeat Le Chiffre at Casino Royale.[155] It is eventually revealed that Dr Noah is Jimmy Bond (Woody Allen), the intimidated nephew of Sir James, and his two-part master plan is to unleash a germ that will make all women beautiful and kill all men shorter than himself, and to replace world leaders with robots under his control. The film ends in a frantic fight at Casino Royale in which all are killed in a gigantic explosion.

Casino Royale had a long, difficult and expensive shoot, such that a contemporary report claimed that the filming "*went on for so long and became a way of life for so many, that few believe it is actually over*" (quoted in Duncan 2012: 132). The press delighted in reporting the confusion surrounding the "*never-ending, ever-spending*" maverick Bond production (*Sun*, 23 July 1966; *Variety*, 10 November 1965).[156] The *Morning Star* labelled the laboured process as "*film-making gone berserk*" (13 April 1967). The original director Joe McGrath was fired at some point, and remaining material and additional 'segments' were shot by John Huston, Val Guest, Ken Hughes and Robert Parrish, an approach rationalised by Feldman as an application of Fordian industrial "*specialisation*" to filmmaking, belatedly claiming that the "*concept of this film has always included not only multiple stars but also multiple directors*" (quoted in the *Guardian*, 4 May 1966). A reporter labelled the novel approach "cinema du cirque" (quoted in Duncan 2012: 132), while Guest described the experience as "*one of the most unique assignments*" of his "*kaleidoscopic career*" (2001: 155). The temperamental star Peter Sellers made life difficult for all concerned and was let go at some point with some of his scenes still to be shot (*Evening Standard*, 15 April 1966),[157] some roles were cast at the very last minute, and there were many delays in production, opportunities producer Feldman took to sign up yet another star who happened to be passing through London to play a cameo.[158] Much material ended up on the cutting room floor and the picture, announced as a three-hour extravaganza with an interval and conceived as the "*Bond movie to end all Bond movies*", was eventually released in a more conventional 131 minutes form with an accomplished score by Burt Bacharach (*Time*, 6 May 1966).[159]

The film attracted universally bad reviews, most critics finding it an ill-judged, rambling and misfiring farce.[160] The *Guardian* judged it a "*big, colourful, noisy, star-studded, plot-less junk-pile of a mess*" (14 April 1967); the *Financial Times* as "*sheer, unadulterated hell*" (14 April 1967); and the American *Village Voice* as "*boringly incoherent*" (15 April 1967). The *Observer* was assaulted by a "*flailing mish-mash*" and complained that every scene is "*ambushed by some preening gag or egomaniacal bit of business*" (16 April 1967). Reporting on what it considered as "*Bond in Bedlam*", the *Daily Mirror* encountered an "*opulent nightmare of plodding puns, ghastly good humour, see-it-a-mile-off buffoonery and over-sexed bedroomery*", the reviewer pronouncing *Casino Royale* the "*worst film I ever enjoyed*" (14 April 1967).

An on-set report in the *Guardian* noted that, "*Even the spoofs are seeking to out-spoof each other*" (4 May 1966); and, as though in comment, the American *Saturday Review* pronounced that it was "*rather difficult to parody something that is already a parody*", declaring in the case of *Casino Royale*, "*the defeat is overwhelming*" (20 May 1967). The *Daily Mail* was conclusive in its judgement, describing the film as the "*biggest, busiest, loudest and most inconsequential of all the Bond pictures. And quite the unfunniest*" (14 April 1967). However, audiences, especially in America, delighted in the zany, star-studded send-up of a very popular genre and the picture made lots of money. It is now a cult film, a camp classic, a psychedelic James Bond, endlessly absorbing in the manner of a train wreck. There is more than a hint of fascination in the *Guardian's* later put down that Feldman's *Casino Royale* was the "*most grotesque and moronic Bond spoof of all*" (20 July 2002). The secret agent spoof in general was not widely popular with critics. The *Sunday Telegraph* in the summer of 1966 complained of a "*genre so enervating*", the reviewer, overcome with the "*urge to mutiny*", muttering: "*I haven't run out of things to say about the hideous spy spoof drama but I've run out of any relish for saying them*" (31 July). In the previous month, *The Telegraph* happily reported on a "*genre which now appears to be at death's door*" (6 May 1966).

Looking back on the spy thriller and its omni-competent heroes since the arrival of James Bond on movie screens in 1962 in *Dr No*, the *Observer* summarised the flamboyant genre as "*that curious no-man's land or adventure playground of the mind that exists between* Playboy *and* Boy's Own Paper" (12 June 1983). This conflation of traditional and modern traits of heroism and masculinity characterised the action-orientated spy story of the period which served as a harbinger and sustainer of the 'Swinging Sixties' and its associated social and stylistic trends. The cycle of secret agent films, beyond an initial curiosity, did not unduly occupy critics who tended to tire of them as too simplistic, too consciously hip, and largely undemanding. In reviewing spy pictures in the second half of the sixties it became standard critical practice to bemoan yet another secret agent melodrama. To take two examples at random from mid-1968, one finds an annoyed *Films and Filming* claiming that, "*Secret agents ... have overstayed their welcome*" (review of *Sebastian*, June: 30), and the *Guardian* stating that, "*it's becoming increasingly difficult to make anything memorable in this genre*" (review of *A Dandy in Aspic*, 5 April). As we have seen, the spy adventure cycle continued on with apparently diminishing returns into the 1980s and by which time it was no longer a vital genre in the British cinema. However, an alternative form of spy story also emerged in the 1960s, one which presented critics with a more serious treatment of espionage, informed by a greater sense of reality and a more complex treatment of morality. In 1967, *Sight and Sound* confessed that as the spy films proliferate, "*one's interest seems to veer towards the men who live in the shadows*" (Spring 1967: 96). Such men with their burdens, anxieties and doubts peopled the espionage drama which is examined in the next chapter.

2.
The Espionage Drama in the Cinema

*Since its popular recognition in the early twentieth century, the spy nov-
el has served as a vehicle to pursue the darker political imaginations of
the Western world.*
(Brett F. Woods 2008: 1)

*It is curious that the novels of Ian Fleming and those of John le Carré
should enjoy popularity simultaneously.*
(*Herald Tribune,* 17 June 1967)

The intelligence historian Adam Svendsen identifies a "*serious*" form of spy
fiction, one which, when explored, "*emerges as a compelling and legitimate
source worthy of study*"; an alternative well of evidence "*which can comple-
ment the contributions made by the non-fiction material*" (2009: 1). Svendsen
sees in the espionage fiction of writers such as Graham Greene and John le
Carré an opportunity for the historian of secret service to capture the "*opera-
tions-focused intelligence world*", a source elucidating many of the "*intangibles*" or "*personal factors*" of the secret world where the archives are often at
their weakest; such as the elusive qualities of "*trust and betrayal*" (2). For
Svendsen, "*realistic and informed espionage novels*" can be "*lightly fictionalised versions of reality*", offering "*Less officially constrained insights*" into the
domain of intelligence and espionage (5, 3, 4). "*Serious*" spy fiction, in contrast to the more frivolous mainstream, poses a greater intellectual challenge,
and provides "*ample opportunities for encouraging (even provoking) in-depth
reflection on intense philosophical, moral and ethical questions, such as regarding trust and betrayal, which are constantly encountered in the intelligence world*" (15). The historian Brett F. Woods has suggested that accomplished spy narratives, drawing on the documentary record and demonstra-
ble geopolitical alignments, and often crafted by former operatives, to all
intents and purposes, "*assume complete historical authority*" (2008: 2); a line
of thought further promoted by former intelligence agents Tod Hoffman and
Frederick Hitz, who have argued how close the fictional accounts of authors
like le Carré can be to factual reality (Hoffman 2001; Hitz 2004).[161]

The espionage drama, in contrast to the spy thriller dealt with in the previous chapter, corresponds to the kind of "*serious*" spy fiction distinguished by
Svendsen and others. In many cases, espionage dramas have been adaptations of the more critically-admired spy stories of such writers as le Carré,
Greene and Len Deighton. In a few instances, new writing for the screen has
been of such merit and ambition, and realised in such praiseworthy productions, that a drama has been raised above the run of the mill thriller. The bulk
of writing in the romantic and adventurous style of spy fiction has been dismissed as 'sub-literary'; however, the espionage drama belongs in the privileged tradition of the 'philosophical' and 'realistic' school of spy fiction, one
commencing with the early writers Joseph Conrad and W. Somerset
Maugham, and proceeding through Eric Ambler, Graham Greene and John le
Carré (Woods 2008: 53-77). Such authors of espionage fiction engage with
issues already evident in the actual world of intelligence, through a process
Svendsen calls "*virtual-reality*": troubling themes which include the murky
realm of trust and betrayal; the duplicity between allies and the morality of
"*friends spying on friends*"; the end of empire and the painful decline in world
status for Britain; and the tendency of agents and agencies of opposing sides,
through professional codes and practices, to begin to resemble one another
(Svendsen 2009: 6). Literary scholar John R. Snyder uses the label "*authentic
spy-story*" to delineate those narratives which represent an "*intellectual enterprise*" and build a "*sophisticated philosophy of how one can or cannot exist
– physically, morally, spiritually – in a realistically apprehended world of complex historical pressures*" (1977: 228); while cultural critic Michael Denning
uses the term "*existential thrillers*" to describe the more thoughtful spy novels
of le Carré and Greene (1987: 34); stories which use, according to Dominic
Sandbrook, "*the issues of secrecy and betrayal to explore wider questions of
identity and morality*" (2006: 623). Joseph Oldham has noted how the serious
spy story draws on elements of the conspiracy thriller, and as a result is more
inclined to be pessimistic, adopt an oppositional perspective and locate "*its
heroes in isolated individuals who resist the corruption of institutions*" (2015).
The historically determined contrast, then, between the James Bond-inspired
spy thriller and the le Carré-Deighton espionage drama, as Toby Miller has
pointed out, has been that the former stood "*for the commodity culture of
youth pleasure and the modern moment, when affluence would effortlessly
continue and develop*", and the latter embodied the "*welfare-state reformism
of post-war Britain*" and its ideals of meritocracy and class mobility (2003:
119).

The new spy story of the early 1960s emerged principally from the pens of
John le Carré and Len Deighton, who developed and updated a tradition of
espionage literature which can be traced through Graham Greene, Eric Ambler and back to Somerset Maugham in the late 1920s and his influential

Ashenden tales. With their ambivalence and resignation, the le Carré and Deighton stories, in the words of literary critic Sam Goodman, shaped the "*core ideological foundations of the period and genre, setting certain, yet distinct, stylistic precedents during the time, based on individual concerns with regard to their wider political context*" (2016: 10). In contrast to Greene and Ian Fleming, the new writing tended to eschew locations in the far-flung empire and to rely on a more restricted space; the stories "*largely enacted in office buildings, down-at-heel areas of London, or drab suburban environments, a dramatic contrast to the established conventions of the genre and the authors that preceded them*" (11). The settings marked out the inconsequentiality and banality of the Secret Service; and for some readers and critics the approach represented a more realistic, at least more credible, treatment of espionage, with the petty rivalries, betrayals and ineptitude seemingly confirmed by recent events. The new secret agent protagonists of le Carré and Deighton were also downgraded from the James Bond archetype, now "*expendable foot soldiers instead of glamorous superspies*" (Maulucci Jnr. 2008: 335). In its responsiveness to "*contextual influences*", the new spy fiction can be revealed as an "*active component of cultural history*", consolidating rather than compensating for, in the manner say of Fleming, the popular anxieties of the period (12).

Case file 1: John le Carré on the big screen in the 1960s

Le Carré knows, from his Foreign Office days, what the world of espionage smells like.
(*Guardian*, 18 October 1982)

For decades to come, the spy world will continue to be the collective couch where the subconscious of each nation is confessed.
(John le Carré, *Guardian*, 16 November 1989)

John le Carré has set himself up as the spychoanalyst of the cold war.
(*Time Magazine*, 27 January 1967)

The year 1963 witnessed two defining events for spy history and spy fiction. In January, former MI6 officer Kim Philby fled to Moscow from Beirut, the culmination of several years of suppressed suspicions and official denials regarding his alleged treachery. The following September, John le Carré published *The Spy Who Came in from the Cold*, a genre-revising story of disillusionment, manipulation, moral ambivalence and betrayal, and a "*stark corrective to the glamorous fantasy of James Bond*" (Sandbrook 2006: 629). Tod Hoffman has claimed that with his sudden defection, Philby took with him the West's confidence in the reliability of the security services. "*How*", it was asked, "*are they to protect us when they were so inadequate at safeguarding themselves?"* (2001: 111).[162] Critic Ron Rosenbaum suggests that the true legacy of Kim Philby was an *"Age of Paranoia"*, a period characterised by a *"plague of suspicion, distrust, disinformation"*, a *"conspiracy consciousness that has emanated like gamma radiation from intelligence agencies East and West, the perverse feeling of unfathomable deceit that has destabilised our confidence in the knowability of history"* (quoted in ibid.).[163] The burgeoning scepticism of the public regarding authority and the government readily produced a readership for morally complex stories and, it has been pointed out, *"le Carré's work satisfied a growing demand for plausibility and a desire for the 'truth' of the spy world that inspired the fiction"* (Goodman 2016: 4). A reviewer has labelled John le Carré the *"historian-cum-psychiatrist of the secrecy business"* (*Daily Mail* 11 April 1991), and it was the seeming authenticity of the stories and the psychologically penetrating narratives which caught the imagination of readers. Le Carré himself has described espionage as the *"secret theatre of our society"*. In the hush-hush back rooms, he has claimed, *"we find out who we are – what we want, what are our ethical priorities, what freedoms we value and what other freedoms we will give up to protect them"* (quoted in Dorril 1993: 428).

The Spy Who Came in from the Cold, a story populated with defectors, double-agents and a disillusioned spy, distilled the feelings of impotency, futility and frustration which many felt in the wake of the endless-seeming security outrages of recent times. Commencing with the flight to Moscow of Guy Burgess and Donald Maclean in May 1951 (but not fully made public until September 1955), the 1950s and early 1960s had visited a number of embarrassing spy scandals on harassed governments and an incredulous public. The frogman Commander Crabb went missing during an unauthorised survey of a Soviet cruiser moored in Britain on a 'goodwill' visit in 1956, only to re-appear dramatically a year later as a headless, handless corpse,[164] and various spies were unearthed in secret establishments: the duplicitous George Blake at MI6 and the blackmailed homosexual John Vassall at the Admiralty. 1963, the year of *Spy*, witnessed the shattering Profumo Affair, in which the Minister of War in the Conservative Government was found to be sharing a call-girl with the Soviet Naval Attaché, the trial of Dr Giuseppe Martelli for the alleged leaking of atom secrets to the Soviets, and, as we have seen, the flight of Kim Philby. Historian Dominic Sandbrook has commented on how the *"series of security scandals in the early sixties ... severely tarnished the reputation not only of the intelligence services but also of Macmillan's Conservative government"* (2006: 633); noting for these years that, *"the issue of espionage was simply more relevant than ever before"* (596). A series of tribunals, reports, commissions and enquiries kept the issues of security and official competence before an excited public.[165] The seeming failures in national security were interpreted in class terms and laid squarely at the feet of the 'Establishment', which it was felt held sway over an antiquated, enfeebled and entrenched social and political system run by and for 'the best people'. Following the revelations about Blake, Vassall and Philby, morale had slumped and suspicions increased inside British Intelligence, and the "*serious*" spy story in the hands of a writer and experienced intelligence officer (although hidden at the time) such as John le Carré could thus function as a meaningful critique of contemporary society.[166] A reviewer once identified that what really seemed to interest le Carré, even more than the mechanics of spying, was the "*mentality of the Intelligence world, its combination of subtlety, complacence and indifference, its deviousness which corrodes everything it touches*" (*Observer*, 3 February 1980). Le Carré's *The Spy Who Came in from the Cold* was the fictional embodiment of Rebecca West's contemporary feeling of the "*dreariness of the cold war*" (1964: 192).

Dominic Sandbrook, the diligent historian of contemporary Britain, has marked down the cultural importance of espionage and the secret agent in the national experience since World War II. On the one hand, the character of James Bond offered readers and later viewers a large dose of fantasy, potency and reassurance. In a different vein, the new novels of Len Deighton and John le Carré spoke to uncertainties harboured by some of the reading public. Sandbrook writes: "*Fear of spies and subversives were often really displaced anxieties about the general decline of British prestige and power, or anxieties about the pace of social changes at home and the threat they seemed to pose to the assumptions of the middle-class spy-story reader*". He goes on to suggest: "*The spy story, then, had proved an excellent vehicle to carry popular resentments, and it was no surprise that the social changes of the post-war world found their expression in a new generation of spy stories in print and on celluloid*" (2006: 595). Le Carré felt some revulsion at the character of James Bond, describing him in 1966 as "*neo-fascistic and totally materialist*", a "*consumer-goods hero*", "*some kind of international gangster*", a figure entirely outside of the political context who in all likelihood "*would have gone through the same antics for any country ... if the girls had been so pretty and the Martini's so dry*" (quoted in the *Radio Times*, 21-27 August 2010: 24; Crutchley 1966: 7). Such strongly felt convictions were likely to influence the author's own spy fiction and eventually impelled him to write a watershed novel. Le Carré saw things in these terms, acknowledging that *The Spy Who Came in from the Cold* "*marked a boundary between two eras: The era of God-is-on-our-side patriotism, of trust in government and in the morality of the West, and the era of paranoia, of conspiracy theory and suspicion of government, of moral drift*" (quoted in Schiff 1989: 98).[167]

The Spy Who Came in from the Cold, John le Carré's third novel, was published to great acclaim in 1963 and proved a major best-seller which ran to 12 impressions in its first six months. Reviewing the novel in the *Guardian*, crime writer Francis Illes called it a "*spy story documentary*" (11 October 1963). At the beginning of the tale, Alec Leamas is at the Berlin Wall as he watches one of his agents being shot dead at a checkpoint between East and West of the city. Leamas has recently seen the destruction of his networks in the German Democratic Republic (DDR) and returns to 'the Circus' in London, the Secret Intelligence Service (SIS). He is pleased to be offered the lead role in an elaborate operation to discredit Mundt, the ruthless head of the East German counter-espionage service. The plan requires Leamas seemingly to turn to drink as a result of his failure in Berlin, to leave the Service under a cloud, and to serve a short spell in prison for assault. A deadbeat former intelligence officer, he attracts the interest of the East German Secret Service as a possible defector, and Leamas is interrogated in Holland and the DDR, where he carefully plants suspicions regarding Mundt. The ambitious Fiedler, the deputy of Mundt, is fed the necessary material and perspective, and calls a tribunal seeking to expose his superior. The court unexpectedly calls a witness, Liz Gold, a young British communist with whom Leamas had become close during his decline, and she inadvertently reveals the plotting of the British, and Mundt is able to turn the tables, and Fiedler and Leamas are arrested. It transpires that British Intelligence, in a plot of Byzantine complexity and without the knowledge of Leamas, actually planned to discredit Fiedler, the loyal German official, taking suspicion away from Mundt, its man in the Abteilung. Secretly, Leamas and Gold are escorted back to the Berlin Wall with arrangements to get them to the West. However, Liz is callously shot while scaling the Wall, Mundt not wishing to risk a civilian outside of the framework of intelligence revealing what she knows, and a disillusioned Leamas allows himself to be killed rather than return to London and a world he no longer believes in. The story thus begins and ends with death at the Berlin Wall, the ominous symbol of a divided world.[168]

The Spy Who Came in from the Cold was written while John le Carré was serving as an intelligence officer in Germany, allegedly quickly over a matter of weeks, and during a period when the author had witnessed the construction of the Berlin Wall.[169] Le Carré has commented on the impact of the Wall on the secret services at the time, recognising that "*the espionage industry was going to become more clandestine, more perilous, more questionable, and certainly more overcrowded than ever before*" (1991: ix). The Wall symbolically brackets the story, it is the place where death is enacted and, in the final outcome, as Gabriel Miller has expressed it, "*merely a barrier between two evils*" (2000: 91). The story was written at a time when le Carré was deeply unhappy in his professional and personal life, and this furnished the mood of the book and the loneliness and bitterness of Leamas. The novel has been widely appreciated as a watershed in the history of spy fiction, sour, cynical and real, an antidote to the glamour of James Bond.[170] The 'Cold' in the title refers to that particular state of aloneness and anxiety that pertains to the agent serving in the field. Le Carré artfully weaves into the story a constant sense of chill, indifference, detachment and aloofness, in atmosphere and characterisation, and provides a fittingly wintry environment for a tale of treachery, deception and betrayal in the Cold War. Leamas is the first of le Carré's important 'outsider' figures, a non-gentleman who didn't go to university, never mind Oxbridge. He is thus available for manipulation, deception, and is expendable; a pawn in a "*filthy, lousy operation*". In his review of the novel, Maurice Richardson felt that the "*homicidal wickedness and unscrupulousness of our side, sacrificing agent after agent, is laid on very strong*" (*Observer*, 15 September 1963). In the history of British espionage fiction, *Spy* is important on two counts: as an espionage novel which imposes a new level of realism on the story, and one that sees no ethical distinction between the intelligence services of East or West. A critic at the *Guardian* once praised the novel as a "*masterpiece of super realism, taut, hard, showing spying's soiled edges, making death hurt, and provoking the reader to a new and chilly vision of one bit of the world he lives in*" (3 September 1970). In terms of ethical practice, we witness the Circus, for operational gain, prepared to destroy the decent, honest, idealistic Jew Fiedler, in order to save the anti-Semitic, former Nazi, mercenary, ruthless killer Mundt. At a prescient moment, Fiedler asks Leamas if London would kill an innocent man, and the latter suggests that it would depend on "*need*". The wise German thus concludes: "*We're all the same you know, that's the joke*". In a magazine piece in 1966, le Carré summed up the mood and values of the ideological conflict: "*There is no victory in the Cold War, only a condition of human illness and a political misery*" (1966: 6).

As le Carré has recorded, *The Spy Who Came in from the Cold* sprung from a remarkable conflation of public and personal experience, confessing: "*I will never forget the time when a disgusting gesture of history coincided with some desperate mechanism inside myself, and in six weeks gave me the book that altered my life*" (1991: x). The novel, which was serialised in the *Sunday Express*, attracted universal acclaim, *Bookman* raving that "*the plot is so absorbing, the characterization so excellent, and the sense of realism so great that one becomes almost reluctant at times to dub it a work of fiction at all*".[171] *Spy* impressed other novelists and writers of spy fiction, and in a famous group of endorsements, Graham Greene claimed it "*The best spy story I have ever read*", Ian Fleming judged it "*A very, very fine spy story*", and J. B. Priestley found it "*Superbly constructed, with an atmosphere of chilly hell*".[172] There have been contrasting views as to the verisimilitude and believability of the story. In an early critique, the West German spy chief Günther Nollau pointed to the many operational and technical defects of the story (1965, quoted in Horn 2013: 261). More recently, a former officer of the Central Intelligence Agency (CIA) judged the story a *"plausible description of the intelligence business. And, with the acceptance of a fair amount of literary license, to which any author is entitled, I concluded that indeed le Carré still presents our world more accurately than most"* (Royden 2009: 11).

The Spy Who Came in from the Cold topped the best-seller list in both Great Britain and the United States, and was much honoured, being the first novel to win both the Gold Dagger Award of the Crime Writers' Association of Great Britain (CWA) and the Edgar Award of the Mystery Writers of America, and later winner of the Dagger of Daggers from the CWA as the all-time stand-out among the winners of the award.

The Spy Who Came in from the Cold (1966) was filmed in Europe for release by Paramount Pictures, directed and produced by Martin Ritt, and starred Richard Burton as Alec Leamas, Oskar Werner as Fiedler, Peter van Eyck as Mundt and Claire Bloom as Nan Perry.[173] The production used locations in London, Ireland, Holland and southern Germany and shot interiors at the Ardmore studios in Dublin. Ritt had bought the story rights while the novel was still in galley-proof and was gratifyingly surprised when he found he had an international best-seller on his hands. Acknowledging the story as *"rough and strong and bitter and critical and tough and sharp"*, the uncompromising director Ritt remained *"determined to shoot it that way"* and buck the dominant trend of escapist-romantic spy thrillers (Miller 2000: 80). Ritt had been a victim of McCarthyism in America in the 1950s, and he was possibly attracted to the story as it reflected his disgust at the cowardice of many of his peers and at the sickening sterility of the Cold War (Sisman 2015: 245). Co-scriptwriter Paul Dehn reported that Ritt insisted that, *"dialogue was keyed-down from melodrama to drama and from drama to flat realism"*, and that subsequently, the performance of the screenplay was *"purposefully pared, pruned, damped, clipped and shorn of even the minor histrionic affectations with which our actors are thought to mirror nature"*. Under the discipline of Ritt, Dehn, a former wartime special operations officer, acknowledged that *"spying had once again become as true as I knew it had differently been true in the 1940s"* (1966: 12-13). The realistic quality of the picture was acknowledged at *Kine Weekly* where it noted the story continuously wore the *"cloak of actuality"* and seldom wielded *"the more exciting dagger of fiction"*. The paper warned exhibitors that the uncompromising film represented a *"hard-ticket proposition"* (13 January 1966). *Spy* won the British Film Academy (BFA) Best British Picture Award.

The film, which attracted the odd unsupportive review on its release,[174] was highly praised for the acting of its leading players, many suggesting that Burton gave his greatest ever screen performance in the picture and for which he earned an Academy Award nomination and won the BFA Best British Actor

Award.[175] Le Carré, however, has always felt the star miscast and too "*noisy*" and too "*theatrical*" for the part (*Guardian*, 5 October 2002).[176] The visual accomplishment of *The Spy Who Came in from the Cold* was also acclaimed. The production was shot on location in black and white during the winter, capturing the sombre grey mood of the story and the shadowy world of spies. As Ritt understood it, "*None of the values in the story were black and white. I wanted rain or greyness in every scene – no sunlight*", an approach that effectively portrayed the sunless world of Cold War espionage (quoted in Miller 2000: 81). As Maulucci Jnr. has noted, such a visual approach conjured up a "*portrayal of international espionage as characterized by death, betrayal, and drabness*" (2008: 337). Oswald Morris shot the movie and his cinematography captured the "*dreariness of the novel's landscape, matching the climate and geography of the film to the emotional weariness of the characters who move through rainy streets in bleak, fog-bound cities*" (85). The *Observer* claimed his work "*deserved a place of honour among the triumphs of black-and-white photography*" (16 January 1966). The great British cinematographer won the BFA Best British Cinematography Award for black and white photography. The film, though, was a commercial disappointment, its dreary *mise-en-scene* and tragic theme out of sync with the dazzling youthful exuberance of the 'swinging' moment. Film historian Robert Murphy has commented that *The Spy Who Came in from the Cold* "*squats like a toad on the zany optimism of the Swinging 60s*" (1992: 224).

The more thoughtful reviewers appreciated that the film was a faithful adaptation of the novel and represented something new and distinct in the spy genre.[177] The *Sunday Times* was pleased to report: "*So at last there is a spy film in which nothing is easy and nobody is adventurous, dashing, acrobatic and nonchalant; in which the official double-cross can come from your own side; in which there are intimations not only of the bizarre but of the shady*" (16 January 1966). The *New Statesman* trumpeted that, "*this is verismo, anti-Bond, the real stuff*"; perceiving in it a reaction to the mainstream, in that: "*There's something almost aggressively seedy and nondescript about both Le Carre's book and the resultant movie, as if part of the inspiration at least had come from a trendy inclination to put down the world of Ian Fleming by turning it, conscientiously, arsy-versy*". And concluding that, "*It must have taken nerve to hold this whole uncommon enterprise so scrupulously down to earth*" (14 January 1966).

It was common to contrast *Spy* with the exuberant thrills of James Bond, *Monthly Film Bulletin* reminding viewers that an important part of the success of the original novel was its timing, "*cold, anti-romantic disenchantment, dry biscuits and railway coffee*" offering a "*necessary antidote to the euphoric champagne confidence of 007*" (February 1966: 19). The *Sun* touted the film as

"*The spy game without martinis*", a "*brilliant injection of antidote into the gasping, glamorous world of Bondism*" (11 January 1966), and the *Evening Standard* welcomed a "*grey ghost among the colourful exploits of current secret agentry*" (13 January 1966). The *Telegraph* asked: "*Is the cult of Bond beginning to fade?*" "*The key to anti-Bondage*" the reviewer informed his readers, is "*disillusion*", pointing out that, "*this curt grey fable of double-think and double-cross is vividly unheroic in its murky contempt for spies and spying*" (14 January 1966). The *People* applauded the "*first attempt to expose the spy trade as the sordid business it is, utterly without glamour or decency*", and recommended a "*film of horrible fascination which I expect to become a classic of its kind*" (16 January 1966). The *Sunday Telegraph* acknowledged the essential cynicism of the story and le Carré's hallmark of professional empathy among secret agents, noting that "*in the spy's world dislike, even hatred, is reserved for the people he knows, but for his enemy there is the friendly recognition of shared expertise*" (16 January 1966). The *Observer* informed its readers to expect "*the bread of espionage, not the circuses of Bondery*" (16 January 1966). A more political tack was adopted at the *Daily Worker*. While judging the picture a "*superbly produced*", "*finely acted ... seedy, squalid film*", it dismissed any possibility of meaningful critique, and, as with all other British espionage films, still felt *Spy* served as a "*contribution to the cold war itself*". "*In the world of spying in the cold war*", the left-wing paper reported, "*its message is: a plague on both your houses – but rather a bigger plague on the Communist house*". The *Daily Worker* also pointed out that following the recent exposure of ex-nazis in leading positions in West Germany, and the prompt way in which the German Democratic Republic has dealt with the very few that have been discovered in high posts there, "*it is no accident that in this film the G.D.R. intelligence chief is supposed to be an ex-nazi*". The reviewer was also far from impressed by the suggested naivety of the Communist Party branch secretary Nan Perry (11 January 1966). In hindsight, though, *The Spy Who Came in from the Cold*, as novel and motion picture, stands as a high-point of the espionage story in one of its greatest periods; a breakthrough tale which has exerted a tremendous influence on the thematics of spy fiction, and brought uncompromisingly to the screen to provide a grim portrayal of modern espionage.[178]

The next screen adaptation of John le Carré was *The Deadly Affair* in 1967, drawn from the 'apprentice' novel *Call for the Dead*, the author's début first published in 1961. The story introduced the author's principal series character George Smiley. Smiley, a former agent-runner in World War II, is now a senior officer at the Circus (SIS) in London. The story takes place in 1959 in and around London. Scandal results from the suicide of Samuel Fennan, a high-ranking civil servant at the Foreign Office, following Smiley's recent routine investigation into the official's communist past. Certain incidental factors lead Smiley to suspect foul play, and assisted by Mendel, a recently retired officer of Special Branch, he begins to unravel a long-standing operation in which the East German Dieter Frey, a former agent of Smiley's during the war, has been acquiring the unsuspecting Fennan's secrets through his wife, Elsa, a survivor of the concentration camps. The ruthless Mundt has killed the now suspicious Fennan and also badly injures Smiley. A trap is laid for Frey and he is killed during a struggle with Smiley. Mundt escapes to East Germany (where he would later feature prominently in *The Spy Who Came in from the Cold*).

Call for the Dead, like its successor *A Murder of Quality* (1962), is very much in the style of a detective novel, with Smiley piecing together the clues and coming to the conclusion of murder. Le Carré was still serving in British Intelligence when he published the story, writing in penny notebooks travelling to and from work and in his lunch hours. The author sought official approval from the Service, and the manuscript was read by the legal adviser who suggested only a single minor alteration to avoid the possibility of libel, and that the author used a pseudonym. The opening chapter provides an overview of George Smiley who would feature or appear in many of le Carré's novels until *Smiley's People* in 1979.[179] Several other characters would also play a part in the novelist's future sagas, Inspector Mendel, Peter Guillam, and the East German Mundt. A tale of treachery, *Call for the Dead* was of its time, making reference to actual traitors such as Klaus Fuchs and Donald Maclean, using a dramatic presentation of Christopher Marlowe's *Edward II* as a commentary within the novel on treachery and murder (and, of course, a play written by a practicing spy), and suggesting Smiley's sense of betrayal in killing Frey, a former student and colleague, who despite the opportunity and his ruthlessness could not come to kill Smiley.

The film version of *Call for the Dead* appeared early in 1967 as *The Deadly Affair*, scripted by Paul Dehn, fresh from *The Spy Who Came in from the Cold*, and produced and directed in London by the American Sidney Lumet for Columbia Pictures. Perhaps influenced by Ritt's *The Spy Who Came in from the Cold*, Lumet had wanted to film the production in black and white as more suitable for a downbeat spy picture, but Columbia with future sales to television in mind would not allow this.[180] So, the director asked Freddie Young the cinematographer to see what he could manage regarding the suppression of colour, and he came up with the solution of 'pre-fogging', exposing the film to 30 per cent of normal before shooting the picture. This had the effect of desaturating the colours without changing their value and the result is a depressing palette enhanced through shooting in outlying districts of London during a wet, bleak late winter. Lumet commented at the time: "*all the glamour is knocked out: everything is real; somehow the glamorous edge is taken off it, which is terribly important"* (*Kine Weekly*, 24 March 1966; *Variety*, 1 February 1967). The American *Saturday Review* judged the colour cinematography as *"so muted as to seem like tinted black-and-white"* (28 January 1967).

Some minor changes to the story were likely to annoy purists. Due to contractual reasons, the protagonist becomes Charles Dobbs (James Mason), as the George Smiley name now belonged to Paramount Pictures which had acquired it with the rights to *The Spy Who Came in from the Cold*; Peter Guillam becomes Bill Appleby (Kenneth Haigh) and Mundt becomes Karel Harek (Les White), presumably for similar reasons; and the central character Dobbs is here working for MI5 rather than SIS. In the film, Mendel and Harek are killed, which does damage to the complicated chronology of the George Smiley saga as both are required in tales set after *Call for the Dead*. A more constructive development to the story is the extra attention given to the marital difficulties of the central character, thereby paralleling the theme of ideological betrayal with an equally important sense of emotional betrayal. Lumet appreciated the film story more widely as about *"life's disappointments"* (Lumet 1995: 86). The result is achieved through having the serially unfaithful Ann (Harriet Andersson[181]) enter into a serious relationship with Dieter Frey (Maximillian Schell), the two people Dobbs loves most, and marking the dual level of the political and the personal in the imaginative title change to *The Deadly Affair*.[182] The appearance of a nymphomaniac wife led to the film attracting an adults-only X-certificate.

The picture attracted generally good reviews, many critics finding it a serious and accomplished treatment of the spiritual loss and exhausted ethics of espionage since the end of World War II. The *Observer* believed *The Deadly Affair* carried *"the real sour taste of the half-century. It is about a world of suave Whitehall coldhearts and sanctioned perfidy, where the double-crossings and killings are undertaken as trivially as the affairs"* (5 February 1967). *Films and Filming* found *The Deadly Affair "quite as good as* The Spy Who Came in from the Cold, *and possibly better"* (April 1967: 7). The *Spectator* felt that the film effectively captured the *"le Carré world of conscience-stricken intelligence agents, the private torment and the professional stab in the back"*, and *"retains its engrossing melancholy"*; the poignant scene between the jaded intelligence agent and the concentration camp victim epitomising *"the real le Carré country, a meeting of middle-aged survivors on the barbed wire of their ideological frontier"* (10 February 1967). *"As a spy story"*, argued the *Financial Times*, *"this is much more intense and serious than the general run; more credible in its pretensions to condemn the moralities of the spy game, to expose the sordid personal tragedies that can ensue from the great impersonal dignities of politics"* (3 March 1967). There was widespread praise for the untypical use of

London locations,[183] Lumet's sympathetic direction, Dehn's intelligent script, and highly professional playing from all concerned. On the latter point, *The Telegraph* enthusiastically referred to a *"feast of acting in the naturalistic style"* (3 February 1967). Just when she thought her patience with spy films had been exhausted, the reviewer at the *Sunday Telegraph* was gratified that *The Deadly Affair* had come along, proving that *"the best of a kind can always overcome resistance built up by the worst of a kind"* (5 February 1967). The usual political objections to a Cold War espionage story were trotted out in the left-wing *Morning Star*. The effort to deglamourise the spy world merely obscured the story's *"outrageous underlying assumptions"*, that *"anyone who has had Communist sympathies must be automatically 'suspect'"*. Ultimately, it was suggested, the picture was *"based on the crude political attitudes it pretends to reject"* (4 February 1967).

When the film was screened in a retrospective at the National Film Theatre, London in 1999, The *Evening Standard* surprisingly claimed it as *"the best film of any John le Carré novel"*, finding it *"far more subtle"* than the earlier *The Spy Who Came in from the Cold*. The reviewer judged that, *"the film's disenchanted, deglamorised texture"* probably accounted for its relative lack of success at the time and accounted for the neglect since as the picture hadn't fit the fashion of the 'Swinging Sixties' (7 January 1999). Film historian Robert Murphy also notes the picture being out of step with the norm, it oddly creating a *"vision of England as a sleepy backwater wherein lurks treachery and brutality rather than tranquillity"* (1992: 226).[184] *The Deadly Affair* was nominated for Best British Film, Best British Actor (Mason), Best British Cinematography (Colour, Freddie Young) and Best Foreign Actress (Simone Signoret as Elsa Fennan) at the British Film Academy Awards.

The Looking-Glass War, first published in 1965, was the eagerly-awaited fourth novel of John le Carré. The author had felt that the operation in his previous novel, *The Spy Who Came in from the Cold*, was too brilliantly conducted, and wanted to correct this impression with a story about a secret department that wasn't as efficient (*Observer*, 19 April 1964). He later confessed that the story was heavily influenced by the disaster of the American Bay of Pigs operation (*Guardian*, 16 November 1989), and that it reflected a lasting impression on the former secret agent of a pervading nostalgia in the Service and in general of British Intelligence living on past glories (Sisman 2015:195). The new story dealt with a small covert intelligence section called the Department, accountable to the Ministry of War. Active and important in World War II, it has declined in significance, losing many of its responsibilities to the Circus (the SIS), which reported to the Foreign Office. Recent intelligence from East Germany is interpreted as indicating a new missile site south of Rostock and the Director, Leclerc, grasps the opportunity to stage an operation, get an agent into the area, and assert the importance of the Department. This aspect of the story also parallels recent events in Cuba. The story is organised in three sections. In the short preliminary 'Taylor's Run', a middle-aged courier, unusually put on an operation, is killed in what might simply be a road accident in Finland while collecting aerial photographs of the area south of Rostock. 'Avery's Run' deals with a young officer in the Department who is sent to Finland to claim the body of Taylor and arrange its return to London. Inexperienced, though idealistic, he is anxious and flustered, annoys the local Consul, and fails to find the film of the overflight. The longer 'Leiser's Run' deals with the preparation of an agent and the operation into East Germany to confirm the existence of the missile site. Fred Leiser, a Pole, is a former agent of the wartime Special Operations Executive, brought back into the Department for this single operation, re-familiarised with radio signalling and unarmed combat, and infiltrated into East Germany. Killing a border guard and incautious in his signalling, counter-espionage is quickly onto Leiser and he is captured in the room of a young woman he has befriended and from which he attempts to signal. Meanwhile, the Department has been ordered to stand-down the operation as ill-judged and for fear of compromising relations with West Germany, and Leiser's final radio message is unheard and unheeded.[185]

The Looking-Glass War was very poorly received in Great Britain, the characters thought too flat and featureless, the absurdity of the Department presented without any ironic humour, and with many feeling disappointed after the brilliance of *The Spy Who Came in from the Cold*.[186] Despite the perceptions of the critics, John le Carré felt his previous novel had been "*fiendishly clever*" rather than realistic, had, in fact, "*glamorized the spy business to kingdom come*". As we have seen, his aim with the new novel was a "*deliberate reversal*", to "*describe a secret service that is not really very good at all; that is eking out its wartime glory; that is feeding itself on Little England fantasies; is isolated, directionless, overprotected and destined ultimately to destroy itself*" (quoted in Cobbs 1998: 65).[187] *The Looking-Glass War* found better favour in the United States, where the delusions of the Service, the muddle and the internecine conflict were readily appreciated after the Bay of Pigs fiasco. Le Carré heads each section of the novel with a short quotation from a classic of espionage or patriotic literature, and these references from Rudyard Kipling, John Buchan's *Mr Standfast* and Rupert Brooke's *1914*, serve ironically to underscore the dishonesty, futility, betrayals and tattered idealism of the tale. There is a constant nostalgic reference in the story to World War II, a time of national assertion, purpose, achievement and pride, and this serves to mark the inertia, decline and atrophy of the post-Suez period.

The operation is mounted according to 'War Rules', the agent being provided with obsolete equipment and trained by wartime personnel in a desperate act to reconnect to past glories. The second major theme of the novel, typical of the author, is that of class, specifically the snobbery and hypocrisy of the social elite. Avery is delighted to be offered entrance to the 'club', only to be witness to its appalling self-interest and indifference to others; finally discerning the *"fatal disproportion between the dream and reality"*. Leiser simply wants to be accepted by the ideal he has constructed of the English gentleman; unfortunately impossible as he is foreign, a tradesman and, in his earnest desire, impertinent, and is callously sacrificed to the exigencies of the Department. Leiser's mythic conception of the British Secret Service is in fact embodied in a seedy sub-section of the Intelligence Service run by war-time relics hungering for another finest hour. Cawelti and Rosenberg were unusual in praising *The Looking-Glass War,* describing it as the *"bleakest and most absurd of all the author's novels"*, and le Carré's *"valedictory to the heroic spy tradition"* (1987: 170). David Monaghan has noted the strong sense of *"spying as an illusionary world inhabited by perpetual children"* in the story (1983: 578), and Eva Horn has suggested that no other story of the Cold War has provided such a *"grim account of the phantasm of the opaque, dangerous, and mysterious enemy territory"* (2013: 254).

Initially, Karel Reisz was interested in directing a film of *The Looking-Glass War* and met le Carré to discuss a possible script (Sisman 2015: 266, 270, 288). The author wrote a screenplay in 1966, now with Jack Clayton slated to direct, but this was not used (*Films and Filming,* April 1965: 37; Sisman 2015: 298).[188] When the film did materialise late in 1969 it was scripted and directed as his début picture by the American Frank R. Pierson, as a Mike Frankovich production for release by Columbia Pictures. The movie takes account of the younger audiences and fresh styles of the new cinemas of the late 1960s and a generation beginning to be disgusted by the war in Vietnam and inspired by the recent youth protests around the world. Accordingly, the producers excitedly announced *"three newcomers"* to the screen: 25-year old cult actor Christopher Jones was cast as Leiser, recently come to prominence as the pop idol President of *Wild in the Streets* (US, 1968) and featured shirtless on the movie's poster, exhorting, *"Why do we listen to them? Why do we fight their wars for them?"*[189]; fresh from the European art house hit *Elvira Madigan* (Swe, 1967) came Pia Degermark; and accomplished stage actor Anthony Hopkins was cast as Avery. Pierson had been attracted to the book by the theme of older men romanticising the war, something he saw as a *"dangerous aspect of the control of the old over the young"*. He sought to intensify this dimension of the story through making the protagonist younger and thereby heightening the sense of sacrifice (*Films and Filming,* September 1969: 30-31).[190]

In the film, Leiser is a young, refugee Pole who will be allowed to stay in Britain with his pregnant girlfriend if he serves the mission. The operation in East Germany is extended in this version and Leiser takes up with a woman (Degermark) and a young boy (Nicholas Stewart) on the road; and a contemporary visual style makes much play of reflections, inverted, distorted and canted images, in an apparent reference to the title of the story. The scenes on the road in East Germany display the fashionable alienation of the European art cinema or the contemporary road movie, enhanced through the unreality of shooting the sequences in the province of Soria, central Spain.[191] At the climax of the picture, Leiser and the girl are blasted to death by the security police, and an ironic cut to a field in Finland shows a group of children finding and playing with the film of the overflight, obvious debts to Arthur Penn's recent *Bonnie and Clyde* (US, 1967) and the cinema of Sam Peckinpah.[192] Another invented sequence has Leiser murder and dispose of an inquisitive lorry driver in a lonely landscape, all the while attempting to hide his activity from a solitary tractor that ploughs a nearby field, and here the debt is to the master of suspense Alfred Hitchcock.[193]

Monthly Film Bulletin found the movie worked well-enough in "*evoking le Carré's picture of Cold War espionage as a world apart, an anachronistic and stubbornly exclusive clan whose members have adopted patriotism as a provisional creed (Avery) or preserve their faith in it through an obstinate nostalgia for the 'War Rules' (Leclerc [Ralph Richardson])*". Although the reviewer was less happy with Pierson's inventions in the latter part of the film dealing with the mission in East Germany, evidence of the writer's "*struggle, against all the odds, to extract some visual impact from a novel which is leisurely, meticulous and progressively internal*" (February 1970: 27). At a time when critical patience with the 007 franchise was wearing thin, several reviewers were happy with an antidote to the more fanciful spy thriller. The *Daily Express* thought *The Looking-Glass War* made a "*welcome change from the glossy world of James Bond*" (31 December 1969) and similarly the *Daily Mail* remarked on "*seedy spies*" which were "*so different from James Bond*" (1 January 1970). However, some critics felt that harm had been done to the intentions and intricacies of John le Carré's novel through the shift in emphasis to a "*trendy tragedy of corrupted middle age versus vulnerable youth*" (*Sunday Telegraph*, 4 January 1970). The *Daily Sketch* considered the film a "*muffled version of the book*" (31 December 1969); the *Evening Standard* thought it a "*breach of faith*" to "*attempt to spruce up and add youth and sex appeal to Le Carré*" (1 January 1970); and the *New Yorker* wondered at this "*youth-oriented spy film*" with some "*painful similarities to* Zabriskie Point" (21 February 1970). The *Spectator* put the failings down to the difficulties posed for adaptation by the original novel. A "*far better book, and far less alluring to the filmmaker, than the sharp, clicking mechanism of* The Spy Who Came in from the

Cold", *The Looking-Glass War* offered only a *"freezingly undramatic exercise in the bunglings of delusional attitudes and until the last chapters almost no action, a book saturated in middle-aged melancholy, elusively useless guilts, and everything least attractive to the mind of the action spy movie"* (10 January 1970). The *Observer* rued the *"spiralling decent into banality"* of the second half of the film which dealt with the doomed young couple in East Germany, during which the carefully built-up sense of authenticity dissipated in a *"welter of incredibly silly dialogue spoken by incredibly silly characters"* (4 January 1970). The same kind of view was taken at the *Sunday Telegraph*, where it was claimed that the *"sense of remembered experiences and allegiances that pulse through le Carré's deep, superb novels and the two previous le Carré films"* had been coarsened and sacrificed for something *"more spectacularly bleak and brutal, more crudely exciting, more obviously aimed at an audience it doesn't credit with the patience to try to understand the drives and fears and frustrations of another generation"* (4 January 1970).

Other reviews praised an *"intriguing, thoughtful film with startling moments of originality"* (*Sunday Mirror*, 11 January 1970), and a picture *"tense, exciting, and splendidly cynical"* (*Daily Sketch*, 31 December 1969). A charitable *Guardian* judged it *"one of those flawed projects one wants to defend rather than attack"* (2 January 1970). A later account is also more favourable to the new direction that the film took with the story, and film historian Robert Murphy highlights the picture's stress on the division between generations. He notes the *"constant sense of the old being parasitic on the young"*, accepts Leiser's irreverence, disrespect and indifference as authentic markers of the contemporary moment, and notes the shocking parallel between the *"recklessly self-destructive young East Europeans and the rigidly repressive state apparatus created by their elders"* and that *"between Leiser (and in the end, Avery) and their elderly, dangerously out-of-touch spymasters"* (1992: 226-7).[194]

There had been an intention to film the only remaining spy novel by le Carré from the 1960s, *A Small Town in Germany*, and both the author and Robert Shaw started writing a screenplay with Karel Reisz in the frame for director. Plans must have progressed for in November 1969 Avco-Embassy announced the production, to be produced by Herb Brodkin in Britain, now with Sydney Pollack set to direct and with advertisements taken out in the trade press.[195] However, for whatever reason the picture never appeared (*Kine Weekly*, 8 November and 21 December 1969; Sisman 2015: 321, 328-29). Shortly after the release of *The Looking-Glass War*, a piece in the *Evening Standard* reported that the *"spy novels of John le Carré don't rouse enthusiasm among the film producers I've talked to"*. It was claimed that the stories were *"too resolutely downbeat, too depressing in showing the shabby lining of espionage, and too short on sex*" for a commercial genre and perhaps this had much to do with the cinema's lack of interest in le Carré throughout the 1970s (1 January 1970).

That said, le Carré had been a phenomenally popular novelist of the 1960s, and accordingly the film adaptations of his stories in that decade were all big-budget, Hollywood-funded productions. Offering as they did a political critique of post-imperial Britain, it was fitting that the pictures were directed by liberal-leaning American filmmakers. Over time, the view has lingered that the stories had been "*ruined by Hollywood*" (*Sunday Times*, 1 November 1987); however, reviewers of the day largely welcomed the pictures as an antidote to the fripperies of the contemporary spy thriller. Le Carré had been part of the secret world (only suspected at the time), and his experiences and insights carried some conviction in his fictions. He had entered the intelligence services "*in the spirit of Buchan*", he has told us, "*and left it in the spirit of Kafka*"; and it is a mood of "*trauma*" that flavoured his tales and reshaped the spy story (quoted in Isaacson and Kelly 1993: 131). The writer's damning view of the Western intelligence agencies did not endear him to the professionals and it has been claimed that the American Richard Helms, the Director of the CIA, and the British Sir Dick White, a head of MI5 and later of MI6, were both critical of his stories (Morgan 2016: 92). As far as the British screen was concerned, though, John le Carré would for the remainder of the Cold War largely be confined to television and principally three classic adaptations as serials in the 1970s and 1980s.[196]

Case file 2: Len Deighton on the big screen in the 1960s and 1970s

Bond meets kitchen sink.
(Report on *The Ipcress File*, *Evening Standard*, 16 October 1964)

This is meant to be spying for real, whereas the Bond films are for glamour-pusses and jokes.
(Report on *The Ipcress File*, *Sunday Telegraph*, 29 November 1964)

Anyone can look good in an Aston Martin but it takes cool to look good getting off a London bus.
('*The Ipcress File* (1965)', *The Times Magazine*, 10 September 1994)

The new spy story of the 1960s also developed in the hands of Len Deighton, a genre novelist who has been called the "*Lord of the Spies*" (*Sunday Times*, 9 October 1988). His story *The Ipcress File* published in 1962 was the first of the new-style secret agent novels to achieve impact and soon considered a breakthrough in spy fiction in terms of characterisation and realism. Deighton, with a more working-class background, was a notable figure in the 1960s and the decade's devotion to style and meritocracy. Having worked in illustration and advertising provided Deighton with a sense of image and flair; and in tourism and cookery with discernment for affluence and the cosmopolitan. Deighton's stories are far less puritanical than *The Spy Who Came in from the Cold*, and fall somewhere between the twin poles represented in contemporary spy fiction by John le Carré and Ian Fleming. A film review in the *New Statesman* commented on this binary arrangement, referring to *Ipcress* as a *"halfway house between squalor and glamour"* (14 January 1966). A central innovation in Deighton's series of spy novels was the nameless agent who narrates the stories. A grammar-school boy from the north, he embodies what Colin Gardner has called a *"mocking counter-trope"* to the James Bond archetype (2006: 188).

As Sam Goodman has noted of Deighton's novels, *"their blend of action and mystery alongside the opportunity to indulge vicariously in fine meals or indeed cups of Nescafé in smart new London coffeehouses"* placed the stories within a *"recognisable"* contemporary context (2016: 5). Brian Baker has referred to the *"affluence narrative"* of the 1950s and 1960s, perhaps exemplified by the James Bond stories, and the emergence of *"bachelor aspirations"*. Such attributes were also evident in Deighton and his secret agent's conscious engagement with 'style', not least of all the contemporary fascination with 'Italian style', and in the agent's connoisseurship regarding food and ingredients (2012: 34-42).[197]

The Ipcress File is narrated by a nameless agent (the device carrying an aura of everyman and anyman) and begins with his transfer from a branch of Military Intelligence to a small but important civilian intelligence outfit, W.O.O.C.(P)., headed by a Colonel Dalby. He is immediately drawn into a conspiracy involving missing 'Security Grade 1's' – scientists, engineers, political advisers and other people essential to the running of the country. An individual code-named JAY is suspected and the investigation shifts between London, Beirut and an American atomic test on a South Pacific atoll. Matters are further complicated when our agent is approached by his former senior officer Colonel Ross who offers secret information for sale, and when he begins to suspect that Dalby is not being straight with him. The only substantial clue that emerges is an audio tape of atonal, electronic sounds.

While witness to an American atomic test on Torke Atoll, our agent is shocked to find that he is under suspicion by both the British and the Americans of leaking information. Discretely following Dalby one night, he is suddenly arrested by the Americans and roughly interrogated, suspected of signalling to a Russian submarine and killing an American officer. He is further shocked when he is told he is being sent to Hungary in exchange for two captive American flyers. Sedated, our agent wakes up in a cell where he is treated brutally by East Europeans and told he will face a trial as an "*enemy of the state*". Summoning up last reserves of strength the British agent subdues a guard, blows a main fuse to the building and escapes through a window, only to be amazed to find himself in Wood Green, London. He soon gets onto Dalby and is unsurprised that his senior officer is in cahoots with JAY. All are caught in a net cast by Ross who had been using our agent to flush out the conspirators. The useful JAY, who had been employing mind manipulation techniques to bring well-placed men under his control, is incorporated into British Intelligence.

Len Deighton was working as a commercial artist when he commenced writing the story as a diversion while on holiday in France. Untutored in literature, he claims he fell into his characteristic first-person style, "*as though I was writing a letter to an old, intimate and trusted friend*" (Deighton 2015: viii). The author also claimed an influence from his time at a smart, London advertising agency, spending his days with highly-educated, witty public school-types. In creating his intelligence unit W.O.O.C.(P)., he later wrote: "*I took the social atmosphere of that sleek and shiny agency and inserted it into some ramshackle offices I once rented in Charlotte Street*" (ix). *The Ipcress File*, subtitled 'Secret File No. 1', incorporates some innovative stylistic devices. Explanatory footnotes and appendices, giving details on characters, operations and technology mentioned in the narrative, provide a 'scholarly apparatus' promoting a sense of authenticity for the story. Each chapter is headed by an extract from a horoscope, which vaguely relates to the proceeding action. Deighton would retain such idiosyncratic stylistic features for subsequent novels featuring the 'agent with no name'. IPCRESS is the acronym for *Experimental Induction of Psychoneuroses in Personality and Behaviour Disorders*, a book our agent consults in researching brainwashing techniques.

The Ipcress File was very well-received, the *Evening Standard* praising it as a "*novel of terrifying originality by an ingenious and idiosyncratic writer of great talent which reveals the double-edged world of espionage as it really is*". Many reviews made a favourable comparison with Ian Fleming, the *Daily Express* finding a thriller that "*outbonds Bond*"; and the *Daily Sketch* spying a "*man to put Bond out of business*".[198] The novel appeared a couple of weeks after the first James Bond film *Dr No* (1962) was screened in Great Britain.

The film version of *The Ipcress File* was produced for Rank-Universal release in 1965 by Harry Saltzman, one of the producers of the James Bond pictures, and conceived as an antidote to the fanciful heroics of 007 (*Kine Weekly*, 17 September 1964).[199] The records show that it was a relatively trouble-free production for the usually volatile and profligate Saltzman (Chapman 2014: 44, 63-65). Despite the aim for differentiation, Saltzman retained the services of several key contributors to the Bond series, composer John Barry, production designer Ken Adam and editor Peter Hunt. On the advice of screenwriter Jimmy Sangster, Saltzman opted for the promising young director Sidney J. Furie (Kremer 2015).[200] The picture was shot on location in the capital and the film story dispenses with the "*Bond-like tourist mobility*" and the 'exotic' locations of Beirut and the South Pacific, which featured in the novel, in favour of a transitional London of warehouses, supermarkets, underground car parks, dingy office buildings, dimly lit libraries and modest apartments (Baker 2012: 43). *Ipcress* took the unusual step of acquiring two huge mansions in Grosvenor Gardens, Victoria as the production base for the picture. The houses, comprising of 40 rooms, provided production offices, canteen and make-up and dressing rooms, as well as studio space for interiors required in the movie (*Kine Weekly*, 8 October 1964). An added advantage was that in the background of scenes shot in the adapted mansions real traffic could be seen through the windows which added to the realism.

The film was made with some style by director Sidney J. Furie, cinematographer Otto Heller and designer Ken Adam, and confirmed Michael Caine, who is provided with the character name of Harry Palmer (agreed by all concerned as a suitably dull and boring name), as a major international film star.[201] Palmer was both an extension of and reaction to the James Bond ideal as created by Ian Fleming and visualised by Broccoli and Saltzman.[202] The historian Dominic Sandbrook sees both agents as reflecting (and generating) the optimism and emerging sense of style of the mid-1960s, in the case of Palmer, circulating in a world of supermarkets, coffee-bars and Italian restaurants; but with Deighton's hero representing the "*cheeky face of lower-middle-class ambition*" (2006: 595). While not particularly admiring the film and its "*general air of Bondishness on the cheap*", *Sight and Sound* acknowledged that with Harry Palmer, for the first time in a British film, "*heroism is no longer the prerogative of a tight-lipped aristocracy imbued with the public school ethos*" (Summer 1965: 150). Palmer was differentiated from the Bond archetype through wearing glasses, something that Furie wittily exploited in the credit sequence when subjective shots from the character of a spectacle-less Palmer are rendered out of focus.[203] Harry Saltzman, though, worried that with 'Palmer' seen cooking, the anti-Bond element might be being taken too far, an activity he felt a little too effeminate (it is Len Deighton's hands preparing the food that the viewer sees in the close-ups).[204] Michael Caine has recalled how Saltzman went off to "*de-gay*" the script before shooting, and pondering as to how to do the cooking "*in a butch way*" (1992: 175); yet, as Colin Gardner has noted, associated traits still attached themselves to the character and left a more "*unconventionally 'feminine' anti-hero*" (2006: 181).[205] The revisionism of the secret agent archetype, was, of course, commented on in the reviews, with the *Spectator*, in its discussion of *The Ipcress File*, a little surprised to find a "*bespectacled Cockney with the current bachelor neatness and a passion for cooking*" (19 March 1965). It is evident that the character of the new secret agent, with his lower-class insubordination and anti-establishment leanings, was calculated to undermine the patrician supremacy of the gentleman secret agent.

The first of the "*new-wave espionage films*" to reach the screen, reviewers had to come to terms with the innovative direction the spy story was taking in the cinema (*Sunday Telegraph*, 29 November 1964), and in the way the "*flip side of the Bond coin*" was imagined on screen (*Sun*, 17 March 1965). Despite a report that claimed the film was "*rapturously received*" at the press screening, some reviews were qualified and others hostile to the inaugural "*contra-Bond*" (*Sunday Express*, 21 March 1965; *Sunday Telegraph*, op.cit.). The *Sunday Telegraph* caught the general expectation when it printed, "*Whatever it was going to be like it had to be* unlike *James Bond*", and critics were divided on a number of points regarding the initial form of the "*anti-Bond reaction*" (op. cit). Whereas many reviewers were impressed and intrigued by Caine's performance as Palmer and believed they were witnessing the birth of a major star, the *Financial Times* felt the attempt to make the character an "*anti-glamorous, anti-dramatic, anti-heroic hero-tough*" had resulted only in a "*rather negative and lifeless centre to the film*" (19 March 1965). The *Sunday Express* complained of a "*blundering hero*", of a "*dreary and colourless performance*", and that the "*whole thing looks like an emasculated James Bond story*" (21 March 1965), and the *Guardian* faulted a thriller "*short on thrills*", and desiring of more excitement and fun concluded: "*give me the Bond films and the Bond books anytime*" (19 March 1965). A more favourably disposed *Evening Standard* praised a spy film which used what looked like "*inside knowledge*", an approach that gripped you "*far more persuasively than the outsize imagination of the Bond adventures*" (18 March 1965). A number of reviewers claimed to have been confounded by an "*incomprehensible*" plot, a problem imported from the original novel (*Sun*, 17 March 1965).

Otto Heller's "*peeping-Tom photography*", with various objects placed in the foreground of eccentric framings in the extreme Techniscope format, excited and annoyed in equal measures (*New Statesman*, 26 March 1965).[206] Sidney J. Furie later suggested that the heavy technique was a result of insecurity and what he felt to be a poor script: "*I was very depressed always when we started shooting, thinking that it was going to be really lousy and I didn't know what to do, so I told myself I would come up with a style of shooting that is different*" (quoted in Kremer 2015). The director's confidence and frame of mind were not helped by the regular bawling outs he received from Harry Saltzman who had envisaged a more conservative approach to filming the picture.[207] The *Guardian* was critical, seeing the approach as the "*sure sign of overweening ambition*" (19 March 1965); *The Times* complained of Furie's "*fidgety style of direction*" in which everything is "*shot from thigh-level around, over, under or through something decorative but irrelevant*" (18 March 1965); while the *Observer* was intrigued by the use of the camera as a "*midget voyeur*" (21 March 1965). The *Evening Standard* had qualified praise for the "*compulsive devices*" of quick cutting, wide-angled lenses and sudden zooms that appropriately distorted relationships and perspectives and effectively reproduced the book's "*obliqueness, density and, sometimes, confusion*"; although it wondered if Furie might have overdone these (18 March 1965). The American *Saturday Review* believed that the director must have had his eye on "*the more experimental of the young French directors*", and had "*applied the techniques with a light, witty, and effective touch, thus adding zest, for those who appreciate such filmic touches, to what otherwise might have been a commonplace suspense yarn*" (31 July 1965); while the American *Newsweek* appositely referred to the picture as the "*thinking man's* Goldfinger" (quoted in Kremer 2015).[208] *The Ipcress File* was invited into competition at the Cannes Film Festival, and elsewhere won British Film Academy Awards for Best British Film, Best Art Direction and Best Colour Photography on a British Film.

Funeral in Berlin was the third spy novel of Len Deighton first published in 1964, but the second to reach the screen. The complex story concerning the defection of a top Soviet scientist is narrated by the nameless protagonist who served as the author's series character in this period and occupies a little over a month in an unspecified autumn. The story, told from the first-person, provides a highly-restricted narrative and the pleasure for the reader lies in the knowledge that our secret agent undoubtedly knows what's going on and is one step ahead of the game even if we are pretty much kept in the dark until the end. A handful of chapters are presented in a more neutral third person narrative to provide sketches of important characters. The action swings back and forth between London and Berlin, and briefly takes in the South of France and Prague, and our hero has to deal with double-crossing agents of various colours and allegiances. Colonel Stok of the KGB promises to deliver the nerve gas specialist for money; Hallam is the fey civil servant at the Home Office who will take receipt of the scientist; the charismatic Johnny Vulkan is the self-serving go-between in Berlin, a man with a dark past; and Samantha Steel is the sexy pick-up who has more than a passing interest in our hero.

The plot hinges on the documents requested for the defecting scientist, seemingly innocuous identity papers in the name of Paul Louis Broum. Our suspicious hero digs into the past and discovers the real Broum worked for the Nazis in France, was exposed as a rich Jew and sent to a concentration camp, and that there he bribed a medical officer to help him assume the identity of a German guard, Johnny Vulkan. The new Vulkan now wants his identity back so that he can acquire his fortune deposited in a Swiss bank before it can be re-appropriated by the authorities following new legislation. The game of bluff and double bluff ends with the devious Stok double-crossing the British, having used the ruse of the defecting scientist to identify key members of West German Intelligence and eliminate them; with Samantha Steele's failure on behalf of Israeli Intelligence in acquiring the scientist to counter Egypt's development of biological weapons; and with our hero pinpointing and killing Hallam as a corrupt civil servant who had connived with Vulkan to acquire the $2 million.

Funeral in Berlin incorporates the stylistic flourishes typical of Deighton's novels in this early period. Chapters are headed by comments on chess moves and strategy, offering a vague commentary on the succeeding narrative; the odd footnote provides additional information; a section of six appendices supply 'factual' information on such topics raised in the story as 'Poisonous Insecticides', 'Soviet Security Systems' and 'The Official Secrets Act 1911'; and a playful self-reflection has a character comment on a cookery article in the *Observer*, items Deighton actually contributed himself. Deighton first visited the Eastern Bloc in the early 1960s shortly after the appearance of the Wall, and he later admitted that he became "*obsessed*" with Berlin, which became a "*second home*" to him and stood as the perfect symbol of a "*divided world*" (Deighton 2009: vi). *Funeral* was Deighton's most successful book, winning praise in *The New York Times* and *Life* magazine, and spending six months on the New York bestseller list.

Funeral in Berlin was the second film of the 'Harry Palmer' movie trilogy of the 1960s, produced by Harry Saltzman for release by Paramount Pictures, directed by Guy Hamilton who had recently completed the hugely successful *Goldfinger*, and starring Michael Caine. Director of Photography Otto Heller and production designer Ken Adam were carried forward from the first Harry Palmer picture. The movie was released in Britain early in 1967 with the humorous tagline, "*It was going to be a lovely funeral. Harry Palmer just hoped it wouldn't be his...*". The simplified version of the tale, in a script by the West Indian poet and novelist Evan Jones,[209] rearranged the story elements so that the essential business of the original novel unfolds in Berlin, with Colonel Stok (Oskar Homolka) being the claimant for defection, a criminal gang specialising in ferrying East Germans to the West being his actual target, and a more developed role for Samantha Steel (Eva Renzi) as the Israeli agent who desires the Broum papers to claim the hidden wealth for Zion.[210] To keep continuity with the first film adaptation of the Len Deighton stories, *The Ipcress File*, *Funeral* has Palmer still working for Colonel Ross at the War Office rather than Dawlish at W.O.O.C.(P), as it is in the novel. As with *Ipcress*, the production undertook extensive location-shooting, here spending eight weeks in both West and East Berlin (*Kine Weekly*, 21 April 1966).[211] The picture was launched with a special showing in West Berlin to which journalists from eight European countries were invited (*Evening News*, 23 February 1967).[212]

It was generally felt to be the case that the sequel was not the equal of the inaugural film in the series. An unimpressed *Morning Star*, rarely a supporter of the spy film, found *Funeral* "*very poor stuff*", the left-wing paper bristling at the portrayal of the "*comic Soviet officer*", the "*tone of facetious cynicism*", and what it regarded as political promiscuity in a story ranging across Western, Soviet and Israeli intelligence (25 February 1967). Some reviewers tended to find the picture flat after the stylistic excitements of *The Ipcress File*. *The Times* claimed the film was "*sadly lacking in the moments of sharply disenchanted observation*" which distinguished *Ipcress*, and that Guy Hamilton's direction was "*plodding*" compared to Sidney J. Furie's "*undisciplined extravagance*" on the previous film (23 February 1967). However, *Funeral* was acknowledged as never less than a thoroughgoing professional production, in which "*the action is shifty, the dialogue pert, the backdrop laid on in a colorful cinemontage of both Berlins*" (*Time Magazine*, 23 December 1966). Several were irritated that the story was even more confusing and inscrutable than *Ipcress*, and, despite the conventions of the spy picture, that scriptwriter Evan Jones had erred by too much "*mystification*" (*The Times*, 23 February 1967; *Financial Times*, 24 February 1967). The *Daily Mail* reported the picture as "*lighter-hearted and less urgent*" than its predecessor, despite all its killings and its grim concern with a fake funeral, perhaps sensing a softening of the cynical style for greater audience-friendliness (23 February 1967). The *Observer* was even more critical on this point, finding *Funeral* "*debilitated*", "*scrappy*" and "*flavourless*", caught between two schools, making only "*gestures*" at the blackness central to the John le Carré originals, and missing completely the "*droll extravagance of the Bond pictures*" (26 February 1967).

While lacking the overt style of *The Ipcress File*, *Funeral in Berlin* does start eye-catchingly. The opening sequence consists of a striking montage, in which a vibrant, colourful and lively West Berlin with its gleaming shopping centres and busy pavement cafés is abruptly replaced by the gaunt silhouettes and dull, grey and oppressive surroundings of the Eastern districts of the divided city. The effect is intensified through filming the West on sunny days and the east in bleak and cloudy conditions. A number of reviewers commented on this promising beginning and juxtaposition of the two Berlins (*Evening News*, 23 February 1967; *Financial Times*, 24 February 1967), as well as on the crisp and neat handling of the mock funeral in the story (*Monthly Film Bulletin*, April 1967: 56).

The film series continued later in the year with an adaptation of Deighton's fourth novel *Billion Dollar Brain* (1966), with the picture released at the end of 1967. In the adventure, the narrator-spy is sent to Helsinki to investigate the unfounded claims of a major operation planned by Western Intelligence. There he finds Harvey Newbegin, a former acquaintance in American military intelligence who had played a part in *Funeral in Berlin* and his young girl-friend Signe, and falls in with a bizarre scheme funded by the Red-hating General Midwinter, a Texan billionaire, to foment an uprising in the Baltic state of Latvia and bring about the end of communism in the Eastern Bloc. The British agent infiltrates the private intelligence organisation, the action ranges across London, Finland, Latvia, Leningrad, New York and Texas, and the hero must prevent some eggs contaminated with a virus stolen from the Microbiological Research Establishment at Porton Down being used in the planned operation or falling into the hands of the Soviets. Newbegin is re-vealed as a renegade lining his own pockets and the KGB's Colonel Stok is weaved throughout the story, helping our agent at several points. Midwinter's intricate scheme is conducted by a massive computer known as the 'Brain'. In typical Deighton fashion, the different sections of the novel are headed by lines from nursery rhymes which vaguely comment on the forthcoming ac-tion and appendices provide details on Soviet Military districts and Soviet and private intelligence agencies.

The 1960s series of Harry Palmer spy pictures was brought to an end with *Billion Dollar Brain*, the film turning out a critical and commercial disap-pointment. *Kine Weekly* had predicted that the picture would "*not be to every-one's taste*" and tentatively informed exhibitors that it constituted a "*thriller for selected situations*" (18 November 1967). The acclaimed art television filmmaker Ken Russell was surprisingly hired to direct the picture which spent five difficult weeks on location in Finland in winter (*Kine Weekly*, 28 January 1966).[213] The cast featured Karl Malden, whose character name is slightly altered to Leo Newbegin, Françoise Dorléac who is given the new name of Anya and is revealed as an agent of Colonel Stok, and Ed Begley as General Midwinter. Honeywell facilities were used for the scenes featuring the main control complex of the Brain.

The modestly spy-fi elements of the story tended to push the film towards 007 territory, the picture's publicity describing it as a "*space-age thriller with a computer-age plot*", a factor reinforced by a modish title sequence designed by Maurice Binder who had already completed comparable work on three James Bond movies (*Billion Dollar Brain* press sheet).[214] Joseph Lanza has claimed that the highly visual and iconoclastic Russell contributed a structure centred on individual scenes that were "*florid, disorientating, and full of enough inside jokes to function independently of the larger story*" (2008: 62). To maintain the continuity of the film series, Palmer is once again working for Ross at the War Office rather than Dawlish at W.O.O.C.(P) as in the novel, and a major addition to the story was a climax featuring an 'invasion' of Latvia by Midwinter and his army which is sent to the bottom of the ice-encrusted Gulf of Finland by Stok.

Critics had already begun to show signs of tiring of the Deighton adaptations at the time of *Funeral in Berlin*. It had been recognised at the *Spectator*, for example, that even "*grown-up thrillers have conventions almost as rigorous as the bang-bang Bond kind*" (10 February 1967). The *Financial Times* had demanded that even at "*this late stage of the cloak-and-dagger cycle*", films needed "*qualities of originality or assurance that* Funeral in Berlin *lacks*", and that even the novelty of the insubordinate secret agent was wearing off, the reviewer breathlessly referring to the "*cheeky cockney, non-conformist, anti-establishment, bolshie, criminal-minded, irrepressible, always justified by eventual success*" Harry Palmer as a "*cliché hero*" (24 February 1967). The *Daily Express*, exhausted by the "*recent orgy of spy films*", had even wished that *Funeral in Berlin* would, once and for all, "*bring the secret-agent vogue to its final resting place*" (26 February 1967).

With *Billion Dollar Brain*, *The Telegraph* suggested, the "*Len Deighton spy stories seem to be going the same way on the screen as the James Bond books – downwards*". As if demonstrating the law of diminishing returns, the reviewer recorded: "*I liked much of* The Ipcress File, *something of* Funeral in Berlin *but little of this scarcely comprehensible rigmarole*" (17 November 1967). *Brain* attracted the usual accusations of being too cryptic, a criticism often levelled at the original novels with their elaborate intrigues and confusing plotlines. For the *Guardian*, it was a case of the "*incomprehensible, which when understood, turns out to be unmemorable*" (17 November 1967). There were complaints that Harry Palmer had "*lost his individuality and become just another insensate sex spy*", and lamented were the once interesting and distinguishing scenes of bachelor pads and secret agent cooking.[215] The *Spectator* wrote of a "*sad falling off*" in the hero (24 November 1967). A promising series had "*gone down the drain*", and, moreover, the films were felt to be "*taking on production values more characteristic of the Fleming series*", the stories now taken over by scenic designers and special-effects departments and "*filled with gadgetry rather than the humorous, subtle suspense of* The Ipcress File". "*And we've really had enough of that by now*" confirmed *Time Magazine* (6 January 1968). *The Times* reported that following the "*dull stodge of* Funeral in Berlin", *Billion Dollar Brain* with its "*incoherent narrative style*" represented a "*further stage in the declining cinematic fortunes of Len Deighton's nameless hero*". While praising the beauty of the winter scenes expertly shot by Billy Williams in Finland, the reviewer denounced the "*dazzle of visual irrelevancies*" insisted upon by Russell (16 November 1967). The obvious nods to Eisenstein's battle on the ice in *Alexander Nevsky* (1938), to Lang's *Siegfried* (1924, the framing of massed troops) and to Godard's *Alphaville* (1965, the scenes set in the grand computer room), were *"terribly pretty, but completely useless"* (*Guardian*, 17 November 1967), and dismissed as an *"indulgence"* (*Spectator*, 24 November 1967). For the reviewer at *Films and Filming* the culminating battle on the ice was *"one of the most ludicrous climaxes"* he had ever sat through (January 1968: 24). For the *New Statesman*, the production was a *"tremendous waste of money and talent"* (17 November 1967).[216]

The left-wing *Morning Star* was more enthusiastic about this recent adaptation of Len Deighton. Praising *Billion Dollar Brain* as a *"spy fantasy with a difference"*, the paper claimed the picture, through making the villain a *"rampaging"* Texan oil tycoon and the intended victims the socialist democracies of Eastern Europe, had turned the *"old formula inside out to make it work against the cold war instead of for it"* (18 November 1967). The *Sunday Times* was less impressed by any revisionism, judging the picture a *"ridiculous fantasy"*, a misfiring *"parody of American anti-Russian lunacy"* (19 November 1967).

As already noted, it was generally felt that the Harry Palmer spy films had become a declining series, from the *"artily composed"* *The Ipcress File*, on to the *"solid sobriety"* of *Funeral in Berlin*, and culminating in the *"incoherence"* of *Billion Dollar Brain* (*Monthly Film Bulletin*, January 1968: 2). *Films and Filming* even wondered if the disappointing *Billion Dollar Brain* represented the *"imminent demise"* of the spy cycle (January 1968: 24). It was therefore unsurprising when announcements to film *Horse Under Water* (1963), the second of Len Deighton's novels to feature the nameless secret agent, came to nothing and the Harry Palmer series was brought to a premature halt (*Kine Weekly*, 1 February and 17 May 1969).[217] The three films, though, were significant and distinct in their clouding of Cold War verities, in placing treachery at the heart of the British establishment, in promoting the KGB's Colonel Stok as the series' most lovable character, and in *Billion Dollar Brain* locating scheming, maniacal lunacy squarely with the Americans. The latter film, in particular, has been seen in terms of contemporary parallels, the Mad Texan Midwinter and his proposed invasion of Latvia a parody of another Texan Coldwarmonger and Lyndon Johnson's intervention in Vietnam.[218]

Harry Palmer, and his nameless counterpart in the novels, was a new type of secret agent for the spy story. He influenced the archetype in two important ways. Firstly, in terms of the 'cool spy', immediately noticeable in the American screen agents Derek Flint (two films 1966-67) and Matt Helm (four films 1966-68), and later a major inspiration for the swinging parodies featuring the International Man of Mystery Austin Powers (three films 1997-2002). In literature, the legacy of the character was immediately apparent in the Adam Diment novels *The Dolly, Dolly Spy* (1967), *The Great Spy Race* and *The Bang Bang Birds* (both 1968), and *Think, Inc* (1971), and the hip, pot-smoking secret agent Philip McAlpine.[219] Secondly, the lower middle-class Palmer led the way for the déclassé spy, and was soon followed by the proletarian Callan who first featured on television (1967-72), and Brian Freemantle's Charlie Muffin who featured in a series of novels (1977-2013) and in a television movie in 1979.[220]

The Len Deighton spy stories with their characteristic first-person narration and the Harry Palmer films with their downbeat hero owed an obvious debt to the American hard-boiled detective story.[221] This had been recognised by reviewers of the film version of *The Ipcress File* who had observed similarities between Palmer and the classic literary detectives Sam Spade and Philip Marlowe (*Sunday Telegraph*, 29 November 1964; *Sunday Times*, 21 March 1965). The critic at *Sight and Sound* argued that Deighton's *The Ipcress File* had been written in "*patchy Chandlerese*" and featured a "*scaled-down Philip Marlowe*" (Summer 1965: 150). Film historian Robert Murphy claims that Deighton's spy stories were an English equivalent of the colloquial American style Chandler and Hammett invented for the thriller, and that it was used to revitalise the spy story in a way that retains a democratic ethos, yet updates it to the slicker, faster, smarter society of the sixties (1992: 221). The literary influences were made more explicit in the film *Billion Dollar Brain*, which has an invented pre-title sequence in which a now independent Palmer is running the H. P. Detective Agency. Unlike Marlowe, he seems to specialise in professionally demeaning divorce work, although this adds to the shabby quality that the series was increasingly bestowing on the character. Tellingly, there is a photograph of Humphrey Bogart on the office wall, the actor most associated with Spade and Marlowe in the cinema.

The 'Harry Palmer' tales marked a departure for the secret agent story in the 1960s, bringing new scrutiny to the hierarchies of class and command and the way the spy genre engaged with changing realities in Britain. Additionally, the legitimisation of a "*narcissistic masculine and heterosexual consumption aligned with 'action' genres and sexual success*" offered a potent "*rebuke to the nepotism, homosexuality and decadence of the Cambridge spies*" and therefore a reassurance against the kind of "*effeminacy*" which had so troubled Harry Saltzman when Palmer was required to enter the kitchen (Baker 2012: 44).

A further attempt to adapt Deighton for the screen occurred in 1976 with *Spy Story*, Len Deighton's sixth spy novel of 1974. It was written in the author's typical style of first-person narrator and hard-boiled dialogue courtesy of the master Raymond Chandler. The complex story centres on former field operative Patrick Armstrong now based at the Studies Centre, London, working on computer-simulated war games involving possible North Atlantic Treaty Organisation-Soviet confrontation in the Arctic Sea. On return from a six-week tour of duty aboard a nuclear submarine, Armstrong encounters a series of strange and unsettling experiences and is inexorably drawn into a dark conspiracy centring on the defection of a senior Russian admiral. He is manipulated by his own security service, by the tough-talking Colonel Schegel of the American CIA recently installed as the new head of the Studies Centre, and by a traitorous Tory MP who has him imprisoned in a remote Scottish house. Armstrong is wounded on the Arctic ice during the supposed exchange with the Russians and in hospital finally learns from the security chief and Schegel that the operation, through undermining the credibility of the main Russian negotiator, had actually been aimed at destroying Soviet-inspired talks intended to bring about the reunification of Germany, an event which would upset the delicate balance of power in Europe.

There has been some speculation that Armstrong is in fact the nameless agent of Len Deighton's earlier spy novels. There are sufficient hints regarding a secretive back-story for the protagonist as well as the re-appearance of characters such as Dawlish of British Intelligence and Colonel Stok of the KGB from the previous stories to give this some credibility, although the author has denied this seeing the character rather as a "*close relative*".[222] Attendance at a naval war game session in a south London school gave Deighton an insight into the dramatic potential of high-tech planning and strategy, and a long-term interest in submarines furnished him with another facet of his story. Typically, the author constructs a 'scholarly apparatus' around his narrative, introducing each chapter with 'notes' and 'rules' pertaining to the gaming conducted at the Studies Centre and allegedly derived from the Institute of War Studies, London. War-gaming serves as an apt metaphor for the tactical and strategic manoeuvring of the Cold War and its furtive clandestine operations, and has been used by other spy writers such as James Mitchell in his 'Callan' stories.

The modestly-budgeted film version of *Spy Story* was directed and produced by Lindsay Shonteff, who had managed some success in the previous decade with the exploitation spy thriller *Licensed to Kill* (1965).[223] The film is a literal account of the original story, only lacking a few scenes – Armstrong's (Michael Petrovitch) desperate night-time flight along some precipitous Scottish cliffs and a rendezvous with the Soviets on the Arctic pack ice, which would have been too expensive to stage on a limited budget.[224] The film was shot entirely on location, the production, for example, filming aboard the training ship HMS Belfast on the Thames, thus giving the picture a raw and authentic quality. The *Daily Mail* was alone in finding *Spy Story* a "*superior looking thriller*", a film of "*pace and a certain throw-away elegance*" (10 July

1976). More typical was the view at the *Daily Express* which found it a *"dreary dramatisation"* in which the cast *"recite their lines as if reluctantly co-opted into an end-of-term play"* (9 July 1976). Most agreed with the *Evening Standard* that the plot was *"totally impenetrable"* (8 July 1976); the *Daily Mirror* uncertain if the script was *"written in code"* (9 July 1976). Battered by the critical onslaught, stung at the remarks concerning his *"clod-hopping direction"* (*The Times*, 9 July 1976), and declaring himself as having *"suffered the critics once too often"*, Shonteff was prompted to publish a letter of complaint in which he berated critics as *"hypocrites"* (*Evening Standard*, 29 July 1976). *Spy Story* was felt to fall well-short of the classic film adaptations of Len Deighton in the 1960s, something essential to the screen spy thriller being neutralised in an overly naturalistic approach through which *"emotion, and above all suspense, has been eliminated"* (*Monthly Film Bulletin*, August 1976: 174). Perhaps with a hint of hope, the *Financial Times* felt the latest adaptation of Deighton looked and sounded like the *"dying gasp of the espionage movie"* (9 July 1976).

The espionage drama in the wider cinema

It is impossible to imagine a spy less like James Bond than Maurice Castle.
(Review of *The Human Factor, Daily Express*, 2 February 1980)

The *"dark business of espionage"* was pursued in a number of films produced outside of the stories written by John le Carré and Len Deighton.[225] Widespread anxiety developed around mind control during the Cold War and fears of indoctrination of the liberal West by the diabolical Reds. The efficacy of thought control was seemingly demonstrated by the startling confessions at Communist show trials and the extraordinary decision of some GI's to remain behind the 'bamboo curtain' after the end of the Korean War in 1953 (Burton 2013). The first British film to treat brainwashing in a scientifically serious and extended manner was Basil Dearden and Michael Relph's *The Mind Benders* (1963), from a story and screenplay written by James Kennaway.[226] The writing began in 1958 at the instigation of Dearden and Relph, with the working titles of *The Visiting Scientist* and *If This Be Treason*, but the topic was thought controversial and production finance was difficult to obtain (Burton and O'Sullivan 2009: 275). The project revived when Dearden was able to persuade the star Dirk Bogarde to take the role of the sacrificing scientist who is prepared to subject himself to experiment and was the first of the new-style, serious spy stories to appear in the cinema. In an unusual move, Kennaway's novel of *The Mind Benders* was published simultaneously with the release of the film.[227]

Major Hall (John Clements), the security officer investigating the strange death of top research scientist Professor Sharpey (Harold Goldblatt), follows the trail to the experiments in the reduction of sensation at an Oxford University laboratory. In an attempt to clear up the mystery, a fellow scientist, Longman (Bogarde), agrees to undergo a 'terminal' experiment in sensory deprivation, during which he is brainwashed into thinking that he hates his wife, Oonagh (Mary Ure). The experiment is thought to be a failure, but unknown to the investigators there follows a period during which the scientist ritually humiliates his wife. Longman is brought back to normal through the emergency of having to deliver their fourth child. It is thus proved that the treasonous Sharpey was not acting according to his own free will, but had succumbed to his own experiments and the Soviets had exploited the situation.

Dearden and Relph were associated with intelligent and responsible screen dramas; however, the critical reception for *The Mind Benders* was not what they had hoped for and Kennaway disappointedly reported that reviews ranged from "*poor*" to "*vitriolic*" (quoted in Royle 1983: 170); while the film's star summed up the general reaction in his autobiography with the headline: "*Bogarde Thriller is Shabby and Nasty*" (Bogarde 1979: 262). The film was criticised for its simple "*Jekyll and Hydism*", evident in the character of the young scientist who is transformed, and for what many felt to be an uneasy blend of science thriller and family melodrama (Burton and O'Sullivan 2009: 280-1). Several aspects of the story caused concern with the censors: the harrowing scenes of the experiment, certain lines of dialogue, and in particular the handling of the birth scene. Negotiation between the film-makers and the British Board of Film Censors led to the film being released with a commercially-restrictive X-certificate, and which almost certainly harmed its performance at the box-office. The American-release movie poster carried the exclamation, "*PERVERTED... SOULLESS! The Most Dangerous and Different Motion Picture Ever Brought To The Screen!*"

Both the novel and the film were at pains to stress the scientific credibility of the story, stating explicitly that it was suggested by experiments in the "*reduction of sensation*" recently carried out at universities in North America. Kennaway was therefore angered when critics dismissed the fanciful nature of the subject. The phenomena of perceptual isolation and sensory deprivation attracted considerable scientific interest through the 1950s and 1960s, revealing that subjects who had been deprived of "*patterned sensory input*" tended to experience "*complicated hallucinations*", showed "*intellectual and perceptual deterioration*", "*became more susceptible to propaganda*", and found the situation to be "*very unpleasant*" (Suedfeld 1969: 3). Each of these elements is carefully made part of the experience of Longman in *The Mind Benders*, confirming the informed and accurate nature of the dramatisation. This is most apparent in the meticulously staged and prolonged sequence of the scientist undergoing sensory deprivation, one sequence at least that many reviewers found both harrowing and impressive. Kennaway drew on the model established by John C. Lilly at the National Institute of Mental Health, Maryland in 1956, the so-called "*water immersion technique*", in which subjects wearing blacked-out head masks were submerged into a tank of tepid water: a "*kind of ultimate in sensory deprivation*" according to one assessment (Solomon and Kleeman 1971: 122).

Kennaway stated the idea behind the story as the "*perennial struggle between humanity and the terrifying advances in science*" (1962: 1). Producer Michael Relph, moved to reply to the poor critical reception, supported his writer in the claim for a serious humanistic message in the film, beyond the demands of a simple spy thriller (letter to *Films and Filming*, April 1963: 3). The story appeared in the year of Kim Philby's defection to Russia and of the Profumo Affair, and offered an imaginative treatment of treachery. The experienced security officer Major Hall is barely in the confines of the research laboratory before his senses are alerting him to "*The whole chilly paraphernalia of treason*".

One of the few novels to attract the kind of attention lavished on John le Carré and Len Deighton was *The Berlin Memorandum* by Adam Hall. First published in 1965, the story introduced the series character Quiller, an agent for the 'Bureau', a covert security organisation which does not officially exist.[228] At the start of the story, he is working in Berlin for the Z Commission, tracking down former Nazi war criminals. He is suddenly returned to the Bureau when the opportunity presents itself of getting to the heart of the secret Phönix organisation, a *renaissant* Nazi group. The bait to entice the reluctant agent is the prospect of unearthing the notorious SS General Zossen. Quiller, acting as Nazi hunter, makes himself a high profile target and is soon abducted by Phönix where he is interrogated by Oktober. Quiller resists truth drugs and is allowed to go free in the hope he will lead Phönix to British Control and expose its intentions. Interposed between the agent and the Nazis is the alluring Inga Lindt, a defector from Phönix, who is tortured in front of Quiller with the aim of getting him to talk, and who later provides the British agent with the secret plans of the Phönix organisation. A subsidiary storyline involves a Jewish biologist; a wartime collaborator of Quiller's who has perfected a deadly plague which he intends to unleash on surviving Nazis in South America. The scientist is murdered by Phönix. Quiller, able to elude his antagonists and return to Control, has realised that the plans which came through Inga are false, that she never fully defected from Phönix, and he is able to lead the German police to the secret hideout of the Nazi organisation.

Quiller then moves in on Zossen, whom he has discovered is a government minister, and extracts the true plans of Phönix to use the plague virus against the Soviets and draw Europe once again into war.

Life Magazine declared *The Berlin Memorandum* "*The best of the new-style spy thrillers*" of the 1960s.[229] The story and the character of the secret agent were influenced by the success of James Bond. Like 007, Quiller is omnicompetent and the reader is informed that he is a known authority on memory, sleep-mechanism, the personality patterns of suicide, fast-driving techniques and ballistics. Quiller is a classic loner; a personal quirk is that he refuses to carry a gun. Much of the effect of the novel is achieved through a first-person narration, recently made fashionable in the spy novel by Len Deighton. Readers are thus rewarded with a precise consideration and practice of tradecraft as Quiller expertly avoids surveillance, rationalises the suspect testimony of former defectors from Phönix, and offers an informed opinion on such things as psychological stress and combating truth drugs. The novel gives a strong impression of residual Nazism in the new Germany and includes some powerful scenes of wartime atrocities perpetrated by the war criminals in the story. The plot of an agent infiltrating a Nazi organisation, of pursuing a private vendetta, of disrupting an atrocity involving germ warfare, and with the suggestion of former Nazis in high places in current West Germany, was later emulated in Frederick Forsyth's *The Odessa File* (1972).[230]

The story was filmed as *The Quiller Memorandum* in 1966 as an Ivan Foxwell production for Rank. It was directed by Michael Anderson, fresh from the wartime secret mission adventure *Operation Crossbow* (1965), starred George Segal as the enigmatic secret agent, and boasted the excellent supporting cast of Alec Guinness as Control, Max von Sydow as Phönix, and Senta Berger as the equivocal love interest. With a script by the celebrated and controversial playwright Harold Pinter, and a score by the brilliant John Barry, the film was a superior spy drama of the 1960s.[231] Publicity for the picture screamed at the audience: "*QUILLER…he's not just another spy – If he shatters your nerves, remember – he's living on his!*" In this streamlined version of the story which reduces the more fanciful aspects of the plot, Quiller is an American, presumably to make the picture more commercial in North America, the back-story of the Z Commission and of Zossen is removed, and the girl Lindt is made a school teacher seemingly unassociated with Phönix. The screenplay is more interpretation than adaptation, and Pinter's response to the intense subjectivity of first-person narration in the novel is to substitute his trademark spare, understated and ominous dialogue in which pauses, silence and stillness allows directors to "*build pictures in the gaps between words*" (David Thomson quoted in the *Guardian*, 4 October 2002). The many confrontations in the story are offered as formal encounters, verbal *pas de deuxs*, with ellipti-cal dialogue mainly suggesting the antagonism and threat seething below the surface, character's motives felt between the lines of everyday small talk, the obscure motivations and complex emotions captured in the sophisticated writing.[232] Anderson bravely constructs the film in a deliberate, mannered style, reinforcing Pinter's oblique dialogue and producing an atmospheric, faintly abstract quality in the film. Extensive location-shooting in Berlin makes the city an important character in the movie,[233] and a telling substitu-tion in the story is the placing of the first meeting of Quiller with Control in the imposing Olympic Stadium in the city, rather than the non-descript thea-tre-setting of the book.[234] Built by the Nazis for the 1936 Games it, therefore, offers a far more symbolic location for a story concerning resurgent Fascism in the new Germany. The picture ends on a more ambiguous note than the novel, with Quiller, in a scene possibly inspired by the famous ending of *The Third Man* (1949), sadly taking leave of Lindt who remains in place in her school, the possibly duplicitous teacher gathering the young children of Ger-many around her, in her custody and within her influence.[235] Producer Ivan Foxwell informed journalists that *The Quiller Memorandum* was not a con-ventional spy thriller and lacked such defining elements as gimmicks and guns (*Sun*, 30 May 1966).[236]

The film opened strongly in metropolitan cinemas, but seemingly trans-ferred poorly to provincial venues and overall performed disappointingly. Reviews of *The Quiller Memorandum* were decidedly mixed, the unusual quality of a spy picture with no gadgets, virtually no gunplay and little physi-cal action seemingly confounding critical expectations. The *Financial Times* found the film "*elusive*", and yet, while acknowledging that the picture broke with the "*depressing convention of invariably identifying the enemy as the Reds*" and presented a "*worrying, anti-conventional dénouement*", the sum of the interesting parts did not add up to a commendable whole. For a thriller, *The Quiller Memorandum* was oddly static, and lacked "*dynamism*", "*pace*" and "*attack*" (11 November 1966). A similar view held at *Monthly Film Bulle-tin* where it was claimed that spy thrillers depended on constant action and narrative twists, which were lacking here, the result of "*plots and Pinter*" simply not mixing (January 1967: 5). The *Observer* thought the picture caught between two schools, unable to "*make up its mind whether it wants to be a post-Bond joke or get its head down and play the Berlin Wall game in the real mud of political intrigue*", and declaring it an uneasy mixture of "*le Carré and Carry-On*". Unseduced by the film's style and ambition, the reviewer dis-missed it as a "*veritable anthology of spy clichés which are treated with a plod-ding reverence*" (13 November 1966). The *Evening News* also sensed some-thing schizophrenic about *The Quiller Memorandum*, and, while "*elegant*", the picture wasn't "*quite believable enough to accept seriously or exciting enough for spy fiction"* (10 November 1966). The *Guardian* found *"something wrong"*, disorientated by a *"very mysterious film"*, and wondered if the intriguing dialogue and excellent performances were let down by an over-glossy style and thin plot? Despite the contribution of Harold Pinter to *The Quiller Memorandum*, *"nothing is going on underneath, and there is not enough surface incident to help us to forget it"* (11 November 1966). The American *Saturday Review* inexplicably found the picture a *"mere orthodox exercise in suspense"* (7 January 1967).

The *Evening Standard* felt no disjunction of styles, praising a *"tremendously efficient new thriller"* which took the *"best of both kinds of spy film – downbeat realism and glamorous fiction"* (10 November 1966). *Films and Filming* was also impressed, praising the picture as a *"rip-snorting thriller"*, and *"stirring up many a deep thought upon life and inhumanity and power and politics"* (January 1967: 29). Other reviewers were in tune with the intentions of the picture, the *People* claiming it a *"refreshingly different kind of spy story rejecting all those gimmicks that were getting so boring"* (13 November 1966), *The Times* noting that after the *"plethora of gimmicks which have assailed us in the last few films of the spy-counter-spy-secret agent cycle, it is extraordinarily refreshing to come back to a film which takes a pure, classical thriller line, based on character and narrative continuity"* (10 November 1966), and *Kine Weekly* declared it *"first-class spy stuff"* (12 November 1966). *The Telegraph* was the most perceptive in recognising the shift in approach in the story, the film dropping what was *"Bond-like"* in the novel and making the secret agent more doubting of his own ability and constructing an intelligent picture of loneliness (11 November 1966). Several reviews noted the topicality of the film when it was released in the week that *"depressing news"* arrived from West Germany of the success in the elections of neo-Nazi candidates in Hesse (*Daily Express*, 9 November 1966; *Evening News*, 10 November 1966).

The left-wing *Morning Star* gave attention untypical of the paper to a spy picture. Welcoming it as a *"spy thriller with a difference"*, the reviewer lauded an attempt to pinpoint a *"real enemy force"*, instead of the *"usual espionage adventure films with their constant stirring up of cold-war hatreds"* (9 November 1966); a move which demonstrated *"courage"* on the part of the filmmakers (12 November 1966). It later reported on the officially enforced changes made to the picture for distribution in West Germany, where all references to the villains as members of a neo-Nazi terror organisation were eliminated, leaving most viewers under the likely impression that it is Communist, and at a time when the German Democratic Republic was continually exposing former Nazis still serving in the Federal authorities (28 February 1967).

Harold Pinter's biographer Michael Billington praises the film as "*superior to most of the Len Deighton-le Carré based films because it latches on to something historically important: the insidious nature of fascism*" (*Guardian*, 4 October 2002). Nicholas Anez, writing in *Films in Review*, later attempted a critical rescue of a film he professed "*unheralded and unjustly neglected*", believing that: "*The intricacies of the multi-levelled storyline combined with an unconventional hero and a melancholy ending doomed the film to an undeserved obscurity*" (1992: 245).[237]

The Naked Runner was a spy novel written by Francis Clifford, first published in 1966 and turned into a film the following year.[238] The story centres on the businessman Sam Laker, who reluctantly agrees to deliver a package for Slattery, a former colleague in wartime special operations and now in British Intelligence, when he is at the trade fair in Leipzig, East Germany (DDR). Of course, once in the DDR things go badly wrong and he is immediately arrested by the state security service and passed over to the ruthless Colonel Hartmann. Using the threat of harm to his son, Patrick, Laker is intimidated into assassinating an East German defector in Denmark. Once in Copenhagen, things again go wrong: Laker rings Slattery in desperation and this alerts Hartmann to his duplicity and London warn the defector who fails to show in the city. Expecting his son to have been killed, Laker returns to Leipzig and contacts the underground and plans are laid for the assassination of the chief of security. Laker shoots the occupant of Hartmann's official car on the autobahn, but is knocked unconscious trying to escape. He later wakes up in a military hospital in Hanover, West Germany. There, Slattery explains that he had been used by British Intelligence in an elaborate masquerade. Patrick was perfectly safe, Hartmann was working for the British, and, as hoped, Laker had killed an American defector badly wanted out of the way by the Western alliance.

Francis Clifford had earned the epithet from *The Telegraph* of a "*thinking man's Ian Fleming*" and his spy thrillers tended to be appreciated as among the more serious of the genre.[239] The use of the executive Laker for intelligence purposes resembles the revelations in the early 1960s regarding Greville Wynne, the British businessman who served as the SIS contact with GRU (Military Intelligence) officer Oleg Penkovsky and visited Eastern Europe on several occasions, and this closeness to actual espionage also colours the tale with a sense of authenticity. *The Naked Runner* is a gripping story, although a reader today might find the 'happy ending' contrived, improbable and disappointing. At the time of publication, *Books and Bookmen* judged it "*One of the finest suspense novels since the war*".[240]

The film rights to *The Naked Runner* were acquired by Frank Sinatra Enterprises shortly before the novel was published, and the picture was produced

in Great Britain, funded and released by Warner Bros., with all-location filming around London and in Copenhagen. Sinatra starred as Sam Laker, Peter
Vaughan as Slattery and Derren Nesbitt as Colonel Hartmann. To
accommodate its star, it was necessary to make Laker an American residing
and working in London, and who had served with the wartime Office of Strategic Services (OSS). Another concession to American sympathies was in
making the target of the assassination a spy caught in Britain, given topicality
through him having escaped from Wormwood Scrubs and being escorted to
Moscow by the KGB, somewhat like the actual George Blake the year previous.
While sticking relatively close to the original plot, the film, scripted by Stanley
Mann, replaced the restricted narrative of the novel, which had ensured the
reader remained as confused, frustrated and tense as Laker, with a more om-
niscient approach, which reveals and closely attends to the machinations of
British Intelligence from the outset. The picture thus sacrifices a good deal of
suspense in favour of prolonged and cynical manipulation of an unsuspecting hero.[241] In such a vein, the movie included some rather crude references
to marionettes, such as a glimpse of a puppet theatre in East Germany. The
picture was released with the tagline, "*They found the key to Sam Laker. They
wound it up good and tight. And then they turned him loose*". *The Naked Runner* stands as a more serious variant of the 'reluctant spy' story that was popular in the latter half of the 1960s and usually embodied in comedy-thrillers
such as *Hot Enough for June!* (1964), *The Liquidator* (1966) and *Otley* (1969).
Here, the narrative is presented in a psychologically-realistic manner and the
unwilling protagonist is subjected to extreme emotional stress and manipulated to perform actions distasteful to his nature.

Critical interest in the film derives from the fact it was directed by Sidney J.
Furie and photographed by Otto Heller, fresh from their achievements on *The
Ipcress File* (1965), one of the most brilliant spy films of the 1960s. Sinatra had
been impressed by *Ipcress*, appreciated that Furie worked creatively in the spy
genre, and that the filmmaker was comfortable working in London. Furie and
Heller carried forward their visual experiments from the previous picture and
The Naked Runner, similarly shot in widescreen Techniscope, is packed full of
'unbalanced' compositions, miscellaneous objects obscuring action occur-
ring in the background, and overblown faces crammed to the front of the
frame. There were many problems during the shoot, mainly stemming from a
temperamental star who despised location shooting. Two weeks before the
production, Sinatra had married the young actress Mia Farrow in a surprise
wedding. Farrow apparently "*haunted*" the set and at one point Furie threatened to quit. There were reports that Sinatra refused to shoot the final scenes
and that the film-makers finished the picture with a stand-in. However, Furie
maintains that despite the tensions the difficult star completed principal
photography and that a stand-in was required to fix some shots during the

editing period as Sinatra was unavailable for re-shoots (Kremer 2015).[242] Either way, such problems explain the rather abrupt and unsatisfying ending to the film.[243]

The film attracted mixed reviews. Some found it an over-complicated spy thriller, while others were prepared to search out a more worthy espionage drama. The *Evening Standard* found it "*bewildering*" (13 July 1967) and the *Financial Times* a "*non-starter in the spy stakes*" (14 July 1967). The *Guardian* believed the over-blown visual techniques only served to "*draw attention to themselves and distract*" (14 July 1967). In America, *Variety* felt that, "*Not only British Intelligence, but anybody's intelligence, is likely to be affronted by this potboiler*" (5 July 1967), and *Time Magazine* complained of an "*amateurish spy film*" played by a cast of "*inept unknowns*" which confused "*tension and pretension*" (28 July 1967).

In contrast, the *Daily Mail* praised a "*taut, tight, fast-moving thriller*" without gadgets and gimmicks (15 July 1976), *Kine Weekly* a "*new angle on spy fiction*" (22 July 1967), the *People* a "*thriller which draws you irresistibly into the plot and moves steadily on to the final punch*" and the *Sunday Times* an "*abrupt, moody, greeny-grey study of tension*" and sufficient to "*stand comparison with Hitchcock*" (both 16 July 1967). *Films and Filming*, while claiming that the adaptation fudged the mystery of the original novel, praised the inventive visuals of Furie and Heller which were "*revitalising*" the thriller form (September 1967: 20-21). The *Evening News* marked *The Naked Runner* down as "*one of those quasi-realistic spy thrillers*" (13 July 1967) and the *Sun* observed that the picture did not hesitate to "*present British security workers as a ruthless, heartless and devious lot*" (13 July 1967). Other reviewers also noted similarities with the recent school of cynical and realistic spy pictures. The *Sunday Telegraph* commended a "*nice straight spy movie*", pointing out that echoes of *The Spy Who Came in from the Cold* included the "*same sort of official double-cross – case-hardened veteran, hired by British Secret Service to assassinate a man, but made to believe he is doing it under duress for the East Germans – and (more to its credit) the same dry style*" (16 July 1967). The left-wing *Morning Star*, not going to be taken in by the supposed critique of the new style anti-heroic spy story, offered a close look at the current vogue of spy films which seem to have as their theme, "*spying for any Government is a ruthless, heartless, iniquitous business*". The paper warned its readers that the message was essentially a "*masquerade*"; that the pictures remained "*heavy-handed, unsubtle cold-war currency dressed up in the 'both-sides-are-just-as-bad' garb*", and, moreover, continued to promote prejudices "*about nasty Communist types*". Such cinema, it concluded, was "*indulging in cold-war propaganda of the most vicious kind*" (15 July 1967).

Film historian Robert Murphy places *The Naked Runner* alongside *The Quiller Memorandum* and *Danger Route* (1967) as "*deeply flawed*", but "*compelling*" films which contribute something to the developing espionage genre. In particular, he found the picture "*satisfying*" at the level of Laker's paranoia and the film's treatment of his miseries as an extended nightmare (1992: 222). However, the French critics Bertrand Tavernier and Jean-Pierre Coursodon are harsher, maintaining that while baroque artifices are acceptable in an unconventional film such as *The Ipcress File*, "*they do nothing for a talky, arbitrary and boring scenario like the detestable* The Naked Runner" (quoted in Kremer 2015). Furie always maintained that the problems lay with the script and that the film never managed to bring comprehensibility to the story. Daniel Kremer notes the difficulty of making stylistically risky films with major stars and sees *The Naked Runner* as the young director's first "*unqualified failure*", one in which it is all too easy to "*perceive the filmmaker struggling to fine-tune his aesthetic in a way that fits the specific film as a whole*" (2015). *The Naked Runner* was the last motion picture produced at Sinatra Enterprises. *The Mind Benders*, *The Quiller Memorandum* and *The Naked Runner* demonstrated that stepping out of the mainstream style of the spy thriller recently established by the James Bond pictures in the 1960s could be tricky, disorientating for some reviewers and audiences, and ultimately commercially risky.

The Human Factor was the final spy novel of Graham Greene and appeared in 1978. For many it is among the last of the truly great spy novels and it heads John G. Cawelti and Bruce A. Rosenberg's list of 'The Greatest Spy Stories', where the literary scholars praise it as a "*compelling tragic novel and one of the most powerful artistic treatments of espionage in the history of the spy story*" (1987: 49). Maurice Castle is in his early sixties and serves as a middle-ranking desk officer in the SIS, heading the small department in London which attends to intelligence in the backwater of southern Africa. Some years earlier, he had served as a field officer in South Africa, but his networks had become compromised and he fled with one of his agents, a black woman named Sarah, whom he married and acted as a father to her then unborn son. Black South African communists had made it possible for Maurice and Sarah to escape, and in gratitude Castle provides intelligence on African matters to the Soviets.

British Intelligence eventually discovers the leak, from a defector in place in Russia, and the department is subjected to a security check led by the newly arrived Colonel Daintry. Circumstantial evidence casts suspicion on Davis, the likeable if innocuous deputy of Castle, and to avoid yet another embarrassing scandal in national security, it is decided to kill the suspected double-agent with a new strain of germ and blame it on cirrhosis of the liver.

The mild Castle is appalled, but sees the death as a chance to step away from his duplicitous role. However, he is suddenly confronted with a former antagonist, Cornelius Müller of the South African Bureau of State Security, and he is now required to work with him as an ally on a joint operation known as Uncle Remus. Appreciating the great cost to himself and his family, Castle passes on to the Soviets the important secrets he acquires, and amid great anxiety and confusion allows himself to be taken to Moscow for safety. Isolated and lonely, he waits there forlornly for his beloved Sarah and their boy, which a vindictive British Secret Service will not allow to join him. It is no comfort when he learns that the intelligence he has been supplying to the Soviets has been of no intrinsic value, but has been used as a cover for a British agent in Moscow who has been doubled by the Russians.

The Human Factor is unusual for the compassion shown to a traitor and for demonising the SIS, and intriguing for the way it blends experience with fiction. In a brief prologue to the novel, Graham Greene disavows any possibility of meaningful overlap of spy fiction and spy reality, but then teasingly quotes from Hans Christian Andersen, that "*out of reality are our tales of imagination fashioned*". The novel, which makes several references to traitor spies such as George Blake, Guy Burgess, Donald Maclean, John Vassall and the Portland Spies, is usually credited as a version of the Kim Philby narrative, Greene having known the double-agent while serving in the wartime SIS, and later controversially acted as a public apologist for him. The author had started the novel shortly after Philby had defected in 1963, but set it aside after he had written the introduction to the double-agent's memoirs *My Silent War* (1968), fearing that the story would be thought of as simply a *roman-à-clef* of the infamous traitor (West 1997: 205). *The Human Factor* contains other elements of the Greene biography, such as 'secret service' in Africa and use of the location of Berkhamsted where Greene had been raised. The character of Davis who dreams of a posting to Lourenço Marques is possibly based on Malcolm Muggeridge who served such a posting in the war and with whom Greene was familiar at that time; the character of the antiquarian bookseller who is Castle's contact in London could have been based on Peter Kroger who spied for Russia in the late 1950s under the cover of dealing in second hand books; and the use of the forename Maurice might have been a sly joke at the expense of Maurice Oldfield the director of SIS (1973-78). Greene returned to the story in the mid-1970s, sent a proof copy of the novel to Kim Philby in Moscow and received some minor suggestions, and there has been speculation that a proof copy was also sent to MI6 which might account for some minor changes in the text as it appeared at publication (West 1997: 236, 240-41).

Greene, the Catholic author, includes a passage in which the emotionally overburdened Castle seeks release through 'confession', suggesting the similarity in the relationships between priest and parishioner, and double-agent and control. Greene, in a riff on the familiar passage by E. M. Forster regarding the choice between loyalty to one's country or to one's friends, was concerned to investigate the 'human factor' in espionage. In his foreword to Kim Philby's *My Silent War* in 1968, Greene had written: "*Who among us had not committed treason to something or someone more important than a country*" (Philby 1979: 7). The friendless Castle chooses allegiance to his family and is told by his wife: "*We have our own country. You and I and Sam. You've never betrayed that country, Maurice*". For anyone other than the most blindly patriotic, the 'betrayed' in *The Human Factor* are not deserving of any loyalty and Castle demonstrates greater integrity. The characters in the story are typically lonely and suffer from solitude, the occupational hazard of the spy, and symbolised by Castle reading *Robinson Crusoe* when isolated in Moscow. For the novelist Anthony Burgess, *The Human Factor*, which Greene claimed to have been one of the most difficult to write, is as "*fine a novel as he has ever written – concise, ironic, acutely observant of contemporary life, funny, shocking, above all compassionate*" (1978). For the film critic at the *Observer*, *The Human Factor* stood as "*Greene's most extensive and subtle meditation on the nature of loyalty, patriotism and treason*" (3 February 1980); and for Quentin Falk the story served as the "*perfect antidote to James Bond*" as it concerned itself "*with the bureaucracy of the Cold War, less minutely than does le Carré but with more humanity*" (1990: 178). A best-selling novel, it was reported that the book sold 200,000 paperback copies in Britain and 2 million books worldwide (*The Times*, 13 December 1979; *New Statesman*, 1 February 1980).

The eminent director Joseph Losey approached Greene for the film rights to *The Human Factor* with the tempting possibility of Harold Pinter to write the script (Caute 1994: 455-56); however, he lost out to the great Hollywood filmmaker Otto Preminger who had acquired the rights at substantial expense and produced and directed the screen version in Great Britain in 1979 with a distinguished cast including John Gielgud, Robert Morley and Richard Attenborough.[244] Greene had been approached to write the screenplay and on his refusal it was passed over to the respected British dramatist Tom Stoppard who in his reverence for the author crafted a faithful treatment of the novel.[245] The picture was made with a deal of trouble during a period of great difficulty in the professional life of Preminger. The production was delayed in starting as there were seemingly problems in putting the financing together (*Variety*, 21 November 1979). These continued to dog the £2.5 million production with the press delightedly reporting a "*never-ending saga of bouncing cheques, writs and enraged thespians*", of crew members stranded in Africa amidst unpaid hotel bills following the completion of location shooting, and enforced cuts to the script (*Daily Express*, 8 August and 15 October 1979; Hirsch 2007[246]; Fujiwara 2008: 414). A new "*sledgehammer blow*" struck when an aggrieved sound editor stole some of the completed film as ransom against unpaid salary (*Daily Express*, 19 September 1979; *Daily Mail*, 20 September 1979). The actors union Equity presented Preminger with two writs in October 1979 on behalf of unpaid members of the cast and threatened to bring in the receiver in November (*Daily Mail*, 19 October 1979; *The Telegraph*, 20 October 1979; *Daily Express*, 13 November 1979).[247] The difficulties arose because investors withdrew support and Preminger was forced to mortgage his house in the South of France and sell some of his valuable art collection to meet the remaining production costs of £1,150,000.[248] The returns on the film were so meagre that financial wrangles were only finally resolved in 1984 following court hearings and a private settlement, and Preminger was reported to have lost a personal stake of £1 million (*Glasgow Herald*, 24 January 1984; Hirsch 2007). There were also reports of clashes between the autocratic "*Otto the Monster*" and the leading man, the brilliant but combustible Nicol Williamson (*Sunday Express*, 15 July 1979; *Evening Standard*, 27 July 1979).[249] The picture was filmed entirely on location with the British scenes shot in Berkhamsted, Market Drayton, Shropshire and London, and the African scenes in and around Nairobi, Kenya (Reynolds 1979: 32). *The Human Factor* turned out to be the director's final film.

The film was vilified in Britain to about the same extent that the novel had been lauded. It was judged as "*unconvincing*" (*Spectator*, 16 February 1980), "*poorly crafted*" and "*wretchedly made*" (*Sunday Express*, 3 February 1980), "*strangely low-key*" (*Guardian*, 31 January 1980), "*suffering from pernicious anaemia*" (*New Statesman*, 1 February 1980), "*old-fashioned*" (*Evening News*, 31 January 1980), "*remarkably dull*" (*Sunday Mirror*, 3 February 1980) and the "*most inept effort to come from the barely competent Preminger*" (*Scotsman*, 9 February 1980). The *Daily Express* was surprised that a filmmaker of the pedigree of Preminger had "*drained the story of all humanity and feeling*" (2 February 1980) and *The Times* was incredulous that the veteran director had turned in something "*verging on the amateurish*" (3 February 1980). Some criticisms centred on miscasting. Maurice Castle in the form of Nicol Williamson lost a couple of decades in age and was now in his late thirties, and it was widely felt that the Somali-born model Iman Abdul Majid who played Sarah was "*gorgeous but incompetent*", and her inability to convey the essential passion in the core scenes with Maurice that represented the 'human factor' in the story tended to leave a dramatic hole in the picture (*Spectator*, 16 February 1980; *Guardian*, 31 January 1980). Bucking the trend, the *Western Mail* found the picture a "*slow but witty and stylish realisation of Graham Greene's recent spy novel*" (6 September 1980).

There were complaints of poor production values which led to unconvincing backdrops for South Africa (filmed in Kenya) and Moscow (filmed in the studio, and done in such "*slapdash style that it resembles a set in a high-school play*", *New Yorker*, 11 February 1980), of poor lighting and framing which the lighting cameraman Mike Molloy attributed to Preminger's lack of interest in the visual aspects of the picture (Fujiwara 2008: 412), and of laboured flashbacks to earlier events in South Africa which were more lightly managed in the book.[250] There were also comments on a curious restraint for a filmmaker celebrated for his mobile framing, that resultantly scenes looked like "*set pieces for a drawing-room play*" (*Evening News*, 31 January 1980), and that Preminger's aim in this regard consisted of little more than "*constantly manoeuvring every pair of speakers into tight two-shots, where they awkwardly sit together exchanging flatly delivered dialogue in long takes*" (*Observer*, 3 February 1980). Quentin Falk, in his study of Graham Greene on screen, echoed all of these criticisms. He found the adaptation a failure of "*staggering proportions – artistically, technically and logistically*", the style "*muted to the point of terminal inertia*", a "*curious mish-mash of casting*" and a production of "*gross artistic miscalculations*" (1990: 178, 183 and 185).

The picture attracted better, sometimes very good notices in the United States. The doyen of auteur criticism Andrew Sarris, long a champion of Preminger, felt the "*conviction*" throughout the film. He respected and admired its "*informed concern for the inescapable ambiguities of the human condition in our time*", and, although a failure in some regards, believed that, "*so much of what Preminger, Stoppard, and Greene were trying to say about the world today came through on the screen that I rejoiced that Preminger had had enough gumption to continue communicating with those of us who have always respected his art*" (1980). Other eminent commentators and critics also printed warm praise. Arthur Schlesinger in the *Saturday Review* heralded *The Human Factor* as Preminger's finest picture for two decades, a view repeated by Vincent Canby at the *The New York Times* (cited in Hirsch 2007). However, *The New Yorker* claimed a "*failure of such serious dimensions*" that it felt impelled to "*reconstruct how it happened, as if preparing a coroner's report*". "*What is major in the book*" it concluded, "*has been blurrily and hastily brushed over in the movie*":

> the lack of relevance in all spying; the dingy, mean-spirited, back-office aura of the Firm; a general deterioration of conviction; the knowledge that 'the other side' is suffering from the very same desultory loss of purpose; the stiff-faced, niggling failures of human understanding, which are linked to rigidities of class.

But, above all, "*the awful universal knowledge – everyone in the story knows it – that class and school and country are no longer to be relied upon, that they very nearly amount to nothing*" (11 February 1980).

In a "*miracle of accidental timing*", the release of the film followed close on the heels of the shock revelation of the double-agent Anthony Blunt in November 1979 (*Scotsman,* 9 February 1980). The exposure had come about due to veiled accusations in Andrew Boyle's *The Climate of Treason* (1979) about the Cambridge Spies, in which Blunt, in a further remarkable coincidence, had been concealed under the name of Maurice.[251] However, the film failed to recoup dividends from the bonus of a topicality which rather seemed to prove Greene's point about class and espionage, and perhaps in the event the media frenzy around Professor Blunt "*upstaged*" what many felt was a slow and staid movie (*Evening Standard,* 31 January 1980).

Recent biographers of Preminger have claimed something of interest and accomplishment in *The Human Factor* and defend the spare style of filming berated by some reviewers. Chris Fujiwara suggests that the "*sense of tiredness, of going through the motions, that pervades much of* The Human Factor, *proves appropriate to the slack and static atmosphere in which Greene's story is set and that gives it its special mood*" (2008: 417). Foster Hirsch acknowledges the "*formality*" as an element of the Preminger style, and that here the director pursued an appropriately "*cool*", "*lean*" even "*barren*" course demanded by the material; a picture "*almost avant-garde in its austerity*" and for which even Iman's "*minimalism*" proved to be appropriate (2007). Graham Greene was less impressed by the adaptation of his novel and refused the film's inclusion in a retrospective of his filmed stories at the National Film Theatre, London in 1984 (*Guardian,* 4 July 1984).

The 'serious' nature of the films considered in this chapter was emphasised through many of the productions seeking explicit connections with the European art cinema and its connotation of depth and sophistication. Spy thrillers tended to feature sexy and nubile continental starlets such as Ursula Andress, Daliah Lavi, Britt Ekland, Camilla Sparv, Elke Sommer, Sylva Koscina and Marisa Mell as part of their appeal. However, espionage dramas preferred to cast performers who had developed reputations in the European cinema, actors like Max von Sydow, who had worked extensively with Ingmar Bergman, and Oskar Werner, who had played for François Truffaut, and actresses such as Françoise Dorléac, who had appeared for Roman Polanski and also for Truffaut, and Pia Degermark, who had been introduced to cinema by Bo Widerberg. The approach is most noticeable in *The Deadly Affair*, which cast the impressive duo of Oscar-winners Maximilian Schell and Simone Signoret, as well as the acclaimed Harriet Andersson (in her first English-speaking role) who had also worked widely with Ingmar Bergman in Sweden.[252]

While the spy thriller often relied on a sense of the exotic for its meaning and pleasures, sending its intrepid agents to the Far East, the Pacific, the Americas and the most glamorous places in Europe, the espionage drama was drawn to more mundane locations, such as drab governmental offices, dreary suburban villas and the miserable fringes of the metropolitan area. A place of special significance and an archetypal "*spyscape*" in the espionage drama was the divided city of Berlin, the liminal divide of the Wall serving as the supreme symbolic setting for the East-West conflict.[253] Literary critic Jürgen Kamm has described the city of the period as the "*spy's perfect playground, his natural habitat, the urban equivalent of the spy's paranoid psyche*" (1996: 65); while biographer Adam Sisman has referred to the city as the "*world capital of espionage*" (2015: 226). The appearance of the Berlin Wall in 1961 coincided with the emergence of the new spy story, and, as Siegfried Mews has argued, the,

> *construction and long-lasting, formidable presence of the Berlin Wall profoundly affected the spy novel itself: it confronted its authors with a new situation that required a re-examination of its generic properties as well as its underlying aesthetic and ideological suppositions.*
> (1996: 51)

Berlin, the front-line city of the Cold War, was the setting of such important stories of the new literature of espionage as *The Quiller Memorandum* and *Funeral in Berlin*, the Berlin Wall or as it was sometimes known in Germany the Todesstreifen (death strip) was the framing motif in *The Spy Who Came in from the Cold*,[254] border-crossing into East Germany was the central narrative act in *The Looking-Glass War* and *The Naked Runner*, and the German Democratic Republic and its pernicious agents remains the 'off-stage' presence directing the malevolence experienced by characters in miserable London locations in *The Deadly Affair*. A special report of the television correspondent of the *Sun* captured the significance of Berlin for the spy story at the time *The Quiller Memorandum* and *Funeral in Berlin* were filming in the city, "*Divided by that obscene communion of bricks and barbed wire we call the Wall, it is the perfect setting for whispers and codes and covers and contacts and things that blow up in the night*". She applauded filmmakers shrewd enough to judge that the "*current appetite for spy fantasy will sharpen into a taste for realistic spy drama and realistic political intrigue*" (30 May 1966).[255]

The spy stories of John le Carré, Len Deighton and a handful of other novelists who mined the anti-heroic tradition captured the popular imagination and convinced some readers that here was a realistic and critical depiction of the clandestine world of spying, in contrast to the fanciful exploits of fictional secret agents like James Bond and his many imitators. The meagre, bland pronouncements on the secret world from official sources meant that the ordinary public had little else to go on, and the 'credible' storylines and more commonplace characters and settings of espionage drama tempted viewers into accepting the fictions as more authentic depictions of intrigue and spying. The alternative tradition also critically examined the 'human factor' in the Cold War, and in the view of Eva Horn shared an awareness that in this war "*humans do not count – unless as a site of unreliability, manipulability, or weakness*" (2013: 251). Reviewers tended to approach espionage dramas in these terms, but were not always convinced that individual pictures succeeded in finding a character, style or narrative that convincingly or adequately portrayed a requisite sense of authenticity or critique. The adaptations of John le Carré succeeded best in these terms; the adaptations of Len Deighton, after a promising start, less so; while there was much qualification about such pictures as *The Quiller Memorandum*, *The Naked Runner* and *The Human Factor*. Historically, there is not the sense that the espionage drama seriously managed to rival the spy thriller as a popular genre; that, indeed, beyond the first flush of hope with *The Spy Who Came in from the Cold* and *The Ipcress File*, the alternative style was by and large simply accepted as a quirky spy thriller, a genre that was running out of steam and outstaying its welcome.

3.
The Spy Thriller on Television

Between implausibility and imbecility falls the shadow of the spy story. In that dim and twisty neighborhood, we fans of the genre are happy to suspend disbelief if only our good will and imagination are not imposed on.
(*The New York Times*, 17 April 1988)

Spy dramas, though unbelievable, make good viewing and appeal to the Bond fantasy buried inside most nine-to-five men.
(*Evening News*, 12 September 1973)

James Chapman has marked the adventure series as one of the "*most distinctive features on the landscape of British television during the 1960s and early 1970s*". Such shows as *Danger Man* (1960-68), *The Saint* (1962-69), *The Avengers* (1961-69), *The Champions* (1968-69), *Man in a Suitcase* (1967-68) and *Department S* (1969-70) featured a variety of secret agents and crime-fighters, lacked any kind of literary pedigree and made little pretence at realism (2002: 1, 3).[256] The adventure series was characterised by its "*pop*" sensibilities, in which style and design were to a greater or lesser extent privileged over content. An embodiment of the social and cultural imperatives of the 1960s around modernity and consumerism, the adventure series absorbed and reflected the same kind of energies and interests located in tourism, conspicuous consumption and sexual pleasure as the James Bond films, Modesty Blaise and other mod secret agent thrillers of the "*high-sixties*" (ibid.: 13-14; Buxton 1990). The spy adventure style of *Danger Man* continued into the 1970s and 1980s in a number of secret agent thrillers which centred on a professional secret agent, but usually in a toned down form and likely derived from a popular spy thriller novel.

An alternative style emerged in the 'spy procedural', which adopted a mode of realistic psychological motivation, naturalistic settings and more convincing storylines.[257] Such shows owed something to the popular form of the police procedural, a sub-genre of the detective story in which   the emphasis is on the investigation of a crime by a law enforcement agency. In the history of literary crime fiction, it represented a shift *"from the efforts of amateur detectives to collective, state activity in the fight against crime, no longer an arbitrary disruption of an organic harmony but a constant, pervasive part of the urban experience"* (Buxton 1990: 120). In Britain, the Inspector Gideon stories of J. J. Marric (John Creasey) and the Inspector Martineau stories of Maurice Proctor were highly influential on the style from the 1950s, and taken up in such television series as *Z-Cars* (1962-78), *Softly, Softly* (1966-76) and *New Scotland Yard* (1972-74), which articulated an accurately rendered description of routine police work. As Joseph Oldham has seen it, the focus is much more strongly on *"procedure, deduction and teamwork"*, with the officers as simple professionals lacking either the glamour of the agents of the spy thrillers or the existential anxiety of the anti-heroes of the John le Carré school (Oldham 2017: 49). According to David Buxton, such police series *"aligned themselves with the technocratic, managerial reformism of the 1960s Labour government"* (1990: 121). The spy procedural with its emphasis on operational practice, the realistic portrayal of professionals at work and recognisable ideological contexts developed a comparable style of *"cloak and dagger realism"* for British television drama. It replaced the adventure series as the dominant form of secret agent thriller on British television in the 1970s and 1980s in such shows as *Special Branch* (1969-74), *Codename* (1970), *Spy Trap* (1972-75), *The Sandbaggers* (1978-80), *Blood Money* (1981) and *Skorpion* (1983).[258]

The period also saw a few comedies making light of secret agents and spy organisations, as well as a handful of dramas specifically aimed at young adults. Spoofs such as *Virgin of the Secret Service* (1968) and *The Top Secret Life of Edgar Briggs* (1974) were not greatly admired and less successful than American TV shows such as *Get Smart* (1965-70). It proved difficult to place espionage in the television schedules for younger audiences and few producers were tempted. *Tightrope* was an unusual example of extended serious drama for young adults and the adventure series *Spyder's Web* (both 1972) proved less popular than its predecessors in the 1960s.

The spy adventure in the 1960s

Escapism is big business. Ever since James Bond hit the jackpot, the trend has been towards crime and spy fantasies.
(*Sun*, 15 October 1965)

The best secret agents are undoubtedly British – Bond on the movie screen, and John Drake, on television, are the two most successful in their respective media.
(George Markstein 1966: 16)

Danger Man was the breakthrough show for the spy adventure in the 1960s and commenced as a series of 39 half-hour episodes produced by the ITC Company and broadcast on commercial television in Great Britain in 1960 and 1961. The series was devised by Ralph Smart who had recently produced *The Invisible Man* series, an updating of the H. G. Wells story that incorporated some espionage elements, which ran for two seasons in 1958 and 1959. Following discussions with Ian Fleming, the idea for a spy thriller emerged which featured the professional agent John Drake who served as a special undercover security operator for the North Atlantic Treaty Organisation and could be appreciated as emerging from the success of the James Bond novels. Smart had been looking for an action drama that ITC could sell in North America, and to bolster the appeal of the show in the United States the *Danger Man* stories were framed in a first-person narration reminiscent of American hard-boiled detective fiction and the American-born Patrick McGoohan was cast as Drake. Under the influence of the actor, the character was sharply distinguished from 007 and emerged as a man of moral standards, who detested violence, used his brains and treated women with respect.[259] As McGoohan stated of Drake at the time, "*He is not a thick ear specialist, a puppet muscle man*". Rather, he saw the agent "*in the heroic mould, like the classic western hero, which means he has to be a good man*" (quoted in Sellers 2006: 43). *Danger Man* was broadcast on the CBS network in America, and although attracting favourable reviews was not sufficiently popular to warrant a further series.

Following the phenomenal success of the early James Bond films from 1962 onwards, ITC returned to *Danger Man* and produced two series totalling 45 one-hour episodes in 1964 and 1965, and a further two colour episodes in 1966, the longer format allowing for more complex plots and character development. These were broadcast in the United States on CBS as *Secret Agent* where it now benefitted from the secret agent craze of the middle-decade and succeeded as a network hit, turning McGoohan into the highest paid actor in British television. Drake was reconfigured in a more British manner, now a Special Security Agent for the fictional M.9, his assignments issued exclusively from Her Majesty's Secret Service. Established cinema directors who worked on the series included Pat Jackson and Charles Crichton, emerging filmmakers included Clive Donner, Peter Yates and Don Chaffey, and these were part of the strategy to raise the quality of the production.[260] Well-known guest performers included Sylvia Syms, John Fraser and Virginia Maskell. In the extended episodes, Drake was sent on a variety of missions of espionage and international criminal intrigue. Tackling an agent suspected of smuggling naval secrets in 'Don't Nail Him Yet' (1964), leading an operation to rescue an agent from an Eastern Bloc embassy in 'A Room in the Basement' and posing as a defector in Singapore in 'A Very Dangerous Game' (both 1965), and investigating the disappearance of a scientist in 'Dangerous Secret' (1966).

A distinguishing feature of *Danger Man* was its puritanical attitude towards sex which stood it in contrast with the approach of James Bond. It was Patrick McGoohan's insistence that there should be no titillation or gratuitous violence, and that the drama should remain suitable for children. The unconventional genre character was promoted as the "*spy with no gun and no girl*".[261] As James Chapman has noted, there was a conscious differentiation between John Drake and James Bond, the former a "*puritan*" and "*traditionalist*", the latter a "*hedonist*" and "*moderniser*". He argues that *Danger Man* with its narratives and backgrounds of recognisable geopolitical conflicts and real political tensions, modest moral imperatives, and manner of taking itself a little more seriously than the typical spy adventure of the decade, fitted the realist lineage of the spy story (2002: 25-27). The show was therefore morally and stylistically conservative in a decade which was to be characterised by permissiveness and stands in contrast with *The Avengers* (1961-69) which, once in its stride, paraded its modish and swinging credentials. In many other regards, though, *Danger Man* happily conformed to the tenets of the escapist spy thriller, absorbing and promoting the archetypal tourist code of the contemporary secret agent narrative and sending Drake off on missions to such trouble spots as Latin America, Central Africa, Eastern Europe and the Balkans (all constructed in a British studio), and especially from the second series onwards, providing the agent with a variety of gadgets – tie-pin cameras, an electric razor which doubles as a tape recorder – to aid him. The moral and realist imperatives of the spy thriller were more fully developed in subsequent secret agent shows, especially the spy procedurals and espionage dramas which began to proliferate from the 1970s. *Danger Man*, popular around the world, was important in the ITC Company's ambition for overseas markets, and helped pioneer associated merchandise and tie-ins for a popular television drama. Alongside James Bond, *Danger Man* "*turned the secret agent adventure series into a prominent vehicle for the economic and cultural export of Britishness*" (Chapman 2002: 51), and in the view of Wesley Britton stood out as both "*one of the best-crafted series in the genre*" and "*one of the best televised time capsules of the Cold War in the 1960s*" (2004: 110).

The spy adventure of the 1960s occupied the television schedules in sometimes more mundane shows. A popular television offering was the lighthearted adventure series *Top Secret*, which ran for two seasons and 26 episodes of one-hour duration on the commercial channel in 1961 and 1962 and starred William Franklyn. Peter Dallas is a British intelligence agent who finds himself in various adventures during a year's leave of absence in Argentina. Essentially a gentleman adventurer in the tradition of The Saint, Dallas tackles crime and wrong-doing in the cities and villages of the South American country. Typical of its day, the series was shot on tape with filmed inserts and Franklyn and a small crew spent eight weeks in Argentina shooting establishing shots and inserts on film.[262] The popular series featured such guest players as Honor Blackman, Hazel Court, Peter Vaughn and Philip Madoc and some episodes were written by Roger Marshall who would later contribute to the spy series *The Avengers* and *Special Branch*. The undemanding show was quite acceptable to the reviewer at the *Guardian* who found it a "*quick and ingenious thriller, with clever dialogue*", presenting an "*unusually entertaining and amusing experience*" (16 September 1961), and felt the BBC had a "*formidable task to draw viewers away*" from the attraction (30 September 1961). However, the American view at *Variety*, which kept a watchful eye on 'foreign' television at this time, was that the series lacked ingenuity and imagination. For its reviewer, *Top Secret* was the "*old secret agent shenanigans all over again, strung along a reach-me-down-storyline, and barnacled with dialog clichés*". The filmed inserts offered "*some mild visual interest*", but a "*guy getting out of a plane in Buenos Aires looks very much like a guy getting out of a plane at London Airport*". Franklyn, though, made a good impression as the gentleman adventurer and was "*pleasantly urbane and laconic*" (23 August 1961). *Variety* remained unimpressed with the second series, which it found "*pedestrian*", "*lightweight*" and "*implausible*". A single shot of Dallas crossing a busy street and back projection to cover a car ride were considered insufficient "*to bring out the steam heat of South America*" (23 May 1962). These were clear signals to British producers that to go over in the States television adventure series needed adequate production values and to be shot on film, lessons learned by ITC and ABC and the successful shows they distributed in America later in the decade.

The Avengers was a hugely popular action series produced by ABC Television and broadcast in seven seasons and 161 episodes from 1961 to 1969, making it the longest-running espionage series on British television before *Spooks* (2002-11). At its height, it attracted an audience of 30 million viewers in 70 countries (Chapman 2000: 38).[263] The show commenced in black and white as a low-key crime series starring Ian Hendry and Patrick Macnee as a wronged doctor and a shadowy agent who engage in a fight against organised crime. Most of these early episodes are lost. Macnee's John Steed was retained for the second season, where the characterisation increasingly became more dandified, embodying a "*foppish style harking back to the Regency and a modish '60s chic*" and symbolic of Britain's romantic past.[264] He was eventually partnered with a series of intelligent, stylish and assertive females: "*hip, leggy, sexy, brilliant, physically competent women who took nonsense from no man*", who typically served as the "*agent of change*" in the series, and who symbolically posed as Britain's modernising future (Miller 2003: 13, 158).[265] Honor Blackman's Mrs Cathy Gale came first, and the storylines for her two seasons more obviously moved into the world of intrigue and espionage. While the stories became increasingly fanciful and fashion-conscious during the third season, and Steed more debonair, it was from the fourth series and the replacement of Blackman (who was away shooting the James Bond picture *Goldfinger*, 1964) by Diana Rigg as Emma Peel that *The Avengers* assumed the characteristic modish, colourful and trendy style so typical of its decade.[266] In 1965, the show, now produced more expensively on film, and from the fifth series in colour, was sold to the American Broadcasting Company and *The Avengers* became one of the first British series to be aired on primetime US television.[267] When Rigg also left to star in a Bond picture, *On Her Majesty's Secret Service* (1969), she was replaced for the final series by Linda Thorson, playing trainee agent Tara King, who it was suggested was "*more likely to arouse the protective instincts of male viewers than her rather Amazonian predecessors*" (*Daily Sketch*, 26 September 1968).[268] Rosie White has argued the show's "*fascination with the idea of mobility*", both in terms of class and gender, marking it out as a key 1960s cultural text. The spy series, she notes, was more open to accommodation of female figures than the private detective genre. *The Avengers* was implicated in the emergence of the 'dolly-bird', a key signifier of the swinging decade and its mythology of a fresh, youthful femininity, symbolising everything that was new, liberated, daring, sexually abandoned, independent and free. "*Spies like Emma Peel*", she asserts, represented a "*1960s femininity, which was physically active, intelligent and sexualised, and yet they were not demonised as femmes fatales*" (2007: 60-68).

The Avengers, especially during the Emma Peel period, was a seminal adventure series of the 1960s, described in its publicity as combining the "*international spy thriller formula with glamour, high-living and the constant surprise of touches of wit and fantasy which make it different from any other TV series of today*" (*The Avengers* press sheet 1965). With its incorporation of fetishistic fashion, mildly kinky sexuality, desirable motor cars, fantasy, parody, formal inventiveness, witticisms and espionage, and its playfulness with the notion of Englishness, the show was emblematic of British style and culture in the decade. The 'formula' of the show as it had been worked up by the fourth season with Emma Peel was described as being "*set against a tongue-in-cheek panorama of the picture-postcard Britain illustrated in tourist brochures*" (*The Avengers* press sheet 1965), and academic Rosie White has commented that the combination of "*pastiche and nostalgia*" and "*playful concern with fashion and artifice*" was part of the show's appeal (2007: 60).The harsher, tougher shows with Cathy Gale dealt with more traditional espionage subjects, a spy within a high-tech defence industry in 'Traitor in Zebra' and a plot to assassinate key government scientists and officials and replace them with *doppelgängers* in 'Man with Two Shadows' (both 1963), and a visiting Eastern Bloc pianist framed for murder in 'Concerto' (1964). The Emma Peel shows moved more towards 'spy-fi', with the duo dealing with killer robots in 'The Cybernauts' and giant alien carnivorous plants in 'The Man-Eater of Surrey Green' (both 1965), as well as overt parodies of popular American action shows, as with *The Man from U.N.C.L.E.* in 'The Girl from AUNTIE' (1966) and *Mission: Impossible* in 'Mission: Highly Improbable' (1967). As Wesley Britton has noted, this was the "*most quirky world of any secret agent*" (2004: 60). The episode 'A Touch of Brimstone' raised some eyebrows with Peel's 'Sin Queen' characterisation and was not shown in the United States at the time.[269] The role of the heroines in *The Avengers* attracted much comment; Cathy Gale and Emma Peel, in particular, being portrayed as modern, intelligent and independent young women, and, unusual for the spy genre, demonstrating through their martial arts abilities 'masculine power'. However, the representation was not, as some have claimed, feminist, as the women were still largely positioned for the male gaze and fetishised through 'kinky' costuming.

The Avengers was not acclaimed by the critics who generally preferred straight thrillers, and, while finding it amusing, were resistant to the self-conscious approach of the series with its knowing winks at the audience. It was common for reviewers to express personal alarm and embarrassment if they found themselves enjoying the show (*Observer*, 7 October 1965), the *Guardian* dismissed it as little more than "*children's television for adults*" (29 September 1967), and the *New Statesman* judged it bland and "*easily experienced and easily forgotten*" (31 January 1964). Towards the end of the run of the third season *The Telegraph* had decided that the show, which was regularly drawing 10 million viewers, could be best described as a "*farcical melodrama*" (9 March 1964), and the following year as "*glorious nonsense*" (29 September 1965). With the advent of the Emma Peel era, the *Observer* worried that *The Avengers* "*could spell death to the realistic thriller*" (3 October 1965), the *Sunday Telegraph* was disappointed that style was beginning to count for everything, the adventures in which its heroes were involved counting "*for less than their mannerisms, their cars and their clothes*" (15 January 1967), while the *Daily Mail* found the new approach "*poetically preposterous*" (15 October 1965).

Still, for many reviewers, *The Avengers* had more "*charm*" than rival shows and proved that, "*style and wit in the stars of a thriller series can make up for any amount of nonsense in the plot*" (*Daily Mail*, 29 September 1967). Eventually, some critics warmed to the show and by the time of the replacement of Emma Peel by Tara King reviewers started to become noticeably sentimental and nostalgic towards *The Avengers*. *The Times* now declared it "*arguably the best series produced by British television*" (10 October 1968) and the critic at the *Observer* announced himself an "*Avengerphile*" and that it would be "*hypocritical to conceal*" one's admiration for the show (29 September 1968).[270]

In retrospect, *The Avengers* is valued for its parody and has developed a significant fan culture which celebrates the show's 'camp', 'excess', 'comic-strip wit', and effortless sixties cool. The series developed a considerable 'afterlife' of stage shows, novels (some by Patrick Macnee) and radio shows. It was eventually resurrected on television as *The New Avengers*, with funding from French and Canadian sources, and which ran for two series in 1976 and 1977 with a total of 26 episodes. It was something of a fraught production and its popularity was harmed by insensitive scheduling in both Britain and North America. This time, John Steed was partnered by the agents Mike Gambit (Gareth Hunt) and Purdey (Joanna Lumley). Although *The New Avengers* retained some of the more fantastical 'spy-fi' qualities of the Emma Peel period of the original series, the drama and thrills were played more realistically, with less emphasis on parody. Most critical attention on the new series, as previously, has centred on the lead female protagonist, Purdey being seen as a response to the increased visibility of feminism in the 1970s. In this respect, the character is typical of the action heroine of the decade, being both an active woman *and* a consumable image. In the sense that Purdey embodied a "*keen, no-nonsense head girl of a secret agent*", she blended English ideals of class, tradition and modernity. While not being feminist, the character traced "*the dynamics around which late-twentieth-century representations of feminism and femininity vacillate*", and the feminism that *The New Avengers* occasionally referenced, "*was a domesticated, consumer-friendly version of the second wave*" (White 2007: 102, 96). *The Avengers* received the Hollywood treatment in 1998, when Warner Bros. released a feature film version starring Ralph Fiennes and Uma Thurman, but the movie was neither a critical nor commercial success.

The Prisoner, starring and created by Patrick McGoohan, was the outstanding cult television spy-fi thriller of the period. The single series of 17 episodes was first broadcast on Independent Television in Great Britain between September 1967 and February 1968, and the surreal storyline immediately attracted and fascinated audiences. An unnamed secret agent resigns, is abducted and finds himself captive in a mysterious and isolated seaside 'village', where he is pressured to reveal the reasons for his resignation and for the knowledge he gained while serving as a secret agent. Inmates are de-individualised and assigned numbers; the protagonist is allocated 'Number Six', but he defies his captors and interrogators, stating: "*I will make no deals with you. I've RESIGNED. I will not be pushed, filed, stamped, indexed, briefed, debriefed, or numbered. My life is my own*". As Wesley Britton has noted, *The Prisoner* was a cautionary parable "*about the rights of free minds in a world seeking conformity and enforced order*" (2004: 14); and Toby Miller has pointed out that secret agent Drake was similarly shown as having to guard against loss of identity in *Danger Man* and frequently seen staring anxiously into mirrors (2003: 95). Viewers were intrigued by the series, yearning to discover the identity of the mysterious and unseen 'Number One' who commands the Village, and the fate of 'The Prisoner' who strives from episode to episode to free himself.

Patrick McGoohan, bored of his role in the popular spy adventure *Danger Man*, formed the production company Everyman Films and used his star power to convince Lew Grade and the ITC Company to back a new, unconventional series for television. For the episode 'View from the Villa' (1960) in the *Danger Man* series, scenes were shot at the Italianate seaside resort at Portmeirion, North Wales, and this fantastical space became the inspiration and 'village' setting for the new show. Similarly, the *Danger Man* episode 'Colony Three' (1965) is seen as having provided inspiration for the new drama series, with textual and thematic elements centred on a village used for social control seemingly a rehearsal for *The Prisoner*. McGoohan as writer, producer, co-director and star, was given unprecedented freedom for *The Prisoner* which was made under unusual conditions of secrecy and there have been claims of megalomania for the difficult and temperamental star. George Markstein, the experienced script editor, and in some versions of the history of the series the co-creator of *The Prisoner*, resigned in exasperation after 13 episodes, claiming that, "*McGoohan would like to be God*" (quoted in Sellers 2006: 127)[271]; while director Robert Tronson's experience on the drama led him to dismiss McGoohan as a "*psychopath*" (quoted in ibid.: 131). *The Prisoner* was lavished with a large budget and some huge James Bond-type sets were constructed at the MGM Studios, Borehamwood.

Executives, bewildered by the storylines and the antics of McGoohan, brought the series to a premature end, and the hastily conceived, some say improvised, final episode number 17 has gone down in history as the "*most controversial television denouement ever*" (ibid.: 134). Audiences, eager to discover the identity of Number One and the ultimate fate of the prisoner, were confused and then felt cheated when in a final confrontation Number Six rips off the mask of his captor to reveal his own face staring back at him. Arguably the biggest anti-climax in television history, switchboards were jammed by angry viewers and Patrick McGoohan was allegedly forced into hiding.

The peculiarities of the unresolved production, narrative and textual issues of the series have meant that *The Prisoner* has developed an enduring fascination for fans, cultists and television scholars and stands as "*surely the most enigmatic television series ever made*" (Chapman 2002: 49). There has been lasting debate whether it is John Drake from *Danger Man* who has entered the Village? Internal textual evidence from the series and production continuity certainly provides credibility for such a view. It is also unclear whether the facility of the Village is under Western or Eastern Bloc control? The show's obsession with captivity, surveillance and espionage certainly marks it out as an intriguing drama series of the Cold War; a "*brilliant mix of Orwell, Kafka and Ian Fleming*" is how Robert Sellers describes it (2006: 126); and the series has been appreciated as in the tradition of dystopian fiction and British classics such as *A Brave New World* (1932) and *Nineteen Eighty-Four* (1949). A major theme of *The Prisoner* is individualism versus collectivism, and George Markstein has claimed he planned the series as a response to "*brainwashing and social control in the post-war era*" (quoted in Seed 2004: 222). Certainly, *The Prisoner* marks itself out as a subversive text, presenting a spy's rebellion against corporate bureaucracy, resistance to a commodified, mass-mediatised society and rejection of the mindless consumption habits of the masses. Cultural historian David Seed notes the self-consciousness of the series, the discourse of "*therapy*" which runs through the episodes, the configuring of 'Number Six' as an "*experimental subject*", and in a chilling observation judges *The Prisoner* "*one of the most surreal applications of a controlled environment for experimentation*" (2004: 222). James Chapman regards *The Prisoner* as defying classification, a hybrid of the 'sensational' and 'realist' forms of the spy thriller, its fantastical qualities blending with conventional elements of deception and interrogation. However, "*What The Prisoner does exemplify in full measure*", he asserts, "*is the sense of paranoia that underpins the thriller: nobody is to be trusted, the protagonist is persecuted by the authorities, and the Village itself represents a form of totalitarianism and social con-*

trol" (2002: 50). Such qualities certainly make it unusual for an adventure series in the 1960s. As such, cultural critic Toby Miller notes the significance of a drama in which social commentary is achieved within a "*pop industrial and generic framework*" (2003: 101). The final word goes to Wesley Britton, who marks down *The Prisoner* as "*the last classic secret agent series of the 1960s*" (2004: 108).[272]

The secret agent thriller

The spy game is catching. Television on all channels is obsessed with it.
(Daily Express, 14 March 1972)

The spy story has taken over from the detective story as family entertainment.
(*The Listener,* 4 May 1972)

I suspect that the ability to enjoy espionage thrillers may be inherited on the Y-chromosome.
(*The Times,* 31 March 1988)

By the middle-1960s, commentators on cinema and television were beginning to talk of "*spy mania*". In 1963-4, the prestigious series *Espionage* had expensively treated intrigue in a number of discrete stories, both historical and contemporary.[273] 1965 was a busy year for spies on the British small screen with the appearance of the serials and series *Contract to Kill* (BBC, a former secret agent turned detective is on the trail of ex-Nazis), *An Enemy of the State* (BBC, a computer manufacturer travels to Moscow on business and ends up on trial for his life when he is accused of espionage), and *The Mask of Janus* (BBC, a thriller set among the British, American and Communist espionage communities in a fictional European country). The cycle of television spy dramas continued in 1966 with *The Spies* (BBC, a spin-off series from *The Mask of Janus*) and *The Rat Catchers* (ITV, a British counter-intelligence unit). Some of these series were purposefully more downbeat than the flamboyant spy adventures which are now better remembered. *The Mask of Janus,* for example, was in a realist style and dealt with the contemporary ideological tensions of the Cold War; while *The Rat Catchers* was conceived of as a "*tough*" drama and offered as a reaction to such fanciful spy adventures series as *The Avengers* (Coke 1966: 3).[274]

As the 1960s died away and American finance for cinema and television production in Britain was being withdrawn, three belated secret agent thrillers made it to the screen. At a more optimistic moment in the summer of

1968, it had been announced that the American Broadcasting Company had agreed a deal with the writer Jimmy Sangster and producer Harold Cohen to distribute two television films. These would be adapted by Sangster from his recent novels *Private I* (1967) and *Foreign Exchange* (1968), featuring the former secret operative John Smith who had descended into the world of the gumshoe (*Variety*, 17 July 1968).[275] Early the next year, ABC announced that it was pulling out of production in the UK, with *The Avengers* winding up with a final season in 1969 and following the recent disappointment of the fantasy series *Journey into the Unknown* (1968), co-produced with Hammer Films. ABC was putting more resources into the made-for-television movie and *The Spy Killer* (1969, from *Private I*) and *Foreign Exchange* (1970) were heralded as the start of a new production trend (*Variety*, 29 January 1969). The pictures were primarily intended for ABC's new showcase 'Movie of the Week', launched stateside in the summer of 1969 with 25 movies averaging $850,000 per film. There was particular satisfaction with the two Sangster productions which were filmed back-to-back and directed by Roy Ward Baker in a hectic 50-day shoot on a single budget, with ABC purring that it had gotten two pictures for the price of one (*Variety*, 13 August 1969).[276]

In *The Spy Killer*, down-at-heel London private eye John Smith is reluctantly returned to the world of cross and double-cross in a plot involving the betrayal of Western agents in the People's Republic of China, while in *Foreign Exchange* he is sent to Soviet Russia to handle a tricky spy swap. Manipulative spy boss Max (Sebastian Cabot) and girlfriend Mary Harper completed the principal characters for both stories. To suit American tastes, Californians Robert Horton and Jill St. John were cast as Smith and Harper respectively, and Smith was made a former CIA agent who had been seconded to British Intelligence before his decision to quit following unsavoury assignments. Sangster's seedy literary sleuth was in a line of investigators which commenced with Len Deighton's 'Harry Palmer' and took in James Mitchell's David Callan and Brian Freemantle's Charlie Muffin. The teleplays considerably softened the vulgar aspects of the character as more suitable for a primetime television drama and correspondingly lost a distinctive aspect of the stories, and foreign locations rendered through stock shots or recreated in the studio made for a cut-price look to the productions.[277] The dramas, though, do pick up on the more critical trend in recent spy fiction of demonising the spy chief, here manipulative, vindictive, and unscrupulous in his use of murder to achieve his ends and to remove bothersome critics and opponents of his actions. An industrial expediency at their time, *The Spy Killer* and *Foreign Exchange* were broadcast for a period throughout the independent television regions in Britain, but then quickly forgotten.

A similar production imperative lay behind *Destiny of a Spy* (1969), a made-for-television movie, shot in Britain at Pinewood studios for Hollywood's Universal Television, and released under the company's 'World Premiere' banner. Universal Pictures was also anxious about its British productions and president Lew Wasserman visited London to calm nerves and reassure the troops, and modestly budgeted television features were clearly a production investment strategy which appealed in straightened times (*Stage and Television Today*, 13 August 1969). *Destiny of a Spy* featured American television star Lorne Greene, supported by such British acting stalwarts as Harry Andrews, Rachel Roberts and Anthony Quayle. Unusually, Greene plays a former Soviet agent (Pater Vanin) brought out of retirement and sent to London on a mission to destroy a new British invention. Drawn into the mysterious death of the inventor, he unexpectedly falls in love with an attractive British double agent (Roberts). The television movie has virtually disappeared without trace; however, it won some plaudits at the time, receiving nominations for Boris Sagal for Outstanding Directorial Achievement in Television from the Directors Guild of America and from the Hollywood Writers Guild for best adaptation (*Stage and Television Today*, 25 February 1970). *Destiny of a Spy* received a British television screening on the BBC in the autumn of 1970 and attracted a respectable viewing figure of over 6 million (*Stage and Television Today*, 26 November 1970).[278]

More substantial than these mid-Atlantic offerings was agent Quiller, the series secret agent in the popular spy novels of Adam Hall who had first appeared in *The Berlin Memorandum* (1965), filmed as *The Quiller Memorandum* in 1966.[279] Adapting *Quiller* to television in 1975 was a notable investment in the spy thriller at the BBC and the single 13 episode season starred the respected actor Michael Jayston. In contrast to the new-style spy procedural, the character conformed to the tradition of the professional lone agent at the service of a department chief, as most famously with James Bond and 'M', except Quiller's relationship with his controller is more fraught and suspicious. *Broadcast* wrote of "*glossily told adventures that even in today's world verge on the incredible*" (15 September 1975). 007 had continued to impress on the big screen in the 1970s in the reformulations of Roger Moore and it was a shrewd investment for a broadcaster to return to the 'sensational' form of spy thriller with one of 007's leading rivals in popular spy literature. The agent was constructed as the classic loner, enigmatic, described in the publicity as "*The Man Who Does Not Officially Exist*", a "*mystery ... obdurate, nihilistic, extremely dangerous*". In contrast to other archetypal secret agents: "*He does not drink or smoke, never carries a gun, rarely smiles*" (*Radio Times*, 23 August 1975: 53).[280] Quiller works for a covert intelligence organisation known as

'The Bureau', which we are similarly informed "*does not officially exist*", and maintains an antagonistic relationship with the manipulative Controller, Angus (Moray Watson); while female interest is occasionally provided by Roz (Sinead Cusack), a Human Rights lawyer.

As befitting the action-oriented spy thriller, Quiller undertakes a variety of dangerous and complex operations in which he is required to be quick-witted, resourceful and ruthless. In 'The Price of Violence' he is assigned to protect an important international visitor from assassination, before discovering the target is himself; in 'Political Jungle' he must rescue a political prisoner; and in 'Mark the File Expendable' Quiller is sent to the Mediterranean after secret rocket technology is stolen from a British base. The episode 'Tango Briefing' was scripted by Adam Hall from his own novel and in the thrilling story Quiller has to locate an aircraft crashed in the Sahara and destroy the secret, deadly and politically sensitive contents on board. The series was in parts stylish and fitted with a dynamic credit sequence over which pulsates a now cult synthesizer rock theme tune by Richard Denton and Martin Cook.[281]

In the summer of 1975, the BBC announced a budget cut of fifteen per cent in its programming (*The Stage and Television Today*, 24 July 1975). The economies affected the production of *Quiller* and the newly agreed budget of £500,000 was now deemed modest for a major series. The filming of exotic locations in the Caribbean and Europe was accomplished, echoes of *Top Secret*, by a sparse two-man crew led by producer-director Peter Graham Scott, and much ingenuity was put to making the series: filming at Virginia Water, Surrey produced scenes set in St. Lucia, at Hayes, Middlesex scenes set in Munich, and a convenient heat wave enabled the English Channel to stand in for the "*beautiful blue Mediterranean*" (*Sun*, 9 August 1975). Contributing writer Brian Clemens has complained of budgetary cutbacks as harming the production, claiming that one story he wrote set in South America, 'Any Last Request', was actually filmed in Hastings on the south coast of England.[282] *The Telegraph* felt the producers had done reasonably well under the circumstances, reporting on a "*high technical competence, much of it devoted to disguising the lack of extras*" (30 August 1975).

Reportedly, audience viewing figures started flagging towards the end of the run, and the producers decided not to re-commission the series. Reviews were generally poor, the spy novelist Joseph Hone writing in *The Listener*, while enjoying it on a '*Boys' Own Paper*' level, found the series "*Light and entirely mindless*", managing an "*absolute conviction in its clichés*" (11 September 1975). The *Evening News* judged the show a "*bit vague and rambling*", believing that British thrillers lacked the "*tautness of script and dialogue of their American counterparts"* (4 September 1975). *The Telegraph* claimed the contemporary *Spy Trap* as the only *"plausible"* espionage series on television, and complained that with *Quiller "we are back to the sub-Bond world of clipped speech, idiotic secret rendezvous, unlikely blondes and frequent mayhem"* (6 September 1975). A damning piece in the *Observer* rejected *Quiller* as *"detestably silly"*, wondered at the *"ineptitude"* of its creators, and found the show *"derivative to the last frame of footage and word of dialogue"* (7 September 1975). In a piece critical of the television thriller in general, *Stage and Television Today* complained of a *"dull, unengaging character"* sailing through *"long-overworked plots reminiscent of many series of the sixties"*. The reviewer noted the forthcoming ITV network premiere of a James Bond film, *Dr No* (1962), and wondered why British television couldn't produce an equivalent fictional character of the seventies to enthral its audiences (23 October 1975). The American trade magazine *Variety* reckoned that as an *"effort at cannibalizing the remains of the superspy genre, it wasn't much better than a long yawn"* (17 September 1975).[283] *Quiller* is now a long forgotten spy series and considering the popularity of the novels a missed opportunity by the BBC.

The alternative tradition of the amateur agent was pursued in *Dangerous Knowledge*, a competent spy thriller untypically produced at the small independent company Southern Television and broadcast over six 30-minute episodes in 1976. The story deals with Bill Kirby (John Gregson), a divorced, middle-aged insurance agent who has money problems and drinks too much. A background in Army Intelligence, he fulfils minor undercover assignments for the extra funds it supplies, and it is during one of these tasks in northern France that he acquires the 'dangerous knowledge' that casts him into a deadly conspiracy. A former resistance worker Madame Lafois (Elisabeth Bergner) has recognised Dr Vincent (Robert Keegan), a key advisor to the British government, as a fellow trainee in a post-war Soviet spy school. A screen is put around Vincent by a misled Roger Fane (Patrick Allen), the civil servant responsible for internal security. Kirby acquires proof of the accusation in the form of a video recording, but his contacts and witnesses are continually being silenced, including a CIA agent who negotiates for the information. When Vincent panics and proposes to shoot Kirby and Fane on a beach in France, the KGB mole is exposed and brought into custody. Gregson had been a popular film star in Great Britain in the 1950s, and this proved to be his final role, dying of a heart attack shortly after shooting aged only 55.

Dangerous Knowledge was shot largely on location around Southampton, the New Forest and in Normandy, northern France in 1974 and produced and directed by Alan Gibson. An expensive production for Southern, the intention was to get the serial onto the ITV network at a peak evening time (*Sun*, 30

November 1974). This proved difficult and time-consuming and an agree-ment was not reached until 1976. The tragic death of Gregson following shooting had also left the networks in a "*dilemma*" as to whether it was ap-propriate to screen the drama (*Sunday People*, 26 January 1975). Eventually, *Dangerous Knowledge* received a network screening on Wednesday evenings at the peak time 8.30 slot, but only following pressure from other regional companies who had argued against a proposed 10.30 late night screening (*The Stage and Television Today*, 29 April 1976). The serial benefited from this accommodation, opening as the ninth most popular show in the network ratings (the second rated show in the south of England), and remaining in the top 20 for its run.[284] It was written by the experienced local television drama-tist N. J. Crisp, who had previously contributed to the spy dramas *Codename* (1970) and *Spy Trap* (1972-73), and who published a handful of spy novels such as *The Gotland Deal* (1976), *The London Deal* (1979) and *Yesterday's Gone* (1983). The drama serial was also notable for featuring Elisabeth Bergner, the great Austrian actress of stage and screen.

Reviews were lukewarm, many finding the serial, old-fashioned, derivative and clichéd. "*Shiny but routine*" was how it was described in the *Guardian* (27 May 1976); the *Sunday Times* referred to it as a "*yarn*" peopled with "*card-board characters*" (30 May 1976); and *Stage and Television Today* dismissed it as a "*stereotype 1950 B picture*" (24 June 1976). The reviewer in the *Daily Mail* recognised the spy serial's debt to a bygone tradition, its pleasures lying in a "*period charm*". He saw Kirby as a "*kind of modern cousin of Richard Hannay*" and the thrills "*Buchanesque*". "*It's all nonsense, of course*", he concluded, "*Boys' Own Paper stuff for adults, and none the worse for that*" (20 May 1976). *Dangerous Knowledge* is largely forgotten and has until recently mainly circu-lated as a re-edited, barely comprehensible 90-minute television film. It does reveal, though, an attempt by a marginal television station to trade in the popularity of the spy thriller.

Running Blind was a further spy thriller centring on a lone professional se-cret agent and first appeared as a novel by Desmond Bagley published in 1970. Former British agent Alan Stewart is coerced into a final operation by Slade, a senior member of the Secret Intelligence Service (SIS). A simple cou-rier job delivering a package in Iceland turns into a nightmare adventure as Stewart is double-crossed and chased by both British and Russian Intelli-gence across the rugged landscape of the inhospitable far northern island. Stewart soon begins to suspect the manipulative and obnoxious Slade and also finds himself up against the ruthless Russian Kennikin, a former adver-sary who has a grudge against the Briton. Stewart in the company of his ca-pable Icelandic girlfriend Elín Ragnarsdóttir is pursued along dangerous mountain tracks, fords swollen rivers and descends into volcanic craters as he tries to piece together the complex mystery; as he expresses it in the story, it is a case of 'Running Blind'.

Eventually, Stewart is able to turn the tables and traps Slade in a hotel room where he forces him to confess he is a double agent; only to be captured in turn by Kennikin who has already abducted Elín. The British agent and his girl shoot their way out, killing Kennikin and wounding Slade, but are injured during the escape. It is explained to Stewart in the hospital that the package he was to deliver, a complex electronic circuit board, was part of an elaborate deception plan hatched by the Americans in collusion with the British aimed at fooling the Russians into thinking the Western allies had developed re-markable new radar capabilities. Slade, ignorant of the deception, had set up Stewart as the fall guy, planning to acquire the gadget for the Soviets without compromising himself.[285]

The story is told in the first-person by Stewart and this intensifies the mystery and suspense as the reader only learns what is going on from the restricted viewpoint of the hard-pressed British agent. Bagley draws on the recent history of treachery in Great Britain in the 1950s and 1960s, and consciously places Slade in the line of traitors listed in the story as *"Maclean, Burgess, Philby, Blake, the Krogers, and Lonsdale"*. The method adopted by the Soviets in *Running Blind* of obtaining papers in Finland of a deceased ex-patriot British youth and thereby acquiring a British identity for Slade is modelled on the 'dead double' technique used for the real spy Gordon Lonsdale (Konon Trofimovich Molody), the agent behind the Portland Spies. The character of Slade re-appeared in Bagley's following novel *The Freedom Trap* (1971) filmed as *The Mackintosh Man* in 1973.[286]

Following failed attempts to turn the story into movies in Hollywood and the UK, *Running Blind* was faithfully adapted into a three-part television serial produced at BBC Scotland in 1979 and starred Stuart Wilson as Alan Stewart, George Sewell as Slade and Ragnheiður Steindórsdóttir as Elín Ragnarsdóttir. It was the first major film made by the BBC in Iceland, produced at a cost of £150,000. One of the difficulties posed by the location was working in almost perpetual daylight making the need for faking night scenes outdoors (*Evening News*, 27 July 1978); and as the winter was barely over when the two-month shoot commenced it presented tough conditions for cast and crew who had to rough-it in tents for the scenes filmed in the remote interior of the island (*Stage and Television Today*, 18 May 1978). Iceland was an unusual setting for a spy story and Bagley used its imposing landscape as a traditional rugged element of a thrilling adventure; glaciers, deep fjords, surging waterfalls, geysers, volcanoes, black sand beaches and otherworldly steaming lava fields also provide a compelling visual interest for the screen drama. The location was judged suitably "*exotic*" for a spy thriller (*The Telegraph*, 13 January 1979).

The *Guardian* was pleased the serial was made on location, that it initially showed promise, but found the problem with the script, "*inexplicably cobbled out of every cliché in the genre*" (6 January 1979). As *The Telegraph* asserted, though, "*there is nothing cliché- ridden about the Icelandic scenery*" (13 January 1979). The *Evening Standard* similarly found Iceland "*striking*" as a location, adding that, "*given the usual willing suspension of disbelief, the action was fast and furious enough to carry one along in a fair old flap of excitement*". Overall, though, it was no better than "*nicely done nonsense*" (8 January 1979). *Stage and Television Today* noted the "*jolly Icelandic scenery*", but asked: "*what else?*"; concluding that the "*general effect of the programme was that of being threatened with an empty gun*" (11 January 1979). The *New Statesman* marked the serial down as "*prep-school-of-Deighton*", an inferior example of a now established secret agent genre with betrayal at the top (12 January 1979).

Running Blind was scripted by Jack Gerson, author of paranormal 'secret state' series *The Ωmega Factor* (1979), and the serial was thought sufficiently successful that he immediately wrote two further espionage serials for BBC Scotland. The three-part thriller *The Assassination Run* (1980) dealt with Mark Fraser (Malcolm Stoddard) a retired British agent whose wife Jill (Mary Tamm) is abducted and taken to Spain, where Fraser is confronted by a complex plot involving the KGB and a German terrorist group. Surprisingly, perhaps, the *Guardian* found this routine series more to its taste (26 January 1980), although a more typical view held at the *Evening News* which dismissed it as "*pulp-magazine material*" and little more than a "*commercial for the Spanish Tourist Industry*" (17 January 1980). Fraser and his wife returned in *The Treachery Game* (1981) set in the Dordogne in France, which involved the death of a British scientist and the holidaying Frasers having to go on the run while trying to solve the mystery. The *Observer* wondered if the plot was "*intricate or hopelessly confused*" (25 January 1981), while the *Guardian* noted that BBC Scotland was "*renowned for its codswallop*", and warned viewers that here was a "*particularly fine wallop of cod*" (16 January 1981). *Running Blind* was the better of the three serials produced at BBC Scotland, but none particularly caught the imagination of reviewers or audiences, and with them, the television spy thriller was failing to rise above the merely routine.

A more unconventional British Secret Service man was *Charlie Muffin* who first appeared in an eponymous novel by Brian Freemantle first published in 1977. In contrast to the archetype secret agent made flesh by James Bond, Muffin is a shabby character. In the story there has recently been a shake-up of British Intelligence, a new military rigour will prevail, and old hands such as the meritocratic Muffin, lower-class and grammar school-educated, are out, in favour of Oxbridge types. However, Muffin is a survivor.

Muffin survives a betrayal by his own Service as he crosses from East to West Berlin, suffers an inferior office, and is refused the credit for the recent break-ing of a Soviet network in the West which has landed the important Russian agent Berenkov in jail. The department seeks to demote him, or better still, remove him. Muffin's native brilliance and his superior's incompetence keep the shrewd agent one step ahead. A senior general of the KGB, Kalenin, is under pressure following the exposure of the Berenkov network, and indicates to the British that he is willing to defect for $500,000. This would be a major coup for the new regime and the American Central Intelligence Agency (CIA) brings pressure to bear to be included as part of the operation. Initially, Char-lie is scrupulously kept out of things, but when two inexperienced agents are lost to Russian counter-espionage, Muffin is recalled and sent to Moscow to negotiate secretly with the general. An elaborate Anglo-American operation is mounted in Austria to bring the valuable defector through from Czechoslo-vakia. All the while, Muffin is dangerously exposed. When Kalenin is wel-comed by the Chief of British Intelligence and the Director of the CIA at a safe house in Vienna, he casually announces that he has no intention of defecting, that he has used the opportunity to round up the 200 Western agents de-ployed on the operation and has the Chief and the Director at his mercy. Brit-ish Intelligence and the CIA have been delivered a serious blow, all in revenge for the destruction of the Soviet network, and the westerners will be ex-changed for Berenkov. Muffin has colluded with the Russian general, will keep the $500,000, and is confident he can keep one step ahead of a vengeful Brit-ish Intelligence and CIA.

With Charlie Muffin, Brian Fremantle created a distinctive secret agent, conceiving of him as a "*quirky, unpredictable, oddball MI5 spy who's a pain in the ass of his Public School colleagues*". The author has described his character as "*dishevelled, cantankerous and disrespectful … a devious, amoral, deter-mined, stop-at-nothing survivor who drinks too much and gambles too hard*"; his axiom: "*to screw anyone from anywhere to avoid it happening to him*".[287] The middle-aged lower-class agent is further characterised by permanently aching feet covered over with comfortable if impractical and scuffed 'Hush Puppy' suede shoes. Muffin is eternally at odds with his higher-class superiors who look down on him with distaste. A true professional, Muffin has more in common with his opponent in the KGB, Berenkov.[288]

Charlie Muffin was produced as a single-drama at Euston Films in 1979 and broadcast in the *Armchair Cinema* strand. The company had previously produced action series like *Special Branch* and *The Sweeney* (1975-78), but now wanted to experiment with one-off films. The spy drama was scripted by the experienced Keith Waterhouse, directed by the talented Jack Gold, and shot on location in London, Vienna and Berlin. The production was acknowledged as "*one of the new wave of British-films-for-TV to be shot as a full-scale feature on 35mm*" and aimed for a theatrical feature quality on a budget of £800,000. This called for some important scenes to be mocked-up on location, such as Berlin's Checkpoint Charlie at London's West India docks (*The Stage and Television Today,* 7 July 1979; *Evening Standard,* 12 December 1979). Selling *Charlie Muffin* as a cinema presentation throughout the rest of the world was part of the distribution strategy and full-page advertisements were taken out in *Variety* in America (9 January 1980).[289]

The television movie is a close adaptation of the novel and lavishly casts film star David Hemmings as the crumpled Muffin. A witty credit sequence presents a restricted view in which only the feet of characters are observed, with smart brogues finally passing onto worn Hush Puppies and the introduction of the misfit protagonist. The critical reaction to the television drama was muted as reviewers had only very recently been bowled over by the BBC television version of John le Carré's *Tinker Tailor Soldier Spy* (1979). The *Sun* noted the contrast, enjoying *Charlie Muffin* as "*pacy, stylish, tense and often very funny*", suggesting that where "*Smiley was an enigma, Charlie was a riot*" (13 December 1979). The *Guardian* liked *Muffin* as a blending of the class war with the Cold War, but suggested it was merely a "*tinier tinker*" (12 December 1979). The *Observer* found the drama a "*wearily familiar story*", and couldn't resist the parting shot: "*Tinkers, tailors, soldiers, cobblers*" (16 December 1979). Other critics saw Charlie Muffin as a seedier relative of Harry Palmer and "*used the early Deighton formula of peed-on cockney sparrer overcoming chinless public-school superiors*" (*New Statesman,* 21-28 December 1979; *Evening News* and *Morning Star,* 12 December 1979). Recent events also set critics thinking, the absurdity of "*the real life Blunt affair*" leading the *Western Mail* to comment that: "*real life could just possibly be more like* Charlie Muffin *than anything else*" (15 December 1979). Those unimpressed by the drama readily drew on baking analogy, the *Evening Standard* finding it "*about as exciting as a half-toasted tea-cake*" (12 December 1979). Drawing together the various threads of critical response to *Charlie Muffin,* The *Telegraph* felt that compared with "*Tinker, Tailor, Soldier, Spy, its conception of espionage seemed childish*", that compared with the "*real life-story of Anthony Blunt it looked totally unsophisticated*", and similarly thought it had landed "*with all the impact of a tepidly toasted tea-cake*" (12 December 1979). Brian Freemantle was impressed by Hemmings's characterisation of Muffin, revealing that, "*Up until that moment I knew how Charlie Muffin thought and how he'd react and what he physically looked like. But I didn't have his facial features. But from then on I did and it's always David Hemmings's face I see when I'm writing, not my blank-canvassed Charlie*".[290] Hemmings was keen to play the character again, some critics were eager to see the return of the unconventional agent, and there had been announcements of further Muffin films. Adaptations of the novels *The Inscrutable Charlie Muffin* (1979) and *Charlie Muffin's Uncle Sam* (1980) were mentioned, but a comparative lack of success of the first production meant that sequels did not materialise (*Evening Standard*, 12 December 1979; *News of the World*, 16 December 1979; *Evening News*, 9 January 1980). Producer Verity Lambert felt that *Charlie Muffin* unfairly lost out to the success of *Tinker Tailor Soldier Spy* which was broadcast around the same time, and a single movie-length production had proved costly and difficult to schedule (Alvarado and Stewart 1985: 97).[291]

A further 1960s film idol was dusted down and wheeled out to star in a television spy drama when sex-symbol Terence Stamp, although previously reluctant to play on the small screen, made his television début as Dr Audley in *Chessgame*.[292] This was a dramatisation of the first three spy novels of Anthony Price, produced at Granada Television and broadcast in 1983. The stories *The Labyrinth Makers* (1970), *The Alamut Ambush* (1971) and *Colonel Butler's Wolf* (1972) feature the series character Dr David Audley, a historian of the medieval Arab world whose scholarly aptitude is used by British Intelligence where he serves as a Middle East analyst and security adviser. He is assisted by Hugh Roskill and Colonel Butler.

In *The Labyrinth Makers*, Audley is required to delve into a mystery dating back to September 1945 and the disappearance of a Royal Air Force transport plane in flight from Berlin to England. The Dakota has recently been found in a lake with the dead body of the pilot and inexplicably the Russians show a keen interest and sniff around the investigation. Audley eventually makes the remarkable discovery that the plane was carrying Schliemann's treasure, plundered from Turkey in the 1870s, deposited in Berlin in 1881, and which disappeared in 1945 during the Russian invasion of Germany. Audley correctly surmises that the Russians are actually after documents which reveal the treachery of the Soviet army in the 1930s, secreted in with the treasure, and which could be used as a powerful bargaining lever in a current power struggle in Russia.

The Alamut Ambush commences with a bomb planted in the car of a senior adviser on Middle-Eastern affairs at the Foreign Office; however, it is a young security technician, Alan Jenkins, who is blown up defusing the device. While Hugh Roskill takes the lead in the investigation, Audley hovers in the background piecing together the complex puzzle. It is cleverly surmised that Jenkins was, in fact, the target of the assassination, having unexpectedly stumbled across secret plans for a cease-fire in the troubled Middle East. A complex plot involving Arab terrorists and Israeli and Egyptian intelligence culminates with Roskill, though wounded, shooting dead three of the terrorists before they can get word to the Middle East. It is at this point that Roskill finally understands that the unfortunate Jenkins had been killed by the Israeli's before he innocently gave the game away.

Colonel Butler's Wolf concerns a plot in which the Soviets are planting young sleeper agents in leading universities in the hope of them attaining positions of power and influence in the future. Colonel Butler leads the investigation, with Audley once again lingering on the fringes pursuing his own discrete enquiries and offering occasional penetrating insights. The conspiracy is pinpointed to Castleshields, an elite educational establishment in the north of England, close to Hadrian's Wall. Butler infiltrates the college posing as a Roman military historian, averts a plot to assassinate a reactionary Portuguese general visiting the Wall, which turns out to be a blind, and uncovers the true conspiracy.

The first three "*intellectual thrillers*" of Anthony Price announced an original talent in British spy fiction who carved out a niche with the "*upper IQ spy story*" (*Western Mail*, 26 November 1983; *Observer*, 4 May 1972). Audley is an eccentric, scholarly figure and echoes the university dons who were recruited into the 'secret war' of deception and black propaganda between 1939 and 1945. Audley is not a man of action, and like George Smiley, more at home, as it was put in the stories, in the "*back room among the files and the reports*", a "*world of possibilities and theories and hypotheses*". He is a man uncomfortable with people, but excited by an intellectual puzzle and exceedingly devious. The stories are full of literary and historical allusions and quotations, there for the educated and intelligent reader to savour.

The television series *Chessgame* comprised of six 55-minutes episodes and treated each novel across two instalments. The story of *The Labyrinth Makers* is necessarily updated to accommodate a production of the early 1980s, the treasure is now the Czar's, and the documents relate to a supposed wartime pact between the Red Army and the Nazis. While Roskill (Robin Sachs) and Colonel Butler (renamed Nick Hannah who uses the cover name of Colonel Butler on the operation, Michael Culver) lead the operations in the dramatisations of *The Alamut Ambush* and *Colonel Butler's Wolf*, in deference to the casting of Stamp, the character of Audley is given greater prominence in these adventures.

The adaptation is quite flat, largely uninvolving and lacks the intellectual challenge of the original novels. The reviews were understandably mixed. For *The Telegraph*, *Chessgame* was a "*disappointment for aficionados of the genre*" (24 November 1983); the *Guardian* thought *Chessgame* had the "*look of a low-rent Le Carré, sexier, but less sonorous*" (19 November 1983); *The Times* found it "*pedestrian*" and succeeded only in "*bringing secondhand material to an already jaded public*" (24 November 1983); and the *Western Mail* believed it unlikely to challenge the "*Smiley sagas*" (26 November 1983). The *Daily Mirror* exhorted that, "*There's nothing like a good spy thriller*", and informed its readers that *Chessgame* was "*nothing like a good spy thriller*". It felt that the series didn't come close to the splendours of the recent *Reilly - Ace of Spies* which had finished its broadcast the previous week (24 November 1983).[293] The casting of Stamp attracted some comment. The *Daily Express* felt the star graced the Audley character with "*ascetic fascination and subtle sex appeal*" (24 November 1983), and the respectful *Daily Mail* wrote of the star's "*quiet authority and elegant presence*" (8 December 1983). However, others felt that the actor's working-class London and sexy persona was hardly ideal for the Cambridge scholar he was playing. More "*Oxton than Oxford*" was how the *Daily Mirror* saw it (24 November 1983.).

Chessgame had been scripted by Murray Smith, who had provided the screenplay for the television movie *Closing Ranks* in 1980. A long-forgotten drama, it was produced at the commercial station Granada and dealt with the anxieties within the Security Service which attended the arrival of a Communist defector. It starred Joss Ackland as the KGB agent Victor Rogachev who defects to England with accusations of a traitor in British Intelligence. It is inferred that Kim Philby is behind the operation. The story echoed the circumstances of Anatoll Golitsyn, a Soviet Intelligence officer who defected to the CIA in 1960. He was brought over to London in 1963 where his accusations about the high-level penetration of MI5 fuelled the paranoia of British officers like Peter Wright and their assumption that the Chief, Roger Hollis, was a Soviet agent, and did tremendous damage. *Stage and Television Today* found it a flawed drama, lacking in credibility. It blamed incomprehensibility for the desertion of the audience by the time of the first commercial break (24 July 1980).[294]

The Secret Servant written by Gavin Lyall and published in 1980 was the first spy thriller to feature Major Harry Maxim, a soldier with experience in the Special Air Service (SAS) who is seconded to the prime minister's office as a special adviser on security. His unexpected appointment follows a scandal resulting from the suicide of Jackaman, a senior civil servant at the Ministry of Defence. Maxim is quickly drawn into a perplexing mystery centred on Prof.

John Tyler a leading government adviser on national security who is preparing for crucial talks on nuclear strategy with European partners. An unstable character named Farthing claims that Tyler was implicated in the death of Jackaman, the latter having acquired an incriminating letter which would destroy the reputation of the professor. Maxim sets about an investigation on which he is aided by Agnes Algar, the MI5 professional stationed at the prime minister's office. Pieces of the puzzle are provided by a Czech defector who had been working on the Tyler file, as well as the wife of Jackaman, and a trail of dead bodies is left in the wake of the investigation.

The roots of the mystery are to be found in a wartime operation led by Tyler who had been an officer in the Long Range Desert Group, which operated behind enemy lines in North Africa. Maxim deduces the shocking truth from a French officer who had served on the patrol, that the survivors had only made it back to Allied lines through the shooting of a wounded French soldier and the cannibalism of his body. Information of great value to the KGB and which could wreck the European talks. The scandal is suppressed, but in a kind of rough justice, Tyler is killed by Farthing whose friend had been one of the survivors on the patrol.

Lyall had been approached to create a "*thriller set in Whitehall*" for television and ending up with masses of material and no immediate prospect of a television drama he turned the story into the novel *The Secret Servant* (*Independent*, 21 January 2003). The story was eventually dramatised for television at BBC Scotland in 1984, starring Charles Dance as Maxim and broadcast as a three-part serial over consecutive evenings and concluding on a Saturday night. The novel was adapted by the experienced Brian Clemens and the production shot entirely on location in Luxemburg, France, Scotland, London, Oxford and Dorset.[295] It is a fast-paced and engaging thriller set in the early 1970s in which hard-working committed professionals are looking after national security and the national interest. In this sense, the story contrasts with such contemporary novels as *A Very British Coup* (1982), also set in 10 Downing Street, and *In the Secret State* (1980), which, as 'secret state' thrillers, offered a critical view of the Security Service and Whitehall. It is revealingly said of Agnes in the novel of *The Secret Servant* that she possessed that most valuable of all talents in the intelligence world: "*loyalty that lasted beyond disillusionment*". Although a supporting character, as a senior, professional officer in the prime minister's office, the capable Agnes holds an unusually important role for a woman in spy fiction of the time. A number of spy stories have featured plots involving dangerous secrets relating to World War II, such as Anthony Price's *The Labyrinth Makers* (1970), which as we have seen was adapted for television as part of the serial *Chessgame* (1983).[296] The press release described *The Secret Servant* as a "*spy film in the genre of John le Carré, only with more action*".

The evening's "*choice*" programme in *The Times, The Secret Servant* was judged a "*thriller with a touch of class*" and without the "*obfuscations*" of John le Carré (6 December 1984). Several reviewers praised the serial as "*pacy*" and "*stylish*", a spy drama done with "*panache*" and "*class*" (*Evening Standard,* 7 December 1984; *The Telegraph,* 10 December 1984). The *Guardian* tautologically informed its readers that, "*If you like this kind of thing you will like this kind of thing. It is shot on location, and better acted, as is often the way with thrillers, than seems strictly necessary*" (7 December 1984). The military bearing and rank of Major Maxim was a throwback for the model of the secret agent, more in the tradition of Commander James Bond and belief in unwavering duty, and untouched by new developments in the genre in the form of the insubordinate sergeant Harry Palmer and his successors. The *Sunday Express* found *The Secret Servant* in the "*best British spy tradition, with plenty of stiff upper lips, public school humour and more bowler hats and umbrellas than I've seen for a long time*". "*The whole thing*", the reviewer confessed, "*had me hooked*" (9 December 1984). It was a view shared at the *Daily Mirror,* which praised BBC Scotland for spinning the "*best TV spy web in ages*", a drama that "*knots with intrigue and sparkles with stylish acting and clever quips*" (8 December 1984). However, the dissenting *Daily Express* dismissed *The Secret Servant* as "*hokum*" (13 December 1984). In an unusual line of development in reviewing spy thrillers, the casting of the 'heart-throb' Charles Dance caused a bit of a stir among female critics. Recently the actor had "*addicted thousands of women*" to the period drama *Jewel in the Crown* (1984, Patricia Finney, *Evening Standard,* 30 November 1984), and the casting of Dance to *The Secret Servant* seemingly increased female interest in a traditionally masculine genre. The *Daily Express* found Dance an "*ideal handsome hero*" and Maxim an "*action man more subtle and stable than Bond*", though "*equally potent*" (Judith Simons, 7 December 1984), and the *Glasgow Herald* marked Dance down as the "*thinking woman's man of action*" (Julie Davidson, 8 December 1984; see also, Hilary Kingsley, *Daily Mirror,* 8 December 1984). "*Not since Sam Neill in Reilly has there been such a hero*" wrote the breathless Nina Myskow in the *News of the World* (9 December 1984), and the lingering scene of Maxim emerging from the ocean early in the first episode seemed to satisfy its intended audience, the *Sunday People* noting its appeal to those "*who wanted to savour every muscle*" (Margaret Forwood, 9 December 1984; see also, Pat Codd, *Daily Star,* 1 December 1984).[297] *The Secret Servant* was popular, with the third and concluding episode attracting nearly 11 million viewers (*The Times,* 18 December 1984).

Mr Palfrey of Westminster was an unusual and thoughtful espionage drama series produced at the commercial Thames Television and broadcast in two seasons of four and six 50-minute episodes in 1984 and 1985 respectively. A pilot drama 'The Traitor' aired as part of Thames Television's *Storyboard* anthology on 23 August 1983. Mr. Palfrey (Alec McCowen) is an officer of the counter-espionage service, a specialised 'spycatcher'. He is not a man of action, but rather an "*inquisitor and an observer*" (*TV Times*, 14-20 April 1984: 18). The pilot and two episodes, 'Once Your Card is Marked' (1984) and 'Official Secret,' (1985) were written by the experienced script-writer and -editor, and sometime author of spy novels, George Markstein. In the first series Palfrey finds himself with a new female boss and a new office. Across the two seasons Palfrey has to deal with such cases as a senior defence official who is carrying on a clandestine affair with a young Czech woman ('The Honeypot and the Bees', 1984), a returning British defector from the Soviet Union ('Return to Sender'), a former senior government official who aims to go public on further moles in British Intelligence ('Official Secret'), and a Soviet informer's claim that a double-agent is operating in British counter-intelligence ('The Baited Trap', all 1985).

Mr Palfrey of Westminster claimed to be an "*authentic*" spy series, the producer Michael Chapman remarking that the "*stories have not necessarily happened, but they could happen*". Chapman pointed to 'The Defector', an episode of the first series broadcast in May 1984, in which Palfrey suspects the motives of a celebrated Soviet author who claims to want to defect, a situation echoed in some respects by the 'Bitov Affair' (*TV Times*, 4-10 May 1985: 31). Oleg Bitov was a Soviet journalist who fled to the West in September 1983, was courted by the British press, and unexpectedly presented himself at the Soviet Embassy and was returned to Moscow in August 1984. The affair remained a mystery for many years and was considered a KGB deception operation.

A distinguishing feature of the series was the casting of the role of Co-ordinator to a woman (Caroline Blakiston) which predates Stella Rimington's ascendency to the top of MI5 by a decade. Critics saw the parallel in terms of contemporary politics, noting the use of the regal name Gloriana for the character of the self-confident Co-ordinator and sarcastically seeing her as "*Thatcher's representative on earth, and more than a bit influenced by her goddess's style*" (*Guardian*, 19 April 1984). A "*brightly satirical creation*" was the judgement at *The Telegraph* (19 April 1984). The character of Palfrey, in his fastidious and obdurate pursuit of truth and security lapses in the Whitehall labyrinth, reminded some reviewers of John le Carré's George Smiley (*The Times*, 19 April 1984; *Daily Express*, 16 April 1984). He was the "*decent spy-man in a world of dirty tricks*" (*The Scotsman*, 21 April 1984). *Mr Palfrey of*

Westminster was an intelligent espionage drama with oblique conflict likely to be played out across conversations, brilliantly so in the initial 'The Traitor', which is effectively a one room drama, and with sparks provided by the friction between authoritarian female head and unconventional, brilliant yet subservient Palfrey. It was reported that George Markstein aimed for television drama which contained "*no bad language, no explicit sex, no shooting, killing, or unnecessary violence*", an unusual approach for a spy thriller, and yet still managed to turn out "*something which will entertain people in a manner both polished and realistic*" (*Daily Mail*, 19 April 1984). The *Guardian* was a little harsh when it rated the series a "*passable hour for spy addicts*" (19 April 1984), while *The Telegraph* was more accepting, welcoming a "*freshness*" in the series, which managed a "*nicely light and cynical touch*" (19 April 1984). Similarly, the *Sunday Express* enjoyed the understatement and a drama series which offered "*quiet but compelling viewing*" (22 April 1984). In a minority view, the *Glasgow Herald* judged it "*camp, rather than naturalistic*" (21 April 1984). The second series was less well-received. The *Daily Mirror* was led to feel that, "*if this is a reasonable portrayal of British Intelligence, thank the Lord we've got no secrets worth having any more, anyway*" (8 May 1985). The *Daily Express* now dismissed the series as "*highly decorative rubbish*" (15 May 1985), while *The Mirror*, still largely supportive, felt the new episodes "*rarely ring true*", and that overall, there was "*too little action, no suspense and the plots become harder to fathom each week*" (29 May 1985). A more recent assessment of Mr Palfrey has praised a "*meticulously paced and unusually cerebral slice of pre-glasnost espionage*" which manages to avoid the "*action, gadgets and glossy accoutrements generally associated with the spy genre*" (*Sight and Sound*, November 2010: 90). The series character of Blair (Clive Wood), a strong arm investigator in Palfrey's department, returned for the one-off play 'A Question of Commitment' in which the watcher suspects he is being watched himself, and broadcast in the *Storyboard* anthology in 1989.

There was a modest flurry of spy thrillers as the Cold War came unexpectedly to an end. *The Man Called Kyril* was a spy novel written by John Trenhaile and first published in 1981. The aged Chief of the KGB, Stanov, is under pressure to unearth the Soviet treachery which is leaking information to the British in London. In a highly secret mission, he deploys the agent known as Kyril to the West in an attempt to expose the traitor and deal with him. The thrilling storyline oscillates between Kyril who is sought by both the British SIS and the KGB which is ignorant of his true mission, the British Secret Service which has been deceived into thinking that Kyril is a possible defector, and the situation in Moscow which has descended into a power struggle between Stanov, his rivals in the senior echelons of the KGB, and the Politburo. The complex game of cat and mouse is further complicated by a highly-placed double-agent in MI6, Royston, who feels compromised by the sudden frenetic activity in London and the widespread suspicion it has generated. The action moves swiftly between Athens, Brussels and London, and the body count begins to climb. Kyril is able to overcome a British SIS agent in Greece, an attempt by the CIA in Belgium to capture him for interrogation in Washington, and a KGB assassination attempt in London. Kyril learns that the senior KGB General Povin is the traitor in Moscow. The deep game finally plays out on a confrontation between Kyril and Royston; the former, on instinct, misinforming the latter that the traitor is General Michaelov of the KGB. Royston shoots Kyril and passes the information onto Moscow. In an ironic ending, the traitors Povin and Royston escape detection and enhance their standing in the Service.

The Man Called Kyril makes mention of actual double-agents within the KGB in London, such as Oleg Lyalin (later a defector), and such notable historical events as the expulsion of 105 Soviet officials from London in 1971. Rather more fancifully, it suggests that Lyalin was eventually tortured and killed by the SIS, when in fact the Russian died of natural causes in the north of England in 1995 after serving the British faithfully. However, the introduction of fact into the story has the effect of making the fiction appear more authentic.[298]

The novel was dramatised for television as the two-part *Codename: Kyril* and broadcast on commercial television in 1988, with the impressive and bankable cast of Edward Woodward as Royston, Ian Charleson as Kyril and Denholm Elliot as Povin. An expensive-looking Anglo-Norwegian production shot in England, Oslo (doubling as Moscow) and Holland with a budget of £3 million, it was scripted by the respected John Hopkins who had previously co-adapted John le Carré's *Smiley's People* (1982). The producers faced some difficulties when star Woodward suffered a heart-attack towards the end of the production and a new character had to be hastily designed and cast to cover uncompleted scenes (*Mirror Weekend*, 7 August 1987).

The Telegraph found the script and direction "*tight-lipped, tense and free of flab*" (30 March 1988), and the *Guardian* judged *Codename: Kyril* a "*superior spy thriller*" (26 March 1988). The production with its bankable cast and international gloss was viewed in some quarters as packaged for worldwide television, and though slick and stylish was resultantly "*heartless, juvenile, and lacking in the le Carré qualities of characterisation and psychological insight which have turned the spy thriller into something more than the sum of its parts*" (*Daily Mail*, 30 March 1988). In a generally favourable review, *The*

New York Times thought the serial veered from *"snappy spy stuff in the bowels of the Kremlin and the arteries of M16 to sappy television chases to Bondlike exploits and back again"*, but felt that ultimately the story was *"closer to Mr le Carré than to Ian Fleming"* (17 April 1988). In a philosophical mood, *The Times* claimed that, *"Spies represent the ultimate in human duplicity. A good spy story should create a world in which actions are predicated upon betrayal and invite meditation on the integrity of human relationships"*. *"There is very little purpose in an espionage drama such as* Codename Kyril", it continued, *"whose ambitions seemed to go no further than looking handsome and giving the audience a few thrills"* (31 March 1988). Of course, excitement was acceptable as entertainment to some reviewers, and the *Sunday Times* found the drama serial *"great, accidental, indecipherable fun"*, adding the coda, though, that, *"it should have been banned under Section Two of the Official Silliness Act"* (31 April 1988). The *Mail on Sunday* was less amenable and dismissed *Codename: Kyril* as *"four turbulent hours of counter-espionage hokum"* and that *"the whole rollicking farrago beggared comprehension"* (31 April 1988), and some reviewers wondered how the upmarket television dramatist Hopkins could be associated with such tosh (*Financial Times*, 6 April 1988). A thoughtful piece in the *Times Educational Supplement* pondered the ironies and absurdities of a spy story like *Codename: Kyril* and the unreal world of espionage. *"This mini-series did advance the diverting, if preposterous thesis that by the end the British and Soviet intelligence services might each be managed by men loyal to the other side"*. *"Would it make any difference if they were?"*, it drily observed. *"Alienated from the official history that will never acknowledge them, deprived of the normal exercise of power in the systems which they serve"*, it continued, *"these agents fall back on the illusion that real power lies on the board where their moves, by some process of astrological transference, determine events in the innocently oblivious lower realms"* (8 April 1988).

The Contract (1988) was the third and final drama serial Yorkshire Television adapted from the novels of Gerald Seymour and followed the acclaimed *Harry's Game* (1982) and the popular *The Glory Boys* (1984).[299] The three-part story, broadcast over consecutive evenings and scripted by Seymour, concerns an operation of the SIS to bring a leading Soviet rocket scientist (Hans Caninenberg) over to the West. Initially the son is brought over by mistake, so a 'contract' agent, Johnny Donoghue (Kevin McNally) a German specialist and former soldier who has suffered a disgrace after shooting an innocent bystander in Northern Ireland, is sent over to East Germany with the difficult task of persuading the scientist along with his daughter to defect and join his son. When the West German Security Service is alerted to the plot and sees it as a violation of the country's sovereignty, the mission is compromised and SIS abandons the agent to his fate. In East Germany, Donoghue has to improvise an escape for his party back to the West. In a tragic ending, the professor is killed on the barbed wire, his daughter refuses to leave him and accompany Johnny to a new life together in England, and the son, mistaken that the British plan to assassinate his father escapes back to the DDR where he is incarcerated. The production was largely filmed in Berlin and along the East-West German border, cast many German actors and astutely allowed the characters to speak in their native language. The *Guardian*, in a nostalgic mood, found it a *"nice old-fashioned Cold War spy story"* (2 January 1988). However, elsewhere there was a feeling that such a tale was losing touch with international events, *Stage and Television Today* wondering why, with Reagan and Gorbachev talking peace and friendship, *"television drama is still embroiled in the Cold War?"* (7 January 1988). Looked at today, the serial is an intelligent espionage drama, unhurried and with an emphasis on the complicated questions of loyalty and decency facing the characters rather than adrenaline-inducing action. The intelligence chiefs are represented as hard-working realists with difficult moral choices to make and complex issues to balance in mounting deniable operations which their political masters wish to succeed, but prefer to be kept in ignorance of and will use against the spymasters if things go wrong. The leader of the operation Henry Carter (Bernard Hepton) is long-weary of putting the Service's objectives above individual sensitivities; while, shown to be living in a brutal and repressive regime, it is no simple matter for the scientist and his daughter to flee to the West and abandon their settled lives.

Finally, *The Endless Game*, published in 1986, was the first in a series of espionage novels written by the acclaimed film-maker Bryan Forbes and introduced the series character of Alec Hillsden, a middle-aged senior agent for a division of MI6. The story commences with the assassination of a prematurely-aged woman in a nursing home by a Soviet hitman named Calder. It transpires that Caroline Oates had been a British agent; a lover of Hillsden's, captured and tortured by the KGB, and returned a vegetable. The killing is seemingly senseless, but when the former traitor Glanville is also murdered following his questioning by Hillsden, the agent decides the answer must lie in the past, in the secret mission to East Germany during which Caroline was taken.[300]

The backdrop to these events is a new Labour government (dating the setting of the story to around 1988) and the harassed Home Secretary Toby Bayldon who is struggling to deal with a breakdown in law and order and especially an intensification of terrorism and bomb outrages. Pamela is a beautiful young woman who serves in a terrorist cell, has recently become the mistress of Sir Charles Belfrage a senior civil servant in the Russian Section of the Foreign Office, and who facilitates his assassination by a member of her group. It emerges that the widespread terror campaign is supported by the Soviets.

In the latter part of the story, Hillsden, acting on a plan hatched by Control, the head of MI6, leaves the Service in disgrace, seemingly deteriorates and is approached by the Soviets for defection. He is secretly flown to Moscow where he is interrogated by the GRU, Soviet Military Intelligence. There he is reunited with Jock, the former leader of the network in Austria which included Hillsden and Caroline, and who was thought dead. It slowly emerges that Jock is the Soviet killer Calder, and before Alec kills him in revenge for his colleague and lover, the Scotsman reveals an extensive infiltration of British Intelligence by the Russians, which includes Control and Bayldon, and which Caroline was beginning to expose. In a bleak ending, Hillsden is left isolated and impotent in Moscow, and, following increased unrest on the streets of Great Britain, Bayldon is elevated to the leadership of a new government.

The Endless Game was one of a number of spy stories that appeared in the 1980s which embodied the conservative anxiety and paranoia regarding national decline, social breakdown, industrial unrest, increased militancy, the suspected existence of a 'supermole', and Soviet plots in the period, and which included Frederick Forsyth's best-seller *The Fourth Protocol* (1984).[301] While arguably cynical and mildly paranoid, *The New York Times* found Forbes an "*intelligent voice that is at its best when evoking an England far removed from any semblance to a demi-paradise*" (12 January 1986). The novel made various references to contemporary events and developments in a typical manoeuvre to suggest immediacy and realism, such as the controversial Special Patrol Group of the London Metropolitan Police which dealt with serious public disorder, and the assassination of the Bulgarian dissident Georgi Markov in London in 1978 by use of a poisoned umbrella tip.[302]

Bryan Forbes scripted and directed a three-hour, two-part British-Italian television dramatisation of *The Endless Game* broadcast on Channel 4 in the summer of 1989, with a distinguished cast which included Albert Finney as Alec Hillsden, George Segal as Jock Calder, Ian Holm as Control, Michael Medwin as Bayldon, Anthony Quayle as Glanville and Kristin Scott Thomas as Caroline. The £4.5 million finance was provided by Rete Italia, the creative talent was British and the production was completed at Shepperton Studios in association with the commercial television company Television South. As a concession to Rete Italia, the part of Caroline Oates was re-written for the Italian actress Monica Guerritore, but these plans for some reason did not materialise (*Screen International*, 16 April and 22 October 1988). The screen drama used extensive locations in London, Devon, Austria and Finland, and included a music score by the renowned Italian film composer Ennio Morricone. The drama is a close approximation of the novel; however, the casting of the American George Segal necessitated a change of origin for Jock Calder who is now credited as a former CIA station head in Austria. The ending of the drama is slightly less bleak than the novel: here, Hillsden, while contentedly watching children ice-skating, gives an ironic smile when he learns that the double-agent Bayldon has succeeded as prime minister.

The reviewer at the *Guardian*, rarely appreciative of spy dramas, worried at the acting getting "*slower and slower*" and the explanations "*longer and longer*" (28 August 1989). Elsewhere, there was muted enthusiasm for the serial, the reviewer at the *Daily Mail*, claiming that "*what Sunday telly really needs are spies*", was clearly more at home with espionage dramas, found *The Endless Game* more comprehensible than both Deighton and le Carré, and declared himself "*happy*" with his time spent in front of the drama (21 August 1989). A view echoed at *Stage and Television Today* which claimed the first instalment captured the interest and promised a "*tense and interesting climax*" (24 August 1989). However, *The Listener* found the pacing "*awry*", the dialogue "*pure suet*", and the score "*peculiarly intermittent*" (17 August 1989).There were tentative plans to film the subsequent Hillsden stories; however, it proved ironic when Forbes had commented on set that, "*if this is a turkey, I guess I'd go back to the word processor*" (quoted in *Screen International*, 22 October 1988). The serial was not a success and it was the last screen drama directed by the veteran Forbes.[303]

The latter part of the story, dealing with the supposed breakdown and defection of Hillsden, owes much to John le Carré's classic *The Spy Who Came in from the Cold* (1963), and 'Alec' Hillsden like 'Alec' Leamas is middle-aged, disillusioned, and betrayed. However, Hillsden is left to fight another day, a story told in subsequent novels, and this optimism coupled with the more reactionary tone of the tale puts *The Endless Game* outside of the territory traced by the espionage drama and the writing of John le Carré. The review in the *Wall Street Journal* pointed to the anachronism of *The Endless Game*, and noting the rapidly changing "*geopolitical situation*", wondered at "*anyone still playing the game by these old rules*" (29 January 1990). This lack of relevance possibly accounted for the limited interest in the expensive and well-cast drama which disappeared almost without trace.

The spy thriller, a popular genre in the cinema in the 1960s, had attempted, with varying degrees of success, to establish itself on television in the 1970s and 1980s. The television spy drama had sought to reproduce the popularity of the literary spy thriller and in the majority of cases TV producers (as with film producers before them) drew directly from the bookshelves for their spies and secret agents, and this was the case with *Quiller, Running Blind, Charlie Muffin, Chessgame, The Secret Servant, Codename: Kyril* and *The Endless Game*. With foreign locations and casting which included Michael Jayston, David Hemmings, Terence Stamp and Albert Finney, there was often an up-market dimension to these television productions which clearly aimed at, if not always convincing as, quality. Original dramas were rarer, the 'presold' secret agent thriller no doubt being considered less risky. However, *Mr Palfrey of Westminster* was an honourable addition to series drama. While interesting in terms of their situation in the line of development of the spy story, caught between the popular spy novel and the glamorous spy picture, the spy thriller on television can be judged only an intermittent success, failing to establish a long-running series character as had been managed in novels, on screen, and in the earlier television adventure series.

A few months after the screening of *The Endless Game*, television was broadcasting demonstrators dismantling the Berlin Wall and Communism was beginning to crumble in Eastern Europe. Creators of secret agent adventures would now be required to rethink the ground rules of the genre.[304] *The Listener* had warned future makers of spy dramas that "*televised spook tales are bound to be measured against the BBC le Carré's, and found wanting*", and some of the recent spy thrillers had indeed failed to impress critics (17 August 1989). The 1980s had witnessed a series of spy scandals and government mishandlings of intelligence and security matters,[305] and established character archetypes and generic conventions of the spy thriller were increasingly unlikely to convince. "*I, for one*", noted the reviewer at the *Western Mail*, "*refuse to believe in all these stiff-lipped Intelligence types, laconic but brilliant, when I remember what we know of British security efforts in real life and in recent years*" (26 November 1983). And it was pointed out at *The Telegraph* that,

> *After reading what we were allowed to read about the case of Michael Bettaney, the solemn misfit and would-be Russian spy employed by British counter-espionage, writers of popular fiction in this area could be excused if they despaired anew of matching the strange ironies of the factual.*

"*Freshness in the well-worn genre*", it warned, "*is difficult to achieve at the best of times*"(19 April 1984).

The spy procedural

We live, the thriller tells us, in precarious times, and we're lucky to be alive.
(John Sutherland, *The Listener*, 21 June 1984)

Writing in 1966, producer and script-editor Cyril Coke feared that, *"Audiences are so used and conditioned to the tinsel variety of secret agent with superhuman intelligence, a tireless, over sexed robot – in fact a superman – that a taste of the real thing can easily prove a terrible let down"*. The problem as he saw it was to *"try to get fairly near the exciting actual truths without showing how really drab and awful that world can be"*. Gambling on the assumption that *"the days of the 'kinky' secret agent stories were numbered and that audiences would soon only respond to stories that, though still exciting, were reasonably within the realms of possibility"*, Coke and his associates at the BBC pioneered a more realistic approach to television espionage with *The Mask of Janus* and *The Rat Catchers* (3). Producer Terence Dudley remarked that *The Mask of Janus* set out to present international espionage as it probably was, *"antiromantic"*, but was disappointed when *"it failed to attract the large audiences enjoyed by the phoney in the genre"* (1966: 15). The grittier approach to the spy thriller resurfaced again a little later in the spy procedural, which came to prominence with *Special Branch*, an innovative police action series which ran to four seasons, broadcast in 1969, 1970, 1973 and 1974, and produced at the commercial Thames Television. The first two series were shot on videotape mainly in the studio with initial episodes in black and white; while the final two series were made on film in colour as the initial productions of Euston Films, an in-house division of Thames, with much material shot on location.[306] The decades of the 1960s and 1970s had witnessed a considerable restructuring and expansion of the actual Special Branch and critics have seen this in terms of a government response to a perceived threat from a *"far and wide left"* which threatened a subversive agenda. Critics of the Branch have seen it as a *"political police force"* (Dorrill 1993: 160-163).

Television executive Lloyd Shirley wanted to move away from the *"mid-Atlantic"* feel of the adventure series of the 1960s and spy shows characterised by adventure and fantasy; an approach, admittedly, which resulted in good sales to the American broadcast networks (Alvarado and Stewart 1985: 32). *"Bridging fiction and fact"*, *Special Branch* consciously drew on an alternative tradition in British television, the naturalistic drama, exemplified in the long-running independent television series *Armchair Theatre* (ITV, 1956-74) (*Sunday Telegraph*, 16 August 1970). The first two series of *Special Branch* comprised of 14 and 13 episodes respectively and starred Wensley Pithy as Detective Chief Superintendent Eden, Derren Nesbitt as Detective Chief Inspector Jordan, Fulton Mackay as Detective Chief Superintendent Inman, and Morris Perry as Charles Moxon of MI5. In an intelligent approach to police drama, there is less emphasis on action and more time spent with the officers at their desks, worrying about retirement, promotion, the intricacies and niceties of police work, and what the ulterior motives of MI5 might be? Star Derren Nesbitt claimed the series was *"going all out for truth"* (quoted in the *Sun*, 11 August 1970). Much care was put into the preparation of each episode. Plots were drawn from the headlines and from reports of old cases dealt with by Special Branch, and were believed to result in stories which *"only rarely over stretched credibility"*. The cast were also invited to dissect the scripts, and in an effort to make the characters more convincing and consistent were invited to alter lines to suit their roles and cut others which they thought were out of character. The outcome of this unusual effort towards realism in the genre, according to *The Telegraph*, was *"some of the most watchable television in the thriller field today"* (12 August 1970).

Eden, Jordan, Inman and their colleagues tackle the varied responsibilities of the Branch, terrorism in 'A Date with Leonides', student agitators in 'A New Face' and providing security for a visiting VIP in 'Visitor from Moscow' (all 1969), and serving undercover to gain information on a traitor in 'Inside' (1970). Stories with a distinct espionage dimension included 'Troika', 'The Kazmirov Affair', 'Reliable Sources', 'Short Change' and 'Care of Her Majesty', (all 1969), and 'Dinner Date', 'The Pleasure of Your Company', 'Error of Judgement' and 'Reported Missing' (all 1970), which involve the officers with defectors, double-agents and confrontations with the KGB. The characterisation of Detective Chief Inspector Jordan was something new in police drama, a hip, post-Carnaby Street dresser, with long hair and an uninhibited girlfriend. The first series of *Special Branch* made the annual list of most popular commercial television programmes, watched on average in 7.7 million homes.

Reviews were initially lukewarm. The *Sun* found it a *"very average series"* (25 September 1969) and *The Telegraph* reported on *"all the clichés of espionage drama"* (18 September 1969). The odd review acknowledged *Special Branch* as something *"original"*, tackling for the *"first time the security arm of Scotland Yard"* and praising the series editor George Markstein for having *"striven so fiercely for authenticity that his programme has achieved a wonderfully true atmosphere of a power game being played across an international chessboard of espionage and national security"* (*Daily Express*, 18 September 1969). The *Financial Times* located *Special Branch* at the better end of series drama with nicely differentiated characters and investigations that were not merely *"possible"*, but *"probable"* (1 October 1969). The *Guardian* placed *Special Branch* in the *"not discreditable little corner in the off-beat law"*, occupied by such other innovative and acclaimed indigenous television series as *Public Eye* (1965-75) and *Callan* (1967-72) (19 August 1970), and the *Observer* recognised an attempt at differentiation, the series trying hard *"to escape the various restrictions of the potentially exportable series"* recently exemplified in the spy adventure series of the 1960s (9 November 1969). The with-it characterisation of Chief Inspector Jordan attracted much comment, marking something new in a *"Sexy and swinging and insubordinate"* senior policeman who sported *"Mr Fish-like clothes"* (*Sun*, 25 September 1969; *Observer*, 9 November 1969).[307]

The second season generally attracted more positive reviews. The *Sunday Times* found the drama *"vigorously prosecuted with due attention to narrative vivacity and local colour"* (27 September 1970). While that reviewer ranked it alongside a quality police procedural like *Softly, Softly*, the *Sun* disagreed and felt it wasn't a *"patch on the realism of Z-Cars or Callan"* (12 August 1970). The *Daily Express* pointed to the quality of writing and praised *"scripts which rarely have to rely on violence for their impact"*. In place of *"thuggery"*, the series attended to the human dimension within the business of special police work, acknowledging that *"the rivalry, the argument between these men in the elite section of the police force is as much a part of the production as the detection in which they are involved"*. The reviewer believed there was a *"true ring about these battles for promotion, or recognition, or merely survival in the tough business of catching the supercrook"* (19 August 1970).

A revamped and more expensive *Special Branch* returned after a three-year break with two £500,000 series of 13 episodes each produced on film at Euston Films. The series adopted an innovative production method, acquiring leases on premises at Redan Place and Colet Court and using these as bases incorporating office, sets and editing suites, and retreating there if the weather was unsuitable for location shooting (Alvarado and Stewart 1985: 45).[308] The new episodes were fronted by the characters of Detective Chief Inspectors Alan Craven (George Sewell) and Tom Haggerty (Patrick Mower), and sought to add *"gritty"* to the show's established *"realism"* (*Morning Star*, 7 April 1973). Max Sexton has argued that the reinvigoration of the series was intended to appeal to younger viewers and that the initial series of *Special Branch* had sometimes appeared *"staid, middle-class and middle-brow"* (2014: 31). The introduction of Craven introduced a sharper class element into the drama, a working-class copper made good, suspicious and resentful of higher-class superiors, he knew the mean streets of London from experience, and Haggerty had a barely concealed vicious streak in his make-up. In the parlance of the force, and substantially adding to the dramatic interaction, the two men had some 'previous' and were openly antagonistic towards each other. Newcomer Mower had been popular in the final two series of the espionage drama *Callan* in 1970 and 1972 and was added for sex appeal.[309] The publicity for *Special Branch* put out by the production company in this period stated the intention of the series as "*hard authenticity, with believable characters in realistic situations, filmed entirely on location against real London backgrounds*" (press pack, 1974). Episodes with an espionage-related story included 'The Other Man' (1973), and 'Jailbait', 'Rendezvous', 'Date of Birth' and 'Diversion' (all 1974). *Special Branch* in this period remained among the most popular of commercial television series, watched on average by around 7.5 million households.

The first episode of the new format dealt with a corruption charge levelled at Craven, and for the *Daily Mail*, true to the tradition of the series, the "*interest lay in following the investigating procedure of the special police and Craven's skill in clearing himself*" (5 April 1973). In contrast, for the *Daily Mirror* it was a disappointing case of the show "*limping back*" (both 5 April 1973). The "*new tough look*" of the series attracted some concern and the *Daily Mail* wondered at how a "*raving psychopath like Chief Inspector Haggerty ever made it to the top*" and worried over his "*vengeful personality*" (26 April 1973). While unconvinced by some of the storylines, *The Telegraph* found it a refreshing change that the production managed to break loose from the studio and range around London and its environs (10 May 1974). The series steered clear of controversial subjects and so avoided the war going on in Ulster and its fallout on the mainland, a considerable irony this as the Branch had its origins in the 19th century in the Special Irish Branch, formed to deal with outrages connected with the campaign for home rule in Ireland.[310] Joseph Oldham has commented on the "*rejection of politics*" in the final two series of *Special Branch*, in which the "*Possibilities of dissent, often with a valid moral case, are flattened into the strict execution of legal procedure*" (2017: 55).

Special Branch, especially the latter two series, was influential on the television action drama in Great Britain which tended to 'toughen up' in the 1970s. The series was dropped by Euston in favour of *The Sweeney* (1975-78) which centred on the Flying Squad, the police division that dealt with serious and organised crime, and which seemed to bear out the *Daily Mail*'s previously noted apprehension about the violent type who would become the "*police hero of the 70s*".[311] As already noted, a shift in style accompanied the change to the tougher law enforcement series, the "*aesthetic of immediacy*" derived from live television through performance and the use of close-ups typical of single-play dramas and the earlier series of *Special Branch* increasingly being jettisoned for single-camera techniques as the marker for 'quality' and 'realism' in the television drama series (Oldham 2017: 47). Euston Films went on to several of the signature action series of the later 1970s, such as *Minder* (1979-84), as well as the historical espionage serial *Reilly – Ace of Spies* (1983).

Codename produced at the BBC was another 'team' series that appeared around the time of *Special Branch*. It was launched with a pilot *Codename: Portcullis* broadcast in the summer of 1969 and followed by a single series early in 1970, for which there were cast and character changes. The drama dealt with the secret department MI17 based at Cambridge University, run by a master of a college and former ex-minister Sir Iain Carfax (Clifford Evans). His manservant Culliford (John White) is a trained killer and a junior don (Peter Jeffrey) is coerced into the outfit. The *Observer* described the initial single-play as a "*gown and dagger thriller*", produced with the "*modernistic trappings*" of fast cutting, but basically an "*old-fashioned ivy-clad whodunit*" and "*passable light entertainment*" (10 August 1969). The series of thirteen 50-minute episodes carried forward Clifford Evans from the pilot who now featured as Sir Iain Dalzell, while Alexandra Bastedo played his daughter Diana Dalzell, and Anthony Valentine and Brian Peck dealt out the rough stuff as the agents Philip West and Culliford. *Codename* was seemingly an attempt by the BBC to produce a challenger to the ITV espionage drama series *Callan*, which had started its successful run in 1967. This was evident in the casting of Valentine who had recently vacated his role as agent Toby Meres in the rival series, and in aping the class antagonism of the earlier show, here between the officer-class West and the other ranks Culliford, which had been such a feature of the relationship between Meres and Callan. *Stage and Television Today* thought that the pilot had some good ideas and attractive settings, but left the impression that it had been "*thrown together*", and that the series had launched quite promisingly, but rapidly deteriorated into "*spy story fodder*", and that the presence of the "*obligatory girl spy*" had "*ruined any chance of absolute realism*" (14 August 1969, and 16 April and 18 June 1970). The BBC did not return to the series.[312]

The spy procedural form developed and consolidated in *Spy Trap*, produced at the BBC and broadcast over three seasons between 1972 and 1975. The drama was devised by the writer Robert Barr who had previously scripted *Spy Catcher* (BBC, 1959-61), a series of true stories of the search for spies in war-time Britain based on the experiences of Lieutenant-Colonel Oreste Pinto. *Spy Trap* centred on 'The Department', a counter-espionage organisation answerable to the Ministry of Defence and headed by Commander Ryan, RN (Paul Daneman) and answerable to Carson (Michael Gwynne), a high-ranking civil servant in Whitehall in overall charge of security operations. Agents in the field were Commander Anderson (Julian Glover) and Lieutenant Saunders, RN (Prentis Hancock), the men who pursue the rogue agents, defectors and other threats to the national interest.

Spy Trap was conceived as a fresh format for a weekday thriller series, with screenings initially broadcast across four early evening slots per week, and storylines such as 'Checkpoint' and 'The Defector' lasted either two or four episodes, before the series settled down to a more conventional bi-weekly presentation. The *Guardian* thought that the introductory four episodes a week was about the *"acceptable threshold of pain"* (23 March 1972) and a cynical *Daily Mirror* thought it a strategy designed to *"breed addicts"* (17 March 1972). Reporting on the first episode 'Checkpoint', about the de-briefing of a British agent following his flight from Moscow after his network was broken-up, *Stage and Television Today* judged the series *"convincingly authentic"*, the *"situations never less than tense"* and the play *"well-written and directed with an uncluttered economy of effort"* (23 March 1972). The first season consisted of 36 short 30-minute episodes.[313]

Screened in the early evening, it was unusual for a spy drama of the period to be broadcast at a time of day suitable for children. The *Daily Mail* admired an attempt *"to make the 7 o'clock spot a little less bleak and predictable"* and a show which tried to *"give us a little politics with our adventure"* (22 March 1972). However, some critics thought the series suffered as a result of an early screening, making for *"anodyne"* drama, *"purged of all reality"*, although the attempt to trade action for thoughtful drama was noted (*Observer*, 16 April 1972).

Spy Trap immediately benefitted from topicality, the screening of the first episode coinciding with sensational news coverage of the trial of real-life spy naval officer David Bingham. In something of a media event, Mrs Bingham offered *"remarkable confessions"* on the 7.30pm News, in which she revealed an *"extraordinary everyday world"* in which she urged her husband on to *"treachery"* to pay off the hire purchase (*Daily Mirror*, 14 March 1972). For *The Telegraph*, Mrs Bingham's *"vivid"* and *"chilling"* revelations *"proved infinitely more compelling and surprising than the clichés of spy fiction"* (14 March 1972).

The second and third seasons adopted the new formula of 15 and 10 longer 45-minute discrete episodes respectively, broadcast once a week but in a later primetime timeslot which allowed for the treatment of individual cases and consequently more developed and mature stories.[314] Relieved star Paul Daneman reported that gone was his earlier portrayal which had necessarily been *"more like a Boy Scout than a secret service boss"* (quoted in the *Sun*, 11 September 1973). In the new seasons, field agent Major Sullivan (Tom Adams) replaced Commander Anderson, while Saunders disappeared from series three. *Spy Trap* depicted a harder-edged world of counter-espionage than had otherwise appeared in spy and thriller series on BBC Television, and was responding to the success of 'team'-oriented investigative dramas such as *Softly, Softly* (BBC) and *Special Branch*. The characterisations in the early series of Commander Anderson, impulsive and insubordinate, and Lieutenant Saunders, younger womaniser, owed something to the successful pairing and personal interaction of Callan and Cross (Patrick Mower) in the final two series of *Callan* which aired in 1970 and 1972. A contributing writer to the second and third series was Kenneth Clark (using the name Ben Bassett), a recently retired Detective Chief Superintendent and former chief of the South-West Regional Crime Squad, who also provided stories for such realistic police series as *Z-Cars* and *Softly, Softly*.

Critics showed signs of having to adjust to the new, naturalistic style of the spy procedural. *The Times* admitted *Spy Trap* was realistic, but found itself wishing for more excitement (14 March 1972). The *Daily Express* believed the television producer was now caught in a "*compromise between the all-action programme which costs money and says nothing and the conversation piece which tries to be a little more subtle*" (14 March 1972). The *Daily Mail* wondered at "*no humour, little animation, and a certain atmosphere of glum dedication*". "*Obviously*", it ascertained, "*the aim is to reject any hint of Bondery and stick to realism*". But, "*Too successfully, as it happens*" (19 May 1972). Becoming more attuned, the *Daily Mirror* felt that the "*world of intrigue where your best friend may be your worst enemy and suspicion goes hand in hand with loyalty was well captured*" (17 March 1972). The reviewer at the *Guardian* gave a thumbs up to the spy procedural, and although "*viewing the proliferation of spy series with every kind of alarm*", she admitted she enjoyed the "*semantics of spying*" in *Spy Trap*, the "*couriers and clearances and contacts who are worked, and covers which are blown*" (23 March 1972). Cultural scholar Raymond Williams, in a thoughtful piece in *The Listener* in which he wondered at the complexity of the spy series in a climate which generally credited the viewing public with little intellectual capacity, remarked that the "*investigators in Spy Trap do not set out to charm*", and, in the ethos of the spy procedural, were merely "*doing a job, as if they were in* Softly, Softly" (1972).

Although having some detractors, *Spy Trap* attracted some very good notices. During the run of the first season, the *Financial Times* found it the "*best fiction on either channel at the moment*", claiming that an "*excellent, simple (and cheap) formula has been found for drawing out the tensions, and it is done with the most easy and relaxed acting from all the principals, a pleasure in itself*" (28 June 1972). However, for the second season, the *Daily Mail* noticed a "*sad decline from the previous quality of bleak authenticity*" (12 September 1973). The *Observer* judged the final season of *Spy Trap*, the "*best series of any kind on television*", admiring the logical plotting, consistently high standard of episodes and the "*satisfyingly complicated stories*" (4 May 1975).[315] The BBC did not return to a long-running counter-espionage series until the hugely successful *Spooks* in 2002.

The spy procedural form was perpetuated in the 'team'-oriented *The Sandbaggers*, the creation of former career naval officer Ian Mackintosh. The series was produced at the commercial Yorkshire Television company and ran for three successful seasons totalling 20 episodes between 1978 and 1980.[316] The stories centred on a small covert team of trouble-shooters within MI6, the Sandbaggers, the 'dirty tricks' outfit which undertakes the tougher and more unsavoury jobs in the world of secret intelligence.[317] The unit is headed by the austere, uncompromising and sometimes ruthless Neil Burnside (Roy Marsden), a tough ex-Royal Marines Officer and the Director of Operations of the Secret Intelligence Service. With the premise of a 'Special Operations Section' within SIS, one would anticipate an action-oriented spy show. Against such expectation, *The Sandbaggers* is at pains to show the routine of the department, the burden of paperwork, office politics, staffing problems and careerism. Mackintosh set out his aims in an early proposal for the series, where he argued that, "*SIS has been the subject of many series and many plays; but never has it been portrayed in real documentary terms*". "*Never*", he reiterated, "*has there been an examination of its methods, priorities, internal struggles and powers within the Whitehall structure. Never has the spotlight been turned on the men who make the decisions, who control the agents, who gamble with the precarious peace of cold war*" (quoted in Oldham 2017: 59). In accordance, the publicity set out the parameters of the show, explaining that, "*The job is not glamorous. There are no high-living James Bonds, beautiful women and mad scientists with plans for taking over the world*". "The Sandbaggers", it claimed, "*is for real*" (*The Sandbaggers* press sheet, 1980). Accordingly, only a short sequence of any episode is devoted to physical deeds and violence, the bulk of the drama taking place behind the scenes in the operations room, in offices and at meetings where characters have intelligent conversations and heated arguments. Much of Burnside's energy and time is spent dealing with inter-service rivalry, the acceptance or rejection of his operations according to political imperatives, battling the bureaucrats, what he sees as the inertia of red tape and an 'old-boys network', and begging and swapping favours with the Americans. The Director of Operations has to liaise with Sir Geoffrey Wellingham (Alan MacNaughtan), the Permanent Undersecretary at the Foreign Office, who operates his own personal political and social agenda, and, to make matters more sensitive, is Burnside's former father-in-law. The *Daily Mail* referred to the two-pronged formula of the series as that of *"inter-departmental intrigue at home, dangerous sorties abroad"* (29 July 1980).

More in the tradition of James Bond than John le Carré, *The Sandbaggers* showed a very productive partnership between the British and the Americans in terms of intelligence. A cordial and supportive rapport holds between Burnside and Jeff Ross (Bob Sherman) of the CIA London Station, and the under-resourced British often call on the 'special secret relationship' to help mount operations, acquire information, and extricate themselves from mission failures.[318] Relations with other European or North Atlantic Treaty Organisation partners are more fraught or hostile, such as with the French ('Special Relationship') and the Norwegians ('First Principles', both 1978). In the world of *The Sandbaggers*, things go wrong, missions fail or are compromised, agents are lost, and allies deceive one another. Joseph Oldham writes of the *"bleak and pessimistic tone"* of the drama, and of *"Mackintosh's drive towards a documentary 'realism', cutting through the more literary ambiguity of the existential novelists"* (2017: 62, 63). Burnside has difficult decisions to make, moral boundaries are crossed, and professional ethics are necessarily flexible. However, it is at a cost. In the latter part of season one, Burnside forges a romantic bond with Laura (Diane Keen), the first female agent of the unit, both of them emotionally damaged by previous relationships. In a tragic denouement in 'Special Relationship', Burnside painfully orders a sniper to shoot Laura dead at the Berlin Wall during an exchange of spies for the greater strategic advantage of safeguarding shared intelligence with the CIA.

Something of a cult has grown around *The Sandbaggers*. At the time of its release on DVD, *The New York Times* referred to it glowingly as the *"best spy series in television history"* (12 October 2003). There is also an ongoing mystique attached to the show, relating to the still unexplained disappearance of writer Mackintosh in a plane crash in fair weather in Alaska in July 1979 while allegedly scouting locations for *The Sandbaggers* (*Guardian*, 12 July 1979). Various oddities pertain to the flight, the crash and subsequent enquiries, and it has been speculated that Mackintosh, who had previously served as an intelligence agent, might have been on a covert mission, even defected to Russia. Certainly, the mysterious Mackintosh's secret background was used in the publicity for the series and picked up by reviewers to explain the seeming authenticity of the series in which there is much intensity but few thrills, and which many came to believe could only have been written by an *"insider"* (Dorril 1993: 424; *Daily Express*, 14 August 1978). Some of the 'quirks' of *The Sandbaggers* include a Director of Operations who prefers Coca Cola to liquor, a lead sandbagger who deplores violence, and a complete absence of flash cars and gadgets.[319]

The Sandbaggers gradually drew to itself approval and critical support. The initially sceptical *Guardian* thought *The Sandbaggers*, "*grew into a nice, gritty, grey series*" (19 September 1978); the *Belfast Telegraph* found it "*nicely tense and plausible*"; and the *Evening News* believed that scriptwriter Mackintosh was to be "*congratulated for his convincing stories, and credible characters*" (26 September 1978). Much of the critical attention centred on the authenticity of the series. The *Evening News* considered that *The Sandbaggers* appealed to people "*who like their spies neither shaken nor stirred*" and that the series "*smacked*" of "*seedy realism*". "*The Sandbaggers live in a world where the most likely violence is GBH of the ear hole in the dark reaches of the corridors of power*" noted the reviewer, "*which indeed is much the way Kim Philby described Secret Intelligence Service work in his book* My Silent War" (9 June 1980). The following month, the same paper observed: "*you don't often get such complex and authoritative plots on television nor such an insight into the real world of Whitehall intrigue*" (29 July 1980). The *Daily Mail* praised a "*credible creation of the deadly mood of diplomacy's secret underworld*" (29 July 1980), and *Stage and Television Today* heaped its praise on the "*splendidly bureaucratic nature of the organisation*" depicted in the series, and believed the originality and strength of *The Sandbaggers* derived from the "*backstabbing Whitehall manoeuvres and interdepartmental wrangling*" central to the drama (19 October 1978).[320]

There was some dismay when it was announced that *The Sandbaggers* would end after its third season. It had developed a loyal following and Ray Lonnen (Sandbagger number 1) and Roy Marsden had acquired a strong female following (*Sun*, 31 July 1980). Ian Mackintosh had not completed the writing of the final series and three scripts had to be provided at short notice by Gidley Wheeler and Arden Winch. The final episode was completed before any decision had been made regarding the future of the series and purposely "*left the door slightly open*" in the storyline; however, the loss of the creator Mackintosh meant that Yorkshire Television ultimately felt it could not proceed with the series (*Evening News*, 28 July 1980). *The Sandbaggers* has continued to draw critical interest and acclaim, Joseph Oldham suggesting that the drama explored "*the ethics of espionage in a much more challenging manner than had been previously achieved*", and managed "*to demystify the bureaucracy and procedures of intelligence work*" (2017: 58).

Spy procedural dramas continued to appear intermittently in the schedules. *Blood Money*, produced at the BBC and broadcast in 1981, was a terrorist thriller serial consisting of six 30-minute episodes devised by the veteran writer Arden Winch, who, as we have seen, had just stepped into the breach at *The Sandbaggers* to help finish off the series.[321] It forms the first part of a loose trilogy with *Skorpion* (1983) and *Cold Warrior* (1984), each drama serial/series featuring the character of Captain Percival (Michael Denison) of the Secret Intelligence Service. *Blood Money* concerned the kidnapping of the child of the Administrator General for the United Nations by the Workers' Revolutionary Army Council, a terrorist cell, and his ransom for £1m and a series of political demands. The police operation to retrieve the boy is led by the down-to-earth Chief Superintendent Meadows (Bernard Hepton) of the Metropolitan Police Anti-Terrorist Branch, popularly known at the time as 'The Bomb Squad', but he reluctantly has to accept the involvement of the more patrician Captain Percival of SIS.[322]

The drama is a tense examination of the Squad's painstaking investigation to identify the gang and the whereabouts of the boy. Meadows insists on a wholly legal and humane operation, but his plans are undermined by Percival who, with official backing, requires that the terrorists are given no opportunity to make political propaganda and are eliminated at the point of their arrest by a unit of the Special Air Service (SAS). The story is focused and intense, points to the tension between the duly constituted police force and the covert Intelligence Service, and doesn't shy from showing the underhanded methods employed by MI6. The drama had originally been titled *Blood Royal* and the kidnap victim had been envisaged as 'The Earl of Balmoral', a distant claimant to the throne. However, there was intervention from Buckingham Palace and the production and its broadcast were delayed while script, character and title changes were made which required two extra days filming at a cost of £10,000. There had been an armed kidnap attempt on Princess Anne in Pall Mall in 1974, and the Royal Family was understandably nervous about a fiction which dramatised a terrorist threat (*Daily Mail*, *The Telegraph* and *Guardian*, 21 November 1980).

Blood Money gathered some very good notices. *The Times* reported that there was "*nothing but enthusiasm about the launch of* Blood Money", the paper praising the dialogue and brisk action (7 September 1981). *The Telegraph* judged it "*just about the best thriller the box has come up with for ages: tense, detailed, credible*", admired the formal structure of the drama which incessantly cut back and forth between the terrorists and their young hostage holed up in a safe house and the patient police investigation, and welcomed the "*glimpse of grinding police routine*" which was thankfully "*worlds away from the 'Bang, you're dead' ethos of* The Professionals" (28 September 1981). The *Daily Mail* was especially vociferous in its admiration, reporting that, "*Without fuss or flourish an unpretentious and unusually intelligent series about a small, kidnapped boy has captivated a sizeable chunk of the viewing public"*. The reviewer marked *Blood Money* down as the *"most engrossing thriller serial of the year"* and Chief Superintendent Meadows as the *"most interesting sleuth on the box since George Smiley"*. With the recent acclaimed *Tinker Tailor Soldier Spy*, the reviewer continued, *Blood Money* shared a *"shadowy, barely accessible world of secrets and subterfuge, where nothing is what it seems, where, as often as not, the loudest sound in a room is a clash of wits"* (29 September 1981). The *Observer* went further and informed its readers to ignore *Tinker* and advised: *"For what real tension looks like, see* Blood Money" (11 October 1981). Many reviewers praised the 'spy procedural' aspects of the serial, the *Sunday Telegraph* commenting that, *"no one has ever dramatised in detail the task of the police in trying even to make a start on locating the victim"* (20 September 1981), the *Evening Standard* remarking that the *"police station scenes all seem absolutely right"*, that the terrorists were depicted with *"chilling realism"*, and that *"Michael Denison, with only occasional appearances, conveys easily the maddening superiority of MI5* (sic)*"* (21 September 1981). In a later assessment of the whole serial, the *Evening Standard* reported that the dialogue throughout had been *"entirely believable; the police procedure meticulous – no false heroics, just plodding work, plus a bit of luck"* (12 October 1981).[323] At the commencement of its run, *Bloody Money* made the third spot in the BBC ratings.

Skorpion was a follow-up thriller by Arden Winch dealing with terrorism, first broadcast in 1983 and similarly consisted of six 30-minute episodes. The drama commences with an assassination attempt on the life of Gabrielle (Marianne Borgo), a senior French international aid worker, and during an effort to flee her light plane crash lands in Scotland. The Metropolitan Anti-Terrorist Branch, now headed by Chief Superintendent Franks (Terrence Hardiman),[324] is directed to the scene where it is joined by Captain Percival who explains that Gabrielle is a reformed terrorist now being sought by her former cell for elimination. The investigation is a race against time to locate the French woman before the ruthless assassin Constant Delangre (Neville Jason) can complete his assignment. In a tense finale, Delangre is shot by Percival at the moment the assassin has Gabrielle in the sights of his hunting rifle. The celebration by the Anti-Terrorist Branch officers is cut short when information is provided through MI5 that Agatha, the old friend who has been providing refuge for Gabrielle, is also a former member of the terrorist cell, and Franks and his team arrive too late to prevent the older woman killing both her former comrade and herself. The 'Skorpion' of the title is the Czech-made machine pistol favoured by the terrorist group in the drama. The serial commenced with strong viewing figures of over 11 million; however, it attracted little critical interest. The review in the *Daily Express* passed over the drama as *"serious, middle-of-the-road thriller stuff"*, found it *"pedantic and slow"*, and wished there was a *"bit more of a sting in this Skorpion's tale"* (13 January 1983). The *Guardian* dismissed the drama as an *"eminently forgettable thriller"* (13 January 1983).

A different approach was taken for *Cold Warrior*, again devised by Arden Winch, which was broadcast in 1984 and consisted of eight pocket spy stories of 30-minute duration. Centre stage is given to Captain Percival, with each episode dealing with a different case, and here assisted by the working-class Danny (Dean Harris) and Jo (Lucy Fleming) at an unnamed, covert intelligence unit.[325] 'Bright Sting' deals with a Soviet attempt to acquire the latest British missile system, 'Dead Wrong' with a murdered journalist who had uncovered a conspiracy, 'The Immigrants' with an assassination attempt on the Israeli Foreign Minister, and 'The Sprat' with a defector from the KGB. To the delight of some reviewers, in the final episode 'Hook, Line and Sinker', Denison was joined by his real-life wife, actress Dulcie Gray, who played a former Special Operations Executive agent from World War Two (*Daily Mirror*, 31 October 1984; *Daily Express*, 1 November 1984). *The Times* referred to the stories as yarns, and, given their short running time, a series that *"moves so fast that it does not have time to worry about little things like plausibility"* (12 September 1984). Other reviewers found a drama in which an *"English gentleman triumphs over sinister foreigners"* quaint and amiable, but old-fashioned (*Evening Standard*, 13 September 1984).[326] The *Daily Star* found *Cold Warrior* a *"pacy, well put-together spy series"*, a kind of *"geriatric version of James Bond"* (14 September 1984); the *Daily Mirror* similarly referred to Percival as the *"pensioner's James Bond"* (6 October 1984); while *The Times*, judged it an *"inventive and entertaining early evening serial"*, made in a technique belonging to the *"pre-Dallas era"* (13 September 1984). One of the interesting features of the three series was the rivalry between the Secret Intelligence Service and the Security Service, something that was common knowledge in Whitehall, and the healthy suspicion of both by the legitimate police service.[327]

A handful of 'law and order' series included, to a greater or lesser extent, espionage narratives. Among the most popular was *The Professionals* (1977-83) which developed the kind of " *'laddish' masculinity which had emerged in the filmed series of* Special Branch *in 1973-74 and proved immensely popular and influential in the police series* The Sweeney" (Sexton 2014: 33). The show, produced at London Weekend Television (LWT), which ran for five seasons and 57 episodes, was initially met with critical hostility but proved immensely popular with viewers. *The Professionals* was created by the veteran Brian Clemens who had previously been involved with *The Avengers* and *The New*

Avengers, and who had been approached for a show to rival Thames Television's popular and influential *The Sweeney*. *The Professionals*, shot on 16mm film with a gritty aesthetic, was clearly inspired by the approach pioneered at Euston Films; although, as Joseph Oldham has noted, it offered a lighter treatment of the counter-terror theme than *Special Branch* (2017: 58). The action of the new series centred on the operatives Bodie (Lewis Collins, who replaced Anthony Andrews at the last minute), formerly of the SAS, and Doyle (Martin Shaw), a former policeman, under the supervision of Cowley (Gordon Jackson) at the recently formed agency CI5 (Criminal Intelligence 5). The team tackle the variety of threats facing law and order and counter-insurgency in the late 1970s and early 1980s, domestic and foreign terrorists, the illegal arms trade, political assassination, armed robbery, political corruption and the odd Soviet attempt at subversion.[328] Actors Collins and Shaw spent time preparing for the series training with the army, air force and navy. The no-nonsense tone of the action series was evident in the call to arms which launched the first episode, spoken over the titles by George Cowley: "*Anarchy, acts of terror, crimes against the public. To combat it I've got special men – experts from the army, the police, from every service – these are the professionals*".

Critics found the series violent and derivative, ploughing a similar furrow as recent 'tough-guy' crime-fighting shows like *The Sweeney* (1975-78) and *Target* (BBC, 1977-78), and in particular perceived it as a home-grown buddy cop show to rival the American originals. For *The Telegraph*, *The Professionals* was "Starsky and Hutch *turned thuggish with chin stubble substituted for sex appeal*" (7 January 1978), and for the *Sunday Telegraph* the series evoked the "*above-the-law arrogance of any strong-arm spy thriller and the cultural values of a soft-porn magazine*" (8 January 1978). The *Evening Standard* dismissed the show as an "*absurd crime series*" (7 November 1979) and the *Evening News* complained of "*plastic heroes*" (1 November 1979). The left-wing press was less than amused. The *Morning Star* found *The Professionals* further evidence of the submerged desire in some for a 'police state' in Britain, with CI5 serving as a "*state police agency answerable to nobody but itself*" (18 October 1978); while *The Leveller* judged the "*nasty*" series the "*perfect visual accompaniment to the eighties*" (January 1981). More recently, Joseph Oldham has marked down the fictional CI5 as "*very much a conservative fantasy of cutting through the 'red tape', providing a vaguely defined official carte blanche for rule-bending cops*" (2017: 58).

The Professionals quickly established itself as a top-rated show with the public. Some episodes attracted viewing figures in excess of 18 million and the series was sold to more than 50 countries. *Marketing Review* later judged

The Professionals, "one of the major success stories in television broadcasting anywhere in the world".[329] In the magazine, Clemens stated his intention with the series from the outset: *"We didn't want something parochial however exciting; we wanted a series that would have an international appeal, even though the action was mainly London-based".*[330] Collins and Shaw quickly established themselves as sex symbols, being voted *"TV's Most Compulsive Male Characters"* in the *TV Times* readers' poll of 1981. 15 novels incorporating storylines from the show and seven picture-book annuals were published up to 1985 and further demonstrated the popularity of *The Professionals.* It wasn't all plain sailing for the production though. During the run of the third series, it was reported that the two action leads wanted to leave the show, the especially outspoken Shaw to pursue a more *"serious"* acting career while Collins was unhappy with the scripts (*Evening Standard,* 7 November and *Daily Mail,* 10 November 1979). *The Professionals* managed two further seasons, the final episode being broadcast on 6 February 1983. Some of the critics were now beginning to change their tune and lamented the loss of a thrilling series. The *Guardian* went so far as to judge *The Professionals "consistently the tautest, slickest thriller series British TV has yet produced"* (10 January 1983), and the *Sunday Express* was now claiming that, *"for a car-chasing, action-packed series Bodie and Doyle can't be beaten"* (18 March 1984).[331]

There was something of an 'afterlife' for *The Professionals.* In 1984, there were premature announcements of an unexpected return of the characters to screens with all the lead actors willing to sign up for a feature-length television movie. However, a change of heart at LWT meant that it opted for Joanna Lumley in a new crime-busting show billed as *The Good Guys,* but which never materialised (*The Sun,* 7 January 1981). Initially, repeats of *The Professionals* were astonishingly popular, attracting up to 10 million viewers. However, concerned about his new serious image as an actor (albeit seemingly less so about his personal popularity), and no longer willing to be seen as a *"violent puppet",* Martin Shaw eventually vetoed these (*Sunday Times,* 10 April and *Daily Mail,* 11 April 1988). Affronted, the *Daily Mail* had now taken to referring to *The Professionals* as that *"excellent series"* (13 April 1988). Shaw relented in the early 1990s and in a *"noble gesture"* was reported to have allowed the screenings so that Gordon Jackson's widow could benefit from the fees paid on repeats (*Today,* 14 October 1991).[332]

The format of an elite crime-fighting agency sanctioned from the Home Office surfaced again in *Rules of Engagement* (ITV, 1997), an unsuccessful pilot for a series which never materialised. In its stead, considerable anticipation met *CI5: The New Professionals* (1999), an updated version of the now 'classic' show masterminded by Brian Clemens and David Wickes (who had directed episodes of the original).[333] A 13-part series was independently-produced with financing from City investors and sold to the world television market.[334] Wickes announced that *The New Professionals* would take account of the revised sensibilities of the times, and that the nineties squad would be "*made up of millennium men and women dealing with millennium problems*" (quoted in the *Daily Mail*, 10 June 1997). To the disappointment of hardcore fans, the new team would include the American agent Chris Keel (Kal Weber) and female agent Tina Backus (played by the Canadian Lexa Doig), while British agent Sam Curtis (Colin Wells) helped shoulder the action stuff. The *Evening Standard* correctly judged matters when it predicted that fans of the show would "*struggle to recognise their heroes*" as served up in the form of a "*clean-cut couple of agents ... and a dose of Nineties-style Girl Power*" (26 August 1999). It had originally been announced, to the great excitement of the fans, that Lewis Collins would take on the role of Malone (*The Telegraph*, 10 June 1997), the new chief of CI5, but for undisclosed reasons the part eventually went to Edward Woodward. CI5 would now be an "*international operation tackling emergencies all over the globe*" and some episodes were shot in South Africa and the United States with the agents dealing with such "*millennial*" threats as the traffic in human organs, ivory poaching and the illegal trade in plutonium (*Evening Standard*, 26 August 1999; *Cable Guide*, September 1999).

CI5: *The New Professionals* sold readily to many territories, but could not find a buyer among terrestrial broadcasters nor among the American networks (*The Telegraph*, 8 August 1998; *Evening Standard*, 26 August 1999). In a last-minute deal, the show was sold to the new cable broadcaster Sky in the UK, received minimal exposure and aired in "*cut-down prints*" from September 1999, well after the show had been broadcast in other territories. Despite the pronouncement from Wickes that he intended to "*keep the unique heart of* The Professionals *so that its loyal following will not be disappointed*" (*Daily Mail*, 10 June 1997), fans of the original series were frustrated by the show and its concessions to political correctness, claiming an abandonment of engaging plots, humour, snappy banter, solid performances and funky music, dull storylines and unimaginative dialogue (*Evening Standard*, 26 August 1999). The 1990s had witnessed a revival of interest in the 'lad culture' of the 1970s and films such as *Get Carter* (1971) and television action series like *The Sweeney* had attained iconic status. CI5: *The New Professionals* flew in the face of this nostalgia, alienating a potential audience for the show, and, as predicted in the *Sunday Times*, suffered from failing to recognise the emergence of cultural irony among certain viewers since the original had aired (15 June 1997). The series also failed to attract new viewers in large numbers. There were complaints of the overt commercialism of an approach which numbed the drama through excessive product placement, following deals with Hugo Boss (male fashions and wristwatches), agnés b, Whistles and Jigsaw (fashion and accessories), and Nissan and Lotus (cars) (*Cable Guide*, September 1999). The *Guardian* judged the show a "*classic of unintended comedy*" (13 September 1999) and there was no follow-up series.

C.A.T.S. Eyes was produced at the commercial station Television South (TVS) and broadcast in three seasons comprising of 30 episodes between 1985 and 1987. It was distinctive in that its team of three agents were women recruited to the Covert Activities Thames Section (C.A.T.S.), the refined and classy Pru Standfast (Rosalyn Landor, replaced by Tessa Robinson [Tracy Louise Ward], after series 1), the streetwise and cheeky Frederica Smith (Leslie Ash), and former police officer Maggie Forbes (Jill Gascoine) to supply legitimate police procedure.[335] Set up by the Home Office and responsible to the civil servant Nigel Beaumont (Don Warrington), the section operated as an all-female detective agency and took on 'official' operations as necessary. The initial feature-length episode 'Goodbye Jenny Wren' gave a good indication of the type of dual narrative thrust the series would provide, cutting between a sanctioned action against a Soviet trawler involved in electronic espionage and a private case involving a philandering businessman whom a wife seeks to catch out. Future episodes tended to feature either espionage or crime stories. The series was filmed on location around the Kent area served by TVS, with a production base in the former Chatham Dockyard.

The show was popular, opened with an audience above 11 million and regularly featured in the ratings. *C.A.T.S. Eyes* figured in speculation that television was depicting women as being "*more aggressive, more assertive and more independent*" than in real life, and the series was singled out as "*influential fiction showing the independent woman in a dominant position*" (*The Stage and Television Today*, 1 August 1985).[336] However, this dimension was seemingly lost on reviewers who were generally not impressed by the show. Bemoaning a lack of a "*really good cops and robbers*" series, *Stage and Television Today* dismissed *C.A.T.S. Eyes* as having "*nothing original about it*" (25 April 1985); and the *Guardian* wondered if the girls' "*Oxfam clothes*" were intended as a joke, and squirmed as Pru blurted out such lines as: "*Since we joined the EEC, the Thames estuary and the Medway towns and ports have become the crossroads of European crime, espionage and terrorism. There's more afoot in the lay-bys and cafes around here than in the Whole of London, Paris and Amsterdam put together*", and offered as justification for the setting of the action in the South East (13 April 1985).[337]

Spy comedies and dramas for young adults and children

Television invested less heavily than did British cinema in spy comedies, and managed little success when it did so. *Virgin of the Secret Service*, an unsuccessful spy adventure series of the 1960s, featured the dashing hero Captain Robert Virgin of the Royal Dragoons (Clinton Greyn), was produced at the commercial ATV company and broadcast in a single season of thirteen one-hour episodes in 1968. The action is set in the early 1900s in the period just before the establishment of a permanent Secret Service in Britain, the regular officer Virgin takes his orders from Whitehall and there is a prominent imperial dimension to the drama, with the hero tackling insurrection, misdeeds and crazed local rulers in far-flung parts of the Empire and beyond. Virgin's nemesis is the evil German masterspy Karl Von Brauner (Alexander Dore) and his demented aide Klaus Striebeck (Peter Swannick), which accorded with the contemporary enmities of the spy fever of the period depicted, and romantic interest was provided by the character of Mrs Virginia Cortez (Veronica Strong), an emancipated Edwardian woman. The series was devised by Ted Willis, better-known as the writer and creator of cosy social dramas featuring good-hearted coppers and plucky charwomen such as *Dixon of Dock Green* (1955-76), *Knock on Any Door* (1965-66) and *Mrs Thursday* (1966-67).[338] The series was not granted a network transmission and was scheduled eccentrically around the different ITV regions, and even within some regions, which harmed its chances of attracting a regular audience.

Virgin tended to perplex reviewers who were unsure as to its intention and proposed audience, and the show attracted some shocking notices. Heralded as a "*blood-and-thunder, cliff-hanging spy adventure*" (*Daily Mail*, 6 December 1967), the producers aimed at market differentiation from the contemporary spy thriller, and pointed out that the drama used "*no ingenious and devilish devices, no fast cars, jet planes, mini cameras, secret radios, laser rays, rockets or any of the paraphernalia of the modern spy story*". Virgin was a product of a bygone era, and, as an English officer and gentleman, the King's agent did not "*stoop to the doubtful methods which are a feature of modern espionage*" (*Stage and Television Today*, 29 February 1968). However, was it nostalgic drama, aimed at children, or a send-up? The recent *Carry On* films *Follow That Camel* (1967) and *Carry On Up the Khyber* (1968) had pretty much exhausted the potential for parody in the imperial epic and *Virgin* fell well short of these.[339] The *Daily Mail* found it "*inconceivable that it was not meant to be funny as well as exciting, and incredible that it managed to be neither*" (25 April 1968). *Stage and Television Today* felt that the series was "*too late to be trendy*", having missed the recent fad for Edwardian bric-a-brac and mock imperial fashions, "*Uniforms with brass buttons, posters of Lord Kitchener, enamel advertisements for Bovril*" (10 April 1968), and in this respect, the *Sunday Telegraph* pointed out that the "*basic idea of juxtaposing the present day fad for spy stories and the morals of yesterday was exploited much more neatly in* Adam Adamant" (2 April 1968). The *Guardian*, while bucking the trend and liking the series, fingered the failing of *Virgin* in that it was simply too close in spirit to the old-fashioned *The Four Feathers-* and *The Prisoner of Zenda*-type stories, that its hero was taken too seriously, lacked an appropriate sense of camp and requisite production values, and, consequently, pleased neither the "*childish looking for action and simple morals nor the sophisticated longing for an evening's 'in' joke*" (19 April 1968). The view was echoed in *Variety*'s foreign television section, which dismissed *Virgin* as outdated, "*the kind of comic book adventure stuff which a decade ago was the staple diet fed to subteen audiences at Saturday morning film shows. By failing to go out for the laughs in the right places, the tendency is to find amusement in the wrong ones*" (24 April 1968). The *Sun* marvelled at "*60 inglorious minutes*" (28 March 1968) and the *Sunday Times* at a "*pantomime so grisly it made me squirm with actual embarrassment*" (31 March 1968).

The spy adventure series of the 1960s lingered on in *Spyder's Web*, an offbeat, light-hearted family adventure show comprising of 13 episodes, devised by Richard Harris, produced at ATV and broadcast in 1972. A documentary film unit in a seedy building in Soho, Arachnid Films, is the cover for a clandestine organisation, the Web, which tackles bizarre operations too befuddling for the conventional police and security forces. The unit is headed by the dynamic Lottie Dean (Patricia Cutts), while the debonair agent seconded from MI5 Clive Hawskworth (Anthony Ainley) assumes most of the cloak and dagger responsibilities. Writer Roy Clarke claimed that he approached *Spyder's Web* "*largely for laughs, and a chance to invent oddball characters*" (*TV Times*, 15-21 January 1972: 8). Hawskworth, for example, was cast as an anachronistic 'Bulldog' Drummond-type, and the modern if authoritative Lottie let in a little female glamour and emancipation. The eccentric stories pitted the team against suspect defectors, murderous conspiracies and bizarre plots to liberate the Isle of Wight, and the eccentric, tongue in cheek approach of the series aligned it with the quirky spy and crime adventures of the 1960s such as *The Avengers* and *Adam Adamant Lives!*, which had also played with the tension between modernity and tradition. The show was popular, appearing in the network ratings and regularly attracting viewing figures of six-seven million.

Cult interest in the series resides in Hammer horror star Veronica Carlson who plays Tolstoy-reading secretary Wallis Ackroyd with an exaggerated northern accent. The reviewer in the *Guardian* discerned a "*camp, clever savagery"* in *Spyder's Web*, which she felt *"might make quite a good strip car-toon"*, but was not sure whether it worked in a television drama series (22 January 1972). Other reviewers, while noting the novelty of having a female head of an espionage outfit, similarly felt the series fell uncertainly between comedy and spy thriller. In two separate reviews, *The Telegraph* offered that the series could be viewed as a *"victory for Women's Lib"*, but that apart, it *"did not send up the whole business of secret agents as thoroughly as* Get Smart, *or create an exotic fantasy world, as in* The Avengers" (22 January 1972), and later dismissing *Spyder's Web* as *"nonsense, without having* The Avengers*'s merit of being elegant nonsense"* (25 March 1972). Shot in colour, all but two of the episodes now only survive in black and white.

The Secret Service, broadcast in 1969, was the final 'Supermarionation' series produced by the Century 21 Television production company established by the legendary Gerry and Sylvia Anderson. It comprised of 13 episodes and followed such successes as *Stingray* (1964-65) and *Thunderbirds* (1965-66). The series was based around the eccentric actor Stanley Unwin, famous for his nonsensical 'gobbledegook' language which so took the fancy of Gerry Anderson. The character of Father Stanley Unwin is a rural parish priest and undercover agent for British Intelligence Service Headquarters, Operation Priest (B.I.S.H.O.P.). Able to miniaturise his assistant Matthew Harding using a device called 'The Minimiser', the pair undertakes a variety of dangerous missions. Unwin serves the intelligence chief 'The Bishop', who is based in Whitehall, and other series characters include Agent Blake and the unsuspecting housekeeper Mrs. Appleby. At least once each episode, Father Unwin uses his 'gobbledegook' to confound some innocent interloper who annoyingly delays him on his mission.

The unusual premise did not go down well with television executives, especially Lew Grade who headed the distribution company ITC, and the show managed only a limited regional broadcast in Great Britain and was quickly forgotten. It did though, despite lingering suspicions to the contrary, sell to the South and North American markets where it managed a limited broadcast, and to such territories as Taiwan and the Philippines (*Back Stage*, 13 February and 6 March 1970; *Variety*, 11 February and 24 June 1970). *The Secret Service* developed the marionette puppetry techniques of its forerunners with a greater use of live action, especially around the character of Unwin. The episodes had Unwin and Harding pitted against a conspiracy, a gang of saboteurs, attempts to steal cutting-edge technology and experimental weapons, and plots to assassinate visiting dignitaries. The formal inventiveness of *The Secret Service*, its idiosyncrasy and quaintness, and its pleasing mock-baroque theme tune by regular Barry Gray, make for an unconventional and rather fun spy drama, but it was poorly received and has attracted only a few defenders. In comparison with the futuristic qualities of previous Supermarionation shows, *The Secret Service*, with its rural parish and frock-coated priest driving an antique 1917 Ford Model T car, seemed old fashioned, even reactionary, and could hardly be expected to appeal greatly to children. The storylines depict a Britain under siege from despicable foreign agents intent on stealing its secrets, and it was perhaps too great a leap of faith to expect an ageing man of the cloth and the invention of an eccentric parishioner to deal with the threat. The conflation of Church and 'secret state' is possibly unique in British spy fiction, and the characterisation of Father Unwin perhaps drew inspiration from G. K. Chesterton's famous amateur sleuth Father Brown. Century 21 had achieved greater success with *Captain Scarlet* (1967-68) and *Joe 90* (1968-69), shows which drew on aspects of Cold War paranoia and secret agent mania.[340]

Tightrope was unusual in being a spy thriller aimed at young adults, the generic requirements of sex and violence allied to a plot centred on complex geopolitical tensions tending to target secret agent stories at more mature readers and viewers, the exceptions being 'family' shows like *Danger Man* and *The Avengers*. The drama was devised and written by Victor Pemberton, produced at the commercial ATV Company in 13 half-hour episodes all ending in a cliff-hanger, and broadcast in 1972. The story is set in a school where sixth form pupil Martin Clifford (Spencer Banks) is drawn into a deadly conspiracy. Regular school educational programmes are interrupted by unscheduled 'Voice of Truth' broadcasts inciting students to take political action; shortly after he warns Martin to be vigilant the headmaster is attacked and killed; several of the teachers begin to behave strangely; a shadowy and eccentric character Forrester (John Savident) claims to serve British Intelligence and asks the sceptical Martin for help; Martin's father is arrested on suspicion of sabotage at a nearby American air force base; a Russian submarine is stationed off the coast of East Anglia; and an American air force security officer is murdered. Martin is drawn into various adventures, in which he is drugged, incarcerated, attacked by a mysterious character in black coat and white gloves, nearly blown-up, and held captive alongside Forrester onboard a Soviet trawler. In a deepening mystery, Martin is unsure whom he can trust and what is the nature of the conspiracy. In the final outcome, the 'Voice of Truth' is revealed as a long-term Soviet plan to revolutionise British youth, the authoritarian teacher Fletcher is the killer with the white gloves, and math's teacher Miss Walker is really Major Svedlov of the KGB, the agent charged with realising the Russian plot.

The complicated story, full of twists and turns, makes unusual demands on the intelligence of a young audience: in terms of awareness of Cold War history and characters such as the atom spy Klaus Fuchs and the traitor Kim Philby; and in terms of geographical and ideological alignments required to understand the position of a school teacher who is a former Hungarian dissident. There is a surprising feeling of conspiracy and paranoia in *Tightrope*, a strong hint of the 'secret state' in this children's drama; in the sense that a sleepy English village is under the sway of official forces, where innocent-seeming school teachers are in fact security officers and enemy agents, the landlord of the pub a double-agent, and the local postmistress a code-breaker and wireless operator. The quirky elements in the story follow in the tradition of such adventure series as *The Avengers* and *The Prisoner*. Ultimately, *Tightrope* portrays a conservative ideology, expressing contemporary anxieties about dissident youth. At one point in the drama, for example, there is a 'sit-in' of sixth form students; however, Martin grows to respect his father, a simple security guard at the air base, and Forrester's aim is to train a cadre of youthful spies to demonstrate the essential soundness and patriotism of young people. The series, produced in colour, only survives in black and white. *Tightrope* was something of a 'star vehicle' for Spencer Banks who had previously scored in the popular children's sci-fi series *Timeslip* (1970-71).

The spy-farce *The Top Secret Life of Edgar Briggs* was produced at the commercial London Weekend Television and broadcast in a series of 13 half-hour episodes in 1974. *Briggs* had been written by Richard Laing and Bernard McKenna especially for comedy actor David Jason who was previously best-known as a comic foil of Ronnie Barker in such series as *Hark at Barker* (1969-70), *Six Dates with Barker* (1971) and *His Lordship Entertains* (1972). Briggs is deputy controller in a branch of the Secret Service and despite his crippling ineptitude and bumbling, and to the eternal surprise of his incredulous associates, he always foils the plot, saves the intended victim, exposes the enemy network or reveals the traitor. The producer Humphrey Barclay called the approach "*crazy and chaotic*" (*Stage and Television Today*, 5 September 1974). The series, which did not parody any specific paratext such as James Bond and simply relied on slapstick and sight gags, was a disappointment and was removed from its network spot on Sunday evenings after only four weeks and replaced by the American filmed series *Planet of the Apes* (1974).[341] The show tended to bemuse reviewers who found the comedy too broad and corny, although the *Guardian* thought it had something going for it as a comedy of the "*absurd*" (30 September 1974). Plaudits tended to be restricted to the performance skills and pratfalls of Jason, as when *Variety* praised his "*plentiful gifts of timing, movement and mugging*" (2 October 1974) and the *Guardian* his "*immaculate deadpan elan*" (30 September 1974). A more recent view following the show's belated release on DVD despaired of a gifted comic actor "*reduced to clowning*" (*Sight and Sound*, June 2015: 100).[342]

The spy thriller thrived on British television from the 1960s through the 1980s, providing thrills and excitement for the popular audience. It assumed a variety of dramatic styles, being central to the adventure series of the 1960s, producing secret agent stories and dispensing team-oriented action in more realist spy procedurals in the 1970s and 1980s, and offering a smattering of comedies and children's entertainment from time to time. The production style of these shows, in line with television more generally, shifted from the 'intimate' aesthetics of the multi-camera television studio, an approach suitable for more parochial storylines and characterisations, to the more 'cinematic' aesthetics of single-camera shooting on film, an approach pioneered in the adventure series of the 1960s, taken-up by some spy thrillers in the 1970s, and dominant by the 1990s as the guarantor of quality for selling dramas on the international market. With the exception of some spy procedurals, these shows rarely attracted serious critical attention at the time; however, reviewers had more to get to grips with in the form of the espionage drama as it transferred to television, especially in the adaptations of 'serious' spy authors like John le Carré into pioneering television drama serials. This work is examined in detail in the following chapter.

4.
The Espionage Drama on Television

Anyway, the whole business of spying is a complete load of nonsense … It is a means by which the State oppresses its own people and has nothing to do with national security at all. If recent events are to be believed, the whole of the spy network works for the other side anyway.
(*The Scotsman*, 21 April 1984)

The new style spy fiction of the early 1960s also found a space for itself in the television schedules. There were major adaptations of both John le Carré and Len Deighton in the 1970s and 1980s, in which the cynical school of espionage drama with its uncertainties, moral complexity, cynicism and characteristic theme of betrayal, found an expression. The approach adopted a populist form in the guise of working-class spy Callan. The eponymous series ran for four seasons between 1967 and 1972 and offered a deglamorised, downbeat treatment of counter-espionage, a world of intimidation, anti-heroism and class consciousness which was tremendously influential and popular with viewers. Leading playwrights like Dennis Potter and Stephen Poliakoff also wrote serious drama for television, exploring complex themes of loyalty, class and exile in the world of the clandestine. Plays such as Potter's 'Traitor' (1971) and *Blade on the Feather* (1980), and Poliakoff's 'Soft Targets' (1982) represent a serious dramatic engagement with the spy story and an ambition for the spy drama well above the run of the mill.

The prestige format for British television drama was the single-play, and a number of respected anthology strands were in place in the schedules by the 1960s. Increasingly discussed and commented on in public during the period, espionage in all its ramifications was a likely subject for television dramatists and a number of plays tackled spying and Cold War tensions. 'The Scent of Fear' was an hour-long drama broadcast in ABC's *Armchair Theatre* series in 1959 and the first full-length television play written by the respected Ted Willis. Allegedly, it was a true story related by former air hostess Mary Higgins Clark and dealt with a stowaway (Neil McCallum) aboard a plane departing from an Iron Curtain country, shielded by a stewardess (Dorothy Tutin) and sought by a secret policeman (Anthony Quayle) before it lands in London (*Stage and Television Today*, 3 September 1959). 'Flight from Treason' (*Arm-*

chair Mystery Theatre, 1960) and 'The Omega Mystery' (*Armchair Theatre*, 1961) seem to have been abortive pilots for a proposed adventure series written by James Mitchell and starred John Gregson and Donald Churchill as unconventional spycatchers. 'Hedgehog' was an hour-long drama broadcast in the BBC *Sunday-Night Play* strand in 1962 starring Muriel Pavlov and Patrick Barr, in which threat is visited on a family by the brother of the East-European wife, and who is seeking secrets from a nearby government establishment. None of these plays was out-of-the-ordinary and reviewed at best politely (see *Stage and Television Today*, 17 September 1959, 14 September 1961 and 6 September 1962). While the single-play offered the prospect of respectability, the critical standing of the spy story at the time tended to pull in the opposite direction. The problem for the espionage drama on television lay with the suspicion in which the genre was held. As was still being noted much later in the *Weekend Telegraph*, even one of its leading writers found it difficult to be taken seriously. "*Because his books have bold, bright covers and sell in large quantities at international airports*" the argument ran, "*there are still people who fondly believe that Len Deighton is little more than a purveyor of pulp*" (1 October 1988). It would be a struggle for the 'up-market' spy story to overturn the prejudices attending the spy thriller.

A critical breakthrough came with the single-play drama 'A Magnum for Schneider', broadcast in February of 1967 as part of the prestigious drama strand *Armchair Theatre*.[343] It was a more successful effort by James Mitchell and dealt with a shadowy counter-intelligence department and its coercion of an agent to liquidate a German arms dealer. The play attracted much better notices than previous espionage dramas, *Stage and Television Today* admiring the script as "*tight, laconic and mercifully unmannered*", noted its close relationship with the "*low-key realism le Carré school of spies*", and correctly predicted that the "*special agent could go far*" (9 February 1967). 'A Magnum for Schneider' stood in contrast to the glossy productions of the contemporary adventure series and managed to attract a respectable 5.7 million viewers. The hardboiled drama was counter to the flamboyant mood of the contemporary spy adventure series and was keyed more to the disillusion of industrial disputes, balance of payment crises, states of emergency, the retreat from 'East of Suez', and the assorted harsher realities that were the flipside of the 'Swinging Sixties' (Burton 2008).[344]

From an early date, there was a view that 'A Magnum for Schneider' would be an appropriate pilot for a secret agent series, and the character of the reluctant spy Callan was revived for four extremely popular seasons, broadcast later in 1967 and in 1969 (black and white), and in 1970 and 1972 (colour). The first series was produced at ABC TV, while the subsequent series were produced at the successor station Thames Television. The lower-class Callan was played by Edward Woodward and the show concentrated on the drama of a situation which had the agent reluctantly working for 'The Section', a 'dirty tricks' department responsible for assassination, extortion and blackmail, all the jobs that are too suspect and sordid for the conventional Security Service. Callan is a specialist, a master safe-cracker and executioner, but also a man with a conscience who has to live with the consequences of his actions. He is a man who is good at what he does, but doesn't like doing it, and uncomfortably for his superiors he is insubordinate and likes to know 'why' a job has to be done. Reginald Colin, who joined the show as a producer from the second series onwards, aimed at a human drama rather than a clichéd spy thriller, claiming that, "*What I tried to do throughout the entire series was to show a human being under pressure. Sometimes under pressure of death, always on the limit of his nerves, because that is what television does best: to see how individuals act under pressure*" (quoted in Pixley 1987: 27).[345] As Joseph Oldham has recently observed, *Callan* was "*one of the first television spy series to extensively site its drama within the conspiratorial workings of the secret state*" and provided an "*unusually psychological focus for a spy drama of the period*" (2017: 17).

The series, with its pronounced class and psychological dimensions and low-key London settings, was an important contribution to the realistic espionage story of the 1960s and 1970s, and stands in a direct line of decent from the Len Deighton stories *The Ipcress File* (1962) and *Funeral in Berlin* (1964). This was noted when the first series of *Callan* was announced in the summer of 1967 and the new "*reluctant spy-hero*" was reckoned to have "*much in common with Harry Palmer, even to the off-London accent and the running feud with his superiors*" (*Stage and Television Today*, 20 July 1967). David Callan was a further drop down the social scale from Deighton's lower-middle class but aspirational secret agent and, at least in Callan's domestic circumstances, marked the appearance, still rare, of the blue collar spy.[346] The reluctant Callan heralded the arrival of the anti-hero on British television. *Stage and Television Today* noted the approach as the "*reversal of the J. Bond formula*", commenting that, "*Callan's spying horizons are altogether more modest, not to say tawdry*". In marking the character as "*lower class in a totally unfashionable, chip-on-shoulder way*", and "*neither functionally callous nor cool and detached*", the reviewer unconsciously exposed Callan's differentiation from Deighton's trendy and of the moment 'Harry Palmer' (18 May 1972). Some years after the initial broadcasts, the *Daily Mail* neatly pinpointed the character as the "*insubordinate, subordinate*": "*working-class, stoical, sadistic, solitary, bloody-minded to a fault, who became a ratings winner by being a perennial loser*" (3 September 1981).[347] As a number of observers have noted, Callan's antagonism with his superior Hunter subverts the tradition within the Ian Fleming stories of James Bond's unswerving loyalty to M. Even in a genre

notable for its masculine qualities, *Callan* was particularly ruthless in its denial of narrative space for women; the only recurring female character being
Liz March (Lisa Langdon), who as Hunter's secretary was only briefly
glimpsed in 31 episodes.[348]

The dynamic of the series had Callan in conflict with Hunter, head of the
Section (the various incarnations were played by Ronald Radd, Michael
Goodliffe, Derek Bond and William Squire), and a strong antagonism exists
between Callan and a rival agent, the public-school bully and socially superior Toby Meres (Anthony Valentine, Peter Bowles in the pilot-play). This rivalry
is temporarily transferred to the cocky younger agent Cross (Patrick Mower)
in the third and part of the fourth series, where age becomes the mark of
contrast and competitiveness, before Meres returned for the final nine episodes.[349] A further significant series character was the insanitary Lonely (Russell Hunter), a petty thief whom Callan intimidates to acquire information
and burgle premises. The offbeat and sometimes touching relationship between Callan and Lonely was a significant factor in the popularity of the show.
The overall approach was unglamorous, the characters, though fascinating,
often unappealing, and there is a sense of unease and moral uncertainty
about much of the work undertaken by the Section. Callan, in stark contrast
to James Bond, is an ordinary Londoner, a man with a stain in his past which
is the leverage that Hunter uses against him. He lives in a dingy flat in Shepherd's Bush, eats at cheap workers' cafés and seemingly leads no kind of social life. The sense of austerity was further maintained by resisting "*all temptations to become gimmicky*" as well as by the complete absence of background music in the screen stories (*Stage and Television Today*, 30 October
1969).

Initially, Callan is an outsider, a former agent now pressured by Hunter to
take on special assignments for the Section. Ordinarily, he works as a lowly
book-keeper. In series two, he returns to the Section where he serves as the
leading operative. During series four, Callan is reluctantly promoted to
Hunter, a role which tests his conscience even further as he now has operational leadership and life and death decisions to take. With the death of Cross
in 'If He Can, So Could I', Callan is returned to operational duty. Throughout,
Callan is involved in a variety of cases and assignments which effectively
traverse the spectrum of Cold War, domestic subversion and terrorist activities and threats. In 'The Good Ones are All Dead' (1967) Callan must determine if a businessman is a wanted war criminal; in 'Red Knight, White Knight'
(1969) he rightly suspects a KGB defector is an assassin intending to kill
Hunter; in 'Amos Green Must Die' (1970) the Section is detailed to guard a
controversial right-wing politician and Callan closes in on a black militant
assassin[350]; and in the three-part 'The Richmond File' (1972), which brought

the series to an end, Callan plays a cat and mouse game with the high-ranking KGB agent.[351]

From the second series onwards, *Callan* was one of the most popular dramas on television. During the 1969 and 1970s seasons the show regularly topped the ratings with as many as 13 million viewers and remained Thames's highest-rated drama success until the police drama *Van der Valk* in 1973 (*Stage and Television Today*, 1 May 1969, 11 June 1970 and 25 October 1973). It was reputedly the favourite show of the two-time Labour Prime Minister Harold Wilson, a politician who held a jaundiced view of British Intelligence.[352] At the culmination of season two, in the story 'Death of a Hunter', Callan had been originally killed at the end of the drama, and when this was leaked to the public, the audience reacted strongly, and there was even a 'Callan Lives' graffiti campaign. The producers backtracked, shot a new ending in which Callan was only wounded and the agent was reinstated (Pixley 1987: 28; Callan: *This Man Alone*, Network DVD 2015). In 1972, the *Daily Mail* was unequivocal in stating Callan, "*Britain's most popular secret agent*" (4 November) and labelled him a "*telefolk hero*" (2 March).

Many reviewers recognised something fresh and original in *Callan* and yet struggled to place it critically and worried about its brutality. The *Sun* captured the ambivalence when it described the characterisation as "*repulsively attractive*" (30 January 1969), as did *The Telegraph* when it portrayed the series as "*sickening, artificial, confusing and gripping*" (6 February 1969). In a similar vein, the *Daily Express*, three years later, wrote of the drama's "*uncompromisingly vicious world of high spying*" and declared David Callan "*one of the most compulsively unattractive, implausible characters ever to reach TV*" (2 March 1972).The *Sun* was still perplexed at the time of the third series, finding the drama "*monstrously unreal*", even "*corny*"; "*Yet*", admitting that, "*it keeps you sitting there unable sometimes to move*" (9 April 1970). The *Daily Mirror* noted the drama's "*seedy menace*" and marked the series as "*brutal, rough, tough stuff*" (30 January 1969). There were comparisons with the downbeat *Public Eye* (1965-75), a show about a moody, embittered private detective, and in the same way *Callan* was appreciated as "*seedy where others are glossy*", a show that flattered "*the plebs by suggesting that a proletarian hero can be every bit as good as the old school tie brigade, if not a bit better*", and made "*the whole horrible business seem somehow cosy and shabby as an old suit*" (*Sunday Times*, 30 March 1969; *The Telegraph*, 9 April 1970).[353] *The Telegraph* was not a fan, but acknowledged a "*loving and meticulous bit of pop mythmaking*" (12 April 1970), while the *Daily Sketch* wondered at the morality of *Callan*, claiming that, "*Callan's world is an unhealthy place where the best people cultivate the worst instincts*" (9 April 1970). Writing at the time of the final series, the *Daily Mail* commented that, "*Production, script and direction were scrupulously true to their chosen idiom and contrived as always a curiously pungent authenticity"* (2 March 1972). In total, there were 43 episodes of *Callan* across four seasons.[354]

James Mitchell eventually lost interest in the drama series form and declared himself *"far more interested in writing a cinema version for Woodward"* (quoted in the *Daily Mail*, 4 November 1972). In 1971, Hammer Films had expressed interest in a *Callan* movie; and American producers sought an option on Mitchell's Callan novel *Russian Roulette* (1973) (Callan: *This Man Alone*, Network DVD 2015). In the outcome, there appeared an eponymously titled British feature film in 1974, directed by Don Sharp, expanded from the original story of 'A Magnum for Schneider', which had Callan assigned to assassinate an arms dealer, and is one of the better spin-offs from the small to big screen in the period. The film critic at the *Observer* found it *"surprisingly enjoyable"*, well-directed and acted, *"entirely gripping"* (26 May 1974), the *Sunday Times* felt the picture deserved *"honourable mention"* and offered a *"sharp neat plot and a good deal more feeling for character than is usual in such exercises in violence"* (26 May 1974), and the *Morning Star* argued that the *"chilling authenticity of* Callan *cannot be dismissed as easily as the wish fulfilment fantasies of James Bond"* (24 May 1974). The *Guardian* admired the barely held tensions between Callan (Edward Woodward) and Hunter (Eric Porter) and Meres (Peter Egan), perfect little *"studies in the subtle gradations of English class viciousness"* (23 May 1974).[355]

The eminent cultural critic Raymond Williams declared a special interest in *Callan* among secret agent shows, as belonging with Len Deighton and John le Carré to the *"anti-romanticism"* of *"disillusioned spy fiction"*. The reversal in direction from *"glamorised intelligence"* he saw as *"sharper"* in *Callan*. In *Callan*, he noted that, *"our introduction to the agent is not in Mayfair or Crete or the Bahamas, with careful allusions to exotic literature or exotic drinks, but in a bleak flat where he has a cold and is trying to clear it with a towel over a basin"*. Williams noted an *"overwhelming, inescapable but unaccepted alienation"* in the drama and saw a *"corroding self-deprecation and irony"* as the real significance of *Callan*. Unexpectedly, then, a secret agent drama series expressed a real *"contempt for the system in which he is trapped"* and for the employers who are *"self-evidently trivial, stylish, unfeeling and dishonest"*. Through serving, Williams asserted, Callan knows he is *"destroying himself and others"* (1972).

A final, belated screen outing for the agent came in 1981 with the feature-length television drama *Wet Job*, made for ATV Television, in which Callan is forced out of retirement to deal with a past antagonist who threatens to expose the former agent in his memoirs, but in fact intends to kill him. A subplot involves a dissident writer, spirited out of Czechoslovakia and now a target for the KGB. Writer James Mitchell had carefully not killed off the character and eventually he met up with Woodward again and discussed what Callan would be like 10 years older (*Wet Job* press sheet). Appealing to fans and the curious, and billed as "*The Return of Callan*", *Wet Job* was popular and made sixth place in the ITV ratings for its week of broadcast, but was poorly received. The *Daily Express* called it a "*wash-out*" and was disappointed that "*such a noble piece of work as the original* Callan *should come to this*" (3 September 1981); and for the reviewer at the *Daily Mail*, it was "*like reaching into the wardrobe for a favourite old sports jacket only to find that the tweed has the moth in it*" (3 September 1981). The *Guardian* summed matters up when it offered: "*There may be a limit to the decrepitude a faithful fan will take and probably Callan should take it no further than this*" (3 August 1981).

Callan was a qualified critical success and the benchmark television spy series of the late 1960s and early 1970s against which all others were measured. Edward Woodward was acclaimed for his portrayal of the disillusioned agent, winning the British Academy of Film and Television Best Actor TV Award, the *Evening Standard* TV Actor of the Year Award, and the *Sun* Best Actor of the Year TV Award all in 1970. Callan was named The Most Compulsive Male TV Character by the *TV Times* in 1972. *Callan* has slowly attracted a cult around it with devoted fans and admirers. When the second and third seasons were re-run on Channel 4 in 1984 it was described as the "*ultimate urban spy series*" (*Callan* press sheet), and the show remains one of the most fondly remembered of all British television spy dramas.[356]

Case file 1: John le Carré on the small screen

There is something about his writing that makes it particularly suitable for television adaption – perhaps its innerness, its feeling of privacy, its introversion. Watching it alone, at home on a small screen, perhaps is the right way to see a drama of personal confusion, personal betrayals and personal understanding.
(Review of *A Perfect Spy*, The Telegraph, 5 November 1987)

Not many authors of distinction have been so well-served by film (or telefilm) as to stunning realization of character and fidelity of atmosphere, nuance and all that jazz. Le Carré should count himself lucky. His fans too.
(Review of *Smiley's People*, Variety, 29 September 1982)

Like most authors, I am a timid creature, and desperately scared of the screen presentation of my work.
(John le Carré, *Sunday Telegraph Magazine*, 21 October 1979)

In the 1960s, John le Carré's genre-revising espionage novels were readily adapted for the cinema, perhaps most successfully with *The Spy Who Came in from the Cold* (1966). Commencing in the 1970s, his phenomenally popular spy stories began to be translated to the small screen where they often set a new benchmark for television drama and established a gold-standard for the representation of *"up-market espionage"* on television (Oldham 2013: 729-738).[357] The author's characteristic setting of the 'Circus', his name for the Secret Intelligence Service (SIS), coupled with the theme of moral ambiguity, were developed in a series of novels which set out the discrepancy between what a country purports to stand for, and what is done in its name. In a world where official secrecy is all-pervasive, he appeared to suggest, the spy novel performs a small, seemingly subversive but necessary democratic function; namely, to *"hold up a mirror, however distorted, to the secret world and demonstrate the monster it could become"* (*Sunday Times*, 1 November 1987).[358]

John le Carré's first work to appear on television was 'The End of the Line', a single-play drama produced at Thames Television which was broadcast in the respected *Armchair Theatre* strand.[359] The only story the author has written specifically for the small screen, it was a wordy and enigmatic piece featuring simply two characters, set on the train journey from Edinburgh to London. A young minister (Ian Holm) unaccountably enters a first-class train compartment reserved solely for a senior government scientist (Robert Harris). The latter nervously engages the former in conversation and the strange encounter switches tone between intimidation, flattery and sexual suggestiveness, authority and dominance shifting around the two characters. It emerges that the scientist has been romantically enticed by a Soviet controller and subsequently given away secrets, and that the clergyman is in fact a MI5 agent drawing on the form of the confessional to extract an admission of guilt from the scientist. The theme of betrayal was typical territory for le Carré, and the claustrophobic setting and mood of submerged threat and aggression were Pinteresque. The reviewer at the *Guardian* accepted the play in this mood, finding it *"dense"* and *"disturbing"* (30 June 1970). For a reviewer at *Stage and Television Today*, jaded by the recent poor quality of ITV programming, 'The End of the Line' *"was like a shining jewel in a sea of mud"*. While le Carré's play was not a great work, the acting of Harris and Holm was judged first-rate, and Alan Cooke's direction took advantage of the confines of the set, making the train compartment as *"big as an average torture chamber, which is exactly what it was"* (2 July 1970). The play is little known and seemingly was granted only a single television broadcast.[360]

Questions of loyalty, betrayal and faithfulness in a faithless world were expanded from the chamber piece of 'The End of the Line' and provided with a grand stage in the novel *Tinker, Tailor, Soldier, Spy,* a highly unusual, complex and influential espionage story, the seventh novel of John le Carré, first published in 1974 and a huge best-seller. Le Carré maintained that for some time he had aimed to reverse the situation in *The Spy Who Came in from the Cold* and deal with a traitor inside our own Service (Deindorfer 1974: 15). The back-story concerns Operation TESTIFY, an aggressive action in Czechoslovakia involving the British agent Jim Prideaux and ostensibly to recruit a Czech general. The operation goes wrong and the resulting scandal brings down Control and those officers most closely associated with him, chiefly George Smiley his deputy. About a year later, an insignificant operative named Ricki Tarr suddenly appears in London with an extraordinary story claiming a Soviet 'mole' in the 'Circus', a deep penetration agent in the higher echelons of the SIS. In a most secret operation, Smiley is brought in out of the cold and charged to investigate Tarr's accusations and review the shambles of Operation TESTIFY to see what light it might throw on the possibility of Soviet penetration. He is assisted by Peter Guillam who heads up the strong arm boys of the Service and who surreptitiously acquires documents and information for Smiley to assess; while Smiley unobtrusively interviews the other casualties of the catastrophe to build up a more precise picture of TESTIFY and try to identify the 'mole' known as 'Gerald'. Smiley is also interested in 'Merlin', a valued Soviet informer who is too good to be believed. A subtext involves the parallel betrayal of Smiley by his promiscuous wife Ann. A version of the traditional nursery rhyme and counting game, 'Tinker, Tailor, Soldier, Spy' is used in the story to code the suspects for the 'mole' in MI6.

Smiley reveals that Control had hoped with TESTIFY to flush out the 'mole', but that Soviet Intelligence was aware of his scheme, scuppered the operation and relied on the resulting scandal to disgrace Control and see a dangerous opponent removed from office. 'Merlin' is also revealed as bogus, a Soviet deception to hide the 'mole' behind a smokescreen of success. The traitor in the ranks is revealed as the glamorous Bill Haydon, one of the most brilliant officers at the 'Circus', who had cruelly carried on an affair with Ann, and is killed by his protégé and possibly former lover Prideaux before he can be exchanged with the Russians.

Tinker, Tailor, Soldier, Spy, the first novel of the Karla trilogy and which introduced the Soviet Spymaster Karla, was followed by *The Honourable Schoolboy* (1977) and *Smiley's People* (1979). The story introduced and helped popularise le Carré's lexicon of the secret world of British Intelligence, terms such as 'mole', 'lamplighters', 'scalphunters', 'ferrets', 'babysitters', the 'Circus', and 'pavement artists'; jargon of the tradecraft and secret world of agents which cast a hue of authenticity on the fiction and more than hinted at the chummy homosocial environments of public-school and gentleman's club.

The novel included characters that had appeared in the author's previous novels, such as Smiley, Guillam and Inspector Mendel formerly of Special Branch.[361]

There is a melancholic aspect to the story, a sense of passing and of looking back, of a former good time when Englishmen could be proud. The nostalgia is shattered by the revelations and the new realities, and the spirit is captured in a character's lament with George Smiley that a generation and class of men were now lost and redundant: "*Poor loves. Trained to Empire, trained to rule the waves. All gone. All taken away*". A pronounced anti-Americanism underpins the sense of loss, of new rivalry and of inferiority. We are told of Control's attitude to the Americans, that he "*despised them and all their works, which he frequently sought to undermine*". For Bill Haydon it was unbearable to witness the passing of British prestige and its replacement by "*greed and constipation*" in the hands of Americans. "*He hated America very deeply*"; and when it came to choose against the United States or Soviet Russia, "*he would prefer it to be the East*". An "*aesthetic judgement*" as much as a "*moral choice*", he maintained. Such anti-Americanism had some historical credibility and was typical of members of the Cambridge Spies, their KGB handler reporting that the group, through demonstrating a profound love of England, never considered themselves unpatriotic, but "*worked tirelessly against the Americans*" (Modin 1994: 272; see also, Boyle 1980: 311, 384).

The great theme of *Tinker, Tailor, Soldier, Spy* is betrayal. "*Haydon had betrayed*", we are told: "*As a lover, a colleague, a friend; as a patriot; as a member of that inestimable body which Ann loosely called the Set: in every capacity, Haydon had overtly pursued one aim and secretly achieved its opposite*". For all that, Haydon is a romantic symbol of Englishness, the last of a type; an inspiration for Guillam, and for Smiley a man to be pitied. After all, had not Haydon been betrayed by the forces of history, "*an ambitious man born to the big canvas*"; "*for whom reality was a poor island with scarcely a voice that could carry across the water*". The review in *Sight and Sound* described *Tinker* as the "*quintessential post-war spy story, which as we know is about betrayal, the fourth and fifth men, the double agent and the double game*" (Winter 1979: 58); and in the character of Bill Haydon, many critics have sensed a mediation on the double-agent Kim Philby, of whom John le Carré, the former MI6 officer, was a harsh critic (Willmetts and Moran 2013; Oldham 2013).[362]

Le Carré has reported that he turned down movie offers for the book because he thought that the condensation necessary would be impossible (*The Listener*, 13 September 1979). *Tinker, Tailor, Soldier, Spy* had first been considered for adaptation for the small screen at the commercial company London Weekend Television in 1975, with producer Richard Bates and writer Julian Bond (*Daily Express*, 12 April 1975; *Stage and Television Today*, 23 January

1975), with possibly Paul Scofield or James Mason playing Smiley (Sisman 2015: 394). The proposal was for a longer format 12-part serial, but when the head of programmes Cyril Bennet died in a fall, the idea was dropped (*Daily Mail*, 8 September 1979).[363] *Tinker Tailor Soldier Spy* (without the commas) was eventually adapted as a £1 million, 7-part television drama serial produced at the BBC in association with the American Paramount Television, and first broadcast in 1979.[364] The distinguished cast was headed by Alec Guinness as George Smiley, and included Ian Richardson, Ian Bannen, Hywel Bennett, Beryl Reid and Michael Jayston.[365]

The television serial form was a revered standard of British television drama, with acclaimed adaptations of the classics of Jane Austen, Charles Dickens, George Elliot and Thomas Hardy. In the 1970s, the strand was updated to include more contemporary authors and novels, such as Rebecca West's *The Birds Fall Down* (BBC, 1978), Vera Brittain's *Testament of Youth* (BBC, 1979) and Evelyn Waugh's *Brideshead Revisited* (ITV, 1981).[366] *Tinker, Tailor, Soldier, Spy* was considered a novel of sufficient literary merit to be dramatised as a classic serial and emerged as "*the BBC's most elaborate and expensive productions ever of a recent best-seller*" (*Sun*, 8 September 1979).[367] The creative team of producer Jonathan Powell, director John Irvin and writer Arthur Hopcraft had recent experience on such acclaimed dramas and adaptations as *Hard Times* (ITV, 1977), *The Nearly Man* (ITV, 1974, 1975) and *The Mayor of Casterbridge* (BBC, 1978).[368] It was reported that le Carré wanted to see *Tinker, Tailor, Soldier, Spy* on screen, but, wary from previous screen treatments of his novels, was "*worried that the novel's complex and impenetrable character would be trivialized or over-simplified by a careless production*" (quoted in the *Daily Mail*, 8 September 1979). *Tinker Tailor Soldier Spy* was the first drama to be shot entirely on film at the BBC, something Powell was insistent on, and used the prestige of the cinema actor Guinness to convince the BBC to shoot with film.[369] Shooting on 16mm film was becoming standard for action series such as *The Sweeney* (1975-78) and the standard was decided on for *Tinker* as it would help denote the contemporary nature of the setting. Principally concerned with quality, the adaptation was not approached primarily in terms of genre, but rather more in terms of the literary value of the classic serial (Oldham 2017: 84, 74). Extensive locations included Portugal, the Austrian/Czech border, Scotland, Oxford, Buckinghamshire, Berkshire, Gloucestershire, Middlesex, Kent, Worcestershire, Hertfordshire, aboard a ferry on the English Channel and numerous sites around London. By pure coincidence, the interiors of the 'Circus' were shot on location at a building on Cork Street, London, which, to the great delight of the author, had formerly been occupied by MI5 and where John le Carré had undergone some of his training (Sisman 2015: 403). A sneak preview at the Edinburgh Festival elicited the comment from a reviewer that the serial promised to be the "*most elegant and poten-*

tially absorbing series the BBC has attempted for a very long time" (*Evening News*, 31 August 1979). The producers were granted the unexpected benefit of a closedown of the rival commercial television service throughout the late summer of 1979 due to an industrial dispute, which had the twin benefit of attracting viewers to BBC 2 who would not normally venture there, and of leaving reviewers fewer options to write about.

Critical response tended to centre on a couple of substantial issues. First, there was near universal praise for the quality of the cast and the brilliance of the acting, stylish presentation, writing and direction. The *Western Mail* claimed it a "*real delight to watch something excellently acted, with a fine, taut script, and directed with a real feeling for suspense*" (15 September 1979). The *Financial Times* found elements of the production cinematic and praised the ambition of the serial which turned out "*unlike anything else I can recall on television*" (3 October 1979). At the conclusion of the serial, the same reviewer could judge that the drama had the "*same sort of satisfying logic and symmetry as a good crossword or a Bach suite*", and had turned out "*one of the truly memorable drama serials I have seen in 10 years viewing*" (24 October 1979). The *Evening Standard* advised its readers to tune into the drama, as "*you will not fail over the next six weeks to experience delights that will make all subsequent spy series seem like anti-climaxes*" (11 September 1979), and the *Guardian* implored its readers: "*Don't dream of missing it. It simply seeps atmosphere*" (11 September 1979). On the completion of *Tinker Tailor Soldier Spy, The Telegraph* declared it a "*master-work*" and "*by several lengths the drama serial of the year*" (23 October 1979).

Critical discussion also focused on the complexity of the narrative. Concern surfaced with the first episode, which dealt with Control launching operation TESTIFY, Jim Prideaux's failed mission in Czechoslovakia and the sudden appearance of Ricki Tarr and his disturbing accusations. The *Morning Star* found it "*confusing, to say the least, even tedious at times*" (12 September 1979), and the same went for the *Spectator* which claimed it "*thoroughly confusing*" (6 October 1979). The *Daily Mail* felt sure that for an "*audience force-fed on James Bondage and* Charlie's Angels, *a spy thriller that refuses to come out of the cold, where there are no car chases, gun battles or even a beddable blonde, must be a source of some bewilderment*", and admitted it found the serial "*not simply demanding viewing, but exhausting*" (2 October 1979). Certainly, the denial of the 'immediacy effect' of contemporary action television could, in important ways, further help position *Tinker* as 'quality'; however, some wondered if comprehension was possible if one hadn't read the novel (*Scotsman*, 15 September 1979) and *Variety* felt duty bound to impress on waverers that the "*excitement of this opus is intellectual*" (3 October 1979). Eventually, some reviewers decided to be thankful for small mercies, accepting that *"the whole thing is so beautifully done that perhaps understanding doesn't matter"*, and settled *"for the fleeting impressionism of beautifully composed scenes and beautifully finished acting"* (*The Telegraph*, 10 October 1979). A further review in the *Daily Mail* spoke of the drama's *"obscure, teasing progress"*, and while unable to claim having *"conquered the complexities of this roundabout tale"*, the reviewer admitted that, *"like half the nation I'm hooked to the thing"* (18 September 1979). Some perplexed reviewers claimed to resort to tape recordings of episodes and the weekend repeats in an attempt to get to grips with the story.[370] Soldiering on into the series, the *Evening News* eventually admitted defeat, finding the drama *"as remote, exclusive and baffling as ever"*, and wondering *"when do the flashbacks end? When are we in the past or the present? And in either case, how are we supposed to translate the obscure jargon of the espionage industry?"* (2 October 1979). Eminent cultural critic Richard Hoggart, in a televised discussion, argued that the strong viewing figures for the serial had demonstrated superior intelligence on the part of the audience and that sceptical television programmers should take note (*Sight and Sound*, Winter 1979: 58). Anticipating difficulties with the American broadcast, the Public Broadcasting Service fronted the screening with host Robert MacNeil coaxing John le Carré to clarify *"the shop talk, psychological banter, and cryptic vocabulary"* which were thought to be a problem for viewers (*Variety*, 1 October 1980). This seemed to work and *Tinker Tailor Soldier Spy* was reported as attracting *"record viewing figures"* on public television in America (*The New York Times*, 20 December 1981; Sisman 2015: 409). In a more recent discussion, television scholar Joseph Oldham has argued that the drama serial was *"able to appeal to a mass audience through striking a careful balance between the underlying simplicity of its whodunit narrative and the pleasures of incomprehensibility"* (2017: 12).[371]

At least a couple of critics delighted in nay-saying *Tinker Tailor Soldier Spy* and took the opportunity to attack the pretensions of le Carré and the adaptation. Clive James in the *Observer*, in an assessment which attracted some comment, reported that the serial was *"not quite as incomprehensible"* as the original novel, but that *"it was equally turgid"* (16 September 1979). By the third episode he concluded that the serial gripped like a marshmallow and judged the adaptation a *"concerted attempt to inflate a thin book into a fat series"* (30 September 1979). By the time of the fourth instalment, James was receiving letters enquiring if he was pursuing a personal vendetta against le Carré and the serial, and feeling castigated he promised to watch to the end, but feared that; *"what should have been a thriller is turning out to be only marginally better than plain dull"* (7 October 1979).[372] Richard Ingrams at the *Spectator* asserted that the adaptation seriously overrated John le Carré's talent and drew too conspicuously on the author's *"pretentious dialogue"* (22 September 1979), and *"for all the brilliant acting and the stylish presentation"* the appeal of the serial "*remained on a superficial Agatha Christie level*" (27 October 1979).

The drama attracted viewer correspondence to the press. The reviewer at *The Telegraph* reported of letters arriving daily from "*distraught readers*" asking for "*enlightenment on who is doing what and to whom in Tinker, Tailor, Soldier, Spy*" (10 October 1979). A correspondent to the *Guardian* wrote in response to the "*alarming joke*" circulating among reviewers and the television public, namely the "*apparent difficulty of following the serial Tinker, Tailor, Soldier, Spy?*" A further letter writer to the paper provided a passionate defence of the dramatisation, declaring it "*compulsive viewing*" and pointed to the important implications of the debate regarding literacy and the mass media (18 October 1979). It prompted a number of tongue-in-cheek letters to the paper from readers who had their own ingenious theories on the identity of the 'mole', one claiming it was, in fact, George Smiley (2 November), and another that accepted George as the double-agent, but that the guiding hand belonged to the "*molemaster*", his wife Ann Smiley (6 November 1979). The argument was laid to rest when the story's author John le Carré, in a spoof letter to the paper, revealed there was no 'mole' and "*outed*" Control and his plot to undermine the 'Circus'. "*Thus under Control's evil guidance*", he confirmed, "*do the victims destroy each other for our public sport*" (7 November 1979).[373]

The television broadcast of *Tinker Tailor Soldier Spy* coincided with new revelations about 'moles' in high places. Andrew Boyle's *The Climate of Treason*, published in January 1979, dealt with the Cambridge Spies, and speculated on the identity of a 'fourth man'. Le Carré's *Tinker, Tailor, Soldier, Spy* had been readily acknowledged as a version of the Guy Burgess, Kim Philby and Donald Maclean narrative, and now the dramatisation hit the screens amid conjecture about further double-agents in British Intelligence and only weeks before Prime Minister Margaret Thatcher exposed Anthony Blunt in parliament as a Soviet agent within the wartime MI5. The critic at the *Scotsman* returned his thoughts to *Tinker Tailor Soldier Spy* in the new year of 1980, now aware of the Blunt saga, declaring that, "*Nothing could have come closer to an idea of what the real thing was like*" (5 January).

The screening of *Tinker Tailor Soldier Spy* brought about some discussion and debate. The eminent historian and former intelligence officer Hugh Trevor-Roper was invited by the *Daily Mail* to comment on 'How real is George Smiley's world?'. Considering that Trevor-Roper and le Carré had previously been involved in an unfortunate business regarding Kim Philby, the normally prickly Regius Professor of Modern History at Oxford University was magnanimous towards the author.[374] The historian now referred to John le Carré as a "*master who knows his way in that labyrinth: who understands its psychology and who also, like Philby himself, repudiates 'that silly James Bond stuff' and knows that, in intelligence work, there are no short cuts*". For Trevor-Roper, the story brought "*many real episodes to mind*" and in 'Gerald' the mole he recognised his "*old friend*" Kim Philby. Overall, *Tinker Tailor Soldier Spy*, the product of a "*sensitive and thoughtful writer*", offered a "*marvellous opportunity to explore the whole psychology of secret services: that 'circus'*"; that "*island of half people with its internal power struggles. Its special morality, its ambiguous loyalties*" (1979).

Tinker Tailor Soldier Spy also became a talking point for the public, in workplaces, shops and pubs. This was encouraged by the popular radio broadcaster Terry Wogan who kept up a running commentary on his breakfast show and who ran a spoof quiz asking "*Does anyone know what's going on?*" (Sisman 2015: 406). The television critic at the *Daily Mail* reported that, "*half the nation has been hooked on the great Mole hunt*" and declared the screening and its public reception a "*national event*" (23 October 1979). "*Hours after the end of Tinker, Tailor, Soldier, Spy*", it was reported that "*people were spotted wearing T-shirts claiming: 'I Knew It Was Bill Haydon'*". While the screening of the omnibus edition of the serial at Christmas was marked by an uncharacteristic "*Official BBC Joke*", the proceeding programme being a wildlife film called *The Undergrounds Movement*, "*about moles*" (*Sun*, 13 December 1979).

Anxious regarding the screen adaptations of his books, John le Carré admitted at the time of the first broadcast that, "*I had no part in it, I was scared of it, and I woke up to find it wonderful*" (quoted in the *Sunday Telegraph Magazine*, 21 October 1979). *Tinker Tailor Soldier Spy* is now widely regarded as one of the most accomplished of British television drama productions and it sold to more than 30 countries. In a recent assessment of the Smiley adaptations, Joseph Oldham has asserted that the serials "*epitomise*" the "*existential/realist*" strand of televised spy fiction, more concerned with the "*intellectual rigours of espionage*", and denoted the understated characteristics textually "*through muted colour palettes, frequently drab, cramped environments, and a marked absence of action and adventure in favour of dialogue and contemplation*". "*Thus*", he maintains, "*Tinker, Tailor, Soldier, Spy was conceived and presented as a drama of conversation in enclosed spaces rather than one of action and excitement*" (2013: 736-37). It was noted by some in the BBC that the drama serial revealed, in the words of the managing director of Television, a "*striking similarity*" between the Corporation and the 'Circus'; and as a historian of the BBC has written: "*Certainly the traffic of files and humdrum bureaucratic record with which Smiley painstakingly unravelled the treachery were Corporation tradecraft too*" (Seaton 2015: 302-3). In part, the comparison was actively sought by director John Irving, who later confessed that he "*based my version on the corridors of the BBC*". "*This Circus*", he admitted, "*was a combination in my imagination really of all the intrigues, jealousies, rivalries within the departments of the BBC and combined with my schoolmasters, my boarding school*".[375] British Academy of Film and Television Arts (BAFTA) TV Awards went to Alec Guinness for Best Actor and Tony Pierce-Roberts for Best Film Cameraman.

Following the critical and popular success of *Tinker Tailor Soldier Spy* it was inevitable that the BBC would look again at adapting John le Carré. The next George Smiley novel was *The Honourable Schoolboy*, which continued the story of the rehabilitated spymaster as he commences to build up the 'Circus' following the shattering exposure of Haydon and which had been published in 1977. However, a massive novel set largely in the Far East, it was unapproachable for British television drama at that time, and ruled out by producer Jonathan Powell as "*too big, too sprawling, and too expensive*" (quoted in the *Sunday Times*, 1 November 1987). The solution was to jump to the third novel in what had become known as the 'Karla Trilogy', *Smiley's People*, first published in 1979, another best-seller and which had already attracted two offers for the film rights (Sisman 2015: 412).[376] In this story, George Smiley is once again brought out of retirement, this time following the murder of one of his former agents on Hampstead Heath. Before his death, General Vladimir had tried to contact Smiley, informing him that it concerned "*the Sandman*", the codename for Karla. Pursuing a personal investigation which takes him to Hamburg and Berne, Smiley discovers Karla's great secret; that he has put love before duty and hidden away his daughter in a Swiss asylum, paid for by KGB funds and without the knowledge of his Soviet superiors. This is the leverage that the British spymaster exerts on the Russian spymaster to force his defection to the West.

The six-part adaptation, made with "*reverential fidelity*" according to the *Times Literary Supplement* (5 November 1982), was again produced by Jonathan Powell at the BBC, with financial contribution from Paramount Television and a budget of £2 million.[377] There had been a problem with the script written by the experienced John Hopkins and le Carré provided a re-write.[378] "*In the first version of the script, which John Hopkins wrote*", reported Powell diplomatically, "*we found ourselves too restrained by the parameters of the book*". A desire to be faithful to the novel, led to a script that didn't work. "*So, we called le Carré in to work with Hopkins to resolve the technical difficulties*". "*It's a strange thing*", the producer concluded, "*that the original writer can often be more free with his material than an adapter*" (quoted in *The New York Times*, 20 December 1981).

Director John Mackenzie spent some months preparing the shoot which was then planned as three two-hour films, but production delays meant that he had to pull out and take up commitments on other projects (*Glasgow Herald*, 12 December 1980; *Daily Express*, 8 January 1981).[379] Simon Langton took over as director and locations included London, Paris, Germany and Switzerland; and unable to shoot at a bridge linking East and West Berlin, the production found an identical structure in Nottingham which doubled as the crossing point for Karla from East to West Berlin which concluded the story.[380] Another impressive cast was gathered for the production, including Bernard Hepton[381] as Toby Esterhase and Beryl Reid as Connie Sachs reprising their roles from the first serial, and Curd Jürgens, in what proved to be his final role, as General Vladimir.[382] *Smiley's People* won BAFTA TV Awards for Best Actor (Guinness), Best Actress (Beryl Reid, playing Connie Sachs), Best Film Cameraman (Kenneth MacMillan) and Best Original Television Music (Patrick Gowers).[383]

Considering the fuss elicited by the plot of *Tinker Tailor Soldier Spy*, reviewers anticipated similar difficulties with *Smiley's People*, willingly in many cases. The author was the "*master of obfuscation*" and "*only God and le Carré*" knew what *Tinker, Tailor* was about asserted the *Guardian* (21 September 1982). "*Baffling, infuriating and a must for millions*", the *Sun* reminded its readers, "*the thriller series Tinker, Tailor, Soldier, Spy was the telly tease we loved to hate*"; and similarly at the *Daily Star*, "*whether you can follow the story of Smiley's People or become completely baffled by its twists and turns, there is one thing for certain you will not be able to stop watching*" (both 20 September 1982). Some reviewers continued to complain of "*confusion*" (*Morning Star*, 23 October 1982). Others reported more positively that *Smiley's People* adopted a "*far less confusing and convoluted route*", and seemed more prepared "*to take the viewer into its confidence from the start*" (*Daily Mail*, 21 September 1982). Equally, the *Sun* judged the sequel "*far less complicated*" (24 September 1982).

However, would *Smiley's People* be as good as *Tinker Tailor Soldier Spy*? When the "*long-awaited moment arrived*", and the sequel was about to hit the screens, the *Mail on Sunday* commented on the critical anticipation, claiming that "*millions of armchair critics were poised to see if they could tick off the failure of a sequel*" (26 September 1982). The *Guardian*, while judging the serial "*less compulsively mysterious*" than its predecessor, sat back and noted how "*simply lovely it is to look forward to something on TV again*" (21 September 1982). The *Financial Times* griped at "*minor disappointments*" and that the scriptwriters had bowed to the "*sleepy ones*" and offered a far more "*conventional narrative full of clues*" (13 October 1982). And presenting the programme-makers with a similar devil you do and the devil you don't kind of dilemma, the *New Statesman* now demanded something more "*lacon-*

ic", claiming that the "*more we're in the dark the better we like it*" (15 October 1982).

Smiley's People was also reviewed in the context of a critical backlash against John le Carré. The *Evening Standard* worked up something of a campaign against the author during the run of the serial. In its opening salvo it declared itself "*highly suspicious of the work of le Carré, especially in film form*", as there was "*considerably less there than meets the eye*". For that reviewer, "*the craft, the skill and expense which has gone into creating his books for television is evidence of how seriously the legend of le Carré is now taken*". While the "*humourless*" le Carré was thought good at plot, "*he appears to have little to say of any great consequence*" (21 September 1982). The following week, the paper judged the production "*Preposterously written*", if "*beautifully directed*" (26 September 1982), and later as a "*farcical series, where form has defeated content all ends up*". It railed at the "*chumps*" who had built a "*literary statue called le Carré so that they might worship at his convoluted genius*" (5 October 1982). Elsewhere, the *Sunday Times* complained of "*Le Carré's self-over rating fiction*", and doubted if *Smiley's People* added up to the "*drama event of the year*" (26 September 1982). For *The Telegraph*, it was only Alec Guinness's George Smiley which transformed "*this second-class literature into first-class television*" (21 September 1982), and the radical *Leveller* magazine remarked on le Carré's "*literary pretensions*" and wondered why had "*so much been spent on it*", and why had a "*spy thriller been given such room to move in?*" (November 1982: 30). Richard Ingrams at the *Spectator* remained hostile at the thought of le Carré on screen and claimed the serial demonstrated "*how a really good actor can transform a rotten script*", and with the story still dense and hard to follow that it was only Alec Guinness who prevented it from "*foundering altogether*" (25 September 1982). The *Guardian* claimed it was wrong to pretend that le Carré's enjoyable fictions were major works of art, and, in a view echoed elsewhere, that to bestow on a television serial "*the kind of prestige treatment accorded to* Tinker, Tailor – *and now to* Smiley's People – *invests the whole Smiley opus with a seriousness, and high-mindedness that, for me, the books do not have*". The reviewer felt that things would have been different, less pretentious, if Arthur Lowe had got the part of Smiley (18 October 1982).

Once again, there was interest in the authenticity of espionage as depicted by John le Carré. The *Mail on Sunday* charged Chapman Pincher, its expert on security and intelligence, to comment on 'how real is Smiley's world?' The result proved less interesting than Hugh Trevor-Roper's engagement with *Tinker Tailor Soldier Spy*, the correspondent largely restricting himself to textual matters in the story, such as the jargon used by spies and what resemblance George Smiley bore to Sir Maurice Oldfield a former head of MI6. In general, he judged the "*atmosphere*" created by le Carré as "*unusually convincing*" (1982).

The reviewer at the *Daily Mail* commented on the "*decidedly haughty attitude*" adopted by some critics towards *Smiley's People*, a serial that seemed "*to have fascinated half the nation and infuriated all the rest*". He noted how an "*identical impatience and animosity*" had greeted the screening of *Tinker Tailor Soldier Spy* and that history was now repeating itself. He predicted that *Smiley's People* "*would survive the slings and arrows of its detractors*"; after all, its predecessor was now "*firmly enshrined as a universally admired landmark in the history of television*". While finding the drama "*forbidding and inaccessible*" and not always sure "*what the hell was going on*", he suggested that the convolutions of the plot and the sparseness of the clues derided by some doubters actually constituted "*the secret of its deeply curious appeal*"; the show creating "*its own hallucinatory world of shadows and omens, where nothing is what it seems, where few voices can be trusted, and the atmosphere is haunted by the ghosts of old scores unsettled and old atrocities unavenged*". He informed his fellow critics that he was "*more than willing to travel with George Smiley along all those tangled twists and turns relishing the serial's heightened mood of threat and malice, its mesmerising photography and its meticulous acting performances*" (14 and 26 October 1982).

There were similarly disposed reviewers who once again acknowledged something special in the adaptation of John le Carré to the small screen. *The Times* praised the "*infinite care*" taken over the production (21 September 1982), and a joyous *Sun* found it "*all so atmospheric and beautifully acted from Sir Alec Guinness downwards, that I could happily watch it three times a week*" (24 September 1982). The *Mail on Sunday* was anxious whether the BBC could not pull off the same trick twice, yet, "*All reservations were swept away by the sheer style and sustained air of self-confidence*", convinced that viewers were "*simply unused to seeing anything like such infinite attention to detail in television thrillers*" (26 September 1982). The *Morning Star*, rarely a supporter of espionage fiction, believed the second le Carré serial had "*lost none of its compulsive style*" and thankfully proved "*less obscure than* Tinker, Tailor" (29 September 1982). Questioning the view that the le Carré dramatisations were over-valued, the *Scotsman* claimed that they did manage "*to suggest more than what is merely eventful; they seem to say something about, life*" (23 October 1982). The *Observer* noted the "*sniffiness among critics with fond memories of* Tinker, Tailor", and declared *Smiley's People* an "*impeccable success*". The new serial had all the virtues of its predecessor, and in addition, "*frequent humour, a wider variety of action and milieu, and a less baffling plot*". For this reviewer, the production "*roundly confirmed television as the ideal medium for the spy story*" (31 October 1982). The *Daily Mirror* declared itself "*gripped*" and worrying about withdrawal, asked, "*Is there a cure for chronic John Le Carre-itis?*" (25 September 1982); and, aware that the saga had now come to an end, T. J. Binyon, the scholar and respected writer on detective fiction, wondered: "*Whither now?*" (*Times Literary Supplement*, 5 November 1982).

The success of *Tinker Tailor Soldier Spy* on American public television meant that *Smiley's People* was granted a wider broadcast, screening as an 'Operation Prime Time' presentation in three two-hour segments on some 100 independent commercial stations across the country (*The New York Times*, 20 December 1981). *The New York Times* judged the drama, although "*not 'easy' television*" and demanding of "*unusual concentration*", "*marvelously riveting*". "*All of which*" it worried, made the prospect of frequent commercial interruptions "*especially worrisome*" (24 October 1982). *Variety* summed-up the situation for the American audience: "*For the mass market, no; for the class market, yes*" (29 September 1982).

The successful transfer to television of *Tinker Tailor Soldier Spy* and *Smiley's People* ensured there was considerable anticipation for the dramatisation of *A Perfect Spy*, John le Carré's eleventh novel, first published in 1986, and the first of his books that was not submitted to the authorities for clearance. The story deals with the complex life of Magnus Pym, a brilliant Secret Intelligence Service officer, latterly Head of Station for Czechoslovakia and based in Vienna, Austria. The British Secret Service is thrown into turmoil when he goes to ground, hiding himself away in a seaside boarding house he has long prepared as a sanctuary. There, he ostensibly writes his memoirs, addressed mainly to his young son and to Jack Brotherhood, a mentor figure and the man who recruited Pym to the Service. It is his account of an extraordinary upbringing, one that had prepared him as a 'perfect spy' and for a lifetime of betrayals, and the theme is that of how the child is father to the spy. It was noted at the *Mail on Sunday* that le Carré's previous novels had "*done more than anything else to show us the grey and ghastly world in which spies end up*", whereas the new work "*offered us the even more secret world in which they may begin*" (8 November 1987).

The complicated narrative cuts back and forth between Pym's reminiscences and the frantic search for the missing intelligence officer by the British, the Czechs and the Americans. The reader discovers the background to Pym, partly from the act of writing the memoirs, and partly from Brotherhood's attempt to discover the secrets of the missing agent: Pym's unusual childhood; the unexplained absences of his trickster father, Rick; time spent at boarding school and university; and his introduction to intelligence work, first unofficially in Switzerland and later during his military service in the British Zone in Austria. It is during his time with the British Army of Occupation that Pym is recruited to serve the Czech Secret Service by Herr Axel, a refugee he had earlier befriended, then betrayed, while temporarily stranded in Berne, Switzerland on an abortive mission for his father, who, as usual, was involved in a scam to obtain money. Axel coaxes Pym into an arrangement whereby the Communist agent receives British secrets and thereby safeguards his own position within the repressive Czech regime, and Pym can advance his career through establishing a seemingly important agent network in Czechoslovakia, which is in fact controlled by the Communists. Pym rises effortlessly in the Service, serving in Berlin, Stockholm and, the greatest prize, Washington. Throughout his life, Pym betrays those around him, his father, his two wives, Axel, Brotherhood, his Service and his country. Eventually, the Americans begin to suspect Pym and his deception, but the British defend him and claim that, if anything, the Czechs are trying to frame a loyal British officer who has long been a thorn in their side. Pym's sudden disappearance thus rocks British Intelligence. Despite the excellence of his tradecraft, Pym is eventually traced to his 'safe-house' by Brotherhood. However, his manuscript completed, the disgraced agent takes his own life, signalling his transition from lonely boyhood to even lonelier death.

A Perfect Spy is an epic tale of personal and professional betrayal. It has been judged John le Carré's most ambitious and autobiographical novel, incorporating as it does a complex series of stories and flashbacks. The West Country childhood, non-conformism, absent mother, public school, Oxford University, Army Intelligence and MI6 belong to the biography of both Pym and le Carré. The author has claimed that writing the story was a cathartic experience, allowing him to come to terms with his own unconventional upbringing in which his remarkable father Ronnie, a swindler and fantasist, played a destructive role. Significantly, in creating the story, le Carré was insistent that the son Magnus Pym should be an even bigger confidence man than his father; one, according to *The New York Times*, "*intimately aware of the dynamics of love and loyalty as tools to be used in the covert manipulation of men, knowledgeable in the uses of the lie, cognizant of the fragility and vulnerability of those whom life, in one way or another, has badly hurt*" (13 April 1986). As Pym writes his memoirs he is constantly reflecting on how early experience taught him "*stealth, subterfuge, dissimulation and tradecraft*", as Eric Homberger as expressed it, and in the process creating a perfect spy (1986: 102).[384]

For some critics, *A Perfect Spy* is an uncharacteristically humorous novel for the author, albeit a darkly comic story. This dimension is largely attributable to the larger-than-life portrait of Rick Pym, who is painted as a kind of endearing monster. In addition, le Carré artfully constructs an insistent framework of doubling and repetition in his story, which, at its most obvious, includes Pym's two wives, two agent runners (and father figures), and two rival Services. These have been taken to stand as metaphors for a "*world divided against itself; a world in which men must constantly struggle to discriminate among conflicting loyalties and shifting identities*" (Laity 1987: 138). *A Perfect Spy* is also concerned with the division within the self, and this accounts for the chameleon-like qualities of Pym, who re-defines himself depending on to whom is he relating or trying to impress. In a sense, the autobiographical story 'outed' John le Carré as a former intelligence officer, confirming what some had suspected, "*namely that earlier le Carré books were based on real incidents in the espionage war*" (*Marxism Today*, November 1987: 41).

A Perfect Spy was produced as a £6 million, seven-part BBC television serial in 1987, directed by Peter Smith and starred Peter Egan as the adult Magnus Pym and Ray McAnally as Rick Pym. The dramatisation saw the return of Arthur Hopcraft who had previously adapted le Carré for television in 1979 with *Tinker Tailor Soldier Spy*, and locations were shot in Corfu, Austria, Switzerland and Great Britain. Jonathan Powell, now head of drama at the BBC, served as executive producer on the production and bought the rights to the novel before it had been published (*Sunday Times*, 24 November 1985). He later pointed to the distinctiveness of the new story, describing it as "*a different kind of book*".

> *It isn't a mystery thriller, it is more of an extended answer to the questions left at the end of Tinker, Tailor. That revealed who the traitor was, and this book tries to explain what it is in the lives of people that makes them grow up to become traitors.*
> (Quoted in the *Sunday Times*, 1 November 1987)

The *Spycatcher* trial which had recently unfolded in Australia at great embarrassment for the British government and intelligence services was thought to have "*revived the nation's interest in the murky world of secrets and betrayal*" and was sure to be a great boost for the new drama (*Today*, 31 October 1987). As the *Times Literary Supplement* commented, "*Broadcast at a time when the government's ban prohibited the BBC from dealing with real-life spies, Peter Smith's stylish production of John le Carré's* A Perfect Spy *took on an enhanced aura of secrecy*" (24 December 1987).

The complex achronological narration of the novel, involving the juxtaposition of Pym's reminisces, Brotherhood's pursuit of the errant spy, and the wife's attempt to discern the personal and professional treachery of her husband, is dispensed with in favour of a linear narrative. The screen story commences with Brotherhood closing in on Pym in his safe haven, and a single flashback takes the viewer back to childhood and then progresses straightforwardly through to the suicide as more suitable for a broad television audience. While some reviewers expressed relief at the concession to comprehensibility (*Times*, 4 November 1987; *Guardian*, 5 November 1987), others felt it a betrayal of the novel and an "*unforgivable error*", and "*more so if it was done to make things 'easier' for the viewers*" (*The Times*, 5 November 1987). There remained concern, however, that John le Carré was difficult to follow, perhaps something inherent in the author's approach to construction, and *The Telegraph* complained that the drama seemed to "*revel in complexity for complexity's sake*" (26 November 1987).

There was wide praise for the outstanding performances in the series and the painstaking recreation of the past; but in other respects the critics were divided. For *The New York Times*, *A Perfect Spy* was "*another very impressive addition to the television record of le Carré explorations*", "*Gloomy and disturbing*", to be sure, "*but singularly absorbing*" (16 October 1988). However, considering the high-level of expectation placed on the adaptation, there was for some a sense of let-down. The novel had been welcomed in quarters as the author's "*espionage masterpiece*", even the "*most intriguing father and son enigma in literature*" (*Daily Mail*, 5 July 1987), but the adaptation for the *Sunday Times* was a "*bit of a disappointment ... a touch directionless*" (29 November 1987). For others, the dramatisation lacked pace, the *Sunday Telegraph* complaining of the "*pedantry*" of the approach, and that the initial episode "*trudged dourly through the early years of the novelist's semi-autobiographical hero, Magnus Pym, explaining how he learned the arts of duplicity and secrecy*" (8 November 1987). While "*marvelling*" at the acting skills on show, the *Sunday Telegraph* was nonplussed at a drama "*moving at the speed of Brezhnev's funeral*" and wanted "*something to happen*" (15 November 1987). The reviewer at the *Scotsman* confessed to "*finding it hard to keep my attention from nodding off or wondering what's on the other channels*" (14 November 1987). The *Daily Mail* concluded that there were "*two distinct schools of thought*" about *A Perfect Spy*: the first, "*frequently conveyed to me by my enthusiastic network of unpaid amateur TV critics, is that following the twists of John le Carré's story is about as fascinating as watching paint drying*"; the second, "*believes that it satisfyingly confirms everything set out by Peter Wright in Spycatcher*" (26 November 1987). In a letter to Alec Guinness, le Carré made out that the television version of *A Perfect Spy* was a major professional disappointment to him, although the confession might have been coloured by the nature of the recipient and their previous work together (Sisman 2015: 450).

At the time of the broadcast of *A Perfect Spy*, when expectation was still high, the question for the BBC was "*what to plunder next from the le Carré canon*". There remained one 'vintage' novel left un-filmed and *A Small Town in Germany* (1968), it was thought, "*would divide perfectly into serialized television drama"*. Both Jonathan Powell and Arthur Hopcraft were keen to take it on and optimistic that it would reach the screen, but the relative failure of the recent dramatisation seemingly ensured that it remained un-shot (*Sunday Times*, 1 November 1987).

The BBC adaptations of John le Carré were notable creative achievements for British television. Taken as a group, they represent a pinnacle of accomplishment for the spy drama on screen; and the legendary *Tinker Tailor Soldier Spy* remains in a class of its own and is widely appreciated as one of the finest attainments of television drama. The dramatisations afforded the opportunity to broadcast to large audiences the author's remarkable view of the secret world of British Intelligence and his characteristic concern to draw parallels between the body politic and the stifling, enclosed ambit of the spy. Viewers were treated to what many considered a more credible portrayal of the Secret Service, while additionally being encouraged to accept the spy genre as capable of filtering wider concerns, "*like class divisions, the decay of post-imperial Britain, and the crisis of faith among its ruling echelons*" (*Guardian*, 18 October 1982). *A Perfect Spy* was a cathartic experience for le Carré, and, as the author has claimed, rid him of the spectres of both his father and that of the Secret Intelligence Service (*Der Spiegel*, 7 August 1989). He would not write so directly about either of these presences for a long-time to come.[385]

Case file 2: Len Deighton on the small screen

Rival espionage author Len Deighton was less well served by television. The big screen had lapped up three 'Harry Palmer' pictures in the 1960s and a further espionage tale with the modest film version of *Spy Story* in 1976. However, the viewing public had to wait until the mid-1980s before a spy story by the leading genre author was represented on the small screen. In between the novels *The Ipcress File* (1962) and *Funeral in Berlin* (1964), Deighton wrote the single play drama 'Long Past Glory' which was broadcast in the *Armchair Theatre* strand late in 1963. However, this had no espionage angle and was rather in the style of Harold Pinter, dealing with two old men who inhabit a decaying sewer pumping station whose world is disrupted by the arrival of an argumentative young man. Much later, the novels *Berlin Game* (1983), *Mexico Set* (1984) and *London Match* (1985) comprised an ambitious espionage saga by Deighton, "*an epic story of treachery in three acts*" (*Game, Set & Match* press book). With these tales the author returned to the espionage story after an absence of seven years and introduced a new series character in Bernard Samson, a former successful field agent in Germany and now a middle-ranking desk officer with the Secret Intelligence Service in London. Samson is a typical Deighton outsider in the Service: he was born and grew up in occupied Berlin; his father was a self-made man who became something in Military Intelligence; the young Samson did not go to university; and he has married into a well-to-do family, his wife Fiona also working as a senior operative in SIS. It was once pointed out that, "*if we are talking about class in British society, Deighton knows what it is to be an Other Rank, and shows it right through his spy books*" (*Guardian*, 18 October 1982). The long three-part story of treachery and betrayal involves Samson in a complex 'game' of intrigue played across the cities of London, Mexico City and Berlin. In *Berlin Game*, Samson has to confront the fact that Fiona has been the suspected double-agent in London. In *Mexico Set*, Samson is sent to Mexico City to assess an important major of the KGB, Erich Stinnes, the officer who had arrested him in East Berlin in the previous story. London wants Stinnes 'enrolled' for defection and Samson is assigned to the tricky task of getting him, even though Stinnes could be part of a plot to ensnare Samson. In *London Match*, the debriefing of Stinnes suggests a further mole in London Central, circumstantial evidence pointing to the Anglo-American Bret Rensselaer, a senior official in SIS and in charge of the interrogation. At great personal and professional risk, Samson demonstrates that Stinnes has been a plant all along; part of a long-term plan of Fiona's aimed at discrediting Rensselaer and Samson and destabilising SIS. Great embarrassment at London Central ensures that the fiasco will largely be buried and Samson can expect little credit from his insights and risk-taking.

With the *Game, Set & Match* trilogy, Len Deighton set out to explore the theme of domestic and professional betrayal at length. He had initially planned to start the story following the initial betrayal by Fiona, at what is now the beginning of *Mexico Set*, but sensing the need for more description of the betrayer, he ended up with the novel *Berlin Game*. Deighton wanted the narration to be highly subjective and wrote the series in his characteristic first-person style. Accordingly, he has warned readers not to take the narrator's words too literally: "*Bernard isn't the awesome genius that he would have us think*" and "*We'll never know exactly what happened that year, and Bernard's story is as near the truth as we can hope to get*" (1993: 5-6). The Samson saga is, though, written in a more detached style than the author's previous spy novels and eschews the deliberate hard-boiled style of *The Ipcress File* and *Funeral in Berlin* that fixes those stories to an earlier period. Deighton is a meticulous planner of his books and required a wall chart to plot the complexity of his three novels. The multi-book format allowed him to take his characters into lives that, "*while being so weird and wonderful, are burdened with the domestic everyday events that we all endure*" (Deighton 2012a: vii). He was erecting a "*boardroom drama*", as he pithily put it, "*in which the consequence of being 'outvoted' was not losing a job, but losing your life*" (Deighton 2012b: vi). Deighton claimed to have drawn on many sources within the intelligence community for his details, delighting in being able to "*test the boundaries of secrecy*" and "*use material ... by those who were gagged by over-assertive officialdom*" (viii). Two more trilogies furthering the story of Bernard Samson appeared as *Spy Hook* (1988), *Spy Line* (1989) and *Spy Sinker* (1990), and *Faith* (1994), *Hope* (1995) and *Charity* (1996).[386]

The television *Game, Set & Match* was produced at Granada Television in 1988 and was Len Deighton's first major drama on television.[387] The 13-part serial was a major undertaking, the company's most expensive drama production to date, and an attempt to break the BBC's recent stranglehold on spy dramas following the success in adapting John le Carré with *Tinker Tailor Soldier Spy*, *Smiley's People* and *A Perfect Spy*. The production was a mammoth undertaking, the publicity claiming a £5 million budget, the transportation of nine and a half tons of equipment some 42,000 miles for location-shooting in London, Berlin and Mexico, a shoot lasting nearly a year and requiring two directors, and backgrounds requiring 3,000 extras. *Game, Set & Match* was the first production allowed to stage drama at the sacred Pyramids of Teotihuacan, the first to film sequences at the military shrine at Chapultepec, and the first to be permitted to enact scenes inside the National Palace, Mexico City. It was also the first time the Americans allowed a crew to film dramatic sequences at Checkpoint Charlie and other crossing places at the Berlin Wall.[388] Denied permission to shoot behind the Iron Curtain, Bolton Town Hall and Manchester Victoria Station doubled convincingly for East Berlin and Gdansk, Poland (*Game, Set & Match* press book; *Daily Mirror*, 23 November 1987). A section of the Berlin Wall nearly 600ft. long, 15ft. high, complete with watch towers, razor wire, savage dogs and arc lamps imported from East Germany, was built at Nether Alderley, Cheshire, although it was required for only seven minutes of screen time (*Daily Mail*, 30 January 1987; *Today*, 27 July 1987; *Stage and Television Today*, 22 December 1988). To off-set some of the investment, the serial was pre-sold to broadcasters in North America (*Stage and Television Today*, 26 March 1987). The impressive logistics were a major feature of the publicity for the serial and Granada television trumpeted the drama as "*The ultimate spy story*" (*Game, Set & Match* press release).[389]

The drama was faithful to the original, the only major revision being the staging of a back-story in the novel, the failed operation into the Eastern Bloc in 1978 which reduced Samson to a desk job, as the opening episode of the series which served to set the scene and orientate viewers. The subjective approach of the novels was translated on screen through having Bernard Samson (Ian Holm) feature in all but four of the drama's 664 scenes and through a voice-over technique which allowed access to his thoughts and anxieties.[390] *Game, Set & Match* was the centre-piece of the ITV network's autumn schedule in 1988, opening with a double episode.

Critical response to the serial was disappointing. As with John le Carré adaptations previously, and even though the *"elliptical tease"* of the former was eschewed *"in favour of treachery with a direct punch"* (*Scotsman*, 3 October 1988), there was much muttering about the plot being too complex and impenetrable. *Today* likened the initial double episode to a *"two-hour IQ test"*, claiming the viewer was *"never quite sure which time zone we're in, with the plot whipping back and forwards from present to past and back and forth over the Berlin Wall"*. Admiring the impressive production values, the reviewer thought it a *"shame we can't follow what they're up to"* (6 October 1988). *The Telegraph*, though finding the serial an *"extremely classy piece of screen drama"*, worried that a *"superbly decorated exterior"* overlay a more questionable *"interior rationale"*, where it was hard to discern what the characters were about (4 October 1988). *The Times*, in contrast, felt the Len Deighton adaptation had the *"advantage over le Carré of a plot that it is, more or less, possible to follow"* (3 October 1988). In terms of plot, the *Independent* reported of *"viewers desperately trying to keep up"*, while in terms of drama the paper warned of *"stylish* angst": a *"world-weary intelligence operative, plangent cello music, grey dawns in Berlin and the twilight of trust"* (4 October 1988). The *Daily Mail* found the serial the *"most wearisomely drawn out epic"*, with the reviewer claiming to have *"scarcely understood a word of the thing from start to finish"* (20 December 1988).

One of the reasons for the critical coolness was that during the long production period the mood of the Cold War changed drastically with the emergence of *glasnost* and *perestroika*, and despite some updating of the drama to include reference to the Solidarity Movement in Poland the story was being overtaken by events. *The Telegraph* complained of a *"dated Cold war adventure"* (25 October 1988), the *Guardian* was quick to note that the story was clearly more 'Andropov' than 'Gorbachev' (4 October 1988), and in interviews Ian Holm acknowledged that the *"whole mood of East-West relations"* had changed since they started making the serial, and wondered whether *"this kind of spy story now seems dated to an audience of the Gorbachev era"* (*Guardian*, 24 September 1988). The *Daily Mail* claimed that spy stories had *"lost their zing since Gorbachev had arrived"*, and that, *"we have spent so much time already at Checkpoint Charlie, watching Richard Burton, Michael Caine and dozens of others slouching through, to be much amazed by Mr Holm doing the same thing all over again"* (4 October 1988). *"If it is the price to be paid for a long pause from spy epics"*, a later issue of the paper asserted, *"I hope Mr Gorbachev will be willing to do the decent thing and pull the Wall down forthwith"* (20 December 1988). There was, however, much admiration for Holm's "*dominating and hypnotically effective performance*" (*Scotsman*, 3 October 1988), a contribution that "*made it all watchable*" (*The Times*, 25 October 1988). A complex drama series, *Game, Set & Match* steadily lost viewers throughout its long run up to the Christmas period in 1988 and attracted on average a modest audience of only six and a half million viewers each episode (*Stage and Television Today*, 22 December 1988).

A review in the *Weekend Telegraph* by an admirer of Len Deighton was more supportive, claiming the large cast of characters "*drawn with meticulous detail*", the dialogue "*hauntingly spare and telling*", and the drama creating a "*terrific sense of atmosphere and place, in particular of Berlin, on both sides of the Wall*". Fearing plans for the deregulation of broadcasting in Britain, readers were warned that *Game, Set & Match* was "*exactly the kind of high quality project that could be most in danger*" (1 October 1988).[391] The *Spectator* informed its readers that the serial was "*time consuming but unmissable*" (8 October 1988). The *Sunday Times* found it "*one of the more intricate and thoughtful serials of the year*", and suspected that a critical snobbery was denying *Game, Set & Match* the praise it deserved. After all, although a "*great plot-writer, terrific at character, a nifty hand at atmosphere and an unchallenged authority on his subject*", Deighton was also "*that most un-Booker Prizeworthy of creatures, a popular novelist in the espionage genre*" (4 December 1988). *Stage and Television Today* questioned some of the liberties taken with the intricate story, but ultimately declared Deighton adaptation-proof and accepted that the production had caught the spirit of the author. In the outcome, the reviewer much preferred the "*people fiction*" of Deighton to the "*dull ciphers*" and "*tricksy plots*" of John le Carré's "*espionage fiction*" (6 October 1988).

As was becoming common for television espionage dramas, a former insider of the intelligence services was approached to comment on the authenticity of the dramatisation. Anthony Cavendish, onetime member of MI6 and author of *Inside Intelligence* which was currently being suppressed by the authorities, found the details of tradecraft and operations questionable; however, he did believe that *Game, Set & Match* gave the "*feeling of the 'true secret service'*": "*the deviousness, the snide way people speak to each other, the way in which officers are constantly trying to score points at the expense of a colleague*", all important markers of the espionage drama style (*Sunday Times*, 9 October 1988).

Ever since he read *Berlin Game* in 1983 and anticipated the trilogy, Brian Armstrong, head of drama at Granada, had been determined to produce a dramatisation (*Stage and Television Today*, 22 December 1988). A wary Len Deighton was finally won over by the company's recent track record with classy television adaptations, especially *Brideshead Revisited* and *Jewel in the*

Crown (1984). While acknowledging the professionalism of the production, however, Deighton was unhappy with the central casting of Ian Holm, a respected actor he felt too old (at 55) and too short (at 5ft 6in) for the role of Bernard Samson.[392] Lacking control, the author felt that *"someone somewhere was inflicting a brutal wound upon the whole project"*, and that the casting was *"bizarre"*: *"the tall became short, the short became tall, the angry became weary, the brunettes became blond, the fat became thin, the Americans became English, the clean-shaven wore beards and those with spectacles shed them"*.[393] Consequently, the author re-acquired the rights to the story and has refused permission for re-broadcasts and for release on DVD. *Game, Set & Match* has become therefore very difficult to see and an intriguing prospect for the fan of the spy drama. It was rumoured around 2009 that cult film-maker Quentin Tarantino, denied a chance to direct a James Bond movie, was contemplating filming the *Game, Set & Match* trilogy for the cinema (*Guardian*, 14 August 2009).

Literary espionage dramas

The subject of espionage had long maintained a powerful grip on the British imagination.
(Dominic Sandbrook 2006: 595)

Most espionage fiction has conventionally been dismissed as 'sub-literate' and unlikely to rise above the simple demands of popular genre stories and their emphasis on sex and action. A handful of novelists, as we have seen, were afforded some critical respect and in this regard Eric Ambler was one of the more admired authors of espionage stories. In the 1930s, his novels had helped transform the spy story into something more respectable, literary and politically credible. The BBC had produced a six-part serial in 1953 of *Epitaph for a Spy* featuring Peter Cushing, from Ambler's classic novel of 1938. *The Schirmer Inheritance*, a novel of 1953, was adapted into a six-part serial at the commercial channel ABC in 1957 starring William Sylvester. The BBC had another go at *Epitaph for a Spy* in 1963 in a dramatisation comprising of four 30-minute episodes broadcast in the regular Sunday serial slot. It starred Colin Jeavons as the unfortunate Joseph Vadassy, an East European on vacation who finds himself embroiled in a web of intrigue at a hotel in the South of France. The serial is now believed to be lost and not too much is known about the production. The story was softened for television, and updated to the 1960s it lost the poignancy of its original interwar setting. The American *Variety* felt the original *"ironic adventure"* had been transformed into a *"facetious spree"* and that the attempt to substitute *"teasing fun for tension did not come off"*. Overall, it judged the production *"artificial"*, that the performances lacked a "*third dimension*", and that Jeavons strove for titters "*to creaking effect*" (29 May 1963). Other critics concurred, *Stage and Television Today* judging the serial "*weak*" (6 June 1963) and the *Television Mail* finding it "*just another cops-and-robbers opus*" (24 May 1963).

A Quiet Conspiracy (1989) was a four-part serialisation of *The Intercom Conspiracy* (1969) and the first of master spy writer Eric Ambler's novels to be dramatised for television in Britain in a quarter of a century. Indeed, the *Weekend Telegraph* took the opportunity to point out that Ambler was "*one of the best and most prolific spy writers ever to be neglected by television*" (25 February 1989). Ambler confessed at the time that he was weary of adaptations of his work, the whole business making him "*feel queasy*". However, he diplomatically declared himself satisfied with the recent translation to the small screen (Anglia press sheet for *A Quiet Conspiracy*). The drama was produced at the regional Anglia Television, shot on location in Strasbourg and starred Joss Ackland. Scriptwriter Alick Rowe had to construct a conventional narrative line from the novel's unusual amalgam of notes, interviews, telegrams, letters, and imaginative 'reconstructions' of important scenes compiled by the writer Charles Latimer for a book about a conspiracy involving a jaded journalist, a right-wing magazine and NATO secrets. *The Telegraph* felt the drama didn't have the "*mesmeric intensity*" of Granada's recent *Game, Set & Match*, but appreciated it as "*certainly more comprehensible*" (4 March 1989). The sister paper the *Weekend Telegraph* found *A Quiet Conspiracy* a "*suspenseful tale with immaculate pacing*" and, with a nod to Ambler, declared it "*entertainment of a well-crafted superior kind*" (25 February 1989). The drama was popular with viewers and kicked off with an audience of well over nine million (*Stage and Television Today*, 9 March 1989).

Anglia immediately followed *A Quiet Conspiracy* with another made-for-television Ambler thriller. *The Care of Time* (1990) was an adaptation of the author's final novel and starred Michael Brandon and Christopher Lee. The story ranges from Pennsylvania, across Europe to the Austrian Alps, and deals with a journalist who is coerced into editing a Russian terrorist's memoirs and ghost-writing an exposé of modern terrorists. Tise Vahimagi has warned of the "*puzzling plotting*" and judges the production an "*ambitious TV film with a reach that was greater than its grasp*".[394]

The first drama to treat a Cambridge spy, albeit tangentially, was 'Traitor', a 60-minute television drama produced within the celebrated *Play for Today* strand at the BBC and first broadcast in 1971. As noted in the *Daily Express*, "*Traitors, however trivial, fascinate the people or societies they betray. Long after the dead-letter boxes and the forged passports are located and explained, we want to know why they did it*" (15 October 1971). Evidently, the Kim Philby, Guy Burgess and Donald Maclean narrative tempted some of the best creative writers on television to treat the theme of espionage, dramatists such as Dennis Potter, Alan Bennett and Stephen Poliakoff.[395] 'Traitor' was written by Potter and starred John Le Mesurier in the role of the title character. The action is set largely in the cheerless, claustrophobic Moscow apartment of Adrian Harris, a former controller in British Intelligence who had defected in face of imminent exposure. The drama revolves around his interview by representatives of the Western press who search for answers as to why the Eton College and Oxford-educated Harris betrayed his country. During the confrontation Harris descends into drunken abusiveness and sprays his guests with tormented talk, the trying experience inter-cut with painful memories of his childhood – humiliation and brutalisation at public school, an unsympathetic and demanding father – and later with Harris's informing on a defecting Soviet and the foreign agent's subsequent liquidation.

The model for Harris was the notorious British traitor Kim Philby who had defected to Russia in 1963 and who for a long period relied heavily on drink. One of Philby's middle-names was Adrian, the domineering father in the drama bore several resemblances to the spy's own parent, the eccentric St. John Philby, and the murder of the Russian defector in the play is similar to Philby's role in the Konstantin Volkov affair. Philby had been interviewed by a British journalist in Moscow in December 1967 and the story appeared in the *Sunday Times*, and this could have provided Potter with the inspiration for his play. Harris, like Philby, has a stutter. The drama is concerned with the meaning of 'Englishness', as distinct from simple notions of patriotism, and what kind of treachery is involved if someone retains a love of one's country but is still prepared to betray it for a higher ideal. Harris repeatedly gazes at an English landscape painting hanging on his wall, one of the few items he was able to spirit away with him. He continues to dress like an English gentleman and trades English literary quotations, Blake, Wordsworth, Tennyson, Auden, with a public school-educated reporter. In one heated exchange, Harris maintains that he might have betrayed his class, but never his country. Yuri Modin, the KGB controller of the Cambridge Spies, later commented on the "*patriotism*" of the traitors, claiming that the men all "*nourished a profound and passionate love of England*", and this complex attitude is something Potter presciently teases out in his drama (Modin 1994: 272). The conclusion of the play is deliberately uncertain. At the point of Harris's near collapse, there is a sudden return to the beginning of the drama. This time, however, Harris discovers a hidden KGB microphone in the apartment, and as he prepares to meet the journalists he repeats to himself: "*Remember the microphones and be careful... For God's sake remember the microphone!*" Was this a flashback, simply revealing that Harris knew he was being recorded, and therefore the viewer had just witnessed a 'performance' for his listeners? Or, had the initial messy interview been the imagination of Harris, part of the subjective framework of the drama? Whichever, Harris is continuing to lie to someone: his new Soviet masters, the journalists, even himself. 'Traitor' stands as a prime example of the new espionage drama of the period, which sought a more complex engagement with the shadowy world of the spy and the moral and ethical questions involved in clandestine activity. Potter stated his intention with the drama as illustrating his belief that the "*worst traitors are the dogmatists who think it a weakness to change their minds*" (quoted in *The Times*, 15 October 1971), while one of his biographers has claimed that the "*fascinating play*" embodied "*Potter's ambiguities about his heritage in the widest sense, the educational, socio-political and literary traditions of England*" (Gilbert 1998: 195).

The reviews were mixed, and this is unsurprising for a television play prone to wordiness, moral complexity, subjectivity and literary allusion. The *Guardian* counted 'Traitor' one of the more memorable dramas in the recent *Play for Today* season (25 February 1972); *The Times* felt there was "*too much psychology and too little sociology*", and that accordingly the play failed to provide a satisfactory answer to the question of what makes a privileged "*Philby-figure*" spend a double-life spying for the Soviet Union?; and the *Observer* declared it the "*drama event of the week*" and "*technically riveting*" (both 17 October 1971). The sense that childhood experience informs character in later life was a central theme in the work of Potter, evident in the celebrated 'Stand Up, Nigel Barton' (1965).[396] Potter, a miner's son who made it to Oxford University, equally had to confront complex personal issues of class loyalty and betrayal, themes he explored in 'Barton' and in 'Traitor'. Critics recognised this. Brian Davies writing in the *Television Mail* judged 'Traitor' a "*deeply-felt emanation from Potter's own experience*". "*As a description of a particular incident*" he found the play "*brilliantly effective*"; although, as an "*exploration of character*", he judged it "*less satisfying*" (22 October 1971). The seriousness with which the drama was greeted was evident in Potter's appearance on the discussion programme *Late Night Line Up* following the broadcast of 'Traitor', where he spoke with "*personal emotion*" and at length about the "*predicament of the uprooted Englishman*" (*Observer*, 17 October 1971; Carpenter 1998: 261). As an adequate summary of the critical views on the play, one can refer to Potter's biographers, who have written contrastingly of the play's "*mesmerising quality*" and "*astonishing emotional impact*" (Gilbert 1998: 196) on the one hand, and of it as merely a "*competent excursion into John le Carré territory*" on the other (Carpenter 1998: 261). Dave Rolinson, a specialist critic on British television drama, has judged 'Traitor' "*one of the most thematically ambitious of Dennis Potter's early plays, tackling family psychology, patriotism and, through nuanced use of literary quotation, the way culture and institutions reinforce political values*".[397]

A few weeks before the broadcast, the Conservative government had expelled 90 Russian diplomats and the *Morning Star* noting the topicality commented that the screening "*slotted neatly into the current Tory spy-mania*" (16 October 1971).There was unanimous praise for Le Mesurier's "*tour-de-force*" performance, from an actor better-known for light comedy roles, with one critic judging this his "*Hamlet*" (*Guardian*, 15 October 1971), and for which he won the British Academy of Film and Television Award for Best TV Actor.

Blade on the Feather, first broadcast in 1980, was a further drama on the theme of espionage and treachery written by Dennis Potter, and which, according to biographer Humphrey Carpenter, improved "*immensely*" on 'Traitor' (1998: 389). The script was originally offered to the filmmaker Joseph Losey, but he left the project when he failed to interest any of the leading theatrical knights, Alec Guinness, John Gielgud or Laurence Olivier, to take on the central role of the Anthony Blunt-like traitor (*Sunday Mirror*, 25 May 1980). Other distinguished performers said to have declined the part were Dirk Bogarde, David Niven, Robert Morley and James Mason, and producer Kenith Trodd felt the actors had "*funked it*", fearing the "*implications*" in the recent atmosphere thrown up following Blunt (quoted in Gilbert 1998: 248). A little later, *Blade on the Feather* appeared as the first of six single-plays by Potter proposed at London Weekend Television (LWT). In the event only three were completed and the association ended in acrimony with LWT claiming budget overruns on the productions (*Guardian*, 29 July 1980; *Stage and Television Today*, 31 July 1980).[398] The drama was shot on location on the Isle of Wight and directed by Richard Loncraine.

Blade on the Feather dealt with the elderly, reclusive, reactionary and authoritarian Prof. Cavendish (Donald Pleasence), a former Cambridge scholar who is working on his memoirs. A mysterious visitor, the symbolically-named Daniel Young (Tom Conti),[399] arrives just in time to provide the kiss of life to the professor who is suddenly stricken by a seizure.[400] Young then ingratiates himself with Cavendish's trophy wife and daughter and is invited to stay for dinner. During the meal, the conversation turns unexpectedly to the Cambridge Spies, Burgess, Philby and Maclean, and it is clearly an awkward moment for the professor, it later being revealed that he recruited them for the Soviets at university. That night, Young secretively seduces the daughter, and the following day he steps uninvited into the shower with the wife, where later she is found brutally murdered. The various events are overseen by the roguish, gun-toting manservant Jack Hill (Denholm Elliot), a guardian figure and intimate of Cavendish.[401] At high-tea, Young reveals his true identity as Cartwright, the son of a Foreign Office official who had been murdered while escorting a Soviet defector and who had been betrayed by Cavendish. Under the guise of retribution and in a reversal of the beginning, the younger Cartwright intimidates Cavendish into taking his own life, effectively proffering a 'kiss of death'. However, in a final twist, it is revealed to Hill, who is in fact a Soviet minder, that Cartwright is a KGB agent and Cavendish had to be eliminated before his memoirs – his 'confession' – reached the wrong hands; additionally that Mrs Cavendish had been an MI6 sleeper agent placed on the inside to discover what she could. The drama is repeatedly punctuated by ominous claps of thunder.

'Blade on the feather' is a line from the famous 'Eton Boating Song', crooned homo-erotically in the drama by Cavendish and Hill, and had been chosen by Potter to comment on the traditional status of Eton as the training ground for Britain's wealthy and privileged elite. Revealingly, the traitors Cavendish, Hill and Young/Cartwright all attended Eton. A key speech is given to Cavendish in the final confrontation with Cartwright in the summer house. Asked about his patriotism, Cavendish observes that he was "*born into a class that loves only what it owns. And we don't own quite enough of it anymore*". As he emphasises: "*That is why all of the renowned traitors came from my class*". In a corruption of the famous saying, Cavendish informs Cartwright that, "*The English have lost more battles on the playing fields of Eton than on any other acre of land this side of Vladivostok*". With *Blade on the Feather* Dennis Potter aimed to convey "*something about my sense of the decay of English life, of it being an over-ripe plum ready to fall – if not already rotting on the ground*" (quoted in Carpenter 1998: 390).

A review in *The New York Times* noted that England seemed "*preoccupied in recent years with stories of treason and treachery*", and described the play as a "*John le Carré thriller as arranged by Harold Pinter*", and this neatly captures the unorthodox, provocative and eccentric qualities of the drama, one which the critic labels a "*quite bizarre and compelling tale*" (19 December 1984).The review in the *Guardian* praised the drama as "*rich in imagery, lavish in cast, seething with scenery and writhing with treachery*" (20 October 1980), and that in *The Times* proposed "*Gold medals all round for the acting, editing and production*" (20 October 1980). A number of critics saw the play as on a higher level to a simple spy drama, appreciating it as a "*moral tale about the dangers and decay of our ruling class*", and "*something richer and more Oresteian than a spy story*" (*Evening News* 20 October; see *Sunday Telegraph*, 26 October 1980). Alexander Walker wrote a long-piece praising the drama in the *Evening Standard*. Disappointed with recent British movies, he argued that the "*British cinema is indeed alive and well, though living in television*", doubted if he would see a better British film than *Blade on the Feather* in the "*orthodox cinema this year*", and one produced at the modest cost of only £350,000. In Walker's assessment, *Blade on the Feather* was an "*all-British success*", a "*grippingly convoluted journey into the heart of a peculiarly English darkness*

– to do with class loyalties, national treachery, the politics of Right and Left, the way that silver spoons, as someone says, tarnish fast in the corroding culture of elitist England" (1980). The *Daily Mail* agreed, finding Potter's play "*masterly*" and rich in "*deliberate ironies*". Part thriller, part fantasy, part political melodrama, *Blade on the Feather* "*offered a mesmerizing view of our deeply soured age*", suggesting for that critic the "*final cry, the death-rattle perhaps of an elitist, public-schooled England unscrupulously embracing even the despised creed of Marxism in a last ditch effort to cling to its traditional feudal overlordship*". While some reviewers refused to accept the play's analysis of treachery or found it a little obscure, the *Daily Express* agreed with the *Mail*, accepting that the three most infamous recruits of Professor Cavendish, Guy Burgess, Kim Philby and Donald Maclean, "*would even now be lording it over the rest of us if the revolution had won in Britain*" (both 20 October 1980).

There were a few dissenters. *Stage and Television Today* declared itself disappointed with the three Potters put out at LWT, finding them "*lacking in sound structure*" (20 November 1980). Some felt the play's thesis about traitors was inadequate, with the *Sunday Times* judging *Blade on the Feather* "*politically unsatisfactory*" (28 October 1980). *The Telegraph* also grumbled on this point, claiming that "*for a play about a man who for reasons of personal belief took the enormous moral risk of living a double life and persuading others to do so, the political and intellectual content was disappointingly flimsy*" and failed to act as an "*allegory of our time*" (20 October 1980).

Blade on the Feather incorporated many of the themes and devices associated with Potter's work: the arrival of a sinister stranger; class and family betrayal; a forceful defence of England, married to a critique of the British class system. Although a murder mystery played out in an English country house is untypical for Potter.[402] "*While the intrusion in literal terms is into the classic venue of the English thriller*", the plot's "*metaphor*", the *Financial Times* argued, "*is that of Tinker Tailor Soldier Spy*". In one of several comparisons to John le Carré, the reviewer judged "*Potter's marrying of the two forms into one pastiche*" as "*masterly*" (22 October 1980; see also, *Times Literary Supplement*, 24 October 1980). On the other hand, while acknowledging a "*story out of le Carré and recent news about moles and how to get rid of them*", the *Scotsman* judged the new play an "*odd work*" (25 October 1980). Reviewers tended to see the Cavendish character as an analogue of the donnish Anthony Blunt who had been exposed as a traitor in the previous year (*The Times*, 20 October 1980; *Financial Times*, 22 October 1980; *Observer*, 26 October 1980).[403] At the time of the broadcast of the play, Potter was subject of the National Film Theatre's first season ever to be devoted to a television playwright, and this unprecedented honour further confirmed the literary credentials of *Blade on the Feather* and its status beyond the mere spy thriller. In this respect, *Variety* declared the play "*extremely highclass fare*" and brimming with "*production and literary values*" (5 November 1980).

The single-play remained a revered form of television drama in Britain, embodying literary credentials largely denied elsewhere on the small screen. 'Soft Targets' was written by the emerging dramatist Stephen Poliakoff and screened in the BBC's celebrated *Play for Today* anthology strand in 1982.[404] At the time of the broadcast, the 29 year-old Poliakoff was referred to as a "*wunderkind*", having had recent critical successes with *Stronger than the Sun* (BBC, 1977), *Bloody Kids* (ITV, 1980) and *Caught on a Train* (BBC, 1980) (*Guardian*, 19 October 1982). A 'quality' television drama, 'Soft Targets' was produced by Kenith Trodd, the long-time associate of the acclaimed television playwright Dennis Potter, directed by Charles Sturridge, who had achieved recent praise with the television serial *Brideshead Revisited* (1981), and starred the accomplished actors Ian Holm and Helen Mirren.

The story concerned a minor Soviet diplomat Alexei Varyov (Holm) stationed at the Russian Embassy in London, who ostensibly writes pieces about England and the English for journals back home, but who spends much of his time taping British television programmes for his Moscow bosses. Alienated and bored, he pines for home. A confusing cycle of events and people convince Alexei that he is the mouse in a cat-and-mouse conspiracy game being played by a Foreign Office smoothie (Nigel Havers) and a spookily attractive pleasure-seeking Celia (Mirren). Alexei's mounting paranoia convinces him that he is the target of some deadly stratagem of British intelligence. He decides to use the unexpected turn of events to his advantage, and, strikingly unconcerned about the KGB, he deliberately behaves suspiciously to bring British Security down on his head and provoke a return home. At one point he believes he has succeeded; but his arrest by MI5 is a mistake, the officers were after a different Soviet official and Alexei is confused and annoyed to be released. The drama ends mutely, with Alexei's visit to hospital to see Celia who is recovering from a suicide attempt, revealing her not as a threat to the Russian, but a kindred 'exile', a lower-class outsider who finds herself amidst chattering society, and an even more serious victim of alienation. Stephen Poliakoff developed the idea for the drama after meeting a Russian journalist in London who was homesick (*Guardian*, 19 October 1982).

Reviewers were generally impressed by the drama and its thoughtful and provocative themes. Broadcast during the inaugural run of *Smiley's People*, 'Soft Targets' was appreciated as a "*brilliant, elaborate joke at the expense of the breed of spy fiction (Le Carré, Fleming, Deighton) in which no voice is to be trusted and a conspiracy lurks beyond every shadow*" (*Daily Mail*, 20 October 1982). All indications are that the drama is "*set in Smiley country*", a place of "*dark hints, seeping suspicion and drifting conspiracy*". Except here, all the mystery and threat is in the mind of Alexei (*Guardian*, 20 October 1982). The *Sunday Telegraph* commented on a "*flipside version*" of the typical spy drama (24 October 1982). The truism of the genre is that a Soviet citizen stationed in London must have come for espionage, a situation troubling to both the foreign national and for home security. So, it is a case of "*Turning Smiley on its head*" (*Morning Star*, 23 October 1982), of Stephen Poliakoff constructing his drama to show "*How revealing it might be to demonstrate this mutual paranoia at work, in a case where it was completely misplaced*" (*The Telegraph*, 20 October 1982). The myth of ever-present espionage is cleverly perpetuated by Poliakoff in the key sequence set at a lavish country house wedding in Sussex. Alexei is a bystander, an outsider figure. The Russian fascinates some of the guests, and he is only half-jokingly asked if he is "*undercover*", and if he would obligingly give the alert when "*they're about to start dropping the big one*". The image of Alexei wandering around the reception snapping away with his camera, ironically sustains the possibility, as Robin Nelson has observed, "*that he might actually be spying*" (2011: 196). *The Times* admired the "*Subtle distortion of the thriller idea*", and the ambiguity of a nightmare of unanswered questions: "*Who is spying on whom, and is anyone spying on anybody? Who is the victim and who is the victimiser?*" (20 October 1982). The reviewer at the *Daily Express* revelled in the "*thrill of tension where no tension exists*", and judged 'Soft Targets' a "*small television masterpiece*" (19 October 1982).

Some reviewers were beguiled by a drama that was "*attractively vague*" (*Sunday Times*, 24 October 1982), a "*funny, dreamy, wry mystery*" (*Guardian*, 20 October 1982), and a "*very classy tease which generated all the mystery and suspense required of a spy thriller before uncovering its purpose as a study in human alienation*" (*The Telegraph*, 20 October 1982). For the *Scotsman*, the play was a "*delightful confidence trick*", a "*play about nothing which keeps us on the edges of our seats almost to the end*" (23 October 1982). Others, more robustly wedded to the conventions of the spy thriller, derided what was perceived as a "*muddle*" and were dismissive of a "*play with so little point*", arguing that, "*Ninety minutes of film where hardly anything happens makes hard work of television*". In the further view of the *Evening Standard*, 'Soft Targets' was a "*dramatic disaster, a play based upon a literary sleight of hand which never convinced for one moment*" (20 October 1982).

Literary scholar Robin Nelson is correct in recognising that Poliakoff is preoccupied with the "*setting up of generic expectations, only to deflate them*". However, he is misguided in his suggestion that the purpose or outcome of such an approach is "*spoof*" (2011: 195). The paranoia, alienated characters, Celia's attempted suicide are not intended as humorous; rather, the dramatist's approach is a serious investigation of the spy thriller form, of the overriding mistrust which clouds East-West mutual understanding. Poliakoff declared himself struck by the idea that "*we're so conditioned by films and television and novels about the confrontation of East and West that we automatically assume the other side is full of intrigue*", and he used the insight to probe the form of the spy thriller.[405] For the writer, the "*emotional journey that the characters go through is what's paramount*", confirming the serious nature of the drama as a "*story about personal alienation*" (quoted in the *Guardian*, 19 October 1982). Alexei tells Celia that he "*plans to write an English ghost story, a combination of Dostoevsky and Sherlock Holmes*". And it is this conflation of the two cultures and two national styles that Poliakoff interrogates in his drama. *The Times* observed that, "*What seemed at first to be a conventional drama turns out to be larger and more convincing than that*": "*We are apparently watching a play which depends upon intrigue and suspense, but in fact we are really being presented with a vision of an English life as absurd and also mysterious, penetrated with a thin air of suspicion that slowly dissolves conventional certainties*". "*In the balance*" the paper calculated, "*between Dostoevsky and Sherlock Holmes, Dostoevsky wins*" (20 October 1982). Taking a more global view, the reviewer at *The Telegraph* suggested the contemporary relevance of the drama, pondering if the "*sharp, witty*" 'Soft Targets', was "*faintly subversive*", sensing at a particularly acute time in Western belligerence to the Communist Bloc an "*implied encouragement of a more relaxed view of the Soviet threat*" (20 October 1982).

The espionage drama on television combined two of the more admired qualities of performance and presentation on the screen: a sense of realism and a literary credibility. The espionage drama also tended to incorporate a greater philosophical and moral complexity when compared with the simplistic, Manichean dualities of the spy thriller. *Callan*, for example, probed a more downbeat world of the secret agent, in which coercion and manipulation were the incentives for serving the state. Dramas from such literary figures as Dennis Potter and Stephen Poliakoff were often formal experiments, confusing, upturning and confounding the conventions of the spy thriller. 'Literary' spy stories from John le Carré and Len Deighton became major television dramatisations of the period, obsessive investigations of truth and deceit, loyalty and betrayal, and, echoed in Potter, serious investigations of the type of treachery recently exemplified by Guy Burgess, Kim Philby, Donald Maclean and Anthony Blunt that had shocked and fascinated the British public in equal measures. The traitors of the recent past hung over British spy fiction of the Cold War, inhabiting its characters and invigorating its themes. The British spyscreen dramatised that history, sometimes in a nostalgic fashion when concerned with traditional heroes, other times in a more critical manner when dealing with real treachery. Historical spy dramas are the subject of the following two chapters.

5.
The Nostalgic Spy Drama

It's no surprise that a country seized with insecurity and ravaged by strikes, should take refuge in hugging its past or dyspeptically trying to shake truths out of its present. It's a way of keeping alive an endangered identity.
(Harlan Kennedy 1985: 55)

It's a very British thing to want to bless the past, because it provides a comparison with the present which doesn't seem to be satisfactory. It's a kind of protective pessimism rather like talking about the weather.
(Chris Morahan, director of *Ashenden* (1991), quoted in *What's on in London*, 27 November 1991)

As newly-established British crafts like bond trading or property speculation are suddenly found to be less than secure, viewers are evidently relishing a reassertion of traditional values. They don't want to hear about collapsing financial institutions, impervious mega-corporations or official cover-ups of government ineptitude. Send for Hannay!
(*Guardian*, 2 March 1989)

Spy/Author: mythologising Ian Fleming

There was much in his personality and way of living that Fleming was to extract for Bond.
(Masters 1987: 150)

Ian Fleming, the author of the James Bond stories, was a glamorous character who shared some traits with his alluring secret agent and who lent himself as subject to romantic screen treatments of his life. Fleming's privileged story has been told in *Goldeneye: The Secret Life of Ian Fleming* (1989) and *Fleming* (2014), two dramas that revel in the opulent and exciting aspects of the Fleming legend.[406] Both dramas dealt with the life of the soon to be famous author before he takes up the pen, mainly focussing on his wartime exploits in naval intelligence and the period up to the invention of the James Bond character in

1953. The feature-length drama *Goldeneye*, released on the 25th anniversary of the death of Fleming, was the first production of Anglia Films, a new film-making subsidiary of the commercial Anglia Television. Budgeted at £2 million, it was filmed on location in London and Jamaica, directed by the maverick Don Boyd, scripted by the experienced writer Reg Gadney and starred Charles Dance (*Screen International*, 8 April and 27 May 1989). The more recent four-part serial *Fleming* starred Dominic Cooper and was produced at the international satellite broadcaster Sky Atlantic, part of a recent £600 million investment in British drama.[407] Both were glossy productions by the standards of television and, bolstered by the exotic attractions of Jamaica, paraded the lavish *mise-en-scene* of the contemporary heritage drama which had come to prominence since the early 1980s. *Goldeneye* was viewed as a "*handsomely mounted concoction of secret service capers and seductive women ... easy on the eye and undemanding of the mind*" (*Stage and Television Today*, 20 August1989). In an even more explicit fashion, *Fleming* invoked the style of the cinematic Bond, opening with stunning *sub aqua* and Alpine ski scenes reminiscent of *Thunderball* (1965) and *The Spy Who Loved Me* (1977), before sauntering on to a glamorous wartime London. *The Telegraph* judged it an "*energetic, enjoyably rollicking romp, not to be taken too seriously*", with the added bonus of a "*lot of sex*" (12 February 2014).

Both dramatisations reputedly drew on John Pearson's lively *The Life of Ian Fleming* (1966), a biography by a long-time acquaintance which appeared soon after the death of the author. Pearson wrote of the "*golden myth*" which grew up around Fleming and his approach was to cement the idea that Fleming's life was "*living fiction*" and that the Bond stories were the "*lethal fantasies of the self he might have been*" (334, 114, 190).[408] A more recent biographer has suggested that Pearson's flattering treatment "*helped establish the myth of Ian as 007 template*" (Lycett 1995: viii). It was no doubt an approach a popular and admiring readership wanted and helped set the legend about the creator of the world's most glamorous secret agent which would later be adopted by television dramatisations.[409] The epithet offered Fleming by Anthony Masters, that of the "*dashing spy*" (1987: 13), perfectly fitted the image of the novelist presented in early biographies, in popular screen dramas of more recent times, and was probably how Fleming would have liked to have seen himself. The myth has been strong enough to find its way into the critical literature, Rosenberg and Stewart claiming that "*few writers have created a fictional character who is so much their author's doppelganger*" (1989: xii).

Goldeneye and *Fleming* did offer themselves for counter-readings. A highly critical review of *Fleming* in the *Guardian*, for example, argued that the "*high gloss*" of a serial that "*looks and feels luxurious*" only masked the unacceptable privilege of Ian Fleming and his class; offered in fact a "*disturbing portrait of violence and predation*", and amply demonstrated, albeit unconsciously, a figure *"cocooned by wealth, arrogance and an assortment of creamy thighs"* (8 February 2014). This, of course, was not at all how the producers wanted the audience to view *Fleming*, and, no doubt, few did. The obvious pleasures in the screen biographies lay in their mythmaking, their sumptuous presentation, in romantic depictions of the past centring on heroism, wealth, easy living and casual seductions; fantasy constructions which arguably removed viewers from the anxieties and trials of their everyday existence into a more reassuring space imbued with the warm glow of nostalgia. The fixing and reproduction of the Ian Fleming legend in dramas such as *Goldeneye* and *Fleming* have served as comforting presentations of 'spy faction'; a heroic secret agentry permeated with glamour, style, class and charm which has long characterised an idealised form of espionage and its practice in Britain. As John Pearson once noted, the collapsing of the fantasy life of Ian Fleming into the Bond stories was profoundly satisfying for the many readers of the novels. For some, the adventures of 007 served as a sort of undercover autobiography of Fleming and subsequent romantic dramas treating the Fleming legend merely extended and fed on public expectations concerning the mortal involvement of the author and his character (1966: 221-2, 232). For cultural critics Tony Bennett and Janet Woollacott, the figure of Fleming has *"typically functioned as merely one more site for the incarnation and expanded reproduction of the figure of Bond"* (1987: 89); and drawing on their terminology, Fleming has been *"Bondianised"* to serve as a dashing figure of romanticised screen biographies to be lapped-up by a willing public (90).

This and the following chapter deal with twin aspects of historical spy fiction. Tana Wollen has noted how popular screen fictions of the period from the late 1970s into the 1980s observed a set of *"ambivalent impulses driving the search for connections to the past"*, the result of anxieties concerning the parlous social and economic conditions of the country. In this chapter, the films and dramas tend to treat the adventurous and romanticised form of spy fiction. Set in the past, both actual and imagined, they evoke a 'nostalgic' sense of history in which heroes and heroines pursue clear moral duties in the service of King and Country, or derive from classics of popular literature which have found a privileged place in the national imagination. The adaptation of literary classics bestows an aura of cultural respectability, and, Wollen has argued, promotes a pleasure of recognition which belongs to memory. This could be a memory of actually reading the novel, or more likely a memory which is generally circulated, *"part of a common cultural 'baggage'"* (1985: 163). The process of adaptation could therefore produce a *"spectacular memory"* of Britain's imperial and aristocratic past, of when the *"British were at their best"* (166). In Wollen's terms, many of these fictions take *"respite in the burrow"*. For the viewer seeking reassurance, the *"straining present can blow itself to bits while we snuggle back"* (1991: 180), with the nostalgic dramas fabricating a *"comforting history for popular spectacle"* (1985: 172). For cultural historian Jeffrey Richards, this process can be understood as a *"politics of nostalgia"*, a manner of looking backwards towards a *"Golden Age"* and the *"return to the pre-existing ideas of national identity"*. Not to be dismissed as simply passive, nostalgia can be appreciated as a *"restructuring of the past into an amalgam of myth, reality and ideal"* (1997: 352, 364).

In the next chapter, history is more problematic, and conscience and duty are conceived in terms of a world ideology rather than a narrow nationalism. Such films and dramas are less celebratory about history and tend to focus on treachery and notorious traitors of the recent past, most obviously the 'Cambridge Spies', and in doing so confront sensitive issues about class, privilege and loyalty. Such fiction can be reassuring, making neat and reasonable the troublesome and inexplicable. Equally, though, the drama is voyeuristic, allowing the viewer access to secret places and hidden motives; the resulting actions less certain, authority more under scrutiny. Wollen suggests that in this second strand of historical screen fiction, *"the present needs explaining, or at least it needs to be placed in a context, so that we can make better sense of what is going on"*; the disturbances of the present-day needing *"to be framed and focused to ease the confusion of our gaze"* (1991: 180).

More generally, historical mystery fiction has in recent decades grown in importance and popularity. Detective stories set in former times are widely read and enjoyed, becoming a distinctive sub-genre of crime fiction and covering many historical periods from antiquity through to the near past. Popular exponents of British historical detective fiction are Lindsey Davis with her Marcus Didius Falco stories set in Ancient Rome, Ellis Peters with her Cadfael stories set in Medieval England, Anne Perry with her William Monk stories set in Victorian London, and Peter Lovesey with his Sergeant Cribb stories located in late-19th century England. Historical spy fiction has not enjoyed as high a profile, but there have been many stories of 'secret service' and intrigue set in the past.

The first classic of historical spy fiction was *The Scarlet Pimpernel* (1905), Baroness Orczy's tale of daring and English decency during the terror of the French Revolution. Later, Dennis Wheatley set his popular series of Roger Brook stories around the time of the French Revolution and Napoleonic Wars in the period 1783-1815. A secret agent of Prime Minister William Pitt the Younger, Brook featured in 12 novels between 1947 and 1974, and though romantic the books are characterised by an impressive historical detail. More recently, there has emerged a minor trend in historical spy fiction. Julian Rathbone, who has written a variety of historical novels, offered up *A Very English Agent* (2002), a romp which covers the period from Waterloo in 1815 to the funeral of the Duke of Wellington in 1852. The improbable but entertaining story is framed as the memoirs of one Charlie Boylan, who claims to have spied for Great Britain and been involved in such events as the Peterloo Massacre in 1819, the Cato Street conspiracy in 1820, and in saving Queen Victoria from assassination at the Great Exhibition in 1851. The 'Mamur Zapt' series of stories by the Anglo-Egyptian-Sudanese Michael Pearce deal with mysteries and intrigues in Egypt under British rule in the early 20th century, the character of 'Mamur Zapt' being the official title of the head of the Cairo secret police and fulfilled by Gareth Cadwallader Owen, a Welsh army captain. Gavin Lyall's 'Honour Quartet' of *Spy's Honour* (1994), *Flight from Honour* (1997), *All Honourable Men* (1998) and *Honourable Intentions* (1999) deal with the fledgling British Secret Service in the years 1912-14, the period immediately before World War I and the pioneering days of modern espionage. The ambitious *Faces of Terror* trilogy by the Anglo-Russian Emanuel Litvinoff charts a pair of young revolutionaries from the streets of East London and the Siege of Sidney Street in 1911, and their political passage over the years through the Bolshevik Revolution, and on to the repression of Stalinist Russia across the novels *A Death Out of Season* (1973), *Blood on the Snow* (1975) and *Face of Terror* (1978).

There have been numerous screen treatments of historical spies and secret agentry. *The Siege of Sidney Street* (film 1960) and *Under Western Eyes* (from the novel by Joseph Conrad, TV, 1962) deal with the period of anarchists and revolutionary terrorism in the period before World War I. The First World War is the setting for the films *I Was a Spy* (1933, from the biographical memoir of Marthe McKenna 1932), *Dark Journey* (1937) and *The Spy in Black* (1939, from the novel by J. Storer Clouston 1917). Major deceptions of the Second World War are subjects of the movies *The Man Who Never Was* (1956) and *I Was Monty's Double* (1958), the fanciful adventures of the World War II spy Eddie Chapman are featured in the picture *Triple Cross* (Fr., 1966), secret operations were resurrected in *Operation Crossbow* (1965, a fanciful interpretation of 'Operation Crossbow', the Allied attempt to discover Germany's progress with the 'V-weapons'), and *The Heroes of Telemark* (1965, a more sober treatment of the raid on the German heavy water plant by SOE-trained Norwegian resistance fighters), and various aspects of the secret war was depicted in such diverse films as *Against the Wind* (1948), *Odette* (1950) and *Orders to Kill* (1958).

The historical spy dramas treated in the first part of this chapter were largely produced across the years of the late 1970s and 1980s. In a broader discussion of "*nostalgic screen fictions*", Tana Wollen has noted the "*new line in the nostalgia which the 1970s had found so marketable*", suggesting that the retrospection of such costume films and television dramas as *Chariots of Fire*

(1981), *Brideshead Revisited* (TV, 1981), *Hope and Glory* (1984) and *Wish You Were Here* (1988), was a reaction to what Patrick Wright has called the *"dislocating experience of modernity"*, and that, correspondingly, what is interesting is *"how such fictions shape collective memories and how they have become part of a wider enterprise, namely the reconstruction of national identity"*. The nostalgic spy fictions of the 1970s and 1980s were part of a broader process of *"looking back and blocking out"* which assuaged anxieties of the time, and contributed to a reassuring sense of the national imaginary, a yearning for belonging and identification with a national ideal located in the past, a place where social status is known and observed, and world-standing acknowledged and honoured (1991: 179-181). Commenting at the end of the decade, the *Guardian* postulated that, *"In the face of social chaos and too much technology, nothing it seems is more refreshing than the adventure yarn"* (2 March 1989).

A prestigious early television series with some historical storylines was *Espionage*, consisting of 24 black and white episodes and broadcast by Associated Television (ATV) in 1963-64. Each episode, budgeted at an expensive £40,000 for a nine-day shoot, lasted 50 minutes and dealt with a complete story, and the anthology dipped into various historical periods, ranging from the American War of Independence to the Second World War. Most episodes though dealt with the contemporary Cold War, with one or two storylines *"Snatched straight from today's headlines"*.[410] The series was initiated by Herbert Hirschman and Herb Brodkin, two producers with long experience in American television drama. *Espionage* was a co-production between ATV and NBC in the States, the first such arrangement between a British producer and an American network (*Stage and Television Today*, 3 October 1963). Largely produced in Britain,[411] the series was overseen by Lew Grade who at that time was Managing Director at ATV and aimed to break into the American television market with his British productions (*Stage and Television Today*, 11 April 1963). British writers and directors were hired to contribute and included old hands like Michael Powell and Seth Holt, and future film-makers such as David Greene, Ken Hughes and the American Stuart Rosenberg.[412] The superior series, mainly shot at Elstree Studios, with locations around London, Europe and North America, featured such well-known British, European and American players as Anthony Quayle, Dennis Hopper, Patricia Neal, Arthur Kennedy, Diane Cilento, Pamela Brown, Martin Balsam, Roger Livesey, Bernard Lee, Ingrid Thulin and Donald Pleasence, while the music was composed by the experienced Britons Malcolm Arnold and Benjamin Frankel.

Originally, it was envisaged that *Espionage* would deal with stories about World War II and would be written and directed by Americans. However, finding this approach too restrictive, the theme and scope of the series was broadened out to one that examined "*human, political and social factors in war and peace*", one that aimed to "*personalize in depth controversial issues and to make each episode as thought-provoking as possible*" (*Kine Weekly*, 12 September 1963). Stories based on historical characters and events were 'He Rises on Sunday, and We on Monday', about the traitor Sir Roger Casement and the Irish Rebellion, and 'The Frantick Rebel', described as a "*fictionalised story based on historical events*", with "*all the characters based on real people*", about an American woman in London who tries to get British military secrets to Benjamin Franklin in Paris during the American War of Independence.[413] The series was launched with some publicity, NBC taking out a two-page advertisement in *Variety* to promote its forthcoming autumn schedule, and for which *Espionage* served as the flagship production (10 April 1963). The show was popular enough and launched in Britain with an audience in excess of 6 million and just about held this figure for the run of the two seasons. The critics, though, were largely unmoved by what they saw. The *Daily Mail* complained of a story "*planted against a tourists' pictorial guide to London*", and found the whole a "*load of rubbish, plainly very expensive, but rubbish nevertheless*" (7 October 1963). The same reviewer, this time writing in *The Telegraph*, complained that, "*You get the feeling that the dialogue is sawn off in great, dead chunks by the script writers*" (24 February 1964). The review in *Stage and Television Today* was even more dismal, the critic declaring his experience of the first episode "*one of the unhappiest hours of my television viewing life*". He found the plot of 'The Incurable One' had little to do with the generic title of the series and dismissed it as "*pretentious tripe*" (10 October 1963). Genre critic Wesley Britton has judged *Espionage* as essentially 1950s in style and crucially out of synch with the new Ian Fleming-inspired pop standard of the day (2004: 179).

The late 1970s saw the adaptation of a cycle of well-loved period spy stories for the screen. A time of social and political turmoil in Britain, it was seemingly reassuring and nostalgic for film and television audiences to experience once again popular tales from an earlier 'golden age' of espionage fiction; a time "*When spies were real gentlemen*" (headline for a review of *The Riddle of the Sands*, *Daily Mail*, 27 April 1979). In the previous decade, when it had been decided to revive the clubman hero 'Bulldog' Drummond, the film producers had been "*emphatic that he can't be brought to the screen in the old form*"; insisting that now "*Hugh and the rest of the gang are impossible caricatures*" (quoted in the *Evening News*, 29 December 1966). The outcome was that the new Drummond was re-imagined as a wannabe James Bond for the 'Swinging Sixties' in the pictures *Deadlier than the Male* (1966) *and Some Girls Do* (1969).[414] The new period dramas of the seventies were touted as being for fans of the spy story; "*not the ludicrous James Bond but grand adventure in the Richard Hannay genre*" (from a review of *Reilly - Ace of Spies*, the *Sunday*

Times, 4 September 1983). Clear cut moral imperatives, upstanding heroes and simple 'derring-do' also contrasted sharply with the recent cynical school of spy fiction and its murky terrains of Cold War disillusionment, unprincipled intelligence organisations and degraded protagonists. Contemporary realism invested in ruthless working-class heroes would be replaced by the "*courage and fair play of the more genteel middle-classes*"; and as Tana Wollen continued to express the distinction: "*Where there is grit, there was pluck*" (1985: 161). Sarah Street has investigated the 1970s cycle of 'heritage crime' films, a series of adaptations of the popular author Agatha Christie produced at EMI Films which commenced with the extremely successful *Murder on the Orient Express* (1974), a film that demonstrated a "*populist approach of adapting older classics*" (Street 2008: 107). The EMI executive producer Nat Cohen explained the rationale of the series: "*I just had the feeling, considering all the doom and gloom in the country, Agatha Christie would go down well*" (quoted in Street: 105); a view seemingly validating the social and commercial value of reassurance and nostalgia for the decade. Street has seen the cycle of 'heritage crime' films as precursors of the significant heritage-themed films of the 1980s, concentrating on middle-class and upper-middle-class characters "*who are frequently not what they seem*", spectacular scenery and sometimes foreign locations (114).

The first of the adaptations of nostalgic spy literature to reach the screen was *Rogue Male*, a classic adventure story written by Geoffrey Household and first published in 1939. The famous tale deals with a nameless English gentleman who, for sport, 'stalks' an unspecified leader of a totalitarian European power, to see if he can evade the tight security and for professional satisfaction get the dictator in his sights. Captured, tortured and cast over a cliff and left for dead, the sportsman manages to crawl away and painfully make his way back to England. Knowing the chase will not abate, he makes plans to retreat into the English countryside, but is forced to kill a foreign agent in the London Underground, adding the police to his list of pursuers. He goes to ground in the remote county of Dorset, but after some months he is identified in a local post-office and the foreign agents and British police are once again on his track. Although the hero elaborately lays a false trail, the determined and resourceful foreign agent Major Quive-Smith, similarly a huntsman, tracks him to his subterranean lair and imprisons him there, demanding a signed false confession of an attempted act of assassination undertaken with the complicity of the British government. The 'Rogue Male' bides his time, fashions a crude weapon based on a Roman *ballista*, and kills Quive-Smith. Destroying all evidence of what took place, he then disappears, now planning a genuine assassination of the dictator. *Rogue Male* is in the tradition of the 'hunted man' adventure established with John Buchan's *The Thirty-Nine Steps* (1915), and like the earlier classic, features the 'double-pursuit' of the hero, by the police and by a dangerous foreign agency, and much recourse to field craft and survival.

The novel had previously been filmed in Hollywood as *Manhunt* (US, 1941), directed by Fritz Lang, but this departed significantly from the original story. A more faithful adaptation was produced by Mark Shivas as a television feature-length drama by the BBC in association with Fox Television in 1976, scripted by the celebrated Frederic Raphael, directed by the experienced Clive Donner, and starring Peter O'Toole as the hero (here named Sir Robert Hunter) and John Standing as the villain Quive-Smith. The largely shot on location drama, in London, the Cotswolds, and with rural Wales standing in for Bavaria,[415] is unequivocal about having Adolf Hitler as the target of the 'sporting' stalk, Raphael framing a subtle accusation against the British for their complacency at the time of the Munich appeasement and their indifference to Nazi Germany. He also introduced the novel's belated revenge aspect early on, presented as fleeting memories and referencing a specifically Jewish fiancé who has been victimised and murdered in the foreign regime, as the motive for Sir Robert's actions. At the end of the screen story Hunter is pointed in the direction of the Special Operations Executive (SOE) and an active role with the resistance movement on the continent. The director Clive Donner was drawn to the gentleman hero, seeing him as "*standing for values much more worthwhile than the brutal, politically and materialistically motivated values of contemporary heroes like James Bond*" (quoted in the *Radio Times*, 18-24 September 1976: 4).

The drama was widely praised as a skilful and authentic adaptation of a popular classic, and as showing signs of maturity for the made-for-television film. *Variety* admired the "*dramatic pace and esthetic value*" of the production, claiming the drama did "*much to tighten a gap between big budget theatrical fare and compact quality television*" (6 October 1976). The review in *The Times* felt O'Toole, Raphael and Donner had perfectly "*captured the disciplined extravagance of the original with affection and skill*" (23 September 1976), *The Telegraph* that they had taken the "*essential period flavour of the piece and nurtured it with a love and distinction*" (23 September 1976), and the *Daily Express* praised an "*elegant adventure yarn*" (23 September 1976). Geoffrey Household seemed genuinely pleased with the adaptation, declaring that the producers had been "*remarkably faithful to the book, and when they add anything, it only improves the original and makes me kick myself for not doing it in the first place*" (quoted in the *Daily Mail*, 17 September 1976).[416] There were some gripes from purists about softening the story, making it more palatable, tasteful. A popularising approach "*doesn't necessarily make a better picture*" argued the *Guardian*, but, adding significantly, it is likely to be more reassuring and "*one you can watch in comfort*" (23 September 1976).

Producer Mark Shivas sensed an opportunity with nostalgia and aimed to *"revive vintage thrillers, charting the development of heroes between the wars"* (quoted in the *Daily Mail*, 17 September 1976). *Rogue Male* was to be the first of five or possibly six productions, presenting the British hero up to the eve of World War II, and other proposed adaptations included classics by John Buchan, Dornford Yates, Sax Rohmer and Francis Beeding (*Daily Express*, 23 September 1976; Hodgson 1978: 70). The *Sunday Telegraph*, correctly labelling the initiative, excitedly reported a forthcoming series of *"Clubland Hero adventures"* (8 January 1978), and *The Telegraph* commented that Shivas and Donner had *"created a corner in upper crust British adventure, 20s vintage"* (28 December 1977). In the event, only two further screen dramas emerged, again directed by Clive Donner, Shivas declaring the making of feature-length period dramas to near-cinematic quality *"very expensive"* (quoted in Hodgson 1978: 71). 'She Fell Among Thieves', broadcast in the BBC's prestigious *Play of the Week* strand in 1978, was from a 1935 thriller by Dornford Yates, but had no discernible espionage angle. *The Three Hostages*, broadcast as a television movie in 1977, was from the famous adventure novel by John Buchan, the fourth of the Richard Hannay stories and first published in 1924.[417] The story centres on a criminal organisation led by the mysterious Medina, manipulating the mass of disturbed and disordered minds left over from the Great War. Once cornered, the sinister group kidnap three children and Hannay, now a country gentleman, is drawn into the affair and gives chase. The *Daily Mail* found this dramatisation by the popular historian John Prebble *"the best of its kind to-date"*, a play *"complementing Buchan's beguiling story-telling with modern polish and techniques"*, that actor Barry Foster had *"responded with the definitive Hannay"*, and the whole represented a *"feast both for those who love Buchan, and newcomers ready to sample adult fairy tales replete with Edwardian snobbery as well as undated excitement"* (28 December 1977). For the *Sunday Telegraph*, Donner's realisation was *"clean and luminous and hugely enjoyable"* (8 January 1978), and the *Guardian* enjoyed a *"rattling good yarn"*, likening the nostalgic viewing experience to *"looking down the wrong end of a telescope"* (28 December 1977).

John Buchan's 1922 adventure novel *Huntingtower* was produced at BBC Scotland as a six-part Sunday serial for children in 1978.[418] Producer Pharic McLaren had been aiming to dramatise the story for some years, but the rights had been until recently held by Walt Disney Productions (*Stage and Television Today*, 18 May 1978). The action takes place in south-west Scotland and centres on Bolshevik agents who imprison a Russian noblewoman. The fight back by the local rural community is led by retired grocer Dickson McCunn (Paul Curran) and includes a group of semi-outcast street urchins from Glasgow. *Stage and Television Today* welcomed a straight-forward adaptation acknowledging that a *"no-nonsense, full-blooded adventure must be played straight and with a strong sense of realism"* (26 October 1978). A later review in the same paper described the serial as an *"enjoyable romp"* and credited the casting and playing of the children (21 December 1978). An unattributed press cutting declared it *"Spiffing fun"*; however, in a moment of civic-mindedness, the reviewer wondered: *"With all the anti-communist and anti-Soviet propaganda lying around in cheap TV thrillers, as well as in current affairs, should we be all that happy about reinforcing the fall out as far as youngsters are concerned by dishing up even this well-done nonsense?"*[419]

John Buchan was the author adapted most frequently in the heritage spy cycle, with his early classic of espionage literature *The Thirty-Nine Steps* being translated to the cinema for the third time in 1978, following the popular film versions of 1935 (directed by Alfred Hitchcock as *The 39 Steps*) and 1959 (directed by Ralph Thomas also as *The 39 Steps*). Starring Robert Powell as Richard Hannay and directed by Don Sharp it was distinct as the first attempt on screen at a period setting for the famous story of the 'accidental hero' falling foul of a nest of spies planning to assassinate a visiting foreign minister and plunge Europe into war.[420] The film follows the original in outline, but invents a Hitchcockian grandstand finale staged atop Big Ben and with a bomb set to go off in the Houses of Parliament, writer Mark Robson believing that the original ending set on a stairway and a beach being too dull (*Film Review*, October 2006). The film was popular in Britain, but left critics unimpressed. *Monthly Film Bulletin* dismissed the picture as a *"series of set-pieces which are distinguished from the surrounding narrative mainly by their sheer preposterousness"* (December 1978: 249).

As Sarah Street has noted of the 'heritage crime' cycle, the legacy of the film adaptations was a tradition of extremely successful television series and dramas (2008: 115), a consequence noted at the *Guardian* which reported in the later 1980s that the *"ether is awash with period sleuths and gentlemen amateurs from a less cynical era"* (2 March 1989). While the demarcation of the heritage spy drama on screen was less clear-cut, the process was evident with *Hannay*, produced at Thames Television in two seasons broadcast in 1988 and 1989, incorporating 13 episodes at a cost of £3 million. Robert Powell satisfyingly reprised the role of John Buchan's popular hero for television. The new adventures recounted in *Hannay* are all dated before World War I and therefore predate the contemporary stories published by Buchan between 1915 and 1936. The series was largely written by Michael Robson, who had scripted the 1978 cinema version of *The Thirty-Nine Steps*, and had the support of the Buchan estate. As in the original novel, Hannay arrives in Great Britain from the Cape Colony and finds himself thrown into adventures. Initially, he is pitted against his arch enemy, Count Otto von Schwabing (Gavin Richards),

as in 'The Fellowship of the Black Stone', in which the German seeks to destroy the British fleet at Scapa Flow, and other episodes deal with period espionage, such as 'Voyage into Fear' and 'The Hazard of the Die' (both 1988), and
'The Terrors of the Earth' (1989). Increasingly though, the storylines divert
toward period crime and detection, as in 'Death with Due Notice' (1988, a
deranged killer), 'Coup de Grace' (1989, blackmail), 'That Rough Music' (1989,
a protection racket) and 'The Good Samaritan' (1989, a variant on *Murder on
the Orient Express*). The episode 'Point of Honour' (1988) was adapted from a
1914 short story by the thriller writer Dornford Yates. "*Why nobody thought of
this earlier I cannot imagine*" wondered *Stage and Television Today*, "*since
John Buchan's intrepid hero is tailor-made for the telly*" (7 January 1988).

   In an article in the *Daily Mail* it was speculated that the moment, well into
the second term of Margaret Thatcher's Conservative government, was propi-
tious for a character like Richard Hannay, the "*most enduring hero of them all:
clean cut, courteous, resourceful, athletic, handsome and resolutely patriotic –
a winner for King and Country and Empire*". The writer Michael Robson
claimed that Hannay represented the "*last years of innocence*" in the British
historical experience, and that the "*values he held then are returning to fashion now*". "*There is none of the sex and violence which have become standard-
ised*" he added, hoping that, "*With any luck we may be on the crest of this new
wave–this desire to return to the old heroic values*". Television reviewer David
Lewin helpfully chipped in, claiming that the "*code of the old hero and his
virtues are returning in a post-AIDS society*". Star Robert Powell agreed, feeling
the time was right for a change in style, commenting that modern heroes of
television drama "*were slick or cynical and not one was from the age of innocence which I think is what audiences want again. Real heroes don't have psychological hang-ups*" (all 28 December 1987). The reviewer at the *Scotman*
also appreciated *Hannay* in its contemporary historical moment, railing at
the present ragged reputation of the "*Unsecret Services*" which seemingly
"*spend their lives and our cash destabilising Harold Wilsons and Russell John-
sons*", and welcoming in its stead a compensatory drama having "*all the right
props from the nostalgic past and a sterling Buchan-based script stuffed with
old-fashioned goings-on and virtues*" (9 January 1988).[421] The *Mail on Sunday*
found the series therapeutic, claiming that, "*after a hard-day's reality, I enjoyed wallowing in its daftness*" (10 January 1988).

   The reviews for the series were mixed, the judgement of the critic depending on whether they were presently inclined towards "*escapist entertainment*"
and prepared to "*suspend disbelief*".[422] The *Times* noted that Powell made a
"*personable Hannay*", and the paper marked the series as a "*modern pastiche
which makes use of the characters and ambience and invents the stories*".
However, the 'Boys Own Adventure' and 'Ripping Yarns' quality of the series

meant that, "*Hannay has such a miraculous facility for getting out of desperate situations which for other mortals mean certain death, that the plot is rather lacking in tension*" (5 January 1988). For *Stage and Television Today*, it was precisely on the level of the Edwardian " '*Boys Own' fantasy*" that made the series "*enjoyable*" (2 February 1989). At the *Guardian*, it was felt that Hannay lacked the "*grit*" to convince as a first-rate period thriller, but the reviewer warmed to the "*gently leg-pulling stories*" (7 January 1988). The *Evening Standard* found the whole thing "*outdated*" (7 January 1988), and for the second series *The Telegraph* complained of "*elegant boredom*" (1 February 1989). There were the usual gripes concerning historical inaccuracies: the reviewer at *The Telegraph*, while seldom having a "*serious objection to well-written drivel*", complained of the production's failing attempt at "*period feel*", finding the costumes wrong, the accents wrong, and the social mores and modes of speech "*ludicrously wrong*" (7 January 1988); while *Today* considered it "*history repackaged for those who get their information on dinosaurs from cornflakes packets and their knowledge of the Second World War from bubble gum cards*" (9 January 1988).

The heritage spy cycle of the late 1970s continued in the cinema with *The Lady Vanishes* (1979), a film version directed by Anthony Page and written by Hollywood's George Axelrod. The classic mystery story was originally published in 1936 as *The Wheel Spins* by Ethel Lina White during the 'Golden Age' of English crime fiction. The heroine Iris Carr is something of a headstrong and spoiled young woman, holidaying boisterously in South-Eastern Europe with a 'crowd' of similarly-minded types. Travelling back to England alone on an express train, she is plunged into a mystery following the disappearance of the elderly British governess Miss Froy. Fearing her sanity and accused of hysterics, and with romantic interest provided by a fellow traveller Max Hare, Iris unearths a conspiracy which seeks to remove Miss Froy who is being abducted as she is aware of a political scandal in the small country where she has been working.

The new production was produced at Hammer Films on a budget of £2.5 million for distribution by Rank and merged the original story with material from the famous Alfred Hitchcock cinema version of 1938. There was no longer any need to be coy about national sensibilities and the Nazis are specifically presented as the enemy; the comic characters of Charters and Caldicott (Arthur Lowe and Ian Carmichael) are imported from the earlier film; and to improve chances in the international film market, the romantic leads (here named Amanda and Robert) are made American, played by Cybil Shepherd and Elliot Gould in a pastiche of the sparring duos of classic 1930s romantic comedy. In the manner of the classic *It Happened One Night* (US, 1934), she is a flighty heiress and he a committed newsman.[423] *Monthly Film*

Bulletin was underwhelmed, suggesting the picture "*shunts the stars through their paces with little saving energy, and uses the incongruous Panavision format to ensure that audiences have plenty of time to appreciate the Austrian locations*" (May 1979: 98-9).

There have been more recent period adaptations of both *The Thirty-Nine Steps* and *The Lady Vanishes*. The former was produced as a feature-length television drama at the BBC and broadcast at Christmas in 2008, starring Rupert Penry-Jones as Richard Hannay. This adaptation, which benefited from extensive location-shooting in Scotland (*Radio Times*, 20 December-2 January 2008: 20-21), is an amalgam of the original story and, with added female interest (a suffragette called Victoria), a night spent over in an inn, and the memorising of secret plans, Hitchcock's classic cinema version of the 1930s. While the screening attracted a respectable 7.3 million viewers, there were a number of complaints regarding historical inaccuracies in the presentation, and reviewers were largely unimpressed. *The Times* felt the "*overall effect was to turn Buchan's blood and thunder tale into a pallid politically correct Enid Blyton story*" (29 December 2008). A similar feature-length television drama of *The Lady Vanishes* was broadcast in 2013 with location-shooting in Budapest, Hungary. This was the closest screen version to the original story and starred Tuppence Middleton as Iris, Tom Hughes as Max Hare, and Selina Cadell as Miss Froy. *The Lady Vanishes* attracted a sizable audience on first broadcast and mildly supportive comments from reviewers who appreciated it as a modest entrant in the classic tradition of the BBC costume drama.

The Riddle of the Sands was arguably the first classic of modern British spy fiction; the only novel written by Erskine Childers it was published in 1903. The story tells of two young gentlemen, Davies and Carruthers, engaged in a yachting expedition on the *Dulcibella* around the desolate northern coast of Holland and Germany. It is Davies's view that a suspicious German, Dollmann, is in fact an Englishman in the service of Kaiser and that military secrets are hidden in the coastal waters of the region. The two patriotic Englishmen decide to investigate, set off to navigate the treacherous waterways and mudflats of the Frisian Islands and solve 'the riddle of the sands'. Their adventures lead them to discover a German plan to float an invasion army to the undefended east coast of England.

In his preface to the novel, Erskine Childers presented *The Riddle of the Sands* as an urgent warning to guard against German militarism. In view of the "*pitiful inadequacy*" of the Secret Service which remained indifferent to the threat, Childers felt duty bound to publicise the narrative so as to "*avert a national danger*". The book was banned in Germany at the insistence of the Kaiser and it has been alleged that when Childers next went sailing in the

Baltic his movements were observed by German spies (Moran and Johnson 2010: 1). The novel had an impact, though, and helped prompt the establishment of a North Sea Fleet and a North Sea naval base to defend Britain's eastern coast. In a famous example of life imitating art, two British naval officers, ostensibly on a yachting holiday in 1910, were arrested, imprisoned and later pardoned in 1913 by the Kaiser while surveying the German naval fortifications at Borkum, the largest and westernmost of the East Frisian Islands in the North Sea. One of the accused, Lieutenant Brandon, revealed in evidence that he was an avid reader of *The Riddle of the Sands* (Seed 1992: 71). Literary historian Robert Giddings notes that *The Riddle of the Sands* has held a "*special place in the affections of thriller aficionados and sailing enthusiasts alike*". He marks the novel's enduring appeal in the "*hauntingly atmospheric backdrop of the fogbound seas and treacherous sands of the Frisian Islands*", wrapped up in a "*tense and gripping story*" (2009: 338).[424]

The Rank Organisation chose the story as its third heritage spy drama in as many years, following on the heels of *The Thirty-Nine Steps* and *The Lady Vanishes*, observing a similar approach as EMI Films with its heritage crime cycle. There had been several plans over the years to film *The Riddle of the Sands*, the great film-maker Michael Powell failing on two attempts to get the picture off the ground. Eventually, a film version co-scripted and directed by feature débutant Tony Maylam was released in 1979, starring Michael York as Carruthers, Simon MacCorkindale as Davies, Alan Badel as Dollmann, and Jenny Agutter as his daughter Clara Dollmann. Appearing seven decades after the novel, the pressing and contemporary story of 1903 is now reconfigured as nostalgic spy fiction. After a long search by the producers, an old motor cruiser was found; converted from an Isle of Wight lifeboat it was similar to what Erskine Childers had sailed at the time of the novel. The picture was shot mainly on location, at Entehuizen in Holland, an unspoilt harbour town which also furnished a period railway, and where the boat's cabin, the setting for many scenes, was mocked-up in a local barn. Other scenes were captured at the unspoilt coastal village of Greetsiel in Germany.[425] Inclement weather made for a difficult shoot and the picture, distinguished by the cinematography of the veteran Christopher Challis, found little support at the distributor Rank and was allowed to slip by. Reviewers were largely underwhelmed, complaining of a dull script and stiff caricatures. The critic at the *Financial Times* grasped for the predictable pun when he claimed, "*The film misses the boat*" (27 April 1979). John Pym at *Monthly Film Bulletin* found the actors playing the English heroes doing their "*well-bred best*"; however, he warned: "*because nobody has taken the trouble to recreate the essential tensions of the period, the whole exercise gives off a musty air which smart production values alone are insufficient to conceal*" (March 1979: 51). The *Observer*, in a generally commendatory review, acknowledged the traditional and nostalgic quality of the adaptation, commenting that, "*It is rare in these post-Watergate days to find upright heroes exposing wicked enemy conspiracies rather than those of their own side*" (29 April 1979). The time-honoured qualities and values of the story were appropriate for its moment, as the picture was released in the final lead up to the general election that saw the return to power of a traditionalist Conservative government under Margaret Thatcher.

The Rank-produced heritage spy films and the EMI-produced heritage crime cycle constituted a plan, of sorts, by the major British producers to reconnect with the traditional family audience and help boost declining cinema revenues.[426] The trend was noted at the *Scotsman*, which commended the return to classic authors such as John Buchan and Erskine Childers. Praised as "*good adventure stories*", they were drawn "*from the reliable schoolboy literature of an earlier, more predictable part of the century, when the Empire was still more or less intact and it wasn't unfashionable for a young man to be patriotic, well-mannered, charming to women, and often foolishly heroic*" (28 April 1979). Some reviewers accepted *The Riddle of the Sands* in this spirit, judging it an "*excellent adventure*" (*Sunday Mirror*, 29 April 1979); that it was "*easy to imagine younger audiences loving it*" (*Sunday Telegraph*, 29 April 1979). However, the economics of the film marketplace seemed to suggest something different. Rank (and EMI) was in difficulty with its cinema division in the later 1970s, straddled with a policy suffering from a "*fatal*" sense of the "*unadventurous*" and a distribution arm reluctant to take pictures it felt it couldn't sell to a fragmenting audience increasingly dominated by more challenging youthful tastes. In this context, Alexander Walker considered *The Thirty-Nine Steps* and *The Lady Vanishes* "*ill-advised remakes of Hitchcock classics, rendered even more pallid by comparison with the earlier films*"; and *The Riddle of the Sands* as only a children's film by default and accordingly missing that audience. Rank failed to sell its pictures to a major American distributor as these found the productions "*dated*" and which were, in any case, reluctant to handle product that couldn't command the loyalty of the company which made them (1986a, 207-208).

Period detectives and secret agents became common in the television schedule in the late 1970s and 1980s. The traditional heroes were "*brave, honourable and independent*", and the *Guardian*, writing at the end of the decade, has adequately summarised their appeal and relevance in terms of clothes, cars, vocabulary and immaculately-appointed homes chiming "*perfectly with the booming heritage industry*". Of course, the critic maintained, these stories have endured down the decades, pointing to their seductive nostalgia; and wondered "*if there's any realistic hope of dragging Britain into the 21st century, when 'conservativism' remains the word which suits us best*" (2 March 1989).

Case file: Reilly – Ace of Spies (1983)

> *Any man who had the nerve to think he could take over revolutionary Russia and run it must be worth a television series any time, don't you think?*
> (Screenwriter Troy Kennedy Martin, quoted in the *Daily Express*, 8 July 1982)

> *Eat your heart out, James Bond. Your days as the top screen superspy are numbered.*
> (*Sunday Mirror*, 8 August 1982)

Sidney Reilly was a legendary British spy of the early 20th century and his extraordinary adventures were recounted in *Ace of Spies* by Robin Bruce Lockhart published in 1967. Lockhart was the son of Robert Bruce Lockhart, a colleague of Reilly's and an important diplomat and secret agent in Russia around the time of World War I, and Robin claimed to write with first-hand knowledge.[427] The account, however, is often hagiographical, embellishing the legend as much as revealing the man and secret agent, boldly claiming Reilly as "*surely not only the master spy of this century but of all time*" (1983: 13). Robin Bruce Lockhart served in Naval Intelligence during World War II where he knew Ian Fleming and it has been suggested that Reilly was a possible model for the fictional super agent James Bond.[428] The tale told in *Ace of Spies* includes Reilly's remarkable exploits for the British Secret Service, his attempts to discover Russian intentions in Persia in 1897, his securing of oil concessions for the British in Persia in 1904, his acquisition of secret German weapons plans in 1909, his joining in disguise of the counsels of the German High Command later in World War I and which led to his meeting with the Kaiser, and finally his various intrigues in Europe and Russia to lead the counter-revolution against the Red Terror after 1917 and depose the Soviets. The latter adventures which lasted between 1918 and 1925 are the best-known of Reilly's colourful activities. Interspersed with the espionage is a larger-than-life appetite for womanising and the making and losing of fortunes. *Ace of Spies* meditates at some length on the complex and perplexing matter of Riley's death as it appeared in the late 1960s.

Reilly – Ace of Spies was a period drama serial of 12 loosely-connected episodes depicting the legendary exploits of Sidney Reilly based on the account by Robin Bruce Lockhart.[429] Starring Sam Neill and written by Troy Kennedy Martin, it was produced for television at Euston Films and broadcast in 1983. The feature-length pilot episode 'An Affair with a Married Woman' is set in 1901 in Baku, Russia, where Reilly (named Rosenblum at this time) is engaged by the British Secret Service on a mission to discover details of the Russian oil survey. Further episodes of 50-minutes duration deal with the adventures of Reilly between 1904 and 1925: 'Prelude to War' is set in Port Arthur in 1904 during the Russo-Japanese War and has the spy aiding the Orientals; 'Dreadnoughts and Crosses' and 'Dreadnoughts and Doublecrosses' are set in 1910 and has Reilly intriguing in the rivalry between Germany and Russia; 'Gambit', 'Endgame' and 'After Moscow' have the agent intriguing in Moscow during the aftermath of the Russian Revolution in 1918 and culminates in a retreat back to Great Britain; and 'Shutdown' is set in 1925 and sees Reilly back in Moscow where he is arrested and later shot.

Reilly - Ace of Spies was a lavish 'blockbuster' production, shot on film with a budget of £4.5 million with the aim of achieving a cinematic quality. Location shooting took place in London and Paris, while Malta stood in quite convincingly for Russia, Persia and Manchuria.[430] There had been intentions to dramatise *Ace of Spies* for many years. Universal Pictures had early on taken option on the story and planned to make a feature film with Laurence Harvey as Reilly, but it never materialised, and the project later floundered at both London Weekend Television and the BBC, before it eventually settled at Euston Films which had been set-up in 1971 as a subsidiary of the ITV broadcaster Thames Television to produce single dramas and series on film.[431] Pre-sales of *Reilly - Ace of Spies* to America, Australia, French-Canada and Holland off-set the risk of Euston's most expensive production to date (Alvarado and Stewart 1985: 14).

The production of *Reilly - Ace of Spies* had to confront various problems regarding historical knowledge and accuracy, a situation not unfamiliar to those trying to reconstruct the secret world. In the long gestation period of the serial the scripts became 'out-of-date' as new insights into the Reilly story emerged and necessitated constant rewrites. The producers, for example, had to respond *tout haste* to Michael Kettle's *Sidney Reilly: The True Story of the World's Greatest Spy* which was published during the latter stages of the production in 1983. A windfall was provided when Euston unexpectedly received the research material compiled for the unrealised film of Reilly planned at Universal (Alvarado and Stewart, 1985: 112).

Subsequent critical interest in the serial has centred mainly on the writer Troy Kennedy Martin, who allegedly nursed the project for a decade and claimed to have written a million words involving 80 script revisions over the final four-year period in creating the drama (Cooke 2007: 145). Denied access to the archives of the British Secret Service, Kennedy Martin had to piece together the life of Reilly from published memoirs and personal reminiscences (*Daily Express*, 8 July 1982); although Bruce-Lockhart remained a key source. With *Reilly - Ace of Spies* he aimed to create "*something that would bear comparison with Somerset Maugham's Ashenden stories or with Graham*

Greene of Stamboul Train" (quoted in Cooke 2007: 142), and would therefore have been gladdened by the comments in the *Guardian* which found a "*Somerset Maugham-ish sense of sex and cynicism about the story*" (6 September 1983). Television scholar Lez Cooke claims that *Reilly _ Ace of Spies* "*attempted a serious approach to history*", was not simply a nostalgic costume drama about the romantic exploits of a British spy, but strove to "*achieve a balance between the serious dramatisation of real historical events, action-adventure and romance*", sufficient to attract a popular audience (2007: 139). This was the view of Verity Lambert, Head of Drama at Thames and executive producer on the serial, who thought the dramatisation was a "*real opportunity to do something about an extraordinary charismatic character against a fascinating historical background ... and also to have some kind of serious underbelly at the same time*" (quoted in Alvarado and Stewart 1985, 110-111). In stylistic terms, Cooke sees the "*matter-of-fact*" narrational voice-over as confirming the "*historical authenticity of the serial*", and as "*ensuring Reilly's activities are seen within a wider political context*" (2007: 140). The problem with this view, of course, is that Robin Bruce Lockhart is hardly a credible historical source. The drama, like the book, fails on many occasions in terms of historical accuracy, makes elementary mistakes such as having Mansfield Cumming (Norman Rodway) involved in the British Secret Service in 1901, when in fact he was appointed to what was a wholly new Service in 1909, and, furthermore, fabricates much new material such as a murderous vendetta Reilly pursues against the powerful arms dealer Basil Zaharov (Leo McKern) following the death of a girlfriend. The tagline for *Reilly _ Ace of Spies*, "*He lived for danger ... and died a legend*", more accurately reflected the intention of the serial.

Sidney Reilly remains a mythic and mysterious figure in espionage and other accounts of his enigmatic life have been more critical, claiming that the agent, referred to by some colleagues in British Intelligence as "*Reckless Reilly*", was no more than a con-man, an adventurer and a rogue, that at one time or another worked for the Japanese, Russian, German and British governments, and more damning, might have been a double-agent. The writer on intelligence Michael Smith offers the sober judgement that, "*Reilly's activities _ in government service, in business and in love _ were exaggerated beyond belief, both by himself and by his biographers. But they were nevertheless colourful*" (1996: 87).[432] Chris Burt the producer of *Reilly _ Ace of Spies* had to admit under questioning: "*What's true and what's not true in the Reilly story is not clear. He was a consummate liar. The series is a piece of entertainment, not historical fact*" (quoted in the *Daily Mail*, 5 September 1983); a view echoed by writer Kennedy Martin who, despite any diligent research, described the approach as "*fiction with a background of history*" (quoted in *The New York Times*, 15 January 1984). The general critical attitude to the drama's supposed treatment of history was captured in a remark at the *Western Mail*, which opined: "*A nearly true story, and preposterous as all spy stories must be*" (10 September 1983); a view that conformed with an old epithet which described Reilly as "*The Scarlet Pimpernel of Red Russia*" (*Sunday Referee*, 30 May 1937).

Interestingly, an element of 'real history' intruded during the broadcast of the serial. The Soviet historian David Golinkov had given an updated account of Reilly in his book *The Secret War Against Revolutionary Russia* (1981), and Moscow's authorised English language newspaper *Soviet Weekly* reproduced edited extracts during the run of *Reilly – Ace of Spies*, suggesting that the British agent, when told he was to be executed, offered his services to Soviet counter-intelligence, and the study confirmed that the death sentence was carried out on the orders of the Soviet Supreme Revolutionary Tribunal on 3 November 1925. Producer Chris Burt declared himself "*astonished the Russians have finally admitted they killed Reilly*" (quoted in the *Daily Star*, 11 November 1983). The dramatisation had had to deal with the difficult issue of the death of Sidney Reilly and the producers felt confident enough that they could "*actually make an accurate guess about when Reilly was killed*", opting to have him shot on the specific orders of Stalin in 1925, something which had long been suspected (Alvarado and Stewart: 112).[433] Following the revelations in *Soviet Weekly*, Burt proudly proclaimed: "*In the programme we did have Reilly shot by the Russians in 1925*", declaring himself "*amazed we got it right because we had little to go on*" (quoted in the *Daily Star*, 11 November 1983). The Soviet newspaper *Izvestia* criticised *Reilly – Ace of Spies* and accused the serial of glorifying Sidney Reilly and of omitting politically sensitive material such as two abortive assassinations of Soviet officials and the plotting to murder Vatslav V. Vorovsky, a Marxist journalist and Soviet diplomat (*The Times*, 17 November 1983). Robin Bruce Lockhart remained unmoved by the various revelations and later published the sensationalist *Reilly: The First Man* (1987), which claimed that Reilly did not die in Russia in 1925, but went on to mastermind other amazing espionage coups, further undermining his credibility as a source.[434]

Reilly – Ace of Spies attracted a lot of press interest and many column inches were put to outlining and discussing the mysterious and controversial career of Reilly.[435] He was often favourably compared with James Bond, both agents being larger-than-life womanisers, and many reviewers enthusiastically extolled Reilly as "*Britain's greatest secret agent*". The *Sun* found *Reilly* "*crackles with style and quality*" (8 September 1983); and the *Daily Mail* praised a "*tautly acted and expertly made epic of intrigue, exotic mistresses, double-crossing and high adventure*" (5 September 1983). A slightly let down *Evening Standard* had expected a treatment a "*great deal grittier, more exciting, and more politically resonant than this frivolous old-fashioned romance*" (6 September 1983), the *Spectator* reflected that *"almost invariably when a lot of money is spent and the publicity machine is wheeled out, the end result is disappointing"* (10 September 1983), *The Times* found *"nothing interesting enough remotely to justify the expense involved"*, and a *"plot which itself deserves to be in a museum"* (13 October 1983), and the *Sunday Times* noted a confused sense of literary origins, *Reilly – Ace of Spies "taking over territory once colonised by Conrad and Kipling, and populating it with characters out of Sax Rohmer and worse"* (11 September 1983). Most acclaim was devoted to the serial's impressive production values, the *Daily Telegraph* lauding that the *"Photography, acting, direction, locations, all come out of the topmost drawer"* (22 September 1983), and the *Daily Express* claiming, *"This handsomely filmed series has a sense of time which makes it a feast for the eyes"* (6 October 1983). Production values were pleasingly high and the characterisation of Reilly was that of a *"spy on the grand scale"* (*Daily Express*, 8 July 1982). *Reilly – Ace of Spies* attracted decent if unspectacular viewing figures, usually over eight million a week, but was judged *"not the triumph"* the producers had hoped for (*Daily Mail*, 17 November 1983).[436]

The serial differed from other nostalgic spy dramas considered in this section due to its more ambiguous hero, a complex character with whom an audience would struggle to identify with too directly, other than as the *"spy you love to hate"*. A critical *The Times* did not see things this way, instead observing that, *"It seems a pity, however, that such a malevolent man should be turned into a hero: if the series were not inept, it might be distasteful"* (13 October 1983). The dramatisation made much of Reilly as a relentless lover and of his *"under-the-covers missions"* (*Daily Star*, 29 August 1983). While the production team took *"much trouble to ensure design and backgrounds suggesting the period in which John Buchan's forthcoming and clean-limbed hero Richard Hannay flourished"*, the dubious morality of Reilly distanced him from the up-standing heroes of early spy fiction, and the characterisation in the series, as noted at the *Daily Telegraph*, was more obviously modern, a *"buttoned, ruthless Reilly, with stoney-faced good looks sufficient to stir the sexual appetite of every passing young woman"*, and *"closer to the style of Ian Fleming's figment, James Bond"* (6 September 1983). And it is this connection with the romantic super-agent 007 which places the discussion of the historical Reilly in a section concerned with nostalgia. In both literary and screen forms, the charismatic agent emerged in mythic terms, and the lavish television drama serial promoted such mythical qualities, as well as a nostalgia for a time long gone. As the historian Jennifer Siegel has written, the escapades of Reilly in Tsarist and Bolshevik Russia were the *"stuff of which legends are made"*, and in all likelihood were *"complete legends themselves"* (1995: 475).

Revisiting the classics

The nostalgic spy dramas discussed so far were largely set in the formative period of early espionage fiction, the years around the First World War, and in the case of *Rogue Male* and *The Lady Vanishes* the eve of the Second World War; overall, three decades which could be taken as the first 'golden age' of the spy story. The films and television dramas were derived from popular classics, novels which had been influential but denied the status of literature. In the self-imposed derogatory terms of the authors John Buchan and Graham Greene, 'shockers' and 'entertainments'. Other costume dramas in the 1970s-1990s drew on further classics of spy fiction; popular stories set in the earlier period of the 19th century as well as more literary works that probed the moral and ethical complexities of the clandestine world. This group related more obviously to the tradition of the 'classic serial', radio and screen dramatisations of British novels predominantly of the Victorian and Edwardian periods. Broadcasters sought cultural respectability with the adaptations and through a two-way process the classic serial became a "*means by which past literature is identified as being worthy of classical status and this contributes to the construction and maintenance of the literary canon*" (Giddings and Selby 2001: ix-x). Through a specific presentation of English literature and heritage, the classic serial also offered an appeal to culturally aware audiences in the world film and television market.

The Scarlet Pimpernel is the most enduring character of historical spy fiction. A creation of Baroness Emma Orczy, he appeared in a play first performed in 1903 and in a novel published in 1905. There were 10 further novels between 1906-1940, collections of short stories in 1919 and 1929, various related novels featuring relatives of the Pimpernel or purporting to be biographical works, numerous movie and television adaptations commencing with an American silent film of 1917, and numerous parodic allusions to the character in other works, most notably perhaps the character of The Black Fingernail in the British spoof *Don't Lose Your Head* (1966), one of the long-running series of 'Carry On' comedy films.

The basic story of the Pimpernel adventures involved the seemingly foppish Sir Percy Blakeney secretly leading a band of English aristocrats as the Scarlet Pimpernel in the rescue of their French counterparts in the 'Reign of Terror' of the French Revolution. Pitted against the Pimpernel is Citizen Chauvelin, a ruthless protector of the revolution. A number of historical individuals appear in the stories, such as Robespierre, Danton, Marat and Saint-Just. The Scarlet Pimpernel, a 'device drawn in red – a little star-shaped flower', is used in the stories as the sign of the secret organisation formed to save the lives of French nobles.[437]

The Pimpernel had been played on screen in Great Britain by Leslie Howard in the classic film *The Scarlet Pimpernel* (1934), by Barry K. Barnes in the film *Return of the Scarlet Pimpernel* (1937), by David Niven in the film *The Elusive Pimpernel* (1950), and by Marius Goring in the television series *The Adventures of the Scarlet Pimpernel* (1956). The Pimpernel was revisited twice on screen in the 1980s and 1990s. The character was played by Anthony Andrews in the television movie *The Scarlet Pimpernel* in 1982, loosely adapted from the novels *The Scarlet Pimpernel* and a later sequel *Eldorado* (1913), and produced at London Films, the company which had made the famous cinema version with Leslie Howard in 1934 and now lingered on with a handful of television dramas. A leisurely running time of three-hours for commercial television, the film was directed by the experienced Clive Donner who had recently acquired experience of costume espionage dramas with *Rogue Male* and *The Three Hostages*. Historical and visual splendour was maintained through filming at such heritage locations as Blenheim Palace, Ragley Hall, Broughton Castle and Milton Manor. The British production, respectfully reviewed, was commissioned by the CBS Network and intended for the American market, but a hoped for series failed to materialise (*Sumter Daily*, 4 July 1986). The Pimpernel was later played by Richard E. Grant in the handsome television series *The Scarlet Pimpernel*, broadcast in six episodes across two seasons in 1999-2000, and yet another attempt by London Films to cash in on a long-held property. Filming took place at historic locations in the Czech Republic and reviewers generally found the production sumptuous and witty (*Variety*, 4 March 1999). The Pimpernel is a melodramatic, escapist figure, akin to such characters as Robin Hood and Zorro, and an archetype of the English gentleman hero. While one of the most enduring characters of historical spy fiction, he is far removed from modern, bureaucratic identifiers of secret agents and espionage, and the simple, daring exploits depicted in the stories firmly belong to the romantic tradition of the genre.

Kim by Rudyard Kipling is a classic of both the literature of Empire and of historical spy fiction and published as a novel in October 1901. The setting is the 'Great Game', an expression coined by Kipling in the novel and referring to the imperial struggle played out between Great Britain and Russia in central Asia in the period of the 1880s-1890s, and which Kipling claimed in the story "*never stops night or day*". Kim is the orphaned son of an Irish soldier, an urchin on the streets of Lahore, India who passes for native. While serving as a disciple of an aged Tibetan Lama, Kim is introduced to the Great Game when he is recruited by Mahbub Ali, a native operative for the British Secret Service, to carry a message to the head of British Intelligence in Umballa. The story ends with the Lama finding his enlightenment and Kim facing the choice between a spiritual and a patriotic future.

While there have been criticisms of *Kim* as a complete fabrication of a supposed British intelligence system in the sub-continent, the scholars Moran and Johnson have pointed to the manner in which the espionage literature of the period reflected contemporary anxieties and aspirations. Thus *Kim* expressed widely held concerns regarding a Russian threat to the landward borders of India, especially through the North-West Frontier and Afghanistan, of a feared Franco-Russian alliance which would unite Britain's main imperial rivals, of internal subversives, and reflected an imperial Islamophobia. An *ad hoc* yet widespread intelligence network was operated by the British in the region, which included the Indian Survey Department, boundary commissions, local native agents and the use of Indian merchants as *"the eyes and ears of the Empire"*. Moran and Johnson refer to Kipling's *"idealized world"* in *Kim*, *"one where British Intelligence is alert to the dangers, operates within the sub-strata of native society, and thwarts the conspirators to maintain British security"* (2010: 7).[438]

There had been a Hollywood movie version of *Kim* (1950) starring Errol Flynn as Mahbub Ali and Dean Stockwell as Kim, and the story was revisited for a British television adaptation in 1984, directed by John Davies, starring Peter O'Toole as the Lama, Bryan Brown as Mahbub Ali, and in his only screen role Ravi Sheth as Kim.[439] It was a fairly faithful adaptation and a further London Films production of a classic of British espionage literature for the American network CBS (*Stage and Television Today*, 29 March 1984). The new production was filmed extensively on location in Northern India.[440] *Variety* judged it an *"engrossing, lovely telefilm not to be missed"*, and praised it as a rousing adventure (23 May 1984). *Kim* was intended as entertainment for children and young adults, while retaining interest for those who enjoyed screen versions of classic literature. As with *The Scarlet Pimpernel*, the story and its tradition now had little immediate connection to the modern espionage story.

In 1928, the novelist and dramatist W. Somerset Maugham published a collection of seven short spy stories as *Ashenden; or, The British Agent* dealing with the adventures of the eponymous agent during World War I. In the preface, Maugham made it clear that the stories were *"founded on experiences of my own during that war"*, but he stressed that they were not "reportage, *but works of fiction"*. He revealed that, *"The works of an agent in the Intelligence Department is on the whole monotonous ... The material it offers for stories is scrappy and pointless"*. This was a radically fresh perspective for spy fiction and the *Ashenden* stories have been acclaimed as offering a new realism in the modern espionage story, in stark contrast to the fanciful heroics of the contemporary spy thriller and the writings of William Le Queux, E. Phillips Oppenheim and Sydney Horler.

The *Ashenden* stories are classics of their type, the best-known and most acclaimed collection of short spy stories, and which singularly have regularly
made appearances in anthologies of spy fiction. While their importance is
appreciable in their 'modern' style, more realistic, less idealised, it is a curiosity that the stories dwell relatively little on the actual business of espionage.
These tales are essentially character studies in which Maugham can comment
on various human foibles and qualities. The secret agent stories have been
immensely influential; Eric Ambler writing in 1964 claimed that there has
been "*no body of work in the field of the same quality written since* Ashenden"
(1974: 17).

The *Ashenden* tales, via the stage play *Ashenden* by Campbell Dixon which
confected romantic aspects for the story, had been the basis for Alfred Hitchcock's film *Secret Agent* of 1935. In 1959, the single tale 'The Traitor' was
dramatised on the BBC starring Stephen Murray, but this is now believed
lost.[441] In 1991, the influential stories were adapted more substantially by
David Pirie as *Ashenden* in a major four-part BBC television mini-series co-
produced with the American cable network Arts & Entertainment, and budgeted at an impressive £4.1m (*Observer*, 17 November 1991). It starred Alex
Jennings as Ashenden and Ian Bannen as spymaster 'R'. Handsomely mounted and shot on location in post-communist Hungary and Yugoslavia, and in
Austria and the UK, the series adapted the four stories most suitable for an
espionage series: 'Giulia Lazzari' (as 'The Dark Woman'),[442] 'The Traitor', 'Mr
Harrington's Washing' and 'The Hairless Mexican'. The first two episodes include material from 'Miss King' so as to provide some necessary background
on the writer Ashenden, his recruitment into the Intelligence Department by
'R', and his stationing in Geneva. The series introduced the real-life character
of Mansfield Cumming into the stories, the first head of the Secret Intelligence Service (SIS), and integrates actual experiences from Somerset
Maugham's life prior to his engagement as an agent in Switzerland. Screenwriter Pirie drew on biographies of Maugham and Cummings as well as the
original short stories, and these bolster the historical realism of the drama.
The novelist William Boyd, writing in the *Sunday Times*, praised the series and
lauded Pirie's use of contemporary sources, as these "*imbue the stories with
an objectivity and a veracity which are completely convincing*" (1991).[443]

The television *Ashenden* is generally a close adaptation of the original material with only minor changes of detail, and stands as a superior television
period drama of its day. The only substantial alteration comes in 'The Hairless
Mexican', the best-known of the stories, which changes the target of the assassination to an American woman for whom Ashenden has come to show some
romantic affection. Her wrongful murder intensifies the emotional impact of
the drama.

Stage and Television Today, worrying that the spy drama "*seems to have little less to play with but clichés*", was enjoyably surprised by the quality and sensitivity of the production and rated *Ashenden* the "*highlight*" of the week's viewing (28 November 1991). Many reviewers found *Ashenden* a classy drama series, if a little slow; at *Time Out*, for instance, it was judged "*stylish and intelligent amusement*" (20 November 1991). As was common with British television costume dramas, there was praise for the meticulous recreation of the past; this was the case at the *Financial Times* which admired *Ashenden's* "*beautifully photographed period reconstructions and the fine performances*" (9 December 1991). For some reviewers, the *mise-en-scène* was all they felt able to commend, *The Telegraph* claiming the series "*memorable chiefly for the lushness of its setting*" (18 November 1991), and the *Mail on Sunday* finding it "*watchable mainly for a nice old boat which steamed slowly back and forth across Lake Geneva*" (24 November 1991). A more overtly critical review at the *Guardian* found the dramatisation "*slenderly-plotted and curiously under-populated, as if all the location shooting had been tackled on a Sunday morning*" (25 November 1991).

A more developed and thoughtful critique appeared in the *Sunday Times*, written by the novelist and sometime spy writer William Boyd.[444] There he somewhat iconoclastically criticised Maugham's "*execrable style*", and was pleased that the adaptation had managed,

> *to save Maugham's Ashenden stories from their own toiling inadequacies, from a tone of voice and manner that virtually guarantees a built-in obsolescence, literature's very own self-destruct mechanism. We have the Ashenden stories made anew here, and can judge – freshly – their real modernity and originality buried beneath the leaden prose.*

He argued that writer David Pirie's decision not to restrict himself to the source stories lifted the curse of "*period*" that hung over the tales, the resulting films emerging as a "*telling and clever amalgam of the fictive world of the stories – plot-lines, settings and characters – and of the realities, both sinister and banal, of the actual time and place, truths which hindsight and history have subsequently provided*" (1991).

Ashenden's origin in the cool tone and "*cynical nonchalance*" of the biographical Somerset Maugham tales sets it apart from the more straightforwardly nostalgic screen dramas derived from the romantic strain of popular spy literature exemplified by John Buchan.[445] The director Chris Morahan pointedly claimed that, "Ashenden *avoids sentimental nostalgia*"; that in the final episode, in contrast to restorative adventures like *The Thirty-Nine Steps*, Ashenden "*turns away from English society*", showing his disenchantment with the manipulation and cynicism of the Secret Service and the class it serves (quoted in *What's on in London*, 27 November 1991). Writer David Pirie was particularly struck by a comment of Mansfield Cumming which he added to the stories, warning of the inevitable drift for the espionage agent from disillusionment, to disaffection, and finally to defection, a strikingly modern idea which is seemingly borne out in Maugham's experience as a secret agent, subsequently written into the short stories collected in *Ashenden*, and which Pirie describes as a "*chronicle of disillusionment*" (quoted in *The Telegraph*, 14 November 1991). William Boyd noted the skilful treatment of the theme in the television *Ashenden*, the "*impending sense of decline and self-disgust*" developed across the four dramas, resulting in a,

> *compelling and cogent portrait of a fundamentally decent man drawn into a world where decent values are redundant, if not plain dangerous; where your best protection, and probably the key to your survival, is the development of a thoroughgoing cynicism, a reliance on the expedient and a refusal to trust.* (1991)

The reviewer at *The Telegraph*, complaining of a "*rather dusty quaintness*" in the television *Ashenden*, "*compared with the sophisticated complexities of John le Carré*", failed to grasp the fundamental modernity in the series, unconsciously exposing his resistance to generic complexity in a period costume drama drawn from stories which originated the sensibilities of modern spy literature (18 November 1991). The alertly-tuned Boyd rightly felt that comparisons with le Carré were "*fair and valid*"; that *Ashenden*, "*as progenitor of this particular seedy ambience*", was not, "*Thankfully*", *Reilly - Ace of Spies* or *Bulldog Drummond*". Instead, the four films "*set their face against any facile period illusion or escape*", conjuring up in their place a "*convincing ring of authority*", and the whole having a "*solid buttress of authenticity to it*" (1991).

The Secret Agent, subtitled 'A Simple Tale,' was a landmark novel by Joseph Conrad. The story is set in 1886 and, in a narrative constructed in a broken chronology, centres on the indolent Adolf Verloc, an *agent provocateur* for a European power and associate of a group of anarchists and terrorists. Verloc, who owns a seedy shop selling pornography, is ordered to carry out a terrorist outrage by his political employer which is intended to lead to the suppression of émigré radicals by the British authorities. A bombing is arranged and it is later revealed that the beloved young brother of the wife Winnie Verloc was killed at the accident, Adolf having exploited the childlike simplicity of the half-witted Stevie. In despair, Winnie stabs Adolf to death, and when her savings are stolen by the manipulative seducer Comrade Ossipon, she drowns herself in the English Channel. The historical context of the story was generally the terrorism and extremist politics of the period which included numerous dynamite outrages on mainland Britain, and specifically the French anarchist Martial Bourdin who died gruesomely when he blew himself up in 1894 in Greenwich Park with explosives possibly intended for the Greenwich Observatory.[446]

The novel did not sell particularly well, but attracted generally favourable reviews; although, for some conservative tastes, the story was 'indecent'. Master spy novelist Eric Ambler later referred to *The Secret Agent* as the *"first attempt by a major novelist to deal realistically with the secret war, with the subworld of conspiracy, sabotage, double-dealing and betrayal, the existence of which had for so long been denied"* (1974: 14). Over time, *The Secret Agent* has come to be seen as one of Joseph Conrad's masterpieces, an artistic achievement of the first rank, and one of the very greatest novels of terrorism. According to two admiring Conrad scholars, *"In its irony and symbolism, its realism, its conjunction of the mainstream novel and the detective story,* The Secret Agent *may well be the modern novel, where every word counts and reverberates not only through the entire novel but in our very consciousness"* (Harkness and Birk 1990: xxiii).

Television producer Colin Tucker once described Joseph Conrad as *"legendarily impossible to film"* and few adaptations have made money (quoted in the *Radio Times*, 24-30 October 1992: 44); however, this has not prevented movie and television producers from trying. *The Secret Agent* was first adapted for the screen as the updated *Sabotage* (1936), directed by Alfred Hitchcock, and this version simplified and sanitised the moral complexities of the original, spared Winnie Verloc, and lightened the tone. *The Secret Agent* was first adapted for television by Alexander Baron in a *"handsome two-part account"* screened on the BBC in 1967 with Nigel Green and Mary Webster as Adolph and Winnie Verloc (*Sunday Telegraph*, 16 July 1967). Conrad's own adaptation of the novel for the stage was produced as a single play drama at the BBC in 1975 starring Anton Rogers and Frances White as the Verlocs, and managed a *"feeling for period drama"* and a *"lovely, fusty, Edwardian atmosphere"* (*Daily Mail*, 2 October 1975).

Two screen versions were produced in the 1990s. A three-part adaptation by Dusty Hughes appeared on the BBC in 1992, starring David Suchet as 'Alfred' Verloc and Cheryl Campbell as Winnie Verloc. It was intended the dramatisation would not be a typical BBC costume drama, that there would be no *"posh frocks"*, and sufficient emphasis would be placed on the *"murky under-world and squalid back streets of Soho"* (*The Telegraph*, 4 January 1991; BBC press sheet 1992).[447] *The Los Angeles Times* accepted the validity of this approach, asserting that espionage had *"never been dingier or less romantic"*, praising *"outstanding performances"*, and claiming to be *"hooked on the interlocking human tragedy and political intrigue"* (14 November 1992). *The Times* found it "*spellbinding*" and wondered if a commercial television company would have financed a project "*so dark, its sets swathed in shadow, its high society scenes so unglamorously low and calculating, its ending so bleak*" (15 November 1992).

However, some British critics were not taken in and still noted the prettifying aesthetic of the classic costume serial, *The Secret Agent* conjuring up a "*gorgeous BBC reconstruction of 19th-century Soho*" that resulted in "*chocolate-box poverty*" (*Independent*, 1 November 1992). The adaptation was generally received as atmospheric yet ponderous, worthy but dreary, *Stage and Television Today* cautiously wondering "*who would dare to find fault with this story of terrorism, deceit and inner conflicts at the turn of the century?*", before admitting that "*it would*", and judging the adaptation "*tortuously slow and very, very dull*" (12 November 1992). The reviewer at *Today*, while claiming the drama "*beautifully scripted, acted and filmed*", found himself nodding-off (29 October 1992); while for the *Independent* a "*surface perfection*" failed to plumb the "*story's depths*" (1 November 1992). The approach to the dramatisation was tragic-comic, and this was appreciated at the *Observer* which wrote of Suchet's "*masterly (and slightly hilarious) portrayal*" (25 October 1992). As befitting the adaptation of a classic of literature, there were the usual comparisons between the original novel and the screen drama. The *Independent* thought the translation "*cautious*", with a "*great cast struggling to invest their characters with character and a fidelity to the original that leave you longing for a philandering adapter*". The conclusion: "*Viewers who'd read the book were probably disappointed; those who hadn't fell asleep*" (1 November 1992).

A movie version of *The Secret Agent* starring Bob Hoskins as Verloc and Patricia Arquette as Winnie, adapted and directed by Christopher Hampton in 1996, was a critical and commercial disaster.[448] The production was a labour of love for co-producer Hoskins who had spent four years putting the project together, and once on-board Hampton set out to be faithful to the "*visual world*" of the novel. After "*fruitless searches in London, Bristol, Liverpool and Dublin*" the filmmakers opted for "*Caroline Amies's gloomy, fetid, muddy, wonderfully atmospheric Soho street*" created at Ealing Studios (*Sunday Telegraph*, 8 February 1998).[449]

The movie opened disastrously in the United States, *The New York Times* calling it a "*drably tasteful*" and "*curiously muted adaptation*" (8 November 1996); and the *Village Voice* dismissing it as "*slack and gloomy*" and "*weirdly sentimental*" (12 November 1996). With box-office receipts reputed to be as low as $106,000 in North America, it was feared the film might go "*straight to video*" in Britain, with an "*industry insider*" quoted as saying, "*It is a terrible film, an embarrassment that should be forgotten as quickly as possible*" (*Sun-*

day Telegraph, 28 December 1997; *Evening Standard*, 5 January 1998). In the event, the picture got a belated release in Britain in 1998 where reviews were little better. Fairly typical was the view at the *Financial Times*, which felt it had all the "*miserablism*" of Joseph Conrad, but with little of the "*wit, terror or hallucination*" (12 February 1998); and some took it as confirmation that Conrad remained 'unfilmable'. The reviewer at *Time Out* advised his readers to "*avoid*", and as with other critics wondered at a "*criminally prosaic flashback structure*" which results in an adaptation that "*travesties the novel*" (11-18 February 1998). It was judged a mistake at the *Sunday Telegraph* that Hampton should adhere to what the screenwriter himself described as the "*curious structure*" of the original (28 December 1997). A more considered examination of the film has praised a "*faithful rendering on the screen of the Conrad original*", and one which therefore "*deserves a prominent place among the better screen versions of Conrad's fiction*" (Phillips 1999: 177).[450] However, Hampton's fidelity to the novel, specifically perhaps it dark, uncompromising vision and mise-en-scene proved to be unattractive to reviewers and audiences.

The immemorial insights and truths of Joseph Conrad's *The Secret Agent* have constantly impressed themselves on observers. The BBC television dramatisation of 1975 struck a reviewer as "*surprisingly up-to-date in its attitudes*", in its manner of being "*profoundly cynical about all parties*" (*Daily Mail*, 2 October 1975). Christopher Hampton judged *The Secret Agent* "*one of the most remarkable and prophetic novels of the century, and one of the most influential*". A story of "*brilliantly paradoxical characters*", the progenitor of a "*new tone appropriate to the atrocities of the coming century*", and the "*ancestor of a whole strain of modern literature*", and not least of all the world of the modern spy fiction of Graham Greene and John le Carré, "*where ideological double-crosses and the oversimplifications of whatever shabby orthodoxy happens to be in the ascendant mirror the hypocrisies and betrayals of private life*" (quoted in the *Sunday Telegraph*, 28 December 1997).

More recent interest has been heaped on the novel following the terrorist attacks on New York and Washington in 2001, which seemed to reject the optimism that the world could be united under the sign of the market, and which seemed to suggest a return to the troubled age of empire. Conrad conjures up the plot to blow-up the Greenwich Observatory as an assault on the rationality of science, society's most cherished beliefs, symbolically embodied in the attack on the Prime Meridian. Modern observers have noted how the strike on the twin towers, symbols of Western trade and finance, can be configured in much the same way, as an attack on the fundamental values of contemporary capitalist society. The philosopher John Gray has gone so far as to claim Joseph Conrad with this novel as the "*first great political novelist of the 21st century*" (2002). The BBC announced plans late in 2014 for a new dramatisation of *The Secret Agent* starring Toby Jones as Verloc, from writer Tony Marchant. The three-part serial was broadcast in the summer of 2016, and there was predictable discussion of the timeliness of the adaptation, following the recent slaughter of innocents in Nice (*The Telegraph*, 18 July 2016), and the now common observation on the contemporary relevance of the story which had established itself as the "*prism through which modern political insecurities are viewed*" (*Guardian*, 16 July 2016). However, true to form, the most recent incarnation of *The Secret Agent* was poorly received. The *Guardian* complained of the "*one-dimensionality*" of the adaptation, in which the complexities of the novel, formal and thematic, were lost to a "*psychological thriller*" (18 July 2016), while the *Daily Mail* cruelly maintained that pairing socks was more "*compelling*" (23 July 2016). Conrad's complex 'simple tale' continues to stimulate readers and remains startlingly germane; it also continues to confound its adapters who have largely failed to find a method of translating it to the screen without losing much of its seduction and effect.

Wartime Myths

Time and distance must take away the edge of pain because, as I look back, I cannot help remembering the 'good' times ... There was the unity we felt during those traumatic years, when we were all together fighting for the same cause, a unity which sadly evaporated with the end of hostilities.
(Former Special Operations Executive agent Noreen Riols 2013: 164)

Will TV ever stop mentioning The War?
(*Sun*, 31 January 1990)

All historical narratives are necessarily tentative and speculative, but they become far more so when spies are involved.
(Hastings 2015: xxv)

World War II and its momentous events has been a common setting for historical spy fiction. True stories of special operations and resistance were the subject of *Odette* (book 1949, film 1950, on Odette Sansom) by Jerrard Tickell and *Carve Her Name with Pride* (book 1956, film 1958, on Violette Szabo) by R. J. Minney. Wartime secret missions and capers thrilled readers in *The Guns of Navarone* (novel 1957, film 1961) and *Where Eagles Dare* (novel 1967, film 1969) by Alistair MacLean. These can be appreciated as part of a wider 'nostalgia' for the Second World War embraced within British popular culture in the period since 1945. As the cultural historian Jeffrey Richards has observed, this was not a nostalgia for the actual experiences of shortages, destruction and loss, but rather a longing for a period of "*shared effort and sacrifice, common purpose and good neighbourliness and justified struggle against a wicked enemy*" (1997: 360). Literary historian John Sutherland noted the "*revival*" of the "*secret history*" style of fiction in the 1970s, especially in best-selling stories of the 'secret war' as found in the exciting adventure yarns *The Eagle Has Landed* (novel 1975, film 1976) by Jack Higgins and *Eye of the Needle* (novel 1978, film 1981) by Ken Follett. Sutherland explains the appearance of this trend in terms of both the "*ineradicable popular belief that the real facts of history are never given*" and the "*relaxation on official records*" which had allowed the publication of factual accounts which fed a public appetite for secret histories (1981: 172-173).[451] Film historian Robert Murphy, discussing the war film more generally, has added that following the 1970s there was a shift from "*violent action*" to "*intimate romance*", allied to a "*greater willingness to question received myths*" about World War II (2000: 239). Films such as *Another Time, Another Place* (1983) and *Hope and Glory* (1987) are framed in terms of a more complex or subjective 'nostalgia' than hitherto, shedding light on experiences previously unrepresented. The BBC television dramas 'Licking Hitler' (*Play for Today*, 1978) and 'Rainy Day Women' (*Play for Today*, 1984) offer a more thoroughgoing "*reassessment*", depicting a "*dirty war*", where the authorities are "*devious and unscrupulous, distorting truth in the name of national security*". In their "*yearning to uncover secrets about the war, to discover what really happened*", Murphy aligns the dramas with the contemporary cycle of 'secret state' thrillers like *Defence of the Realm* (1986) (262). A series of 50th anniversaries of key events in World War Two commenced in 1989 and ran through to 1996, bringing renewed focus onto the war, both in terms of nostalgia and critique.

Of this small group of revisionist war dramas of the 1970s and 1980s, 'The Imitation Game' (1980) dealt most directly with the secret war; specifically, the code-breakers at Bletchley Park engaging with the German wireless traffic coded through the Enigma enciphering machines, and the crucial intelligence derived from this operation known as ULTRA. The elaborate operation was one of the most closely guarded secrets of the war. The play had been written by Ian McEwan at the invitation of the director Richard Eyre, filmed on location in Essex and Suffolk, and broadcast in the *Play for Today* drama anthology strand on the BBC in 1980. McEwan brought together three elements that were preoccupying him at the time. The first was the Women's Movement and the wish to write about society not in terms of economic classes but as a patriarchy; the second was an interest in the mathematician and wartime code-breaker Alan Turing[452]; and the third was Mozart's *Fantasia in C Minor*, K475. 'The Imitation Game' begins early in the summer of 1940. Cathy Raine (Harriet Walter) is an intelligent and head-strong young woman who joins the Auxiliary Territorial Service (ATS) in preference to working in a munitions factory and opts to serve in the exciting-sounding role of 'special operator'. She is posted to a wireless intercept centre (Y-station) where she laboriously records incoming coded messages. At each stage of her aim to be independent and do something more fulfilling, her ambition is hampered by an external sexual appraisal of her role, from her father, her boyfriend or a senior officer (Head 2007: 53). After assaulting a chauvinistic publican, she is re-assigned to Bletchley Park where she is put on general duties in the mess. Turner, a Cambridge don, is intrigued by the young woman's independence, invites her to his rooms for tea, and their attempt at lovemaking ends in humiliation for the man. He angrily storms out and the curious Cathy is caught looking over some of his secret papers. Accused of "*knowing more about Ultra than any woman alive*" she is incarcerated for the rest of the war by a nervous security organisation. Our final view of Cathy is through the barred window of her cell, reading the score to Mozart's *Fantasia in C Minor* sent by Turner, the musical motif which fascinates Cathy and runs through the drama (McEwan, 1981). As Hayes and Groes assert: "*We leave Cathy forced to retreat into the realm of the imaginary, literally and figuratively imprisoned and excluded from reality*" (2009: 36).

Finding it difficult to research Turing at that time, McEwan decided that his Turing "*would have to be invented*", and appeared as the character of Turner. However, the writer did discover that the majority of personnel who worked at Bletchley Park were women, doing vital but repetitive jobs, that women in the early war years were thought incapable of keeping a secret, and, with the observation that "*Secrecy and power go hand in hand*", that he could ally this to his intended theme of patriarchy (1981: 18). Film historian Robert Murphy has argued how 'The Imitation Game' revised the ideology of such wartime consensual dramas as *The Gentle Sex* (1943, about the ATS) and *Millions Like Us* (1943, about women conscripted into an aircraft factory). Cathy refuses to act with traditional deference to men and is accordingly disgraced and punished; there is no suggestion of the emerging equality of the earlier films; and the revisionist interpretation of wartime circumstances is that of chauvinism and discrimination, that "*all male-female relationships are troubled by misunderstandings, hostility and prejudice*" (2000: 263).

A number of former ATS women wrote to the BBC's listings magazine *Radio Times*, "*mostly in a critical vein*". Ian McEwan graciously replied to the correspondents, pointing out that it had not been his intention to "*impugn the ATS*". He claimed to have researched 'The Imitation Game' for four months, to have interviewed many former ATS women, and that despite a "*total refusal of co-operation from the Ministry of Defence*" had tried to get the period details right. He revealed that by the end of the war there were over 10,000 women working in and around Bletchley; a great proportion of them in vital but mechanical tasks. "*The closer you moved to the centre of 'Ultra*", he pointed out, "*the more men you found; the further out, the more women*". In terms of sex and power, he confided, ULTRA suggested to him a microcosm of a whole society. "*If there were no women mathematicians in the universities at the time, then it is worth asking why*". His play, he asserted, "*exploited a series of accidents and coincidences in order to move the heroine from the periphery of Ultra to its centre where she was to be destroyed*". The author expressed his hope that, "*viewers would be prompted to consider that they live in a patriarchy and that its values are perverse*" (17 May 1980: 71). 'The Imitation Game' received a limited theatrical release and as such was reviewed at the *Monthly Film Bulletin.* It was judged there that the intelligent drama ignored the great social changes that took place in the war, and that Cathy's "*solitude, sullen silences and aggressive sarcasm – the result of her frustrated ambitions – undermine any notion of incipient female solidarity*". This, of course, could be where the writers to the *Radio Times* felt a personal affront. The review also took into consideration class, embedded in the setting in the echelons of intelligence and code-breaking. As it noted, the Bletchley Park elite are all Cambridge graduates, their power residing in their ability alone to break the codes; after all, Turner is not disciplined for having secret files in his room as he is "*indispensible*", a privilege denied to those providing the massive support structure around him and his colleagues (June 1983: 160-161).[453] 'The Imitation Game' remains unusual as both a critique of the wartime myth and of the venerated achievement of Bletchley, and reminds us that it would be wrong to idealise blindly the remarkable successes of wartime code-breaking. Like many centres of wartime activity, intercept stations, dissemination stations and their like suffered problems of absenteeism and staff discontent at working conditions and motivation, not least among women who resented their low pay and status, and who were often unenlightened about their vital contribution to the war effort (Hastings 2015: 406-7).[454]

A more direct, yet much more fanciful and venerating treatment of Alan Turing at Bletchley Park, was provided in the glossy American-financed film *The Imitation Game* (US, 2014). This was loosely based on the biography *Alan Turing: The Enigma* (1983) by Andrew Hodges, which had previously been the inspiration for Hugh Whitemore's stage play *Breaking the Code* (1986) about Alan Turing and his eventual suicide in 1954 and which had been dramatised for television in 1996. The new film which starred Benedict Cumberbatch as Turing was very popular and well-received as a conventionally dramatic wartime thriller set among the boffins (*Empire,* 27 November 2013; *Guardian,* 16 November 2014; *Independent,* 8 December 2014). *The Critique* summarised the picture as a "*highly digestible, emotionally compelling depiction of how Turing's intellectual and technological achievements contributed to winning WWII, followed by the tragedy of Turing being unfairly convicted for his homosexuality*" (20 January 2015). The movie did though attract a lot of comment and criticism regarding its *"glossing-up of the story"*[455] and for a cavalier treatment of historical fact, especially in the downplaying of Turing's homosexuality, the playing-up of the *"romance"* between Turing and fellow code-breaker Joan Clarke (Keira Knightley), the over-emphasis to Turing's centrality to the breaking of codes and the physical creation of the mechanical bombe, and numerous other inaccuracies relating to Bletchley and its characters (*The New York Review of Books*, 19 December 2014; *Slate*, 3 December 2014). Max Hastings, the popular historian of the secret war, dismisses the picture as *"absurd"* and a *"travesty"* (2015: xxvii, 546).

The story presented in the film *Enigma* also attracted some controversy, further demonstrating the concern for accuracy in historical fiction and that the depiction of wartime code-breaking and the (mis)attribution of clandestine successes and scientific breakthroughs could still ruffle national pride. A popular spy thriller set in early 1943 in World War II, *Enigma* was written by Robert Harris and first published in 1995. The setting is once again Bletchley Park, but this time more obviously fictional, the story centring on a brilliant young mathematician Tom Jericho who is recovering from a breakdown and the monumental effort to break into the German naval code used by the U-boats (SHARK).[456] The thriller element of the story concerns Jericho's efforts to locate Claire, his former lover, who has disappeared after having taken some German signals communications. Jericho investigates the mystery with the help of Hester, Claire's roommate, and stays one step ahead of the official investigation led by the oily Wigram of the Security Service. The mystery centres on the massacre of 10,000 Polish officers by Soviet forces in the Katyn Forest, something the British authorities had sought to suppress so as not to embarrass its new ally. It is suspected that Claire had obtained the decrypts for her latest lover, the Polish cryptanalyst Pukowski, who aims to get the secret back to the Germans as payback for the massacre by the Soviets, and which would expose to the enemy that the Allies had broken into ENIGMA. It is eventually revealed that Claire is in fact a British agent and that Tom had stumbled onto a security operation. While he ponders if Claire had ever loved him and if he will meet her again, he discovers that his latest efforts at Bletchley had once again got a foothold into SHARK and this could turn the tide in the Battle of the Atlantic.[457]

The blending of history with imagination is characteristic of British spy fiction, yet one cannot but feel that here the extraordinary achievements of the Government Code and Cypher School at Bletchley Park are lost to a commercial story in which the thriller element and the melodramatic are primary concerns. *Enigma* works principally as a romantic mystery thriller and as such gripped a large readership.[458]

The film rights to the novel were bought by rock star Mick Jagger in 1995 who intended to use the picture to launch his new company Jagged Films (*The Times*, 21 November 1995). In the event, *Enigma* the movie proved a troubled project and cameras only began rolling in April 2000, with Tom Stoppard as screenwriter, Michael Apted as director, John Barry as composer, and stars Dougray Scott as Jericho and Kate Winslett as Hester. Production finance was eventually found in Germany and Holland.[459] Chicheley Hall, Buckinghamshire, stood in for Bletchley, and other scenes were shot in London, Devon, Scotland and Holland.[460]

While keeping the basic story, the movie, released in 2001, opted for an even more populist approach than the best-selling novel. This is evident in the revised ending, which rejects the book's uncompromising sexual attraction of Hester for Claire in favour of a more traditionally satisfying romantic coupling of the hero and heroine, Jericho and Hester, in the final reel. This necessitates a certain demonisation of Claire, who here is portrayed as helping Pukowski out of love and has to disappear with the British Secret Service seeking her as a traitor. In perhaps an obvious move, the dramatisation turns Claire into one of the enigmas of the title, the one code Tom couldn't break.

The ENIGMA and ULTRA successes were highly classified and largely remained secret until the publication of F. W. Winterbotham's *The Ultra Secret* in 1974.[461] The book was published amidst much trepidation in Whitehall and the history of ULTRA, as of much of the history of the secret world, remained contentious for some time to come (Moran 2013: 255-80; Aldrich 2004). Unsurprisingly, the interpretation of the past in *Enigma* ruffled some feathers and caused some controversy. Producer Mick Jagger saw it as his responsibility to Bletchley Park, to be "*honourable to the memory of the people who worked there*" and not to "*trivialize*" history (quoted in the *Evening Standard*, 27 September 2001). In particular, *Enigma* would serve as a riposte to the recent American *U-571* (2000), a "*Hollywood travesty of historical fact*" and which, according to the *Evening Standard*, "*incorrectly depicted Americans as the wartime heroes of the great Enigma code-breaking coup*". In comparison, *Enigma* would be a "*wholesale reconstruction of the period and the technology that led to the all-important breaking of the Enigma code*" and "*set within a framework of assiduously researched facts and personalities*" (7 July 2000). When *Enigma* was premiered at the Sundance Film Festival, it was pointedly reported that the producers had decided to add one especially pertinent scene to *Enigma*. "*We talk about the British seamen who died retrieving U-boat code books*", stated director Apted, and we wanted to "*set the record straight*" The scene was viewed as a "*stinging rebuke*" to the previous year's Hollywood blockbuster *U-571*, which had American servicemen finding the code book (quoted in *The Telegraph*, 27 January 2001).

The *Evening Standard*, fed-up at the British film industry for "*allowing Hollywood to steal, traduce and fictionalize some of our finest hours for its own gung-ho glory*", declared its national pride restored with *Enigma*, adding that, "*Seldom have I been so fascinated by a view of one of Britain's wartime achievements*" (27 September 2001). The nationalistic *Sun* breathed a sigh of relief, and exclaimed: "*At last a film about World War Two that doesn't make the Brits out to be toffee-nosed twits who sat around sipping tea until the Americans showed us how to hammer Hitler*" (29 September 2001).

However, *Enigma* hardly "*set the record straight*" as far as Polish national honour was concerned. The Polish ambassador boycotted the high-profile British premier in London, and a spokesman for Mr Komorowski explained that the ambassador was absent from the screening because he found the film "*outrageous*". "*The only Polish character in the film is a traitor, but he is fictitious*". It was pointed out that, "*There was no traitor among the many Polish cryptoanalysts who shared their knowledge with the French and British from 1939 and worked with them to break the code*". "*Of course*", it was recognised, "*the film is not a document, but we think there is no explanation for breaking the limit of fiction. The young spectators learn history not at school but at the movies. Fiction should not make us upset*" (quoted in *The Times*, 26 September 2001). In a letter to The *Evening Standard*, the ambassador dismissed the picture as a "*falsification of history*" (4 October 2001). The distinguished Oxford historian Norman Davies wrote to *The Telegraph*, acknowledging that *Enigma* was a "*welcome antidote to previous distortions*", but warned that readers should beware: "*For the liberties taken in the making of* Enigma *are every bit as misleading as other films of the genre. What is more, the argument for welding a fictional scenario to a genuine historical setting does not hold good if the historical setting is anything but genuine*". To put the record straight, he stated: "*In reality, there were no Poles working at Bletchley during the war; and there were no known Polish traitors or secret collaborators operating in wartime Britain*" (27 September 2001). Andrzej Morawicz, president of the Federation of Poles in Great Britain, denigrated *Enigma* as a "*gratuitous slur on Poles who fought side by side with their British allies*" (quoted in *The Telegraph*, 28 September 2001). In a letter to the *Evening Standard*, he confirmed that the film had raised a great deal of disquiet and consternation among the Polish community, spelling out that what seems unacceptable is the fact that,

> there is only one brief mention that it was the Poles who made the Enigma machine available to British Intelligence. The overall impression is of a Polish traitor at Bletchley Park, when no Pole ever actually worked there, let alone was a traitor.
> (1 October 2001)

Robert Harris reported his surprise at what he called the *"organised letter-writing campaign mounted by some members of the Polish community against the film of my novel* Enigma", and specifically addressed accusations made by a Jozef Garlinski which had appeared in a letter printed in *The Telegraph* on 3 October 2001. In his own letter, Harris claimed that he knew that no Pole ever worked at wartime Bletchley, and that the character that was causing such indignation was clearly indicated in the story as holding a British passport, and is the son of an English mother and a Polish father. He further claimed that Pukowski, the fictional Pole who discovers the existence of a great crime in 1943, was based on the real-life Walter Ettinghausen, a German-born Jew who worked in the Naval Section at Bletchley and who, in 1943, translated a decoded intercept referring to the Final Solution. *"Far from seeking to be gratuitously offensive about the Polish contribution to the breaking of Enigma"*, Harris claimed, *"it was partly my anger at British disregard for Polish suffering that fuelled the novel"* (*The Telegraph*, 4 October 2001). Embarrassed that Robert Harris was getting some of his *"flak"*, Tom Stoppard also replied to Garlinski in the same newspaper. He pointed out that the screenplay of *Enigma*. unlike the novel, had space for only a passing mention of the Poles' early and invaluable part in cracking the Enigma code and that Garlinski was wrong in his assertions that the film suggested that everyone knew about the machine at Bletchley Park, and that ULTRA was the name of the code-breaking unit. *"As for the most significant 'blunder'"*, Stoppard continued,

> *that Harris invented a Pole at Bletchley Park when in fact there were no Poles there, this can be termed a 'blunder' only in the sense of upsetting someone who takes a fictitious Pole to be a slur on Poland's heroism and sacrifices in the war".*[462]

An uncredited historical consultant on the picture was Mavis Batey, who as a young Mavis Lever was one of only three skilled female cryptanalysts at the Government Code & Cypher School throughout the war, and who advised Kate Winslett about life at Bletchley Park and on her characterisation of Hester.[463] Through Mavis, the producers and Dougray Scott were able to meet her husband Keith Batey, a mathematician at wartime Bletchley. Following the release of the film, Mavis reported that she had been required to do a lot of *"Pole-soothing"*, and that Keith was upset by factual errors. For herself, she claimed diplomatically that she had been *"enchanted by the way it captured the mood of Bletchley and her feeling of being very young and working on something of great importance"* (quoted in *The Telegraph*, 4 October 2001).[464] That Hester has to remind Jerrico in the story, that brainy men summoned to Bletchley all become cryptanalysts, but that brainy women, like her, have to make do as clerks and typists, seems not to have bothered Mavis; and on this point of gender inequality the commercial film differed substantially from quality television's 'The Imitation Game'.[465] Writer Hugh Sebag-Montefiore, author of the recent *Enigma: The Battle for the Code* (2000), praised the historical accuracy of the picture as far as SHARK was concerned, reporting that, "*The Bletchley Park codebreakers really were blacked out and this really did lead to multiple sinkings of Allied ships in mid-Atlantic after the Germans altered their naval code*". Furthermore, he confirmed the "*authenticity of the main characters*", noting observable likenesses in the picture to Mavis Lever (Winslett), Alan Turing, Harry Hinsley and Dilly Knox (Scott), Frank Birch (the character of Skynner played by Robert Pugh), and Sir Dudley Pound (the character of Admiral Trowbridge played by Corin Redgrave) (2001).

Released into cinemas at the time of a strong trend for teen movies, some reviewers welcomed a picture that placed at least a limited demand on the viewer, the *New Statesman* claiming *Enigma* "*about twice as intelligent as the average Brit film*" (17 September, 2001).[466] It was typical of critics to mark the film as respectable, though schizophrenic, the story getting "*caught between the demands of psychologically compelling history and crowd-thrilling adventure*" (*Time Out*, 26 September-3 October 2001). Swerving, it was noted at *The Times*, between an "*intelligently executed, coldly precise, brains-before-brawn portrayal of those whose mathematical prowess helped to win the war for Britain*", and "*ration-book glamour*", "*which whirls with passion, murder, femmes fatales and espionage*" (27 September 2001). Other reviewers found the film old-fashioned, even wistful. The *Independent* claimed that, "*At its most nostalgic, the film seems like a wartime flagwaver made half a century too late*" (25 September 2001), the *Observer* informed its readers that, "*Enigma is an enjoyable, well-dressed and polite British thriller that your grandmother would like*" (30 September 2001), and *The Times* commented: "*It may be a sign of the times that, while it's illogical to be nostalgic for a time, a war, a Britishness you never knew, with Enigma you almost manage it*" (27 September 2001). *Sight and Sound* declared the picture a "*ghost from a bygone, stiff-upper-lip era of British film-making*", and like others pointed to the descents into John Buchan country in the finale set in the Scottish Highlands where Tom apprehends Pukowski and in the Miss Marple-type sleuthing of Hester, as "*Kate Winslet's plucky investigator pedals furiously around the English countryside with a secret code concealed in her knickers*" (October 2001: 47).[467]

Some reviewers argued over the film's revisionism. the *Independent* viewed *Enigma* in terms of critique, with Bletchley Park serving as a "*paradigm of the English class system*". "*It is represented as a hive of voyeurism, eavesdropping and bureaucracy. Snobbery and sexism are rife*" he claimed (25 September 2001). However, few others saw in *Enigma* the kind of cutting re-evaluation present in 'The Imitation Game'. The *Guardian*, for example, declared *Enigma* "*handsome, if simplistic*", and suggested the picture had shirked the opportunity for true revisionism, studiously avoiding the "*depressing story of suicidal cottaging boffins*", and turning in "*preposterous Boy's Own stuff which is light years away from the closeted realities of Bletchley Park*" (28 September 2001). Robert Harris replied to accusations that his story had glossed over the "*homosexuality of the real-life mathematician on which it is based*". He denied that Tom Jerrico was based on Turing, "*who was, in any case, in America during the crisis described in the story*", and pointed out that, "*there were several hundred other codebreakers at Bletchley Park, apart from Turing: statistically it seems highly unlikely that a majority were gay*" (quoted in the *Guardian*, 23 February 2002).[468] The *Sun* lumped *Enigma* in with conventional heritage movies, declaring it "*thespionage*", a "*spy story that's only worth watching for the acting*" (29 September 2001). More than one reviewer felt that the ENIGMA story would have been better and fuller-served in the form of a classic television serial (*New Statesman*, 17 September 2001; *Independent on Sunday*, 30 September 2001).

The wartime code-breakers' story has attracted much comment and interest. The popular historian Max Hastings for one has identified the legend of the signals war; after all, he asserts, "*here was something Churchill's people did better than anybody else*" (2015: xxvii). The screen treatments of Bletchley Park have largely and comfortably fitted the achievements into the wartime myth of the Second World War as Britain's 'finest hour'. Certainly, the ENIGMA triumph is more deserving of such veneration than most other aspects of the wartime experience. However, the gloss, thrills and melodrama have tended to detract from the accomplishments of the dedicated staff based at the Park. In contrast, 'The Imitation Game' reminded audiences that many women were frustrated by lack of real opportunities to serve the war effort. That some former ATS personnel should complain of the drama's revisionism demonstrates the centrality of the myth to British culture.

Another aspect of the secret war which came in for imaginative treatment was the Special Operations Executive (SOE), which had been formed in July 1940 to conduct espionage, sabotage and reconnaissance in occupied Europe, and to support local resistance movements. Various accounts and memoirs of the men and women of SOE began to appear in the years following the conflict, and the majority of these centred on France.[469] The burgeoning interest in special operations was also evident in a spate of novels dealing with the secret war and sabotage, such as Peter Churchill's *Glières* (1958), C. S. Forester's *The Nightmare* (1954) and Jerrard Tickell's *Villa Mimosa* (1960). Where women were central in the forthcoming screen representations of this secret wartime activity, these were less radical and more populist in intention than McEwan's 'The Imitation Game'; more myth-making than de-mythologizing. Historian Max Hastings has commented that many of the memoirs and stories incorporate invention and melodrama, maintaining that, "*Most accounts of wartime SOE agents, particularly women and especially in France, contain large doses of romantic twaddle*" (2015: xxvi).

The television drama serials *The White Rabbit* (1967), *The Fourth Arm* (1983) and *Wish Me Luck* (1988-1990) dealt with special missions and agents parachuted into occupied Europe. *The White Rabbit* by Bruce Marshall had first appeared in print in 1952 as an account of Wing Commander F. F. E. Yeo-Thomas's gruelling exploits as a network leader in France and later incarceration in Buchenwald concentration camp. Aspiring producer Michael Deeley had hoped to film the story in the early 1960s. He gained verbal approval from Bruce Marshall, sounded out the actors Dirk Bogarde, John Mills and James Mason, as well as the directors Guy Green, Robert Siodmak and Roy Baker. Once he had the commitment of star Kenneth More, Deeley floated the idea at British Lion Films, but was dismayed when board member John Boulting when behind his back, bought the script rights and signed up More. To add insult to injury, Boulting never made the picture (Deeley 2008: 24-25). The project resurfaced a couple of years later when Kenneth More put the idea to David Attenborough, who as controller of the new television service BBC 2 was looking for flagship dramas and *The White Rabbit* was commissioned as a four-part serial.[470] More, then working on the prestige BBC drama serial *The Forsyte Saga* (1967), was a considerable coup for the new channel. The rights to the *The White Rabbit* had now passed to the American film producer Hal Chester, who refused to relinquish them. In an unusual move, Attenborough exploited the BBC's legal entitlement to film the story for a single domestic broadcast, and this probably accounts for the enduring lack of awareness about the prestige serial (More 1978: 211-13).[471] The main worry over the dramatisation stemmed from the numerous and lengthy scenes of torture in the story. Screenwriter Michael Voysey commented on the difficulties posed by the narrative, but bravely reported that it was necessary not to "*pull our punches ... if we are to successfully portray this man's tremendous courage*" (quoted in *Stage and Television Today*, 22 September 1966). Reviews picked up on the problem of depicting the hideous brutality of the Nazis and the camps. The *Guardian*, while not wishing to impugn the integrity of the producers, felt *The White Rabbit* had fallen into a moral "*trap*" and that sadism "*played too big a role*" in the production. Showing the torturers going to work on Kenneth More in a bath tub in the first episode was quite enough (More reported that being dragged with shackles through a bath of water nearly drowned him, 1978: 212); however, interspersing the drama with historic footage depicting the horrors of the camps was "*going too far*", believing that using "*pieces of old newsreel that shows real suffering*" was questionable, "*both artistically and aesthetically*". "*One cannot help wondering*", it grumbled, "*if the people who get up in arms every time a bit of bare tit is shown on the screen will ever com-*

plain about this true obscenity" (18 September 1967). *Stage and Television Today* was less squeamish, believing that from the evidence of the first episode visual violence was kept to a minimum, suggested rather than shown, and that, *"tension was built unbearably by the restless to-ing and fro-ing of the guards"* during the scenes of torture. The reviewer commended the understated performance of More, the multiplicity of atmospheric sets, and felt the drama offered much promise (21 September 1967).

The Fourth Arm was produced at the BBC by the veteran Gerald Glaister, who had a track record with successful World War II drama series such as *Colditz* (1972-74), *Secret Army* (1977-79), and *Kessler* (1981).[472] The 12-part serial starring Paul Shelley and Philip Latham dealt with the recruitment and training of an elite group and the operation against a V1 rocket site in France. The 'fourth arm', denoting a clandestine military force alongside the regulars of the army, navy and air force, was an early term for military activities of sabotage, subversion and black propaganda in the Second World War. *The Telegraph* judged the now forgotten serial a *"good, uncomplicated, reasonably scripted action tale"* (8 January 1983).[473]

Wish Me Luck was produced at the commercial London Weekend Television (LWT) and broadcast in three seasons of 23 episodes in 1988, 1989 and 1990. Created by Lavinia Warner and Jill Hyem, who had previously been involved with the hugely successful World War Two female-centred drama series *Tenko* (1981-84), the serial dealt with the French section (F-section) of the SOE, with particular attention to the women agents who served in occupied France. It was felt that at the time of production their story was *"little known and their heroism understated"* (*YOU* magazine, *Mail on Sunday*, 3 January 1988); and the reviewer at the *Scotsman* informed his readers who he suspected might be becoming a little bored with Second World War dramas that, "Wish Me Luck *will stand out among records of Second World War heroism, because its fearless spies and infiltrators are all women"*: *"It is really an untold part of the story of the war"* (16 January 1988).[474] The trade paper *Stage and Television Today* rated the prospects of such a serial, noting that the *"Woman's role in the war, apart from that of the waiting or grieving wife, mother or girlfriend"*, remained largely untouched, *"so it is little wonder that LWT fell on the idea of a drama about female secret agents with an enthusiasm matched by a generous budget and hefty on screen and off screen promotion"* (21 January 1988). The first season concentrated on the recruitment and training of two female agents: the upper middle-class Liz Grainger (Kate Buffery) and Jewish cockney Matty Firman (Suzanna Hamilton). They are dropped into France where eventually Matty is captured. The second season focused on two new agents Vivienne (Lynn Farleigh) and Emily (Jane Snowden) who are dropped into Southern France to work with a resistance network. Liz eventually joins them and personal issues complicate their dangerous wartime mission. The final season shifted ground a little away from the relations between the British agents, and concentrated more on the atrocities inflicted on innocent French people by the Nazis. The action switches to a Resistance stronghold in the French Alps where a new agent Virginia Mitchell (Catherine Schell) is infiltrated. It is shortly before D-Day and an uprising is encouraged from London; however, unknown to SOE, it will not be supported by Allied military forces.[475] Colonel Cadogan (Julian Glover) and Faith Ashley (Jane Asher) who staff F-section back at command were based on the real-life figures of Colonel Maurice Buckmaster and Vera Atkins.[476] The historical adviser on the drama was Yvonne Cormeau, a former heroine of F-section who had been the second female wireless operator to be sent to France, where she served on the 'Wheelwright Circuit' in Gascony 1943-45, and completed 400 transmissions. The drama was filmed at locations in France. *Wish Me Luck* was a top-rated show and nearly 14 million viewers tuned in for the second season. While this figure fell for the final season it still attracted an audience of nearly 10 million.

The critic at the *Independent* approached the first season warily, suspicious of an element of "*glamour*", and what it judged as "*brisk and over-lit action and schematic characterisation*". Warning that, "*Beyond the gloss, the serial needs to be true to the extraordinary courage of the women whose lives it fictionalises*" (18 January 1988). Reviewers worried that television schedules had become clogged with World War Two dramas, and the *Scotsman* dryly commented on the "*invaluable*" Second World War, "*which, had it not happened, it would have been necessary for television to have waged it*" (23 January 1988). The *Telegraph* judged that, "*Like most wartime drama series, 'Wish Me Luck' is fiction based on mistily-remembered history*", and found the heroics to be a little too "*Girl's Own Paper-ish*". However, it correctly conceded that *Wish Me Luck* was likely to find an audience: "*For the middle-aged, it's sure-fire nostalgia, for the young, it's action-adventure history, and for all concerned, it's good box office*" (18 January 1988).[477]

Charlotte Gray, another wartime story of a female agent, was a best-selling novel by the acclaimed author Sebastian Faulks published in 1999. The title character is a young Scottish woman who is reluctantly persuaded to join a clandestine unit known as G-section and trains to serve as a courier with the resistance in France.[478] The lengthy novel develops along several narrative strands, unfolding across the years 1942-43. There is Charlotte's mission with the resistance, and her independent efforts to track down her lover Peter Gregory, an RAF pilot who has been shot down over France. There is the injured Peter who must painfully make his way back to friendly lines. There is Julien the local resistance leader who falls under the spell of Charlotte; and there is his father and two young Jewish boys who are eventually rounded up by the authorities for despatch to a concentration camp. In the final outcome Charlotte and Peter are reunited in England.

Faulks spent a year in Burgundy while he was writing *Charlotte Gray,* fascinated by the prospect of communicating the experience of recent history, the author aimed to provide readers with an *"imaginative access to the past"* (quoted in the *Independent,* 28 August 1998). Critics tended to find the novel two-faced: a rather improbable love story set in rural France; and a somewhat more serious treatment of the human condition in the complex context of occupation. The driving motivation of romance deflects from the credibility of a story about women in the secret war, and although it has been claimed that *Charlotte Gray* draws on the actual experiences of brave agents such as Nancy Wake and Pearl Cornioley, and there is an observable influence from the classic account rendered in *Odette* (1949), the novel is a missed opportunity to present an imaginative treatment of a remarkable set of female experiences from World War II.

The story was adapted into the movie *Charlotte Gray* in 2002, largely made by the team which had produced the successful historical picture *Mrs Brown* (1997), screenwriter Jeremy Brock and producers Sarah Curtis and Douglas Rae, and produced at Film 4. Directed by Gilliam Armstrong, *Charlotte Gray* starred Cate Blanchett and was shot on location in London, Scotland and the village of St Antonin-Noble-Val in southwest France.[479] The film story centres more on the heroine, and each of the strands of the book, Peter, Julien and his father, the Jewish boys, are experienced from the character of the protagonist. Some material is lost to simplification, for example the issues Charlotte has with her father, while others are changed, such that the picture ends with the heroine returning to France after the war to take up her romance with Julien. The effect is to enhance further the romantic and melodramatic aspects of the story, and package these alongside the visual pleasures of a contemporary heritage film experience. The picture was premiered at the Odeon, Leicester Square, London, in the presence of Sonya D'Artois (Sonya Esmée Florence Butt) and Nancy Wake, *"two of the 39 women agents who risked torture and death in Nazi-occupied France during the Second World War"* (*The Times,* 20 February 2002).[480]

It was widely felt that the movie fudged the matter of language and accents, as no character actually speaks French, some like Julien (Billy Crudup) speak English with a modest French accent, and others such as his father (Michael Gambon) *"with a French accent bought from the* 'Allo 'Allo *surplus store"* (*Financial Times,* 21 February 2002).[481] The approach was judged *"faintly ridiculous"* in *Time Out,* an old-fashioned convention which *"strips the drama of a lot of its suspense"* (20-27 February 2002).[482] The *Evening Standard* pointed out that, "*No film today has any chance of registering a truthful impression of espionage being conducted on enemy territory if this outworn convention of making everyone Anglophone continuously sabotages all daily intercourse, covert operations, risks of exposure and even the tension of being an endangered stranger*". It dismissed the picture as a "*turnip*", or, as it might best be expressed in the circumstances, "*un navet*" (21 February 2002).

Charlotte Gray was also felt to have poorly served history, heroism and sacrifice. Patrick Marnham, author of *The Death of Jean Moulin* (2000), a biography of a French resistance leader, judged the picture a "*simplification of history*"; such that it "*manages to obscure the real achievements of the women who risked torture and death to fight beside the Resistance*". He pointed out that, "*Unlike Charlotte Gray, the women of SOE did not go to war to rescue their boyfriends. And if they were volunteering for a dangerous mission, it was not to help them 'heal their inner conflicts'*"; adding that in real life, "*Charlotte Gray would have been weeded out at the preliminary interview*". "*'Basket cases' were too unpredictable under pressure*" he soberly recalled. Marnham quoted the veterans Francis Cammaerts, who commented that, "*The lives of SOE agents have been terribly romanticised. What we were risking was our skins, but for the French it was their homes, their families, their children. It was everything*", and Pearl Witherington, who confessed she found the "*modern obsession with the romantic and the personal 'offensive'*". He further made the distinction that, "*Nancy Wake used to kill German sentries with a knife*", while Charlotte Gray "*spends more time falling in and out of love*"; and concluded: "*The 13 SOE women agents who died deserved a better tribute than this preposterous fable*" (quoted in the *Evening Standard*, 22 February 2002).

The film was also not well-received more generally. In a slightly later assessment at *Time Out*, Geoffrey MacNab pointed out that when compared to *The Sorrow and The Pity* (Sw/Fr/W Ger., 1969), Marcel Ophuls' "*majestic documentary about the Vichy years*", "*Armstrong's recreation of the era can't help but seem kitsch in the extreme*" (6-13 October 2004). *The Times* felt that "*credibility*" had been "*pushed out of the window to make way for wild romantic claims and sheer box-office vanity*", and that audiences had been served up with a "*thriller which is stubbornly unrevealing about the war*" (21 February 2002). The *Financial Times* complained of "*two hours of feel-my-beating-heart schmaltz*", and the *Evening Standard* of a "*fagged-out romanticism*" (both 21 February 2002). *The New York Times* found the film "*lumbering*" and complained of an "*incoherence and lack of credibility in a movie that leaves an emotional void*" (28 December 2001). The *Independent* captured the sentiment of many, when it concluded: "*It must have seemed a fine idea at the time; sadly, it looks like a missed opportunity now*" (22 February 2002). There was common complaint that *Charlotte Gray* put visual allure above plausibility. The reviewer at the *Independent on Sunday* informed readers who had seen the recent *Enigma* and *Captain Corelli's Mandolin* (2001) that they would know what to expect: "*some classy acting, some Forties tailoring, some tourist brochure countryside and a sweeping score, just to underline how epic it all is. You'll also expect the film to be bleakly uninvolving*" (24 February 2002). The *Sunday Telegraph* was bemused at "*how wonderful wartime looks*", and declared itself "*overwhelmed with fake nostalgia*" (24 February 2002). At least one reviewer unfavourably compared the movie with a former classic, suggesting that, "Carve Her Name with Pride *sets a very high standard that Charlotte Gray never really approaches*" (*Quadrant* July-August 2002: 98).

Charlotte Gray was an expensive flop. Costing around $25 million, it only returned a fatally disappointing $700,000 in the American market, where it had been hurriedly launched in time for anticipated Academy Award success (*The Telegraph*, 29 September 2001).[483] Debating whether *Charlotte Gray* "*really deserves its place in British cinema's hall of infamy*", *Time Out* reminded readers that, "*Certain films are now remembered as much for the damage which they did to the companies that made them as they are for their own merits*", reporting that the main funder Film 4 was closed down as a standalone film operation with its own distribution arm following the failure of *Charlotte Gray* (6-13 October 2004; *Evening Standard*, 21 March 2002).[484]

The wartime achievements of the SOE have recently come in for criticism. A record of "*follies, failures and embarrassments*" has been unearthed, in which extravagances and criminal miscalculation led to agent capture and deaths. A historian of the secret war has argued that such revisionism should not be allowed to mask the towering historical reality of numerous SOE agents and local people risking everything for Resistance. The contribution, it has been claimed, "*should be judged much more by the magnitude of their stakes and sacrifices than by the military achievements*", and while the military contribution might have been small, the "*moral*" contribution was "*beyond price*". While the activities for a field agent might have been an "*indisputably romantic adventure*", film treatments such as *Charlotte Gray* tipped the balance in favour of the melodramatic and lost sight of the grim reality of the forfeit made by so many young people (Hastings 2015: 281-82, 557).

War, Treacheries and Betrayals

Restless, a novel by the acclaimed William Boyd published in 2006, is an important recent example of historical spy fiction, in which murky exploits in the secret war leave a troubling legacy in the present. The story was adapted by Boyd into a three-hour, two-part television drama and broadcast on the BBC in 2012, starring Hayley Atwell, Charlotte Rampling, Rufus Sewell and Michael Gambon. The historical location scenes were shot in South Africa, and filming also took place at sites in Oxfordshire, Cambridge and London. The story is structured in two time frames: the 'present' is the long hot summer of 1976 which centres on Ruth Gilmartin, a young single mother and postgraduate student at Oxford University; while the 'past' is the period encompassing 1939-42, an account of Eva Delectorskaya, a young exiled Russian woman recruited to British Intelligence in pre-war Paris. Ruth is shocked to learn that Eva is the real identity of her widowed mother Sally, who has presented her daughter with a 'memoir' of her wartime experiences. The narrative cross-cuts between Ruth reading the manuscript and coming to terms with her mother's mounting paranoia, and the story of Eva, her training in Scotland in signals, combat and survival techniques, her wartime service in espionage and propaganda in Belgium, London and America, and most importantly her relationship with the enigmatic, yet attractive and self-assured, Lucas Romer, head of a small intelligence unit attached to the Government Code and Cypher School. The unit's most important mission is in the neutral United States, the objective to encourage America to join the fight against Nazi Germany.[485] On a supposedly simple courier's job in New Mexico, Eva narrowly escapes being murdered, and when a colleague is found dead she goes to ground in Canada, later London, and disappears under the new identity of Sally Gilmartin. Eva has long-suspected Lucas Romer and enlists the help of Ruth in locating and confronting him. An old, respectable and ennobled man, Romer is finally exposed and chooses death to disgrace; it made to appear to the world as a heart attack.

William Boyd has stated that with *Restless* he aimed to "*explore the human consequences of what it is to be a spy. What price do you pay when you have to live in a world where nobody can be trusted, even those people you love?*"[486] Trust is a major theme of the story, a point ironically made by Romer when he knowingly advises Eva early in the timeframe: "*Don't trust anyone, ever*". For the secret agent it is "*The one and only rule*": "*Always suspect. Always mistrust*". The human consequence of this fact is the eternally vigilant, suspicious, even paranoid Sally Gilmartin, noting down the details of new cars that come into the district, surveying with binoculars the woods opposite her house where she feels threat lurks, forced to live in a world without trust. A state of "*restless watchfulness of someone living a totally secret, underground existence*" is how Boyd later expressed it.[487]

Eva's story unfolds against a backdrop of real historical incidents, organisations and characters, such as the catastrophic Venlo Incident (1939, renamed Prenslo in the story) in which two British Secret Intelligence Service officers were lured to German captivity in Holland, the British Security Coordination in New York, the Soviet defector Walter Krivitsky (renamed Aleksandr Nekich in the story), and the Japanese attack on Pearl Harbor in December 1941.

Romer's treachery, of course, is analogous to that of Cambridge Spy Kim Phil- by, and, indeed, the drama has been seen as the "*latest in a long line of dra- mas to engage with the story of the Cambridge Five, depicting the activities of a fictitious 'sixth man' in the 1940s and 1970s*" (Oldham 2014: 94). Boyd con- ceived of Romer as an amalgamation of Kim Philby and Anthony Blunt, imag- ining "*someone with Philby's charm and easy charisma but someone who hadn't had to defect and had gone on, like Blunt, to receive all the laurels, sta- tus and privilege that a grateful nation could bestow*" (quoted in the *Guardian,* 22 December 2012). The story also points up some parallels between mother and daughter, wartime spy against Fascism and 1970s radical against capital- ism and state dictatorships. The critical response to *Restless* was largely fa- vourable with reviewers praising Boyd's attempt to use the spy story to treat such serious themes as the relation between past and present, shifting identi- ties, illusion versus reality, and the generation gap. Some critics have suggest- ed that a source for a story about a quiet, elderly woman suddenly being re- vealed as a spy would be the exposure of Melita Norwood in 1999, the so- called 'Spy Who Came in from the Co-op'.[488]

The *Guardian* wondered at "*so many inconsistencies in the storyline*", but found the drama "*well-acted, well-written, well-paced and well-filmed*" (27 December 2012). *The New York Times* felt that, "*unimaginative direction and the show's lulling, pedestrian rhythms forestall any danger of being truly en- gaged with either plot*", yet conceded that the traditional strengths of British drama, an "*understated script free of hackneyed dialogue or florid emotion*" and "*niceties of language*", should be enough for "*devout fans of the British espionage thriller or the British cozy mystery*" (6 December 2012). Once again a drama placed a woman at the centre of the secret war. However, with its betrayals and paranoia, and radical student Ruth, *Restless* was closer to the more activist 'The Imitation Game' and its critique of the secret war than the essentially cautious *Wish Me Luck* and *Charlotte Gray*. It was also written in the knowledge of the infamous true stories of wartime treachery examined in the following chapter.

The secret war was allied to television detective fiction in the later series of *Foyle's War* (2002-2015), a popular historical detective series set in the area around the historic town of Hastings during World War II and broadcast on commercial television. Detective Chief Superintendent Christopher Foyle (Michael Kitchen) tackles a variety of serious wartime crimes, across six sea- sons of the show and spanning the period of the war. He confronts such mis- deeds as murder, sabotage, profiteering, the black market, art theft, fraud, fifth columnists, Nazi sympathisers and racial problems at an American army base. Foyle often comes up against high-ranking officials in Military and Brit- ish Intelligence who would prefer that he mind his own business, but he is tenacious in seeking justice. The episodes 'The French Drop', 'Bad Blood', and 'The Russian House' draw Foyle into specific aspects of the secret war. The popular series was unexpectedly dropped after season five by the commercial television network and hastily brought to an end in 2008. Angry response from loyal viewers saw the series resurrected in 2010 and more wartime cases for Detective Chief Superintendent Foyle.

Season seven, broadcast in 2013, is set in the months of July to September 1946 and the recently retired Chief Superintendent Foyle is pressured into relocating to London and joining MI5, where he is to help tackle the new, terrifying implications of the emerging Cold War. In 'The Eternity Ring' Foyle deals with atom bomb spies, in 'The Cage' he is drawn into the sinister workings of a secret military establishment, and in 'Sunflower' the security officer investigates a former Nazi now serving the Western alliance. The review in the *Guardian* found the new series a *"lot of fun, gripping without taking itself too seriously – the cold war with a twinkle. And the Big Upheaval – of place, time, enemy, employer – isn't just pulled off, it actually breathes new life into* Foyle's War" (25 March 2013). The recent eighth and allegedly final series broadcast in January 2015, features Foyle in three further cases with MI5. 'High Castle' involves dark secrets from the middle period of the war, 'Trespass' deals with the conflicts and complications surrounding the future of Palestine, and 'Elise' has Foyle investigating a wartime traitor who gave away agents to the Nazis.[489]

The two-part television dramatisation *Spies of Warsaw* was a further example of the literary derived 'heritage' spy drama. This had a distinctive pedigree, being based on the novel by the American Alan Furst, a leading practitioner of recent spy fiction, and offering the unusual historical frame of French-Polish-German intrigues on the eve of World War Two. A BBC co-production with European partners, the serial aired on the arts channel BBC 4 in 2013. It told the story of French military attaché Colonel Jean-François Mercier (David Tennant) serving in Warsaw who realises that war is imminent, but cannot convince his superiors. He is drawn into intrigue and romance which ultimately leads to his dawning realisation that after dealing with Poland the Germans intend to invade France through the Ardennes. The general view was that *Spies of Warsaw* was old-fashioned, sedate and lacking in tension. *The New York Times* found it an *"enjoyable, straightforward espionage tale without a lot of twists or extra layers"*; but that it felt *"oddly like an English countryside whodunit"* and exhibited an *"almost comic-book adherence to stereotype"* (2 April 2013). The *Guardian* wondered at a drama which could present a hero as a *"latter-day Scarlet Pimpernel"*, *"Yet here was Tennant fencing in 19th-century palaces by day and going out at night to give the beastly Boche a bloody nose or two, and lingering under showers after bedding various miladies when he had a spare moment, before slipping into a silk dressing-gown in between"* (9 January 2013).

The impending doom of an earlier world conflict was the context of *Pascali's Island*, set in the Aegean in the period before the Great War. It derived from a literary spy novel written by Barry Unsworth, published in 1980, and had a greater claim for 'Britishness' than *Spies of Warsaw* in deriving from an English author and featuring an Englishman as a central character. The film adaptation was released in 1988, the feature début of writer-director James Dearden and starred Ben Kingsley and Charles Dance.[490] The story takes place in 1908 at the time of the insurgency of the Young Turks on the small Turkish administered island of Nisi in the Greek Aegean Sea, and centres on the shabby Basil Pascali (Kingsley), a 45 years old Levanter descended from an Irish mother, who for the last 20 years has diligently forwarded unheeded intelligence reports to the Sultan in Istanbul. One day, he senses that the local Greeks have begun to show him hostility, and this is coincidental with the unheralded arrival on the island of a mysterious English gentleman, Anthony Bowles (Dance), who claims to be an amateur archaeologist. Pascali is engaged to act as guide and interpreter for Bowles who seeks a lease to survey a classical site on land under the protection of the local Pasha. The watchful Pascali comes to suspect a conspiracy and that Bowles is a charlatan seeking to swindle the authorities over false claims for riches in the earth. When Bowles actually makes an amazing find the Englishman attempts to remove the treasure secretly with the help of an American skipper of a boat who is in league with local Greek rebels. Pascali, fearing his own position with the local authorities, betrays Bowles, and the Englishman and his confederates are killed while excavating and before they can escape.

The picture out of necessity for the popular market had to move away from the epistolary form of the novel and opt for a more traditional objective narration. Accordingly, time spent with Pascali writing and narrating his reports is kept to a minimum. The movie was shot on the Greek islands of Rhodes and Simi by the accomplished Roger Deakins, where the locals were still sensitive about having characters moving about dressed as Turks, and the picture managed to conjure up a strong pictorial sense of time and place. Interviewed at the Cannes Film Festival where the film was in competition, Dearden summed up the story as "*ultimately about trust and betrayal, and that's what leads to tragedy*" (quoted in Kennedy 1988: 17). The tale of intrigues weaves together the themes of the fading of the old order in face of insurgent nationalists and the imperial assertions of the new European powers, stultifying bureaucracy and its corruption, and the jaded loyalty of forgotten subjects.[491] Dark ironies of trust and loyalty, of deceit and betrayal, of honour and friendship, of sham pose turning into bright reality, and dramatic conflicts played out in an exotic setting, bring to mind Joseph Conrad. Pascali, the nominal spy, is obsessively voyeuristic towards Bowles, trying to decipher what he is up to, an activity not without a degree of homoerotic longing, and professional and private motivations are collapsed in the character of the forgotten agent. The story points up the parallels between the narrator and the Englishman, "*kindred spirits*" is how Pascali describes it in the novel, both actors in their way; and it is with painful irony that the loyal islander ultimately betrays Bowles while the fraudulent Englishman remains true to his word and intended to do the decent thing by Basil and reward him.

The *Observer* found *Pascali's Island* a "*quietly ironic costume piece*", and, sensing a lineage to an earlier tradition of British spy fiction, judged Pascali and Bowles as "*Ambler characters trapped in Edwardian amber*" (15 January 1989). Other critics made a comparison, usually unfavourable, with the films of 'international intrigue' produced in Hollywood in the 1940s, pictures like *Casablanca* (US, 1942) and *The Mask of Dimitrios* (US, 1944) (*New Yorker*, 15 August 1988). *What's On* found the picture a "*delightful period fable for adults*" (11 January 1989). A more critical view tended to prevail elsewhere, with *Monthly Film Bulletin* finding the telling of the story for the cinema "*muffled*", the narrative "*gratuitously padded out*" with "*unnecessary amplification of the material*", and the *Guardian* bemoaning a lack of narrative drive to match the accomplished playing and dismissing the picture as a "*lethargic exercise in emotional atmospherics*" (12 January 1989). Reviewers were becoming weary of the seemingly endless parade of 'Brit-lit' pictures, and were not well-disposed towards yet another costume picture set at the end of empire, and it was common to find *Pascali's Island* dismissed as yet another example of the "*Laura Ashley school of filmmaking*" (*Hampstead and Highgate Express*, 20 January 1989), as a "*post-colonial fantasy*", and as such simply "*pretty and pretty pointless*" (*New Statesman*, 20 January 1989).

A tale of conspiracy, an atmosphere of paranoia, and a set of personal misfortunes set *Pascali's Island* in the tradition of the espionage drama. Such qualities of illusion, deception, suspicion, unease and corruption provided for "*fascination*" at the *Daily Mail*, which praised a cynical and pessimistic story in which "*everyone is lying to somebody else; deceptions and cross purposes, eventually tragic, persist to the end*" (13 January 1989). In a generally supportive review, the *New Musical Express* noted, "*Everything is about appearance and surface, the codes of politeness glossing over the intrigue which eventually spills over into something more dangerous*" (14 January 1989). A period drama, *Pascali's Island* was quite modern in its sensibilities, a "*world at the point of change, as nervously poised for peace or war as the world today in the era of Reagachev arms talks*" (Kennedy 1988: 18); or rather, it belonged to a tradition of spy literature which emerged in the more recent past.

The Heat of the Day, first published as a novel in 1948 by the acclaimed author Elizabeth Bowen, was adapted for television in 1989, by which time its contemporary post-war setting now counted it as a period drama. It is a complex and literary story with multiple flashbacks, in which Harrison a counter-espionage agent confronts the beautiful and sophisticated Stella Rodney with the accusation that her lover Robert Kelway is spying for the Germans. Harrison proposes that he will remain silent about the treachery if he can replace Kelway in Stella's affections. Although Robert denies the allegation, Harrison informs Stella that his prediction that Kelway would change his behaviour once alerted to his perfidy is confirmed. Robert eventually returns to Stella and confesses his treachery. Robert dies but Stella, at some cost to her reputation, is able to hide his guilty secret. Much later, Harrison visits Stella and reveals that his first name is also Robert, but the resolution of their relationship is left ambiguous.

The Heat of the Day was dramatised for television at the commercial Granada Television, directed by the experienced Christopher Morahan and starred Patricia Hodge as Stella, Michael Gambon as Harrison, and Michael York as Robert.[492] The edgy literary novel was appropriately scripted by the acclaimed dramatist Harold Pinter, who no doubt relished a story set in a *"weird half-lit wartime world where nothing was quite as it seemed"* (*Daily Mail*, 1 January 1990); but the film is surprisingly little-known and Pinter later complained that, *"it was shown at 10pm on a Sunday night the day after Boxing Day and about three people saw it"* (quoted in the *Guardian*, 4 October 2002). The adaptation is a little stagey, but impressive for its performances and literate screenplay, the latter endowed with the menace, indirect conversations and the not-quite-what-it-seems quality characteristic of the playwright. Roy Foster has commented on the *"ominous and liberating"* story of the novel, a sense of the *"uncanny"*, a *"preoccupation with the fracture of things below a surface just beginning to crack, the progress of slippage and collapse, the psychology of hurt and betrayal"*, a style *"tense, nervy, jumpy"*, dialogue *"risky, inverted, interrogative"*: ideal terrain for an adapter such as Pinter (1998: 2, 4, 6). The drama draws on imagery and motifs of *film noir*, supplied in part by the original novel, and of the gothic which aptly suggest the threat and anxiety at the heart of a story in which identity is suspect and motives unclear. Critics who had a liking for atmosphere above pace found the dramatisation gripping. Lighting and visual design came in for praise, and the heavy ambience of the piece had a suffocating effect at the *Guardian*: *"Oxygen seems to leave the air. You asphyxiate with doubt"* (1 January 1990). The TV critic at the *Daily Mail*, perched on the edge of her seat, found *The Heat of the Day "superb"*, a production which had *"assembled more talent in one sitting than we'd probably seen over the whole year"* (1 January 1990); and similarly *The Listener* enjoyed a *"luxurious dramatisation"* which offered a *"fair shot at matching the voluptuous grace of Bowen's writing"* (21 December 1989).

The Times pinpointed the Pinter influence, "*in conversations constructed from spare, precise dialogue and significant pauses in which the viewer is consistently invited to find more than lies on the surface*" (30 December 1989). Harold Pinter's biographer Michael Billington, writing in the *Guardian*, rated *The Heat of the Day* as "*one of his finest studies of obsession and betrayal*", and praised Morahan's "*masterly recreation of wartime London*" (2002).[493] There is little sense of the sentiment or wistfulness of nostalgia in *The Heat of the Day*, a story of coercion and infidelity. In its darker themes and more pessimistic treatment of wartime Britain, the fiction was keyed into the legacy of guilt and anxiety which hung over recent experience as much as did the sense of relief and achievement. The story, then, belongs to the "*psychopathology of wartime*" and the history of treachery and figures like William Joyce and John Amery, and the novel could be appreciated as an imaginative companion to Rebecca West's factual *The Meaning of Treason* published in 1945 (Stonebridge 2007). As a historical drama it was in closer alliance with those that have treated the history of treachery in post-war Britain, the atom spies, the Cambridge Spies and the Portland Spies, dubious characters who featured in numerous screen representations.

The national past has been a staple of screen art and entertainment in Britain. Literary classics, popular potboilers and contemporary bestsellers have readily been adapted as costume dramas, encompassing the spectrum of spy fiction, from Erskine Childers and Joseph Conrad, through John Buchan and Somerset Maugham, onto Geoffrey Household and Elizabeth Bowen, and bringing things up-to-date with the more recent Sebastian Faulks and William Boyd. The imaginative treatment of spying and espionage in Britain, bolstered by a strong sense of authenticity, has given particular attention to the Second World War, a conflict and national experience that has widely attracted a strong sense of myth and nostalgia, qualities which have been reinforced, on occasion interrogated, in screen fictions. While the nostalgia of some historical spy fictions equates with the affirmation characteristic of the spy thriller, a less comforting history of espionage has also featured in the national imaginary, one centred on actual historical figures, real spy cases and national scandals, detailing a darker history more typical of the espionage drama. The history of treachery and betrayal, incompetence and humiliation, has found fascination with the British public, and indeed some of the "*imaginative*" fictions, such as 'The Imitation Game', *Restless* and *The Heat of the Day*, encapsulated the mood of despair, deceit and perfidy pertaining to the shame of personal and national disgrace associated with traitors. The treatment of national dishonour on screen has not been without controversy and is examined in the following chapter which deals with dramatisations of the troubled history of spies and spying in Britain.

6.
The Historical Spy Drama

Secret service history may be a health hazard ... People turn out to be not what they seemed; institutions do not function as they were supposed to; accepted truths may be deliberate disinformation; spies and moles are everywhere; and the cleverest and most dangerous of them are those who appear most unlikely and innocent.
(Bernard Porter 1989: 228)

Our defectors to Moscow have become an established mythology, to be exploited not only by biographers and social historians but by inquirers into the semantics of 'treason' and the morality of a nation, a class and a generation.
(Anthony Burgess, *Observer*, 19 March 1978)

The series of spy scandals and humiliations which surfaced in the 1950s and early 1960s were, to a considerable extent, the rationale for the new-style spy stories of John le Carré and Len Deighton, and which later figured as espionage dramas on screen from the mid-sixties onwards. Some of the cases and their characters were more directly articulated for the screen in a series of dramas which dealt with actual spies and treachery from history. The smashing of the Portland Spy Ring was the sensational news story in 1961 and the first true-life espionage tale to make it to the screen in the new decade of the 1960s; the recent history being recounted in the modest film *Ring of Spies* released in 1964, directed by Robert Tronson and initially distributed on a double-bill with the aging thriller *State Secret* (1950). The Portland Spies case was a seeming success in a period of humiliation and public concern for the security and intelligence services. The Ring was headed by a KGB agent posing as Canadian businessman Gordon Lonsdale; a photographic and communications centre was established in a house in Ruislip by the American traitors Morris and Lona Cohen posing as antiquarian booksellers Peter and Helen Kroger; and vital naval secrets were supplied by the Britons Harry Houghton and Ethel Gee who worked at the Admiralty Underwater Weapons Research Establishment at Portland in the south of England. The Russians eagerly sought Western secrets regarding the tracking of Soviet submarines and the espionage cell had been operating in Great Britain for five years before its discovery. A contemporary account of the saga described the Portland Spy Ring as the "*most successful and extraordinary spy network ever known in Britain*" (Bulloch and Miller 1961: 19).

The producers of the picture had access to unprecedented detail of the affair as the trial at the Old Bailey had, unusually for a spy case, been public. The script material was compiled by a crime reporter who had sat through the trial, co-scriptwriter Frank Launder was present at a key session in court, and the production claimed to have shot scenes at many of the actual places featured in the events, such as the Old Vic theatre and a suburban bungalow in Ruislip (*Kine Weekly*, 29 August 1963; Brown 1977: 149).[494] In the dramatisation, Houghton (Bernard Lee) is returned home in disgrace from the British Embassy in Warsaw and is re-employed at the Admiralty's secret establishment at Portland. He is soon contacted by the Polish Secret Service which blackmails him into providing secrets. Houghton, with the encouragement of Gordon Lonsdale (William Sylvester), secures these through flattering Miss Gee (Margaret Tyzack) who has access to the safe in the Record's Office. Documents are retrieved for Lonsdale who passes them onto the Kroger's for transmission to Moscow. Spending freely of his ill-gotten gains, Houghton comes to the attention of the Security Service and is put under surveillance. An intricate police operation unearths the activities of the spy ring and the principals are arrested and convicted.

For *Kine Weekly*, this "*slice of recent history*" proved that, "*truth can be as exciting as fiction*" (2 April 1964). However, many reviewers found such a conscientious documentary approach to the subject a little dull and pedestrian. *Monthly Film Bulletin* felt it had the "*effect of a newspaper serialisation, in which facts and times are carefully recorded, but no one has gone very far with speculation about how the people concerned might actually talk and feel*" (May 1964: 77). In America, *Time* complained of "*drab middle-class doings*" (12 June 1964),[495] while in Britain *The Telegraph* reported that, "*It is all from life, but less than lively*" (20 March 1964). Reviewers who were now coming to terms with the screen excitement of *Dr No* (1962) and *From Russia, With Love* (1963) speculated that with the spy genre, a documentary realism, devoid of "*drama, thrills or sex*", made a poor comparison with thrills and action (*Time*, 12 June 1964). The *Daily Herald* duly noted that the "*activities of real agents, with their copies of Punch and shopping baskets, are not nearly as exciting to watch as those in the Bond world of fantasy*", and that "*reality*" as far as espionage was concerned, should be left to "*the courts*" (17 March 1964).

Film historian Robert Murphy has been more impressed, finding the picture a "*splendid apotheosis of the Cold War melodrama*", Houghton and Gee "*fascinating, almost tragic figures*", and noted how, unwitting of the producers,

The story of how they rationalize away their scruples, overcome their fear, exult in getting the better of their patronising superiors and then drift into greed and discontent and carelessness, comes to seem like a warning less of the corrupting power of Communism than of the dangers awaiting those who shed the bonds of conventional morality and assume the amoral attitudes of the classless, materialistic affluent society.
(1992: 220-1)

Cold War historian Tony Shaw concurs, believing Lonsdale's sleazy parties in the picture serve to feed the *"pleasure-seeking desires of an increasingly materialistic and valueless society"*, and that the *"corrupting power of communism"* is displaced by the *"temptations of Western affluence and promiscuity"* (2001: 59). Murphy sees *Ring of Spies* and its unintended critique as foreshadowing on screen the sad, bitter and lonely world of espionage of John le Carré. A contemporary reviewer at the *Guardian*, in the wake of a series of spy scandals and failures in British Intelligence, assumed a more cynical stance, judging *Ring of Spies* a *"very romanticised picture of British counter-spying"*, and wondered if the British *"really were as nimble as this?"* (31 May 1965). The *Daily Worker* also warily noted the story's consensual, uncritical attitude to security, judging the film *"tiresome and tasteless and should never have made"* (21 March 1964).

The public informational style of the picture was manifest in the short sequences which bookended the movie. The first provided a potted history of espionage, while the latter called for vigilance, where the viewer is warned of the continuing threat of Soviet espionage. The *Daily Worker* predictably railed against *"obnoxious commentary at the beginning and end, which does its jovial best to whip up hatred and fear"* (ibid.). The main false historical note is the inclusion of George Blake into the story. The Soviet mole in MI6, also exposed in 1961, is here seen attempting to warn a Soviet Embassy official about the imminent arrests, but actually played no part in the Portland operation. As might be expected, the film fails to be critical regarding the obvious failures in security pertaining to the case and which were mildly raised in the official Romer Report (1961).[496] Houghton later claimed that he was not overly liberal in his spending and it has since become clear that his treachery only came to light through the revelations of the Polish defector Colonel Michael Goleniewski – overall, a very poor indictment of British security. Houghton and Gee were sentenced to 15 years in prison; the Krogers and Lonsdale also received long jail sentences, but were later exchanged with the British subjects Gerald Brooke and Greville Wynne held on espionage charges in the Soviet Union. Acting on their notoriety, Harry Houghton later published *Operation Portland, the Autobiography of a Spy* (1972) and Gordon Lonsdale *Spy, Mem-*

oirs of Gordon Lonsdale (1965, actually ghost-written by Kim Philby). The immediate neighbours of the Kroger's in Ruislip were the subject of Hugh Whitemore's television play 'Act of Betrayal', which was broadcast in the BBC's *Play of the Month* anthology in 1971. The drama starred Alan MacNaughtan and Mary Wimbush as the Krogers, and Gertan Klauber as Lonsdale. The 'act of betrayal' of the title ironically relates to the solicited entrapment of friends and neighbours by the security services. The play thus posed serious questions: are not personal relationships more important than policies? And if we stoop to lies and deceit to counter lies and deceit, do we not degrade ourselves? *Stage and Television Today*, in a lengthy review, appreciated the acting and the conviction of the play, but even more the complex moral issues that were raised. Especially it asked: "*To what extent is the State entitled to force its citizens into actions that may conflict with their consciences, on the grounds that the safety of the realm may conceivably be threatened?*" (7 January 1971).[497]

Ring of Spies was the first picture of the 1960s to deal with an actual case of British traitors. The film attracted modest scrutiny and comment regarding the practice and representation of treachery, the effectiveness of the Security Service, and the accuracy of historical recreation. In the coming decades, there would be many further depictions of notorious traitors and security scandals in British cinema and television, which often created considerable controversy and around which such questions and issues would be debated much more fiercely and passionately.

Journalist David Leitch has written of the "*forbidden, almost voyeuristic thrill*" of suddenly being able to see into the secret world, the consequence of an espionage controversy which unexpectedly cracks open ('Introduction' in Modin 1994: 1). Similarly, the television reviewer at *The Telegraph* has commented on the "*deep pleasure*" that espionage drama can dispense through "*seeming to let us into state secrets*" (review of *Spooks*, 13 September 2005). The satisfaction and to some extent the social and political meaning of historical spy fiction is this revelation of a hitherto secret past. At their most intriguing, historical spy stories revisit previously hidden or obscured events, and defamiliarise and disrupt the "*collective memory*"; a process, as Victoria Stewart has observed, that can lead the reader into questioning why aspects of the national past have been concealed and neglected (2011). Historical spy fiction assuages the curiosity in the reader or viewer as they enter previously obstructed or elided domains, a desire reinforced by the wish for revelation already figured in readerly pleasure. The World War II and Cold War periods were characterised by official secrecy, and the authorities in Britain endeavoured to maintain a strict silence on important wartime and operational secrets, a process equating to the management of recent history. Through denying access to documents and invoking the Official Secrets Act to gag potential commentators, the secret world only leaked out piecemeal and intermittently into the public domain (Moran 2013; Aldrich 2004).[498] As the writer Rebecca West once observed, the public knows little of treachery and espionage, "*except what it hears from the lips of ministers in the Houses of Parliament, or from counsel and judges at the trials of persons charged with offences against treason or Official Secrets Acts, or from the press*". "*Of these three sources*", she maintained, "*the last has been much the most reliable*" (1964: 368); and in such an environment, fictional sources can assert much credibility with a sceptical public.

The study and writing of intelligence history has changed gradually over the years. Secret Service history has certainly posed a problem for historians, Bernard Porter declaring it a "*bewildering world*" (Bernard Porter 1989: 228). More recently, Christopher Moran has traced the altering "*trajectory*" of writing about the Secret Service in Britain: from its virtual "*absence*" for much of British history, "*walled off from public view*"; through the period, beginning in the 1960s, of the "*airport bookstall school of intelligence historiography*" written by "*exposé merchants ... peddling tall tales of treachery, betrayal, murder, and whatnot*", which fed a public fascination denied satisfaction resulting from official silence and denial; the gradual opening of the archives in the 1970s allowing for the revealing of the secret war of deception and code breakers; the emergence of the "para-*historians*" in the early 1980s, their conspiracy theories and representation of the intelligence services as right-wing plotters and a threat to democracy; onto the upsurge in academic interest in intelligence studies commencing in the middle of the 1980s and the appearance of specialised periodicals such as *Intelligence and National Security*; and crowned by a new era of "*openness*", which has witnessed a greater willingness to declassify documents, resulted in the unprecedented appearance of a spate of official histories of the leading branches of the intelligence service, and marked the confirmation of the subject's "*newfound legitimacy*" (2011a).[499] However, former wartime intelligence officer Malcolm Muggeridge has warned from experience, that diplomats and intelligence officers are even "*bigger liars than journalists, and the historians who try to reconstruct the past out of their records, are, for the most part, dealing with fantasy*" (quoted in Carter 2001: 250). While the films and dramas of historical spy fiction show no direct alignment with the shifting historiography – although there is a tendency for stories to affiliate with the "*sensation-seeking writers*" treating treachery – the increasing professionalisation of the writing on espionage has provided a cogent framework for critiquing historical spy fiction for any inadequacies, distortions and bias.[500]

The historical stories discussed in the following chapter are invariably structured as 'realist fiction', confident in a direct access to the past, and, unlike doubting postmodern historical narratives and their suspicions of the metanarratives of history, unconcerned with the possibility of unreliability in the narration of the past and with the problems of access to an historical truth. That, as we shall see, does not mean that the films and dramas and their depictions of espionage history were free from criticism. In many cases, they attracted fierce condemnation as biased, distorted, selective and far from authoritative in their treatment of the past; and did so despite the partial and subjective nature of much of the historical record in the field.

Their Trade is Treachery[501]

Secret war replaces actual combat. Consequently, the real combatants of the Cold War are spies and traitors.
(Horn 2013: 230)

In British television, the activities of Kim Philby and his fellow traitors have always been the extreme opposite of a secret. Indeed, it has sometimes seemed hard to shut writers up on the subject.
(*Guardian*, 28 April 2003)

Treachery in the Cold War period has been of equal fascination for both authors and the public. The atom spies of the 1940s were the inspiration for such novelists as Nigel Balchin and his story *A Sort of Traitors* (1949, filmed as *Suspect* 1960) and Robert Harling and his story *The Enormous Shadow* (1956); and notorious figures such as the double-agents Kim Philby and Anthony Blunt have inspired a number of novels. *The Untouchable* (1997) by John Banville is clearly based on Blunt; an imaginative engagement with the characters of Guy Burgess, Philby and Blunt is offered in David Mure's novel *The Last Temptation* (1984); the back-story to Michael Hartland's *The Third Betrayal* (1986) is the remarkable Soviet agent 'Sonya' (Ursula Ruth Kuczynski) who operated undetected in Britain as a naturalised British subject in the 1940s; while *Red Joan* (2013) was inspired by the long-term Soviet agent Melita Norwood publicly exposed in 1999, and who the newspapers dubbed "*The Spy Who Came in from the Co-op*".[502] The press and its readers were spellbound and scandalised in equal parts by the treachery of educated and well-connected figures. The peculiar matter of sex and sexuality attached to the homosexual Burgess, the bi-sexual Donald Maclean and Blunt, and the supposed libidinous heterosexuality of Philby has also ensured a healthy curiosity in the men's activities and motives, and effectively mapped the discourse of "*sexual deviance*" on to that of "*ideological deviance*" (Baker 2012: 31). A series of spy scandals in the late 1950s and early 1960s, culminating in the 'Profumo Affair' which ran its course across 1962 and 1963, and the defection of Kim Philby to Moscow in January 1963, ensured that the British press and its public remained fascinated by espionage in the period and indignant at the seemingly endless failures of the security services. As we have seen, treachery in the period was the essential backdrop of the new espionage literature of John le Carré and Len Deighton, and fresh, more cynical and critical stories of British Security and Intelligence. The scandals and revelations of the period were also the source for a number of original screen dramas which reflected the public's fascination for (usually) well-born traitors and double-agents.

In 2003, the *Evening Standard* commented jadedly that, "*Every few years, someone in a position of authority in the television world gets nostalgic for that louche and traitorous group of young men who infested Cambridge University in the Thirties*" (10 May 2003); and, indeed, the screen has paid particular attention to the infamous 'Cambridge Spies', the collective term for five graduates of Cambridge University who attained senior positions in the British Secret Service or government office where they systematically spied for the Soviets. In a wider cultural sense, Willmetts and Moran have noted that, "*Few intelligence failures have been more enduring or produced more press headlines, more history books or more works of fiction than the treachery of the 'Cambridge Five*'" (2013: 49). For the public, these figures became "*subjects of grim fascination*" (*The Telegraph*, 25 April 2003). Kim Philby (codenames: SÖHNCHEN, STANLEY, SYNOK, TOM), served at the War Office, at the Secret Intelligence Service (SIS) from September 1941, and in a senior intelligence role in Washington in the late 1940s. Under suspicion from the early 1950s, he was distanced from sensitive information and eventually defected to Moscow in 1963. Guy Burgess (codenames: MÄDCHEN, HICKS, JIM, PAUL), who for a time served at the BBC, War Office and Foreign Service, and developed a peripheral role in the SIS, and Donald Maclean (codenames: HOMER, LYRIC, SIROTA, WAISE, STUART), who became a senior diplomat at the Foreign Office, both spending time in Washington, fled Great Britain for Soviet Russia in 1951, moments before the exposure of Maclean.[503] Anthony Blunt (codenames: TONY, FRED, JOHNSON, YAN) served in the wartime MI5 before returning to academic life after the conflict, from where he occasionally performed services for the Soviets for several years. He came under suspicion in the early 1950s, eventually confessed on the promise of immunity from prosecution in 1964, and was publicly 'outed' in 1979 in a damaging exposure for the government. John Cairncross (codenames: LISZT, MOLIÈRE, KAREL) served at the Foreign Office, the Treasury, at the code-breaking centre at Bletchley Park, with SIS, at the Cabinet Office, and the Ministry of Supply, a remarkable collection of offices from where he could obtain classified documents. He came under suspicion following the defection of Burgess and Maclean and quietly left government office. On investigation he made a partial admission, but it was only on the release of Soviet documents in the 1990s that the true extent of his treachery and his importance to the Soviets were revealed. The assessment of the intelligence historians Nigel West and Oleg Tsarev is that the "*damage inflicted by Philby, Burgess and Maclean can only be described as colossal*" (1998: 186). Add to these the names of Blunt and Cairncross, of the group as a whole the latter passing the most classified documents to the Soviets in the period 1941-45, it is unsurprising that the Soviets referred to the men as 'The Magnificent Five' and the remarkable intelligence they provided over many years as 'The Crown Jewels'.[504]

The Cambridge Spies or 'Stalin's Englishmen' as they have been called, stand as the index of Cold War treachery in Britain. They have attained a considerable mystique in British culture, the story offering a compelling insight into the "*most embarrassing episode in British secret service history*" (review of *Cambridge Spies*, *Guardian*, 5 August 2002). As such, mere mention of the group or an individual in British spy fiction summons up the very depths of perfidy and delineate the territory of the traitor. As the historians Willmetts and Moran have recently asserted, "*Few Cold War stories have captured the British public's imagination with such frenzied intensity and lengthy duration as the saga of the Cambridge Five*" (2013: 51). Spy novels as diverse as *The Enormous Shadow* (1955), *From Russia, With Love* (1957), *The Ipcress File* (1962), *The Naked Runner* (1966), *Colonel Butler's Wolf* (1972), *Disorderly Elements* (1985), *Legacy* (2001), *Restless* (2006) and *Free Agent* (2009) make mention of one or more of the traitors, both as a mark of the fiction's supposed authenticity or realism, and in some cases as part of a wider critique of the British establishment and political society.[505] The popular fascination with the "*Cambridge Comintern*" (Cecil 1984) has been encapsulated in the epithets: "*Spies, Lies, Buggery and Betrayal*" and "*Toffs, Queers and Traitors*"; a seductive perversion of the British secret agent as heroic, patriotic and heteronormative.[506]

Cinema and television in Britain have shown considerable interest in the nation's past. Although much attention has been paid to the British experience of the early part of the twentieth century, screen historian John Hill has noted how film and television-makers from around the 1980s began to show increased interest in the decades following World War Two. These productions, interestingly, tended to revise the common representation of the period as stable and contented, and pose a more critical view, one characterised in terms of repression and privation. Historical biopics such as *Dance with a Stranger* (1985), *Personal Services* (1986) and *The Krays* (1990) were populated with "*criminals, deviants and misfits*", and "*seem to offer a set of characters who are in protest against the drabness and conformity of the society around them*" (1999: 125).[507] This places the pictures in stark contrast to the celebrated cycle of 'heritage films' which tended to be drawn from the nation's classic literature and promoted the more pictorial aspects of the British countryside, its better families and their impressive homes. The historical spy dramas dealing with the Cambridge Spies occupy an interesting space between the 'revisionist' and the more mainstream historical films. On the one hand, a film like *Another Country* (1984), and television biopics such as 'Philby, Burgess & Maclean' (1977) and *Cambridge Spies* (2003), deal with a privileged group of young men, an ancient and venerable public school and university, and the corridors of power in the national institutions of the Foreign Service, the Secret Service, and the BBC, staples of the heritage genre; and on the other hand, with a disreputable collection of traitors, ambiguously in protest against their social and political surroundings, and who, by the standards of their time, displayed a deviancy in their sexuality and general behaviour. It is this mixing of privilege and sordidness, of social and sexual transgressions, of the inter-relation of perversion and subversion that explains the long-standing public fascination with these 'respectable spies', and the inducement to film and television producers to explore a colourful and unconventional group of young gentlemen engaged in treachery.[508] The initial group of 'Cambridge Spies' dramas were clustered around the early 1980s, a period of transition from traditional Labour to new-style Toryism. It was a politically complex period of hope countered with disillusion, of tradition contradicted by adjustment, and of a market-inspired morality flying in the face of customs believed immemorial. As American film critic Harlan Kennedy has observed of this moment and its cultural representations: "*Just as Watergate in America in the Seventies lit the blue touch-paper to a whole epoch of Paranoia and Conspiracy cinema ... so the political leakiness of modern Britain is opening up a new era of* films traiteurs" (1984: 9).

The single play television drama 'Philby, Burgess & Maclean' was written by Ian Curteis, produced at the commercial television company Granada, and first broadcast in May 1977 in the anthology series *ITV Playhouse*. It addressed the dramatic period during which the realisation emerged within the British Secret Service that senior officers and diplomats were spying for the Communists, and *Stage and Television Today* declared itself surprised that the story had not been told in dramatic form on television before (10 June 1977). Suspicion first falls on Donald Maclean and then by association on Guy Burgess and Kim Philby. The drama covers the decade beginning with the Volkov incident in 1945, the erstwhile Soviet defector in Istanbul who offers to name spies in the Foreign Office and in the SIS, the VENONA decrypts of Soviet radio traffic which implicate Maclean and lead to the defection of Burgess and Maclean to Moscow in 1951, and ends with Philby's public denial in 1955 that he was the 'Third Man' in the spy ring. Anthony Bate plays Philby as a resolute character under increasing strain, Derek Jacobi essays a camp and twitching Burgess, and Michael Culver portrays an unnerved Maclean coming apart at the seams.[509] 'Philby, Burgess & Maclean' was Granada's entry into the 1978 Monte Carlo Festival and was a British Academy of Film and Television Awards Best Play nominee. It was subsequently broadcast in 48 countries, with an estimated audience in excess of 100 million.[510] Explaining his drama, Curteis said that he wrote the play "*chiefly as an exciting spy story, but also to investigate the motives of the men, and to try to get the feel of what it must have been like to be them*", and pointed to its exploration of whether we "*owe a loyalty stronger and deeper than to our own country*" (quoted in the *TV Times*, 26 May 1977: 3). The play suggests that the Soviets regarded Maclean as their most important source, having provided atomic secrets of incalculable value from his post in Washington towards the end of World War II, and that it was the grave implications of atomic weaponry which provided the self-justification for the men in their treachery against the Allies at this time.

Reviews were largely positive, noting Granada's progress with the drama-documentary format and praising the quality of the play's writing, acting and staging (*Guardian*, 28 May 1977). The *Daily Mail* found 'Philby, Burgess & Maclean' an "*imaginative yet restrained reconstruction ... an absorbing and satisfying project*" (1 June 1977). The *Guardian* praised the script as "*literate, perceptive and alive with irony*" (1 June 1977), and *The Times* judged the drama a "*stylish piece of demonography ... resisting all the excesses of 'nostalgia*'" (1 June 1977). The *Daily Express* admiring the drama-documentary approach, felt: "*We could do with a lot more spy thrillers based on this kind of reality in place of most of the fictionalised rubbish television usually serves*" (1 June 1977). The dramatisation prompted some probing of the apathy of an establishment which failed to spot the traitors in its midst, and which many felt had not been adequately explained, even concealed. The conclusion of course lay with class, the *New Statesman* sensing, if a little crudely, that, "*In the sealed-off world of the FO [Foreign Office] it would have been easier to persuade the spymasters that Herbert Morrison had been flogging secrets than to finger fellows you'd only ever fingered once before, at school*" (3 June 1977)[511]; and the *Sunday Telegraph* was convinced that:

> *Philby and Co. got away with it because as products of the ruling class, public school and Cambridge they were thought to be incapable of deviation from the loyalties planted deep into their genes by centuries of cold baths, construing Ovid, playing games, shooting things and a little sodomy.* (5 June 1977)[512]

The historical consultant for 'Philby, Burgess & Maclean' was Philip Knightley, a journalist who had co-authored *Philby: The Spy Who Betrayed a Genera-*

tion back in 1968. The teleplay was marginally premature to the revelations in 1979 which led to the public exposure of Anthony Blunt, a fourth member of the Cambridge Spies; and following the new scandal, Granada took the opportunity to re-distribute the drama and it was picked up by new territories and re-shown in others (press sheet issued 7 January 1980). There was little of the clamour around 'Philby, Burgess & Maclean' that would attend future Cambridge Spies dramas regarding historical interpretation and accuracy. The left-wing *Morning Star* was critical in part, the reviewer sourly complaining that the play offered "*no new information, no new concept or insight*", and was unsurprised that, "*Nothing at all was conveyed, however, of those shared anti-fascist pre-war days which persuaded these and many other bright young intellectuals to support the socialist cause*" (1 June 1977). A couple of years later Curteis received an unexpected endorsement of his historical drama, reporting that: "*I got a message from Kim Philby. His daughter who lives in London saw the play and wrote to him about it. He wrote back saying my guesses were right*" (quoted in the Anglia Television press sheet for *The Atom Spies*, 1979).

Ian Curteis scripted a number of historical television dramas in the 1970s and 1980s, including *The Atom Spies* in 1979, described in its press sheet as a "*real life thriller about some of the most important and chilling events of our time*". The drama was produced at Anglia Television, dealt with the treachery of Alan Nunn May (Edward Wilson), Bruno Pontecorvo (Michael Craig) and Klaus Fuchs (Andrew Ray), and covered the period from 1945 when the Soviet defector Igor Gouzenko put Western security onto Nunn May through to the arrest of Fuchs in 1949. It was claimed that some scenes were shot at Harwell, the Government's Atomic Energy Research Establishment, established on 1 January 1946, and the workplace of Fuchs and Pontecorvo (*Atom Spies* press sheet). The drama was well-received. *Stage and Television Today* greatly admired the production and judged the play the "*real reward from a week's viewing*" (14 June 1979), and the *Observer* found it convincing and a "*first-class TV drama*" (3 June 1979). It surprisingly remains the only dramatisation of the treachery of Nunn May, Pontecorvo and Fuchs and this significant aspect of British treachery.[513]

The theatrical play *Another Country*, written by Julian Mitchell, premiered on 5 November 1981 at the Greenwich Theatre in southeast London and successfully transferred to the West End in March 1982. It launched a quartet of aspiring and hugely talented young actors, Rupert Everett, Colin Firth, Daniel Day-Lewis and Kenneth Branagh. The drama, a "*well-made piece about buggery, barratry and bolshevism at a leading British public school of the 1930s*", deals with the two outsiders Guy Bennett and Tommy Judd (*Observer*, 10 June 1984). The former is openly homosexual and the latter Marxist. Following the scandal of a fellow pupil's suicide after he is discovered having sex with another boy, there is a crackdown on loose, immoral and unconventional behaviour. Bennett is persecuted and Judd is ultimately disillusioned in his bid to wrest some control from within the structures of power. The play ends on a vaguely optimistic note, with the two young men contemplating future rebellion and with Bennett picking up a copy of *Das Kapital*, and musing, *"Wouldn't it be wonderful if all this was true?"* The title of the play is taken from the patriotic song *I Vow to Thee, My Country*, which includes the lines: *"And there's another country, I've heard of long ago; Most dear to them that love her, most great to them that know"*. The notion of 'another country' in the play could allude to Soviet Russia, as well as the secretive world of the homosexual in the 1930s. The drama won the Society of West End Theatre Awards Play of the Year for 1982 and was one of the theatrical events of the decade. *Another Country* is an imaginative treatment of the (de)formative schooldays of Guy Burgess, who had attended public school at the privileged Eton College, and later was a controversial figure on the London social scene for his drinking, unchecked homosexuality and outrageous behaviour.[514]

In 1984, Julian Mitchell opened out his stage play of eight characters and four sets for the cinema. The picture was modestly budgeted at £1.2 million, directed by Marek Kanievska who had previously worked in television, and with Rupert Everett as Guy Bennett and Colin Firth as Tommy Judd. Colin Firth considered the film *"far more cool and darker"* than the stage play (quoted in *The Times*, 2 June 1984), the most significant additions being two brief episodes set in Moscow in 1983 in which the elderly Bennett is interviewed by a journalist and which bookend the historical scenes at school. The new material alludes to Guy Burgess, who had in fact died in Moscow in 1963, more strongly than anything in the original play.[515] The most interesting line of dialogue as far as parallels with Burgess are concerned comes late in the drama when Bennett reflects on recent events and utters, *"What better cover for somebody like me than total indiscretion"*. This is an apt assessment of the future spy submerged under the dissolute and seemingly incautious Guy Burgess.[516] The picture has largely been appreciated as part of the emerging 'heritage cinema' of the early 1980s, films treating Great Britain's national and literary past, with important contemporary examples being *Chariots of Fire* (1981) and *Heat and Dust* (1982). *Another Country*, in line with other heritage films, has been seen to transform the ostensive object of the criticism – here the repression of the authoritarian public school – into a source of visual pleasure. Thus, any critique is lost to the fascination and seductive allure for the viewer of the picturesque and the ceremonial of a selective national past.[517] Such a view should be balanced with the fact that both Eton College and Charterhouse School, seemingly aware of the drama's critical stance, refused to allow location filming at their institution (*Daily Mirror*, 25 May 1983).[518]

The film *Another Country* can be usefully compared to Lindsay Anderson's masterful *If....* (1968), as both pictures deal with the theme of revolt in the setting of a public school. *If....* treats the contemporary scene of youthful revolt in the late 1960s; while *Another Country* examines the repressions and abuses which led to a generation of traitors in the British establishment. In her biography of Anthony Blunt, Miranda Carter discusses the culture of dissent evident in public schools in the 1920s. This tended to manifest itself in "*aestheticism*", a certain preciousness in attitude and feyness in behaviour, and a provocative intellectual arrogance, all of which are apparent in Bennett. As she states, the public-school system "*offered an excellent training ground in dissidence. It inadvertently fostered a questioning and subversive attitude and a profound distrust of authority, necessary for any intellectual class and vital to the manufacture of an artist, writer or spy*" (2001: 25-26). The drama was also seemingly credible in showing the "*traditional pastime*" of the aesthetes of "*finding a younger boy to admire*" (39). Kanievska was drawn to the drama's extraordinary quality of obsession, "*That whole environment, all those formative years spent with kids already obsessed with power. Obviously that affects the sort of society we live in because these people end up governing, end up in control and have done so for generations*" (quoted in Marshall 1985: 32).

Another Country was widely praised, considered a "*remarkably assured first feature*" from Kanievska, and "*brilliantly well acted by a fine young cast*" (*Glasgow Herald*, 5 May 1984). It was a British entry to the Cannes Film Festival where it won a 'Best Artistic Contribution' Award for cinematographer Peter Biziou. The approach to the story was original in that the "*seeds of treachery*" in the Cambridge Spies saga "*were shown to be sown not as generally thought at university but at public school*" (*The Telegraph*, 15 May 1984). In a review of Graham Greene's *The Human Factor*, the *Guardian* had earlier mused on the British establishment's fascination, even "*sneaking respect, verging on affection*", with its own traitors. The reason for this, it speculated, was that, "*adult life is simply a sequel, usually disappointing, to the only five years that really count in a man's life, the years in a public school*". There was a widespread recognition, it maintained, that a boy of independent outlook "*might very well, and with no small justification, rebel against the whole thing, and do his worst*" (16 March 1978). *The Telegraph*, reviewing *Another Country*, felt such a thesis "*carries weight*", and that the school's "*conservative traditions*", and Guy's "*homosexual promiscuity*" combine to make a "*convincing picture of a highly unstable character who needs only the influence of his best friend, a dedicated Marxist, to turn him against the class-ridden Brit-*

ish system as he sees it" (15 May 1984). *Newsweek*, which found the picture "*troubling and powerful*", was sufficiently convinced that scorn and betrayal by schoolmates could, in an impressionable youth, fuel a lifelong hatred of the hypocritical British class system; "*just as it did in the case of MacLean*" it suggested (28 May 1984). The *Evening Standard* dutifully sat through a "*lesson*" in the "*genealogy of treason*", prepared to accept that the "*road to Moscow is paved with English hypocrisy and public-school vice*", a fact "*made plausibly persuasive in the stifling atmosphere created in a school where a spy system already operates and moral blackmail (backed by a big cane) is the norm*" (7 June 1984). The *Daily Mirror* praised an intelligent and compelling film: "*Savage, funny, cynical in its observations of an educational system that created leaders and destroyers of an empire*" (8 June 1984).

Other critics were far from persuaded. The *Daily Express* confessed it found the idea that a hedonistic, politically uncommitted, cynical, homosexual youth would plan to betray his country out of a fit of schoolboy pique "*quite unconvincing*" (8 June 1984); the *Observer* dismissed the "*theory*" as "*simpleminded*" (10 June 1984); and the *New Statesman* dismissed a "*glib bit of motivation*" (8 June 1984). Some felt the addition of the prologue and epilogue superfluous; "*cataleptically inauspicious*" was how it was described at the *Financial Times* (8 June 1984), it being quite obvious that the story was drawn from Burgess, and "*rather crude in its abrupt and unqualified leap of thought from an unhappy homosexual outsider to a Red Spy*" (*The Times*, 8 June 1984).[519] The *Telegraph* felt the adaptation of *Another Country* to the screen, while a "*gain to the eye*", was a "*loss to the argument*" (8 June 1984). A poor review in *Monthly Film Bulletin* found it dispiriting that the most influential philosophy of the twentieth century was reduced to the cavortings of a few frivolous adherents. Here the view was that "*eccentrics*" such as Kim Philby, Guy Burgess, Donald McLean and Anthony Blunt simply could not support the ideological weight brought to bear on them in the drama (June 1984: 173-174). In contrast, Derek Malcolm writing in the *Guardian*, a former pupil at Eton, felt the film tempted the viewer into delving into the assumptions which lay behind the elite institution and its privileged education, "*the reasons for the ridiculous and demeaning pecking order of the system and for the traditional clap-trap that goes with it which sucks the weak and the foolish, even the strong and the less foolish, into such loyalty and admiration*". He concluded that, "Another Country *may not be entirely convincing in its new format, but it smacks of the truth all the same*" (1984).[520] In this perspective, the humiliating outsider status of the Marxist and flagrantly homosexual in the repressive structure of the public school might just be a reasonable motive for the betrayal of one's class. Others questioned the romantic outsider status afforded Guy Bennett who dared to be different, "*instead of being the somewhat squalid hypocrite and liar which his equivalents in what is called real life undoubtedly are"* (*Spectator,* 16 June 1984); a dramatic course it was felt which steered too close to justification of the Cambridge Spies' treachery. The left-wing *Morning Star* made its usual interjection with regard to Cambridge Spies dramas, noting a lack of historical context for explaining the treachery, and complaining that there *"could have surely been scenes of the rise of fascism and the mass unemployment of the era"* (11 June 1984).

Marek Kanievska and Rupert Everett revisited the Cambridge Spies in 2004 with *A Different Loyalty,* a £10 million British-Canadian co-production shot on location in London, Malta, Montreal and Moscow inspired by the story of British traitor Kim Philby's love affair and marriage to Eleanor Brewer (Sharon Stone) in Beirut and his sudden defection to the Soviet Union in 1963.[521] The producers pitched the film as *"parallel stories of one woman's obsession with a man, and that man's equally passionate adherence to communism"* and immediately invoked an angry response that, *"one of Britain's most notorious and damaging traitors"* would be portrayed as a *"romantic husband motivated by idealism".* *"Expert witnesses"* were immediately invited to comment. Former Foreign Office official newly turned spy writer Alan Judd remarked that, *"We are living in a perverted moral universe if we make heroes out of people like this";* and intelligence historian Christopher Andrew chipped in that, *"If this film is only carefully selecting parts of the story that appeal to Hollywood, it will not give a very rounded impression. It is unlikely to convey the brutalisation of Philby's personality that his spying caused him"* (all *The Telegraph,* 19 May 2002).

Video Business was mildly impressed, promising its readers a *"good evening's entertainment for those who enjoy discussions of geopolitics presented with the occasional trench-coated spy lurking in the corners".* On the other hand, *Variety* found the romantic-thriller a *"disappointing companion piece"* to the earlier *Another Country,* a *"creakily mechanical star vehicle"* for Stone and Everett, and unconvincing in its mixing of *"Cold War, John le Carré-style intrigue with woman's picture passion"* (2-8 August 2004). The approach of the picture was summed up by the eye-popping scene in which Eleanor Philby rips open her blouse and shouts, *"Can you choose Communism over these?"* In the late 1960s, the public was interested in the experiences of Eleanor Philby, the wife of a traitor and defector who successfully published her story as the Ian Fleming sounding *The Spy I Loved* in 1968 and which was serialised in the *Sunday Times.* Audiences were clearly less interested in the romance and tragedy to be extracted from such a situation in the new millennium and the film came and went quickly and left little lasting impression.

In 1979, following the revelations contained in Andrew Boyle's best-selling account *The Climate of Treason: Five Who Spied for Russia* (1979), the disloyalty of Anthony Blunt was made public by Prime Minister Margaret Thatcher.[522]

This greatly changed the context for treating the Cambridge Spies and the public understanding of their treachery. The single-play 'Blunt' was broadcast in 1987 as part of the BBC's prestigious drama strand *Screen Two*. It dealt with the circumstances surrounding the flight of the 'diplomats' Guy Burgess and Donald Maclean in 1951, and therefore covered similar territory as the earlier 'Philby, Burgess & Maclean', the culmination of the period which has been considered a 'golden age' of Soviet intelligence operations in Great Britain. However, the arrangement in 'Blunt' was quite different as it concentrated on the three characters of Guy Burgess (Anthony Hopkins), a minor Foreign Office official, Anthony Blunt (Ian Richardson), Surveyor of the King's Pictures, and Goronwy Rees (Michael Williams), a fellow of All Souls College, Oxford University. The screening commences with a series of newspaper headlines dealing with the shock unmasking of Blunt as a Soviet spy in 1979. The story then flashes back to May 1951 as Guy Burgess reacquaints himself with Blunt having returned from Washington in disgrace. The men are former lovers and still retain a strong bond of affection. The Foreign Office diplomat Donald Maclean is about to be exposed as a traitor and Blunt instructs Burgess to convince Maclean to defect to Moscow. As arrangements are being made, Burgess confides in his onetime friend and former communist Goronwy Rees. Rees's wife becomes suspicious and Goronwy is forced to tell her the truth. Blunt is shocked to discover that Burgess has accompanied Maclean to Russia leaving him in a highly compromised position. Following the disappearance of Burgess and Maclean, Rees is called into MI5 for questioning, and, to cover his own back, Blunt cleverly casts doubt onto Rees's character and loyalty.

'Blunt' was written by Roger Chapman who had a Cambridge University background and had recently written the play *One of Us* which had been staged at Greenwich and similarly dealt with Blunt. The television drama in dealing with the Burgess-Maclean defection takes the unusual point of focus of Blunt and his later unmasking in the late 1970s.[523] Producer Martin Thompson commented on this decision, explaining that, "*We shall use the events of 1979 as a way into the story and look at the episode that caused it a bit more coolly. That does not mean condoning what he did, but it will include his point-of-view*" (quoted in *Broadcast*, 16 August 1985).[524] Inspired by the frenzy of publicity surrounding the unmasking of Blunt, Thompson set about a proposed 6-7 hour serial about Anthony Blunt and the group that spied for Russia, possibly covering the period from Cambridge in the 1930s up to the exposure of Blunt, and with the working title of *The Age of Treason* (*Stage and Television Today*, 17 November 1983). Thompson claimed to have conducted over 80 interviews with relatives and people who knew Blunt, although he reports that those "*who knew Blunt best declined to speak to the writer Robin Chapman or to Ian Richardson, who plays the title role*". Furthermore, the production was refused permission to shoot at Windsor Castle and the Reform Club, two important locations in the story (quoted in the *Sunday Times*, 15 June 1986).

Arguably, the drama played fairly freely with the historical facts and attributed a far greater role to Anthony Blunt in the 'missing diplomats' affair than was sometimes accorded. One reviewer referred to the "*dramatic hypotheses*" of the film, which made Blunt a more important Soviet spy than previously thought, put Blunt on much closer terms with Guy Burgess than ever admitted, and stressed Blunt's emotional devastation and professional betrayal as a spy (*Morning Star*, 10 January 1987). The *Sunday Telegraph* was one which was prepared to accept the "*dramatic reconstruction of fact and opinion which shows the traitors as they really were*" (11 January 1987). The producers, though, correctly anticipated some criticism, especially in regard of the "*'reality' of the script's depiction of events*" (Roger Chapman quoted in the *Sunday Times*, 15 June 1986). With the Blunt affair still a sensitive subject, the drama did indeed attract considerable censure regarding alleged historical inaccuracy, and passionate debate raged across the press regarding the acceptable limits of the drama-documentary form. In fact, an unseemly argument broke out between a former researcher on the production, the writer and producer of the drama, and sundry other voices which reigned in through the columns of newspapers.[525]

The eminent intelligence historian Christopher Andrew claimed that 'Blunt', "*dramatically effective and highly improbable ... rewrites the history of 1951*"; he jibed at the publicised "*several years of expensive research (much of it apparently wasted)*"; and found the drama in poor contrast with Alan Bennett's *An Englishman Abroad* (1983) which had showed "*scrupulous respect for the historical record*" (1987). The art historian, former pupil and apologist Brian Sewell found the characterisation of Anthony Blunt "*preposterous*", claiming that, "*Some may feel that treachery does not merit a fair hearing, and that grotesque caricature is all the man deserves*" (1987).[526] A more tolerant view held at *The Telegraph*, which believed a dramatisation intended to entertain did no real "*harm*" (16 January 1987). The paper was immediately jumped on by a reader who strongly disagreed in a letter to its columns; and further, contested the accuracy of the representation, asserting that, "*Chapman's version of the damaging interview with Burgess in which Rees was apparently told of the coming defection of Maclean is simply not true*", and surprisingly claiming to have been present throughout the meeting (M. M. Hardy, 16 and 21 January 1987).[527] Roger Chapman answered Christopher Andrew in a letter published in *The Telegraph*, confirming that 'Blunt' was "*based on wide reading and was tested against the meticulous research of the producer Martin Thompson*". Suggesting the difference in opinion could be put down to a "*matter of emphasis and interpretation*", Chapman claimed as "*much regard for the historical truth as Dr Andrew"*, but was equally aware of his *"obliga-tions to the validity of dramatic truth"* (21 January 1987). Previously, Chapman had explained: *"The fascinating thing is that we still don't know what Blunt actually did. He admitted that he was a traitor but the extent of the havoc he created is only known to MI5"* (quoted in the *Daily Mail*, 6 September 1985). The creative team on 'Blunt' also had to answer allegations from Cherry Hughes, a former researcher on the production who found a champion in Corinna Honan at the *Daily Mail*. Hughes claimed that her exhaustive re-search was *"ignored"* and consequently the drama was full of *"major errors"*. Clearly aggrieved, she reported: *"My original research was so detailed that I cannot understand how they've got so much wrong in this film". "I can't see that any of my research has been used at all"* she asserted (quoted in the *Daily Mail*, 6 January 1987).[528] Peter Goodchild, Head of Television Drama at the BBC, replied to the accusations, claiming an unjustified attempt to *"discredit the integrity of the BBC film 'Blunt'"*, stood by the research conducted for the drama, and stated for the record that the film was,

> *patently not a detailed chronicle of Blunt's life. Instead Robin Chapman has used first-hand accounts from the main participants in those cru-cial events of May 1951 – when Burgess and Maclean fled to Moscow – to explore dramatically the motivations and personal and political in-volvements of this most enigmatic of men.* (1987)

In her reply published in the same column, Corinna Honan reasserted the criticisms of Hughes and Sewell, and clearly indicated that she considered Goodchild's arguments disingenuous (*Daily Mail*, 10 January 1987).[529]

As 'Blunt' dealt with the shadowy world of espionage, some reviewers al-lowed the historical reconstruction a degree of slack. At the *Western Mail* it was recognised that, *"Facts still lack solidity in the history of defection, so there is plenty of scope for the inventions of screenwriter Robin Chapman"* (10 Janu-ary 1987). The trusting *Independent* sought to fit 'Blunt' into the tradition of spy literature, acknowledging: *"If this were fiction, it would mark the point in time where espionage left the pages of John Buchan and entered the grimier realist world of Le Carrè. But this is fact, however impossible it seems"* (8 Janu-ary 1987). Several critics remarked on the contemporary significance of a story of monumental establishment cover-ups, *"made more believable by the recent court case in Australia"* as it was pointedly expressed in the left-wing *Morning Star* (10 January 1987). The ongoing *'Spycatcher* Affair' provided a *"topicality"* to 'Blunt', confirming that, *"fascination with the shadowy world of betrayals and secret agents is as potent as ever"* (*Western Mail*, 10 January 1987). *Stage and Television Today* welcomed 'Blunt' as a corrective to the farce taking place in Sydney, restoring the balance somewhat *"by taking espionage seriously*" (15 January 1987). As a drama, most reviewers praised the production and the acting, and some felt duty bound to comment on the screen kiss between Burgess and Blunt.[530]

A main source for the dramatic interpretation was Goronwy Rees's controversial *A Chapter of Accidents* (1972), and this furnishes the essential material for the play concerning friendship, patriotism and betrayal.[531] The controversial Goronwy Rees, who had severed links with the Reds after the Nazi-Soviet Pact of 1939, played the telling role in the Cambridge Spies saga of informing on Anthony Blunt during his own interrogation by MI5 in 1951, and later putting the journalist Andrew Boyle onto Blunt which led to the art historian's public exposure in 1979. His daughter has claimed that Goronwy became "*obsessed*" with exposing Blunt as a spy (Rees 1994: 168). It has more recently emerged that during World War II Burgess offered to kill Rees who he now considered a security threat, but was flatly turned down by his Soviet handlers (West and Tsarev 1998: 162).[532] The play was broadcast in America as *Blunt: The Fourth Man*, for which a preface was added explaining the background of the characters. Unfortunately it erroneously listed Guy Burgess and Donald Maclean as members of British Intelligence rather than as diplomats, and over-confidently claimed Blunt recruited Burgess and Maclean to Communism, when it was more likely, as several writers had claimed by that point, that the art historian was recruited by Burgess as late as 1936 (Andrew 1987; Carter 2001: 162-3).

Two notorious Cambridge Spies were the subject of *Single Spies*, a double-bill of one-act plays by Alan Bennett and first performed at the National Theatre in 1988. *An Englishman Abroad*, set in Moscow in 1958 with Guy Burgess, was originally written as a television drama and broadcast on the BBC in 1983[533]; while *A Question of Attribution*, which deals with Anthony Blunt as Surveyor of the Queen's Pictures and played by Bennett on stage, was first performed within *Single Spies* and later adapted for television and broadcast on the BBC in 1991.[534] Both television dramas were directed by John Schlesinger, who returned to the BBC after an absence of nearly a quarter of a century, and produced by Innes Lloyd.[535] A critic has referred to *Single Spies* as an "*exquisite pair of miniatures*" (*Guardian*, 3 March 1989).

An Englishman Abroad is a dramatisation of an actual meeting in Moscow between "*highly theatrical actress Coral Browne and the equally theatrical spy Guy Burgess*" while she was on tour with the Shakespeare Memorial Company with a performance of *Hamlet* (*Mail on Sunday*, 4 December 1983).[536] The screen version of the play commences with a drunken Burgess (Alan Bates) attending a performance, gaining entry to Browne's (playing herself) dressing room (where he steals her soap, cigarettes and vodka), and inviting her to lunch at his seedy apartment. The actress perseveres against the warnings of the British embassy not to meet the disgraced diplomat, struggles across the forbidding city and arrives at the apartment. The stage version of the play commences at this point in the narrative. The pair swaps stories and chat about the old country before Burgess asks her to visit his tailor in London, order and send on a suit. The scene shifts briefly to London with Browne fulfilling the request in a handful of gentleman's outfitters, before the story returns to Moscow and a now sartorially splendid Burgess parading the streets of the city. Real life and theatre, putting on an act and playing a part, catch at each other throughout the play. *An Englishman Abroad* was shot on locations in Glasgow and Dundee which credibly stand in for Soviet Moscow.[537]

An Englishman Abroad attracted extremely favourable reviews, the television critic at the *Mail on Sunday* referring to the "*overwhelming, almost hysterical, praise it has received*" (4 December 1983). The *Guardian* found the drama "*extremely beautiful and funny and sad and marvellous and silly*", and claimed it "*one of those experiences so captivating they alter the way you see things*", forcing one into "*thinking about the nature of treachery and exile and acting*" (30 November 1983). The reviewer at the *Evening Standard* believed it threw "*more light on that cold world inhabited by defectors than any other film I've watched*", that the play featured "*some of the funniest lines ever written or spoken about the nature of treason*", and judged it the "*most perfectly achieved film this year*" (17 November 1983). *An Englishman Abroad* was compared to 'Traitor' (1971), Dennis Potter's anguished study of Kim Philby in exile, although Bennett's approach was tragic-comic.[538] A rare poor notice in the *Spectator* complained that the "*film did not come to life*" (3 December 1983). Typical of responses to the screen treatments of the Cambridge Spies, there was unease regarding the "*miniaturisation*" of the enormity of the crime, the "*softening*" of the treachery into a cosier "*domestic side of treason: the traitor as charming shambles*", and discomfort in the way Burgess "*came over as more of a delightful old queen than the dreadful monster that he was*" (*Sunday Telegraph* and *Observer*, 4 December 1983; *Spectator*, 3 December 1983). The *New Statesman* despaired that, "*It looks as though Guy Burgess has finally been welcomed into the pantheon of popular British traitors, that reassuring Chamber of Horrors with which we neutralise the meaning of treachery*" (9 December 1983). Speaking generally about the Cambridge Spies, the *Telegraph Magazine* claimed, "*they cut pathetic figures for whom one can, at times, almost feel sorry*", and for this commentator Bennett's drama seemed to operate at this level (25 April 2003).

Alan Bennett has claimed to have been more interested in the theme of exile than that of espionage (1988: 217), and that is borne out by *An Englishman Abroad* and by an earlier stage play, *The Old Country* (1977), about a British traitor wanting to return from Russia.[539] It was during the staging of the latter drama that Bennett casually learned from Browne that she had met Burgess in Moscow. The theme of Englishness and exile is explored and presented in a variety of ways in *An Englishman Abroad*. Peter Wolfe has suggested that Burgess's exile has made him even more English than he was at home (1999: 144). It is Bennett's view that irony and scepticism are the English gentleman's heritage, "*And so, by extension*", he claims, "*is the decision to betray it. It is irony activated*" (1988: 219). The writing and staging of *An Englishman Abroad* coincided with the Falklands War in 1982 and this tempted Bennett to consider patriotism and treachery and made him more appreciative of the motives of characters such as Burgess and Blunt, over whom he could no longer conjure any "*patriotic indignation*" (ibid.). Bennett's own ambivalence about his country and the concept of patriotism was expressed in a line given to Burgess in the play: "*I can say I love London. I can say I love England. I can't say I love my country, because I don't know what this means*". Burgess, he suggests, was relatively harmless, seemingly implying that Burgess's rebellion turned political more or less by accident and that a different nudge by fate might have turned it in a purely artistic direction (ibid.: 219-20). The writing of the play is witty, as is the choice of musical accompaniment, as when Browne and Burgess listen to his one record, appropriately Jack Buchanan's 'Who Stole My Heart Away?'[540]; and a well-dressed Burgess attracts the stares of fellow Muscovites over-laid with 'For He Is An Englishman' from Gilbert and Sullivan's *HMS Pinafore*.[541] Through various devices, Bennett presents a man who has only one thing left to hang on to – his Englishness; and illustrates the adage that you may take an Englishman out of England, but you can't take England out of an Englishman.

Between the time of the initial broadcast of *An Englishman Abroad* in 1983 and the staging of *Single Spies* in 1989, the five years that were the "*prime of Mrs Thatcher*", Bennett's attitude towards his country and correspondingly the treachery of his subjects had on his own admission "*hardened*". For the stage dramas he added to the original preface, now claiming that it suits governments to make treachery the crime of crimes. However, the world is smaller than it was, he maintained, and to conceal information can be as culpable as to betray it. He pointed to emerging evidence of a nuclear accident at Windscale in 1957, the full extent of which was hidden from the public. "*Were the politicians and civil servants responsible for this less culpable than our Cambridge villains?*, he asked: "*Because for the spies it can at least be said that they were risking their own skins, whereas the politicians were risking someone else's*". The Cambridge Spies had the advantage of us in that they still had illusions. "*They had somewhere to turn*". "*The trouble with treachery nowadays is that if one does want to betray one's country there is no one satisfactory to betray it to*". "*If there were*", he added cynically, "*more people would be doing it*" (Bennett 1994: 214).[542]

The highly honoured drama won major awards from the British Academy of Film and Television Arts (nine), the David Wark Griffith Awards, the Broadcasting Press Guild (three), the Royal Television Society (two), Barcelona's Setmana International de Cinema, and the Critics' Award at the Prix Italia.

The screen drama *A Question of Attribution* commences with a senior counter-espionage officer wanting to know why the long-running interrogation of Sir Anthony Blunt (James Fox) has revealed no new significant information; the action then shifting between Blunt's office and lectures at the Courtauld Institute in London, and a picture gallery at Buckingham Palace. A new investigator, Chubb (David Calder), is put onto Blunt and questions the art historian on several occasions, but without being able to unearth any substantial details.[543] In the end, it is decided to let Blunt's treachery become public, after all, only immunity from prosecution had been promised the spy, not anonymity.[544] Blunt, in disgrace, loses his posts at the Courtauld Institute and his honours.[545] The stage drama largely restricts itself to the exchanges between Blunt and Chubb at the Courtauld Institute, and between Blunt and Her Majesty the Queen (Prunella Scales in both stage and screen versions) at the Palace,[546] and is concerned with the period of Blunt's extended interrogation by MI5, well before his public unmasking to the House of Commons in 1979. The transition to the screen was thought to have "*enhanced*" the drama, transforming it from an "*amusing comedy of manners*" into "*something far more complex about the nature of truth and fakery*": a "*masterpiece in miniature*" (*Time Out*, 16 October 1991).[547]

As Kara McKechnie has pointed out, "*Where Englishman draws parallels between spying and acting, Question is concerned with art and its forgeries*" (2007: 96); as such, *A Question of Attribution* explores Anthony Blunt's public world of art history as a metaphor for his world as a spy, and the brilliance of the drama is found in the parallels Bennett invokes between the secret, submerged identities of Blunt, and the hidden characters in a painting – third, fourth and fifth men – which are being revealed through restoration; and further probed in a witty exchange between Blunt and Her Majesty the Queen regarding fakes and forgeries in art in which the historian is unnervingly uncertain as to the subtext of the discussion.[548] The painting is *Titian and the Venetian Senator* (*The Triple Portrait*), part of the royal collection and indeed investigated by Blunt as part of his duties. The screen drama also includes a sub-plot in which Blunt is x-rayed, like the painting undergoing restoration, for traces of a recent cancer, a further neat parallel and hinting at the 'hidden' identities lying beneath his establishment surface.[549] Other witty observations on identity and deception, and pointed parallels are subtly planted, as with the personality of the Queen, minor characters forever asking Blunt "*What's she really like?*", in the situation of Blunt investigating a puzzling painting while he is being investigated by MI5 interrogator Chubb, and Blunt peering curiously at the painting *The Martyrdom of St. Laurence* before rushing off to another bout of interrogation with MI5. Bennett initially became interested in Blunt as a subject at the time of his unmasking and jotted down a few notes. He returned to the subject in 1986 when he read about the investigation of the Titian and considered it "*such an obvious metaphor*" (quoted in the *Radio Times*, 19-25 October 1991: 20-21; *Sunday Telegraph*, 11 August 1991).

Once again an Alan Bennett drama garnered excellent reviews. The *Western Mail* thought *A Question of Attribution* the "*Beeb at its splendid best*" (26 October 1991). For the *Mail on Sunday* it was a "*delicious play*" and the "*best television*" in a long time (27 October 1991); the *Independent* praised a drama infused with themes "*substantial enough to fill half a dozen films*" (21 October 1991); and *The Telegraph* marvelled at a drama "*packed with clever art historical metaphor and analogies*" (21 October 1991). There was particular praise for the witty exchange between Blunt and Her Majesty in the Palace; for the *Guardian* "*one of the strongest scenes I have ever seen, full of laughter and danger*" (22 October 1991). Typical for the Cambridge Spies dramas, some felt *A Question of Attribution* was a charitable treatment of its subject and his "*unsavoury yet poignant story*" (*Mail on Sunday*, 27 October 1991). In the longer view, Bennett scholar Peter Wolfe has judged that the play "*makes most other spy dramas look clumsy and mean spirited*" (1999: 158).

There was the usual speculation and criticism concerning the accuracy of the characterisation of Anthony Blunt. *The Telegraph* accepted a "*genuine work of the dramatic imagination*", and, in a swipe at the BBC's rivals, was cheered that the dramatisation "*wasn't one of those dreary drama-documentary reconstructions beloved of the Northern ITV companies*" (21 October 1991).[550] The *Evening Standard* thought the production managed a more "*rounded portrait*" of the notorious character than the earlier 'Blunt'. It was revealed in that newspaper that James Fox had approached the paper's art critic and former pupil of Blunt Brian Sewell for character notes, who "*contributed the missing human elements, as well as authoritative information on his lecturing technique and other details*" (17 October 1991), and the actor was generally praised for his performance.[551] However, while on this occasion Sewell remained silent on the portrayal of his scholarly hero, another former student Robin Simon was impelled to speak out at the "*grotesque*" and "*unbearable*" depiction of the "*tolerant*", "*courteous*", "*humorous*" and "*gentle*" tutor he had actually known. Judged a "*prolonged parody*" and a play that "*got it all wrong*", his complaints centred on an "*extraordinary wardrobe*", a "*crass lecture*" and, the "*most glaring and unpleasant inaccuracy*" –

the character's voice.[552] Simon acknowledged that allowance had to be given for "*dramatic licence*"; that "*a play is a play ... and not history*", and accepted that in the final reckoning Blunt appears to have been a "*master of deception*"; not least amongst those who thought they knew him best. Therefore, in its own "*bizarre way*" this misleading film "*may be as apt an epitaph as any*" (quoted in the *Spectator*, 2 November 1991).[553] *A Question of Attribution* won the British Academy of Film and Television Awards TV Award for Best Single Drama.

Alan Bennett has consistently shown some sympathy for Kim Philby, Guy Burgess, Donald Maclean and Anthony Blunt, claiming impishly that he "*liked the notion of the Cambridge spies betraying their class; I liked them two-timing it*". Such a view stemmed from a recognition of an "*ambiguity about England ... about being, in many ways, very conservative with a small 'c' about England, yet knowing there's so much wrong with it*" (quoted in the *Independent*, 6 May 2014). The dramatist has confessed that the treason the spies are supposed to have committed "*doesn't nowadays seem to me to be a particularly important crime*", claiming that: "*I think spies have done far less damage to this country than people who've been knighted and awarded the Queen's Award for industry when you think of the total destruction of the fabric of this country and the cities and the mess we've made of it*" (quoted in *The New York Times*, 28 October 1984).[554] With regard to the undignified hounding of Blunt after his exposure, Bennett has claimed more sympathy with the hunted than with the hunters. Actor James Fox believed the altering historical context crucial in determining a revised perspective on Anthony Blunt, claiming that, "*Now that there isn't the Cold War context against which Blunt's acts of treachery were seen, we can judge things more objectively*" (quoted in the *Sunday Telegraph*, 11 August, 1991). A sympathetic view towards the Cambridge Spies was not always widely shared.

Case file: "where the facts end and legend takes off", *Cambridge Spies* (2003)[555]

> *We're the Trinity Soviet-ski, You bet-ski!*
> *Just let-ski, Us sing our little song-i-vitch.*
> *Not long-i-vitch, But strong-i-vitch.*
> (Jingle, published in *The Trinity Magazine*, Cambridge University, 1930)

> *For more than four decades the world has been mesmerized by the story of the Cambridge Five; and with good reason, for it is an extraordinary tale which will remain in the collective memory long after we who took part in it are all dead.*
> (Yuri Modin 1994: 268)

I can't recall a programme getting as much hostile pre-publicity as Cambridge Spies, not since the controversial daytime chat show Talking Politics with Rudolf Hess.
(Paul Hoggart, *The Times*, 12 May 2003)

Don't send your boy to Cambridge.
(Review of 'Philby, Burgess & Maclean', *Variety*, 8 June 1977)

Reviewing the Cambridge Spies drama 'Philby, Burgess & Maclean', *The Times* felt the involved and complex story could not be adequately fitted into a 90-minute play, suggesting the requirement of a *"four-part series, going back to Cambridge and forward to Moscow"* (1 June 1977). Its wish was eventually granted with *Cambridge Spies*, a requisite four-part historical drama produced at the BBC and broadcast in 2003, written by Peter Moffatt, directed by Tim Fywell and produced by Mark Shivas.[556] It dealt with the four best-known of the Cambridge Spies, Guy Burgess (Tom Hollander), Donald Maclean (Rupert Penry-Jones), Kim Philby (Toby Stephens) and Anthony Blunt (Samuel West), but only covered the narrower period 1934 to 1951, the point where Burgess and Maclean disappear to the Soviet Union. Episode one treats the 'probationer-spies', being set mainly in 1934 and deals with the 'talent-spotting' of Philby and Maclean by Burgess and Blunt at Cambridge University, and with Philby's period in 'Red Vienna' where he witnesses Nazi brutalities and returns with a communist wife Litzi Friedman (Lisa Dillon). Episode two treats the young men's outward commitment to Nazi Germany and Fascism as they prepare a long-term cover to hide their communist sympathies, the beginnings of their penetration of the British establishment, Burgess at the BBC and on the fringes of MI5, Blunt making an impression at the Royal Palace, Maclean at the Foreign Office, and Philby as a journalist at *The Times* covering the civil war in Spain before joining the War Office, and ends with the confusion caused the Cambridge men by the German-Soviet Pact in 1939. Episode three covers the wartime period, with Blunt more deeply ensconced at the Palace and serving for much of the period at MI5, Maclean's marriage to the American Melinda Marling (Anna Louise-Plowman) and his mounting instability, the treachery of John Cairncross, another Cambridge graduate, at the code-breaking centre at Bletchley Park, and Philby now rising through the ranks at MI6. Episode four commences in 1948, with Maclean at an important post in Washington with access to atomic secrets, the closing in on Maclean by the Americans led by James Jesus Angleton (John Light) of the newly established Central Intelligence Agency (CIA), and the desperate efforts of the four English traitors to manage the defection of Maclean to Moscow in face of a mounting suspicion in British Intelligence.

For authenticity, the producers had wanted to shoot the early parts of the drama at Trinity College, Cambridge, where three of the men had studied. However, it was reported that "*shame still burns*" at the *alma mater* of the spies, Trinity College refusing to allow filming on its premises, and another college had to be used, and even then on the strict condition that it would not be identified (*Variety*, 20 April 2003; *Televisual*, April 2003).[557] Many reviewers commented on the conventionally high production values peopled by "*our finest aristocratic actors*" (*Time Out*, 26 March 2003).[558] It was also rather excitedly noted that, "*While some previous dramatisations tiptoed discreetly round the more salacious elements of the story*", *Cambridge Spies* had no such "*qualms*" (*Guardian*, 8 April 2003). A BBC drama "*high on sex and espionage*" was widely perceived as an audience pleaser, and readers were warned that it was less "*Reds under the Bed*" and more a case of "*Reds in the Bed*" (*Independent*, 3 May 2003). Some marvelled at the prospect of a "*Bolshevik version of* Brideshead Revisited" (*Sunday Telegraph*, 11 May 2003).[559]

From the outset, the producers of *Cambridge Spies* knew there would be troubled waters ahead. Even before filming started the BBC received letters accusing it of "*squandering licence-payers*" money on "*aggrandising scoundrels*" (*Telegraph Magazine*, 25 April 2003). There were "*howls of outrage*" at the *Daily Mail* and shrill criticism in the right-wing press that *Cambridge Spies* glamorised Guy Burgess, Donald Maclean, Kim Philby and Anthony Blunt; that it indeed "*glorifies treachery*" (*Independent*, 3 May 2003). The Soviet defector Oleg Gordievsky, widely reported in reviews, questioned the representation of the Cambridge Spies as "*idealists*" when they were "*traitors*" and denounced the production as "*KGB propaganda*" (quoted in *The Telegraph*, 13 April 2003).[560] *The Times* complained that events had been changed to "*protect the guilty*", and found it nauseating to see the BBC "*whitewashing people who contributed to the murder of millions by their treachery*" (9 May 2003). It had been unfortunate that at a press screening a reference to the Cambridge Spies as "*brave*" and "*heroic*" had been let to slip.[561] The *Times Literary Supplement* believed it had witnessed a "*mythology*" in which British figures of authority were universally presented as "*cretinous*" while Soviet case officers seem, on the other hand, "*sober and businesslike*", suggesting that the drama conformed to what might be called the "*Old Left Interpretation of history*" (23 May 2003).

The BBC was forced to defend its controversial drama against the claim that it aimed to rehabilitate the traitors, and Jane Tranter, head of BBC drama, argued that it would be a "*very bland drama which just said these men were heinous traitors and we hate them*".

> *We show their humanity and fallibility and the passions that drove them to betrayal and huge personal sacrifice. We do want viewers to stay*

*with the characters for four episodes, and they won't if they are one di-
mensional.*
(Quoted in *The Times*, 23 April 2003)

In such an atmosphere something was made of actor Samuel West's political
leanings, that he was a supporter of Social Alliance and was a former member
of the Workers' Revolutionary Party (ibid.). A number of considered voices
challenged some of the accusations, the writer on espionage Phillip Knightley
warning that critics tend to *"overlook the KGB spies'"* main motivation: to
counter the influence of powerful people in Britain in the 1930s – 'Hitler's
Englishmen'" (2003). The *Guardian* argued the *"need to understand the social
and political context of treachery"*. Simply to portray traitors as evil would be
"simplistic, dangerous and wrong". Mass unemployment, great hardship, a
huge imbalance of wealth and poverty, and a British political system that
seemed to offer no means of redressing these evils, it stressed, meant some
looked to Soviet Communism for hope. A tiny few were prepared to spy for
Moscow (8 May 2003).[562] The same point in defence of the serial and the
Cambridge Spies had been made by the BBC's Jane Tranter, who claimed: *"We
are not trying to rehabilitate them; we are trying to put their treachery into
context"* (quoted in *The Telegraph*, 23 April 2003).

There was widespread criticism of *Cambridge Spies* as a historical drama
and much complaint regarding factual inaccuracies in the serial. It was the
first dramatisation of the saga since the end of the Cold War and came in the
wake of a new historiography detailing British espionage.[563] The apparent
greater knowledge of the Secret Service made the production more vulnerable
to accusations of errors, wilful or otherwise, and in this respect the production took something of a *"battering"*.[564] The *Times Literary Supplement* felt its
readers would hardly have the patience were it to list *"all the instances in
which this series creates a misleading impression, adds an uncalled-for spin,
ignores pertinent material or just plain invents things to fit the missing pieces"*
(23 May 2003). The distinguished historian Michael Burleigh *"inveighed
against the BBC's abandonment of facts and issues and the portrayal of these
'pathetic Peter Pans' as heroes"*. Writer on espionage Tom Bower allegedly
*"steamed his windows with indignation at this insult to the memory of all
those brave British agents whose lives were put at peril by the Cambridge spies"*
(both quoted in the *Evening Standard*, 6 May 2003). Intelligence historian
Nigel West denounced the serial as an *"attempt to rewrite history"*, that it
presented a *"naive view of a pretty complex topic"*, and warned the public
that, *"We must be on guard against the revisionism of these characters"* (quoted in *The Times*, 20 April 2003). Miranda Carter, a recent biographer of Blunt,
claimed that it *"changes, fudges and messes around with pretty much every
single event that actually took place, and in so doing, both misrepresents the*

relationship between [the Cambridge Spies], and makes them less interesting". She dismissed the serial as *"just an expensive soap"* (2003). The judgement of the *Independent* was that, *"if you're going to take liberties with the facts, they really shouldn't be stupid ones"* (12 May 2003). The 'softening' of the principals and their notoriety to win viewer sympathy, through emphasis on the vigorous heterosexuality of Kim Philby at the expense of any discomfiting homosexuality practiced by Guy Burgess and Anthony Blunt, and a general attribution of Jewish sympathy to the men, *"when the likelihood is that Philby, Burgess, Blunt and Maclean shared the standard anti-semitism of their circle at the time"*, did not go unnoticed (*Guardian*, 28 April 2003).[565] Art critic Brian Sewell, never far from debate centring on the Cambridge Spies, once again rallied to the defence of his mentor Anthony Blunt, *"whose death 20 years ago I still mourn"*. Exasperated and wondering, *"Where is the Blunt I knew?"*, he railed: *"never was there a more mistaken personification, in every conceivable way"*. In place of a drama of *"false characterisations"* alarmingly *"insistent in their error"*, Sewell had hoped to see an examination of the *"transition from idealism to the drudgery of servitude – but that would have been complex, subtle, difficult"* (2003). The *Guardian* wondered *"whether we can believe anything the characters say"*; and noted a substantial irony: *"given that one of the drama's points is the British establishment's almost comic lack of suspicion of Philby and chums, we find ourselves questioning everything they say"*. It concluded that: "Cambridge Spies *is high-class drama, but historically it's best regarded as a cover story"* (28 April 2003).

In defence against the critical onslaught, the publicity material indicated that the intention had been a *"fictional drama inspired by real events"*, and the screening carried the *"now-standard V-sign to historians and lawyers"*: *"Certain events and characters have been created or changed for dramatic effect"* (quoted in ibid.). The writer Peter Moffat, who researched and wrote the serial over a four year period, had stated the difficulties of reconstructing events: *"The spies were so self-serving that many accounts of the same events were contradictory. This made it difficult to discern the truth, because theirs is a world full of liars"* (quoted in the *Independent*, 4 May 2003). Producer Mark Shivas chipped in that in a case where historical interpretation was contested and complex the production simply adopted the *"most likely story that would make the most dramatic sense"* (*Cambridge Spies* press sheet). This was an approach acceptable at the *Independent*, which was satisfied that, *"Overall, this well-executed drama should be taken as capturing the texture and the disposition of the era rather than being a historically accurate account of this quartet"* (4 May 2003). A later issue of the *Independent* invited its readers to consider where to apportion blame, suggesting the *"real twits in this treachery are not the obviously-communist quartet; it is the British spook recruiters who entrusted them with our secrets"*. The paper claimed that *"much of the criti-*

cism has been misdirected"; adding that it was true, "*as the Daily Mail never tires of telling us*", that,

> *Burgess, Maclean, Philby and Blunt were not heroes. But neither were they bloodthirsty villains. It was naiveté, not evil, which motivated them. In prolonging the establishment's convenient vilification of Moscow's Men, the tabloids enable the real villains, once again, to slip away scot free*
> (11 May 2003)

The more observant critics noticed the link to the BBC's history website in the final credits. While it was tempting to draw from this a certain reservation on behalf of the producers in the veracity of their drama, the *Guardian* felt it might offer an "*answer*", suggesting that: "*If internet links were to provide detailed script notes establishing what is and isn't fact, then drama documentary could become a safe form as well as an enthralling one*" (28 April 2003).

Arguments about historical distortion and idealisation of treachery aside, reviewers were largely dismissive of the serial. For some, the treatment was too simplistic. Expecting to be "*swept up in the strange and revealing truths of their lives*", *The Times* felt it had been served up "*The Ladybird Book of Defectors*", and that consequently *Cambridge Spies* was a "*big fat double-first of a missed opportunity*" (12 May 2003). *The Telegraph* noted that, "*even disregarding historical inaccuracies, Cambridge Spies turned out to be exceptionally thin TV drama*", a shallow dramatisation that was only "*superficially glamorous*" and "*utterly uninvolving*" (12 May 2005). For the *Guardian*, it was simply "*cold, unappealing and often quite dull*" (10 May 2003), for the *Independent* there was a "*dogged pedestrianism about Moffat's narrative*" which did "*little to illuminate character*" (3 May 2003), and the *Observer* complained of a "*script of potentially disabling silliness*" (11 May 2003).

A rare positive view was expounded in *The Telegraph* where *Cambridge Spies* was judged "*nicely scripted*", "*beautifully acted*" and a "*thoroughly absorbing drama*" (9 May 2003). A scene of Anthony Blunt confronting the Queen Mother reminded some of a similar exchange in an earlier Cambridge Spies drama, a relatively "*painful*" experience here compared with the "*brilliant exchange of Aesopian indirection and double-jointed innuendo with which Alan Bennett delighted us in* A Question of Attribution" (*Times Literary Supplement*, 23 May 2003).

The Cambridge Spies dramas dealt with privileged classes and characters invested with a certain cinematic glamour. Commentators noted the national fascination with "*class and our cherished little group of Cambridge spies*" (*The Times*, 16 May 1984); the "*nostalgic fascination for period glamour*" and widespread interest in "*spy scandals, past and present*" (*The Times*, 2 June 1984);

and a public "*mesmerised by their traitors*", "*maybe even tolerant of them*" (*Glasgow Herald*, 3 December 1983). The *Observer* wondered what the rehabilitation of the four men from "*spies to pin-ups*" said about "*our society*" (27 April 2003). In an important sense, the dramas, though often criticised, were not "*unpatriotic*", and were, as argued in the *New Statesman*, "*deeply in love with England, Englanders and Englishness*" (12 May 2003).[566] The appeal of the Cambridge Spies has been put down to their "*extraordinary success*" and the fact that they "*remained unmasked for a bafflingly long time*" (*Telegraph Magazine*, 25 April 2003). Some have admired the fact that they got away with it for so long, the historical saga pleasingly unfurling like a prolonged television serial, a third man, a fourth man, a fifth? The allure of the story has been put down to the voyeuristic appeal of "*gilded youth gone wrong*", and biographer Miranda Carter has noted how, in *Cambridge Spies*, the historically important John Cairncross was relegated in the story because he was working-class (ibid.).[567] In perhaps a surprising intervention, the widow of Cairncross felt compelled to correct the "*travesty of John's portrayal*" as a "*snivelling coward*" who buckles under the intimidation of the "*superior*" Anthony Blunt. In an action she defended as setting the record straight, Gayle Cairncross-Gow asserted that in a falsification of history, *Cambridge Spies* claimed the credit for Blunt in securing ENIGMA for the Soviets when in fact it squarely resided with John Cairncross. She was unsurprised at such a representation in a series "*which largely treats spying as an upper-class English sport*" (2003). The screening of *Cambridge Spies* also provided the opportunity to question the representation of the spy ring as a "*purely masculine elite*", it being pointed out that significant women such as talent spotter Edith Tudor-Hart, handler Kitty Harris, and wives Litzi Friedman and Melinda Maclean were either left out or relegated in the story (*Guardian*, 10 May 2003).

The chief dramatic concern of *Cambridge Spies* is friendship, and treachery and betrayal are figured principally for the four men in terms of their loyalty to each other as comrades in a struggle for their shared beliefs.[568] Of course, this is a highly selective sense of loyalty and elides the ideal of allegiance to one's nation and country folk. The script shamelessly plants in Philby's mouth E. M. Forster's famous pronouncement: "*If I had to choose between betraying my country and betraying my friend, I hope I should have the guts to betray my country*" (noted in the *New Statesman*, 12 May 2003). This left the serial open to attack on the simple point of accuracy that arguably all four men were not as friendly or familiar as a group in real life.[569] The earlier drama 'Blunt' similarly had the title character referring to the famous remarks of E. M. Forster, and producer Roger Chapman had early on explained that the "*core*" of the play would be the exploration of Forster's priority of loyalty (quoted in the *Daily Mail*, 6 September 1985). In that story, Goronwy Rees (who had claimed that Blunt had uttered the words to try to dissuade him from denouncing Guy

Burgess to MI5 in 1951) finds it near impossible to explain to his wife why he owes loyalty to such an unpleasant figure as Burgess; and Blunt cannot forgive Rees for his eventual act of betrayal to a former friend and an ideal.[570] It is revealing of the established code of behaviour and the emotional issue at stake that Rees was all but ostracised by his personal and professional group when he 'ratted' on Burgess in a series of articles in the *People* in 1956 (see Rees 1994: 181-209). The Forster statement has reverberated around British spy fiction as well as the Cambridge Spies for many years, and when exposed in 1979, Blunt lamely invoked the lines as an explanation for his treachery (Carter 2001: 178).[571]

Willmetts and Moran have asserted that the lasting cultural influence of the Cambridge Spies is not only simply as a "*historical event*" but more in terms of its status as a "*narrative*", resonating core themes of national identity in the context of the Cold War and of imperial decline. In such a way, "*Spy film and television functioned not merely as a cultural mirror of the "real history" of the Cambridge Five, but formed the narrative frame, the pre-existent structure, through which the story of the Cambridge spies was rendered to the public at large*" (2013: 55).

Greatest spies and scandals of the century

Even nowadays, when the tradition of silence has long since been broken by a series of espionage memoirs from both sides, it is still more necessarily the case that there are 'more things true than are told', and most probably, 'more things told than are true'.
(Review of Greville Wynne, *The Man from Moscow, The Listener*, 21 September 1967)

I feel it right to warn the House that hostile intrigue and espionage are being relentlessly maintained on a large scale.
(The Prime Minister, 14 November 1962)

There are scandals. And there are SCANDALS.
('This Is the Scandal That Was', *You Magazine, Mail on Sunday*, 31 July 1988)

Historical espionage occasionally treated characters and events other than the Cambridge Spies. In 1967, the English businessman and sometime secret agent Greville Wynne published the harrowing account of his interrogation, trial and incarceration at the hands of the Soviets as *The Man from Moscow*.[572] The story, briefly considered for a movie in the late-60s, was dramatised at the BBC, broadcast across three consecutive nights in 1985 and re-published in book form as *Wynne & Penkovsky*. Wynne claimed to have served with MI5 in World War II and afterwards traded in electrical and machine goods. In the summer of 1955, he was approached by MI6 and agreed to serve as an 'asset', providing occasional assistance to British Intelligence. Later, he was central as an intermediary in a particularly sensitive operation in which a high-ranking Soviet intelligence officer provided secrets to the West. Oleg Vladimirovich Penkovsky was a colonel in the GRU (Military Intelligence) who served on the important Scientific Research Committee with access to major secrets, and who it was believed was disenchanted with the Soviet regime. As a business-man, Wynne was able to seek to develop trade with the Eastern Bloc and eventually request a meeting with the Scientific Research Committee, at which point he could make contact with Oleg Penkovsky. Wynne's published account details the extraordinary experience, with emphasis on his capture in Budapest, his interrogation in the infamous Lubyanka prison, his public trial along with Penkovsky in Moscow in May 1963, his incarceration in the equally notorious Vladimir prison on an eight year sentence, and his famous release 11 months later when he was exchanged for the captured Soviet spy Gordon Lonsdale. Interspersed with this personal tale of human spirit in the face of degradation, are the meetings in London and Paris, under the cover of trade missions, in which Penkovsky was debriefed by British and American Intelli-gence.

The Penkovsky case held an extraordinary importance, taking place be-tween the major crises of Berlin in 1961 and Cuba in 1962; having, according to one observer, the "*highest stakes of any espionage operation during the Cold War*", and leading to the Soviet officer being described as the "*spy of the cen-tury*" (Duns 2013: 14).[573] Wynne's account of the Oleg Penkovsky affair is a heroic and flattering treatment of British espionage at a time in the 1960s, under the influence of fiction writers such as John le Carré and Len Deighton, when a cynical and pessimistic view was beginning to emerge. The experi-ence of Greville Wynne, later described as a "*tale of espionage and intrigue as gripping as any spy novel*" (*Mail on Sunday*, 5 August 1984), provided the inspiration for the BBC television thriller serial *An Enemy of the State* broad-cast in 1965, and the stories *The Naked Runner* by Francis Clifford (novel 1966, film 1967) and *The Russia House* by John le Carré (novel 1989, film 1990).[574]

The dramatisation *Wynne & Penkovsky* by Andrew Carr drew additional ma-terial for the story from Wynne's *The Man from Odessa*, a broader account of his experiences in espionage published in 1981, and like the drama organised in a simpler chronological narrative.[575] The first episode covers Greville Wynne's (David Calder) activities as a businessman in Eastern Europe, his contact with Oleg Penkovsky (Christopher Rozycki), and the first trip to London where the debriefings with the Soviet colonel commence. The second episode centres on the trade mission and debriefing in Paris, the plans to get an increasingly compromised Penkovsky to the West, and ends with Wynne's arrest in Budapest. The final episode deals with the interrogations and trials of Wynne and Penkovsky and the exchange of Wynne for Gordon Lonsdale at checkpoint Heerstrasse straddling East and West Berlin. The treatment thus puts more emphasis on the operation to run Penkovsky and greatly reduces the attention given to the trial and imprisonment of Wynne in Russia which occupies the bulk of *The Man from Moscow*. The otherwise excellent drama makes some extraordinary inventions, as in suggesting Penkovsky met with President Kennedy and the Queen, actually unfulfilled requests of the Russian, and in portraying the colonel's death as suicide in a remote Soviet prison camp, a pet theory of Wynne's who was interviewed at length by the writer Andrew Carr and was a visitor to the set (*Daily Express*, 29 December 1984; *Evening Standard*, 28 December 1984; Wynne 1983: 278).[576] The Russian and Berlin locations in the story were filmed around Glasgow, the Adelphi Hotel, Liverpool doubled for the ornate Praga restaurant in Moscow, and that city's Town Hall provided further interiors for locations behind the Iron Curtain (*Glasgow Herald*, 15 August 1984; *The Telegraph*, 3 January 1985; *Mail on Sunday*, 5 August 1984).

The television dramatisation attracted only modest critical attention. While the *Guardian* passed it over as merely a "*good yarn*" (29 December 1984), other reviewers flagged up the drama's authenticity and credibility. *The Telegraph* felt that *Wynne & Penkovsky* had "*just about everything: the robust feel of authenticity, sturdy narrative thrust, and a* 1984 *whiff to chill the bones*" (5 January 1985); and *The New York Times* found the serial "*evocative and moody*", reporting that: "*Verisimilitude and understatement are everywhere*" (1 February 1985). The *Daily Mail* wished to "*applaud the painstaking fidelity with which the real-life spy story of Wynne and Penkovsky is being brought to the screen*". Noting that, "*compared with the usual run of spy fiction, the series lacks drama, car chases, gunplay*", the paper requested its readers not to mind, after all, "*This is how it really happened*" (4 January 1985). In a rare sour review, the *Mail on Sunday* complained that the true story was told in a "*pretentiously complicated way*", the disorientated critic losing himself in the "*three-way mirror triple flashbacks*" (6 January 1985).

Subsequent accounts of Oleg Penkovsky have differed in important ways. It has emerged that the Soviet colonel, more mercenary in these versions, had approached the West on three occasions which were dismissed as provocations, before he was taken on by the British Secret Service. There has remained a suspicion of the 'defector' account of Penkovsky's actions, with the suggestion that he was in fact a 'plant' feeding misinformation or was part of an elaborate deception operation. It has been claimed on the one hand that Penkovsky was cremated alive as a warning to other traitors; alternatively, that his death was 'staged' and that the agent was removed to a quiet part of Russia away from prying eyes. A less-flattering view has also been presented of Greville Wynne, described in one general history as a "*middle-aged alcoholic of dubious reliability*" (Sandbrook 2006: 606). Shortly after the return of Wynne to the West, *The Penkovsky Papers* was published purporting to be notes and thoughts of the Soviet colonel and these were challenged as an exercise in CIA propaganda.[577] *The Man from Moscow* has been claimed as one of the first accounts of espionage to escape government censure; however, given that Wynne authenticated *The Penkovsky Papers*, it could be that his published story formed part of a propaganda initiative of the British, as perhaps did the later and even more fanciful *The Man from Odessa*.[578]

The Oleg Penkovsky case was one of the most celebrated of all double agent operations and competently portrayed in the drama *Wynne & Penkovsky*. In contrast to the stories centred on the Cambridge Spies, the drama serial detailed a success story of British Intelligence, one that has largely remained outside the reach of a battering revisionism. The early 1960s also witnessed one of the most damaging political scandals of the 20th century. This also had at its centre a GRU officer; however, Captain Yevgeny Mikhailovich Ivanov was more interested in acquiring rather than betraying secrets.

The Profumo Affair was a sensational sex and espionage scandal which rocked British society of the early 1960s. A popular journalistic account of the time spoke of its "*odious proliferations*" enmeshing the "*worlds of politics, the law, Society, property manipulation and the Press*" in a chain reaction suffused with the "*notoriety of crime and the polemics of outraged morality*" (Irving, Hall and Wallington 1963: 1). The affair involved the sociable osteopath Stephen Ward who had a roving eye for the ladies, a beautiful young exotic dancer Christine Keeler and her friend Mandy Rice-Davies, Captain Eugene Ivanov an assistant naval attaché at the Russian embassy, and the Right Honourable John Profumo, the Secretary of State for War in the Conservative government. Ward introduced Keeler to both Ivanov and Profumo at Cliveden, the ancestral home of Lord Astor, and she entered into affairs with both men. Eventually the press got onto the story and the scandal broke in the spring of 1963. It followed in the wake of a series of humiliating revelations concerning national security: the exposure of George Blake the Soviet spy in MI6, and the Portland Spies case, both in 1961; the discovery of the Navy spy John Vassall in 1962; the impending trial of atom scientist Dr Martelli on espionage charges; and the defection of Kim Philby to Russia early in 1963: all of which had been damaging for the government and the Security Service. Profumo denied in parliament any impropriety with Keeler and was eventually caught in a lie.

The year-long crisis has been described as the "*most public shaming a Government has endured this century*" (Summers and Dorril 1987: 3); and the "*tarts, titles, and tits*" aspect of the saga dominated the front pages of newspapers (Finney 1996: 148). The press made much of the possibility of 'Jack the Lad' Profumo being indiscreet in his pillow talk with Keeler, who in turn might pass on secrets to Ivanov. In the words of a contemporary television news report the Affair brought the British government to the "*brink of shabby disaster*"; and the social commentator Christopher Booker has written of the "*boundless fantasy ... in which not only every member of the Government but the entire upper class of England seemed to have been caught up in an orgy of model girls, perversions and fancy dress sexual frolics*" (1969: 192).

The "*scandal that swung the sixties*" was the subject of the contemporary low budget exploitation film *The Keeler Affair* (1963) (*Guardian*, 14 February 1989). This was quickly, cheaply and safely produced in Denmark to take advantage of the intense interest in the recent events and briefly involved the two women at the heart of the scandal: Keeler provided a filmed introduction to the picture; while Mandy Rice-Davies appeared as a showgirl in a clubroom scene. The narrative is organised as the guilt-induced dream of Keeler (Yvonne Buckingham) in which she is cross-examined by an over-bearing and moralising judge, and this allows for a quite pretentious treatment in certain scenes, something later charitably described as "*pseudo-Brechtian stylisation*" (*Financial Times*, 5 February 1971) and less benevolently as "*ham-fisted expressionism*" (*Observer*, 7 February 1971). In classic exploitation fashion *The Keeler Affair* salaciously ran through the notorious activities which had so enthralled the British public: wild drinking; dope-smoking in low dives; impromptu stripteases; daring towel parties; and shootings involving jealous boyfriends. Despite the fact that the picture was "*comically moral in its insistence on horrible warnings of how the Big City can ruin a Young Girl*", the film was rejected by the British Board of Film Censors and therefore denied legitimate screenings in Great Britain (*Financial Times*, 5 February 1971).

The Keeler Affair resurfaced in the early 1970s when the film featured in a battle between the New Cinema Club, London, and the British Board of Film Censors.[579] The picture was once again denied a certificate by the censors, later supported by the Greater London Council, an action, according to the left-wing *Morning Star*, providing "*further evidence of the folly and the dangers of censorship, which in this case obviously has more to do with the protection of political interests than with the so-called protection of public morality*" (5 February 1971). Few found the film obscene; all considered it inept; and most concurred in the judgment that the censorship was politically motivated. Typical was the view at *The Listener*, which regarded the film as a "*cau-

tionary tale", and *"totally harmless apart from its tendency to derange and concuss with boredom"* (11 February 1971).

The Profumo Affair was revisited a quarter of a century after it first shook British society in the historical feature film *Scandal*. The movie was immediately marked down as the *"year's most controversial film"* (*Daily Mail*, 29 July 1988) and destined to *"divide and disturb"* (*Evening Standard*, 5 December 1988). The concept was brought to Palace Pictures by Joe Boyd and scriptwriter Michael Thomas, produced at a cost of £3.5 million, directed by the débutant Michael Caton-Jones and released in 1989, with crucial funding coming from the American independent Miramax Company which secured the distribution rights for North America. *Scandal*, six tortuous years in the making, had originally been proposed as a television mini-series, and had been put into development at the BBC before it was later vetoed in the boardroom. ITV companies were warned off the subject by the Independent Broadcasting Authority, and so the potentially lucrative production was rejected at Thames, Granada, Southern, TVS and Channel 4 (*Sunday Times*, 19 February 1989).[580] The reduction of the scope of the production to a feature film meant that the picture had to focus on the Stephen Ward and Christine Keeler stories, and, allegedly, shed *"much of the more contentious material that had been planned for the television series"* (*Sunday Times*, 19 February 1989). Despite that, the announcement of the film production immediately invoked a storm of protests and warnings, and the filmmakers discovered that in the case of Profumo, *"the Establishment closes ranks even today"* (*You Magazine*, *Mail on Sunday*, 31 July 1988). It was reported that, *"Many Establishment figures have expressed displeasure at the re-opening of the Profumo affair"*, and that several distinguished actors had declined to play the disgraced politician (*Daily Mail*, 4 June 1988).[581] Veteran film star Douglas Fairbanks Jnr, whose name had been bandied around in the original trial of Stephen Ward, threatened to sue the producers if he was named in the film (*Daily Mail*, 7 July 1988).[582]

The screenwriter and producers drew on a large body of writing and expertise in the preparation of the picture. The publicity reported that *Scandal* was *"based in part"* on the following publications: *Nothing But ...* by Christine Keeler and Sandy Fawkes (1983), *Mandy* by Mandy Rice-Davies and Shirley Flack (1980), *Stephen Ward Speaks* by Warwick Charlton (1963), *The Profumo Affair, A Summing Up* by Judge Sparrow (1963), and *Scandal '63* by Clive Irving, Ron Hall and Jeremy Wallington (1963). The investigative reporters Anthony Summers and Stephen Dorril, authors of the recent *Honeytrap: The Secret Worlds of Stephen Ward* were credited with *"special thanks"* (*'Scandal'* press sheet, Palace Pictures 1989). Mandy Rice-Davies and Christine Keeler were both reported as *"supportive"* of the production. Davies claimed to have corrected the script for certain errors, but still complained that, *"I'm in places*

*that I was never in, saying things I didn't say and doing things I didn't do be-
cause it helps the narrative*"; and Christine Keeler was reported as a "*paid
adviser*" to the production (Rice-Davies quoted in the *Independent*, 3 March
1989; *Today*, 7 February 1989).[583]

Scandal concentrated on the figure of Stephen Ward (John Hurt), who first
notices Keeler (Joanne Whalley-Kilmer) in an exotic revue in Soho, London in
1959. Keeler moves into Ward's mews house and he introduces her to the
high-life of swimming parties at Cliveden, as well as the seedier side of the
social scene such as sex parties and dope smoking. In Ward's home she sleeps
with Ivanov (Jeroen Krabbe) from time to time, as she does with Profumo (Ian
McKellan), with whom she starts a more serious affair.[584] Trouble between
Keeler and a West Indian boyfriend culminates in a shooting incident outside
of the mews house. Alarmed by her increasingly wayward behaviour, Ward
drops Keeler and she responds by telling her story to the press. Ivanov returns
to Russia, Profumo is eventually forced to resign, and Ward is abandoned by
his influential social circle. Needing a scapegoat, the Conservative Party elite,
British Intelligence and Scotland Yard serve up Ward as the sacrificial lamb,
and he is prosecuted for living off immoral earnings. The disgraced doctor
takes a fatal overdose of barbiturates on the eve of the court's expected verdict
of guilty.[585]

Scandal, "*The most talked-about British film for years*", was the subject of
tremendous pre-release hype, and benefitted from an exceptionally widespread launch for a British film, opening in 215 cinemas across Britain. The
film was also relatively successful in America, but only following an initial
scare when the Motion Picture Association of America imposed an X-
certificate on the picture, which would have spelt commercial death. Failing
in an appeal, Miramax cut some material from the 'Man in the Mask' orgy
scene to receive a more audience-friendly R-certificate (*Daily Mirror*, 27
March 1989; *Independent*, 6 April 1989; *Sunday Times*, 9 April 1989; *Evening
Standard*, 17 April 1989; *Time*, 1 May 1989).[586] *Time* magazine in America
vividly described *Scandal* as an "*express tour of the Profumo affair that moves
with a pop historian's revisionist swagger and plays like* News of the World
headlines set to early '60s rock 'n' roll" (ibid).

Australian scriptwriter Michael Thomas was keen to rile the British Establishment, highlight the hypocrisy surrounding the Affair, and redeem Christine Keeler, who had "*been taking the punishment for many years for what had
happened*" (quoted in Finney 1996: 148). In explaining his approach to the
story, director Michael Caton-Jones claimed: "*I wanted to dispel the myths
and to deal with it all not in a sensational way but in a way that would explain
how the characters got into the trouble they did*" (quoted in the *Scotsman*, 3
March 1989). Following a heavy-drinking session with producer Stephen

Woolley, the proletarian Scottish director expressed his intention more colourfully, as a "*mission to make people fucking feel what they should have felt
at the time that this poor bastard Ward was shafted. Nobody lifted a finger, and
it was all because of these fucks who are still running the country today*" (quoted in Finney 1996: 162). Executive producer Joe Boyd took the unusual step of
writing an essay justifying the production of a motion picture of the Profumo
Affair. 'Scandal: A Historical Perspective' was appended to the press sheet
issued with the film. While acknowledging that the "*bringing up again of the
events of that period may be hurtful or embarrassing*", the paper stressed that
the issue transcended the questions of "*personal honour, shame or morality*".
For Boyd and his generation, "*the affair was one of the most important in
modern British socio-political history*", and many who were young at the time
"*recall the tremendous impact those events had on their view of the world and
its hypocrisies*". The significant social, political and Cold War implications of
the affair gave, according to Boyd, "*the lie to the oft-stated view that Profumo's
'indiscretion' with Keeler was a relatively innocent albeit foolish act, for which
his subsequent disgrace has been ample if not excessive punishment*". While
the producers maintained that any distress the film caused the former politician and his family was to be regretted, they also pointed out that, "*When
John Profumo asked Christine Keeler for her telephone number, he stepped into
history*", and that consequently, "Scandal *belongs not just to him and Christine Keeler, but to history*" ('*Scandal*' press sheet, Palace Pictures 1989).

There had been a long process of rehabilitation for John Profumo since the
scandal had destroyed his political career in the early 1960s, and it was reported in the *Daily Mail* at the time of the film's production that there had
been a "*tremendous groundswell of sympathy for a man who has remained
dignified in disgrace*".[587] There was now widespread debate regarding whether the former Secretary's humiliation should be raked over once again in a
popular film (29 July 1988). The Bishop of Stepney was particularly vocal in
this regard, asking in an extended piece published in *The Telegraph*: "*Hasn't
John Profumo suffered enough?*"; pleading that, "*Surely, it is time for the punishment to stop?*" (*Weekend Magazine*, 4 February 1989). The Bishop wrote to
both John Hurt and Ian McKellen asking them to consider withdrawing from
the production (*Evening Standard*, 8 July and 11 July 1988).[588] Elements of the
right-wing press were predictably hostile in their dismissal of the film, clock-
ing up the inaccuracies in the historical depiction, and claiming the unacceptable invasion of a man's private disgrace. The *Daily Mail* wondered, "*Will
this torture never end?*", and asserted that, "*actors purporting to be real people
speak lines written by a script writer for the purpose of making entertainment
and money, without care for the suffering of those people whose lives are being
exploited*". In claiming that, "*since the law in Britain says that this is perfectly
permissible then I suggest that there is something very wrong with the British*

legal system", the correspondent revealed a remarkable insensitivity to the shabby treatment of Stephen Ward at his trial (8 February 1989).[589]

"Already the Establishment is on the attack" was how the *Daily Mail* reported the conservative response to the announcement of the film (27 January 1989). Lord Rees-Mogg, the new head of the Broadcasting Standards Council, made it known that, *"such a film is bound to defame many people, some of them still alive. It cannot tell the story without doing so"*. He also complained on the grounds that no-one had the right to *"renew the agony of offences years after they have been expiated"* (quoted in the *Scotsman*, 3 March 1989). Lord Denning was interviewed on television, where he maintained that history had already been *"properly given and presented"* by his official enquiry published in 1963, and that any media treatment of the events were bound to be *"distorted"* (ibid.). In acts of obstruction, Lord Hailsham, the Tory Grandee, refused the filmmakers permission to use a clip from his famously choleric interview with Robert Mackenzie on BBC TV at the time of the scandal (*Evening Standard*, 2 March 1989), and London Regional Transport refused a poster featuring the classic image of Keeler astride a chair on its sites as it celebrated a *"convicted criminal"* (Finney 1996: 165).[590] Several stately homes refused permission for location shooting, and the requisite scenes set at Cliveden were completed at the accommodating Longleat House, Wiltshire. When it was revealed that Palace Pictures would receive funding from the official British Screen Finance towards the production of *Scandal*, Kenneth Warren, the Conservative Party chairman of the Commons select committee on trade and industry, threatened to bring the matter before his committee. He claimed it a *"sad waste of public money"*, and that, *"Surely there are better stories to tell which the country would like to hear?"* (quoted in *The Times*, 11 June 1988).

Typical critiques of *Scandal* in the right-wing press were delivered by Paul Johnson in the *Daily Mail* and Anthony Hartley in the *Sunday Telegraph*. Johnson dismissed the picture as an *"exploitation of the scandal"*, and claimed that the film industry had failed to learn the lessons of the Profumo Affair, preferring to think that *"sex, notoriety and cheap sensationalism are the things that matter most in life"*. This kind of wrong attitude, he blamed squarely on the failings of the 1960s. A thoroughly Thatcherite sentiment, and a neat bit of deflection, he offered an *"indictment of the decade that cost Britain dear"*, claiming that, *"We paid for the follies of the Sixties in the painful decade which followed"*. Thatcherism, he asserted, had laid stress *"increasingly on high standards of public behaviour"*, and had made Britain a more sane and sensible place – *"and I think a more honest one too"*. *"It has been a case, in the 1980s, of national self-redemption"* he trumpeted. The scandal he claimed as a *"fascinating but ultimately unimportant episode of 1963"*, and the movie would have been *"more in tune with the spirit of today if it had concentrated on its one ennobling feature, the survival and recovery of Jack Profumo himself"*. The disgraced Secretary of State for War, in a contortionist piece of revisionism, he judged as *"The one heroic figure of this sorry tale"*, and a *"shining example of quiet, self-effacing public service"*. And in an astonishingly misguided appreciation of popular cinema, he claimed the story of Profumo's subsequent dedication to the poor of the East End as *"the material for a truly notable film"*. However, this he claimed was *"probably outside the sex-blinkered vision of our showbiz industry which is still, to a large and depressing extent, stuck in the cultural groove of the Sixties"* (1989).

Hartley echoed this kind of partisan thinking, attacking the *"paranoic imagination"* of *"liberal intellectuals"* and what he called *"the myth, which the film perpetuates, that the prosecution of Dr Ward was an Establishment conspiracy"*. In a counter-revisionist manner, he praised *"Lord Denning's convincingly factual account"* of the scandal, claimed that, *"the security risk in the affair was minimal"*, and that Ward *"did not suffer an 'actual injustice"*. He was, after all, *"convicted by a jury, and his suicide was his own decision"*. The *"legend"* of Stephen Ward, he maintained, *"bears little resemblance to historical truth or even probability. The victimisation of Ward would seem to have required the collaboration of the Cabinet and the Commissioner of Police, the Head of the Security Service and Lord Denning in a quite elaborate deception"*, and stressed that, *"Conspiracy theories are always a misleading approach to history"*. From this general standpoint, the posthumous martyrdom of Ward could be denied and he could be dismissed as *"just a patriotic pimp"* (1989).

The *Guardian*, sagely wrote that the *"more those flies now buzz around decrying the movie, the more we'll know it has served its purpose"* (2 March 1989). The screen story, in its sympathy for Stephen Ward and its critique of the Establishment, echoed a historiographical trend which had commenced with Ludovic Kennedy's *The Trial of Stephen Ward* (1964),[591] and more recently developed in Philip Knightley and Caroline Kennedy's *An Affair of State: The Profumo Case and the Framing of Stephen Ward* (1987)[592] and Anthony Summers and Stephen Dorril's *Honeytrap: The Secret Worlds of Stephen Ward*. The viewpoint that emerged on this side was of a 'mockery' of a trial and a conspiracy managed by politicians, the police and the Security Service to serve Ward up as a sacrificial lamb.[593] Advocates of freedom of speech and critics of the Establishment accordingly made their defence of the film *Scandal*. The *Observer* reminded readers that, *"Until a Privacy Bill becomes law there is nothing, thank goodness, to stop people making films about historical events"*, and then stressing the increasingly felt view that, *"it tends to be forgotten that the real victim of the scandal was not Mr Profumo but Dr Stephen Ward"* (12 February 1989). And it was on this latter point that producer Stephen Woolley claimed justification for his movie. *"It should never be forgotten"*, he said, *"that Stephen Ward was made the scapegoat by the Establishment for the scandal, ruined, driven to despair and finally suicide. He has a right to be heard, even after his death"* (quoted in the *Daily Mail*, 29 July 1988). The *Mail on Sunday* fanfared that, *"Profumo cannot escape the blame"*, campaigned to rehabilitate Christine Keeler who had done *"nothing more immoral than chasing good times"*, and vilified the FOPs (*"Friends of Profumo"*), claiming that: *"The class system and the old boy network buffer and protect them from the womb to the tomb"*. *"It is only with their trousers down"*, it appropriately noted, *"that they are reduced to size"* (12 February 1989). "Scandal", chimed in star Ian McKellen, *"is a vital British film about British society – its snobbery, its hypocrisy, its corruption and its gaiety"*. Advising that, *"You must see it, before those who would prefer its story untold tell you that things have changed since the Sixties"* (quoted in the *Sunday Telegraph*, 5 March 1989).

Some surviving participants in the Profumo Affair took the opportunity to air their views in the press. Richard Du Cann QC, a junior barrister in defence counsel James Burge's chambers at the time of the Stephen Ward trial, dismissed *Scandal* as a *"sad, bad film"*, a *"grotesque bowdlerization of the trial"*, and a version that, *"squanders the truth"* (1989).[594] Logan Gourlay had been a *Daily Express* columnist who covered the scandal at the time. In a long piece defending Stephen Ward, the veteran newsman complained that, *"too often* Scandal *sinks to a soft porn level"*; however, while acknowledging that it offers no answers, he did constructively point out that the film raises several questions about society's hypocritical attitude to scandal and sexual misdemeanours in high places, and how it has changed, if at all, since the Sixties. His conclusion:

> *Judging from the reactions to the revelations about Cecil Parkinson and more recently Sir Ralph Halpern, Major Ron Ferguson and Frank Bough, the depressing answer is that hypocrisy and sanctimoniousness about such matters have not lessened; if anything they have been increasing in the less liberal Eighties.*[595]

In a lesson for the present, he warned that the present Government's dangerous passion for secrecy, as demonstrated by the '*Spycatcher* Affair', could mean that, *"without the unusually melodramatic factors which drove the Profumo affair into the open, a Minister's barefaced lie to Parliament about a vital subject might never be detected"* (1989). Another *Express* man, Ian Aitken, who had broken the story of Profumo offering his resignation, worried that the squalid affair was being offered up as *"entertainment for a popcorn-munching audience of teenagers"* (1989). R. Barry O'Brien had covered the Profumo Affair for *The Telegraph* and his view of *Scandal* was that, *"The film does not tell the whole story, but does tell it the way it was"*. While claiming that, *"Many of the questions posed by the affair are left unanswered"*, he believed the picture made a contribution to the controversy on whether or not Ward was framed, *"in its portrayal of the police officers whose investigations led to his arrest the day after Mr Profumo resigned"* (1989).[596] Lord Rawlinson, the government Solicitor-General at the time of the Profumo affair, found *Scandal "sleazy ... a total distortion of the truth"*. *"The film makes it appear the Government was responsible for the investigation and prosecution of Stephen Ward"*, he asserted, *"which is not only untrue but very stupid ... the last thing the Government wanted was to involve Ward in a sensational trial"*. The claim that the *"investigation and prosecution of Ward was an act of political malice and revenge"*, he dismissed as *"absurd"* (quoted in the *Daily Mail*, 15 March 1989).

Scandal was one of a growing number of movies which re-examined and re-assessed recent British history and which took as their subject the repression, lies, corruption, injustices and hypocrisy of the 1950s and early 1960s, and the seedier side of the underworld; other examples being *Dance With a Stranger* (1985), *Prick Up Your Ears*, *White Mischief* and *Personal Services* (all 1987), *The Krays* (1990) and *Let Him Have It* (1992) (*Village Voice*, 9 August 1988).[597] *Scandal* has been seen especially in terms of exposing the hypocrisies of British justice and upper-class sexual profligacy (Aldgate 1999: 222). Some claimed the historical message of the film as relevant to its own day and a continuing sense of corrupt Conservativism. The reviewer at *The Telegraph* noted that, *"Released amid the new Puritanism of the late Eighties one has the uncomfortable feeling that if similar events occurred today the ruling classes would react in exactly the same way"* (2 March 1989). The Conservative government had equally witnessed its own damaging spy scandals with the 'Spy-catcher', Michael Bettaney, Cathy Massiter and Geoffrey Prime affairs, and its own share of sleaze and corruption with the falls from grace of Jeffrey Archer and Cecil Parkinson. The topicality of *Scandal* was confirmed by the breaking Pamela Bordes affair, a similar sex and security debacle involving a high-class call girl, ministers, Establishment figures and Libyan intelligence officers. The *Evening Standard* praised *Scandal* as a *"morality play for today"*; *"intriguing and instructive for the bizarrely close parallel it draws between 1963 and 1989"*. *"Both eras"*, it observed, *"had a Tory government fast losing popularity and showing the strain of long office ... Scandal won't take anyone's breath away nowadays. But it will take many of us revealingly back to the way we were and, for all purposes of political and moral expediency, the way we still are"* (5 December 1988 and 2 March 1989). The *Observer* acknowledged a story that finds in 1963 a society much like our own, a:

> *political party too long in office; a Prime Minister arrogantly out of touch with currents of opinion; the police and the law used for political purposes; the secret service going about its business without having to give a public account of itself; a Press largely cowed, craven and prudishly prurient.*
> (5 March 1989)

The *Village Voice* similarly offered the historical parallel, observing that the early 1960s "*was a period of repression, of lies and hypocrisy, of one rule for the rich, another for the poor – none of which is very different today, under a more right-wing, Conservative government*" (9 August 1988). The *Observer* could make the telling observation: "*If the film brings home to certain people how quickly an apparently well-entrenched and long-serving Tory Prime Minister can be subverted by smugness and scandal then it may well serve a useful purpose*" (12 February 1989).[598]

As might be expected, the reviews of *Scandal* were mixed. For the *Daily Mail* it was the "*most accomplished British commercial film in a long time*", a picture in which "*Entire sequences grasp the look, sound and feel of that era*", and one "*especially strong on the sad, tacky ambience of loveless sex*" (3 March 1989). For the *Observer*, *Scandal* was a "*sober and responsible movie*", which was neither "*moralising*" nor "*judgmental*", but was "*angry about hypocrisy, scapegoating and bad faith*" (5 March 1989). The film attracted positive reviews in the music press, which was always receptive to a cinema of pop cultural interest and class critique. The American *Rolling Stone* magazine praised *Scandal* as a "*major, boldly original work*", a picture that "*provoked*". Accepting that the film "*could have exploited the tawdry surface of the tale for a quick box-office killing*", the reviewer happily reported that the producers "*dug deeper to illuminate character and incident within a vivid historical context*" (18 May 1989). The British *New Musical Express* acknowledged the original affair as "*irresistible*". "Scandal *pays unfussy attention to its era*", it proceeded, "*and it is this evocation entwined with good old British hypocrisy that gives the film a look and a feel like no other homegrown movie before it*". There was also purpose to the picture: "*to redress the balance, rewrite history and show how Ward was brutally treated by his former friends in high places*"; and further, "*to expose the repressed and neurotic English attitude to sex, particularly when it impinges on public life*" (4 March 1989).

Other reviewers were more critical. The *Scotsman* complained of a "*Bland travesty of truth*" and a "*superficiality that hides more than it knows*" (6 March 1989); while "*passably entertaining*" with some "*gloriously funny moments*", the film, according to *Today* magazine, "*constantly sweeps across the smutty action at full flight without pausing to give the story depth or the characters motivation*". There was, correspondingly, "*too much flesh and not enough fleshing out*" (3 March 1989). The *New Yorker*, while sympathetic to the "*tasteful*" approach of the film, was not impressed by an "*exhausted dramatic format*", dismissed the general approach as "*intellectually mediocre*", felt there must be a "*better angle on the Profumo affair than humanizing Stephen Ward*", and passed over the picture as "*just one more English film about the cruelty of the class system*" (15 March 1989). Although "*interesting as a reminder of events*", the picture, according to the *Village Voice*, was "*thin stuff*", and "*wasn't intense or shrewd or skilful*" (2 May 1989).

Scandal did not treat the national security aspects of the Profumo Affair in any great detail. Defence was the issue with which Labour leader of the opposition Harold Wilson adroitly castigated the Conservatives at the time of the scandal. It was also the ostensible subject of the official enquiry led by Lord Denning, who was instructed to investigate whether the Profumo case had endangered national security, and to examine the performance of British Intelligence.[599] Subsequent investigations of the affair have unearthed connections to both the Royal Family and the Kennedy administration, and claimed a specific intelligence role for Ward and his part in a possible entrapment of Ivanov.[600] In the view of writers such as Summers and Dorril, the scandal was stage-managed to keep these damaging aspects of the affair secret. As they have written, "*The Alarming possibility of active espionage in the Profumo case was not considered in any depth in the Denning Report. Nor were a string of questions concerning the role of British Intelligence*" (1987: 6).[601] And it is at this level of secrecy, suppression and the unresolved that *Scandal* could intrigue and confirm relevance to its own time.

Today was disappointed that the picture "*only hints in passing that there might have been something more sinister going on*" (3 March 1989). The *Western Mail*, affirming that, "*Public interest in the Profumo affair was justified because of its implications for national security*", criticised that, "*The connection – in the shadowy figure of Russian attaché Ivanov – remains unresolved in the film, and Ward's connections with MI5 are only touched upon. What we are left with is a shallow depiction of Keeler's involvement with Ward*" (4 March 1989).[602] Several reviewers understood that the producers had shown "*legal caution*" in their approach to the story, and that revisionist literature such as *An Affair of State*, could reveal the extent of the frame-up against Ward in a way that the film didn't dare (*Evening Standard*, 2 March 1989; *Village Voice*, 2 May 1989). "*Regardless of artistic merit and ethical standing*", *Scandal* demonstrated one invaluable thing. Stephen Ward "*messed with the Establishment, dangerous today, fatal a quarter-century ago*". The film, in the judgment of the *Daily Mail*, was "*worth seeing for that reminder alone*" (3 March 1989).

The historical spy dramas discussed in this chapter addressed an intricate and shifting terrain of political and emotional choices and decisions, caught up in questions of loyalty and betrayal, idealism and self-interest, guilt and innocence. The treatment of treachery and political indiscretion often came in for criticism; however, on the other hand, as Harlan Kennedy has pointed out, the very roundness of the individual portraits is a "*reflection of the extent to which we now empathize with, rather than simply praise or condemn, the complex choices and emotional contortions of the men who choose to become traitors*" (1984: 10). The subject of treachery brought into question the nature of Englishness and several of the screen representations tended to be flavoured by a sense of nostalgia. For heritage dramas like *Cambridge Spies* the nostalgia was likely to be visual and superficial, for dramatists like Alan Bennett and plays like *An Englishman Abroad* the flawed protagonist longed for a bygone England, "*when everyday life was more decent and humane; when the Tories were benevolent; and when Londoners could find a Lyons within walking distance of job and home to serve them a good cup of tea*" (Wolfe 1999: 159).[603] This type of filtered longing was equally a component of espionage dramas which incorporated the Cambridge Spies narrative and such plays as Dennis Potter's 'Traitor' and *Blade on the Feather*.[604] The subject of indiscretion on the part of John Profumo proved a battleground for conservatives and liberals, both sides arguing fiercely over who was victim, who was honourable and who deserved rehabilitation. The role of the secret services in the murky affair had remained shrouded in the mists of official secrecy and occupied observers. At the time of the movie *Scandal*, the *New Statesman* suggested that the real interest of the film lay in the unanswered questions: Did MI5 set the whole thing up with Ward working for them? Were they trying to get Ivanov to defect? Did they murder Ward as some have suggested? And the biggest question of all, "*what happens when politicians lose control of their own security services? What happens when 'British Intelligence' is responsible to no one but itself?*" (3 March 1989). Such questions and concerns reverberated throughout the 1980s, and are the focus of the following chapter which examines the screen's response to the 'secret state' and concerns regarding politics, intelligence and the abuse of power.

7.
The 'Secret State' Thriller of the 1980s

When a ship of state springs leaks – as Britain's has been doing like a colander in the last four years of Thatcher Government, with old spies being unmasked, top-secret documents fed to the Press and media, and mini-Watergates opening up from Westminster to Wapping – astounding things start happening to the state's popular culture.
(Kennedy 1984: 9)

We always have to be aware of the enemy within, which is much more difficult to fight and more dangerous to liberty.
(Prime Minister Margaret Thatcher 1984)[605]

State paranoia is an epistemological crisis of secret state knowledge and its usage, a crisis that runs both ways: as a distrust of the state against its citizens, and as a distrust of the citizens against the state.
(Eva Horn 2013: 279)

Even paranoids have enemies.
(Golda Meir to Henry Kissinger 1973)

In January 1986, the BBC commenced broadcast of the four-part drama *Dead Head*, an irreverently comic anti-establishment conspiracy thriller by the controversial playwright Howard Brenton. It starred Denis Lawson as luckless small-time crook Eddie Cass who is mercilessly set-up as the fall guy for a murder scandal which stretches to the very pinnacle of society. The not-too-bright Cass is, in his fashion, patriotic and a dedicated royalist, and is at a loss as to why the 'secret state' should seek to frame him for a series of Jack-the-Ripper-style killings of London prostitutes. The vengeful Cass is ultimately bought off by the Establishment. When he is told that the actual killer is a member of the royal household, his sense of patriotic duty wins him over to silence. In an ironic denouement, the drama serial ends with the crook reconciled with his estranged wife (Lindsay Duncan, seemingly configured as the *femme fatale*, but actually Eddie's guardian angel throughout the story), enjoying at the state's expense the luxury of retirement in the Caribbean from where he has been narrating the tale. In classic mystery style, the story is constructed as the restricted narrative of the confused protagonist; this serves to crank up the sense of paranoia in the drama as the viewer is as equally befuddled as the hero as to the motivation and nature of the malevolence. As Eddie tellingly utters at one point, "*I'm in a country I don't understand, on a quest I don't know what for*"; summing up his experience as "*A season in Hell*". Brenton claimed his intention was to write a comedy which turned fierce and dangerous (Commentary, *Dead Head*, Eureka DVD 2012).[606]

The stylised serial operates as a homage to the classic 1940s Hollywood thriller. Brenton claimed the intention as "*taking film noir to a different level in television*" (Commentary, *Dead Head*); and as such, key characters parade about in trench coats, fedoras and cocktail dresses against the backdrop of a decaying, unstable, race-torn, and corrupt Thatcherite Britain, and Cass spins a fine line in trademark hard-boiled voice-over dialogue. A contemporary synthesiser soundtrack with more than the odd nod to the classic thriller scores of Bernard Herrmann adds to the incongruence. The drama clearly drew narrative and generic inspiration from a variety of texts of mystery fiction, most obviously such paranoid *film noirs* as *Detour* (US, 1945) and *Desperate* (US, 1947), Alfred Hitchcock's classic *The 39 Steps* (1935) and *Psycho* (US, 1960), the head in a hatbox psychological thriller *Night Must Fall* (play 1935, film 1964), the picaresque state-of-the-nation odyssey *O Lucky Man!* (1973), the violent revisionist crime movie *Bonnie and Clyde* (US, 1967), and the quirky New Hollywood conspiracy thriller *Winter Kills* (US, 1979). Brenton beat Dennis Potter to the punch with a drama of studied *noir*ishness, *Dead Head* airing slightly before the similarly 'authored' drama serial *The Singing Detective* (TV, 1986), an acclaimed 'singalong' pastiche of the classic hard-boiled thriller. Howard Brenton, who later described the high-style of *Dead Head* as the "*poetry of tosh*", added "*stinging social commentary*" to his drama serial, akin to the "*European tradition that stretches from the French film-noir of the Thirties to Fassbinder's underrated* Berlin Alexanderplatz": the outcome being highly distinct from the "*slick, narrative house-style typical of nearly all British television drama*" (commentary, *Dead Head*; *Guardian*, 11 January 1986).

Dead Head caused a stir among the tabloids, which responded with "*TV Orgy Shocker*" headlines to some kinky sex involving an otherwise naked débutant in Wellington boots forcing herself on the handcuffed anti-hero, and reacted with similar synthetic horror to a severed head plotline. Reviews for such an original thriller were understandably mixed and some praised it as ambitious, witty and provocative. *The Times* judged it an "*intriguing tale*": "*neither a pleasant thriller to watch nor to contemplate*"; the playwright doing a "*terrific job of creating a sinful world in which severed heads, official corrup-*

tion and two-legged and four-legged scavengers are almost de rigueur" (15 January 1986). In a later assessment, the *Evening Standard* claimed *Deadhead* as the "*only British series that came close to* Twin Peaks' *jocular malice*" (4 January 1996). The *Guardian* felt that *Dead Head* had "*lashings of panache and style*", and was funny enough to "*neutralise any mild offence it might offer even the most squeamish*". However, it believed Brenton failed properly to understand the "*thriller model*" he was clearly fascinated by, and was therefore unable to "*parody its effects in a really satisfying way*" (16 January 1986).

In interview, writer Howard Brenton has since claimed that there was felt to be some "*disgrace*" to be involved with the serial, it only receiving a single broadcast and the unfortunate director Rob Walker unable to work again on television for two years (BBC Radio 4 *Front Row*, 3 April 2011).[607] Brenton, who himself had to wait for 16 years before writing further for television, resurfaced with contributions to 13 scripts of the hit thriller series *Spooks* (2002-2011), and has stressed a strong interest in the literary potential of intrigue, claiming that spy stories "*give you a sense of what is happening beneath. That is why they are so strong*"; and it is in this sense of burrowing to a heart of darkness, a rottenness at the centre of British society, that *Dead Head* displays its ideological intent.[608] As the playwright later observed: "*You often write something extreme for fun and it turns out to be horribly near the truth*"; and a drama that had originally been jokey and playful ultimately turned into something more incisive and relevant (Commentary, *Dead Head*). Brenton perceived Eddie Cass as an everyman figure, a hero for the 1980s on whom the forces of contemporary history are directed. Ordinarily, according to Brenton, the two worlds of Thatcher's Britain never meet each other, although they exist in the same space; here however, the boundaries are melted as the petty criminal is startlingly jerked into the world of privilege and influence, where he is intimidated, tormented, battered, and tortured, but ultimately rewarded: bought off to keep silent by the Establishment. Ironically, Cass is a working-class Thatcherite, selfish, exploitative and traditionally nationalistic. A quality the powerful recognise and take advantage of, cheaply buying Eddie's silence and avoiding the scandal that would rock the constitution. A paranoid drama of manipulation and abuse, in which democratically enshrined liberties and individual freedoms are systematically perverted, and the madness of the privileged is covered-up by a lapdog Security Service, *Dead Head* was an archetypal if stylised 'secret state' thriller of the socially and politically divided 1980s. It was joined by several other films and television dramas which sought through their imaginative representations to expose the hypocrisy and malevolence which many liberals and civil libertarians felt characterised politics and society in the decade.

A complex chain of developments centring on immigration, student militancy, crime and permissiveness, later coupled with increased industrial militancy and armed insurrection in Northern Ireland, led to a situation in which society became increasingly polarised into 'authority' and its 'enemies'. The resulting 'crisis' brought about an effort on the part of the authorities to produce a 'disciplined' society and a sense in some quarters that the 'emergency' was to be explained by interlocking 'conspiracies' (Gill 1994: 71). Out of this emerged a 'deep suspicion' of the traditional social and political elite in Britain and its links with the Secret Service (Smith 1996: 17); to the extent in fact that a "*paranoid style*" has been claimed for British political culture for the decades of the 1970s and 1980s (Moran 2014).[609] Conventionally 'off-limits' to the press, a slew of security scandals in the late 1940s to 1960s – the atom spies Alan Nunn May, Klaus Fuchs and Bruno Pontecorvo, the 'missing diplomats' Guy Burgess and Donald Maclean, the missing frogman Commander Crabb, the espionage trials of George Blake, the Portland Spies and John Vassall, and the operation of official secrecy through a discredited 'D-Notice' system – forced secret government and its management into the spotlight and cast doubt on the competence of the intelligence services, their fitness for duty, and the need for press vigilance (Moran 2013).[610] Later, anxieties regarding the 'strong government' ethos of the administrations of Conservative Margaret Thatcher and their intention to keep a firm lid on the secret world, corporate corruption, and mounting concerns regarding abuses by the Secret Service and loss of civil liberties were a feature of the politically troubled 1980s in Britain.[611] Disturbingly for the post-war political consensus, it began to be claimed that during the 1970s activists and groups to the left of centre of the Labour Party had been targeted for intimidation, black propaganda and covert action, activity aimed at demonising radicals, tainting by association legitimate social democratic politicians, and ultimately consolidating the hold on power of conservatives and reactionaries. That the security services were acting, in fact, not as a counter-espionage body, but as a politically partisan 'secret police', and in a sense represented a 'covert state', unaffected by changes in elected officials and unconcerned with constitutional niceties. The 'hidden hand' was believed to be an alliance of the Secret Service (MI6, MI5 and Special Branch), 'permanent government' (the mandarins of the civil service), and some Conservative MPs, businessmen, 'friendly' journalists and various 'agents of influence'. A 'culture of secrecy' pervaded the practice of government in Britain, a situation neatly encapsulated in historian Bernard Porter's observation that, "*Insiders could not speak out, and outsiders could not look in*" (1989: 217). Even a Right wing journalist such as Chapman Pincher could write of an MI5 that was "*constitutionally opposed to revealing anything ever*" (1991: 191). As the Labour politician Richard Crossman remarked in 1971, "*One result of this secrecy is to make the British electorate feel it is being deliberately kept in the dark and increasingly to suspect the very worst of its rulers"* (quoted in Moran 2013: 14). It is unsurprising that such circumstances contributed to a climate of conspiracy.[612]

Criticism of government, security and intelligence fell on three main areas: the inadequacy of political control by ministers; lack of accountability of the Secret Service to Parliament and the public; and abuses of civil liberties. Political manipulation by the agencies of national security stretches back at least to the early decades of the twentieth century and the infamous 'Zinoviev Letter' of 1924, in which British communists were seemingly urged by the Soviet Comintern to court favour in the Labour Party, promote an Anglo-Soviet treaty, and to encourage 'agitation-propaganda' in the armed forces. This has since been revealed as a plot to destroy confidence in the first Labour government in which MI5, MI6, Conservative Party Central Office and the right-wing press had a hand. A clear example of what later has been termed *"active party political malice"* (Leigh 1988: 20), and which could stand as the first instance in the modern age of 'secret state' interference in the British political process (Porter 1989: 167; Smith 1996: 52-53; *Guardian* 4 February 1999).[613] Gradually the security services began to extend their interference and mischief in political and governmental processes, for example through vetting procedures for the recruitment of staff required to handle classified material or for work deemed sensitive, although in reality, as critics have pointed out, a practice that actually extended to seemingly innocent posts at the state broadcaster the BBC, the British Library and at the Post Office, the latter having technical links with the intelligence services. The brief was interpreted liberally, operated secretively, and gave extensive influence and powers for prying, intrusion and blacklisting.[614] The historian Bernard Porter has written of how, traditionally, the secret services had *"remained hidden in the deepest shadows of British political life"* (1989: 194), and that only once previously in history, with the hated 'spy system' of the Tory Prime Minister Lord Sidmouth in the 1810s, had the Secret Service provoked as great a storm of resentment. Following the mass-expulsion of 105 Soviet 'diplomats' in 1971, KGB operations in mainland Britain were dealt a crippling blow from which it never recovered. It has been alleged that the security services were accordingly released to target a supposed domestic subversive threat, referred to as the *"far and wide left"*, and fears regarding a *"political surveillance role"* mounted (Dorril 1993: 6, 9). A government adviser has revealed the anxious mindset of traditional politicians in the early 1970s faced with rising industrial unrest: *"At this time many of those in positions of influence looked into the abyss and saw only a few days away the possibility of the country being plunged into a state of chaos not so very far removed from that which might prevail after a minor nuclear attack"* (Brendon Sewill quoted in Dorril 1993: 7). The Security Service had on hand the Watchers Unit, the 'heavy mob', the 'Tinkerbell squad' and the 'Rat Catchers', for purposes of surveillance, burglary, telephone monitoring and postal interception. It has also been claimed that the Security Service used private detectives for a range of illegal activities such as breaking and entering and bugging, as well as to infiltrate trade unions where they served as undercover operators for the purpose of surveillance and destabilisation (Murray 1993: 22-35, 85-121). As Peter Gill has noted, such allegations of surveillance, disruption, disinformation and extreme countering policies are conduct which was arguably *"more 'subversive' of the democratic process than anything targeted as such by the Security Service during this period"* (1994: 37).

Awareness and concern regarding the 'secret state' began to grow during the 1970s. A significant context for this were the unsettling revelations coming from America regarding the Watergate scandal and where the American Central Intelligence Agency (CIA) and Federal Bureau of Investigation (FBI) were subjected to unprecedented and intense scrutiny by a series of official committees and reports which exposed a culture of illegality, unethical practice and anti-democratic activity.[615] In Britain, suspicions began to mount concerning a 'Wilson Plot', a 'paranoid' conspiracy to discredit the Leader of the Labour Party and eventual four-time Prime Minister Harold Wilson through disinformation, harassment, surveillance and media manipulation. In its most extreme form, it was claimed that Wilson was an agent of the KGB working directly for the aims of the Soviet Union. The author and journalist David Leigh has commented on the *"climate of deceitfulness, paranoia and mutual denunciation of which Harold Wilson became a victim in 1974"* (1988: 19). An important historical and theoretical engagement with the operations of secret government came with an article written for State Research by E. P. Thompson, first published in 1978. There, the radical historian revealed the long tradition in Britain of *"ruling-class institutions"* and their invigilation of the people, their use of informants and surveillance, their unaccountability, and warned that in their present formations of MI5, MI6 and Special Branch, *"they are larger and more powerful, and less subject to, ministerial or parliamentary control than they have ever been"* (1978: i). Thompson commented that, *"The ruling group within the State in Britain has a kind of arrogance about it which may be historically unique"*. *"It has a settled habit of power, a composure of power"*, he observes, *"inherited from generations of rule, renewed by imperial authority, and refreshed perennially from the springs of the best public schools"*. *"It is a group which does not bother, or need to bother, to get itself elected"*. He further warns:

> *It knows what 'British interests' are, and defends these through every change of political weather. It decides whether you or I are subversive, and whether our actions should be watched. It does not have to justify*

its decisions in any public arena. It rules, unobtrusively, from within. (vi)[616]

Mounting fears regarding phone-tapping, illegal surveillance, and infiltration by security officers into legitimate democratic organisations fuelled interest in the covert and malignant activities of secret government. For some, the paranoia was justified. It was leaked that the files of the Special Branch were expanding at 2,000 new names a month in the 1970s, and that the Branch's new computer held the names and details of 1.25 million individuals (Aubrey 1981: 28); and it has been claimed that the Security Service had established by 1980 the largest computer centre in Europe (Dorrill 1993: 145). The worry for liberals was the security services' policies of collecting intelligence on the basis of suspicion, speculation and prejudice, their cavalier definitions of suspects and subversives, and the potential for political interference this afforded them. Historian Bernard Porter has commented on the mindset created by such apparent or potential intrusion, noting that, "*nearly anyone in Britain who was in the slightest degree radical had come to assume, or to suspect, that he or she was on an MI5 or Special Branch list somewhere*" (1989: 206). According to Porter: "*In one way or another, Britons were far more spied upon in the 1970s and 1980s than they had been for 200 years at least, and possibly for the whole of their history*" (208). "*A state within a state*" was how the unfortunate John Berry described it at his trial for offences under the Official Secrets Act in 1978 (quoted in Aubrey 1981: 56). It is instructive to the main subject of the discussion here, the conspiracy thriller in Britain in the 1970s and 1980s, that conservatives regularly attacked the BBC for being politically subversive across the period, which developed into something approaching a paranoid fever during the Thatcher administrations of the eighties (Seaton 2015).

A series of public exposures and controversies through the 1970s and 1980s ensured that the machinations of the 'secret state' regularly made the front pages of the newspapers.[617] In November 1976, the Labour government announced that it intended to deport two American writers, Philip Agee and Mark Hosenball, who had displeased Western intelligence agencies with their revelations about the CIA and signals intelligence.[618] There quickly followed the political scandal known as the 'ABC trial' in 1978, when the two journalists Crispin Aubrey and Duncan Campbell were prosecuted for "*unauthorised receipt of classified information*" after interviewing John Berry a former corporal in signals intelligence. The case brought into public awareness the existence of the "*secret watchers*" and their phone-tapping, examination of mail, and interference with democratic freedoms; not least in the revelation of jury-rigging at the trial (Aubrey 1981; Campbell 1979). The affair was badly managed by the authorities, and as Christopher Moran has summarised it, "*For the state, what started out as an attempt to clip the wings of two journalists turned into a horror show and ended in farce*" (2013: 187).[619] For liberals, by the 1980s, MI5 was turning from a counter-espionage organisation to a domestic surveillance agency that compiled reports on the "*enemy within*": "*radical trade unionists, students, feminists, black-power activists, pacifists, MPs and particularly teachers*" (Hollingsworth and Fielding 1999: 27).

The 1970s and 1980s were the decades of the 'whistle blower', a neo-logism coined to cover principled men and women who breached confidentiality and risked prosecution in deciding to leak classified information or speak out against malpractice, lies, cover-ups and deceit within government. Attention first centred on American whistle blowers. These included Daniel Ellsberg, a former Pentagon official who leaked 'The Pentagon Papers' in 1971 which showed how the American public had been misled for decades over foreign policy in Indo-China; and such renegades of the CIA as Victor Marchetti, who exposed the Agency's covert operations in the co-authored *The CIA and the Cult of Intelligence* (1974), and Philip Agee, who had published the exposé *Inside the Company* in 1975. In Britain, the term applied to John Berry of signals intelligence who found himself embroiled in the 'ABC Trial', Clive Ponting a civil servant in the Ministry of Defence who leaked politically embarrassing secrets in 1984 regarding military cover-ups in the recent Falklands War, Cathy Massiter an officer of MI5 who revealed that the Security Service spied on trade unions and civil liberties groups, and most controversially Peter Wright the former officer of MI5 who published his memoirs which exposed the whole panoply of 'dirty tricks' employed by a Security Service that was seemingly running amok. In the words of one writer on intelligence and security, it was clear from various accusations and revelations that, "*not only was MI5 bugging people's telephone calls and opening their letters, but many of those put under surveillance were not even guilty of the very broad definition of subversion that the service was using as a benchmark*" (Smith 1996: 68).

Of greatest significance, though, were revelations which began to emerge in the early-1970s about a 'Wilson Plot', which culminated in the seismic convulsions of the '*Spycatcher* Affair' in 1986-87, a highly public and prolonged legal case in which an anxious Conservative government, already accused of excessive secrecy, sought desperately to suppress the disclosures of former secret servant Peter Wright who described a Security Service seemingly "*out of control*".[620] Among the many disturbing activities revealed was the hounding of the Labour Prime Minister Harold Wilson and his confidants, the sensational boast that while at MI5 "*we bugged and burgled our way across London at the State's behest, while pompous bowler-hatted civil servants in Whitehall pretended to look the other way*", and that obtaining "*intelligence about do-*

mestic subversion", as opposed to catching spies, became "*our overriding priority*" (Wright 1987: 54, 359; Pincher 1987a).[621] A legal overview of the debacle described *Spycatcher* as a "*personal revelation of incompetence and illegality in the British Security Service*" (Fysh 1989: v).[622] The origins of the 'Wilson Plot' lay in the late-1940s and the politician's dealings with Soviet Russia at the Board of Trade, which in the eyes of some within British and American Intelligence cast dangerous suspicions onto him. A leading figure of the left-wing of the Labour Party, Wilson, during the period of Conservative hegemony in the 1950s, had represented British firms in their trading with the Eastern Bloc and made several visits behind the Iron Curtain. The businesses were run by such émigré East Europeans as Montague Meyer, Rudy Sternberg, Harry Kissin and Joseph Kagan, making Wilson further suspect in the view of the security services, and MI5 began to compile a secret file on the Labour politician.[623] In a suspicious climate of Cold War conspiracy and paranoia, the sudden and unusual death of the Labour leader Hugh Gaitskell and his replacement by Wilson could be construed as a KGB plot; something hinted at by the Soviet defector Anatoli Golitsyn and eagerly pounced upon by partisan sections within MI5 and the CIA. The paranoid head of counter-intelligence at the CIA, James Jesus Angleton, was a leading advocate of Wilson's guilt, and it wasn't a large step to tie the sex and security scandal of 1963 known as the 'Profumo Affair' into the supposed Soviet conspiracy as this rocked the creaking Conservative Party and opened the doors for a Labour election victory and the elevation of Wilson to the premiership.[624] It was suspected that Wilson had been compromised by a Russian 'honeytrap' operation, had exposed himself to blackmail by the KGB, and that this possibly involved his political secretary Marcia Williams who exercised seemingly unnatural power and influence over the party leader. This led to claims of a 'Communist cell' within Downing Street taking its orders from the Kremlin. Further defectors such as Josef Frolik and Oleg Lyalin added fuel to the fire, accusing other labour politicians of serving Eastern Bloc masters, the backbencher Will Owen, the junior minister John Stonehouse, and the old-stager Tom Driberg, a disreputable bunch of grasping politicians, shady businessmen and reprobates, but sufficient to whet the appetites of the reactionaries in MI5 who remained convinced of subversives at the heart of government (Leigh 1988; Dorril and Ramsay 1992).[625] Shortly after Wilson's sudden resignation in 1976, it was reported that MI5 had bugged the prime minister both at Downing Street and in his private office at the House of Commons, but in the turmoil of political change and national crisis the story attracted little attention at the time (Aubrey 1981: 43).[626]

The general political and economic turmoil of the 1970s meant that military diehards, reactionaries and powerful business interests sensed Armageddon in the tide of subversion, militancy and permissiveness which swept Britain across the decade.[627] Superannuated generals, titled financiers, knighted press tycoons, the madder elements of the Tory party, and disgruntled former intelligence officers surreptitiously met in cloistered groups to discuss the 'treachery' of Harold Wilson and his advisors, how to deal with the paralysis of Britain by the trade unions and militant labour, and how to maintain essential services in face of national breakdown.[628] Ultra-right-wing patriotic groups such as Civil Assistance, the National Association for Freedom, the Unison Committee for Action, GB75, Red Alert and the British Military Volunteer Force sprang up to gather together kindred spirits, 'private armies' and 'vigilante groups' caught the imagination of some nationalists, and sections of the Conservative Party moved appreciably rightwards under the sway of a new philosophy championing market forces and the leadership of Margaret Thatcher. In such a climate, there was talk of military coups, of dealing with the 'enemy within', of 'regime change' and the forced replacement of a non-functioning democracy by an authoritarian government. George Young, former deputy chief of MI6 and leading figure of Unison, mused over "*When Treason Can be Right*", pondering at what point patriotic sections of the nation in face of a government in the sway of a foreign ideology "*should grab their Top Secret files and head – if not for the hills – at least for the United States embassy*" (quoted in Leigh 1988: 223).[629] Taking stock of the 1970s, historian Bernard Porter has noted: "*This was the time when the Right finally reasserted itself in British politics, after decades in the wilderness, and began pushing back the 'socialist' tide which had been steadily engulfing Britain for all those years*" (1989: 201-202). The first of the supposed coups that can be taken seriously centred on the newspaper magnate and banker Cecil King, who envisaged a "*government of national unity*" nominally headed by Lord Mountbatten, a figure acceptable to the army and the royal household. Meanwhile, dissident officers at MI5 mischievously sent documents to publications like the satirical *Private Eye* which smeared Wilson and his circle and built up a suspicion of deep penetration of the Labour party by the Soviets.[630] Bernard Porter was made anxious by such activities at the Security Service. "*In view of its social composition, its political tendencies, its virtual unaccountability and the secrecy which shielded all its activities, this could be ominous*" he subsequently warned (1989: 196). In the same period, David Leigh commented on the considerable power of the security services and worried over their unaccountability. "*Only once in the entire post-war history of MI5 was an outside body allowed to publish a report on its conduct and methods – the Denning Report on the Profumo affair, which was scarcely critical*", he notes.

> *No minister was prepared to answer questions in Parliament about what MI5 did. No independent political or judicial body had oversight over it. It was part of the secret apparatus of perpetual war with which the British populace had been blessed without ever being consulted.*
> (1988: 98-99)

Lord Carver, former chief of the defence staff, fretted to Parliament in 1988 about politically unsophisticated MI5 officers who *"appeared to savour Sherlock Holmes, Richard Hannay, Bulldog Drummond or even James Bond"*, and *"lived in a completely closed world whereby what really went on and what people actually thought and did, they just did not understand"* (quoted in Hollingsworth and Fielding 1999: 25). The author and journalist Francis Wheen has summarised the *"strange days"* of the 1970s in Britain, a time when *"retired generals formed private armies to save the country from anarchy, industrial moguls plotted coups against the government and malcontents in the security services bugged and burgled their way across London in a quest for proof that the Prime Minister was employed by the KGB"* (2009: 10). In such a climate, it was unsurprising that journalist and writer David Leigh could assert that, *"The real subversive rot was never in the British Labour Party"*. Rather, that, *"it was in the supposedly 'patriotic' secret organisations of the Cold War"* and despaired of the *"sick fantasies"* of MI5 (1988: 3, 235).[631]

Unease and disquiet regarding the encroachment of the 'secret state' in the period was apparent in the emergence of new libertarian groups and activity, and expressed in a variety of publications, legal and cultural. In the 1950s, there emerged the Campaign for the Limitation of Secret Police Powers, which published such accounts as *The Secret Police and You* (1956) and *A Year with the Secret Police* (1957), and claimed that 500 people had become the innocent victims of repression. A landmark study examining official secrecy was Sir David William's *Not in the Public Interest: The Problem of Secrecy in a Democracy* published in 1965, and several groups crusaded in the 1970s against excessive secrecy in government and for reform of the Official Secrets Act, such as the Campaign for the Revelation of Secret Information, Public Secrets, and the Freedom of Information Campaign. State Research (1977-82) was an independent group of researchers collecting and publishing information from public sources on developments in state policy in a monthly *Bulletin*, and was succeeded by Statewatch (1991-). State Research effectively served as a watchdog, particular attention being paid to the fields of law, the police, internal security, espionage and the military, and the links between the agencies operating in these fields on the one hand, and industry, right-wing and para-military organisations on the other (*State Research Bulletin* 1: 18). *The Political Police in Britain* (1976) was an exposé of the *"social and political control that lie behind the liberal facade of British society"*, written by

Tony Bunyan (later to establish Statewatch), a journalist who specialised in civil liberties and political trials; while *The Technology of Political Control* (1977) by Carol Ackroyd, Karen Margolis, Johnathan Rosenhead and Tim Shallice argued that communities were now confronted by a "*new type of weaponry*" which had social and political control as its main target (11). *The Pencourt File* (1978) was the published account of the extraordinary events which led from recently resigned Prime Minister Harold Wilson's unprecedented disclosures and suspicions to the BBC journalists Barrie Penrose and Roger Courtiour regarding interference in national democratic processes by South African Intelligence and the British Security Service.[632] *The Lobster* (later simply *Lobster*) began as a bi-monthly mimeographed newsletter that first appeared in September 1983, initially put together by Stephen Dorril and Robin Ramsay, and which reported on issues of intelligence, "*parapolitics*" and state structures.[633] *Their Trade is Treachery* (1981), which faced considerable obstruction, was the first airing of 'rogue' officer Peter Wright's activities at MI5 in the post-war decades, written by the well-known right-wing journalist and dedicated 'mole-hunter' Chapman Pincher.[634] Wright's full account later appeared in *Spycatcher*, written with the journalist Paul Greengrass, which was held up for publication until 1987, but which had generated considerable interest and speculation since 1985. Following the lifting of the ban on media discussion of Peter Wright's memoirs, the *Observer* led with an "*Exclusive*" on Sunday 16 October 1988 revealing the 'Wilson Plot Secrets', and the door was now wide open for further detailed enquiries into the 'British Watergate', such as David Leigh's *The Wilson Plot* (1988) and Stephen Dorril and Robin Ramsay's *Smear! Wilson and the Secret State* (1992).[635]

The clandestine services in Britain operated according to a remarkable set of double standards. While the establishment traitor Anthony Blunt was provided with immunity and hidden from public scrutiny, the democratically elected socialist prime minister with nothing proven against him was seemingly secretly subjected to surveillance and investigation, his character smeared and his authority challenged. For some, the class element of the Blunt affair was self-evident: a long-line of clerks, non-commissioned officers and 'foreign' outsiders like George Blake had been marched to the Old Bailey for summary punishment as traitors; while upper-class spies like Blunt and Kim Philby were afforded special treatment and privileges. Wilson and his office were kept in the dark concerning the Blunt scandal, as well as the internal rifts within MI5 which had led some to suspect that its chief Roger Hollis was a Soviet spy. Amazingly, such information and suspicions were shared with the CIA, a representative of a foreign power.

The widespread interest and concern regarding the abuse of power and privilege within secret government manifested itself in a group of paranoid fictions; novels, films and television dramas which can be termed 'secret state' thrillers; stories concerned with the exercise of power in contemporary Britain.[636] The political thriller has been part of the popular literary scene in Great Britain since the mid-19th century. An important formative novel is Disraeli's *Sybil* (1845), a story of class antagonism with a conspiracy at its heart, and by a future prime minister no less. Literary historian Christopher Harvie has identified three key moments of the political thriller: the turn of the century and the period up to World War I in which patriotic authors such as William Le Queux warned of invasion threats from the continent in stories such as *The Great War in England in 1897* (1894) and *The Invasion of 1910* (1906); the 1930s and the reinvention of the political thriller as a reaction to fascism in the hands of a writer such as Eric Ambler and his novels *Uncommon Danger* (1937) and *Epitaph of a Spy* (1938); and the period since 1970, at which point by the 1980s, the *"political thriller becomes the chief contribution to printed fiction about British politics"* (1990: 220).[637] One notable trend of the spy story in the decades of the seventies and eighties was its alignment with the right-wing thriller and the emergence of such novels as Chapman Pincher's *Dirty Tricks* (1980), Michael Shea's *Tomorrow's Men* (1981), Sir David Fraser's *August 1988* (1983), Hardiman Scott's *No Exit* (1984), Frederick Forsyth's *The Fourth Protocol* (1984) and Bryan Forbes' *The Endless Game* (1986). The stories construct a narrative backdrop of a divided and decaying country, of trouble and strife on the streets of Britain, the disturbing presence of terrorism and social breakdown, of power-cuts and rubbish strewn streets as civilisation ceases to function (Harvie 1990: 236-240). Representative of the many political thrillers published in the period were *The Chilean Club* (1971) by George Shipway, a story of four elderly ex-army *"super patriots"* helped by a loyal Secret Service to take on student agitators, trendy bishops and trade union bosses with links to Moscow, and return Britain into the hands of *"the bosses"* (aptly described by Bernard Porter as a *"political wet dream"*, 1989: 203), and *The Special Collection* (1975) and *All Our Tomorrows* (1982) by Ted Allbeury, which detail Soviet attempts to bring social and industrial chaos to Britain and the Soviet assumption of control in Britain following its breakdown into anarchy respectively.

The political thriller on the left developed in a different direction and aligned itself to an alternative tradition.[638] Apprehension regarding secret research and restricted government establishments initially surfaced in science-fiction, part of the Cold War anxieties attending atomic science, biological warfare and mind manipulation. Important examples were *Quatermass II* (TV, 1955), *Legend of Death* (TV, 1965), *A Clockwork Orange* (novel, 1962, film 1972), *The Damned* (film, 1963), and *Doomwatch* (TV, 1970-72, film, 1972). Lindsay Anderson's disturbing odyssey *O Lucky Man!* (film, 1971) has its unfortunate anti-hero Mick Travis stumble across both a secret military establishment and a creepy private centre of medical research. A formative television action series which seemed to express anxiety at repressive authoritarianism and a powerful yet submerged 'secret state' was *The Prisoner* (ITC 1967-68); while the ominous use of research by government and shadowy organisations is at the heart of *The Ωmega Factor* (BBC, 1979), a television thriller series dramatising the sinister link between spymasters and parapsychologists.[639] The futuristic drama series *1990* (TV, 1977-78) depicted an Orwellian nightmare of state repression and surveillance and the later drama serial *The Detective* (BBC, 1985) engaged with such themes as the "*covert growth of a national police force, illegal surveillance of the 'enemy within' and corruption at high levels of government*" (Petley 1988: 95). The political historian Steven Fielding sees the transformations taking place in broadcasting in the 1980s as significant, with opportunities for socially critical drama and in particular the acclaimed 'single-play' declining, there was created a radical space for the left political thriller to occupy (2014: 188). Also influential on the British 'secret state' drama were the cycle of conspiracy thrillers such as *Executive Action* (US, 1973), *The Conversation* (US, 1974) and *Three Days of the Condor* (US, 1975) which characterised the New Hollywood cinema of the 1970s, and the tradition of political thrillers in the recent Europe cinema by such committed film-makers as Costa Gavras (*Z*, Fr./Algeria, 1969, *State of Siege*, Fr./It./W.Ger., 1972) and Francesco Rosi (*The Mattei Affair* (*Il caso Mattei*), It., 1972, *Illustrious Corpses* (*Cadaveri eccellenti*), It./Fr., 1976).

A proto-type political thriller in the period before Thatcherism, and one adapted for television, was *Scotch on the Rocks*, which dealt with a revolt in Scotland seeking home rule away from England. It was written by the politician Douglas Hurd and the journalist Andrew Osmond, the third novel in a loose trilogy which began with *Send Him Victorious* (1968), set against the political rumpus caused by the declaration of independence in Rhodesia, and *The Smile on the Face of the Tiger* (1969), which dealt with a Chinese plot to reclaim Hong Kong.[640] The story is set in the near future, Great Britain is ruled by a King, and in a recent general election the leading party, the Conservatives, has no overall majority and must seek a coalition. The Scottish National Party has won the largest number of seats in Scotland, but also has no overall majority. MI5 is in Glasgow and working in tandem with the local Special Branch to unearth the conspiracy. MacNair, a mercenary and explosives specialist, has been infiltrated into the Scottish Liberation Army (SLA) in an attempt to discover the intentions of the plotters. The leaders of the Conservative and Scottish Nationalist Parties agree a formula for peace and a degree of autonomy for Scotland; however, extremists in the movement promote direct action and terrorism in furtherance of complete independence, and an armed insurrection is mounted around Fort William in the Highlands which attracts many supporters to its banner. Politicians at Westminster are prepared to pull out of Scotland, but the prime minister holds steady and is eventually able to act on secret information supplied by MacNair that French communists are providing the SLA with arms and money, and when exposed popular support for the rebellion evaporates. The novel ends on the unexpected note of seeming Dominion status for Scotland and the swearing in of a Scottish prime minister.

The novel was written in the late 1960s, but, a controversial subject, it didn't make it into print until 1971. It attracted some reasonable comments, the *Daily Mirror* marking it down as "*one of the best of its recent kind*" (12 May 1975) and the *Spectator* praising it as "*compelling reading*" (19 May 1973).[641] *Scotch on the Rocks* was an early indication of fears surfacing regarding subversion which would dominate national security concerns in Britain in the 1970s and 1980s, and its theme has once again become pertinent considering recent political history in Scotland, devolution and the rapid rise of nationalism.

The novel was adapted for television as a five-part serial by James MacTaggart at BBC Scotland. The production had been shot on location in Glasgow, Inverness, the West Highlands and Blackpool in the spring of 1972 (*Stage and Television Today*, 20 January and 4 May 1972), but a seemingly nervous broadcaster held back from screening *Scotch on the Rocks* until the late spring of 1973. A spokesman for the serial dutifully stepped forward to deny accusations that the programme "*might be thought to be cashing in on violent events in Northern Ireland*", but the suggestion of a lack of contemporary political relevance would come to haunt the producers (*Daily Mail*, 17 March 1973). The *Guardian* passed over the dramatisation as "*heavy going*" and felt that the adaptation process had weighed down the drama with exposition (12 May 1973). *The Telegraph* believed the opening episode promised "*excitement and wit*", and when it revisited the serial later in the run found it "*fast-moving*", "*decisive and plausible*", the reviewer claiming that, "*Not for some time have I enjoyed anything on television more than* Scotch on the Rocks" (9 June 1973).

With a background of nationalist 'Troubles' in Northern Ireland, a recent Scottish Conservative Party Conference arguing about the need for more independence north of the border, and the "*possibility of a National Assembly for Scotland in the political air*", *Scotch on the Rocks* grabbed attention for its topicality (*Daily Mirror*, 12 May 1973; *Spectator*, 19 May 1973). The suggestion of "*tartan terrorism*" caused a stir and the Scottish National Party (SNP) branded the serial "*reckless*" (*Guardian*, 4 May 1973), and *The Listener* wondered "*what possessed the BBC to put on this fantasy about Scottish Nationalists – a group whose historical record is predominantly decent and restrained – linking up with Glasgow street gangs and dynamiting public buildings. In the context of the Irish horrors, it seems an irresponsible and provocative gesture*"

(17 May 1973). The SNP claimed unfair treatment in the serial in a submission to the BBC Programme Complaints Commission. Specifically, the complaint was in four areas: that the Party was shown favouring violence; had extreme left-wing associations; derived funds from extreme groups in foreign countries; and that the serial constituted propaganda calculated to damage the Party. In its defence, the BBC argued that the serial was "*political fantasy in a realistic setting*" and believed that viewers could be in no doubt that what they were seeing was "*entertainment, not a political tract*". While holding some sympathy with the producer's claim for the drama as entertainment and fiction, the Commission upheld the complaint (*Stage and Television Today*, 11 October 1973; *The Times*, *The Listener* and *Guardian*, 4 October 1973).[642] *Scotch on the Rocks* appeared in the higher ratings in the Scottish broadcast region; however, the broadcaster promised at the time never to screen the drama again.[643] Interviewed in 1973, Douglas Hurd admitted that, "*I was a bit afraid that the book might have caused some alarm, but in fact it didn't*". He was mistaken in adding: "*I very much doubt if the television play will prove disturbing*" (quoted in the *Radio Times*, 5-11 May, 1973: 4).[644]

As a political thriller of the troubled 1970s, *Scotch on the Rocks* introduced some of the qualities that would later be associated with the 'secret state' thriller of the 1980s. These were principally, the drama's association with writers close to politics, a rare view into a secret world of security and intelligence at grip with presumed radicals and subversives, and attracting to itself a degree of controversy and a welter of complaints.

Inside secret government

MI5's eleventh commandment was 'Thou shall not get caught'.
(Sir John Cuckney, former training officer at MI5, quoted in Dorril 1993: 47)

It is always difficult to suggest, even in the silhouette of fiction, the definitive mood of a particular time or period. But if our present era in Britain has two characterising obsessions, they are perhaps the mushrooming of information technology and a scepticism about the benevolence of the state and its secrets.
(Review of 'In the Secret State', *The Listener*, 1 March 1985)

A group of 'secret state' thrillers were set within the ramifications of secret government, framing an inside perspective on the misuse of power. *In the Secret State* was the début novel of Robert McCrum and first published in 1980. Michael Denning has marked the significance of this novel for the genre, noting that McCrum had taken "*the story of the spy betrayed by his own organisation to reconstruct the thriller of the 'secret service' as a thriller of the 'secret state'"* (1987: 141). Of his approach, the novelist later stated: "*I took the familiar genre of the spy thriller and made it carry much more of a load than it normally would*" (quoted in *The Times*, 9 March 1985). The story deals with a security department that collects and processes data. The setting is C Directorate, a top secret data collection and analysis section within the British Security Service. Frank Strange, the honourable section head, is given the push by his seniors, and deeply suspicious commences his own inquiry into the recent suicide of Lister an analyst. He is aided by the donnish Quitman, his young protégé, who is able to provide his former boss with classified information. Against strong resistance, Strange reveals that the sensitive data compiled at C Directorate is being used by an unscrupulous colleague and new section head for commercial gain, even to the extent of providing arms dealers with details of terrorists as potential future customers. Lister had been murdered because he had stumbled onto the scam and had to be silenced. In addition, the Chief of the Directorate is a dangerous reactionary who sees the 'real war' as being with the 'subversives' who seek to undermine the country and his way of life. He therefore attempts to use information held within the data bank to discredit left-wing MPs and anyone who would oppose a clamp down on civil liberties and promote open democracy. Strange is killed by a car bomb, but not before he can get the details of the conspiracies to Quitman, a responsible senior officer. The story drew together the connections between recession and unrest which manifested themselves in the 1970s, and the mounting suspicions regarding the country's secret servants. *In the Secret State* attracted some good reviews, "*hailed as a novel which took a piercing look at government corruption and the cynicism of power*" (*The Listener*, 2 September 1982).

The television adaptation of 'In the Secret State' aired in the BBC's prestigious *Screen Two* single-play drama strand in 1985, was impressively produced on a budget of £600,000, and filmed in Cornwall, Southampton, Dorset and Whitehall, London (*Sunday Times*, 16 December 1984).[645] The drama starred Frank Finlay as Strange and Matthew Marsh as Quitman, and was directed by the experienced Christopher Morahan. The setting is the near future of 1986 and a Britain in social and economic breakdown. Strikes, street crime, social unrest, rubbish-strewn streets and terrorism provide a backdrop of fear, decay, riots, shortages and disillusionment to the story. A symbolic contrast is offered between Quitman's scholarly interest in knightly chivalry and the corrupt Machiavellian world of the British Secret Service. At one point in the story, a character cynically volunteers that, "*Telling lies for the state is what we do all the time, isn't it, Frank?*" 'In the Secret State' dramatised the emerging fears regarding accountability of secret government departments, the misuse of personal data, the prying of the state into the private lives of citizens, the selfish actions of those in positions of authority who claim to serve the national interest, the abandonment of 'liberal democratic niceties', and assorted 'dirty tricks' perpetrated by the security services. The story also dramatised the intense professional ambition and competition of those serving in British Intelligence. Careerism and envy drive staff that ruthlessly seek promotion, power and influence, and delight in putting down a rival. 'In the Secret State' was described as a "*thriller, with keyboards, entry-codes and telephones as its lethal weapons*" (*Radio Times*, 9-15 March 1985: 84), and the drama adds to this presentation of technology an apprehension regarding excessive secrecy, and warns of a government that is more concerned to increase its already centralised authority than its citizen's standard of living. The *finale* of the dramatisation is more chilling than the novel, ending with Quitman, as with Strange before him, the object of permanent scrutiny, retreating indoors away from the constant gaze of sinister men with binoculars. Only two days before transmission of 'In the Secret State', the current affairs series *20/20 Vision* screened the episode 'MI5's Official Secrets ', featuring the accusations of Cathy Massiter, a disaffected former MI5 officer who claimed politicised surveillance on the peace movement and trade unions by the Security Service, and thus providing a thought-provoking context for the drama.

'In the Secret State' attracted some good notices. *The Telegraph* believed the quality of the drama recalled the heyday of the single-play in the 1970s. Judging the character of Frank Strange a "*kind of losing and unsmiling Smiley*", the reviewer noted the contemporary relevance of the drama, the background of an increasingly divided society and a "*government machine using the new weapons of the information technology to increase its power by unaccountable stealth*" (11 March 1985). The *Daily Express*, although less impressed by the drama, also found the backdrop of social breakdown "*believable*", as was the "*concept of a government department above the law that kept files on radical citizens and ruined their lives in the name of national security*" (11 March 1985). *The Times* marked the drama's presentation of Britain as an incipient police state, in which technology and barbarism are fatally combined, and pointed to the sinister double-meaning of 'secret state' in the play, noting: "*This was a 'secret state' not only because its real powers remained undisclosed but also because it discovered the secrets of others through the bewildering procedures of electronic surveillance*" (11 March 1985). A problem for the *Scotsman*, was that 'In the Secret State' was insufficient in its critique of the "*fearful creeps in the Secret Service*", claiming: "*Its weakness was that they were shown using their nasty powers for their own personal gain whereas what's sinister about the ghastly swines is that they serve their political masters and are part of the growing process of turning Great Britain into a fascist state*" (16 March 1985). On a less political and emotional level, the *Guardian* enjoyed a "*hard-driving good-looking thriller*"; though finding the story complicated, it appreciated the novel situation of an "*aging man investigating with accelerating horror his life's work*", and welcomed this as a "*touching variation on the ordinary thriller*" (11 March 1985). 'In the Secret State' shifted the target of who was the 'enemy within'. This was recognised at *The Listener*, which warned: "*The real enemy is the world of the secret state itself – the unaccounted and unaccountable web of bureaucrats and institutions which make up the security services into whose hands have been placed an ever-growing range of electronic gadgetry and information-collating capacity*" (7 March 1985).

The rise of information technology and concomitant technological anxiety was central to a number of political thrillers in the 1980s. *Bird of Prey*, an original television drama, was a techno-thriller written by Ron Hutchinson, produced at the BBC and broadcast in two four-part serials in 1982 and 1984. *Bird of Prey* (1982) and its sequel *Bird of Prey 2* (1984) dealt with emerging anxieties regarding new information technology.[646] In the first of these dramas, an expert in computer fraud within a government ministry stumbles on 'Le Pouvoir', a conspiratorial organisation uniting financiers, a foreign crime syndicate, politicians, civil servants and rogue intelligence officers. Henry Jay (Richard Griffiths) is an inconspicuous civil servant; an innocuous Principal Scientific Officer employed at the Department of Commercial Development (DCD) who is working on a report, 'Computer Fraud in the Age of Electronic Accounting', for a Whitehall Trade Ministry.[647] Off the record, Jay shares information with Detective Inspector Richardson of the Fraud Squad (Jim Broadbent), and when his report is tampered with and buried behind a veil of security and Richardson is brutally killed, Jay is thrown into an international conspiracy organised by the shadowy 'Le Pouvoir' (The Power), and which operates according to the age-old method of favours. Jay is undeterred and goes to ground where he continues his investigation, using his expertise with computers to hack into official sources. The conspiracy Jay unearths involves a powerful financial and crime syndicate which is manipulating a project to construct a Euro Tunnel connecting Great Britain with Continental Europe, a venture worth billions of pounds. Jay kidnaps a key Euro politician (Christopher Loague) on the eve of the meeting which will secure the permissions for the tunnel, and ransoms him for his wife (Carole Nimmons) who is now held by a rogue intelligence officer who is looking after the project's interest in Britain. At the exchange, the politician and the intelligence officer are shot dead on the orders of the crime syndicate as Jay has arranged for the conspiracy to be exposed if he and his wife were harmed.

The *Morning Star* wrote of a "*most impressive drama*" and reported that the series had been so "*hugely successful*" that the BBC contemplated a further series (19 May 1982).[648] *Bird of Prey 2* duly followed, further "*dragged the thriller into the age of microtechnology*" (*Radio Times*, 1-7 September 1984:

11), and picked up the story with the Jay's anxious whether the conspirators will break the computer code which guards their dangerous knowledge, forms their insurance and thus make them vulnerable again. Following a murder attempt, Jay and his wife assume new identities and flee to a safe flat he has prepared on the coast where he commences to prepare a new assault on his antagonists. Through his investigation, Jay learns that Le Pouvoir aims to use the European-wide measures to integrate electronic banking to pull off a gigantic financial fraud, in which the Member of Parliament Greggory (Bob Peck) is central. Roche (Lee Montague), a dangerous rogue operator for Le Pouvoir, takes Jay hostage and forces him under threat to his wife to detect the technical arrangements for the fraud and to break through the computer security arrangements to take personal benefit from the theft. At the last minute, the resourceful Jay is able to break free, taking with him the details of the financial fraud. Pursued by Roche to his safe flat, the assassin is killed by Mrs Jay, at this point a nervous wreck. Jay sensitively explains to his wife that they will have to continue to live anonymously, but that they will no longer want for money. The second series made even greater use of innovative video graphic techniques and computer imagery which would soon be more widely employed in television output and drama (Oldham 2017: 114-17).

The well-received *Bird of Prey* serials were among the first dramas to stress the anxieties that attended the rise of computers in terms of fraud, security and external threats. It was reckoned at the time of broadcast that £1.4 billion a year was electronically misappropriated. The producers stressed the "*up-to-the-minute*" nature of the series, a "*thriller for the electronic age*" as the press sheet described it, and financial expert Colleen Toomey, the technical adviser on the drama, stressed that,

> *We wanted the series to be as authentic as possible, which meant researching everything from computer-talk to the pubs where someone like Henry would go for lunch. Most official bodies were extremely helpful once they realised the information was only to be used in a work of fiction.*
> (Quoted in the *Radio Times*, 17-23 April 1982: 23)

Bird of Prey appeared at the moment when concerns to frame data protection legislation were emerging and fears regarding financial security in a digital environment were mounting, and which led eventually to wider global concerns regarding privacy, surveillance and accountability. It can also be suggested that the *Bird of Prey* serials expressed the emerging anxieties pertaining to the extreme free market economy philosophies of the new Conservativism. Joseph Oldham has drawn the parallel between unfettered market forces and ‘gangster capitalism’ as represented in *Bird of Prey*, an "*all-*

too-efficient force that has abandoned the public interest in favour of a monstrous private agenda, exploiting British society for 'profit maximisation and accelerated acquisition'" (2017: 110-11).

Reviews of the two seasons were generally very good. Many approved of the fresh and intriguing storyline, as well as the unlikely casting of the portly Richard Griffiths as the Billy Bunterish, stubbornly persistent hero engaged in a David and Goliath confrontation. *The Telegraph* admired a *"gripping thriller which builds up the tension as quietly and efficiently as a digital watch"* (24 April 1982) and the *Glasgow Herald* praised a *"sophisticated script"* and an *"atmosphere of contemporary menace"* (1 May 1982). *The Times* was satisfied that the drama had overshadowed the potentially distracting electronic aspects of the narrative with a suitably comic and resolutely downbeat plot, and managed an atmosphere that remained parochially seedy (23 April 1982); while the *Daily Mail* expressed the consensus when it exalted a *"baffling series"* that has *"surprised everyone by emerging as the thriller hit of the year"* (14 May 1982). The *Glasgow Herald* praised *Bird of Prey 2*, enjoying the *"exhilarating pace, sharp tension, courageous editing ... and a sense of humour"*. In Henry Jay, the reviewer felt the drama had furnished for the thriller, *"the most original leading man since John le Carré gave us George Smiley"* (8 September 1984). *The Times* thought the second serial capped the first, provided a *"welcome lift to thriller-writing"*, and waited expectantly for a *Bird of Prey 3* (28 September 1984).

Case file 1: *A Very British Coup* (1988)

> *We were an effective, well run, legally based and overseen organisation, of which the country could and should be proud.*
> (Stella Rimington, former Director-General of MI5, 2002: 254)

> *I believe that working for a secret intelligence service almost always brings about a state of mind which permits anything if it is done for the benefit of the service and hence for the good of one's country.*
> (Former MI6 officer Anthony Cavendish 1990: 2)

> *A major new TV series looks set to have the Tories foaming at the mouth.*
> (*Mail on Sunday*, 21 June 1988)

A Very British Coup was first published as a novel in 1982 by Chris Mullin, a Labour Party insider and editor of the left-wing newspaper *Tribune* (1982-84), which, in the view of Julian Petley, *"put flesh, in fictional form, on some of the rumours and allegations about plots to destabilise the Labour government, which were then generally dismissed as mere paranoia on the part of Harold*

Wilson and his associates" (1988: 96). It was adapted for television in 1988, and again in an updated form as *Secret State* in 2012. *A Very British Coup* is set at the heart of political power at 10 Downing Street, where a newly-elected radical Labour prime minister is undermined by the entrenched forces of permanent and secret government which conspire to return British politics to 'normality' and re-assert their own privileged positions. The original story, set in the near future of 1989, commences with the landslide election of an extremist Labour government, headed by former Sheffield steel worker and trade unionist Harry Perkins. The establishment is appalled at the proposed radical programme of withdrawal from the North Atlantic Treaty Organisation, the dismantling of the nuclear deterrent, public control of finance, the abolition of the House of Lords and an end to private newspaper monopolies. The 'counter-revolution' is organised through the Security Service and incorporates the press barons, high finance and senior civil servants, which do all in their power to intimidate, distort, destabilise, blacken and hamper the democratically-elected government. The forces of reaction in Britain are aided by the American State Department and CIA, which bring to bear their considerable influence and resources to return Britain to 'sanity'. In the final outcome, the Security Service is able to unearth a past romantic involvement of Perkin's which is shaped to compromise him and force his resignation. He is replaced as leader of the government by a moderate Labour man in the pocket of MI5.

The novel includes a frontispiece, a segment from an article by the right-wing journalist Peregrine Worsthorne titled 'When Treason Can Be Right' (echoes of George Young), published in 1979.[649] It commences with the candid if unsettling confession: "*I could easily imagine myself being tempted into a treasonable disposition under a Labour government dominated by the Marxist Left*". The story then proceeds to fictionalise and to some extent satirise an essential contradiction within the reactionary position which would unhesitatingly bring down a democratically-elected government in the name of 'democracy'. Labour politician Tony Benn had commented on the sinister inertia in the British social and political system, claiming that, "*As a minister, I experienced the power of industrialists and bankers to get their way by use of the crudest form of economic pressure, even blackmail, against a Labour Government*". These lessons led him to the conclusion that,

> the UK is only superficially governed by MPs and the voters who elect them. Parliamentary democracy is, in truth, little more than a means of securing a periodical change in the management team, which is then allowed to preside over a system that remains in essence intact. (Quoted at http://spiritofcontradiction.eu/rowan-duffy/2013/01/23/a-very-british- coup, accessed 18 July 2015)

The story was conceived by Mullin in 1980 when he was on a train returning from a Labour Party conference at Blackpool and wondered how the establishment would react to a left-wing Labour government.[650] The right-wing Mrs Thatcher had only uncertainly established her position in office at the time, Labour was high in the opinion polls and there was a felt possibility that, come an election, the Labour Party would be led by the radical Tony Benn. A recent announcement that the Americans were planning to install Cruise missiles on their British bases had given a new lease of life to the extremist position on the Left (*Guardian* 7 March 2006), and demonstrations arranged by the Campaign for Nuclear Disarmament which were attracting crowds in excess of 200,000 made the material even more topical.[651] *A Very British Coup* was one of the most high-profile political novels of the decade and represented an early fictional engagement with the 'secret state', a mounting conviction on the Left that the power of the traditional establishment was protected and maintained by a shadowy collusion of security, business and political interests. In the story, it is the Director-General of DI5 (a designation sometimes used for MI5) who co-ordinates the struggle against Perkins and his administration; for example, engineering a smear campaign against an able Foreign Secretary and forcing his resignation. Meanwhile, the Americans have in their pocket a moderate trade unionist who is used to foment industrial unrest in the crucial power industry and bring great resentment against the government. Mullin has pointed to revelations later in the 1980s, the supposed plot to undermine Harold Wilson's Labour government in the 1970s and MI5 vetting of employment and promotion at the BBC, as offering belated credibility for his story. As he commented: "*Suddenly the possibility that the British establishment might conspire with its friends across the Atlantic to destabilise the elected government could no longer be dismissed as left-wing paranoia*" (quoted in the *Guardian* 7 March 2006).[652]

As early as 1984, *A Very British Coup* was conceived as a feature film, part of the Film 4 initiative, perhaps with the radical Ken Loach directing. Reconceived for television, it was reportedly rejected by the state broadcaster the BBC, but eventually materialised as a three-part serial in 1988, scripted by the talented Alan Plater back at Channel 4 Television, which at that time was tasked with championing new voices and alternative perspectives.[653] It was reported that Tony Benn helped producer Ann Skinner through "*pointing out what was realistic in the script and what was not*" (quoted in the *Mail on Sunday*, 2 June 1988).[654] The filmed story is set in the near-future of the early 1990s. Following the exposures of the '*Spycatcher* Affair' of 1987-88 and the revelations that the Security Service interfered in domestic politics, the story was toughened up, made harder and sharper, emerged as even more credible, and benefitted from "*uncanny topicality*" (*The Times*, 18 June 1988). *A Very British Coup* is a sympathetic adaptation, directed with verve by Mick Jackson and resulting in a witty yet chilling drama; a "*dangerous series*" is how the director referred to it (quoted in Petley 1988: 96). The only major revision to the original story is a re-drawing of the ending, where Plater has Perkins out-manoeuvre the 'secret state', make a prime ministerial broadcast on national television exposing the machinations of the Security Service to undermine democracy, and call an election to gain the support of the British public. Amid these optimistic scenes there are brief, almost subliminal images and sounds which suggest the preparation of a military coup, with echoes of the 1973 CIA-engineered coup in Chile, and that the establishment is about to get very serious. The reviewer at the *Independent* sensed the novel approach of the series, claiming that political drama on television tended to pursue the view that Labour leaders willingly surrendered their beliefs when in power, while *A Very British Coup* is about something darker, "*the theft of good intentions*" (20 June 1988).

The drama attracted a lot of interest in the press, in the political and media columns, the letters pages, as well as the television reviews. The political correspondent at the *Sunday Telegraph* predictably reported, on rumours circulating before the broadcast, that, "*Tory MPs see the drama, A Very British Coup, as a vehicle for side-stepping the courts and raising the same questions as the* Spycatcher *book. They believe that the drama is unbalanced and deeply hostile to the Conservative Party*". A spokesman for Channel 4 rejected Tory accusations that *A Very British Coup* was "*anti-Conservative*". Claiming: "*It is a fictional piece and we are very proud of it. It is a drama first and foremost and we did not set out to make a film that made out how good the Left is and how bad the Right is*". The MP Sir John Biggs-Davison, in something that was becoming a mantra for the Tories at the time, rather limply commented: "*It would be nice if some of these television dramas about spies and politics were less Left-wing*" (all 8 May 1988). *A Very British Coup* proved an "*irresistible talking point*" for the politically-minded. For a columnist at the centre-left *Guardian*, the serial gave a "*powerful description of the power of the state apparatus*" and exposed the "*contempt which its real masters have for democracy*". For this writer the message of the drama seemed credible, and it was depressing, "*Facing up to the deeply entrenched anti-democratic character of the British state*" (8 August 1988). The *Observer* confirmed that the serial "*provoked some serious constitutional speculation*", claiming that the '*Spycatcher* Affair' and the current Tory White Paper on official secrecy has "*made many more wonder whether there are any more depths to which official Britain would not stoop in order to keep us in our place*" (10 July 1988).[655]

The hard-left was more ambivalent about *A Very British Coup*. Predictably, the radicals bemoaned the suggestion that revolutionary change would result from the "*courage and determination of individuals*" rather than the "*mass action of the people"*. The *Morning Star* pointed to the necessity of *"mass ex-tra-parliamentary action"* in support of Labour to bring about radical change and griped that, *"it wasn't the case in the film"* (9 July 1988); a view expounded in such fringe journals as *Labour Briefing* and *Socialist Worker* (see *The Times*, 29 July 1988 and Keighron 1991: 216). Left firebrand Ken Livingstone took the opportunity of the political furore created by *A Very British Coup* to berate the *"wets"* at the centre of the Labour Party.[656] For him, the plot of the drama confirmed *"every left-wing conspiracy theory"* concerning MI5, the press barons and Establishment links with America, and in the outcome propounding its message to a *"vastly larger audience than all the tens of thousands who over the years have listened to Tony Benn expound on this theme in meetings throughout the length and breadth of the country"* (1988). Livingstone took to task the *"unjustified abuse"* from Labour deputy Prime Minister and moderate Roy Hattersley who had reviewed *A Very British Coup* in *The Listener*, where he had declared the story *"immensely exciting but wholly unbelievable"*, at times *"politically ridiculous"*: *"all too obvious and fantastical"* (1988). The left-winger accused Hattersley of doing the work of the Conservative faithful, claiming that the *"Tories are more than happy to leave it to Labour right-wingers to rush in to defend the status quo and savage the work of author and MP Chris Mullin"*. Even worse, from Hattersley's viewpoint, Livingstone argued, was, *"the knowledge that to publicly concede the truth about where power lies in Britain would mean that the Labour leadership would have to draw up a package of reforms to make us a more open and accountable democracy"*. Even to admit such things, claimed Livingston, would shift the Labour party to the radical left and strengthen progressive forces throughout British society. *"That is quite definitely not on the agenda for Labour's present deputy leader"*.[657] Highly supportive of the serial, Livingston claimed that *A Very British Coup* was a *"brilliantly produced and acted drama"* which had managed *"to get across to the general public the very shallow hold of democracy and freedom in Britain today in a much more effective way than any socialist theoretical tract could have done"* (ibid.). The old left-stager Tony Benn was reported as saying that the plot (of the novel) *"describes in a very realistic manner what would happen to any future Labour Government which tried to carry its policy through"* (quoted in the *Scotsman*, 2 July 1982).[658] Glenys Kinnock, the wife of the Labour Party leader, also gave A *Very British Coup* a vote of support. She praised the drama's *"sustained tension, rattling speed, fact running through the fiction, hope mixed with menace, the clash of right with might, compelling acting"*, and claimed the serial depicted *"what people of all political persuasions know to be real about British politics and what people of all persuasions who believe in elected government hope is unreal"* (1988).

Although the Conservative Party response was muted, the right-wing press was largely hostile to the drama serial. The general critique was framed in terms of fantasy, many commentators evoking the metaphor of a dream. The *Sunday Times* claimed only a "*veneer of political relevance*" and dismissed it as having "*little to do with reality*" (26 June 1988). The *Daily Mail* derided it as "*wishful thinking*" (20 June 1988); the *Sun* calmly claimed it "*too flawed by left-wing fantasies to be taken seriously*" (22 June 1988); the *Financial Times* passed it over as a "*slick and sexy re-telling of old myths which people would like to go on believing, but cannot*" (6 July 1988); and the *Mail on Sunday* dismissed it as "*lurid*" (2 June 1988).[659] The setting of the drama for some seemed pre-Thatcher, a socialist left "*returned to a blissful, Garden of Eden-like state of purity*". The *Sunday Telegraph* sought to reassure its readers, asserting that, "*It's a little difficult to accept a drama as futuristic, when its politics are so plainly antediluvian*" (26 June 1988), and the *Sunday Times* asserted that the "*basic notion that there could be electoral victory for an ultra-left party had shallow verisimilitude in 1980 if you were blind, deaf and uncritical. In 1988 it is strictly for the adventure playground*". It warned leftists who enjoyed the drama that, "*Politics is going to be boring and capitalist*" (3 July 1988). *The Telegraph* reported that *A Very British Coup* raised the same allegations made in *Spycatcher*, and quoted Chris Mullin who claimed the adaptation as an "*attempt to smuggle the message to a fairly wide audience that any government which threatened the status quo would still be illegally destabilised by the British establishment*" (9 May 1988).[660] The *Daily Mail* praised a "*first-class production*", but dismissed a "*second-rate story*" (4 July 1988), and the *News of the World* wrote of "*fantastic tosh*" (26 June 1988).[661] Norris McWhirter, co-founder of the right-wing Freedom Association, wrote a letter to the *Guardian* registering his suspicion that a "*comparable parable slanted to the Right would not be given air time – let alone two transmissions per week*" (25 June 1988). Musing on the lack of comment from the official Labour Party, the liberal *Guardian* asked its readers to imagine a "*three-part drama starring a female prime minister, who plotted with her henchmen to abolish the NHS and with the Americans to bomb Iran, and was then brought down by revelations, manufactured by the lefty BBC, about a financial scandal inside her own family*". This, it contended, bore a similar relationship to reality as *A Very British Coup* and claimed would never pass protest from the Tory Party and would not get made (21 June 1988). It was reported that Mrs Thatcher's advisers had refused permission for filming in Downing Street (*Mail on Sunday*, 2 June 1988).[662]

Many reviews of the serial were good, not least for the acting of Ray McAnally as Harry Perkins, a talent called "*awe-inspiring*" at *The Telegraph* (4 July 1988). The *Scotsman* informed its readers that, "*Everything in this short Channel Four series, Alan Plater's screenplay, the screen itself, bursts with televisual intelligence*" (25 June 1988). The *Observer* praised a "*slick, witty and utterly compelling production*" (26 June 1988); the *Guardian* found it full of "*vigour, exhilaration and jokes*" (20 June 1988); and the *Times Literary Supplement* enjoyed a "*series of rare power*", believing it a "*genuine improvement on the original*" (1-7 July 1988). The American magazine *Village Voice* judged *A Very British Coup* "*gutsy, galvanizing political fiction of the highest order*", and claimed it "*the most relevant in a recent line of superior British conspiracy-theory thrillers*" which traded "*not in paranoia but in unacceptable truths*" (17 January 1989). *The New York Times* declared it a "*riveting, walloping, unapologetic celebration of left-of-center politics*" (13 January 1989) and *Time Magazine*, after a "*disillusioning presidential campaign*", welcomed a "*TV political drama for adults*" (16 January 1989).

Some critics, however, seemed offended by the subject matter, possibly the case at *The Times* where the review rather sourly complained of Plater's script as the "*dullest he has produced in years*" (20 June 1988). The rejoinder to this is stated on a militant website, where it is observed that the attention paid by the drama,

> to collusion between the 'secret state', industrialists and the media was unusual as it is often understated by the left. The left tends not to want to get lumped together with mad conspiracy theorists and in doing so often errs too far on the side of credulity.

It adds that any attempt to take a democratic road to socialism needs to assess seriously how it can deal with the 'secret state'.

> MI5, MI6 and the CIA are not something that is (sic) easily controlled or easily eliminated; they have their own agendas and are often quite willing to work with finance and industry in order to keep democracy in check.
> (http://spiritofcontradiction.eu/rowan-duffy/2013/01/23/a-very-british-coup, accessed 18 July 2015)

Peter Keighron has assessed the critical response to *A Very British Coup*, both from the Left and from the Right. He reports that in confronting such a directly political proposal, mainstream reviews attempted to reaffirm the gap between fact and fiction, politics and culture, which the film was attempting to narrow. He writes of the urgency which mainstream critics applied to the task of denouncing *A Very British Coup*; and from the Right perspective, the task of denying the programme's political content was imperative and partly achieved through deflection; that is, as we have seen, by praising the serial's artistic form. Left periodicals surprisingly ignored the radical drama; *Marxism Today, Socialist Review* nor *Tribune* having anything at all to say about the programme. A major failing of Left criticism Keighron sees as the lack of discussion of the politics of culture itself, a crucial development on the tendency simply to discuss politics within the cultural space of the journals. In summary of the Left critical response, he writes of both its 'quantitative' and 'qualitative' failures (1991). The brave, radical nature of *A Very British Coup* did not receive the encouragement from the Left that it deserved. However, in what might be construed as politically motivated, or at least politically meaningful, in artistic terms, *A Very British Coup* won British Academy of Film and Television Arts Television Awards for Best Drama Series and Best Actor (Ray McAnally), and an International Emmy for Best Drama.

Corporate corruption and illegality

Where the world of law enforcement overlaps the world of political expediency, where monied interests override the future safety of human beings – this is the Edge of Darkness, the crumbling cliff-top where Western society is beginning to teeter.
(*Western Mail*, 2 November 1985)

Nothing is what it seems, all statements are ambiguous, distinctions between good and evil dissolve in expediency, and the ground beneath the feet is always quicksand. Across this quicksand crawls one honest man hoping to survive long enough to comprehend the forces that manipulate him.
(Review of *Edge of Darkness*, *Mail on Sunday*, 15 December 1985)

Edge of Darkness (1985) and *Secret State* (2012) deal with complex conspiracies involving corporate wrongdoing and irresponsibility, the television dramas concentrating on the blatant disregard for the environment by business corporations and the collusion which binds international finance, permanent government and intelligence in a sinister alliance.[663] *Edge of Darkness*, produced by the BBC in association with the American Lionheart Television and first broadcast on BBC 2 in 1985, is a terrifying odyssey into the dark heart of the secret nuclear state of Thatcher's Britain, and a classic of both the serial form of television drama and of the conspiracy thriller. The complex story of murder and of government and corporate cover-ups involving the nuclear industry unfolds across six episodes. *Edge of Darkness* was written by the accomplished Troy Kennedy Martin, who had previously scripted the historical spy series *Reilly – Ace of Spies* (1983), directed by Martin Campbell who had also worked on *Reilly*, and produced by Michael Wearing, who had recently fashioned the *Bird of Prey* 'secret state' thrillers.[664] Kennedy Martin set out to shape a political thriller about "*our obsession with official secrecy*", but after hearing President Reagan's 'Star Wars' speech on nuclear defence in 1983, he reshaped the material away from a domestic political thriller towards a global political narrative dealing more directly with nuclear concerns and the survival of the planet (Cooke 2007: 156; Pixley 2003a: 53; *Stage and Television Today*, 24 October 1985). He called the focus of the anxieties in *Edge of Darkness* the "*'silhouette' of modern British politics*" (quoted in the *Radio Times*, 2-8 November 1985: 85). The serial was budgeted at an expensive £2 million and filmed over a six-month period on location in Yorkshire, Scotland, North Wales and London. BBC Bristol's design team built a sinister goods train mocked for carrying nuclear waste on a private line on the outskirts of Leeds and the outline of a submerged nuclear city in the heart of a Welsh slate mine. The BBC trumpeted the serial as a powerful thriller for the nuclear age, "*concerned with modern man's most dangerous collective addiction – nuclear power and the obsessive apparatus of state security and interlocking business interests which ensure its restless expansion*". Producer Michael Wearing claimed it an "*elemental story for our time*" and a production "*which only an independently minded and traditionally funded BBC would have chosen to initiate*" (*Edge of Darkness* press release).[665]

Ron Craven (Bob Peck) is a policeman assigned to investigate allegations of election fraud in the Miner's Union involving its leader Godbolt (Jack Watson). One night he is confronted by a gunman on his doorstep and his daughter Emma (Joanne Whalley) is tragically shot dead.[666] It is assumed that Ron had been the intended victim; however, the distraught Craven discovers a hidden side to Emma: that of an environmental activist and of her confrontation with International Irradiated Fuels (IIF) and its secret Northmoor site for dumping nuclear waste. Ron is officially informed that Emma was known to be a terrorist, a member of a subversive anti-nuclear group called 'GAIA' which had previously broken into Northmoor. Various complicating strands are woven into the plot, including dangerous characters from Craven's time serving in Northern Ireland, the loose cannon American CIA officer Darius Jedburgh (Joe Don Baker) with his own curiosity regarding Northmoor,[667] the American businessman Jerry Grogan (Kenneth Nelson) and his intention of acquiring IIF, and Clementine (Zoë Wanamaker) a sometime associate of Jedburgh who helps Craven. Pendleton (Charles Kay) is the shady security advisor attached to the Cabinet Office. Later, Craven and Jedburgh gain entry to Northmoor where they find evidence of a nuclear accident and of secret weapons research. The American makes off with a sample of plutonium and confronts Grogan at a 'Star Wars'-like military conference on 'directed energy weapons', where he irradiates him. Craven traces Jedburgh to a remote cottage; ill from radiation poisoning they discuss the coming struggle between mankind and the Earth. Jedburgh is killed when the house is stormed, but Craven is let go, only to die from his exposure to radioactive material. The 'Edge of Darkness' stated by the title refers both to Ron's oedipal tragedy at the loss of his beloved daughter and the nuclear catastrophe facing the world.[668] The American *Village Voice* acknowledged this merging of personal loss with an entire ecosystem come to grief, commenting that the drama combined the "*scope and poetic force of King Lear with the obsessive effect of Vertigo*" (22 March 1988).

The producers felt they had something out of the ordinary with *Edge of Darkness*: arranging a special screening for an invited audience at the British Academy of Film and Television Arts, London, with the creative team and cast in attendance and the production billed as a "*unique event in BBC history*"; and scheduling the first public screening at the Cornerhouse art cinema in Manchester with introductions by producer Michael Wearing and director Martin Campbell.[669] "*What the serial does suggest*", claimed Wearing at the time, "*is that the nuclear state is a state-within-a-state, and has grown up without public debate or democratic control, and threatens the very survival of our planet*" (quoted in the *Daily Mail*, 2 November 1985).[670]

Reviews of the initial episodes of *Edge of Darkness* tended to be cautious, claimed bafflement and were sometimes disappointed given the pre-broadcast hype; but it soon became apparent that many critics were becoming mesmerised by the serial. This was evident at the *Sun*, where the reviewer claimed he "*fought it for weeks*", but conceded that, "*eventually* Edge of Darkness *got a grip on me*" (12 December 1985). The *Scotsman* wrote of television drama "*beyond the normal calls of duty*", claimed that *Edge of Darkness* heralded a "*new TV era*", and, commenting on the drama's frenetic stylisation, reported that, "*Nothing so visual, so auditory, so consummately noisy, busy to the eye, so exciting to see and hear, has ever appeared on the British box*" (9 November 1985). The same paper in a later review described the serial as a "*chilling, engrossing image of Thatcher-Land*" (16 November 1985). The *Evening Standard* labelled the drama "*gloomily stylish*" (19 November 1985), and the *News of the World* summarised the production as stunningly filmed and the viewing experience as "*hypnotic: menacing, intense and at times heart-rendingly moving*" (24 November 1985). *The Telegraph* praised *Edge of Darkness* as a "*masterpiece*" and "*one of those very rare television creations so rich in form and content that the spectator wishes there was some way of prolonging it indefinitely*" (26 November 1985). The *Daily Express* saluted a "*rare drama which demands that the mind be engaged while enjoying the thrill-a-minute adventure*" and "*created with such brutal reality that it feels all too true*" (5 December 1985) and the *Glasgow Herald* commended a "*stunning, sophisticated multi-layered thriller*" (14 December 1985). Echoing a number of reviewers, the *Mail on Sunday* praised *Edge of Darkness* as the "*best drama series of the year*", a thriller "*enriched by humanity, a tragedy enhanced by wit, a fantasy endorsed by grisly reality*" (15 December 1985). Following its critical success, *Edge of Darkness* was hastily and uniquely scheduled for a repeat screening on the more popular BBC 1only a month after its conclusion on BBC 2 (*The Telegraph*, 26 November 1985).[671]

The left-wing *Morning Star* found the serial *"gripping, suspenseful television"*, although it questioned the need to have an election scandal in the miners' union and one of its officials implicated in the conspiracy (4 November 1985). On the opposite side of the political spectrum, the *Daily Express* praised *Edge of Darkness* as *"brilliant television"*, but wished the *"brilliance had been devoted to a better cause"*, one demonising the Soviet Union rather than the United States as the main threat and enemy (13 December 1985). There was also mild criticism that *Edge of Darkness* had simplified and misrepresented the theory of Professor Lovelock, who had recently proposed that all living things on the earth interact and interrelate, like parts of a single organism in a way aimed at keeping the planet fit for life. This view had been propounded in his book *Gaia: A New Look at Life on Earth* (1979) (*You Magazine, Mail on Sunday*, 10 November 1985). Troy Kennedy Martin acknowledged at the time that the shift in his thriller towards a more serious theme was influenced by his reading of Lovelock (*Stage and Television Today*, 24 October 1985). A representative of Gaia Books wrote to the *Guardian* and complained of the wrong-headed image of Gaia in the serial, complaining that, "*The group in* Edge of Darkness *with its extremist politics and feminism, CIA connections, secrecy and confused doom-ridden science is a distorted parody of a new movement that is just reaching public awareness*" (22 November 1985).[672] The BBC as a consequence was forced to issue a statement that the terrorist group called Gaia in the drama was *"entirely fictional, and has no connection with the Gaia movement"* (*Guardian*, 19 November and *Observer*, 20 November 1985).[673]

The cultural anxiety regarding nuclear catastrophe at the time was expressed in such dramas as *The China Syndrome* (US, film, 1978), *Silkwood* (US, film, 1983) and *Threads* (TV, 1984). Television scholar John Caughie argues that anxiety found its form in "*narratives of paranoia in which dark influences were at work, and in which the interests of states and corporations were mysteriously intertwined, operating outside the normal process of politics, commerce and law*" (2007: 37).[674] *Edge of Darkness* conforms to this scheme, and its dramatic confrontations centred on energy, power and the environment fits it into the main political struggles of the time, those between the Thatcher government and the miners on one hand, and Thatcher and the anti-nuclear protestors on the other. It has been suggested, for example, that the Security Service targeted for investigation organisations such as Greenpeace, Friends of the Earth and the Campaign for Nuclear Disarmament among many, and in some cases subjected individuals to harassment, intimidation and physical abuse, such as the peace campaigners Dora Russell,

Madeline Haigh, Pat Davis, Dr Di McDonald, Jane Powell and Hazel Rennie (Murray 1993: 122-142, 209-240). Critics have also pointed to the strange deaths of the elderly environmental activist Hilda Murrell in 1984 and of the radical solicitor Willie McRae in 1985,[675] with claims of a cover-up, corporate conspiracy, and even of possible state murder (Green 2013; Murray 1993: 143-208). Accordingly, the targeting and elimination of the anti-nuclear campaigner Emma Craven in *Edge of Darkness* might not have seemed far-fetched to some at the time. The *Daily Express* believed that *Edge of Darkness* "*superbly focused the mind on the dilemmas of the nuclear age*" (10 December 1985).

Writer Troy Kennedy Martin claimed that there was no reluctance at the BBC to take on a "*controversial or hot subject*". In fact, he recorded, the Head of Drama Jonathan Powell was "*looking for an original contemporary drama, perhaps with that aim, to change the direction and nature of the department's output*" (quoted in *Stage and Television Today*, 24 October 1985).[676] Some reviews noted the "*formal risks unusual for television*" taken by the drama (*Evening Standard*, 5 November 1985), and the general advance from naturalism making the serial "*something new to the TV thriller genre*" (*The Telegraph*, 26 November 1985). There was also acknowledgement of the unusual generic-hybridity of *Edge of Darkness*, the *Guardian* observing how the programme set out to "*break every rule in the book*", combining "*Black comedy with revenge tragedy, a ghost story with political intrigue*" (4 November 1985). John Caughie comments on the unusual narrative complexity and ambiguity of *Edge of Darkness*, the unexpected "*avant-garde sensibility in a popular thriller*" which pushed the serial form of television drama to its limits (2007: 6); the reviewer at the *Guardian* claimed a "*mixture of Costa Gavras and Nicolas Roeg*" in the unusual combination of political thriller and metaphysics (4 November 1985); and *You Magazine* praised a drama tinged with "*apocalypse but also with poetry, myth and mystery*" (*Mail on Sunday*, 10 November 1985). Troy Kennedy Martin has commented on the maturing of the serial form of popular television and that "*serious*" drama was no longer seen as solely being the province of the single play. He suggested that *Edge of Darkness*, in dealing "*with a conflation of worrying trends – the increase in official secrecy, the growth of the nuclear industry and the power of Whitehall*", struck a nerve in audiences. He continued: "*In our story we show that plutonium has become a means whereby civil servants can maintain and increase their power base, and this produces a momentum which leads inexorably towards the growth of the state within the state*" (quoted in Petley 1988: 96). Such views were endorsed at the *Financial Times*, which proclaimed that it was:

Kennedy Martin's deep concern about nuclear proliferation and about the implications of Reagan's Star Wars plans for the future of mankind

which lifts this series out of the general run of the crime thriller and jus-
tifies its comparison with the single plays of the 1960s.
(11 December 1985)

The American *Village Voice*, although disappointed at the drama's gender politics constrained within a traditional "*nuclear family*", was bowled over by the serial's narrative complexity and maturity, claiming it as "*television's first major dramatic work, structured specifically in terms of the medium's possibilities and limitations*" (22 March 1988).[677] The *Independent* boldly claimed that, "*After* Darkness *people wrote differently for television*" (17 May 1992), and television historian Andrew Pixley has gone so far as to judge *Edge of Darkness* "*possibly the finest BBC drama ever made*" (2003a: 52). The acclaimed serial was nominated for 11 British Academy of Film and Television Arts Television Awards, winning six, including Best Drama Series/Serial and Best Actor for Bob Peck.[678]

Secret State, a four-part dramatisation broadcast on Channel 4 in 2012, was adapted from the novel *A Very British Coup*. The drama was updated to make it relevant to the political landscape of the new millennium, and one which could no longer tolerate the idea of a traditional socialist Labour leader winning a landslide election victory. It plays as an exciting modern conspiracy thriller, in which a newly installed prime minister, Tom Dawkins (Gabriel Byrne), has to deal with the criminal irresponsibility of an American multinational oil corporation which seeks to suppress a major tragedy at one of its plants in the north-east of England. Dawkins, trying to establish the truth and gain fair compensation for local families, and which also includes the killing of the previous prime minister in a seeming terrorist attack, is drawn into a web of deceit involving his own Secret Intelligence Service (SIS), senior military figures, Cabinet colleagues and leading financiers. Although the party he represents is not named, Dawkins is a populist who strives for transparent government and accountability; however, the forces of reaction in collusion with powerful multi-nationals conspire to frustrate him and pursue an agenda of selfish, unregulated finance capitalism. The thoughtful Byrne was attracted to a drama that raised questions; one that touches on almost imperceptible, subterranean changes in the British political landscape, such as the collusion between government and big business; the nature of the relationship between the media and government; the rise of terrorism and the equivalent rise of surveillance; what constitutes integrity in a politician; what does a government choose to reveal, and how does it cover up; what is and is not in the interests of the public; can there be transparency in politics; and the influence of a huge corporate interest on government. And, in this particular story, "*the development of a highly dangerous fuel*".[679]

Reviewers were generally unimpressed, finding the politics and political characterisations improbable, and were unnecessarily harsh towards a sometimes thoughtful drama in the judgment that the *"real world has been abandoned. It's been sexed-up and Spookified for the attention-deficit 21st century, with big explosions and downed planes, spy-cams pointing every which way, and glamorous young staff at GCHQ. Heaps of fun, but not a whole lot more"* (*Guardian*, 7 November 2012). *Secret State* launched with a disappointing viewing figure of 1.25 million, well down on Channel 4's recent average market share (*Guardian*, 8 November 2012). Joseph Oldham maintains that the failure of *Secret State* lies in its wedding to the traditional conspiracy thriller-style of the 1980s, coming over as rather *"bland"* in the post-*24* age, but that it does reveal that the *"sense that the conspiracy embedded in the political culture has shifted from a fundamental vision of how Britain should be run, as in* A Very British Coup, *to one in which the British politics are simply a tool for private agendas that lie somewhere entirely separate from national concerns"* (2014: 99).

A few good men

The Official Secrets Act is not used against those who cause genuine breaches of security. It is used as a deterrent against those whose words might set in motion criticism of the privileges, inefficiency and arbitrary power of the secret security bureaucracy.
(Jock Kane, whistle blower and former officer of the Government Communications Headquarters, GCHQ, 1980, quoted in Aubrey 1981: 140)

Spyship (1983), *Defence of the Realm* (1986), *The Whistle Blower* (1987), *Hidden City* (1988) and *Hidden Agenda* (1991) feature individual investigators – journalists, a bereaved father, an educational statistician, an honest policeman – who turn up malpractice; with their efforts and sometimes self-sacrifice leading to the public exposure of government cover-ups and security abuses. As Joseph Oldham has commented, the

> *classic form of the conspiracy thriller is frequently characterised by narratives in which the protagonist, in addition to uncovering the truth, must also strive to put it into the public domain, with the implication that the subsequent public reaction may prove the most productive force for affecting positive change.*
> (2017: 151)

The form, therefore, promotes the importance of the free press, and journalists are, unsurprisingly, prominent in the genre. The New Hollywood's *All*

The President's Men (US, 1976) is typical, yet influential, in this respect. That is certainly the case in the dramas discussed in this section; however, the oppression is such that the narrative often silences the protagonist and typically feels able to offer only a mildly optimistic ending.

Spyship initially appeared as a novel written by Tom Keene and Brian Haynes first published in 1980. The story takes place early in 1974 when a state of the art fishing trawler *Arctic Pilgrim* is mysteriously lost with all hands in the inhospitable northern waters of the Barents Sea. The ship had been unofficially conducting top secret electronic surveillance on behalf of Naval Intelligence as a part of an ongoing TROJAN programme and had been involved in an incident with a Soviet submarine and a Royal Naval frigate.[680] British Intelligence, in collusion with Soviet Intelligence, mounts a cover-up to avoid an embarrassing and damaging scandal. The local townspeople of Hull, the home port of the ship, begin to ask difficult questions and Colonel Francis Mann–Quartermain, the Deputy of Intelligence, strives to contain the potentially harmful secrets. A brother of a shipmate who launches a public campaign to investigate the tragedy is framed and silenced through having stolen goods planted on him; an awkward girlfriend of a trawler man is murdered and crucial evidence is destroyed; a partisan chairman is appointed to the official inquiry into the shipwreck; and a secretary at the trawler company is killed in a car crash to keep her from speaking with the press.

The investigation into the disaster is taken up by Martin Taylor, a local journalist who lost his father on the *Arctic Pilgrim*. He soon attracts the attention of Mann–Quartermain and the deadly killer Evans is put onto him. Taylor fights off a murderous attack in his apartment, his girlfriend Suzy is abused when she refuses to tell Evans where Taylor is hiding, and the reporter narrowly avoids being run over at the docks before he escapes to North Norway to pursue his investigation. There, he is able to piece together the final clues to the mystery, kill Evans during yet another murderous attack, and return to Hull to confront the conspiracy. Back home, Taylor is interviewed by Sir Peter Hillmore, the Head of SIS who is appalled at Mann–Quartermain's unauthorised and illegal methods, and who appeals to the journalist to suspend his investigation in the national interest. Meanwhile, Mann–Quartermain, who has privately been told by Sir Peter that he is quietly to retire, kills the head of the Service with a car bomb made to look like a terrorist attack, and assumes the leadership of the SIS at the behest of a government ignorant of his crimes. Sometime in the future and in an ambiguous ending, Martin Taylor sits at his typewriter and nervously begins to compose the tragedy of the *Arctic Pilgrim*.

In an 'Author's Note' which precedes the novel, Keene and Haynes point to the "*facts and rumours*" relating to several sinking's, collisions and disappearances of ships off British shores; especially the loss of the Hull trawler *Gaul* in 1974 with 36 lives, a modern 1,106-ton factory freezer vessel specially designed for Arctic waters, and which some local people claimed was gathering intelligence, carried Royal Navy personnel, was involved in electronic warfare and had been boarded by the Soviet Navy.[681] The ship disappeared at the time of a NATO exercise in the area.[682] This was seemingly the reverse of the case of the famous 'Whisky on the Rocks' incident in 1981, when a Soviet Whisky-class submarine engaged in a surreptitious probe near a Swedish naval base ran aground and enabled the Swedes to conduct an inspection. Keene and Haynes had been the researchers on the television investigative documentary 'The Mystery of the *Gaul*' (BBC, 1975). More widely, it was claimed that deliberate provocation has in fact become a regular feature of SIGINT work itself. Allegedly, ships and aircraft have been sent into foreign sea- and airspace, often with the frightening intention of triggering the other side's defence communications into action, thus giving the distant monitors a truer picture of enemy capability. "*In some cases*", it has been asserted, "*ships have been attacked, submarines have collided and planes have been shot down in this deadly game of cat and mouse*" (Aubrey 1981: 136).

In *Spyship*, the cover-up of the tragedy and the perpetration of a deception is a collusion between British Intelligence, the government, the Royal Navy and the Russians; while the policy of intimidation and murder is that of an independently operating Deputy of SIS, acting on his own initiative and warped sense of the national interest. The rogue nature of Mann–Quartermain slightly mutes the 'secret state' element of the story; however, a chilling irony is that Mann–Quartermain is able to outwit Sir Peter Hillmore and assume the role of Head of SIS from where he will be able to continue his covert and illegal operations in the complete ignorance of the politicians.[683]

The six-part television drama serial *Spyship* was broadcast on the BBC in 1983, adapted by Keene and Haynes with the help of the experienced James Mitchell and Robert Smith. The drama followed the story quite closely, but interestingly imposed a bleaker ending. Colonel Main (the name is simplified for the drama, and the name of the trawler is altered to the *Caistor*) is able to assume the leadership of SIS through convincing his political superiors that it was Hillmore who ran the network of illegal agents. He is then left free to continue his murderous campaign and the final scene of the drama has Martin Taylor and Suzy blown-up in their car to silence them forever. The drama, shot on location around the fishing port of Hull and in Norway, is approached in a naturalistic manner. Producer Colin Rogers claimed at the time that all got involved in it,

> *because we saw it as a drama about real people facing up to things*
> *which take place at a much higher level, which they never get a chance*
> *to confront, even though they're affected – people reacting to a situation*
> *they're put in, and fighting back.*
> (Quoted in the *Radio Times*, 5-11 November 1983)

Commenting at the time of the broadcast, writer Brian Haynes reiterated that, "*A lot of very strange things happened in the Gaul inquiry*", adding that, "*People were persuaded to stop asking questions*" (quoted in the *Daily Express*, 5 November 1983). The broadcast of *Spyship* came in the wake of the mystery shrouding Korean Air Lines Flight 007 shot down in Soviet airspace on 1 September 1983 which granted topicality to the serial.

Reviews of *Spyship* were varied. With nautical puns ready to hand, the *Daily Mail* thought the first episode was "*well launched*" and admirably concentrated on "*depth of characterisation*" rather than "*Boy's Own shenanigans*"; while the *Daily Express* experienced "*that sinking feeling*", in contrast finding the first episode "*workmanlike*" and "*distinctly underwhelming … for such a thundering good story*" (both 10 November 1983). The *Guardian* felt *Spyship* was produced "*with more love and money than thrillers usually get unless they are written by Le Carré*", and made effective use of locations. However, "*exception*" was taken regarding the use of "*real tragedy*" for "*entertainment*", the critic "*unpersuaded that the loss of a real ship and real people is a suitable subject, even a suitable starting point, for a spy thriller*"; and while this seems to ignore the potential for political critique in the drama, the reviewer conceded that such an approach gave "*this thriller unusual tenderness and perhaps, truth*" (10 November 1983). Once it had digested the whole serial, the *Daily Mail* noted the "*chilling simplicity and painful presentation of human loss in the face of bureaucratic cold-bloodedness*" which left the viewer "*in no doubt about the presence of evil*" (24 November 1983).

Case file 2: *Defence of the Realm* (1986)

> *The Security Service is part of the Defence Forces of the country. Its task*
> *is the Defence of the Realm as a whole, from external and internal dangers arising from attempts at espionage and sabotage, or from actions of persons and organisations whether directed from within or without the country, which may be judged to be subversive to the state.*
> (Directive of the Home Secretary to the Director-General of the Security Service, 24 September 1952)
>
> *MI5 does not kill people.*
> (Stella Rimington 2002: 163)

National Security is what Her Majesty's Government say it is.
(Gill 1994: 98)

In 1984, Lord Fraser, a senior law lord, had stated that in his view, "*The deci-sion on whether the requirements of national security outweigh the duty of fairness in any particular case is for the government and not for the courts*" (quoted in Hollingsworth and Fielding 1999: 248). Two years later, the brood-ing conspiracy thriller *Defence of the Realm* was released into cinemas, a mo-tion picture which dramatised the extrajudicial tendencies of the 'secret state'. The film was directed by David Drury, produced at David Puttnam's Enigma Films, from an original screenplay by Martin Stellman dating back in part to 1980. Hack journalist Nick Mullen (Gabriel Byrne) is doggedly pursuing a sex and politics scandal involving a prominent left-wing politician, Dennis Mark-ham (Ian Bannen), who, echoes of Profumo, has seemingly been sharing the favours of a young woman with an East German embassy official. Fellow journalist Vernon Bayliss (Denholm Elliot), a friend of Markham and former communist, disbelieves the accusations and mysteriously dies while secre-tively pursuing his own enquiry. Mullen, realising he could be a tool for disin-formation, now switches his attention to the conspiracy, discovers material previously supplied to Bayliss by a whistle blower within government which reveals that Markham has been framed by MI5 to silence him from asking awkward questions in parliament, and slowly unravels a massive government cover-up of a near-nuclear accident at an American USAF base in East Anglia. Business interests being more important than the truth, Mullen is prevented from publishing his explosive story by the owner of the newspaper who has a financial stake in defence contracts, and the reporter is brought in for interro-gation by the Security Service. Refusing to answer its questions and maintaining the right for freedom of information, the reporter is unexpected-ly released. In a shock ending, Mullen and Nina Beckman (Greta Scacchi), Markham's secretary who has reluctantly come to help the investigation, die in a mysterious explosion in Nick's apartment, seemingly the victims of bu-reaucratic murder. However, Nina has been able to post evidence of the con-spiracy to French and German newspapers and a major scandal is visited on the Conservative government. The movie's publicity provocatively asked: "*How far will some people go in defence of the realm?*"

The film counts as a minor triumph in the British film renaissance of the first half of the 1980s. However, it stands as a leading example of the 'secret state' thriller which came to prominence in the same period and the picture has been designated by Julian Petley as "*Britain's first fully-fledged contempo-rary paranoia movie*" (1988: 95). *Defence of the Realm* drew on the tradition of European political thrillers, the film-makers specifically acknowledging the influence of Francesco Rosi's *Illustrious Corpses* (screened as a model for the cast and crew on the eve of production), and reconfigured the style for a British political and security context which had created a persecution mania among liberals and leftists. *Defence of the Realm*, as John Hill has pointed out, also drew on a liberal Hollywood tradition of journalist movies in which a reporter-hero exposes wrongdoing in high places (1999: 147).[684] The debt is made evident through the placing of a still on a notice board in the newsroom from the most successful of these films, *All The President's Men*, featuring Robert Redford and Dustin Hoffman as the legendary investigative reporters Woodward and Bernstein.[685] It has since emerged that the Security Service did indeed target leftists in the media who were seen as subversive and a threat to 'national interests' (Murray 1993: 91, 99, 251-271).

The picture attracted generally favourable reviews, with widespread praise for the performances of Byrne and Elliot, although there were some quibbles regarding a disjointed narrative structure (*Daily Express*, 3 January 1986). The *Financial Times* judged it the "*best film yet to show us how our liberties are being picked off*". An effective dissection of the "*moral crumminess*" of political integrity in Britain, the story, while seeming "*far-fetched*", managed a "*subversive coherence that is truly disturbing*" (3 January 1986). *The Times* found *Defence of the Realm* "*something quite new for the national cinema*", an accurate record of contemporary paranoia, with the portrayal of menace "*in cosily familiar characters and circumstances*" and orders to kill "*uttered in cultivated English voices*" (3 January 1986). The populist *Star* praised a "*sharp, all-too-believable attack on Press power, political trickery and Secret Service skullduggery in modern Britain*" (4 January 1986) and the *Observer* found the picture a superior British example of the paranoid thriller (5 January 1986). The *Spectator* commended "*one of the best political thrillers in recent years*", a "*purely cinematic*" achievement who's "*preoccupations with the secret state make for effective drama*", and which possessed "*imaginative force*" precisely because it represented a "*powerful unease*" (11 January 1986). The *New Musical Express* welcomed an "*absorbing and thought-provoking film, whose hard-edged visuals are matched by its incisive insights*" (4 January 1986).

Defence of the Realm was less-well received in America. The *Village Voice* judged it "*Atmospheric but flimsy*": "*not the sort of thriller that holds up to reasonable analysis*" (3 February 1987). The *New York Times* was even harsher, dismissing the film as a "*breathless but largely incomprehensible mess*" (16 January 1987). The *New Yorker* recognised the movie as an example of paranoiac realism: an English equivalent of *All the President's Men*, "*but darker and more oppressive*". However, it found the picture lacked action, "*just about all plot*", which failed "*to give you a good time*" (9 March 1987).

The *Monthly Film Bulletin* was surprised to find a film prepared to broach all sorts of political questions. In particular, the *"politicisation of the security services, the issues raised by the presence of American nuclear bases in Great Britain, and the reasons why Britain's press is so monolithically conservative"*. In the process, *Defence of the Realm "sheds light on a vast web of unsavoury events, ranging from the American bases to Fleet Street, from the hushed world of gentleman's clubs where secret political deals are struck to the anonymous, windowless rooms and corridors where faceless functionaries deal with those deemed a threat to the defence of the realm"* (November 1985: 338). The film, as with *Edge of Darkness, The Whistle Blower* and *A Very British Coup*, expressed an anxiety regarding the consequences of the American presence and its effect on the British system of government, and apprehension about Britain becoming an *"increasingly secretive and authoritarian American satellite"* (Petley 1988: 95). The acting is uniformly excellent in the picture and the cinematography and staging create an artfully *noir*ish ambience for the paranoid theme. Roger Deakins who photographed the picture and an admirer of the French crime films of Jean-Pierre Melville aimed to make *Defence of the Realm* visually unlike anything that had come out of Britain recently (*Sight and Sound*, Summer 1985: 191). A case in point is the scene of Nick's abduction and interrogation, which bears some similarity to the treatment of Agee and Hosenball who had to present themselves to an officially appointed committee at a gentleman's club in Pall Mall, *"A vast, eerily empty building of endless carpeted corridors, decorated ceilings and crystal chandeliers"*. In judgement sat the *"three wise men"*, and incredibly, *"There was no evidence, no witness from the security services, no legal structure whatsoever"* (Aubrey 1981: 104).[686] The visual stylistics of *noir* was ideal for the expression of largely hidden, repressive and manipulative states in British political culture, and for the ill-defined anxieties and sense of impotence of the public.

While boldly political during a controversial period for British Intelligence and the service's questionable relationship with the government – there was a Commons Home Affairs Committee inquiry into Special Branch early in 1985 at which there was repeated questioning about the nature and extent of files kept by the force and during which a senior police officer expressed the hope of *"repolishing the image"* of the Branch (*Guardian*, 24 January 1985) – it is perhaps reassuring, or at least ironic, of the true strength of democracy that *Defence of the Realm* was completed with government finance channelled through the National Film Finance Corporation. The title derives from the Defence of the Realm Act passed in 1914 at the outset of World War I and relates to wide-ranging powers assumed by the government, which some have criticised as authoritarian and mostly aimed at social control. *Films and Filming* commented on the rarity of a *"good British political thriller"*, finding that *Defence of the Realm "neatly skirts most of the traps that make British thrillers dull and predictable*" (December 1985: 40-41). The *Observer* felt the timely film fed "*our current fears and anxieties into its nightmarish narrative*" (5 January 1986).

The novel *The Whistle Blower* was the first thriller by John Hale and published in 1984. At the heart of the story is a major security breach at GCHQ in Cheltenham, the agency responsible for providing signals intelligence. Dodgson, a senior mathematician, has been trading secrets with the Soviets for 10 years. This only comes to light when the man is arrested for possessing child pornography. The British and American intelligence services suspect two further officials within GCHQ, but cannot agree on their identity. The British, moreover, fear a KGB disinformation plot designed to drive a wedge between the Atlantic partners. However, on the prompting of the Americans who are acting on information supplied by two defectors, two of the suspects meet with 'accidents'.[687] Into this scenario of treachery and retribution drops Frank Jones, whose son Bob is a Russian linguist at GCHQ. The young man dies unexpectedly after falling from the roof of his apartment. Gradually, Frank begins to piece together a conspiracy, in which it is revealed that Bob had become disillusioned with the ways of Western intelligence and consequently a security risk. The two storylines slowly begin to merge for the father. He learns that Bob had intended to publish an exposé of the secret work of GCHQ and reveal all he knew about 'dirty tricks'. Frank is 'warned off' his investigation, but slowly compiles damning evidence against the Security Service. Meanwhile, Dodgson is further interrogated, and through a mixture of deceit and mind manipulation, he finally reveals the two other traitors. As a consequence a minor official of GCHQ is 'posted' to Cyprus, and although protesting a frame-up is arrested for dealing in heroin and incarcerated in a Turkish prison; while a junior minister is afforded greater courtesy and unexpectedly 'retires' for health reasons. Finally, Frank draws the two threads together: Bob had been suspected of giving secrets to the Soviets, and the authorities, fearing another scandal and further embarrassment with the Americans, had 'removed' the problem. Virtually impotent, Frank arranges with a radical journalist and television filmmaker to produce a hard-hitting television drama exposing the tragedy of his son and the sickness at the heart of the British Security Service and its allies. It was, after all, "*the best an ordinary man could do*".

The Whistle Blower drew together several of the stock elements of the 'secret state' thriller. There is a complete evasion of private rights and civil liberties in an ubiquity of surveillance, eavesdropping and phone-tapping; a dramatic representation of the 'panoptic state' in which "*the subject of control is seen without seeing, while the agents of control see without being seen*" (Gill 1994: 81). There is a virtual absence of ethical and moral standards within the intelligence services, and widespread use is made of criminals, illegal entries, destruction of evidence, intimidation and liquidation. In an outburst that is part of the back-story, Bob states: "*They are not answerable. And they know they are not*". The narrative makes mention of contemporary events and individuals, which adds to the realism and authenticity of the material. There is reference to the 'whistle blower' Philip Agee, the 'defector' from the CIA who had taken the lid off American intelligence with his *Inside the Company* in 1975. The actions of Bob Jones mirror those of John Berry, the disillusioned former signals operative who was prosecuted in the 'ABC Trial' of 1978 for daring to talk with journalists, of Jock Kane a former SIGINT officer who published revelations in the *New Statesman* in 1980 concerning inefficiency and corruption at GCHQ, and of Dennis Mitchell who had resigned from GCHQ in 1984 in protest of the trade union ban and was publicly critical of the service before a court injunction was imposed on him. The 'faked' escape of Dodgson from jail is based on the famous breakout by George Blake in 1966 (it is even the same prison, Wormwood Scrubs), and Dodgson is based on Geoffrey Prime, a signals officer at GCHQ convicted in the early 1980s of charges of espionage and child sexual abuse. An immediate context for the story was the successful prosecution of Sarah Tisdall for leaking secrets from the Foreign Office in 1983. The critique of security, intelligence and privilege is channelled through the character of Frank Jones, "*ordinary taxpayer, Tory voter*", an undemonstrative patriot who had completed his national service and flew in the Korean War, and who until recently had "*lived in a state of innocence*". He serves as a surrogate for the 'innocent' reader who is likely to be shocked out of their complacency. *The Listener* judged the book "*excellent*", claiming that there had not been a "*more chilling first thriller for years*" (10 January 1985).

The Whistle Blower was filmed in 1987, starred Michael Caine as Frank Jones and was directed by Simon Langton who had previously directed the acclaimed television dramatisation of John le Carré's novel *Smiley's People* for the BBC in 1982. It retains many of the settings, dialogue and characterisations from the novel. The most substantial revisions now have Bob Jones (Nigel Havers) killed so that the Americans can be presented with a scapegoat and the British can shield a more highly placed traitor whose exposure would cause a major embarrassment, a more active role for the lefty journalist Bill Pickett who is eliminated for his pains, and a new more activist ending which has Frank confront the high-ranking 'mole' within British Intelligence, extract a confession and symbolically disappear into the crowds of Remembrance Day with the possibility that he will publish the truth.[688] Some critics noted a similarity with the Hollywood political thriller *Missing* (US, 1982), as both feature a father's impatience with their son's leftism and who initially hold a touching faith in their country and government (*Films and Filming*, May

1987: 43). The location shooting in Cheltenham caused some embarrassment when GCHQ advised staff against taking part as extras in the production. It was reported that management at the base, in a manner not inconsistent with events in the film, had "*warned all 6,000 workers that the film is anti-GCHQ and to take part would be 'undesirable'*". Jack Hart, spokesman for the banned unions at the facility at Cheltenham replied: "*It is a typically stupid and silly move by the management – what possible harm could it do for employees to take part?*" (*Guardian* and *Mirror*, 28 October 1985).

Reviews were mixed but largely supportive and many felt that the overexposed Caine had returned to form with his sympathetic portrayal of Frank. *Monthly Film Bulletin* judged *The Whistle Blower* a "*fairly tough outing in an apposite genre*" (May 1987: 158-159) and the *Daily Mail* applauded a "*mainstream thriller by, for, and about adults*" (29 May 1987). Some critics remarked on the contemporary relevance of the picture. *The Telegraph* appreciated a script that aimed "*consistently sharp comments on the state of the nation since Blunt*" (29 May 1987), the *Sunday Express* the artful construction of a "*sinister sense of an unelected secret elite*", while the *Sunday Times* claimed that the shock effect of the film had been "*softened by recent revelations*" (both 31 May 1987). The left-wing *Morning Star* appreciated an "*air of authenticity*" which put the film "*streets ahead of the many formula spy-thrillers*". Given the history of official manipulation, the reviewer "*found no difficulty in swallowing all the devious dirty tricks shown in the film*" (12 June 1987).[689] In a longer and more thoughtful piece, the *Evening Standard* noted the "*cynicism*" and "*secrets*" that had recently spilled out all over the press. It accepted the "*creepy plausibility*" of the story and the film's imaginative portrayal of an England where the intelligence elite "*obey no law but their own class ties in fixing the Who's Who of political murder*". In indicting "*obsessive Government secrecy and unmonitored Intelligence dirty tricks*", the paper boldly claimed: "*it identifies real places, raises specific security issues and all but names actual people*". In conclusion, it suggested that: "*if the rulers of the 'Secret State' see fit, we ourselves as well as our liberties will be done in without so much as an official blush*" (28 May 1987). *Sunday Today* judged *The Whistle Blower* a "*gutsy, moving and exciting film*", and admitted to be sufficiently convinced, "*that our real security forces could behave in this way. Indeed, it makes us wonder whether they are doing so already*" (31 May 1987). Reporting on a "*fine political thriller*", *What's On* noted that the filmmakers cleverly avoided the stock conventions of *film noir* and set the story in ordinary, day-lit, seemingly-innocent locations. After all, it noted,

> it is the half-lies, procrastinations and dissemblings of apparently 'ordinary' people, Government agents of the most trivial kind, that create an atmosphere of unease, distrust and eventually naked danger, that

somehows packs an even greater punch than an ambiance of thugs and melodramatic shadows.

"*That it is the more credible*" it continued, "*heightens the unease of the viewer, for the acts portrayed are doubtless but the tip of an iceberg as far as British 'official' secrecy is concerned*" (25 August 1987).

Not all papers were accepting of the picture's thesis, *The Telegraph*, while admiring a competent "*anti-heroic political thriller*", couldn't stomach the claim that the intelligence services, to preserve the American connection, would murder British citizens. "*The idea may chime with current paranoia about 'the secret world' and unease in the Atlantic Alliance*" it asserted, but the idea "*robs The Whistle Blower of any claim to be more than inverted James Bondery in which friends are turned into foes*" (31 May 1987).[690] Larry Ceplair writing in *Cineaste*, coming from the opposite political spectrum, also rejected the "*conceptual flaw*" of the picture. "*Common sense, John le Carré's novels and a host of memoirs*", he asserted:

> *make it impossible for a reasonably intelligent viewer to believe that the apparatus that promoted and protected Philby, Maclean, Burgess, Blunt and, in all likelihood, a fifth, higher-ranking mole, and that has failed to keep its loyal 'spycatchers' quiet, is capable of a decisive, efficient elimination of civil servants and civilians who have become suspicious.*

Suspicion of incompetence in the intelligence apparatus, he maintained, "*is cause for much more than a haughty public denial and a private sigh*" (1987/88: 74). On balance, Ceplair's observations are worth heeding. After all, the standard leftist critique of the Security Service was that it was officered by incompetents protected by a veil of secrecy. If so, it was hard to credit the 'secret state' as a ruthless perpetrator of bureaucratic murder, efficiently going about the elimination of subversives and irritants. This, in fact, was an observation made in *Hidden City*, discussed presently. There is the possibility, of course, that the Left was misguided and MI5 was happy to maintain the smokescreen of ineptitude and bungling?

Hidden City, a Film 4 production written and directed by Stephen Poliakoff, was first screened on Channel 4 in 1988. A quirky variant on the 'secret state' thriller, the story concerned James Richards (Charles Dance), a stuffy yet modestly famous educational statistician who is dragooned into a web of intrigue by the excitable and pushy former film librarian Sharon Newton (Cassie Stuart). Newton has come across mysterious and sinister footage seemingly depicting the abduction of a woman, spliced into government films with such innocuous titles as *The Hedgerows of England* and *Hop Pickers in Kent*, and requires the well-connected Richards to unlock some of the doors obstructing the path to solving the mystery. Very soon, heavies from the Security Service are intimidating the statistician, and both Richards and Newton's apartments are roughly turned over in an unauthorised search. Eventually, the unlikely pair piece together the secreted film, and trace the mysterious hospital ward, now deserted, which features in the final chilling scenes. The evidence seems to reveal a massive government cover-up of an atomic accident in the 1940s, the ward used to house the injured men, and the abducted woman a wife who is brought to confront the horror inflicted on her husband. Other menacing scenes in films dating from the 1950s, of a man and a woman blindfolded, interrogated and seemingly killed, remain unexplained, but hint at sinister experiments conducted under the title of OPERATION MAGNIFICAT. Richards and Newton discard the evidence they have collected and wander onto the streets of London dreaming of other official secrets they might uncover.

Hidden City is an unconventional conspiracy thriller, the emphasis less on credible thrills and more on *"uncanny coincidences"*, the eccentric pairing of Richards and Newton and their unusual adventure, and art film aspirations (Nelson 2011: 203). Sharon intuits the likely meaning of the drama when she realises that the authorities are, *"So drowning in secrets, they can't remember where the important ones are anymore"*. The search for evidence by the amateur investigators reveals the 'hidden city', extensive tunnel systems below the streets of London, a city of forgotten secrets, in which are stored enormous quantities of low-grade government documents, a huge municipal incinerator that consumes the excreta of government departments, and above ground a vast refuse tip to which classified papers and records are mistakenly consigned. It is at the rubbish tip looking for a missing film that Richards absently picks up some discarded medical records which constitute the secret evidence about the accident which the authorities wish to remain hidden.[691] The story and imagery are obsessive about 'waste'. The drama constantly hints at secret, submerged worlds below the streets of the city: a decrepit section of the London Underground which holds government waste waiting to be disposed of; secretive masons disappearing into their underground lair[692]; a derelict briefly glimpsed lying in a storm drain; each image suggestive of an unacknowledged labyrinth stretching beneath our feet, an apt metaphor for the clandestine secret services which operate silently, invisibly and subterraneanly. As Poliakoff expressed his motivation, *"if you scratch the surface the city becomes a dark and strangely glamorous place full of hidden tunnels and alleyways, built by a society that is addicted to secrecy"* (*Hidden City* press book). A possible influence on this aspect of the drama could be Paul Laurie's *Beneath the City Streets*, the recently updated edition of 1979 falling foul of the 'secret state' for divulging sensitive information regarding the network of underground communications and survival tunnels to be activated in the event of a nuclear attack or accident. While the inspiration for the clinic treating the victims of the radioactive accident came from a designer Poliakoff had previously worked with, whose father had worked at the Dounreay Nuclear Power Development Establishment and had become contaminated whilst cleaning out a pipe. As a consequence "*he was put in some kind of special unit and this turned out to be in Bond Street*" (*Guardian*, 7 July 1988). The film was premiered at the Venice Film Festival in 1987.

Hidden City was largely judged as a flawed directorial début for Stephen Poliakoff. Many were put off by the "*crass*" acting of Cassie Stuart, perhaps unaided by an inexperienced director (*The Telegraph*, 3 September 1987; *Independent*, 23 June 1988). For the *Guardian*, the film was "*dramatically rather ramshackle*", although, in terms of the filmmaker's "*open attack on a society which permits its bureaucrats so many official secrets*", it constituted a "*brave attempt to make a thriller that is relevant both to the times we live in and the city in which it is set*" (23 June 1988). The *Financial Times* was annoyed at a "*portentous essay in Teach Yourself Paranoia*" (24 June 1988); the *Sunday Telegraph* was more receptive to "*wild unsubstantiated allegations about hushed-up nuclear accidents*". "*Still, as paranoia goes*", it delighted, "*this simply whizzes*"; the *Scotsman* despaired of the "*depressing scene of police statism*" (27 June 1988); and the *Sunday Times* recommended it as "*Good fodder for paranoids*" (both 26 June 1988). The *New Musical Express* dismissed the picture as a "*lumpen version of Terry Gilliam's Brazil*" (25 June 1988) and further commentary in the *Guardian* noted down the picture as a "*parable for the Peter Wright era*" (7 July 1988). The *Times Literary Supplement* felt that a promising situation somewhat lost its way, "*as if Klute … were turning into an adventure of Enid Blyton's Famous Five*" (1-7 July 1988). As for several other 'secret state' thrillers, some of the most insightful commentaries came from Alexander Walker who wrote two pieces on the film at the *Evening Standard*. He enthusiastically embraced *Hidden City* as a "*jabbing drama about the obsessive secrecy of England*", of the authorities "*endlessly trying to cover up the past by destroying it*", and the picture offering a "*powerful metaphor for the masonic secrecy cloaking our rulers*" (1987). In a review following the film's television broadcast, Walker noted the contemporary relevance of the drama, pointing out that: "*If the Official Secrets Act needed any more reduction to absurdity than it is receiving at the moment, this film supplies it. If the Government won't let the facts be published, then it will get the fiction it deserves*". His conclusion that, "*Poliakoff's vision works so well because deference to authority and a passion for secrecy are imbedded in the bones of the Brits*" (1988).

In contrast to the typical paranoid thriller, the malevolent forces of secret government in *Hidden City* are not ruthlessly proficient. In the time-honoured tradition of British bureaucracy, the secret servants are bungling and inefficient, classified documents are misfiled, mislaid, misdesignated and inadvertently sent for disposal, and a security officer, in time-honoured civil service tradition, casually interrupts a suspenseful search, which almost nabs him Richards, for a scheduled tea-break. A number of insiders and politicians have referred to the incompetence of the security services. The persecuted journalist Crispin Aubrey has made the point that it is "*only through their mistakes*" that anything emerges from the secret world (1981: 50), and there has long been a suspicion that the intelligence services were the dumping ground for the lesser-able public-school-types who couldn't make it in Whitehall or the City (Deacon 1984: 446). Even the official Radcliffe Report (1962-64) on the intelligence services referred to MI5 and MI6 as the "*natural home of the incompetent*" (quoted in Carter 2001: 399).

Obvious influences on *Hidden City* are Antonioni's *Blow-Up* (1966), a classic of 1960s art cinema and another enigmatic London film that similarly involved a possible conspiracy/mystery embedded within a piece of film, and Terry Gilliam's *Brazil* (1985), in which a malevolent state, waste and administrative inefficiency combine.[693] "*Ultimately*", as Robin Nelson has observed, "*the outcome of the mystery ... is of secondary importance to* Hidden City's *cinematic evocation of a time and place*" (2011: 206): London in the 1980s and its sense of entropy; of frustrated potential, of leaky buildings, accumulated waste and inept bureaucracy, captured in images desaturated of life and vitality.

In contrast to *Hidden City*, the film *Hidden Agenda* was defiantly social-realist in style. Released in 1991, the picture was written by the Marxist Jim Allen and directed by Ken Loach, Britain's most political filmmaker and proclaimed "*enemy of the Establishment*" (*Guardian*, 8 February 1990). The hard-hitting drama is set in the context of 'The Troubles' in Northern Ireland in the early 1980s. Only two years previously the espionage writer and former spy Anthony Cavendish had remarked on the difficulty of dramatising intelligence issues in the Province, commenting that, "*Ireland, where so much of today's intelligence effort is concentrated, is dangerous ground for film-makers, given the government's hypersensitivity*" (1988).[694] Loach boldly stepped into the breach with a story that involved the shooting in Ulster of Paul Sullivan (Brad Dourif), an American civil liberties lawyer, and the follow-up investigation by Paul Kerrigan (Brian Cox), a senior British police officer with a reputation for honesty and incorruptibility. The Royal Ulster Constabulary (RUC) is obstructive and Kerrigan, working with Ingrid Jessner (Frances McDormand) a civil liberties activist, immediately suspects a cover-up.[695] Paul Harris (Maurice Roëves), a former Military Intelligence officer who had spearheaded controversial 'psy-ops' operations in the Province aimed at blackening the republicans and their supporters, has evidence on tape of a high-level conspiracy and which had been promised to Sullivan. Before Kerrigan can acquire the tape, he is warned off by a senior officer in MI5 and a leading Conservative politician who threaten to ruin the policeman's career and also his marriage through some innocent though potentially compromising photographs of Kerrigan with Jessner. Kerrigan returns to mainland Britain with the names and confessions of the men who carried out the killing of Sullivan offered as scapegoats to protect the wider interests. Meanwhile, Harris is snatched and murdered by the British Security Service; his death made to look like an Irish Republican Army (IRA) retribution killing. Jessner has managed to acquire the tape and in an open ending is in a position to expose the cover-up and conspiracy.

The idea for the picture originated with producer David Puttnam who proposed a film about the John Stalker affair, the senior policeman who headed an inquiry into the alleged shoot-to-kill policy in Northern Ireland. The impetus was lost when Puttnam was dethroned from Columbia Pictures and the project was rescued by the small film company Hemdale (*Observer*, 6 May 1990). Ken Loach had wanted to make a film about the Province for some time, and had recently completed a short documentary for the BBC's *Open Space* series on behalf of the 'Time to Go!' campaign which aimed to get the troops out of Northern Ireland.[696] *Hidden Agenda* was made in a degree of secrecy with the producers fearing adverse reaction and some time passed by as the legal team agonised over the known facts and the implications of the story. Loach had intended to shoot the picture in Northern Ireland, but this was not possible as the producers could not get the necessary financial insurance. Eventually, the guarantors agreed that some of the filming could take place in Belfast providing that it did not involve major dialogue sequences, and some additional shooting also took place in Dublin. As a result, many key scenes were shot in an abandoned Victorian school in Kings Cross, London, which was convenient, provided plenty of natural light, privacy, large rooms and was used for both indoor and outdoor scenes, especially those set at RUC headquarters. Typical of Loach's celebrated method, some local Irish nonactors were used in the production, including local Sinn Fein councillor Jim McAllister. This was ironic as McAllister was banned from speaking on British TV under then current government broadcasting restrictions (*Hidden Agenda* press book).

The backdrop to *Hidden Agenda* was the introduction and extension of 'low intensity' and 'psy-ops' responses by the security forces in Northern Ireland in the 1970s in their dealing with the mounting insurgency and unrest.[697] Among the 'dirty tricks' attributed to the various British intelligence agencies in the province were fabrication of evidence, torture, murder faked to look like 'sectarian' killings, the planting of bombs in Dublin to provoke the Republican Irish government into tougher anti-IRA laws, homosexual seduction and blackmail, 'black' propaganda and disinformation, the use of *agent provocateurs*, fabricating evidence and 'covering up' (Porter 1989: 199). As we have seen, the film drew its specific inspiration from the official inquiry which commenced in 1984, led by John Stalker the Deputy Chief Constable of the Greater Manchester Police, into an alleged 'shoot-to-kill' policy by the Security Service and RUC in Northern Ireland.[698] Stalker was faced with substantial 'non-co-operation' in the Province, not least of all around a tape recording key evidence, and, in what could be construed as obstruction, was removed from the Inquiry following allegations of corruption, charges of which he was later cleared, and significantly no prosecutions followed the publication of the final report.[699] The conspiracy threatened with exposure in the film involved Harris and his 'psy-ops' teams detailed by extremists in the Security Service, business and politics to undermine Edward Heath, the moderate leader of the Conservative Party, destabilise the Labour governments of the mid-1970s, and to blacken the name of the Labour Party leader and sometime Prime Minister Harold Wilson. The aim being to smooth a path for the election of an extreme right-wing leader of the Conservatives, something which came to pass in the late 1970s when Margaret Thatcher assumed the party leadership and became prime minister in 1979. Such treasonable scheming, claimed to have been the rationale of a secret 'psy-ops' operation codenamed 'Clockwork Orange', was alleged in such radical journals as *Lobster*,[700] and argued in such books as *Smear! Wilson and the Secret State*.[701] Several of the characters in the drama have their counterparts in the actual events of the 1970s and 1980s: Harris is a composite of Colin Wallace and Fred Holroyd,[702] two 'whistle blowers' who had served in Military Intelligence; and the smug Tory politician Alec Nevin is a barely-concealed portrait of Airey Neave, a senior advisor to Margaret Thatcher before he was killed by the IRA in 1979. In interview, Ken Loach has made clear his intentions with the film. "*What we tried to do with* Hidden Agenda", he has volunteered, "*was say very clearly to people*",

> '*Look, the British have death squads in Northern Ireland. They have behaved like terrorists and they've used terrorists to carry out killings. They've been involved in the torture of political suspects. And some elements of British Intelligence have used the same black propaganda techniques against British politicians that they've used against the IRA. Now what are we going to do about it?*'
> (Quoted in Fuller 1998: 82)

With regard to the specific security dimension, Loach argued the "*need to reassert the idea of democratic control over intelligence services and security forces who are supposed to be acting on our behalf*" (quoted in the *Guardian*, 8 February 1990). The filmmaker was bound to raise controversy in claiming that British security agencies served the political status quo in the same way as its counter-parts in the right-wing regimes of Nicaragua and Chile. In a separate review in the same newspaper, Derek Malcolm admitted to the "*grim feeling*" engendered by the film that, "*Ulster is Latin America without the weather*". In defence of the controversial viewpoint, co-producer Eric Fellner claimed the story drew on a recent Amnesty International report which concluded that the Third World was not alone in offending against civil liberties and that First World countries were clandestinely infringing rights too. He dismissed accusations that the picture was pro-IRA, stressing that, "*It's about the security forces, not sectarian problems*" (quoted in the *Independent*, 19 April 1990).

Hidden Agenda caused outrage when it was selected as the British entry to the Cannes Film Festival in 1990 and the "*rent-a-quote*" Conservative MP Ivor Stanbrook was wheeled out by the tabloid press where he dutifully declared the film the "*IRA entry*" to the Festival (quoted in the *Sun*, 21 April 1990; *Guardian* 6 May 1990).[703] At the heart of the unseemly public rows and cross-denunciations of an unruly press conference, Ulster-born Alexander Walker, the eminent film critic of the *Evening Standard*, in the words of another journalist, "*extravagantly blew a fuse*" (*City Limits*, 10 January 1991). Walker claimed that *Hidden Agenda* had been rightly received with "*periodic derisive laughter*" by the small group who turned up. However, the left French paper *Libération* refuted the allegation, stating that Walker was "*lying*" and that, "*never before had a press showing been so well attended and an audience so attentive, calm and respectful*" (quoted in the *Guardian*, 28 May 1990).[704] There was a concerted attempt to get the picture withdrawn from Cannes, supposedly led by a Fleet Street newspaper, and a delegation of journalists implored the festival director to withdraw *Hidden Agenda* because they claimed it did not accurately represent Britain (*City Limits*, 10 January 1991). The left-wing *Morning Star* reported on the orchestrated "*smear campaign*" targeting the film (17 May 1990) and European journalists sympathetic to the film took to calling the British tabloids the "*hooligans of the press*" (quoted in the *Guardian*, 28 May 1990). A statement presented at the Festival by the filmmakers claimed it was an "*honest film about the excesses on both sides*", and left it up to the audience to decide who was right (quoted in the *Daily Mail*, 21 April 1990). Fuelling the controversy, *Hidden Agenda* won the Special Jury Prize at the Festival, an act, according to *The Telegraph*, "*inexplicable except as an anti-British gesture*" (13 January 1991).

In Britain, the film was attacked, before it had even been screened, in a "*furore-a-minute campaign*" in the right-wing press (*Financial Times*, 19 May

1990). There were allegations that some cinemas were pressured not to show it (*Guardian*, 17 May 1990). During the time of the Festival screening, the incensed Alexander Walker condemned *Hidden Agenda* as a "*warmed-over dish of virtually every conspiracy theory that has been left on the doorstep of Stormont or Downing Street in the last 20 years*". For him, "*Scarcely a scene in the film has the ring of truth*", and he pointedly dismissed it as an "*absurd film that trades on paranoia but delivers only one political gaffe after another*" (1990). It was common to write off the film as an exercise in left-wing obsession. The *Financial Times* found the whole "*hopelessly overcooked*", with a plot which descended into an "*All-Weather conspiracy Zone*" (19 May 1990). *The Times* felt that the dramatic content remained "*stillborn, smothered in words and the monotonous sound of tubs being thumped*"; *The Telegraph* trumpeted the film as the "*Hard Left version of the Troubles*"; and *Today* complained of the "*worst kind of simplistic, leftist claptrap*" (all 10 January 1991).[705] A further review in *The Telegraph* credited *Hidden Agenda* as "*some bizarre form of science-fiction fantasy*", and that its only future significance "*will be as a museum-piece, to show how sections of the left were, as late as 1990, unable to explain the collapse of Socialism except in terms of half-baked conspiracy theory*" (13 January 1991).[706]

Counter-reviews accepted that there was "*ample evidence*" that something was "*very rotten in the state of Northern Ireland*" (*Time Out*, 9 January 1991). David Pailister, a reporter on Northern Ireland affairs since 1974, confirmed that Ken Loach's research had been "*impeccable*" (1991); while the *Morning Star* believed the story had a "*well established and disturbing parallel in fact*" (11 January 1991). Other critics, sympathetic to the crusading achievements and commitment of Loach, tended to support *Hidden Agenda* as a brave but imperfect film: *The Times* finding it a "*gripping thriller*", but that it tended to "*harangue*" (18 May 1990); *Time Out* considering it an "*important film that deserves to be seen and discussed*", "*urgent*", "*intriguing*" and yet "*flawed*" (2 January 1991); and *City Limits* commending a "*courageous attempt to use the thriller format to criticise the British presence in Northern Ireland, a subject rarely touched upon in the cinema*", but that ultimately, the picture was only "*partially successful*" (10 January 1991). In an unqualified review, the *Scotsman Weekend* praised a work of "*impressive honesty*", a film of "*strength and dignity*", and an "*outstanding thriller*" made with Loach's trademark "*authenticity*" (19 January 1991). Critics tended, though, to prefer recent television dramatisations and docudramas such as *Shoot to Kill, Death on the Rock* (TV 1988) and *Who Bombed Birmingham?* (TV 1990) as more notable critiques of security and of miscarriages of justice.

Hidden Agenda hit the headlines again in 1993 when its premiere on television was abruptly cancelled in the wake of an IRA outrage in Warrington. To some this smacked of censorship. It was argued at the *Guardian* that: "*If there was ever a good time to show a serious political thriller about Northern Ireland on television, it was after the attack*" (23 March 1993); and the *Observer* believed the screening had been "*censored at the very time when it might have had maximum impact*" (28 March 1993). The broadcaster received over 100 calls of protest and a number of readers wrote letters of complaint to the press (*The Times*, 24 March 1993; *Guardian* 24, 25 and 27 March 1993). In a different vein, an inflamed columnist in the tabloid *Sun* lumped "*the worm*" Loach in with the "*TV trendies*" who sprang to the defence of "*convicted killers*", asserting that such men "*should be on trial for treason not drawing fat salaries*" and deserved the "*bullet or the rope*" (7 April 1993).

The individual investigators in this group of stories, the journalists Martin Taylor and Nick Mullen, the statistician James Richards, and the honest policeman Paul Kerrigan are significantly aided and abetted by female companions. The girlfriend Suzy in *Spyship*, the quirky Sharon in *Hidden City*, the civil liberties activist Ingrid Jessner in *Hidden Agenda*, and the personal secretary Nina Beckman in *Defence of the Realm* equally face threat and intimidation. Suzy and Nina pay the ultimate sacrifice; while Ingrid is the final hope for justice.[707] The conceiving of opposition to the state in primarily individual terms, encouraged by the individualising logic of mainstream narrative conventions, is seen as a weakness of such dramas. When cast in the form of a crime thriller with its archetypal character of the investigator as loner, it has been judged a particular problem, "*downplaying more organized, or collective, forms of political protest and opposition*" (Hill 1999: 150-151). A 'few good men', even with female help, are, in the terms of such critical analysis, unlikely to bring about fundamental change outside of the fantasy of fiction.

Conspiracy dramas have also commonly been criticised for their limited diagnosis of the political maladies they deal with. For rightists, they are stories simply to be dismissed as liberal hysteria. In a more sophisticated critique, the commercial thriller and its attachment to narrative conventions of individual agency, inter-personal relations and surface realities are unable to penetrate beyond some vague conspiracy theory to the actual social, economic and political structures which determine the complexity the stories seek to expose. As a consequence, political film historian John Hill asserts, "*it is the idea of a 'conspiracy' that typically becomes the preferred form of 'explanation' in accounting for how the 'secret state' works*"; this, he argues, limits the ideological effectiveness of political thrillers in which nameless conspirators remain a mystery and merely encourages a sense of political powerlessness and paranoia (1999: 152-53). Other critics have followed a similar line of thinking. Larry Ceplair writing in *Cineaste* has claimed that such thrillers "*lack political intelligence*", and that "*maze-like exercises*" in depicting bureaucratic corruption are more likely to be harmful, failing to indict the system and suggesting that the problem lies with personnel and personnel practices, "*A few words of admonition, a little public exposure, and the apparatus will be debugged and ready to continue on its respectable, necessary anticommunist path*" (1987/88: 74). Jerry White, dealing more specifically with *Hidden Agenda*, has suggested a simplification of a complex situation to ensure an appeal to as large an audience as possible; thereby sacrificing the integrity of the significant accusations it poses (1993: 18). The general critique, though, needs to take note of the often hostile responses from right-wing vested interests, especially apparent in the case of *Hidden Agenda*, which seek to prohibit the making and screening of radical dramas, a reaction that suggests such fictions are taken seriously by their opponents. Possible exceptions to the type of criticism offered by Hill, Ceplair and White are the novels *The Volunteers* by Raymond Williams and *The Rebels and the Hostage* by David Craig and Nigel Gray (both 1978), left-cultural thinkers who use the genre to "*explore the dilemma of a left confronted with a coercive bureaucracy and a collusive media*" (Harvie 1990: 237). *The Volunteers*, for example, is a near-future story that inverts the usual alignment of political forces, and here a radical journalist following up the violent death of a government minister unearths a left-wing conspiracy to take power, thus confronting the reporter with a considerable quandary. The story has been called a "*British* All the President's Men, *only much more politically astute*" (*New Internationalist*, July 1991). In another vein, television scholar Joseph Oldham has argued the significance of the conspiracy thriller, claiming that the political qualities of these dramas are best situated in their use of 'genre deconstruction '. In this analysis, the loss of shared cultural values through the abandonment of the social-democratic consensus characteristic of the period is dramatised by means of the collapse of earlier generic certainties, most readily achieved in the extended paranoid narrative of the serial form of such dramas as *Edge of Darkness* and *A Very British Coup* (2017: 127).

Academic historians working in the field of intelligence studies have been wary of conspiracy theories born of excessive levels of official secrecy drawn well beyond operational needs. As biographer Miranda Carter has noted though, "*Espionage seems naturally to attract conspiracy theorists and fantasists*" (2001: xv); and Richard Thurlow has added, "*the unsatisfactory nature of political accountability, which often led to denial of knowledge of operations by the relevant ministers, produced a climate in which conspiracy theories flourished about the alleged illegal activities of MI5 and MI6*" (2000: 183). In the main, however, the accusations, for example, that Sir Roger Hollis, the Director-General of MI5 (1956-65), was a Soviet agent, and that the Security Service mounted a plot against Harold Wilson, have been vigorously dismissed by intelligence academics as "*fictions*" that fail to stand up to rigorous objective scrutiny (Andrew 2010: xx). Political and intelligence scholars tend to invert the conventional arrangements and see circumstances the other way around. Thus, Christopher Andrew and Christopher Moran, in line with traditional right-wing journalists and commentators such as Chapman Pincher, write of Wilson's "*conspiracy paranoia*", "*mania for conspiracy*", "*chronic insecurity*", "*paranoiac suspicions*" and "*persecution mania*" (Andrew 2010: 627-643; Moran 2013: 138-142; Pincher 1991: 67-158).[708] And for Andrew, writing in his 'authorised' history of MI5, the supposed plot against Wilson is dismissed as the "*passionately held but intellectually threadbare conspiracy theories of a disruptive minority*" (2010: 520).[709] Similarly, academic historians have been critical of the 'parapolitics' tradition of writing about the secret services. Christopher Moran describes the aim of the "*Civil Liberties Project*" as investigating the "*heartless aspects of the secret state*", in the process, "*upending established orthodoxy by rendering Western and Eastern European intelligence services as equally contemptuous and equally corrupt*" (2011a: 47). Elsewhere, he complains of the "*para-historian's attempt to annex intelligence to the domain of airport bookstall literature, replete with wayward charges, dubious sourcing and a general tenor of sensationalism*" (2013: 328).[710] Right-wing journalists such as Chapman Pincher explain-away the paranoia and conspiracy-mindedness of leftists and liberals as a natural "*deep distrust of anything savouring of secret police*" (1991: 77).

Such entrenched thinking among specialist scholars has continued to be resisted by critics of the security services, and has recently been challenged by intelligence historian Jon Moran. He argues that to single out Wilson as paranoid is to misjudge the general climate of political paranoia in Britain at the time; that indeed, "*state security was as paranoid as any other actor*" in the period with its obsessions about mole-hunting and in seeing subversives everywhere (2014: 175). The idea of a 'Wilson Plot' has failed to be simply brushed off and credibility has been seen to rest with the "*cumulative evidence*" that has built up over time of a suspected conspiracy (173). The authorised history of MI5 by Christopher Andrew has also been criticised, not least in its dismissive treatment of the 'Wilson Plot', and that evidence was withheld from the study by official command, making it tainted and unreliable.[711] Jon Moran has correctly noted the "*continuing power of ideas of right wing plotting against Wilson*" (161), and in a wider sense, Len Scott and Peter Jackson have reminded us that, "*One reason why there are conspiracy theories is because there are conspiracies*" (2004: 19).

The 'secret state' thriller of the 1980s embodied the political and social anxieties of leftists and civil libertarians in face of the revelations regarding an unchecked and unprincipled secret government; an alliance of intelligence officers, official servants and political reactionaries who failed to conform to the myth of gentlemanly integrity, and construed and promoted a 'national interest' which equated to a blatantly selfish class interest. The alleged nefarious activities of this sinister group were perpetrated behind the impenetrable screen of 'national security' and 'official secrecy', and controversies such as the '*Spycatcher* Affair' briefly lifted the veil and allowed a curious yet anxious public to peek in on the secret world. It was in the very nature of the 'secret state', with its suppressions and denials, that the allegations of foul play could not be dismissed out of hand. Sally Hibbin, the producer of Channel 4's *A Very British Coup*, argued that the vogue for conspiracy thrillers in the 1980s could be explained by the public's changing perceptions of the state. Under Thatcherism and the breakdown of political consensus and the drawing up of battle lines, she suggested, the entity of the state had become more tangible, "*something more obviously* there". The state, its motives and power, was now more of a "*force to be reckoned with*" (quoted in Petley 1988: 96, emphasis in the original). Mick Jackson, the director of *A Very British Coup*, also commented on the relevancy of the conspiracy cycle, noting the "*vague anxiety*" and sense that "*things are spinning out of control*" throughout society. "*Films like* A Very British Coup, Defence of the Realm *and* Edge of Darkness", he claimed, "*helped to legitimise such feelings. They help people to realise that they are not alone in their worries, that they are not crazy or paranoid, and that there really is a hidden, unanswerable face of authority beneath the acceptable public mask*" (quoted in Petley 1988: 96). Intelligence historian Jon Moran has commented on the "*cultural power*" of the central motivating element of left paranoia across the period, the 'Wilson Plot', and that this manifested itself in a variety of conspiracy thrillers in the 1980s (2014: 175).

Many of the screen dramas, such as 'In the Secret State', *Spyship*, *A Very British Coup* and *The Whistle Blower*, were based on novels; while a handful, such as *Defence of the Realm*, *Bird of Prey* (1 and 2), *Hidden City*, *Edge of Darkness* and *Hidden Agenda*, were new fictions produced for cinema and television. Surprisingly, the screen versions, as in the case of *Spyship*, *A Very British Coup* and 'In the Secret State', and in an inversion of typical practice, were often bleaker than the literary originals, promoting a deeply pessimistic vision of a malevolent and omnipotent Security Service, ruthless in the pursuit of its objectives, and unhesitating in its methods.[712] While such viewpoints might indeed be 'fictions', it is not sufficient simply to dismiss them as 'conspiracy thinking', wayward theories without empirical foundation. While critical of their political effectiveness, John Hill acknowledges the 'secret state' thriller with its dramatic mix of conspiracy and paranoia as a "*perfect*" embodiment of the 1980s, noting that the "*sense of helplessness which these thrillers characteristically created, was also a good expression of the strong sense of political impotence (and the inability to effect change) that was felt by so many liberals and the left during this period*" (1999: 153). As television historian Lez Cooke has reminded us, the dramas were produced in a "*far more reactionary politi-cal climate*" than previously, the debate about progressive television drama in the context of Thatcherism being "*not so much about how socialism could be achieved, as it had been in the previous two decades, but about how a total hegemony of right-wing ideology could be averted*" (2007: 167). It is important to remember that the 'secret state' reached into the very corridors of the state broadcaster, the BBC. In 1985, there was great controversy when it was re-vealed that BBC staff were vetted on behalf of the Security Service, which in turn regularly briefed the broadcaster on subversives in the industry. At a time of considerable tension, hostility and confrontation between the broadcaster and the government, the level of paranoia and mutual suspicion was indexed in the regular sweeping for bugs of the offices of the Director-General and the Chairman of the BBC (Seaton 2015: 8, 291). In what a historian of the BBC has described as the "*most existentially challenging period since its inception*", it is unsurprising that programme-makers responded with conspiracy fictions portraying the dark machinations of the state and its secret servants (26).

The mood of pessimism and powerlessness was often captured in the re-views, the dramas conjuring up a "*frightening world where honest coppers and ordinary folk are kept in the dark by politicians, union men and secret services of all kinds. The men with power are all corrupt and all in collusion*" (Review of *Edge of Darkness*, *Evening Standard*, 5 November 1985). The screen dramas discussed in this chapter, and the novels from which some derived, were popularly viewed and read, and fed into a climate of opinion, widely circulat-ed in the media, that distrusted the intelligence services and their intimate relationship with the traditional power base in the country. The 'structure of feeling' expressed in the dramas was real enough, and in the absence of an alternative perspective on the 'secret state', the consequence of official silence and denial, it is unsurprising that many in Britain could accept that the secu-rity and intelligence services engaged in unlawful surveillance, black propa-ganda, intimidation, and the removal of awkward citizens, its critics and op-ponents. Bernard Porter has concluded that, in view of the security controver-sies, blanket secrecy, the anti-democratic tenor of the administration and consequent public anxieties during the 1980s, "*it was difficult to reassure many people that the security services were not corrupt and tyrannical*" (1989: 219). Thus was opened up a dramatic space to express audience uncertainty, mistrust and doubt. In the summary of the critic Julian Petley, "*the message from A Very British Coup and its predecessors is that in a country that has spawned Peter Wright and his cronies no one can justly be called paranoid: it's all true*" (1988: 96).

8.

The Spy Drama Following the End of the Cold War

Things are changing so fast in Eastern Europe these days that yesterday's espionage thriller may be positively obsolete. With no cold to come in out of, with no Iron Curtain to tunnel under, what's the point of having a bunch of guys running around with cloaks and daggers?
(*Wall Street Journal*, 29 January 1990)

My country has done a terrible thing to you. We have deprived you of an enemy.
(Eduard Shevardnadze, Soviet Foreign Minister, *Sunday Times* 9 October 1988)

An old Security Service joke tells of how MI5's motto 'Regnum Defendre' (Defence of the Realm) would better read 'Rectum Defendre' (Defend your Backside!).

In 1989, John le Carré, referring to the Cold War, the archetypal setting of his espionage fiction, had confessed that there was a "*limit, after all, to the extent to which you can dramatise a stalemate*" (quoted in the *Guardian*, 16 November). In April 1991, the BBC re-broadcast le Carré's classic Cold War serial *Tinker Tailor Soldier Spy* (1979). Reviewers speculated on how the current audience would take the drama as it came in "*out of the cold*", in a world climate that was now much changed, and where "*East and West are no longer locked in a bitter cold war*" (*Daily Mail*, 27 April 1991). Eminent spy author le Carré is a suitable subject to begin an examination of espionage, drama, the break-up of the Soviet Union and potential redundancy. The context and circumstances of intelligence and security in Britain has certainly altered since the late 1980s, when the collapse of the Berlin Wall had removed the central adversary which had dominated the landscape of the Free World since the end of the Second World War. Despite the government's desire for a 'peace dividend', though, the demise of the Warsaw Pact, which many saw as signal-

ling the end of the spy, and indeed the spy writer, had only increased the need
for intelligence,

> *as fragile new democracies threaten to plunge back into totalitarianism,*
> *weapons-grade nuclear materials are traded on the black market, and*
> *Third World countries that were previously kept in check by their super-*
> *power mentors turn into dangerous mavericks.*
> (Michael Smith 1996: 13)

Active terrorism has kept the West on its toes, provided a potent 'enemy image', and put the security services on a permanent war-footing once again;
and following the devastating attacks in America in September 1991, there
has been a major revision in global intelligence policy and approach. According to Sir Andrew Turnbull, the Cabinet Secretary:

> *The whole demands of security had changed, in that we had gone away*
> *from a world where you kind of knew your enemy; in the Cold War or*
> *Republican terrorism, you knew kind of what they intended to do and*
> *the degree of violence they could inflict upon you. We are not in that*
> *world anymore – we haven't the faintest idea what are the limits.*
> (Quoted in Hennessey and Thomas 2011: 220)

The clandestine services, admittedly, had to fight a rear-guard action to
stave off drastic cuts to their budgets. They were not helped by the fact that
their reputations were at an "*all-time low*" following the very public revelations and accusations in the 1980s by whistle blowers such as Peter Wright
and Cathy Massiter, disquiet regarding alleged "*shoot-to-kill*" policies in
Northern Ireland and Gibraltar, lingering suspicions of widespread surveillance, an ill-defined understanding of subversion, systematic law-breaking
and assorted "*dirty tricks*" in the name of national security, and inefficiency
derived from years of operating in excessive secrecy (Smith 1996: 68; Dorril
1993: 75-108). The British intelligence community had very visibly been seen
to have been caught napping over the fall of the Shah of Iran, the invasion of
the Falklands, the invasion of Kuwait, and even over the unexpected end of
the long stand-off between the Eastern Bloc and the West in 1989. Despite
criticism, though, the transformation of the 'Cold War' into a 'Hot Peace' ensured that MI5, MI6, the Government Communications Headquarters
(GCHQ), and other agencies readily and eagerly found new threats to be
monitored or countered in their strivings to justify their existence.

Critics of the intelligence framework in Britain have long complained of the
national obsession with secrecy and a policy which maintained the "*tightest*
system of administrative secrecy in the Western world" (Hennessy and Townsend 1987: 291). However, the more uncertain circumstances in which the

security services found themselves in the 1990s meant that pressure increased for more openness and accountability, which has led to a "*managed and partial disclosure*" of historical secrets, and which it was expected would go some way to re-kindle public faith in the security agencies (Thurlow 2000: 184).[713] The updated Official Secrets Act, the Security Services Act of 1989 and the Intelligence Services Act of 1994 provided a new framework for the secrecy laws, legislative and public recognition of MI5, MI6 and GCHQ for the first time, and established an Intelligence and Security Committee to provide a degree of parliamentary oversight.[714] A modest Open Government Initiative fuelled further expectations for reform, and official publications, such as *The Security Services: MI5* (1993), *Central Intelligence Machinery* (1993) and *National Intelligence Machinery* (2000), have provided simple overviews of hitherto secret organisations, and helped explain the changing nature and structures of intelligence and security in Britain. Furthermore, there has been a relaxation in the policy of releasing official documents into the Public Records Office, which has led to a revolution in the historiography of the Secret Service. The 'creeping liberalisation' has seen the publication of collections of formerly secret documents, such as *MI5: The First Ten Years, 1909-19 - An Introduction to the Newly Released Records of the British Counter Intelligence Security Service at the Public Record Office* (1997), *British Intelligence: Secrets, Spies and Sources* (2008), and *Spying on the World: The Declassified Documents of the Joint Intelligence Committee, 1936-2013* (2014). Furthermore, previously restricted internal histories such as *The Security Service 1908-1945: The Official History* (1999, originally completed in 1944) and *The Secret History of S.O.E.: Special Operations Executive 1940-1945* (2000, originally completed in 1947) have now been made available in published editions. In an unprecedented action designed to suggest greater transparency, the authorities have sanctioned the publication of authorised centenary histories of both the Security Service and the Secret Intelligence Service (SIS), with Christopher Andrew's *The Defence of the Realm: The Authorized History of MI5* (2009) and Keith Jeffrey's *MI6: The History of the Secret Intelligence Service 1909-1949* (2010).[715] The period following the Cold War has certainly witnessed a re-examination in Britain of the tricky balance between the public's right to know and the 'necessary evil' of the state's need to keep certain things secret.

There have been various initiatives to modernise the intelligence services, to shed the traditional cloak of secrecy, and to provide a more public face to the secret world. The process has required a degree of corporate image-building. The appointment of the first woman to head the Security Service, Stella Rimington (1991-96), provided a welcome opportunity to improve the Service's public reputation, to gain a "*good 'equality' angle*" from the story, and embark, as she put it, on a "*mission to inform*" (Rimington 2002: 242, 253). Rimington became the first senior MI5 officer openly to visit Moscow (to advise on how to run a Security Service in a democracy), the first Director-General (D-G) whose name was publicised on appointment, the first D-G of MI5 to pose openly for cameras at the launch of a brochure outlining the organisation's activities, and the first to present a series of public lectures, including a television lecture entitled 'Security and Democracy: Is There a Conflict?'[716] The intelligence services now routinely place job advertisements in the press, make career presentations at recruitment fairs, are available to candidates who generally apply for the Civil Service, promote themselves as modern, equal opportunities employers, and have moved into imposing new corporate headquarters at Thames House (MI5) and Vauxhall Cross (MI6).[717] Rimington signalled the significant change in culture when she commented on her appointment: "*Our detractors who accuse us of being conservative, old-fashioned, Cold War warriors are a very long way from the truth. We would like to see such myths blown away*" (quoted in Staniforth 2013: 98).[718]

In a "*new world order*" where the "*clarity which the Cold War brought has gone*", the need for intelligence has remained a priority, and in the process of re-tasking the intelligence and security agencies the emphasis has shifted from the traditional function of counter-espionage and counter-subversion to that of a more focused counter-terrorism.[719] Eliza Manningham-Buller, the Director-General of MI5 in the early 2000s, in assessing the new global terror-ist threat after 9/11, spoke of the vulnerability of sophisticated Western socie-ties, and the new challenges posed: "*Challenges of scale, geography, culture and language*", and described the international terrorist organisation Al Qaeda as a "*complex and diverse target, capable of real harm to our way of life*" (quoted in Hennessey and Thomas 2011: 222). However, the effects of "*globalisation*", the increased inter-dependency of nation states in terms of communications and finance, has also meant new challenges for the Security Service, notably in countering "*complex clandestine networks*", transnational organised crime engaged in narcotics, money laundering, people trafficking, war-lordism, nuclear proliferation and the illegal weapons trade (Aldrich 2009: 759-60). This has meant new resources in the fight against international organised crime and to secure the e-infrastructure essential for commerce and finance.[720] The consolidation of a British 'security state' took on a fresh urgency in face of the 'new terrorism' which had surfaced with the attacks in New York on 9 September 2001 and London on 7 July 2005, and efforts were increasingly devoted to protective security and turning Britain into a 'hard target'. By 2007, MI5 had overwhelmingly become a counter-terrorist agency and only a small fraction of its budget was now being devoted to counter-espionage. Similarly, after the fall of the Berlin Wall at the end of 1989, the Secret Intelligence Service had to re-assess its intelligence role. According to the official website, the intelligence challenges which are now dominant are headed by "*regional instability, terrorism, the proliferation of weapons of mass destruction and serious international crime*". This was essentially a new intelligence environment in Britain in which openness and image-management were the fresh realities. The writer on intelligence Nigel West has since, perhaps generously, claimed that not very much is left secret about MI5, SIS, or GCHQ. As he reports, the three agencies have established themselves in ostentatiously plush landmark buildings in recent years, with vast budget overruns, public affairs units, and, in the cases of MI5 and GCHQ, impressive websites. Gone are the days of,

> *anonymous, dingy offices in Victoria, or antiseptic, unmarked tower blocks in Waterloo. John le Carré, Len Deighton, and Ian Fleming would be lost in the present environment, but at least their spymasters did not brief journalists or develop cozy relationships with ministers or, worse, with their spin doctors.*
> (2005: 30)

The changes in the structures of intelligence and security in Britain since the late 1980s have not come about without comment or critique. Many have refused to be taken in by the "*charm offensive*" or the seeming "*new cloak of respectability*", seeing the trumpeted transformations as cosmetic. Some have been anxious about the increased scope of the services, the likely extension of surveillance of the public, have doubted the claims for a new accountability, questioned the seeming "*self-regulation*" of the services, and worried that steps were being taken by a Conservative government to create a "*secret police*" (Smith 1996: 82). Sensing once more a trampling of the rights of the individual in favour of the security of the state. As the *Guardian* worried, would not the "*war against terror*" conducted in an atmosphere of menace "*end up being as much a threat to our freedoms as terrorism itself*"? (17 October 2002). In restating that "*Secrecy is our absolute stock in trade, our most precious asset*", Sir Colin McColl head of SIS seemed to indicate that MI6 would not be going as far as its sister organisation MI5 in offering a new openness (quoted in Smith 1996: 164); and for many critics the veil of secrecy has traditionally served as a cover for illegal activities or simply ineptitude. As the popular historian Max Hastings has asserted, "*The record suggests that official secrecy does more to protect intelligence agencies from domestic accountancy for their own follies than to shield them from enemy penetration*" (2015: xvii). Meanwhile, the Security Service, which had previously come in for some criticism and embarrassment following the Bettaney scandal in 1984, had more recently become embroiled in the Shayler affair in 1997. The report of the Security Commission set up in the wake of Bettaney was critical of the Service's management; and this was reiterated by whistle blower David Shayler who pointed to the Security Service's sometimes bungling incompetency, profligacy, complacency, failure to modernise, inflexible bureaucracy, excessive secrecy and consequent widespread disaffection among younger staff. Shayler, a former MI5 officer who was prosecuted by the authorities, commenting on his unfair treatment, pointed out that, "*Anthony Blunt got immunity and he was a KGB spy*", while he was persecuted despite the fact that, "*All the disclosures I have made have been in the public interest in an attempt to improve efficiency in MI5 and better protect the public*" (quoted in Hollingsworth and Fielding 1999: 204).[721] Marjorie Thompson, former chair of the Campaign for Nuclear Disarmament and surveillance victim of the 'secret state', has been critical of the supposed new openness, making the telling comparison that it is "*Shocking to think that we can find out now what the Stasi were up to, but not our own people*" (quoted in ibid.: 112).[722] It has not gone without notice that a new Security Service Tribunal, established to hear complaints by the public into intrusion and invasion of privacy, reviewed 275 complaints between 1989 and 1997, and upheld none of them (ibid.: 250). It is difficult to square up the stated experiences of David Shayler and the views of many critics, with Stella Rimington's assessment of her four years as Director-General, a tenure which: "*saw as much change as any previous period. By the time I left in 1996, I was confident that anyone joining would feel that they had become part of a modern, accountable and respected organisation, clear about its role and responsibilities and professionally competent to carry them out with probity, imagination and drive*" (2002: 268).[723]

The spy drama comes in from the cold

If we are no longer to be scared of Reds under the bed, what on earth are we going to read before we turn out the light?
(Review of *Game, Set & Match, Sunday Times*, 9 October 1988)

I am often asked whether the genre is now dead with the apparent ending of the Cold War ... It is not. The new situation between East and West is an intriguing and fertile field for ideas in fiction, and even more so in reality.
(Pincher 1991: 332)

Intelligence insider Anthony Cavendish claimed late in 1988 that the "*future of the television spy looks troubled*". For him, there was little prospect that modern taste would tolerate the traditional stereotype of the gentleman spy or that the bureaucratic and technological nature of today's espionage would lend themselves to drama (1988). And indeed, television scholar Joseph Oldham has declared the 1990s a "*moribund period for the British television spy series*" (2017: 162). The critic at the *Spectator*, nearer the mark perhaps, was more reassuring, though, arguing for the continuing philosophical, structural and political relevance of espionage literature for the modern author as well as for the broad readership which remained faithful to stories of intrigue and revelation. Spy novels, he asserted,

> *continue their obsessive grip on our imagination, even after the end of the Cold War, because they demonstrate, like a formal dance, some of the most haunting philosophies of indeterminacy and mutually shifting positions.*
> (27 December 2003)

The first television spy drama to be screened in face of the imminent demise of the Soviet Union was the situation comedy series *The Piglet Files*. This was produced at the commercial company London Weekend Television as a vehicle for the popular comedy actor Nicholas Lyndhurst who played Peter Chapman, a polytechnic lecturer recruited into MI5 with codename 'Piglet' to train the operatives in the finer arts of gadgetry. The problem is that the agents are all incompetent and Chapman finds himself in a series of uncomfortable positions, the target for a Russian hit man, the penetration agent inside an animal rights activist cell, and left with a dangerous East German agent when a surveillance operation goes wrong. The running gag is that he can't tell his wife (Serena Evans) about his new role, even when she is kidnapped by the Soviets and offered in a trade for state secrets. The comedy, less manic than in the earlier television comedy *The Top Secret Life of Edgar Briggs* (1974), is typically centred on bungling agents, failing equipment and anachronistic old-school-tie types at the top of the hierarchy. *The Piglet Files* ran for three seasons of 21 episodes in total between 1990 and 1992. It was relatively popular, appearing in the lower rungs of the ratings and attracting viewing figures of 6-8 million, most likely due to the well-liked Lyndhurst who was all the rage at the time due to his success in *Only Fools and Horses* (1981-2003).[724] The show, coming so soon after the fall of the Berlin Wall, made only perfunctory reference to the epic changes taking place in Eastern Europe and continued to pit the Security Service against the machinations of the Communist regimes. *Stage and Television Today* judged *The Piglet Files* a "*Carry On secret agent type comedy*", and a show to watch "*with the brain shut down and funny bone at the ready*" (13 September 1990).

The four-part serial *Sleepers*, broadcast at the dying moment of the Soviet Union in the Spring of 1991, was a further humorous yet more topical treatment of the new state of affairs confronting the foreign intelligence and domestic security services, which now had to adjust mind-sets and practices, and sweep away some of the embarrassing debris of the Cold War. In the story, the modern Russian intelligence service stumbles onto a 1960s time-capsule buried beneath Moscow. It slowly dawns that this had been a most secret operation to train and then settle two 'sleeper' agents in Britain in 1966, and which had long since been forgotten. A dishy and ambitious intelligence Major (Joanna Kanska) is sent to London to try and locate the agents and determine if they are still active. A vital piece of evidence is a secret Soviet film of the 1966 World Cup which confirms the presence of the agents in London, and which, to the astonishment of the Russian Head of Station (David Calder), solves the long-standing dispute about whether England's goal in extra-time crossed the line. He sets off to find a sports journalist and a lucrative deal. The CIA is thrown into panic by the sudden appearance of a Russian intelligence officer in the West, and MI5 sense a plot in the Soviet Union's sudden interest in sports broadcasting which it interprets as an intervention into the hooligan problem aimed at undermining British society. Meanwhile, the two agents, Zelenski (Albert, Warren Clarke) and Rublev (Jeremy, Nigel Havers), have completely assimilated into British society: Albert as a family man and shop steward in a Lancashire brewery ironically having trouble with the hard-liners; Jeremy, equally ironically, as a yuppie investment banker in the City. The distraught Jeremy, with a Ferrari, an expensive flat in London, a place in the country and a share in a racehorse, despairingly declares: "*I don't want to go back to a bowl of red cabbage and a bedsit in Vladivostok*".

Sleepers, witty, clever and fast-moving, was universally well-received by critics who had clearly become a little jaded with the "*tired, stereotypical spy series*" of the Cold War period (*Western Mail*, 20 April 1991), and welcomed a "Ninotchka *for the Nineties*" (*Evening Standard* 11 April 1991). *Today* judged the comedy-thriller the "*liveliest new drama on screen*" (11 April 1991); a view echoed at the *Sun*, which admired a "*brilliant series*" (18 April 1991); while the *Evening Standard* commended a "*comedy of almost beautiful precision*" (18 April 1991). The *Daily Mail* was moved to declare a "*rare and wonderful object, a television comedy containing a brilliant, dramatic idea worked out with enthusiasm and flair*" (11 April 1991), and *Stage and Television Today* praised a "*near flawless blend of humour and drama*" (18 April 1991). Reviewers also heaped praise on the BBC, which some felt had been flagging recently. The *Sun* punning that with *Sleepers* the broadcaster had "*finally woken up to the competition and come in from the cold*"; while *Today* claimed the serial as "*one of the best things they've screened for a long time*" (both 18 April 1991). It was felt that *Sleepers* nicely balanced thrills and jokes, and in its "*retro*" qualities caught the "*tongue-in-cheek breeziness of shows such as* The Avengers *and* Adam Adamant" (*The Times*, 11 April 1991).[725]

Actor Warren Clarke had commissioned *Sleepers* in the mid-1980s, but it was only following his success in the drama *Nice Work* in 1989 that the new serial was picked up for production at the BBC after doing the rounds at several ITV companies (*Time Out*, 17 April 1991; *Stage and Television Today*, 18 April 1991).[726] There were fears that the drama had lost its moment, that in a fluid historical situation it might become a "*Victim of Cold War vacillations*", with one of the writers John Flanagan worrying that: "*Had* Sleepers *been released last year, it would have been ideal. As it is, there may not even be a Soviet Union when the series begins*" (quoted in the *Daily Telegraph*, 4 April 1991). In fact, *Sleepers* seemingly accidentally found its moment, the prospect of sleeper agents left stranded after the thaw coming to the mind of more than one reviewer. The disorientating shift in world affairs prompted the *Scotsman* to acknowledge an "*aptly contemporary sub-text*". Noting that, "*While old hats and cold war junkies are still looking for reds under beds, or for capitalists and colonialists in them, your ordinary spy in the street just wants to settle down with a jar and a Maserati and have a good time*" (27 April 1991). The main disappointment with *Sleepers* is the audience-pleasing happy ending, which involves the unlikely rescue of the pair from Russia and the firing-squad of a moribund KGB keen to bury a historical embarrassment, and their return to England, to the bosom of his family for Albert, and to a proposal of marriage and a commitment to settling down for the formerly womanising Jeremy. However, television drama had now clearly begun to mark out the new geopolitical realities.

Another television spy thriller to explore the implications of the past on the radically revised present was *The Waiting Time*, a two-part television drama from Carlton Television broadcast in Britain in 1999 and adapted from a recent novel by Gerald Seymour.[727] In the story, a former member of the East German security police now helping the Western alliance is viciously attacked in the officer's mess while visiting a British Military Intelligence base. Corporal Tracy Barnes who had served in Berlin claims that Hauptman Dieter Krause was the officer responsible for the illegal killing of Hans Becker, an agent being run in the German Democratic Republic late in 1988. Barnes in the company of Joshua Mantle, a sympathetic legal clerk, travels to Rostock, East Germany to find evidence of the crime; while Krause and others implicated in the killing desperately try to remove witnesses and impede the investigation. German Intelligence now seeks to use Krause, who had important connections with the Soviets, to gain influence with the Americans. Meanwhile, the British SIS plays a devious game, egging Tracy on with the intention of embarrassing the upstart new reunified Germany, and using sensitive material which has come out of investigating Krause to compromise an influential Russian colonel of intelligence with prospects for the state presidency. The two British amateurs narrowly win the race against time and force the arrest of Krause; however, in a shock ending, Mantle catches Barnes in a lie and exposes her as a reluctant agent for the communists during the Cold War after being caught returning from the mission which had seen the death of Becker.

The Waiting Time, starring the popular John Thaw as Mantle and Zara Turner as Barnes, was filmed on location in London, and in difficult winter conditions in the Mecklenburg-Pomerania region of the former German Democratic Republic, the Baltic port of Stralsund and in Berlin (*TV Times*, 23-29 October 1999: 13). It was touted as the first "*post-Cold War thriller*", the producer Chris Burt attracted to a story which "*deals with a time which has not been featured on television. The hangover of the Stasi, the East German secret police, their files being made public and the whole era since the Wall came down – that's what fascinated me*".[728]

The drama was not well-received, reviewers finding it, despite its novel setting and time-frame, curiously old-fashioned. The *Observer*, expecting something of interest in a timely story dealing with the "*fallout of political espionage*" in post-Wall East Germany, was disappointed by "*clunky*" dialogue, an "*unpleasant*" female lead character, a plot full of holes, and overall providing "*irritation rather than excitement*" (24 October 1999). *The Telegraph* found little original in *The Waiting Time* other than its setting: "*Everything else about it is familiar from plain old Cold War thrillers – and, indeed, thrillers of all kinds through the ages*" (29 October 1999); while the *Independent* was unexcited by the boundless stereotypes of "*militaristic Russians, ruthless Germans and sturdy British heroes*" (29 October 1999). The large budget and location filming were duly acknowledged, and a generally grudging reviewer at *The Telegraph* felt that the "*ugly, impoverished East German locations added an extra poignancy to the background politics, by making it savagely clear that all the human-rights abuses, all the ruining of lives by the Stasi, had been for nothing*" (5 November 1999).

The novel of *The Waiting Time* is elevated above the routine commercial thriller, though, through a sustained interest in the legacy of the recent pasts for the modern Germany. During a school visit to a museum exhibition on the Stasi, a girl complains, "*The past is boring ... The past is gone, why do we have to know the past?*" The story examines such resistance and inertia in relation to the quest for justice for the murdered Becker and his like, and Barnes and Mantle continually confront the view that, "*There is no will in the new Germany to examine old crimes*". The more mature Mantle sees in this attitude a repeat of the situation that followed World War II and the attempt to bury guilt in a national silence, an awareness of which is forcefully brought to him at the museum at Peenemünde where the Germans using slave labour developed the deadly V2 rocket. The adventure is merely a hollow victory for Mantle who knows the secret world will keep the lid on the recent events and it will remain a private knowledge. At the end of the story, standing on the street observing the German public passing by, he is left worrying if anybody actually "*cared for the forgotten past and the forgotten history?*" Seymour, a meticulous researcher of his novels, has defended the suspense novel, seeing in the thriller genre the *"capability of informing an audience, giving them more insight into the problems we are all talking about, than a forest of newspapers and a cloud of TV newscasts"* (quoted in Simon 2010: 56). These more serious dimensions to the fiction were considerably softened in the screen adaptation.

The collapse of communism in Eastern Europe had to be faced by the leading writers of the spy genre. John le Carré responded to the altering circumstances thrown up by *glasnost* and *perestroika* in his novel *The Russia House*, published in the summer of 1989. In preparation, the author visited the Soviet Union twice in 1987, and aware of rapidly changing circumstances he fixed his story in this year. The story deals with a British publisher, Barley, familiar with Russia, who is approached by a dissident Soviet scientist to publish damaging military secrets. The manuscript falls into the hands of MI6 which convinces the reluctant Barley to return to Russia to verify the document. The dissident is taken into custody by the KGB and the publisher trades what he has with the Russians to secure the release of his go-between Katya with whom he has fallen in love. The story was influenced by the famous Oleg Penkovsky affair of the early 1960s when Western Intelligence had used the British businessman Greville Wynne to liaise with a Soviet intelligence officer who was providing invaluable military secrets at the time of the Cuban Missile Crisis.[729] The novel was adapted by Hollywood's MGM starring Sean Connery and Michelle Pfeiffer in 1990, and became the first major Western production to film in the Soviet Union.

Len Deighton was nominally represented in the changing new world order in the made-for-television movies *Bullet to Beijing* (1995) and *Midnight in St. Petersburg* (1996), which brought his 1960s secret agent Harry Palmer back to the screen after a period of 28 years. The author was not enthusiastic about *"retreading"* the character, but agreed to give his consent to the films if Michael Caine could be coaxed back to the role. Deighton was surprised that the actor signed to the project and was not involved in any way other than his consent for the character rights.[730] The films were put together by Harry Alan Towers with the $11 million finance from Canada, Russia and the UK, shot back to back in post-communist St. Petersburg and London, and sold to the world television market. In the first story, Palmer is retired from British Intelligence as part of Ministry of Defence cutbacks and mysteriously invited to Russia where he becomes involved in a complex conspiracy organised by former KGB spymaster Alex (Michael Gambon), centring on a deadly biochemical weapon being transported by train to Beijing, China and destined for North Korea. In the second story, Palmer has decided to stay in Russia and open a private investigation agency using some of the agents he had encountered in the previous adventure (Jason Connery, Michael Sarrazin, Lev Pry-gunov). This time he foils a plot by Alex to sell stolen weapons-grade plutonium and to steal art treasures from the Hermitage.

The films make a nod to the earlier Harry Palmer pictures: *Bullet to Beijing* begins, as did *The Ipcress File* (1965), with Palmer at a 'static' observation post, provides Harry with a telephone conversation with his sexy secretary Jean Courtney (still played by Sue Lloyd), later reprises the obligatory scene of the agent's insubordination with a senior officer as Harry is given the sack, and in places rewards the aficionado through alluding to dialogue in the earlier picture; while *Midnight in St. Petersburg* reverts Harry to the role of private detective with which he had commenced the film version of *Billion Dollar Brain* (1967). However, such references seem perfunctory and hardly add up to an intelligent engagement with the iconic status of the original films or develop the character in an interesting way. In fact, in the new stories, Palmer's character has undergone a fundamental change, and in the place of the irreverent, rebellious agent is a more paternal figure, especially to the younger agent Nick (Connery). The fate of Western and Soviet agents following the thaw in the Cold War, the rise of organised crime in the new Russia, and the prospect of reviving an iconic spy from the golden-age of spy movies in the 1960s were intriguing notions for the new espionage cinema, but the plodding Harry Alan Towers was not the filmmaker to bring these themes to life on screen and *Bullet to Beijing* and *Midnight in St. Petersburg* remain little more than footnotes in the history of the spy film. Unfortunately, the return of Harry Palmer in these movies did not excite too much attention and, typical of the wider reviewing, *Variety* found *Bullet to Beijing* "*strictly a low-tech thriller*" which "*lumbers along much in the fashion of the train transporting the spies*" (26 June 1995: 82).[731]

Ethics, terrorism and the new world order

No ethics in the world can get round the fact that the achievement of 'good' ends is in many cases tied to the necessity of employing morally suspect or at least morally dangerous means.
(Max Weber, 'The Profession and Vocation of Politics', 1919)

The new political world order which followed the break-up of the Eastern Bloc led to wider public consciousness and expectations regarding the practice of security and intelligence. As Len Scott and Peter Jackson have noted, "*Ethics seemed destined to be ever more closely entwined with public debate and discourse concerning intelligence*" (2004: 17), and there emerged a concern for 'Just Espionage' and 'Just Intelligence' in dealing with threats and terrorist suspects (Bellaby 2012). The new world order threw up an 'intelligence dilemma' in which the provision of good security had to be balanced with respecting civil liberties and ensuring the continued support of the population for security and intelligence policy (Richards 2012). The new sensitivity towards ethics and intelligence was evident in a viewer response to the commercial film *Enigma* (2001), about wartime code-breakers. In a letter to the *Evening Standard*, Maurice Price maintained that the story was not so much about "*outing*" a traitor, a purely "*fictional*" aspect of the plot, but "*about the murky ethical issues that arise in war where temporary alliances are forged*". The story was about "*expediency*", of ignoring the "*fact*" that Britain's wartime ally, Russia, was responsible for the massacre of thousands of Polish officers. The dilemma "*surely has a resonance today*", Price maintained, in the Gulf War and in the recent revelations of atrocities. Who is the traitor in the story, asked Mr Price?: "*The man who is called a traitor by some, or those who hid the mass killing of his countrymen? And where is the morality that measures one evil against another to reach an end*" (4 October 2001).[732]

The mounting concerns regarding espionage, intelligence, geopolitics and ethics found expression in a trio of linked dramas. *Page Eight* (2011), and *Turks & Caicos* and *Salting the Battlefield* (both 2014), were sequential feature-length espionage dramas written and directed by David Hare, produced for the BBC and since referred to as 'The Worricker Trilogy'.[733] The central character is Johnny Worricker (Bill Nighy), a principled, affable, much-married, long-serving senior intelligence analyst at MI5. In *Page Eight*, a secret source, known only to Benedict Baron, the Director-General of the Security Service (Michael Gambon), reveals that the British Prime Minister Alec Beasley (Ralph Fiennes) has been operating a personal intelligence unit and has withheld sensitive information supplied through the Americans about secret detention centres and suspect terrorists, thereby endangering the country. When Baron dies of a heart attack, Worricker is left to discover the source and get to the heart of the conspiracy. Unsure who he can trust, Johnny befriends a neighbour, Nancy Pierpan (Rachel Weisz), a publisher and daughter of a Middle-Eastern radical, and whose brother has been illegally killed by the Israelis. Worricker refuses to bow down to the prime minister and is deserted by both Jill Tankard (Judy Davis) an intelligence colleague and the Home Secretary Anthea Catcheside (Saskia Reeves) who accept senior posts and keep quiet. Johnny leaks the officially suppressed report of the killing of Nancy's brother and is last seen at London Airport, selecting a flight out of the country, alone, with an uncertain future but in possession of the dangerous knowledge regarding the illegal detention centres. *Page Eight* premiered at the Edinburgh Film Festival.

The Turks & Caicos Islands are where Johnny Worricker lands up in the second instalment of the drama. There, he hopes to remain anonymous and enjoy a pleasant lifestyle. However, he is recognized by the American Curtis Pelissier (Christopher Walken), one of a group of shady American business-men. Pelissier finally reveals he is ex-Central Intelligence Agency (CIA), that he is onto a corrupt group of entrepreneurs who have excessively profited from the construction of detention camps in the world's trouble-zones and wants Johnny's help to extort some of the money back for the Agency. A paral-lel story involves the wealthy British financier Stirling Rogers (Rupert Graves) who is set to host a symposium on Turks & Caicos. Worricker relies on a for-mer girlfriend, Margot Tyrrell (Helena Bonham Carter), now a confidant of Stirling, to provide details of his ambitions and dealings, and it is this knowledge which Worricker and Pelissier use to lever the $200 million out of the syndicate. Stirling has managed a secret fund to be used by his friend the British prime minister in philanthropic work following his withdrawal from public life. The money has come from the profits from building detention camps, information that must not be made public. Pelissier, in fact a serving CIA officer, reneges on his promise to maintain Worricker's anonymity and intends to expose him to MI5 and the prime minister in return for future favours. Worricker, with Tyrrell, leaves the islands secretly into yet another uncertain future.

Salting the Battlefield picks up the story in Germany where Johnny and Margot are in hiding from the British Security Service, insecure, restless, their families under surveillance, running out of money and confronting a vengeful prime minister. Worricker needing to bring matters to a conclusion ap-proaches a newspaper editor with the full story on Alec Beasley. Meanwhile, Jill Tankard is quietly working a deal with Anthea Catcheside to prepare the ground and feather their own nests should the prime minister fall. When the story breaks, the wily Alec Beasley manoeuvres himself into a new role of international statesman as peacemaker in Iran; Catcheside becomes prime minister; and Tankard now has a friend and supporter at the top of British government and senses the dawn of a new golden age for the Security Service. Johnny Worricker is welcomed back in from the cold.

The Worricker Trilogy is one of the most substantial achievements of recent British spy fiction, the review in the *Observer* claiming Hare a "*master of the new espionage, surely a proud successor to Ambler and Le Carré*" (22 March 2014). Across the three dramas, Hare depicts the world of politics, security and intelligence as it settles into a new pattern following the terror of 11 Sep-tember 2001 (9/11) New York and 7 July 2005 (7/7) London, the silences and frustrations of the Hutton, Gibson and Chilcott Enquiries, the disgracing of the outspoken diplomat Craig Murray, the attempted prosecution of Derek Pasquill for leaking sensitive information from the Foreign Office about the government's attitude to secret CIA rendition flights, and, specifically for a subplot in *Page Eight*, the criminal tragedies of Tom Hurndall and Rachel Corrie, the student activists killed by Israeli defence forces on the Gaza Strip. From sources within MI5, Hare had discerned that tension existed within the Security Service following the invasion of Iraq and 7/7, and with his interest piqued the dramatist constructed a story around that supposed apprehension and the criticism that the government had been effectively "*outsourcing torture*" in its activities with some foreign intelligence services. He believed that intelligence and security had moved on since the existential spy fiction of the 1960s, where one side is as bad as the other. "*Johnny is not like that*", he claimed, "*He'd love to go on doing his job if he was allowed to do it*" (quoted in the *Radio Times*, 27 August 2011). Johnny is not somebody to beat the system, but neither is he going to be crushed by it; he's simply "*doing a dishonourable job in an honourable way*" (*The Telegraph*, 28 August 2011). Reviews of *Page Eight* were mixed. A stylised production, *The Telegraph* admired the "noir-*ish, retro mood*" which suited the drama and characterisations (ibid.); while conversely the *Independent* felt the sense of "*retro pastiche*" led the viewer into genre territory that was "*worryingly familiar*" (29 August 2011). The *Guardian* was reassured by a "*film of maturity and intelligence*" (19 June 2011).

Following the completion of *Page Eight*, Hare decided to stay with the character, believing that the "*themes and moral issues raised by the war on terror, and the way in which government and security either do or don't work together, seem incredibly near the knuckle of what's happening in society at the moment*". The dramatist claimed to be "*really drawn to the subject of spies, in a way I've never been in the rest of my life*" (quoted in *The Telegraph*, 27 August 2011). With *Turks & Caicos* and *Salting the Battlefield* former sceptics warmed to the character of Worricker and the ambition of the series, in which Hare explored how, "*Politics is just a function of business now, just a tributary of the great entrepreneurial capitalist system*"; and how the Security Service makes the "*lives of the people who blow the whistle against them unliveable*" (*Guardian*, 21 February 2014). Critics generally admired the dramatist and filmmaker's critique of the intelligence services and modern government, balanced with just enough Hollywood glamour to keep the viewer entertained.

British intelligence agents have been singled out for criticism for taking part in interrogations, contributing questions during torture sessions and benefiting from the intelligence gained, and such activities widely understood as implicitly condoning inhuman treatment. The moral and ethical issues involved have been treated dramatically. *The Whistleblowers* was a glossy independent television series intended to rival the BBC's *Spooks*. The show ran for a single season in 2007 and featured two crusading personal injury lawyers who set about exposing a range of criminal, environmental and corrupt business practices. In the first episode, Ben Graham (Richard Coyle) and Alisha Cole (Indira Varma) happen across the severe interrogation of a suspect by rogue British security agents. *The Telegraph* was critical, complaining that as the *"pace got faster and faster* The Whistleblowers *just got thicker and thicker"* (28 September 2007).

All together more thoughtful and thought-provoking was *Complicit*, a feature-length drama broadcast on Channel 4 in 2013. An original piece for television, the forceful central issue was whether illegal torture was an ethical option in the face of imminent terrorist attack. In the story, black MI5 officer Edward Ekubo (David Oyelowo) travels to Egypt to question a young suspect Waleed Ahmed (Arsher Ali) he believes is planning a terrorist attack using ricin. Ahmed and his colleagues have clearly been tortured by the local security officers, and the victim pointedly tells the British intelligence officer, *"I'm a British citizen and it's your job to look after my constitutional rights"*; but lacking information and convinced that a UK attack is imminent, Ekubo connives in the further torture of the suspect. The leads given by Ahmed under duress prove false and Ekubo's gamble backfires as his connection with the torturers has been pinpointed by a civil rights activist. He is ushered from the Service and there is still the possibility of a terror attack. The idea for the drama occurred to producer Kevin Toolis when Prime Minister Gordon Brown made a statement in 2009 saying that the British state was not involved in torture.[734] With the situation becoming unstable in Egypt, location filming took place in Morocco.[735]

Complicit attracted some good reviews, many critics finding it an intelligent treatment of the complex moral issues involved and a refreshing contrast to the *"torture as a heroic shortcut"* convention of many recent action dramas. Viewers were left in a quandary about the officer's actions and a sense of the right, or even best, thing to do. Was Ekubo's mistake simply to be found out? Were viewers 'complicit' if they rooted for Ekubo to be proved right? The *Independent* maintained that the drama was essentially about this kind of uncertainty, and *"perhaps the best thing about it was that it will have left viewers uncertain and unsatisfied themselves. That's what terror is"* (18 February 2013). The *Guardian* was invigorated by a challenging drama that *"had us readjusting our moral bearings at every turn"* (23 February 2013). The drama, in contrast to series like *Spooks*, emphasised the dullness of intelligence work, with Ekubo spending the small hours scrolling through email intercepts or dully watching footage of a minicab office on the off-chance that something will break for the investigation. *The Telegraph* described the fascinating tension of the non-action as the *"most tentative, particular, sometimes wilfully boring edge-of-the-seat drama I have seen in a long while"* (17 February 2013). Joseph Oldham has praised *Complicit* as a *"very different and more psycholog-*

ical example of a spy thriller"; a new type of *"cultural narrative of the 'war on terror'"*; and through dismissing the fast-paced heroics and simplistic morals of conventional spy fiction, the *"slower and more contemplative approach of Complicit"* provided a *"new and unsettling approach"* towards its depicted longstanding anxieties (2014: 95-97).

The intractable problems of the Near East and the long-suffering peace process between Israel and Palestine were the backdrop to the television drama *The Honourable Woman*. The lavish eight-part serial, typical of recent high-end dramas a cross-Atlantic co-production, was written by Hugo Blick and first broadcast in 2014, on the BBC in the United Kingdom and on the Sundance Channel in America. The complex story, partly revealed through flashback, deals with the Jewish Stein family, headed by Nessa Stein (Maggie Gyllenhaal), which funds a foundation to bring reconciliation and peace to the region. The immediate plan is to connect the West Bank with optical fibre cables; meanwhile, assassinations, kidnappings, sexual abuse and violence, hamper and undermine the philanthropic work. The internecine politics of the region naturally attracts the involvement of the secret services of the Israelis, the Americans and the British, which all have interests to promote and to protect. The rogue MI6 officer Monica Chatwin (Eve Best) manipulates the situation in a bid to secure the top office in the British Secret Service; while Sir Hugh Hayden-Hoyle (Stephen Rea), the unpopular and outgoing head of MI6's Middle East desk, shows greater integrity and manages to unravel the mysteries and free the hostages. The drama commences with the killing in the past of the patriarch Eli Stein (Aidan Stephenson), over which a statement is uttered by Nessa: '*Who do you trust?, and How do you know?*'; and the Stein family endure great tragedy in their bid to bring peace to the troubled region. The drama serial was shot on locations in the UK, America and the Middle-East.

The Honourable Woman works more obviously as a political and family drama rather than a spy thriller. It is riven with family secrets as well as with the obstinate geopolitical problems of the region. The lurking public distrust of the intelligence services is apparent in the story and embodied in the character of the deceitful Monica Chatwin; however, some balance is restored through Sir Hugh Hayden-Hoyle, a flawed figure despised by senior colleagues and estranged from his wife. The serial was highly praised in both Britain and the United States, and won awards and accolades at the Golden Globes, the Screen Actors Guild, and the Emmys.

The security services in Britain have become increasingly occupied with terrorism since the 1970s, when domestic and international terrorist groups often supported by hostile states greatly expanded their activities of hijacking airliners, bombings and shootings (Rimington 2002: 211-19). A small number of screen dramas engaged with the threat posed by terrorists, although films such as *Juggernaut* and *Ransom* (both 1974), dealing with bombs aboard a luxury liner and an airliner respectively, largely focused on the terror as a crime and confront the antagonists with conventional representatives of the police or the army. A more central role was granted the Security Service in *Hennessy* (1975), directed by the efficient Don Sharp for American International Pictures (AIP). In this story a sympathetic IRA bomber (Rod Steiger), whose wife and child have been innocently shot down in Northern Ireland, plans to blow up the Queen at the state opening of Parliament, and opposed to him is the psychotic Inspector Hollis of Special Branch (Richard Johnson), an officer warped by his intimidation and torture at the hands of the republicans in Ulster. While finding the picture imperfect, *Monthly Film Bulletin* was intrigued by a "*well observed and absorbing film*" which presented "*facts of British life which are usually ignored as peripheral or too hot to handle*" (January 1975: 199). *Hennessy* raised a hornet's nest and was refused for exhibition by the two main cinema circuits in Britain. There was some queasiness regarding making entertainment out of the situation in Northern Ireland and embarrassment at the picture's use of newsreel footage featuring the Queen's opening of Parliament. AIP's hastily added statement to the beginning of the film that the "*Royal Family took no part in the making of this film*" and removal at the request of the Palace of six-seconds of offending footage did nothing to assuage the circuits (*Guardian*, 24 June 1975). The picture attracted mixed reviews, it largely being accepted as a competent thriller with some Hitchcockian ambitions (*Guardian*, 17 July 1975; *Observer*, 20 July 1975). The controversy over *Hennessy* meant that first, audiences in Britain were largely denied the opportunity to view the film, and secondly, that producers would be wise to steer clear of Irish terrorism as a subject for commercial cinema.

The excellent television serial *Harry's Game*, about an undercover agent sent into Belfast to track down an IRA gunman, and the feature film *Who Dares Wins* (both 1982), inspired by the Iranian Embassy siege of 1980, were stories centring essentially on army operations and so fall outside of a study primarily concerned with the intelligence services. However, Yorkshire Television (YTV) followed up *Harry's Game* with *The Glory Boys* (1984), another three-part dramatisation by Gerald Seymour from his own novel.[736] The story deals with Israeli nuclear scientist Professor David Sokarev (Rod Steiger) who is visiting London from America and is targeted for murder by a Palestinian assassin (Gary Brown) who is quarter mastered by an IRA contact man (Aaron Harris). Jimmy, a former British agent with a drink problem (Anthony Perkins) is brought out of retirement to manage the protection of Sokarev and neutralise the terrorists. The first assassination attempt at the University of London fails and the IRA man is cornered and captured. Under pressure, he reveals that the Palestinian will try a final effort at Heathrow Airport and the assassin is gunned down on the tarmac before he can fulfil his mission. Following orders, Jimmy 'executes' him but it is caught on camera and there is no way back for the agent into the department. In an ironic ending, Sokarev suffers a fatal heart attack on the journey to Israel.

Following new investment in the company, YTV announced plans to expand it production of drama (*Guardian*, 13 July 1984). *The Glory Boys* was one of the first fruits of this new policy, co-financed from America and at £2 million the most expensive production mounted by YTV to that time (*Stage and Screen Today*, 24 November 1983). The serial commenced a company strategy of seeking international co-financing for its showcase dramas (*Stage and Television Today*, 22 March 1984). *The Glory Boys*, with action ranging across the Middle East, Northern France, Britain and America, was extremely popular and YTV took out advertisements in the trade papers fanfaring its achievement of attracting an overall viewing public of 38.55 million (*Stage and Screen Today*, 1 November 1984). However, *The Glory Boys* was poorly received by the critics, the *Guardian* annoyed at the "*method*" posturing of the lead American actors (29 September 1984), and in a later review dismissing it as "*soap opera for men*" (2 October 1984). In an uncomradely act, Linda Agran of Euston Films ranted against the adaptation on the BBC's review show *Did You See?* She damned the script, lack of suspense and claimed she found it "*dreadful*" and "*laughable*" (quoted in *Stage and Screen Today*, 11 October 1984). *The Glory Boys* is the weakest of YTV's trio of serial dramas, the mild and anxious persona of Perkins being inappropriate for the role of a hard-drinking, chain-smoking, trench coat-wearing special agent. The inexperience and bickering of the two terrorists is a refreshing twist for the genre, but tends to undermine the heavy-handed comparisons the drama keeps insisting on between the murderous terrorists and the equally destructive security forces (at one time or another both are referred to as "*the glory boys*").

There have been a number of dramas dealing with millennial terrorism, but films such as *The Hamburg Cell* (TV, 2004), about the 9/11 hijackers, and *Four Lions* (2010), an unconventional comedy about four incompetent British jihadists who set out to train for and commit an act of terror, have little or no discernible British Secret Service element. More typical have been a slew of action films and television dramas which promote a swift, sharp, violent response to terrorism and terrorists. *Strike Back* (2010-15) dealt with the special operations unit 'Section 20' and sent it agents on high-risk missions across the globe. Originally appearing as a novel by former Special Air Service soldier Chris Ryan, a popular Anglo-American series was produced at the satellite broadcaster Sky Television. *Strike Back* has run for five seasons and there are plans for a further series and possibly a feature film. The team largely confronts terrorist-related threats, preventing weapons of mass-destruction falling into the wrong hands, dealing with the illegal arms trade and various planned terror attacks.

The lone agent bent on justice and retribution was the subject of *Cleanskin* (2012), a brutal, blue collar thriller written, directed and produced by Hadi Hajaig.[737] Bodyguard and grizzled ex-soldier Ewan (Sean Bean) is tasked by British Intelligence to locate and neutralise the Islamic terrorists who have just killed his employer and stolen a quantity of Semtex explosive. Although betrayed by rogue operatives in the Security Service, Ewan kills the terrorists, but is helpless as the bomb kills its intended target. Ewan then despatches his controller Charlotte (Charlotte Rampling) who has been using the operation to remove the traces of her illegal covert activities. Allegedly produced on a budget of under £2 million, some critics sensed a talent submerged beneath an overly-complex flashback structure and an unbalancing corridors-of-power conspiracy subplot (*Empire*, 5 March 2012). It was felt that Hajaig had tentatively managed to examine just why young British Muslims become radicalised, but that this promising excursion was largely lost to the conventions of the action thriller. Ultimately, though *Cleanskin* was so "*shot through with contradictions and non-sequiturs that it struggles to stay afloat*" (*Sight and Sound*, May 2012: 60). A savage review in the *Guardian* dismissed the picture as a "*leaden*", "*laboriously-acted*", "*lad-mag fantasy*" (8 March 2012).[738]

The secret and illegal arms trade was an area of mounting anxiety in the post-Cold War period and a threat that the security services were tasked to deal with. John le Carré had treated the subject in *The Night Manager*, his first novel of the new era in world politics. This was adapted, with some changes in locations, into a highly-successful six-part television drama serial in 2016, co-produced by the BBC and the American cable network AMC with a reputed budget of a lavish £20 million. Le Carré's more recent *A Most Wanted Man* (2008) had been filmed in 2014, a British, American and German co-production. Set in Germany with a covert German intelligence unit, it compassionately treats an innocent political refugee from Muslim Chechnya caught up in the deadly games of counter-terrorism.[739] Brad Pitt had originally acquired an option on *The Night Manager* (*The Telegraph*, 31 August 2010), and there had been a deal which involved Paramount and a plan for Sydney Pollack to direct with a script from Robert Towne (*Salon*, 21 October 1996). The story centres on the character of Jonathan Pine (Tom Hiddleston), a former soldier, now a night manager in a luxury hotel. With personal reasons of his own, Pine allows himself to be persuaded by a small intelligence unit operating out of the Foreign Office to infiltrate the organisation of slippery millionaire arms trader Richard Onslow Roper (Hugh Laurie), a man styled the "*worst man in the world*". A long and dangerous assignment, Pine unearths a major arms deal involving buyers in the Middle East and proof that Roper is in cahoots with rogue officers in MI6. A big-budget production, locations were shot in Switzerland, Morocco, Mallorca and various sites around the UK.

In a discussion of the massive arms deals of the late eighties, Stephen Dorril has written of the *"mysterious world of 'people who knew people', with intelligence links, with access to Whitehall and even Downing Street, and who now moved into the arms world"*; and of the *"grey market"* involving arms deals that were not public, and not officially approved by governments, but having tacit or sometimes secret government backing (1993: 340-41, 345). This was the world depicted in le Carré's *The Night Manager*. The strange events pertaining to 'Project Babylon' and the Iraqi Supergun, and the Matrix Churchill Affair, which also involved suspect arm sales to Iraq, provided chilling context for the story and the drama.

The *Guardian* believed *The Night Manager* was as *"sexed up as television drama comes"* (21 February 2016). For the populist *Sun* this was fine and judged it, *"One of the greatest series of all time"* (28 March 2016). Eye-poppingly in terms of television, the production prioritised the action and glamour of the spy thriller element of the story. This was noticed at the *Guardian*, which, in its review of television for the year, reported on a *"budget-bustingly grand epic of subterfuge and deceit ... full of inconsequential impossibilities"* (13 December 2016). At the time of the screening of the final episode, the reviewer at the paper concluded that the serial,

> *may have been a stylish and trenchant espionage drama of, no doubt, award-garnering brilliance. It may have explored the nature of good and evil, arms smuggling, the refugee crisis, the aftermath of the Arab spring, and Britain's post-colonial role in the world. But I couldn't take it entirely seriously.*
> (28 March 2016)

The Night Manager was an international success, selling to 180 countries. Viewers found Hiddleston appealing and attractive, and there was serious discussion of his potential to replace Daniel Craig and assume the role of James Bond (*Independent*, 11 October 2016).

Case file: "Terror with a twinkle", *Spooks* (2002-11)[740]

> *The attacks on America last September signalled the beginning of terrorism on a new terrifying scale. In March this year, MI6 announced it was doubling recruitment of front-line officers for the new 'war against terrorists'. Back at home, we officially face the biggest threat to national security since the Second World War. For the first time since the end of*

the Cold War, a spotlight is shining on our national Security Service,
MI5. And for the first time since the early 80s, spies are back on our TV
screens in Spooks *– a drama about the highly-charged modern world of*
'five'.
(*Spooks* press sheet, BBC)

Now that medics, detectives and pathologists have been done to death,
television dramatists have turned to MI5 for inspiration in their search
for the next big thing on television.
(*Guardian*, 23 November 2001)

It would be nice to believe that Spooks, *glamorous, exciting and packed*
to the gills with chisel-featured decision-makers of both sexes, is drag-
ging MI5 into an era of positive change.
(Spooks. *Behind the Scenes*, 2006: 22)

As Joseph Oldham has reported, "*In the first decade of the 21st century,* Spooks
dramatised the domestic front of Britain's involvement in the 'War on Ter-
ror'".[741] Spooks *was an extremely popular action series running for 10 seasons, consisting of 86 episodes, produced at Kudos Productions, filmed on
location in and around London and the South East, and broadcast on the BBC
between 2002 and 2011.[742] Kudos' brief from the BBC was to develop the
programme as an "*intelligent action series which really deals with big spy
issues and big subjects*" (quoted in Oldham 2017: 167). Mainly set in the capital, the series conveys a strong sense of the nation at risk by setting scenes
conspicuously within, or in front of, iconic buildings like the Houses of Parliament and St Paul's Cathedral. The drama, created by David Wolstencroft,
centred on 'Section B' of the Counter-Terrorism Department of MI5, and the
storylines addressed the various security concerns and myriad threats confronting a contemporary intelligence organisation. According to producer
Andrew Woodhead, the script policy was to "*take current reality and just ask
the question 'What if?'*" (quoted in the *Radio Times*, 22 September 2006: 21).
The series was hailed as a "*step out of the shadows for MI5*", promised to "*let
you in to a world that you've never seen before*", and represented the "*first time
that life in the modern security service has been the subject of a television drama*" (unattributed press cutting, 23 November 2001; *Guardian*, 23 November
2001). *Spooks* was trumpeted as a spy drama for a "*new millennium, a new
world order*" (Spooks. *Behind the Scenes*, 2006: 9).

The first show aired on 13 May 2002, only months after the terrorist outrage
on the Twin Towers, New York on 9 September 2001; a coincidence which
marked *Spooks* as a timely series.[743] The publicists for the show made much
of this topicality, declaring "*MI5 are in the news everyday – they're in the front*

line of the war against terrorism" (quoted in the *Radio Times*, 11-17 May 2002: 20); a view echoed in sections of the press which noted: "*Not since the Cold War has there been a time when the existence of the security services has seemed more essential or their activities more credible*" (*The Telegraph*, 14 May 2002). Authenticity, it was claimed, was guaranteed by advisers Nick Day, a former MI5 officer, and Mike Baker, an ex-CIA agent (*Radio Times*, 11-17 May 2002: 20), and there was clearly an attempt with the series to improve the standing of the Security Service at such a sensitive period and after more than a decade of public suspicion and disquiet since the notorious '*Spycatcher* Affair' of the mid-1980s. Advisor Mike Baker was at pains to stress: "*In the past, we didn't always make an effort to show our good work. So anything that can be done to generate a balanced view of the services is terrific*" (quoted in ibid.).[744] *Spooks* helped shape a fresh popular image for the intelligence services in the 21st century, at a moment when MI5 was in the process of defining a new role for itself. It promised to "*unlock*" the secret world of the contemporary Security Service and "*update*" the popular notions of what makes a spy (*Spooks* press sheet, BBC). Although it was stressed that there was "*no official cooperation from serving officers*", an "*intelligence source*" commented on an initially pleased MI5: "*I think they are just glad that they are being shown in a positive light for a change, instead of total bastards playing dirty tricks*" (quoted in the *Guardian*, 23 November 2001; *Observer*, 26 May 2002).

Spooks aimed to portray the "*passion, jeopardy and intrigue of people who have to lie for a living*", and, according to Jane Featherstone the head of drama at Kudos, it would provide a "*unique insight*" into the "*human dilemmas that spooks face in their everyday lives*" (quoted in unattributed press cutting, 23 November 2001; *Spooks* press sheet, BBC). The long run of the show meant that characters were lost and replaced as the series unfolded; and in an affront to the basic tenets of 'series narrativity', the promising young agent Helen Flynn (Lisa Faulkner) is shockingly killed off in the second episode. Sir Harry Pearce KBE (Peter Firth), the Head of Counter-Terrorism, remained in place for the entire 10 seasons, and Senior Intelligence Analyst Ruth Evershed (Nicola Walker) appeared in series two-five, reappeared in series eight and then stayed the course until her murder in series 10. Chief of Section and Senior Case Officer Tom Quinn (Matthew MacFadyen) served up the action stuff part-way into series three and then was replaced by Adam Carter (Rupert Penry-Jones) who shouldered his way on to series 7 before he was blown-up in a car bomb. Other significant characters included Case Officers Zoe Reynolds (Keeley Hawes), Fiona Carter (Olga Sosnovska), Jo Portman (Miranda Raison), Ros Myers (Hermione Norris) and Danny Hunter (David Oyelowo).

Creator David Wolstencroft claimed that the series essentially "*followed the contours of society's response to 9/11*". The first season was about defending the realm, "*in the context of a catastrophe that everybody was still absorbing*"; the second season explored the landscape of counter-terrorism, "*now we've got to go and get the bad guys*"; the third season was about how society was going to live with the threat, "*how does it affect our own lives*"; the fourth season dealt with civil liberties, "*how far should the intelligence services really go to protect people*"; and the fifth season was concerned with democratic government, "*can it continue to function in the face of the huge problems – terrorism, fuel crises, immigration, the environmental issues*".[745] According to the publicity machine, *Spooks* had "*trained a hard eye on the morals of both state and Security Service, questioning and probing the major issues of the time*" (Spooks. *Behind the Scenes*: 12-13, 22). However, critics were largely unconvinced by the supposed realism of *Spooks*, or indeed the lofty claims for the series. The show was dismissed as "*shiny and insubstantial*" at the *Guardian* and as "*frothy nonsense*" at the *Observer* (both 14 May 2002). The *Independent* saw it as a "Danger Man *for the post-Cool Britannia generation*", the *Sunday Telegraph* as "*More Thunderbirds International Rescue than John le Carré*" (both 19 May 2002), and the *Guardian* as essentially "The Professionals *with a couple of A-levels and a degree in graphic design*" (13 May 2003). The *Evening Standard* warned of "*Teflon drama – glib and glossy with nothing to stick in the mind*", and in a further review wearied of the clichés and found it all "*spookily familiar*" (13 and 20 May 2002). The *New Statesman* wondered if the endless clichés were deliberate mockery, claiming the dialogue so terrible that you "*wonder if it is deliberate*" (20 May 2002). Things had not improved by the sixth season for this critic, but at least he could claim some compensation in that now "Spooks' *dialogue is so bad that it is almost poetic*" (*The Times*, 5 December 2007). Communications scholar Paul Cobley remarks on the "*paradoxical mix of glamour and realism*" and how the narratives of *Spooks* "*almost entirely bracket out the squalor of much of contemporary London*" (2009: 40, 38). Other onlookers, according to the *Observer*, were wearied by the "*relentlessly positive image of the intelligence service*" (26 May 2002); and some were troubled by the "*spy is cool*" and "*Spies-Who-Shop-At Gap*" approach of the series (*Evening Standard*, 20 May 2002). There was more than a faint implication, it was suggested at the *Independent*, that, "*just five photogenic agents are responsible for the security of the entire country rather than a large and anxiously self-sustaining bureaucracy*" (14 May 2002). Former MI5 officer and latter whistle blower David Shayler, an early, discarded adviser to the production, complained of "*silly plotlines*" and, echoing others, claimed that strikingly handsome, touchingly young, Armani-suited agents (albeit significantly multi-racial and mixed gender) couldn't be further from the truth.[746] Shayler slyly pointed out that adviser Nick Day had served at MI5 for less than two years, and that the "*proposed plotlines of violent anti-abortionists and international rightwing extremist conspiracies were the stuff of liberal-left fantasy rather than any reflection of the real and vital work MI5 does in protection of our security and our democracy*" (2002).[747] The left-liberal view was, in fact, critical of the absence of the "*traditional enemies of the intelligence services*", for it the typical targets of a partisan Security Service: "*Labour back-benchers, East London Imams, Greenpeace members, and people who pick up laptops left behind on the 4.50 from Hassocks*" (*Independent*, 19 May 2002). For those who enjoyed a fast-moving thriller series, *Spooks* was enjoyed as "*high-class hokum*", in which "*MI5 threw off its veil of secrecy and emerged as an ultra-high-tech, forward thinking security organisation populated by attractive young whizz- kids whose lives are devoted to protecting ordinary folk from the hordes of terrorist nasties in our midst*" (*The Telegraph*, 14 May 2002). Overall, as Joseph Oldham has observed, *Spooks* offered-up contemporary, aspirational agents and represented a "*high-image-conscious imagining of MI5*" (2017: 174, 171).

Spooks turned out to be a major hit thriller series, the opening episode being watched by more than nine million viewers, and the inaugural series claiming an impressive 41.2 per cent of audience share (*The Telegraph*, 15 May 2002; *Evening Standard*, 18 June 2002).[748] Released with the strapline "*MI5, not 9 to 5*", a configuration hardly suggestive of realism, the series caught the public's imagination and served up a pleasurable balance of topicality, stylish drama and excitement. The impact of the show was demonstrated in the dramatic increase in hits on the official MI5 website, numbers soaring to 10,000 a week during the run of the show, and 2,500 logging on at the end of the weekly episode. Visitation was helpfully facilitated through a link on the BBC's *Spooks* website entitled "*How do I become a real life spy?*" The public mood was expressed at the *Guardian* where a reviewer claimed *Spooks* "*so good it makes you want to be a spy*" (28 May 2002), and there had indeed been a doubling of applications for jobs in counter-espionage in the two weeks following the launch of the series, something welcomed by the Security Service which had launched several recruitment campaigns since September 11. It was reported in the *People* that around 85 graduates applied for jobs within hours of the screening of the first episode and the paper quoted a senior Whitehall spokesperson who enthused: "*The programme generated a fantastic response from the sort of people MI5 wants to recruit*" (quoted in, 19 May 2002). In an innovative attempt to align fantasy with reality, the BBC accompanied the first series with an interactive website where participants could "*sign up*" as an MI5 officer, uncover a conspiracy and save the world (*Guardian*, 13 May 2002; *Observer*, 26 May 2002). Service recruitment hit the headlines once again during the run of the fourth season in 2005, when it was reported that, "*The violent death of two female characters in the* Spooks *drama series is putting young women off joining MI5*". The concern about the shortage of female applicants coincided with MI5's drive to expand its staff from 2000 to 3000 following the recent terror attacks on the capital. Having to put renewed efforts into explaining to women applicants that a career in the agency was not going to lead to an early grave, the Security Service took out advertisements in the magazines *She* and *Cosmopolitan* (*The Times*, 31 October 2005).[749]

While *Spooks* was generally felt to help the profile of MI5, there were also some concerns at the Security Service about the "*overdramatic portrayal of the organisation*". Although "*entertaining fiction*", there was unease that *Spooks* might give a completely false impression of life inside the Service and its activities. No less than the Director-General of MI5, Eliza Manningham-Buller, lamented that the real world of intelligence was not like it was on television in *Spooks*, "*where everything is (a) knowable, and (b) soluble by six people*" (quoted in Hennessey and Thomas 2011: 251). Specific concern was signalled over the manner in which characters regularly acted outside the law in pursuit of their investigations, for example an episode that, "*depicted MI5 agents murdering an enemy spy, something which is strictly forbidden by law*", and similar alarm was expressed at the depiction of agents "*having sex in the corridors of its headquarters*" (*Sunday Telegraph*, 26 May). "*The programme may be acting as a recruiting sergeant*", a former spook was reported as saying, "*but MI5 will want to be sure they are not attracting fantasists who think they will swan around the world killing bad guys*" (quoted in the *Sunday Telegraph* 16 June 2002). Troubled that the series was encouraging the wrong kind of people to apply to join MI5, the Service website was revised with a "*beefed up 'myths and misunderstandings' section*" which specifically rebutted the "*wilder claims of the BBC series*" (*Spooks: Behind the Scenes*: 36). Overall, though, the Security Service was likely best pleased with the effect *Spooks* was having on its image, and would have been quietly gratified with the assessment of actor Peter Firth, who claimed that, "*People love anything to do with the world of MI5. It's in the public domain so much more now*" (quoted in the *TV Times*, 15 October 2004: 13).

Drama lines of *Spooks* caused public controversy from time to time. Concern began with the opening episode, which dealt with a case of "*boutique terrorism*" undertaken by an American pro-life activist, and this was criticised for "*demonising*" an essentially non-violent organisation (*The Telegraph*, 15 May 2002). In the second episode, in "*one of the most shocking deaths ever depicted in TV fiction*", rookie agent Helen Flynn has her face forced into boiling oil before being shot in the head and killed. Such brutality drew an unprecedented 334 complaints from viewers and according to executive producer Stephen Garrett, who was required to reply to criticism, "*our foes and our fans were shocked in equal measure*" by such an unexpected and violent occurrence (quoted in the *Guardian*, 3 June 2002). The BBC defended the scene, saying it was shown after the watershed at 10pm, a warning was screened beforehand and the camera panned away for the most graphic moments of the agent's suffering *(Sunday Telegraph,* 26 May 2002).[750] Further problems followed the screening of the second episode in series two (2003) that dealt with a 'suicide bomb school' in a British mosque, which was watched by nearly eight million viewers and attracted fierce criticism from the Muslim community. The BBC received nearly 1000 complaints, rebuke from the Muslim Council of Britain for what was seen as a *"distortion of the reality of Muslim life in Britain and an incitement to religious hatred"*, and an e-mail campaign challenging Islamophobia in the media. The morning following the broadcast a young Asian student was beaten by two white youths who claimed he had been *"spooked"*, and the Central Mosque in Birmingham, which had featured in the episode, was daubed with racist graffiti which read: *"Suicide bombers inside – kill the bombers"*. A spokesman for the broadcaster claimed the episode had been *"extensively researched"* and that advice had been obtained from Islamic experts (quoted in the *Guardian, The Times* and *The Telegraph,* 11 June 2003). In the drama, the terrorist cell is infiltrated by a *"sympathetic Muslim character"* based on the *"true story of an Algerian agent who assisted the British Security Services undercover"*, and subsequently the BBC was cleared of inciting violence and hatred by the Broadcasting Standards Commission (*The Times,* 31 July 2003).

As *Spooks* settled into its groove in subsequent seasons, critics tended to soften to its charms. Elaborate claims for realism and relevance tended to be forgotten and the series was now largely tolerated as glamorous and thrilling, a *"smart well-made, human series, which manages to enthral as well as thrill"* (*The Times,* 5 August 2003).[751] Reviewers were now prepared to abide *Spooks* as simply a *"very polished espionage series along James Bond lines"*, and it was *"all so fabulously complicated and implausible, you just have to go with it"* (*Guardian,* 12 June 2003 and 13 September 2005). Indeed, television scholar Joseph Oldham has asserted that, the war on terror aside, *Spooks* must be appreciated in terms of continuity with previous espionage dramas, believing it was conceived as an *"heir to specifically British traditions of spy thriller"* (2017: 163). In an important sense, *Spooks* was in the line of the spy procedural, also aligning itself with the recent form of the 'precinct drama ' and the ideal of the familiar workplace family, as well as ' life-style ' dramas featuring young, aspirational characters. In *Spooks,* though, the drama was presented more dynamically and visually. The popularity of the show meant a higher budget, a *"lot more explosions, boat chases and helicopters"*, and consequently a greater emphasis on action (*TV Times,* 15 October 2004: 13). It had been stressed that it was *"hard to make exciting television about the genuine lives of MI5 staff, when most of them do jobs no more life-threatening than monitoring the output of radio stations in countries you have never heard of, or listening to thousands of hours of crackly telephone traffic on the off-chance of hearing the words bin Laden"* (*The Times*, 3 June 2003). And this was a practical reality increasingly acceptable to the production team, which began to infiltrate James Bond-style self-referential knowingness into storylines; an episode in season two, for example, having a dangerous Serbian agent declare: "*I'm not a fan of spy stories. They always make espionage seem so exciting. And if you ask me, it's probably quite the opposite. The actual job, I mean".* By the time of season seven, *Spooks* was appreciated as a "*programming brand*", a "*resilient ratings winner*" and attracting both a mass audience and a cult following (*The Telegraph*, 8 August 2008).

In the view of the *Guardian*, the show provided a "*glossy, Bondish look combined with genuine ethical dilemmas*" and was perfectly acceptable as a "*designer espionage series*" (26 May 2003). Academic Barbara Korte has recently emphasised the "*prominence of ethics in the series*", believing that *Spooks* functioned as a "*morality play for the early twenty-first century*". She stresses storylines which pinpoint the crisis in confidence of some agents, the moral dilemmas they navigate, a sceptical representation of politicians, a series which devoted "*much attention to matters of political ethics and how moral principles are compromised by politicians, out of personal ambition and for the sake of doubtful political aims*", and an engagement "*in a topical debate about greater transparency and accountability of the secret services and the necessity for stricter oversight by the government to ensure consistency with their legal mandate*".[752] She attributes some of this seriousness to political dramatist Howard Brenton who scripted a selection of the early shows.

Spooks was an important renewal of the form of the spy thriller after the uncertainty cast on the genre following the break-up of the Soviet Union and in terms of the show's adoption of the paranoia and focus on 'terrorism as crime' in the contemporary world. In this respect the series aligned itself with such hit North American films and shows as *The Sum of all Fears* (US, 2002), *Alias* (US, TV, 2001-2006) and *The Agency* (US, TV, 2001-2003). In particular, *Spooks* was (largely unfavourably) compared with the American spy thriller *24* (US, TV, 2001-2010), from which it absorbed its modish stylisation, "*fetishism for technology*" (Erickson 2008: 344), and appearing as a "*state-of-the-art, hip, slick, fast-moving, decidedly gripping drama series with split-screen moments and a restless camera always on the move*" (*The Telegraph*, 18 May 2002). For those receptive to the "*lightning-paced, information-heavy*" approach of the contemporary thriller, *Spooks* was "*one of the coolest home-grown series for years*" (*Time Out*, 15 May 2002); however, despite the claims of publicity, it was an approach "*not really concerned to tell us the truth*" (*The Telegraph*, 18 May 2002). The first season of *Spooks* won the Best Drama Series Award from the British Academy of Film and Television Arts, and future seasons racked up nominations for BAFTA TV awards.

In a critique of recent spy dramas, Joseph Oldham has summarised how *Spooks* initially concerned itself with the combat of terrorists, "*thereby reviving the "counter-terror"* narrative model of *The Professionals* (1977-82), and combined this with a more "*realist tone*", the series then evolving into a "*complex meditation*" on contemporary concerns such as the "*erosion of civil liberties*", the "*growing culture of surveillance*", and "*systemic political corruption*". *Spooks* thus became a "*hybrid*", incorporating traits of the "*conspiracy thriller into the traditional spy thriller model*"; yet any critique was "*limited by the fundamental narrative impulse of spy fiction towards maintaining the status quo*".[753] The *New Statesman* expressed the tension created by such a contradiction another way, suggesting that *Spooks* operated in a "*no man's land between spy genre and real-world espionage*" (20 May 2002). A point critically examined at the *Guardian* following the screening of the final episode of *Spooks* in 2011, where it was concluded that events of the last decade had reduced the distance between the laughably implausible and the horribly real to a very thin line.

> *Spooks's brilliance has been to tiptoe along that line from start to finish. It was first aired six months after 9/11, and ever since then a combination of actual events, political rhetoric and pandemic paranoia has lent it just enough credibility to perturb.*
> (23 October)

"*With a cast of fresh-faces and a budget of several pounds*", Kudos and the BBC embarked in 2008 on the spin-off series *Spooks: Code 9* (*The Times*, 11 August 2008).[754] Disparagingly referred to as '*Baby Spooks*', the drama was set in the near future of 2013 and dealt with a country and Security Service decimated by nuclear attack, where it falls on the younger generation to pick up the pieces and carry on the fight. Unsurprisingly, there were claims that *Spooks: Code 9* was just a cynical exercise in audience manipulation, and that the broadcasters were simply 'cashing in' on the success of the parent show.[755] Executive producer Karen Wilson acknowledged that there was "*negativity*" around the appearance of the drama. "*I don't expect anyone to approach a spin-off series and say really positive things about it*", she admitted (quoted in *The Telegraph*, 8 August 2008). The series aired on BBC 3, a channel serving younger viewers, with the intention to "*appeal to the original spy show's fan base and also to a younger audience*" (*TV Times*, 15 August 2009: 23). The story arc of *Spooks: Code 9* reflected the proposed audience demographic, who would be introduced to a "*new age of ID cards and checkpoints*", the drama suggesting that the "*secret services would be forced to recruit younger, university-aged agents in a desperate bid to infiltrate the ranks of ever younger terrorists and anarchists*" (*The Telegraph*, 8 August 2008). The series of six episodes failed to woo viewers or critics and ran for only a single season. In the judgment of *The Times*, *Spooks: Code 9* fancied itself as "*gritty and hip, combining state torture with a boozy, flirty* This Life *house-share for the torturers, yet it lacks the balls to link the 'code-9' attack with either the Olympics or al-Qaeda*" (11 August 2008).[756]

In another effort to mine the popularity of the show, a movie version of *Spooks* was officially announced in November 2013 and was released in May 2015 as *Spooks: The Greater Good*. The film involved production personnel from the television series, director Bharat Nalluri, writers Jonathan Brackley and Sam Vincent, and producers Jane Featherstone and Stephen Garrett, and carried over actor Peter Firth who plays spy chief Sir Harry Pearce. The story, dealing with both modern terrorism and betrayal in the Service, centres on a threat to the capital, and was shot on location in Berlin, Moscow, the Isle of Man and London. While keeping the emphasis on visual action and style, in several ways the movie version inverts the approach of the established television series. The focus now is on the maverick Pearce, decommissioned from the Service following the loss from custody of a high-profile terrorist, and pursuing a personal agenda to expose the traitor in MI5 he suspects of treachery. Too old for credible physical heroics, Pearce manipulates a young officer who he had earlier shunted to the sidelines of espionage (Kit Harrington) and who can deliver the action stuff. With its barely concealed professional animosities and traitors in the ranks, *Spooks: The Greater Good* presents a forceful critique of the Security Service and hardly polishes the image of MI5 in the manner of the original, which had kept treachery and betrayal largely at the fringes. Reviewers were unimpressed with the upgrade to the big screen. *Variety* dismissed the picture as a "*strained, superfluous spinoff*", which "*plays less as an organic extension of the series' universe than an all-purpose genre piece nominally tailored to fit the 'Spooks' franchise*"; while *Empire* could only rate it as a "*decent, mid-list spy thriller, suspended somewhere between le Carré and Bond but with a budgetary austerity in keeping with UK government spending cuts that keeps it out of the real high-stakes game*" (both 8 May 2015).

The spies who went back into the cold

The cold war may be over, but as a genre for films and fiction it has survived. Thriller writers have returned to their old hunting grounds, as if the Wall never came down.
(*Guardian*, 10 November 1995)

It says something ominous about the state of the world that the Cold War – with its rigid ideological convictions, clearly defined adversaries, and Mutually Assured Destruction –would invoke a sense of wistfulness.
(James Kirchick 2016)

The spy thriller still pines for the Soviet Union.
(John Updike, *The New Yorker*, 13 June 2005)

The immediate consequence of the fall of the Berlin Wall was that spy authors went in "*search of new territory*". However, as Mark Lawson writing in 1995 noted: "*like 'sleepers' planted in enemy territory ... British spy writers have been gradually reactivated*". In what Lawson has classified as the "*evolutionary*" trend of the new spy fiction, John le Carré examined the instabilities in the new global order in *The Night Manager* (1993) and *Our Game* (1995), and as we have seen the new environment was explored in dramas such as *Sleepers*, *The Waiting Time*, *Bullet to Beijing* and *Midnight in St. Petersburg*; while, in what Lawson has classified as the "*museum*" trend, Len Deighton, for example, "*froze time*" and sought to turn the spy story from a contemporary to a historical genre with a new spy trilogy *Faith*, *Hope* and *Charity* (1994-96), set in 1987 when the embers of the Cold War were beginning to dim.[757] At the moment of the post-Cold War thaw, Lawson sensed that the writing in both the evolutionary and museum modes was tending to look over its shoulder, serving up "*elegies for an epoch and a genre, elegant endings rather than new beginnings*" (1995).

The incentive to set spy stories in the past, Lawson's 'museum trend', has proved enduring. *Booklist* has commented on the "*remarkable resurgence in mystery and espionage fiction set prior to and during World War II*" for example (1 May 2011), evident with such writers as David Downing with the '*Station*' series, Aly Monroe with the Peter Cotton series and William Boyd with *Restless* (2006), who have set their stories in the wartime and the later 1940s period. Jeremy Duns with the Paul Dark series, Ian McEwan with *The Innocent* (1990) and *Sweet Tooth* (2012), Alan Judd with *Legacy* (2001), and Jonathan Coe with *Expo 58* (2013) have sent their spies back into the cold, using the Cold War period for a nostalgic evocation of classic espionage settings. The author John Lawton has treated an extended history of the wartime and post war decades in such novels as *Blackout* (1995), *Old Flames* (1996), *A Little White Death* (1998) and *Riptide* (2001), in which a London detective becomes involved in such sensational intelligence and security events as the 'Buster' Crabb and the 'Profumo' Affairs. The recent spy dramas set in the Cold War are in the lineage ploughed by earlier films and serials such as 'Philby, Burgess & Maclean' (TV, 1977), *Wynne & Penkovsky* (TV, 1985) and *Scandal* (film, 1989),[758] and they have been paralleled by American mini-series dealing with Cold War espionage such as *The Company* (US, TV, 2007) and *The Americans* (US, TV, 2013-), the films *Argo* (US, 2012) and *Bridge of Spies* (US, 2015), and the German television serial *Deutschland 83* (Ger, TV, 2015).

It has been suggested that the "*nostalgia*" for the Cold War could be "*comforting*" and "*familiar*" in a security environment which had become more uncertain. That espionage of the recent past could appear *"clean"* and bound by *"rules"* in comparison with contemporary terrorism which in contrast seemed *"dirty"* and *"unpredictable"*.[759] As the *New Yorker* has asserted, *"There was an intelligibility if not a friendly intimacy in the old contest, one between two large, idealistic, rough-mannered nations seeking to maintain their spheres of influence short of tripping nuclear war"* (13 June 2005). Indeed, it has recently been noted that the spy genre has been *"returning to the moral ambiguity of its cold war heights"*, and understood as a reaction to the trend following 9/11 for rather simplistic *"tough macho thrillers about special forces heroes"* dealing with terrorists in a black and white world (*Guardian*, 10 May 2015). Many critics have observed that modern espionage is technology intensive and essentially static, the front-line now manned by charmless computer geeks staring at monitors and engaged in an activity essentially nondramatic. This is why, as *The Telegraph* has expressed it, *"so many new spy dramas are old ones"* (2 May 2015). James Kirchick has posited that the renewed interest in Cold War culture and politics isn't a fad. *"It points to a deeper longing for an earlier, simpler time"*, he maintains, *"when the nature of global conflict was bipolar – as opposed to the confusing, multipolar mess we have today"*. During the Cold War the West knew who its enemies were. *"The borders delineating that enmity were as obvious, and as physically stark, as the Berlin Wall. Tense and dangerous as those times were, at least we could distinguish good guys from bad – for the most part"* (2016).

As early as 1990, shortly after the Berlin Wall had first been breached, a spy story looked back to the Cold War period. *The Innocent* was an espionage novel written by Ian McEwan, a major British writer of the late 20th century.[760] The action is set in the mid-1950s and tells the story of Leonard Marnham, a young Post Office technician sent to Berlin where he is seconded to the American CIA under the supervision of Bob Glass and instructed to work on a highly secret project, a tunnel beneath the city under the Russian sector from which the Anglo-American alliance will tap into Soviet military telephone and telegraph communications. Lonely and repetitive work, the shy and immature Leonard, literally an 'innocent abroad', finds companionship, romance and a sexual awakening with the divorced Maria, a Berliner who lives in periodic fear of her abusive former husband, Otto. Leonard's settled world collapses when Otto steals into their bedroom, fights with Leonard and is killed by Maria. Fearing the police, the couple decides to dispose of the body; there follows a grisly scene in which the corpse is dismembered, and a confused Leonard ends up stowing two cases of body parts in the tunnel. Worrying that they will be discovered by the Allies, Leonard gives away the location of the tunnel. The passageway is stormed by the Russians and the Briton has a nervous wait to see if the Soviets will make public the grisly discovery. Leonard and Maria are estranged by the recent experience and he flies home to London and a new life.

A postscript brings the story forward to the summer of 1987. Leonard is visiting Berlin and looking over his old haunts. He has been prompted by a letter from Maria in which she discloses the events in Berlin following the departure of Leonard and her life in America where she settled with Bob Glass. She reveals that the secret of the tunnel was betrayed by George Blake, a British (SIS) official in Berlin who Leonard had casually told about the 'decoding equipment' and who had passed this onto the Soviets and thus provoked the raid. Leonard resolves to visit the recently widowed Maria in America and possibly return with her to Berlin.

The Berlin Tunnel, codenamed GOLD by the SIS and STOPWATCH by the CIA, occupied a *"historic and honoured place in the story of the Cold War"* (Stafford 2002: 3). The initial planning commenced in 1953 and followed similar successful smaller British operations in Vienna codenamed CLASSIFICATION.[761] The complex construction and technical challenge of the 1,476 feet long tunnel was largely met by the Americans and communications interception was achieved between May 1955 and April 1956 (11 months and 11 days in total) at which point Russian and East German engineers stumbled across the chamber. When the story of the tunnel broke in the American press in 1956, the *New York Herald Tribune* described the venture as the *"stuff of which thriller films are made"* (quoted in Stafford 2002: 11). Ian McEwan drew the details of his story from David C. Martin's *Wilderness of Mirrors* (1980), and used two historical characters in William Harvey, the legendary CIA station chief in Berlin, and George Blake, the MI6 officer who betrayed the tunnel.[762]

The Innocent is an unconventional love story, a black comedy and historical spy fiction; and in this unusual combination the story draws together the three main elements of McEwan's literary style and concerns as they had developed to that point: the dark nightmares, power of love and the possibility of redemption of the early writing; the greater social, political and historical awareness of more recent years; and an optimism in the hope of renewal, the promise of reunion. Sanford Sternlicht has pin-pointed *The Innocent* as a *"macabre comedy of manners about twentieth-century nationality, sexuality, and political mores"*,[763] and Kiernan Ryan as a *"spy yarn within which is concealed a wry historical novel about the twilight of British supremacy, the triumph of American cultural imperialism and the ice age of the cold war"* (quoted in Head 2007: 96). The two main themes of the story are the suspicions, prejudices and tensions at the heart of the Anglo-American alliance and innocence in its varied guises.[764]

The film rights had originally been acquired by Paramount and set to star Kyle MacLachlan, Willem Dafoe and Lena Olin. However, the studio put the property in turnaround and *The Innocent* emerged as an Anglo-German film adaptation with a script by Ian McEwan. Produced in 1993, it did not appear in English-speaking countries until 1995. The picture suffered from some bizarre casting, with the Welshman Anthony Hopkins playing the American CIA agent Bob Glass, the American Campbell Scott playing the Englishman Leonard Marnham, and the Italian Isabella Rossellini playing the German Maria. Hopkins in particular was accused of an uncertain, wandering accent. By all accounts the production was an unhappy experience, with the producers demanding changes in the presentation of the story to foreground the love affair and downplay the "*dark elements*" (Mann 2005: 536). The director was the acclaimed John Schlesinger, who had brilliantly contributed to *An Englishman Abroad* (TV, 1983) and *A Question of Attribution* (TV, 1991), but described *The Innocent* as a "*ghastly experience*" (quoted in ibid.: 537).[765] For some obscure reason, the spy George Blake is here named Geoffrey Black. The ending of the story is altered in two significant ways: first, there is an airport scene added where Len and Maria painfully separate, and this seems a gratuitous nod to a similar scene in *Casablanca* (US, 1942) in which Rossellini's mother, the great Hollywood actress Ingrid Bergman, had played her most famous role; and second, the reuniting of the couple in Berlin amidst the joyous scenes of the Wall dividing East and West coming down in 1989 provides the definite happy ending which the producers seemingly required. The film's tagline, "*At a time of intrigue. In a world of secrets. The only thing you can trust is your heart*", aptly captured the intention of the producers. McEwan had been disappointed that script revisions meant that the story lost some of the emphasis on the spy tunnel, and it must be concluded that a fascinating historical event of the Cold War had been more robustly captured in the novel, but was squandered in the movie (Mann 2005: 536).

By far the most high-profile return to the Cold War for a British screen entertainment was the motion picture version of John le Carré's *Tinker Tailor Soldier Spy* (once again without the commas), released with much fanfare in 2011, produced at Working Title, directed by the Swede Tomas Alfredson and which starred an ensemble of prime British acting talent, including Gary Oldman cast against type as George Smiley, John Hurt as Control, Benedict Cumberbatch as Peter Guillam and Colin Firth as the mole Bill Haydon.[766] Locations were shot in London, Budapest, Hungary and Istanbul, Turkey, and a disused army barracks in north London was taken over by the production as an economical space to shoot the picture (*The Telegraph*, 3 September 2011). It was thought a gamble to adapt a novel notorious for its complex plot and lack of physical action, and make a period picture, a "*slow-burn spy thriller*", which would be difficult to sell to the multiplex audience (*Sight and Sound*, October 2011: 16). As actor Gary Oldman anxiously expressed it: "*It's not Bourne or Bond*" (quoted in the *Radio Times*, 10-16 September 2011: 32).

However, co-star Colin Firth seemed to judge the *zeitgeist* about right when he commented, "*One can be almost nostalgic about the Cold War now*" (quoted in *The Telegraph*, 3 September 2011). Working Title was encouraged by the critical and commercial success of the recent German film *The Lives of Others* (Ger, *Das Leben der Anderen*, 2006), set in 1984 and dealing with the surveillance of East German citizens by the state police (*The Times, Culture Magazine*, 11 September 2011); although the producers might have been made a little more anxious by the commercial disappointment of the American *The Good Shepherd* (US, 2006), about the early days of the CIA. The "*sexing up*" of the attraction meant a darker approach to the story and a tougher, more menacing Smiley, producing a "*lean and tightly wound period piece*" (*The Telegraph*, 29 July 2011). There was also the obvious anxiety regarding the existing adaptation for television which was revered as a classic against which a new film was sure to be compared.[767] Some distance was created between the two versions through the architectural re-imagining of the 1970s in terms of hi-tech modernism, especially so in the case of the Circus, which now exists as a modernist seventies block *within* a complex of historical buildings.[768] The cinematic Circus exterior was filmed at Blythe House in London's West Kensington, now part of another British state institution, the Victoria and Albert Museum. The spatial design of the picture centred on frames, grids and cages, suggestive of isolation and entrapment.[769]

The picture was a commercial and critical success, although much of the texture of the original had to be jettisoned to accommodate a standard two-hour commercial movie. The adaptation for the small screen as a leisurely serial allowing for time and space had indeed been praised. "*This, really, is the joy of filming a story of such complexity in seven 50-minute slices, rather than trying to cram it all into a 90-minute feature film. No nuance need be lost, no tiny detail overlooked*" lauded the *Evening News* at the time of the original television serial (11 September 1979). But it was the case here, as John le Carré colourfully expressed it, that the producers had to "*turn a cow into an Oxo cube*" (quoted in *Sight and Sound*, October 2011: 19). The few critical detractors made something of the unfortunate condensation required for a two-hour commercial movie. The review in *The Atlantic*, largely favourable, felt that to "*strip down or minimalize le Carré, however, is to sacrifice the almost Tolkienesque grain and depth of his created world: the decades-long back-story, the lingo, the arcana, the liturgical repetitions of names and functions*" (December 2011); *Sight and Sound* felt that the picture lost some dramatic and emotional impact as there was too little time to build up the characters of the potential moles and thereby develop tension at the final unmasking (October 2011: 79); and *Film Quarterly* believed the picture failed to "*compellingly reimagine the story*", that Oldman's reading of Smiley's blankness was "*far less sophisticated than Guinness's*", and the outcome was a "*depoliticized film*"

(Winter 2011: 37, 38, 41). Elsewhere, the picture found acclaim as a "*marvellously chill and acrid cold war thriller*" (*Guardian*, 5 September 2011); a "*beautifully-judged thriller whose relationship with its predecessor simply gives it another layer of interest*" (*Guardian*, 9 September 2011); and a "*hugely successful treatment of formidably resistant materials*" (*Sight and Sound*, October 2011: 20). There was also widespread praise for the film's evocation of the 1970s, John Naughton noting the picture's "*unsparing accuracy of its vision of a near-bankrupt, early-'70s England*" (*The Word*, January 2012: 48). *Tinker Tailor Soldier Spy* won British Academy of Film and Television Arts Awards for Best British Film and Best Adapted Screenplay.

The eminent film scholar David Bordwell has declared himself "*fascinated by a film that can succeed both critically and financially and still leave its audience puzzled about its plot*". He sees *Tinker Tailor Soldier Spy* as a refute to the "*dumbing down*" of recent cinema; as one of a group of contemporary movies from ambitious film-makers who aim at sectors of the audience who are willing to exert some intellectual effort, creating films which seek to balance novelty with intelligibility. Appropriately, the narrative style of the picture harked back to the more elliptical storytelling of the 1960s and 1970s and such "*self-consciously wrought genre films*" as *Blow-Up* (1966) and *The Conversation* (US, 1974).[770] There were hopes in some quarters that Alfredson would be assigned to the two remaining parts of the trilogy and plans were announced that Working Title was considering another John le Carré adaptation, but so far nothing has materialised (*Sight and Sound*, October 2011: 20).[771] The dramatic return to the Cold War, especially those stories based in the 1970s, was no doubt a legacy of the success and importance of the BBC's *Tinker Tailor Soldier Spy* of 1979, and the classic serial provided narrative and iconography that would influence subsequent treatments of the decade. As Douglas McNaughton has commented, feeling of a decaying Britain embedded in the committee rooms and corridors of the Circus, depressing Fleet Street restaurants, faded hotel rooms and shabby safe houses, constructed a "*drab, confining chronotope of post-imperial 1970s Cold War England*", and it was a representation that lingered in the cultural imagination.[772]

A further evocation of espionage in the 1970s came with *Legacy*, a spy novel written by Alan Judd (Alan Adwin Petty), a former official in the Foreign Office and once Personal Assistant to the Chief of the Secret Intelligence Service Sir Colin McColl. It was first published in 2001 and later adapted for television in 2013. It continues the story of Charles Thoroughgood who had first appeared in Judd's prize-winning début novel *A Breed of Heroes* (1981). The character has now left the army after service in Northern Ireland in the early-1970s and is undergoing initial training at MI6: a noticeable shift from 'hot' war to 'cold' war for the character. He is detailed to make contact with a former university acquaintance, Viktor Koslov, a new appointment in the Russian Embassy who might possibly be 'turned' as he has been observed frequenting a prostitute. In the event, Charles is stunned to learn from Koslov that his recently deceased father, a surveyor who worked on secret government establishments, was a long-standing Soviet agent. Shaken by the revelation, he further discovers that his father was also implicated in LEGACY, a long-term KGB operation to create a network of secret caches at strategic locations in Western countries. Thoroughgood, wanting to get to the bottom of his father's treachery, continues as case officer for Koslov. Using the latter, who has bits of the puzzle, Charles is able to locate two secret caches of sabotage materials, as well as steer away two KGB heavies who are closing in on the Russian. In a final revelation, a relieved Thoroughgood is informed that is father was in fact a double-agent, feeding the Soviets disinformation.

Legacy is a story of betrayal, of one's country and, seemingly, of one's family. With its deliberate plotting and careful attention to the routine of espionage work, much of which necessarily takes place behind a desk in an office, *Legacy* is in the tradition of the realistic espionage story and many have compared it with the writing of John le Carré. The resemblance is made even more apparent in Alan Judd's setting the story in the 1970s, a clear reference back to a 'Golden Age' of the British spy novel, although the story lacks much of the social and moral critique to be found in the le Carré school. *Legacy* draws on the recognisable ideological landscape and characterisations of the middle-Cold War, and in this regard, there is the necessary reference in the story to historical reality, the industrial unrest, the expulsion of 105 Soviet diplomats from Great Britain in 1971, the immediate legacy of the 'Profumo Affair', the double-agent Oleg Penkovsky, the defector Lyalin, and, with the caches of armaments, the contemporary anxieties regarding guerrilla-style *Spetsnaz* operations.[773] Judd later wrote that he,

> *wanted to show that spying involves talking to people rather than killing them, that intelligence organisations are characterised far more by loyalty than betrayal, that humour is more common than backstabbing but that nevertheless the work can have personal costs.*[774]

The reviewer of the novel at *The Telegraph* noted an essential cosiness in the construction:

> *This is a Secret Intelligence Service run by avuncular civil servants who commute from Kent and Surrey, spend the weekends digging their gardens, and, in the sleepy and indirect manner of well-clubbed gentlemen, play brilliant endgames that protect us against enemies without and within.*

As such, the paper found *Legacy* a "*dense and satisfying thriller*", but, with its "*understated flair and essential British decency*" and ultimate denial of treachery, the story was removed from the critical tradition of British spy fiction of the previous generation (29 September 2001).[775]

The BBC television drama *Legacy*, starring Charlie Cox and Andrew Scott, was broadcast in 2013 and was a truncated and simplified version of the original story. For reasons of dramatic excitement, much of the drudgery and routine of training, office life and family obligations are excised in favour of operational procedure, chases and some gunplay. The outcome, shot in a murky, restless, washed-out style, edges more towards being a spy thriller, much complexity being lost to a restricted 90-minute format. Critics were far from impressed, finding the drama stranded somewhere between the adrenaline-rush excitement of the very contemporary *Spooks* and the brilliant BBC adaptations of John le Carré around the turn of the 1980s. In the summary of the *Guardian*, the dramatisation lacked the "*sophistication, the genius and complexity of character and plot*" of a le Carré, or the "*feeling that this is actually what it was all like*" (29 November 2013). A significant revision in the television adaptation was a suggestion that in the dénouement the Service lies to Charles about his father, who probably *was* a Soviet agent, and this suggestion of penetration and betrayal is the obvious legacy of the le Carré narratives on the dramatisation.[776] The *Independent* acknowledged *Legacy* as an "*exercise in Cold War nostalgia*", unfortunately for that reviewer, the "*only thing it managed to make me feel nostalgic about was* Spooks", unintentionally generating a hankering for more contemporary spy stories (29 November 2013).

The Game is an original drama serial written for television consisting of six episodes and produced at the BBC. Unusually, it premiered on BBC America towards the end of 2014, then on BBC First, Australia early in 2015, before receiving its UK broadcast on BBC 2 in April 2015. Location filming took place in London, Birmingham and Derbyshire, with the infamously 1970s 'brutalist' Central Library in Birmingham standing in for MI5 headquarters. The action takes place at the heart of MI5 in 1972, when a team is assembled to look into 'Operation GLASS', in which the Soviets are activating sleeper agents for some unknown purpose. Headed by 'Daddy', the chief of MI5 (Brian Cox), the taskforce also includes his deputy Sarah Montag (Victoria Hamilton), her husband and technical expert Alan Montag (Jonathan Aris), and the operative Joe Lambe (Tom Hughes) with a back-story which puts a question mark on his loyalty. With the Russians always seemingly one step ahead of the Security Service and the deadly assassin 'Odin' (Jevgenij Sitochin) silencing important leads, it is concluded there is a mole in the team codenamed Phoenix. Suspicion initially falls on Alan, but he has been covering for his wife and she is eventually trapped. Sleeper agents are traced to the highest levels of government and a planned *coup d'état* is averted.

The storyline is similar to a number of spy tales published in the period depicted, dealing with highly-placed Soviet agents and which reflected a widespread fear of communist subversion in society.[777] And indeed, alarmist voices on the Right had warned of the actual threat of the type of 'sleeper' agent depicted in the drama, *"apparently perfectly respectable people who have instructions about what to do if called upon in an emergency"* (Pincher 1991: 28). Former spy chief Stella Rimington has given some insight into this world, more prosaic than usually treated in spy fiction, but which consisted of the Soviets seeking to recruit agents of influence and who sometimes MI5 was able to turn around and report back to the British (Rimington 2002: 154).

For creator and co-writer Toby Whitehouse the 1970s didn't feel very far away, and, influenced by a recent reading of John le Carré's *The Spy Who Came in from the Cold*, what attracted him to the period was the *"idea of this secret war where great victories could never be celebrated or conspicuously rewarded and great losses were dealt with in private"*. *"I wanted to look at an entire war"*, he explained, *"conducted in the shadows and the effect that would have on personalities. There's also a romantic element – the whole idea of secret codes and rendezvous and the low-fi nature of the work"* (quoted in the *Guardian*, 10 May 2015). Nicholas Barnett has suggested that *The Game* evoked a *"nostalgia for how spying used to be done"* and *"reminisces for the security of the Cold War and for a form of espionage familiar through the genre of spy drama"*. He sees the nostalgic lens of the drama focusing in particular on depictions of the family, with the counter-espionage team headed by the symbolically-named 'Daddy', and on class, with the 1970s characterised by division between the classes and referenced in repeated asides to such conflicts as the miner's strike and resultant blackouts of 1974. As he asserts, *"the nineteen-seventies are situated as an interregnum during which instability rose and between a golden age of consensus between political parties and the 'revolution' of the Thatcher years"*.[778] *The Game* attracted mixed reviews, *The Telegraph* referring to the drama as a *"nicotine-stained wallow in Cold War spy nostalgia"*, and found it a little pointless, a kind of *"Tinker Tailor Soldier Why?"* (2 May 2015). The *"particularly British"* *The Game* won plaudits at the *Hollywood Reporter* which hoped that success of the serial would create interest in more spy dramas set in the recent past (11 May 2014). In the summer of 2015, a clearly disappointed Toby Whitehouse tweeted that *The Game* would not be returning for a second series, a clear indication that the expensive serial had not been enough of a critical or ratings success.

The metaphor of 'the game' has been commonplace in the genre of spy fiction. It harks back at least as far as Kipling's notion of the 'Great Game' fought out on the frontier of Empire between the British and the Russians in the 19th century, a *"mixture of child's play and theatrics, sports and adventure, a seemingly lighthearted form of war"* (Horn 2013: 121). Eva Horn extends this idea to consider the place of the game and play in the hypothetical conflict of the Cold War. In such a condition, she maintains, battle occurs at the level of simulation and 'playing' *"entails the suspension of real war and its transfer into the Great Game of espionage and military scenarios"* (239). Wesley Britton has indicated that the metaphor has been especially potent for British espionage novels, films and television series, in which a *"tone of civility was seen in images of gamesmanship such as animal hunts, chess, card games and jigsaw puzzles"*. It was an imaginative world in which *"Agents fought deadly obstacle courses in literal mazes"* (2004: 11), and explicitly present in the stories of, for example, Len Deighton (chess in *Funeral in Berlin*, 1964, high-tec war gaming in *Spy Story*, 1974), and the Callan adventures of James Mitchell (military gaming).

The most recent of the historical dramas, *Tinker Tailor Soldier Spy*, *Legacy* and *The Game*, have been set in the 1970s. This follows trends elsewhere in popular culture, in popular music, fashion and the wider screen drama, which has brought a new fascination for a decade until recently dismissed as tacky and tasteless. British films such as *Velvet Goldmine* (1998), *The Look of Love* (2013) and *24 Hour Party People* (2002), and the television series *Life on Mars* (TV, 2006) and *Red Riding* (TV, 2009) have fed an interest in the seventies, for older viewers one motivated by nostalgia, and for younger viewers one led by a curiosity in style. While there has continued to be a healthy fascination in the popular culture of the 1960s, thus far in recent times this decade has only been available for spoofing as far as espionage dramas have been concerned, the result, no doubt, of the huge success of the *Austin Powers* films (US, 1997-2002), and helped by the popular repeats on British television in the 1990s of *The Avengers* (TV, 1961-69).

Conspiracy thrillers

The Thatcher/Reagan Eighties were a fertile time for paranoid political thrillers such as Edge of Darkness. *In our post-11 September world, conspiracy drama is set to make a comeback.*
(*Independent Review*, 10 May 2002)

Surveillance is an inescapable part of life in the UK. Every time we make a telephone call, send an email, browse the internet, or even walk down our local high street, our actions may be monitored and recorded. To respond to crime, combat the threat of terrorism, and improve administrative efficiency, successive UK governments have gradually construct-

ed one of the most extensive and technologically advanced surveillance systems in the world.
(*Surveillance: Citizens and the State*, House of Lords Select Committee on the Constitution 2009)

We have learnt in recent years to translate almost all of political life in terms of conspiracy.
(John le Carré, quoted in Barber 1978: 48)

Joseph Oldham has recently asserted that the conspiracy genre became "*diluted*" once the political turbulence of the 1980s passed into the calmer period of the 1990s. The ousting of Margaret Thatcher from the role of prime minister by her own party in November 1990 was symbolic of this shift and the serial *A Very British Coup* (1988) marked the "*culmination of a paranoid narrative about the thwarted hopes of socialism*" (2017: 153-55, 189). However, paranoid and conspiracy themes have remained central in spy fiction, continuing to cast a darker, more pessimistic hue across the range of stories dealing with the secret world. Anxieties of institutional conspiracy have recently entered period drama treating espionage, as with the film adaptation of *Tinker Tailor Soldier Spy* (2011) and the television series *The Hour* (2011), providing a historical dimension to what Joseph Oldham has argued as a "*crisis*" in the image of post-Cold War optimism. A darker turn in such screen dramas as *Skyfall* (2013) and *Hunted* (2012) have continued the development of conspiratorial tropes within the spy genre, "*challenging its tendency towards optimism and closure, and this tension offers the potential to engage with new political contexts in a contemporary framework*" (Oldham 2015).

State of Play was a conspiracy thriller written by Paul Abbott and broadcast by the BBC over six episodes in 2003. The story concerned the investigation of the seemingly unrelated killings of a black youth on the streets of London and a young woman commuting on the Underground who works as a research assistant for Labour Member of Parliament Stephen Collins (David Morrissey). The news story is pursued at *The Herald* by the investigative journalist Cal McCaffrey (John Simm), a former campaign manager for Collins, who slowly unearths damning evidence of an affair between the politician and his assistant, and a deep-seated conspiracy involving the oil industry seeking official concessions through the government's Energy Select Committee chaired by Collins. The serial, according to Beth Johnson, engages with the "*complex language of 'spin', persuasion and political and personal exposé*" (2013: 87).

The drama weaved a heady and complex blend of ambition, infidelity, personal and professional treachery, with underground spaces serving as metaphors for underhand deeds, and occasional *noir* styling, in the words of Beth

Jonhson, resonant of "*clandestine deals, espionage, personal betrayal and political and corporate wrongdoing*" (91). *State of Play* has been seen as an early indication of the end of the cautious love affair between the media and New Labour which had come to power with much fanfare in 1997. The serial dramatised the betrayal felt by some of the new 'ethical politics' which the Party had trumpeted, and suggested that sleaze, scandals and political spin were part of the normal business of politics. Abbott later claimed: "*The thing I wanted to tackle within a big, six-part drama was the way in which modern government has become so attached to big business*" (quoted in *TV Zone Special* 58, 2003: 53). As a conspiracy thriller, *State of Play* organised its narrative as an investigation, in the tradition Francesco Rosi's classic *Cadaveri eccellenti* (*Illustrious Corpses*, It/Fr, 1976), and, in centring on a journalist as a 'pursuer of truth,' in the tradition of *All the President's Men* (US, 1976) and *Defence of the Realm* (1986).

The series gathered generally excellent reviews and plaudits for the acting of Morrissey, Simm, Bill Nighy (as the newspaper editor) and Kelly Macdonald (as a fellow reporter). The reviewer at the *Radio Times* writing on the eve of the final episode breathlessly claimed that, "*It's been a heck of a ride these past six weeks, hasn't it?* State of Play *has been a seriously good drama ... the script fairly crackled and the story has been gripping, grown-up stuff*".[779] Abbott meticulously researched the drama, spending much time at the House of Commons and relied for insights on parliamentary correspondents Simon Hoggart of the *Guardian* and Norman Lane the deputy editor of *The Times* (*Radio Times*, 17-23 May 2003: 26).

State of Play attracted favourable comparisons with the classic television conspiracy thriller *Edge of Darkness* (TV, 1985) and cynical political drama *House of Cards* (TV, 1990), and it is now regarded as one of the finest of all television conspiracy serials. While plans for a sequel were announced, a "*particularly provocative theme involving the government and the royal family*" (*TV Zone Special* 58, 2003: 55), the climate at the BBC following the *Hutton Report* (2004) criticising the Corporation following its editorial handling of the death of former weapons inspector David Kelly and the issue of 'weapons of mass destruction' in Iran, made this unlikely and the new production never materialised. Although a Hollywood feature film was adapted from the original story and released in 2009 starring Ben Affleck and Russell Crowe.

Science-fiction has long reflected the anxieties attending new technologies and their dystopian potential. The television serial *1990* (1977-78) posited a nightmarish 1984-style future of a tyrannical Public Control Department which denies the rights of the individual and maintains control through ID cards, rationing, censorship and electronic/audio/physical surveillance, and anticipated the unease which would become more widespread in the new millennium when digital technologies greatly enhanced the potential of the authorities for snooping and indexing. *Bugs* (TV, 1995-99), which ran for five seasons, incorporated the fashion for technology, and its team of young investigators moulded into a high-tech crime unit fed the taste for *"futuristic espionage"*.[780] While *Bugs* tended to *"reassure about the realities of surveillance"* and *"support the view that surveillance is a necessary dimension of life today"*, *The Last Enemy* was more serious and critical. A five-part conspiracy thriller produced at the BBC and broadcast in 2008, it is set in the near future when Great Britain has been transformed into a security state following a terrorist outrage and new technology is being developed providing the authorities with total surveillance. A brilliant, unconventional and obsessive mathematician Stephen Ezard (Benedict Cumberbatch) returns to London from China after a four year absence to attend the funeral of his idealist brother Michael (Max Beesely). Allied with Yasim Anwar (Anamaria Marinca), the wife he didn't know his brother had, Ezard is immediately plunged into a conspiracy relating to the mysterious death of Michael, an overseas aid worker, is drawn into the government's controversial new surveillance scheme, becomes the target then ally of rogue agent David Russell (Robert Carlyle), and pursues the truth about a tainted vaccine dispensed in the aid camp. Using his privileged access to the government's experimental TIA (Total Information Awareness) technology, Ezard is able to discover the crisis at the laboratory which led to the contaminated vaccine, and is shocked to find his brother on the same trail, although it is soon learned that Michael is dying from having taken the vaccine. Ezard, with help from Russell and Yasmin, forges on to expose the monumental cover-up.

A complicated story shot in London and Romania, *The Last Enemy* attracted only modest viewing figures which declined through the run of the drama and generally poor notices from the press which found the drama implausible. The writer Peter Berry aimed for a breakneck thriller of contemporary relevance, and the serial dramatised the anxieties which attended the expansion and intensification of security and surveillance following the terrorist outrages in New York in September 2001 and London in July 2005 (*Radio Times*, 12-16 February 2008: 29-30).[781] *"With phone-taps dominating the news of late, along with database leaks, security threats and identity card legislation, the thriller wades head on into some of the most contentious items on the political agenda"* was how *The Telegraph* summarised the timeliness of the drama (16 February 2008). As the intelligence scholars Richard Aldrich and Antony Field have recorded, *"The evolution of the global terrorist threat has led to a fundamental reconsideration of attitudes towards surveillance practices in the United Kingdom"* (Aldrich and Field 2011: 292). There was some unease following the introduction of Suspicious Activity Reports (SARs) which placed a legal requirement on private institutions such as banks, accountants and solicitors to co-operate with the network of security agencies regarding suspicious financial transactions. This resulted in the filing of 278,665 reports in 2012 and critics worried that some people might appear suspicious "*because a number of chance activities have coalesced to generate something which a computer thinks is a problem*" (296). SARs are part of a wider regime of electronic surveillance of British citizens, a situation covered by the new term 'dataveillance', which also includes the requirement of mobile phone companies and internet service providers to retain 'communications data', a vast archive of people's telephone calls, e-mails and web pages accessed. Over half a million requests for information from nearly 800 public bodies were made to data holders in 2008, and many felt such mind-boggling activity constituted an unacceptable intrusion into privacy and confidentiality. In August 2004, the Information Commissioner Richard Thomas had warned against the possibility of the UK sleepwalking into what he referred to as a "*surveillance society*" (*The Times*, 16 August 2004). Concern was registered in the number of official and semi-official reports which examined the issues and dangers, such as *A Report on the Surveillance Society* (Surveillance Studies Network 2006), *Dilemmas of Privacy and Surveillance: Challenges of Technological Change* (Royal Academy of Engineering 2007) and *Surveillance: Citizens and the State* (House of Lords 2009).

The TIA initiative in *The Last Enemy* resembled the government's Intercept Modernisation Programme (IMP), a new domestic intercept plan unveiled in 2008 at a projected cost of £12 billion, and fearfully described as a "*vast government-run silo*" storing the "*details of every phone call, email, text and instance of web access by each person in the UK*" (Aldrich and Field 2011: 294). *The Last Enemy* thus dramatised the "*new intelligence ecology*" of the post-9/11 and -7/7 worlds, in which "*knowledge-intensive security*" is seen as premium, and in which, as Aldrich and Field express it, the "*basic currency is huge volumes of personal data*" (301). The question which legislators and liberal watchdogs puzzle over is how society in a period of threat can ensure accountability and rights alongside safety and protection.

"*For a thriller about surveillance*", the *Guardian* reported, "The Last Enemy is surprisingly unwatchable", the reviewer finding the story "*bewildering, dreary and dull*", and the characters "*incredible*" (18 February 2008). Screened on Public Broadcasting Stations in America, *The New York Times* judged it "*mysterious – but not in the least interesting*", the exposition "*murky*" and the violence "*generic with a heavily recycled feel*" (4 October 2008). *The Last Enemy*, though, attracted a strong endorsement at *Variety*, where it was claimed that, "*The British excel when it comes to paranoid TV thrillers*", and that this, the most recent, "*comes close to being a masterpiece and could hardly feel more contemporary or timely*" (2 October 2008).

Hunted was an action-oriented conspiracy thriller broadcast across eight one-hour episodes in 2012. The story centres on Sam Hunter (Melissa George), a female operative for Byzantium, a private intelligence and security agency which serves the business elite: *"the one per cent that matters"*. In an opening action sequence, Sam rescues a British scientist held captive in Tangiers, but is shortly afterwards set up and shot. Thought dead, she convalesces in Scotland and returns to Byzantium a year later, where she is put undercover as a nanny in the household of Jack Turner (Patrick Malahide), a criminal millionaire. There follows a complex series of plot twists, turns and revelations relating to the securing of a huge contract for a dam in Pakistan, various corporate crimes and conspiracies, murders, continuing unexplained attempts on Sam's life, and her pregnancy. The ruthless Turner is eventually subdued, but shadowy conspirators remain, and to protect Sam her death is faked and she returns to Scotland with her new-born child.

Hunted was created by the American Frank Spotnitz, produced by Kudos Productions, and made for the BBC and the American cable broadcaster Cinemax. Spotnitz had enjoyed a long association with *The X-Files* (US, TV, 1995-2002) and Kudos had previously made the hugely successful espionage series *Spooks* (TV, 2002-2011). *Hunted* posed many interesting moral issues regarding security and private interests in the 21st century, and followed in the wake of public-private partnerships in security in the effort to establish 'resilience' in the face of strategic terrorism and threats to national infrastructure and economic well-being. The public face of which is the government's Project Griffin. Byzantium operates according to some arrangement with MI6 and under a framework of 'official governance', but in a more fanciful element its agents appear to have a license to kill and are expendable for the sake of the mission. Spotnitz wanted to explore the world of corporate power and responsibility, especially how matters of accountability were likely to be subverted in the framework of privatised security and intelligence. He expressed his concern in an interview, where he pointed out that in private security you're being paid to do a job and that right and wrong don't figure into it. *"You're not even told who your client is"*; and perhaps *"you don't know if you're working for a good guy or a bad guy"*. *"Maybe you shouldn't succeed. Maybe it would be a bad thing for the world if you did"* (quoted in the *Guardian*, 28 September 2012). In the drama, the chief executive of Byzantium expounds on contemporary corporations and political power, explaining to an MI6 officer: *"The men who employ me use their power and influence to appoint the government whose orders you follow. You've been bought and paid for ... just as I have!"*

Hunted was expensively produced, shot on location in Morocco, Scotland, Wales and London, and featured elaborate action sequences. *The Telegraph* likened the show to the "Bourne *films wearing lipstick and a floaty scarf*', and indeed Spotnitz had started with the idea of a female Jason Bourne (5 October 2012). The character of Sam Hunter stands in a lineage of action women traceable back to Modesty Blaise and Emma Peel, and more recently evident in *Nikita* (US, TV, 2010-13), and *Kill Bill* (US, 2003 and 2004). Reviews in Great Britain tended to be poor, criticising the underpowered acting and some clichéd writing and characterisation; but were better in the United States where the *"slick suspense"* was appreciated and the show was felt to be thoughtful (*Entertainment Weekly*, 19 October 2012). *Hunted* was only moderately popular in Britain and ratings declined during the run of the serial. Kudos had aimed for a 'returnable brand' with the show and there were plans to shoot a second series centred on Berlin; however, the BBC eventually declined on this. While Cinemax announced it would go forward alone, possibly with a spinoff series featuring the character of Sam Hunter, this has failed to happen. Joseph Oldham has classified *Hunted* as a *"post-patriotic clandestine narrative"*, a spy thriller in which the agency and its operatives are not bound within state institutions. He finds that the resulting generic uncertainty produced a *"somewhat confused and incoherent use of many conventions of spy fiction"*, and though the drama reflected the common anxiety of the contemporary conspiracy thriller, the *"unethical extremes of excessive capitalism"* in this case, this could account for the disappointment for its traditional audience and lack of popularity of the show (2013: 99-100). For Oldham, *Hunted* offered little in the place of the conventional elements of an espionage directed by state agencies, offering instead, *"a bleak world of powerless complicity and self-interest, which it fails to glamorise enough to be engaging"* (2014: 103).

An eagerly-awaited drama was *London Spy*, a five-part serial produced by Working Title Television for the BBC and the American NBC network, written by the novelist Tom Rob Smith and broadcast in 2015. What made the spy drama unusual was that at its centre was a sensitively portrayed gay relationship, and *"surely the first such intrigue in a mainstream TV spy drama"* noted the *Guardian* (9 November 2015). Danny (Ben Whishaw) is a rootless and aimless twenty-something who accidentally bumps into handsome jogger Alex (Edward Holcroft), allegedly an investment banker. Falling in love, the relationship is shattered when Alex is killed in some sort of bizarre sex act, his body sealed in a packing case, with circumstantial evidence pointing at Danny.[782] A conspiracy emerges and it is revealed that Alex was a brilliant agent for MI6 and that Danny is being framed. The young man is aided by his protector Scottie (Jim Broadbent) who has experience of the secret world and the ill-equipped Danny sets about clearing the name of his dead lover. The press refuses to print his allegations; he is misled about Alex's parents, and when he does confront them, they lie about their son; and later Danny is charged with Alex's murder. With Scottie's help, it is discovered that Alex had been working on a method of determining if someone is lying from their speech patterns, a technique invaluable and yet dangerous in the world of espionage. Danny is given the shocking news that he is HIV positive, seemingly deliberately infected giving a blood test while in custody. Meeting again with Alex's mother Frances (Charlotte Rampling), Danny learns of her son's unusual upbringing, her thwarted career in MI6, and the killing of his lover by the Secret Intelligence Service to suppress his secret research. The drama ends with Danny and Frances teaming up with the resolution to clear the name of Alex and bring the Secret Service to account.

The *Radio Times* trumpeted *London Spy* as a conspiracy thriller to put alongside *State of Play* (7-13 November 2015: 15). However, the unusual premise of the spy drama tended to divide critics and viewers alike. The *Guardian* reported that the BBC had "*gathered up its money and its writerly and actorly talent and poured it all*" into the new drama: "*an unutterably delicious, satisfying dish*" it salivated, praising the love story in equal measure as the spy story (10 November 2015). *The Telegraph* was more severe, believing that the serial started off like a "*plodding old carthorse lacking intrigue, charm or plausibility*" (9 November 2015), and that as it progressed it became "*ever more ridiculous*" (23 November 2015). Many who enjoyed *London Spy* felt let down by a serial which ended "*daftly and implausibly*" (*Guardian*, 7 December 2015). The feelings at *The Telegraph* summed up the divided response, finding a drama which "*scaled giddy heights and then plumbed ludicrous depths*", which went "*from being completely gripping to turgid as hell by turns wonderful and infuriating*", and one minute was *Tinker, Tailor, Soldier, Spy*, the next it was *The Bourne Identity* (8 December 2015).

Historically, homosexuality had been an absolute bar to a security clearance in the intelligence services. In the closet had been Sir Maurice Oldfield, head of SIS from 1973-1980 and Alex Kellar, head of MI5's F Branch in the 1960s. The traitors Guy Burgess and Anthony Blunt were widely known to be gay or bi-sexual and this tended to equate, in the mind of the press and the public, 'subversion' with 'perversion'. The *Guardian* found *London Spy* refreshing, "*worlds away from your typical trope-riddled spooks-in-suits*" and a surprising inversion of the "*typically macho world of the spy thriller*". "*Every generation has a different concept of the spy drama*", it claimed, and "*this series feels like the most contemporary version to date*" (9 November 2015).

In a brief discussion of recent television espionage and conspiracy dramas, Joseph Oldham has commented on the aim of producers to "*advance television clandestinity into new territories*" (2014: 103). With mixed success, *The Last Enemy*, *Hunted* and *London Spy* have refreshed the genre, absorbing current anxieties about surveillance, privatisation and sexuality within a dramatic framework incorporating more traditional elements from the conspiracy thriller, such as the malevolence of the 'secret state' which had inspired numerous paranoid thrillers in the previous generation. Disappointed with the tension and credibility of *The Last Enemy*, the *Guardian* had wondered if popular scepticism about almost everything had rendered the conspiracy thriller redundant. Recent dramas such as *Hunted* and *London Spy* have seemingly belied that view (18 February 2008).

Johnny English and James Bond reborn

Rather than espionage fiction concluding along with the Cold War, the genre has instead sustained itself with a range of revisions, reinventions and revelations, intimating that the public appetite for the clandestine is as strong as ever.
(Goodman 2016: 5)

Big-budget, lucrative spy pictures continued to be produced in the new millennium. In Britain, this was most apparent in the screen adventures of Johnny English and James Bond. The two *Johnny English* films (2003 and 2011) were produced by Working Title, a British film production company which has a track record of success in the international film market.[783] The spy spoofs featured Rowan Atkinson, who had gathered a worldwide audience for his 'Mr Bean' comedies, as an inept agent of Her Majesty's Government who, in the absence of anyone else, has to safeguard the interests of Queen and Country.[784] The tagline for *Johnny English* warned the audience, "*He Knows No Fear. He Knows No Danger. He Knows Nothing*". In the first film, English is on the trail of the Crown Jewels stolen at a reception following their recent refurbishment. There follows a series of calamities in which the hapless agent, accompanied by his sidekick Bough (Ben Miller, humorously pronounced 'Boff'), mistakes targets, enters the wrong buildings, and confuses himself with his own gadgets; however, he uncovers a conspiracy which has the French businessman Pascal Sauvage (John Malkovich) a frustrated claimant to the English throne who has stolen the jewels in a preliminary to announcing himself King. However, English is taken off the case for gross incompetence. Having forced the Queen to abdicate by threatening to shoot one of Her corgis, Sauvage gracefully accepts the invitation of the unsuspecting British government to assume the throne. Johnny is reassigned to the operation by the beautiful Lorna Campbell (Natalie Imbruglia), a special agent of Interpol, and the intrepid pair head for Westminster Abbey to disrupt the coronation of the new King. During the farcical attempt to prevent the ceremony, Sauvage is revealed as an anti-British megalomaniac and following a struggle English is crowned King by mistake.

The sequel *Johnny English Reborn* picks up the story of English seven years on. Following a botched operation in Mozambique, the bungling agent is in disgrace, dismissed from the Secret Service and undergoing a personal rehabilitation in a Shaolin monastery in Tibet. A new crisis demands his recall to MI7 and he is sent to the Far East with the novice agent Tucker (Daniel Kaluuya) to prevent an attempt on the life of the Chinese Premier during important talks with the British. There follows the expected series of mishaps, misfortunes and calamities. In the midst of these failings, English discovers that the duplicitous agent inside MI7 turns out to be Simon Ambrose (Dominic West), the brilliant and handsome Agent Number 1, star of British Intelligence, and infiltrates the Anglo-Chinese talks being held in Switzerland and saves the life of the Premier.

Critics were predictably unimpressed by the antics on show, dismissing the pictures as infantile parodies in which "[Mr] *Bean does 007*" (*Observer*, 30 March 2003); the results "*depressing*" and which failed to rise above a "*student revue-grade Bond film skit*" (*The Telegraph*, 6 October 2011).[785] However, the *Johnny English* films were tremendous popular successes, the first instalment earning over $160m in the world market and proving the most popular European film of 2003. With their impressive pre-credit action sequences, stylish titles, muscular music scores, and outrageous gadgets, the movies effectively drew their parody from the ever-influential James Bond archetype. As the reviewer in the *Guardian* reminded readers, "*No genre has been more exhaustively spoofed than 007*" (11 April 2003), and individual set-pieces in the *English* films were readily recognisable from *Dr No* (1962), *Goldfinger* (1964), *On Her Majesty's Secret Service* (1969) and *The Spy Who Loved Me* (1977). The screenwriters Robert Wade and Neal Purvis were regular contributors to the official James Bond films, from *The World is Not Enough* (1999) to *Spectre* (2015), and this experience and familiarity is evident in the effective and affectionate parody of *Johnny English*. There is also a strong nod to the 'Boy's Own' adventure *Where Eagles Dare* (1969) in the staging of a thrilling fight on board an Alpine cable car; while the *English* pictures similarly owe a debt to more recent action cinema, especially the *Mission Impossible* films (US, 1996-2011), the classic *Pink Panther* comedies (1963-1978) featuring the incomparable Peter Sellers as the bungling French detective Inspector Clouzot, and, for *Reborn*, the exotic martial arts-espionage thriller *Enter the Dragon* (HK/US, 1973).

It has been claimed that the 1990s had been an "*uneasy time for spy films*", in that the secret agent genre had become detached from its traditional underpinnings in terms of established enemy and associated masculinity (Bartlett 2013: 19). "*Initially*", in Joseph Oldham's view, "*such developments were largely ignored by the Bond films*", and the franchise was "*able to retain an optimistic tone into the 1990s, helped by a nostalgic 'retro' revival of 1960s spy fiction in this decade"*. In the form of Pierce Brosnan, *"Bond seemed to embody a sense of post-Cold War optimism and, as a charismatic and informal figure with an interventionist stance on world affairs, arguably reflected the contemporary image and popularity of then-Prime Minister Tony Blair"* (Oldham 2015). James Bond though, in the hands of Brosnan, has been appreciated as becoming *"increasingly cartoonish"*, and that post-Cold War the series had begun to slip into *"daft fantasy"* (Bartlett, 2013: 19). To some extent, there has been the need for a reconfiguration of Bond's masculinity in light of the 'New Man' phenomenon since the 1980s.[786] Equally, the producers have needed to address how the new Bond films speak to the post-7/7 context.[787] Both of these imperatives have ensured that in cultural-political terms 007 has been moved in a more serious direction, and this was possible with the re-launching of the series after an enforced hiatus of four years with *Casino Royale* in 2006 and the casting of Daniel Craig as James Bond.

Casino Royale first published in 1953 was the début novel of Ian Fleming and the first adventure featuring secret agent James Bond. The story was soon dramatised as an American television film (US, 1955) and serialised as a comic-strip in the *Daily Express* (1957), and later adapted into two films: in 1967 as a riotous spoof, and in 2006 as an important re-invention of James Bond for the 21st century starring Daniel Craig.[788] The outline story of *Casino Royale* has James Bond sent on a mission by the Secret Intelligence Service to engage the criminal Le Chiffre in a high stakes card game. The aim is to bankrupt the villain and bring down his crooked empire, and to deliver a serious blow to SMERSH, the department of extortion and murder of the Soviet KGB for which Le Chiffre serves as a banker. Bond is assisted on the operation by the beautiful Vesper Lynd. In the initial engagement at the card table, things do not go too well for Bond, but with additional funds provided by the American CIA the British agent comprehensively defeats and ruins his opponent. Following two assassination attempts on Bond, Le Chiffre, desperate, kidnaps Lynd, and lures the agent into a trap. In a notorious scene, Bond is subjected to humiliating torture in an attempt to get him to reveal the whereabouts of his winnings. Bond escapes, but is embittered when he discovers that Lynd had been working for Le Chiffre under the threat of blackmail. The guilt-ridden Lynd commits suicide.

In the novel, the story is set in the casino town of Royale-Les-Eaux, Normandy in northern France. Important characters are introduced who will continue to play a significant part in the series of Bond stories: M, the Chief of SIS; Miss Moneypenny, M's secretary; Felix Leiter of the CIA; Q of weapons branch; as well as a colourful master villain and the all-important 'Bond Girl'. *Casino Royale* has been judged highly by other mystery writers and Ian Fleming admirers. Both Raymond Chandler and Kingsley Amis considered it the best of the Bond adventures, and current spy novelist Jeremy Duns finds it "*intense, almost feverishly so, and richer in characterisation and atmosphere than many of the others*" (quoted in *The Telegraph*, 13 April 2013).

The latest screen version of *Casino Royale* (2006) was eagerly anticipated. Pierce Brosnan had stepped down as James Bond with *Die Another Day* (2002), and the new film offered a distinctive interpreter in the form of Daniel Craig who publicly stated that he wanted to connect with the character's "*dark side*" (quoted in *The Telegraph*, 7 November 2006). In the form of Craig, 007 shifts appreciably from the public-school spy ideal. While entirely contemporary, the movie reverts chronologically to the commencement of Bond's career as a secret agent. In the obligatory pre-credit sequence, we see Bond earning his 'double-0' status through killing a duplicitous MI6 agent in Prague, and therefore the audience gets a young, inexperienced 007. In a calculated audience-pleasing delay, it is not until the final frames of the film, following a remarkable series of action sequences, displays of heroism, and a maturing of the character, that Craig utters the immortal words, "*Bond … James Bond*", thereby finally assuming/confirming his identity as the icon of secret agents. Similarly, composer David Arnold teasingly held back the James Bond theme in his score. Another significant 'modernisation' of the franchise was the jettisoning of the standard Cold War and master villain bent on world domination themes of the series, for the more contemporary fears regarding terrorism. In the revised story, Le Chiffre (Mads Mikkelsen) is the banker and investor for international terrorists. Other notable developments are seen to be the 'eroticising' of Bond as a masculine sex object, principally in the lingering shots where he steps out of the ocean displaying his muscular physique, which seemed to help win female audiences to the film; and the reinvention of the 'Bond Girl' for post-feminist times, one who holds down a professional role as a Treasury agent and who can quip on equal terms with the hero. A major surprise of the movie was its retention of the most notorious line from the book, when Bond, disillusioned by the treachery of Vesper Lynd (Eva Green), consoles himself with the thought that, "*The bitch is dead*". Another was the presentation of the notorious torture sequence in vaguely homoerotic terms. *Casino Royale* emerged into a cinema space informed by the Jason Bourne films (US, 2002 and 2004), reflecting a greater psychological realism than the recent films in the Bond series, and which had in fact been present to a degree in the original novel.[789]

Following its release, *Casino Royale* was widely praised by both critics and fans, and became the most commercially successful Bond film to that date, grossing around $1 billion from all revenues. The film has attracted unprecedented critical and academic interest, and was surprisingly nominated for nine British Academy of Film and Television Arts awards. Christoph Linder has claimed the importance of the picture in that, "Casino Royale *is not just a revising of 007, it is also a reimagining, a reintroduction, a re-evaluation, a reinvention and a renewal*" (2009: 7). With *Casino Royale*, the Bond franchise was seen to shift decisively from the geopolitics of the Cold War to a "*new world order of asymmetrical threats*", and the characterisation was appreciated as tougher, grittier, less Jokey, more psychological, realistic and complex (Hochscherf 2013: 299, 303, 305, 317). It was intended to take the character 'back to basics', and at least for the moment, this was Bond 'unplugged'.

While much of the new-style Bond franchise was carried forward to *Quantum of Solace* (2008), the movie was thought disappointing after the remarkable revisioning and success of *Casino Royale*. For some, 007 working independently and pursuing a personal revenge following the death of Vesper was unacceptable, and the picture, at well under two hours, was also unconventionally short in running time. However, the narrative run-over between the two films introduced an element of seriality, borrowed no doubt from the popularity of recent television dramas, and which has begun to replace the traditional episodic structure of the franchise (Hochscherf 2013: 316). Despite the gripes, *Quantum of Solace* earned nearly as much as *Casino Royale*.

Another unwanted hiatus halted the Craig series of 007 pictures, once again centring on the financial problems of the studio MGM. However, the two most recent James Bond films have confirmed the popularity of the new approach to the franchise, *Skyfall* (2012) and *Spectre* (2015) continuing to break box-office records and the former winning the Alexander Korda Award for Best British Film of the British Academy of Film and Television Arts.[790] Once again, there was a degree of narrative run-over across the films and a new 'vulnerability' for the character of Bond, although there has been a sense that innovation has now been held in check. This was particularly the case with *Skyfall*, which in terms of the recent 007 pictures has been appreciated as a "*deeply conservative film*", and even shifting the "*franchise away from the brave new path forged by* Casino Royale". Myke Bartlett has claimed that the "*primary purpose of the film is to reset the franchise to its 'classic' mode*". Bond reports to a male superior (Mallory played by Ralph Fiennes), flirts with Moneypenny (Naomie Harris), has meaningless sex with exotic women and scores gadgets from Q (Ben Whishaw) in the basement. "*The world has changed*", he asserts, "*but Bond doesn't have to*" (2013: 19). The 'conservative' nature of *Skyfall* has also been maintained by Sam Goodman, who sees the movie as a "*celebration of history and cultural memory, drawing on the tropes of the James Bond series such as the customised Aston Martin and the reintroduction of the character of Q in particular, in a nostalgic, almost elegiac, tribute to the franchise's history*" (2016: 3).[791] *Skyfall* was a landmark in that it marked the 50th anniversary of the Bond series in the cinema, and its coincidence with the London Olympics and the Queen's Diamond Jubilee tied the picture even more tightly with discourses and iconography of Britishness and the nation.[792] In a conscious effort, London was presented as a spectacular setting as never before in a Bond movie. *Spectre* similarly re-deploys the trappings of the franchise, but does engage with contemporary concerns with the surveillance society. In the story, Bond has to deal with the implications of a new electronic global surveillance system known as "*Nine Eyes*", and which threatens the '00' section with closure as the need for human intelligence, agents on the ground, would be made redundant. The film, it has been claimed, argues the risk an amalgamated intelligence society could have for global civil liberties, leaving the audience in no doubt as to the "*dangers of a surveillance state from a civil liberties perspective*", and even being described as "*pro-Snowden*", in reference to the American whistle blower Edward Snowden, whose unauthorised disclosures revealed numerous surveillance programmes, many run by the National Security Agency and the "*Five Eyes*" Intelligence Alliance (Australia, Canada, New Zealand, the United Kingdom and the United States), with the cooperation of telecommunication companies and European governments (Dymydiuk 2016).

The James Bond and Johnny English films demonstrated that the spy film remained an essential genre for the admittedly depleted British cinema in the new millennium. The recent 007 films confirmed that Bond, tailored to the new realities and preferences of the period, could be as seductive and effective as ever; while Johnny English, in a tradition stretching back to the mid-1960s, showed that only one step behind the greatest of all fictional secret agents was a wannabe, an imitator who was prepared to risk all for Queen and Country, however hapless they might be. The continuing popularity and relevance of the spy genre has also been evident in such hit television series as *Spooks* and recent drama serials as *London Spy* and *The Night Manager*, and it has been claimed more widely that there was an upsurge in spy dramas following the attack on America in September 2001, referred to as "*A Season of Spies*" by genre critic Wesley Britton (2004: 252). Some of these films, series and serials have been part of what has been termed a new "*counterterror genre*", dramas touching on themes raised by the dynamics of terrorism and counterterrorism (Erickson 2008: 354-55). Such visual narratives, it has been proposed, can serve to "*legitimise*" and "*normalise*" the practice and impact of a "*highly intrusive and adept security apparatus*", manufacturing acceptance of the range and extent of intelligence activities, and "*making these agents and agencies appear to have a legitimate and normal function in a democratic polity*" (345). Another characteristic of the recent spy genre has been a stepping back from the global war on terror, and, perhaps, a surprising retreat into a familiar, reassuring framework of Cold War certainty and nostalgia. The modern spy story in its second century has proved enduring; vigorous enough to withstand the disappearance of the communist menace in the 1990s, find new threats and a new relevance, and such that it is likely to provide meaning and pleasure for at least the next 100 years. British secret agents and spies, their characteristics, traditions and historical sources have been at the forefront of the literature of the clandestine, and they are set to remain there for some time to come.

Conclusion

Fiction is the most lucid way of shedding light onto the structure of the modern political secret.
(Horn 2013: 25)

In the climate of ideological conflict, the spy is king. From Bulldog Drummond to James Bond, from Kipling's Kim to Kim Philby is the course our world has run.
(Malcolm Muggeridge, *Esquire*, September 1967)

The German literary critic Eva Horn has suggested that spies and traitors have become "*one of the most pervasive motives and fantasies of the twentieth century*". The reason for this lies in the state secrets, intrusion, concealment and public control of a modern society "*that cannot do without secrecy and betrayal*" (2013: 37). In a secret world where much remains "*invisible and unknowable*", fictions offer a welcome "*lucidity*" and "*plausibility*"; a version of the "*truth*" in a landscape where much is concealed, denied and silenced (39-40). In such a sense, she argues, espionage fictions are political, "*because they are often the only way the most secret and dangerous state knowledge can be addressed in public*". At their best and most valuable, such fictions offer an "*insightful critique*" of the secretive structure of modern state power (41). "*If modernity is engaged in suppressing the state secret*" she asserts, "*then fictions dealing with the latter are, no doubt, a symptom of this suppression*" (99). In the important case of traitors and betrayal, spy stories can served as an "*alternative historiography*"; hypothetically reconstructing past, silenced events which the authorities intend to remain buried (40).

Cinema and television's productive and continual engagement with spy fiction certainly suggests the relevance of espionage tales to the cultural imaginary in the period since 1960. The popularity of the spy thriller and espionage drama on both the large and small screen seemingly fed a public appetite for stories of intrigue and served up characters that assuaged anxieties resulting from the Cold War, state security and later the threats of international terrorism. Such narratives could reassure in a global situation in which British prestige was in decline; or could offer plausible insights into secret diplomacy and government double-dealing. In some cases, film and television dramas could allow audiences a view into recent troubling events centring on treachery and scandal. Making visible what was traditionally denied and obscured could be both pleasing and enlightening, and imaginative access could at least provide a sense of the democratic where suppression reigned. The origin point of this cultural outpouring for the modern period was, of course, James Bond. As Bennett and Woollacott have shown, the popularity of 007 peaked in the mid-1960s, and the secret agent clearly functioned "*as either an explicit or an implied point of reference for the rival spy thrillers which flooded the bookstalls, the cinema and the television screens, in both Britain and America*" (1987: 36).

A century of British spy fiction produced its share of classics and it is unsurprising that the British screen should explore this rich legacy of stories. It is interesting and suggestive that film and television should be so active and engaged with canonical spy literature in the later 1970s and through the 1980s, a period embracing a return to traditional values and generating nostalgic views about the greatness of Britain past. Nostalgia has often been assumed to be naive and simplistic, and has consequently suffered from intellectual delegitimation as something uncritical, immature and trivial. It is also often thought of as conservative, with critics asserting its escapist, romantic and sentimental appeal embodied in a longing for an imaginary past that never was and in unease with the sterility of modernity. Unsurprisingly, given such a view, the 'nostalgic' spy dramas of the seventies and eighties have received little critical regard and are given substantial attention for the first time in this study.

It is sometimes noted that the spy thrillers of the 1960s were infused with a "*nostalgia for the old order*", presenting a "*fantasy England in which the establishment is challenged but ultimately triumphant*" (White 2007: 58). While this should not be overstated, after all, Bennett and Woollacott have convincingly established that James Bond "*functioned* above all *as a hero of modernisation*" (1987: 20-21, see also 111-12, emphasis added), the element of nostalgia brings the contemporary spy story of the sixties into alignment with the classic spy tale, and unsurprisingly nostalgia has also figured more recently in considerations of the new world order and its attendant terrors.

> *Trans-national terrorism, homegrown radicalization, loose nukes, a rising China, the disruptive potentials of climate change, political populism, vast migratory waves ... threaten to upend the liberal world order many assumed had been set in stone at the end of the twilight struggle.*

In response to such pressing anxieties, James Kirchick has commented on a contemporary "*resurgent Cold War nostalgia*", a longing for a more unitary, settled and balanced period of struggle (2016). As we have seen, this has resulted in a number of recent dramas setting their action in the Cold War of the 1970s. A decade fixed in the public mind with John le Carré's tale of *Tinker,*

Tailor, Soldier, Spy (1974), a story which furnished the iconography and class and character conflicts of the classic modern espionage tale.

However, nostalgic fiction could not entirely assuage the feeling of anxiety which emerged in the period. A sense of paranoia was produced by the imperative of zealous official secrecy and suspicions of wayward clandestine services, and this manifested itself in a counter tradition of 'secret state' thrillers. As Joseph Oldham has recently asserted, the *"fierce adherence to state secrecy provided much material for paranoid thrillers"* (2017: 12). Eva Horn writes of the *"secrecy effect"*, a process which *"opens up a space of speculation, conflicting versions, distrust, and paranoia"* (2013: 97). Horn has observed that the decades of the 1950s-1980s, the period substantially addressed in this study, were a golden age of political thrillers and spy movies, and, not coincidentally, of conspiracy theories and great scandals (99). Unease over the accountability of the intelligence services and suspected 'rogue' operations opened up space for thrillers dealing with plots against leftists, progressives and sundry democratic organisations, and figured a Security Service seemingly out of control, or, worse, the lap-dog of reactionary forces in the country.

This study has examined in detail spy fiction on British screens since 1960. From that date, the secret agent story underwent a significant genre transformation, under the sway on the one hand of the exploits of super agent James Bond, and on the other under the influence of the new-style espionage writing of Len Deighton and John le Carré. The new impetus was carried into a major cycle of spy stories in the British cinema of the 1960s and later picked up on television in the 1970s. Typical of genre revisionism in the period, the regular use of the spy story led to ready-familiarisation among audiences and the emergence of spoof forms which knowledgeable viewers could pleasingly decode and chase the traits and characteristics back to well-known and popular prototexts. The process of genre transformation has been presented as a fundamental aspect of the celebrated New Hollywood cinema of the 1960s and 1970s. Wider cultural and social changes meant that the essential myth-making of popular cinema was revised and classical cinema and its genres was transformed under the influence of artistic foreign cinemas, younger core audiences, new independence for filmmakers and the emergence of *auteur* directors (Cawelti 2012). Genre transformation has hardly been considered outside the framework of American cinema, but we can see that a similar course of development occurred in the case of spy fiction and the spy screen in Britain across the same period.[793]

Spy thrillers and espionage dramas seemingly brought much pleasure to viewers, and a number of these generated considerable discussion. The historical Cambridge Spies have attracted much fascination and the dramatisation of these notorious traitors has caused great controversy. This was particularly the case with the four-part serial *Cambridge Spies* produced at the BBC and broadcast in 2003, a drama criticised both for a poor appreciation of history and for glorifying a reprehensible quartet of conspirators. It does, though, reflect a lingering sense of the Cambridge Five as 'folk legends' in some quarters of British culture, the traitors as exemplars of the rottenness of the national class system, or even as renegades within that structure, who in some perverted way stood out against its injustices and subverted its values and practices. Similar concern regarding historical accuracy and fairness attended to screen treatments of the secret war. As we have seen, movies such as *Enigma* (2001) and *The Imitation Game* (2014) drew the scorn of some historians, ruffled national pride, and attracted angry letters to the press; while others, such as *Charlotte Gray* (2002), were felt to have poorly served the sacrifices of female agents in World War Two. Other dramas critical of the intelligence services and security activities, such as *A Very British Coup* (1988) and *Hidden Agenda* (1990), also raised hackles and drew columns in the newspapers in which spokesmen for authority and the establishment vented their displeasure. Unavoidably, it would seem, the treatment of the secret world guaranteed an engagement with controversial topics and inevitably led to public debate and argument. At the very least, this ideological aspect of the spy drama justifies its exploration and examination.

In important ways, spy dramas have been taken seriously. This study has paid close attention to the critical reception of spy series, serials and dramas, as reviews and critical discussion of representations of espionage on screen provide a valuable insight into the social meaning of popular culture. As we have seen, critics commonly made reference to actual espionage in reviews, making constructive comparison between fiction and fact, and inspecting the sometimes close relationship of dramas to real spy characters and events. The critical response has also been revealing in terms of the understanding and appreciation of the spy genre, reviewers often comparing and contrasting fictional secret agents, testing new characters against established archetypes such as 'Bulldog' Drummond, James Bond and Harry Palmer, and fitting new stories into archetypal secret agent narratives as established by writers such as Ian Fleming, John le Carré and Len Deighton.

While in many respects populist, the spy screen has also produced some of the most acclaimed modern dramas to be put before an audience. Dramatists of the calibre of Alan Bennett, Dennis Potter, Stephen Poliakoff and David Hare have enriched the small screen with their espionage plays, exploring form as well as the complex nature of treachery. In the cases of the serials *Tinker Tailor Soldier Spy* (1979) and *Edge of Darkness* (1985), the BBC produced two of the most highly-praised dramas in television history. Quality is another substantial reason for the inspection and discussion of recent spy fiction on screen.

Where now for the spy drama? On the big screen, the spy story has become a marginal product for the British cinema. James Bond and the odd spoof have rolled on; and the periodic adaptation of John le Carré has meant the appearance of some espionage in the movies, most obviously with the remake of *Tinker Tailor Soldier Spy* (2011). The development of the spy story on the small screen has, taken generally, been a narrative development from the 'episodic series', characteristic of the 1960s adventure series, the existential spy series *Callan* (1967-72), the spy thriller such as *Quiller* (1975), and the spy procedural of the 1970s such as *Special Branch* (1969-74) and *The Sandbaggers* (1978-80), to the 'novelistic' form embodied in drama serials such as *Tinker Tailor Soldier Spy* (1979) and *Edge of Darkness* (1985). Although the adventure series is an exception, the shift is marked both aesthetically, from shooting in a television studio to shooting with single-camera continuity on film, and qualitatively, the 'novelistic' approach attracting to it a firmer sense of 'quality'. The episodic form has recently been revived by the successful and long-running *Spooks* (2002-11), but according to the imperatives of current 'quality' television drama, it was shot on film with a generous budget to allow for a glossy, glamorous presentation. Elsewhere, the 'novelistic' form has reigned, with literary adaptations of William Boyd's *Restless* (2012), period serials such as *The Game* (2014), and contemporary explorations of conspiracy and treachery in the richly cast *London Spy* (2015) and *The Night Manager* (2016); where high-end production values have been deployed, a degree of artistic self-consciousness and prestige is present, and making for a commercial product saleable in the international market. As Joseph Oldham has asserted, recent spy dramas "*seem progressively pitched more towards an international audience and guided by the 'quality' priorities of overseas pay-per-view channels*" (2017: 199). One commentator has pointed to the potential for "*feminist spy fiction, and for spy fiction with significant female characters written into it*"; but while this trend is apparent in the novels *Restless* (2006), *Charlotte Gray* (1998), *Sweet Tooth* (2012) and *Red Joan* (1999), this has not emerged to the extent it has been evident in crime fiction (Wark 1990: 10). There clearly is room for intelligent female-centred spy dramas on British screens.

So far, there has been no successful episodic series to replace *Spooks*; however, the precinct drama remains a staple of the schedules and it is not inconceivable that a successor might eventually appear. The 'novelistic' drama equally remains a standard dramatic form for television, suitable for period recreations and intelligent conspiracy thrillers. Spy dramas will no doubt continue to appear in this form. With the recent publication of John le Carré's

A Legacy of Spies, in which the author revisits the terrain of the Cold War and the secret world of George Smiley, it is tempting to hope that British television will mount a further serial adaptation of the genre's greatest living author, and treat the modern generation of viewers to a characteristically complex, intelligent, critical and thrilling imaginative treatment of espionage.

This study began with an examination of the world of James Bond and 007's enormous influence on the spy thriller. Appropriately enough, it ends with a consideration of the secret agent's re-alignment for the popular audience in the new millennial form of Daniel Craig. The popularity of the character has been re-confirmed and, bucking the usual trend, has shown a robust upward trajectory never before witnessed in franchise history. There is no reason to disagree with producer Michael Wilson that, "*There will always be a Bond*" (quoted in Field and Chowdhury 2015: 606). And as with 007, there is no reason to doubt that there will always be spy dramas. After all, they are exciting and thrilling, speak to public anxieties about security, secrecy and state control, and offer dramatists and film and television programme-makers a framework for investigating important contemporary issues such as power, surveillance, suppression, treachery, betrayal and democratic freedoms. Long live the spy screen.

Bibliography

Periodicals

Films and Filming
Intelligence and National Security
Journal of Intelligence History
Kinematograph Weekly
The Lobster (later *Lobster*)
Monthly Film Bulletin
Sight and Sound

Books, monographs and articles

Ackroyd, Carol, Karen Margolis, Johnathan Rosenhead, and Tim Shallice (1977), *The Technology of Political Control*, London: Penguin.

Adrian, Jack (1996), 'John Gardner: Overview', in Pederson, Jay P., *St. James Guide to Crime & Mystery Writers*, 4th edition, Detroit: St. James Press.

Aitken, Ian (27 May 1989), 'Keeler, Profumo and me in between', *Guardian*.

Aldgate, Anthony (1999), 'Remembrance of Times Past: *Scandal*', in Aldgate, Anthony, and Jeffrey Richards, *Best of British. Cinema and Society from 1930 to the Present*, London: I. B. Tauris, pp. 220-33.

Aldrich, Richard J. (2004), 'Policing the Past: Official History, Secrecy and British Intelligence since 1945', *English Historical Review*, 119 (483), pp. 922-53.

— (2009), 'The Security State', in Flinders, Matthew, Andrew Gamble, Colin Hay, and Michael Kenny (eds.), *The Oxford Handbook of British Politics*, Oxford: Oxford University Press, pp. 752-72.

— GCHQ (2010), *The Uncensored Story of Britain's Most Secret Intelligence Agency*. London: HarperPress.

Aldrich, Richard J., and Antony Field (2011), 'Security and Surveillance in Britain', in Heffernan, Richard, Philip Cowley, and Colin Hay, *Developments in British Politics* 9, Houndmills, Basingstoke: Palgrave Macmillan.

Altman, Rick (1999), *Film/Genre*, London: BFI Publishing.

Alvarado, Manuel, and John Stewart (ed.) (1985), *Made for Television. Euston Films Limited*, London: BFI Publishing.

Ambler, Eric (ed.) (1974), *To Catch a Spy*, London: Fontana.

Andrew, Christopher (1985), *Secret Service: The Making of the British Intelligence Community*, London: Heinemann.

— (12 January 1987), 'Defecting From the Truth', *The Telegraph*.

— (2010), *The Defence of the Realm: The Authorized History of MI5*, London: Penguin.

Anez, Nicholas (August 1992), ' *The Quiller Memorandum* ', *Films in Review*, pp. 237–45.

Atkins, John (1984), *The British Spy Novel: Styles in Treachery*, London: John Calder.

Aubrey, Crispin (1981), *Who's Watching You? Britain's Security Services & the Official Secrets Act*, Harmondsworth, Middlesex: Penguin.

Babington, Bruce (2005), '*Scandal*', in McFarlane, Brian (ed.), *The Cinema of Britain and Ireland*, London: Wallflower, pp. 197-205.

Baker, Brian (2012), '"You're quite a gourmet, aren't you, Palmer?": Masculinity and Food in the Spy Fiction of Len Deighton', *The Yearbook of English Studies*, 42, pp. 30-48.

Baker, William and Stephen Ely Tabachnick (1973), *Harold Pinter*, New York: Barnes & Noble.

Balio, Tino (1987), *United Artists: The Company That Changed the Film Industry*, Madison, Wisconsin: University of Wisconsin Press.

Barber, Michael (1978), 'Hong Kong Was a "Halfway House"', in Bruccoli, Matthew J., and Judith S. Baughman (eds.) (2004), *Conversations with John le Carré*, Jackson, Mississippi: University Press of Mississippi, pp. 47-52.

Bartlett, Myke (Winter 2013), 'Spyfall: *Tinker Tailor Soldier Spy, Zero Dark Thirty, Argo* and the Contemporary Spy Film', *Screen Education*, 70, pp. 18-23.

Basinger, Jeanine (2007), *Anthony Mann* (new expanded edition), Middletown, Conn.: Wesleyan University Press.

Batey, Mavis (2009), *Dilly. The Man Who Broke Enigmas*, London: Biteback Publishing.

Baxter, John (1973), *An Appalling Talent. Ken Russell*, London: Michael Joseph.

Bellaby, Rose (2012), 'What's the Harm? The Ethics of Intelligence Collection', *Intelligence and National Security*, 27(1), pp. 93-117.

Bennett, Alan (1988), *Objects of Affection and other plays for television*, London: BBC Books.

— (1994), *Writing Home*, London: Faber and Faber.

Bennett, Tony and Janet Woollacott (1987), *Bond and Beyond. The Political Career of a Popular Hero*, Houndmills, Basingstoke: Macmillan Education.

Bergonzi, Bernard (1978), *Reading the Thirties*, London: Macmillan.

Billington, Michael (4 October 2002), 'And You Thought His Plays Were Great", *Guardian*.

Birkinshaw, Patrick (1990), *Reforming the Secret State*, Milton Keynes: Open University Press.

Birner, Louis (1968), 'The James Bond Phenomenon', *Journal of Contemporary Psychotherapy*, 1(1), pp. 13-18.

Black, Jeremy (2004), 'The Geopolitics of James Bond', in Scott, L. V., and P. D. Jackson (eds.), *Understanding Intelligence in the Twenty-First Century: Journeys in Shadows*, London: Routledge, pp. 135-46.

Blake, Matt and David Deal (2008), *The Eurospy Guide*, Baltimore, Maryland: Luminary Press.

Bloom, Clive (ed.) (1990), *Spy Thrillers: From Buchan to Le Carré*, Basingstoke, Hants: Macmillan.

Bogarde, Dirk (1979), *Snakes and Ladders*, St. Albans: Triad/Panther.

Bold, Christine (1990), 'Secret negotiations: The Spy figure in Nineteenth-century American popular fiction', *Intelligence and National Security*, 5 (4), pp. 17-29.

Boltanski, Luc (2014), *Mysteries and Conspiracies. Detective Stories, Spy Novels and the Making of Modern Societies*, Cambridge: Polity.

Booker, Christopher (1969), *The Neophiliacs. A Study of the Revolution in English Life in the Fifties and Sixties*, London: Collins.

Booth, Alan R. (1991), 'The Development of the Espionage Film', in Wark, Wesley K. (ed.), *Spy Fiction, Spy Films and Real Intelligence*, Abingdon, Oxon: Routledge, pp. 136-60.

Box, Betty (2000), *Lifting the Lid. The Autobiography of Film Producer Betty Box, OBE*, Lewes, Sussex: Book Guild.

Boyd, William (10 November 1991), 'A Singular Spy', *Sunday Times*.

Boyle, Andrew (1980), *The Climate of Treason* (rev. ed.), London: Coronet.

Britton, Wesley (2004), *Spy Television*, Westport, Connecticut: Praeger.

Brooke, Allen (2004), 'Furst among Equals', *Contemporary Literary Criticism*, 255, Detroit: Gale, pp. 19-26.

Brown, Anthony Cave (1997), *Treason in the Blood. H. St. John Philby, Kim Philby, and the Spy Case of the Century*, Black Bay, Boston: Houghton Mifflin.

Brown, Geoff (1977), *Launder and Gilliat*, London: BFI.

Bruccoli, Matthew J., and Judith S. Baughman (eds.) (2004), *Conversations with John le Carré*, Jackson, Mississippi: University Press of Mississippi.

Buckton, Oliver S. (2015), *Espionage in British Fiction and Film since 1900*, Lanham, Maryland: Rowman & Littlefield.

Bulloch, John, and Henry Miller (1961), *Spy Ring. The Full Story of the Naval Secrets Case*, London: Secker & Warburg.

Burgess, Anthony (19 March 1978), 'The Quiet Defector', *Observer*.

Burke, David (2008), *The Spy Who Came in from the Co-op. Melita Norwood and the Ending of Cold War Espionage*, Woodbridge, Worcestershire: Boydell Press.

Burton, Alan (2008), 'From Summer of Love to Winter of Discontent: New Directions in the British Television Action Series in the late 1960s', in Helbig, Jörg (ed.), *Summer of Love. The Beatles, Art and Culture in the Sixties*, Trier: WVT, pp. 179-91.

— (2013), 'Mind Bending, Mental Seduction and Menticide: Brainwashing in British Spy Dramas of the 1960s', *Journal of British Cinema and Television*, 10 (1), pp. 27-48.

— (2016), *Historical Dictionary of British Spy Fiction*, Lanham, Maryland: Rowman & Littlefield.

— (2017), 'Uncommon Dangers: Alfred Hitchcock and the Literary Contexts of the British Spy Thriller', in Schwanebeck, Wieland (ed.), *Reassessing the Hitchcock Touch: Industry, Collaboration, and Filmmaking*, London: Palgrave, pp. 221-40.

Burton, Alan and Tony Shaw (2013), *Cinema, Television and the Cold War,* special issue of *Journal of British Cinema and Television,* 10(1).

Burton, Alan and Tim O'Sullivan (2009), *The Cinema of Basil Dearden and Micheal Relph,* Edinburgh: Edinburgh University Press.

Buxton, David (1990), *From* The Avengers *to* Miami Vice: *Form and Ideology in Television Series,* Manchester: Manchester University Press.

Caine, Michael (1992), *What's It All About?,* London: Random House.

Cairncross-Gow, Gayle (15 May 2003), 'Secrets and Spies', *Guardian.*

Campbell, Duncan (1979), 'Official Secrecy and British Libertarianism', *Socialist Register,* 16, pp. 75-88.

Cardiff, Jack (1996), *Magic Hour: The Life of a Cameraman,* London: Faber and Faber.

Carpenter, Humphrey (1998), *Dennis Potter: The Authorized Biography,* London: Faber and Faber.

Carter, Miranda (2001), *Anthony Blunt. His Lives,* London: Macmillan.

— (10 May 2003), 'First person singular: Cambridge Spies? The truth is far more interesting', *The Telegraph.*

Caughie, John (2007), *Edge of Darkness,* London: British Film Institute.

Caute, David (1994), *Joseph Losey. A Revenge on Life,* London: Faber and Faber.

Cavendish, Anthony (1990), *Inside Intelligence,* London: Collins.

Cawelti, John G. and Bruce A. Rosenberg (1987), *The Spy Story,* Chicago: University of Chicago Press.

Cawelti, John (2012), '*Chinatown* and Generic Transformation in Recent American Films', in Grant, Barry Keith (ed.), *Film Genre Reader IV,* Austin: University of Texas Press, pp.279-97.

Cecil, Robert (1984), 'The Cambridge Comintern', in Andrew, Christopher, and David Dilks (eds.), *The Missing Dimension. Governments and Intelligence Communities in the Twentieth Century,* London and Basingstoke: Macmillan, pp. 169-98.

— (1988), *A Divided Life. A Biography of Donald Maclean,* London: Bodley Head.

Central Intelligence Machinery (1993), London: The Stationary Office.

Challis, Christopher (1995), *Are They So Awful? A Cameraman's Chronicle,* London: Janus.

Chapman, James (1996), 'Our Finest Hour Revisited: The Second World War in British feature films since 1945', *Journal of Popular British Cinema,* 1, pp. 63-75.

— (2000), '*The Avengers:* Television and Popular Culture during the "High Sixties"', in Aldgate, Anthony, James Chapman and Arthur Marwick (eds.), *Windows on the Sixties. Exploring Key Texts of Media and Culture,* London: I. B. Tauris, pp. 37-69.

— (2002), *Saints and Avengers. British Adventure Series of the 1960s,* London: I. B. Tauris.

— (2007), *Licence to Thrill: A Cultural History of the James Bond Films,* London: I. B. Tauris.

— (2013), *Film and History*, Houndmills, Basingstoke: Palgrave Macmillan.

— (2014), 'The Trouble with Harry: The Difficult Relationship of Harry Saltzman and Film Finances', *Historical Journal of Film, Radio and Television*, 34(1), pp. 43-71.

Chibnall, Steve (2000), *J. Lee Thompson*, Manchester: Manchester University Press.

Ciment, Michel (1985), *Conversations with Losey*, London: Methuen.

Cobley, Paul (2009), '"It's a fine line between safety and terror": crime and anxiety redrawn in *Spooks*', *Film International*, 7(2), pp.36-45.

Cobbs, John L. (1998), *Understanding John le Carré*, Columbia, South Carolina: University of South Carolina Press.

Coke, Cyril (1966), 'First, Catch Your Spy', *Journal of the Society of Film and Television Arts*, 24, pp. 2-3.

Coldstream, John (2005), *Dirk Bogarde. The Authorised Biography*, London: Phoenix.

Cooke, Lez (2007), *Troy Kennedy Martin*, Manchester: Manchester University Press.

Costello, John (1988), *Mask of Treachery. The First Documented Dossier on Anthony Blunt's Cambridge Spy Ring*, New York: William Morrow.

Cramer, Steve (2016), 'Ideological Anxiety, National Transition and the Uncanny in *The Omega Factor*', *Journal of British Cinema and Television*, 13(1), pp. 61–79.

Crossley, Laura (2016), 'Seeing Isn't Believing: The Fallacy of Vision in *The Ipcress File* and *Skyfall*', in Crossley, Laura, and Clara Sitbon (eds.), *Deception. Spies, Lies and Forgeries*, Oxford: Inter-Disciplinary Press, pp. 11-18.

Crutchley, Leigh (1966), 'The Fictional World of Espionage', in Bruccoli, Matthew J., and Judith S. Baughman (eds.) (2004), *Conversations with John le Carré*, Jackson, Mississippi: University Press of Mississippi, pp. 6-9.

Cunningham, Frank R. (1991), *Sidney Lumet. Film and Literary Vision*, Lexington, Kentucky: University Press of Kentucky.

Deacon, Richard (1984), *A History of British Secret Service*, London: Granada.

Deeley, Michael, with Matthew Field (2008), *Blade Runners, Deer Hunters & Blowing the Bloody Doors Off. My Life in Cult Movies*, London: Faber and Faber.

Dehn, Paul (1966), 'The Spy Who Came in from the Cold', *Journal of the Society of Film and Television Arts*, 24, pp. 12-13.

Deighton, Len (1993), 'Preface', in *Len Deighton. Three Complete Novels: Berlin Game, Mexico Set, London Match*, New York: Wings Books.

— (1994), 'The Worlds of Harry Saltzman', *Sight and Sound*, 4(11), pp. 20-21.

— (2009), 'Preface', in *Funeral in Berlin*, Sterling: New York.

— (2012a), 'Introduction', in *Mexico Set*, Sterling: New York.

— (2012b), 'Introduction', in *London Match*, Sterling: New York.

— (2015), 'Introduction', in *The Ipcress File*, London: Harper.

Deindorfer, Robert G. (1974), 'A Conversation with John le Carré', in Bruccoli, Matthew J., and Judith S. Baughman (eds.) (2004), *Conversations with John le Carré*, Jackson, Mississippi: University Press of Mississippi, pp. 15-17.

Denning, Michael (1987), *Cover Stories: Narrative and Ideology in the British Spy Thriller*, London: Routledge & Kagan Paul.

Dorril, Stephen (1993), *The Silent Conspiracy. Inside the Intelligence Services in the 1990s*, London: William Heinemann.

Dorril, Stephen, and Robin Ramsay (1992), *Smear! Wilson and the Secret State*, London: Grafton.

Du Cann, Richard (2 March 1989), *Independent.*

Dudley, Terence (1966), 'Not in Single Spies, but in Flippin' Battalions', *Journal of the Society of Film and Television Arts*, 24, pp.13-15.

Duncan, Paul (ed.) (2012), *The James Bond Archives*, Cologne: Taschen.

Duns, Jeremy (2013), *Dead Drop: The True Story of Oleg Penkovsky and the Cold War's Most Dangerous Operation*, London: Simon & Schuster.

Durgnat, Raymond (1969), 'Spies and Ideologies', *Cinema*, March, pp. 5-13.

Dymydiuk, Jason (2016), '*Spectre* (2015)', *Journal of Intelligence History*, 15(1), pp. 59-60.

Erickson, Christian William (2008), 'Thematics of counterterrorism: comparing *24* and *MI-5/Spooks*', *Critical Studies on Terrorism*, 1(3), pp. 343-58.

Erisman, Fred (1977), 'Romantic Reality in the Spy Stories of Len Deighton', *Armchair Detective*, 10, pp. 101-05.

Erwin, Kim (1985), *Franklin J.Schaffner*, Metuchen, NJ: Scarecrow Press.

Falk, Quentin (1990), *Travels in Greeneland. The Cinema of Graham Greene*, London: Quartet.

Field, Matthew and Ajay Chowdhury (2015), *Some Kind of Hero. The Remarkable Story of the James Bond Films*, Stroud, Gloucestershire: The History Press.

Fielding, Steven (2014), *A State of Play: British Politics on Screen, Stage and Page, from Anthony Trollope to* The Thick of It, London: Bloomsbury Academic.

Finney, Angus (1996), *The Egos Have Landed. The Rise and Fall of Palace Pictures*, London: Heinemann.

Fletcher, Katy (1987), 'Evolution of the Modern American Spy Novel', *Journal of Contemporary History*, 22 (2), pp. 319-331.

Foot, Paul (1990), *Who Framed Colin Wallace?*, London: Pan Books.

Foster, Roy (1998), 'Introduction', in Bowen, Elizabeth, *The Heat of the Day*, London: Vintage.

French, David (1978), 'Spy Fever in Britain, 1900-1915', *The Historical Journal*, 21(2), pp. 355-70.

Fuller, Graham (ed.) (1998), *Loach on Loach*, London: Faber and Faber.

Fujiwara, Chris (2008), *The World and its Double. The Life and Work of Otto Preminger*, London: Faber and Faber.

Fysh, Michael (ed.) (1989), *The* Spycatcher *Cases*, London: European Law Centre.

Gardner, Colin (2006), 'From Mimicry to Mockery: Cold War Hybridity in Evan Jones's *The Damned*, *Modesty Blaise* and *Funeral in Berlin*', *Media History*, 12 (2), 177-91.

Gelber, Harry G. (1989), 'The Hunt for Spies: Another Inside Story', *Intelligence and National Security*, 4(2), pp. 385-400.

Giddings, Robert (2009), 'Case Notes', in Childers, Erskine, *The Riddle of the Sands*, London: Atlantic Books.

Giddings, Robert, and Keith Selby (2001), *The Classic Serial on Television and Radio*, Houndmills, Basingstoke: Palgrave.

Gifford, Denis (1966), 'Silent Spies', *Journal of the Society of Film and Television Arts*, 24, pp. 6-10.

Gilbert, W. Stephen (1998), *The Life and Work of Dennis Potter*, Woodstock and New York: Overlook Press.

Gill, Peter (1994), *Policing Politics. Security Intelligence and the Liberal Democratic State*, London: Frank Cass.

— (1996), 'Reasserting Control: Recent changes in the oversight of the UK intelligence community', *Intelligence and National Security*, 11(2), pp. 313-31.

Godat, Chris (1997), 'John Gardner: Overview', in Mote, Dave (ed.), *Contemporary Popular Writers*, Detroit: St. James Press. [*Literature Resource Center*, accessed 11 Jan. 2013]

Goodchild, Peter (10 January 1987), 'The Blunt Truth: What the BBC says', *Daily Mail*.

Goodman, Michael S (2014), *The Official History of the Joint Intelligence Committee: Volume I: From the Approach of the Second World War to the Suez Crisis*, Abingdon, Oxon: Routledge.

Goodman, Sam (2016), *British Spy Fiction and the End of Empire*, Abingdon, Oxon: Routledge.

Gourlay, Logan (25 February 1989), 'Scandal's real victim', *Weekend Guardian*.

Gray, John (29 April, 2002), 'The NS Essay - A target for destructive ferocity', *New Statesman*.

Green, Robert, with Kate Dewes (2013), *A Thorn in Their Side*, London: John Blake.

Greene, Hugh (2007), 'Epilogue'. in Greene, Hugh, and Graham Greene (eds.), *The Spy's Bedside Book*, London: Hutchinson, pp. 235-36.

Greenspan, L. G. (17 June 1965), 'Big Step Forward with "Licensed to Kill"', *Kinematograph Weekly*, p.88.

Guest, Val (2001), *So You Want To Be In Pictures: The Autobiography of Val Guest*, Richmond, Surrey: Reynolds & Hearn.

Guy, Stephen (2000), '"Someone presses a button and it's goodbye Sally": *Seven Days to Noon* and the threat of the atomic bomb', in Burton, Alan et al (eds.), *The Family Way: The Boulting Brothers and British Film Culture*, Trowbridge, Wilts: Flicks Books, pp.143-54.

Hagopian, Kevin J. (2009), 'Flint and Satyriasis: The Bond Parodies of the 1960s', in Packer, Jeremy (ed.), *Secret Agents: Popular Icons Beyond James Bond*, Bern: Peter Lang, pp. 21-52.

Hamrick, S. J. 2004), *Deceiving the Deceivers. Kim Philby, Donald Maclean and Guy Burgess*, New Haven: Yale University Press.

Harkness, Bruce, and Nancy Birk (eds.) (1990), The Secret Agent. *A Simple Tale*, Cambridge: Cambridge University Press.

Harper, Ralph (1969), *The World of the Thriller*, Cleveland: The Press of Case Western Reserve University.

Harries, Dan (2000), *Film Parody*, London: BFI Publishing.

Hartley, Anthony (5 March 1989), 'Scandal of Stephen Ward as scapegoat', *Mail on Sunday*.

Harvie, Christopher (1990), 'Political thrillers and the condition of England from the 1840s to the 1980s', in Marwick, Arthur (ed.), *The Arts, Literature, and Society*, London: Routledge, pp. 217-48.

Hastings, Max (2015), *The Secret War. Spies, Codes and Guerrillas 1939-1945*, London: William Collins.

Hattersley, Roy (23 June 1988), 'Let's Pretend Politics', *The Listener*.

Hayes, M. Hunter, and Sebastian Groes (2009), '"Profoundly dislocating and infinite in possibility": Ian McEwan's Screenwriting', in Groes, Sebastian (ed.), *Ian McEwan*, London: Continuum, pp. 26-42.

Head, Dominic (2007), *Ian McEwan*, Manchester: Manchester University Press.

Hennessy, Peter, and Kathleen Townsend (1987), 'The documentary spoor of Burgess and Maclean', *Intelligence and National Security*, 2(2), pp. 291-301.

Hennessey, Thomas, and Claire Thomas (2011), *Spooks. The Unofficial History of MI5 From the First Atom Spy to 7/7, 1945-2009*, Stroud, Gloucestershire: Amberley.

Higson, Andrew (2003), *English Heritage, English Cinema: Costume Drama Since 1980*, Oxford: Oxford University Press.

Hiley, Nicholas (1990), 'Decoding German Spies: British Spy Fiction 1908–1918', *Intelligence and National Security*, 5(4), pp. 55–79.

Hill, John (1999), *British Cinema in the 1980s*, Oxford: OUP.

Hinsley, F. H., E. E. Thomas, C. F. G. Ransom and R. C. Knight (1981), *British Intelligence in the Second World War, Volume 2*, London: Her Majesty's Stationary Office.

Hirsch, Foster (2007), *Otto Preminger. The Man Who Would be King*, New York: Alfred A. Knopf.

Hitz, Frederick (2004), *The Great Game: The Myth and Reality of Espionage*, New York: Alfred A. Knopf.

Hochscherf, Tobias (2013), 'Bond for the Age of Global Crises: 007 in the Daniel Craig Era', *Journal of British Cinema and Television*, 10(2), pp. 298–320.

Hodgson, Clive (April 1978), 'An Interview with Mark Shivas', *London Magazine*, 18(1), pp. 68-72.

Hoffman, Tod (2001), *Le Carré's Landscape*, Montreal & Kingston: McGill-Queen's University Press.

Hofstadter, Richard (November 1964), 'The Paranoid Style in American Politics', *Harper's Magazine*, pp. 77-86.

Hollingsworth, Mark and Nick Fielding (1999), *Defending the Realm. MI5 and the Shayler Affair*, London: André Deutsch.

Holzman, Michael H (2012), *Guy Burgess: Revolutionary in an Old School Tie*, New York: Chelmsford Press.

Homberger, Eric (1986). *John le Carré*, London: Methuen.

— (1988), '"Uncle Max" and his Thrillers', *Intelligence and National Security*, 3(2), pp. 312-21.

— (1991), 'English Spy Thrillers in the Age of Appeasement', *Intelligence and National Security*, 5(4), pp. 80-91.

Horn, Eva (2013), *The Secret War. Treason, Espionage, and Modern Fiction*, Evanston, Illinois: Northwestern University Press.

Houston, Penelope (1964/1965), '007', *Sight and Sound*, 34(1), pp.14-16.

— (1966), 'Joseph Losey's Paper Handkerchief', *Sight and Sound*, 35(3), pp.142-43.

Howarth, Patrick (1973), *Play Up and Play the Game. The Heroes of Popular Culture*, London: Methuen.

Hugo, Grant (1972), 'The Political Influence of the Thriller', *Contemporary Review*, 221, pp. 284-89.

Irving, Clive, Ron Hall and Jeremy Wallington (1963), *Scandal '63. A Study of the Profumo Affair*, London: Heinemann.

Isaacson, Walter and James Kelly (1993), 'We Distorted Our Own Minds', in Bruccoli, Matthew J., and Judith S. Baughman (eds.) (2004), *Conversations with John le Carré*, Jackson, Mississippi: University Press of Mississippi, pp. 128-32.

Jeffrey, Keith (2010), *MI6. The History of the Secret Intelligence Service, 1909-1949*, London: Bloomsbury.

Jenkins, Philip (1990), 'Spy fiction and terrorism', *Intelligence and National Security*, 5(4), pp. 185-203.

Johnson, Beth (2013), *Paul Abbott*, Manchester: Manchester University Press.

Johnson, Ian (October 1965), '007 + 4', *Films and Filming*, pp. 5-8.

Johnson, Paul (5 April 1958), 'Sex, Snobbery and Sadism', *New Statesman*, pp. 430-32.

— (4 March 1989), 'The Real Scandal', *Daily Mail*.

Kamm, Jürgen (1996), 'The Berlin Wall and Cold-War Espionage: Visions of a Divided Germany in the Novels of Len Deighton', in Schürer, E. et al (eds.), *The Berlin Wall: Representations and Perspectives*, New York: Peter Lang, pp. 61-73.

Keighron, Peter (1991), 'Condition critical', *Screen*, 32(2), pp. 209-19.

Kennaway, James (1962), *The Mind Benders, Shooting Script*.

Kennedy, Harlan (July-August 1984), 'Treasons of the Heart', *Film Comment*, pp. 9-14.

— (July-August 1985), 'The Brits have gone nuts', *Film Comment*, pp. 51-55.

— (July-August 1988), 'Dearden's Island', *Film Comment*, pp.17-22.

Kinnock, Glenys (18-24 June 1988), *TV Times*, p. 6.

Kirchick, James (2016), 'Cold War Nostalgia', posted at http://www.foreignpolicyi.org/content/cold-war-nostalgia, accessed May 2017.

Klein, Amanda Ann (2011), *American Film Cycles: Reframing Genres, Screening Social Problems, and Defining Subcultures*, Austin: University of Texas Press.

Klein, Joanne (1985), *Making Pictures: The Pinter Screenplays*, Columbus, Ohio: Ohio State University Press.

Knightley, Phillip (1988), *Philby. The Life and Views of the KGB Masterspy*, London: Andre Deutsch.

— (10 May 2003), 'The truth about the Cambridge spies', *Independent*.

Kremer, Daniel (2015), *Sidney J. Furie. Life and Films*, Lexington, Kentucky: University Press of Kentucky.

Lacquer, Walter (1983), 'Le Carré's Fantasies', *Commentary*, 75(6), pp. 62-67.

Laity, Susan (1987), ' "The Second Burden of a Former Child": Doubling and Repetition in *A Perfect Spy*', in Bloom, Harold (ed.), *John le Carré*, New York: Chelsea House, pp. 137-64.

Landy, Marcia (1991), *British Genres: Cinema and Society, 1930-1960*, Princeton, NJ: Princeton University Press.

Lane, Sheldon (ed.) (1965), *For Bond Lovers Only*, London: Panther.

Lanza, Joseph (2008), *Phallic Frenzy. Ken Russell and His Films*, London: Aurum.

Leahy, James (1967), *The Cinema of Joseph Losey*, London: Zwemmer.

Le Carré, John (May 1966), 'To Russia, with Greetings', *Encounter*, pp. 3-6.

— (1991), 'Introduction', in *The Spy Who Came in from the Cold*, New York: Pocket Books.

— (2014), 'Afterword', in Macintyre, Ben, *A Spy Among Friends. Kim Philby and the Great Betrayal*, London: Bloomsbury.

Leigh, David (1988), *The Wilson Plot: How the Spycatchers and Their American Allies Tried to Overthrow the British Government*, New York: Pantheon.

Lindner, Christoph (ed.) (2009), 'Introduction', in *Revisioning 007. James Bond and Casino Royale*, London: Wallflower, pp. 1-7.

Lockhart, Robin Bruce (1983), *Reilly _ Ace of Spies*, London: Futura.

Low, Rachel (1950), *The History of the British Film 1914-1918*, London: Allen & Unwin.

Lumet, Sidney (1995), *Making Movies*, New York: Alfred A. Knopf.

Lycett, Andrew (1995), *Ian Fleming. The Man Behind James Bond*, Atlanta, Georgia: Turner Publishing.

MacArthur, Colin (1985), 'British film reviewing a complaint', *Screen*, 26(1), pp. 79-85.

Madden, Paul and David Wilson (Summer 1974), 'Getting in Close. An Interview with Jack Gold', *Sight and Sound*, pp. 134-37.

Malcolm, Derek (7 June 1984), *Guardian*.

Mann, William J. (2005), *Edge of Midnight: The Life of John Schlesinger*, New York: Billboard.

Markstein, George (1966), 'Projecting a Spy', *Journal of the Society of Film and Television Arts*, 24, pp. 16-17.

Marshall, Alan (March 1985), 'Kanievska's Country', *AIP & Co.*, 52, pp. 31-35.

Masters, Anthony (1987), *Literary Agents: The Novelist as Spy*, Oxford: Blackwell.

Mather, John S. (ed.) (1955), *The Great Spy Scandal. Inside Story of Burgess and Maclean*, London: Daily Express.

Maulucci Jr., Thomas W. (2008), 'Cold War Berlin in the Movies: From *The Big Lift* to *The Promise*', in Rollins, Peter C., and John E. O'Connor (eds.), *Why*

We Fought. America's Wars in Film and History, Lexington, Kentucky, pp. 317-48.

McCormick, Donald (1979), *Who's Who in Spy Fiction*, London: Sphere Books.

McCormick, Donald and Katy Fletcher (1990), *Spy Fiction: A Connoisseur's Guide*, Oxford: Facts on File.

McEwan, Ian (1981), 'Introduction', *'The Imitation Game'. Three Plays for Television*, London: Jonathan Cape.

McKechnie, Kara (2007), *Alan Bennett*, Manchester: Manchester University Press.

McMahon, Gary (2012), 'The Ipcress File: Part 2, supplement', *Film International*, 58-59, pp. 18-38.

Melvin, David Skene (1978), 'The Secret Eye: The Spy in Literature: The Evolution of Espionage Literature – A Survey of the History and Development of the Spy and Espionage Novel', *Pacific Quarterly*, 3, pp. 11-26.

Merry, Bruce (1976), 'The Spy Thriller', *London Magazine*, 16(1), pp. 8-27.

— (1977), *Anatomy of the Spy Thriller*, Dublin: Gill and Macmillan.

Mews, Siegfried (1996), 'The Spies Are Coming in from the Cold: The Berlin Wall in the Espionage Novel', in Schürer, E. et al (eds.), *The Berlin Wall: Representations and Perspectives*, New York: Peter Lang, pp. 50-60.

Miller, Gabriel (2000), *The Films of Martin Ritt. Fanfare for the Common Man*, Jackson, Mississippi: University Press of Mississippi.

Miller, Toby (2003), *Spyscreen: Espionage on Film and TV from the 1930s to the 1960s*, Oxford: Oxford University Press.

Modin, Yuri (1994), *My Five Cambridge Friends*, London: Headline.

Monaghan, David (1983), 'John le Carré and England: A Spy's-Eye View', *Modern Fiction Studies*, 29(3), pp. 569-82.

Moore, Roger (2008), *My Word is My Bond. The Autobiography*, London: Michael O'Mara.

Moran, Christopher R. and Robert Johnson (2010), 'In the Service of Empire: Imperialism and the British Spy Thriller 1901-1914', *Studies in Intelligence*, 54(2), pp. 1-22.

Moran, Christopher (2011a), 'The Pursuit of Intelligence History: Methods, Sources, and Trajectories in the United Kingdom', *Studies in Intelligence*, 55(2), pp. 33-55.

— (2011b), 'Intelligence and the Media: The Press, Government Secrecy and the "Buster" Crabb Affair', *Intelligence and National Security*, 26(5), pp. 676-700.

— (2013), *Classified. Secrecy and the State in Modern Britain*, Cambridge: CUP.

Moran, Jon (2014), 'Conspiracy and contemporary history: revisiting MI5 and the Wilson plot[s]', *Journal of Intelligence History*, 13(2), pp. 161-75.

More, Kenneth (1978), *More or Less. An Autobiography*, London: Hodder and Stoughton.

Morgan, Eric J. (2016), 'Whores and angels of our striving selves: the cold war films of John le Carré, then and now', *Historical Journal of Film, Radio and Television*, 36(1), pp. 88-103.

Murphy, Robert (1992), *Sixties British Cinema*, London: BFI Publishing.

— (2000), *British Cinema and the Second World War*, London: Continuum.

Murray, Gary (1993), *Enemies of the State*, London: Simon & Shuster.

National Intelligence Machinery (2000), London: The Stationary Office.

Neale, Steve (2000), *Genre and Hollywood*, Routledge: Abingdon, Oxon.

Nelson, Robin (2011), *Stephen Poliakoff: On Stage and Screen*, London: Methuen.

Newton, Verne W. (1991), *The Butcher's Embrace. The Philby Conspirators in Washington*, London: Macdonald and Co.

Norton-Taylor, Richard (1990), *In Defence of the Realm? The Case for Accountable Security Services*, London: Civil Liberties Trust.

O'Brien, R. Barry (3 March 1989), 'Keeler sees her scandal revived at the cinema', *The Telegraph*.

O'Connor, John, and Martin Jackson (eds.) (1979), *American history/American film: interpreting the Hollywood image*, New York: Ungar Publishing.

Oldham, Joseph (2013), '"Disappointed romantics": Troubled Heritage in the BBC's John le Carré Adaptations', *Journal of British Cinema and Television*, 10(4), pp. 727-45.

— (2014), 'Changing narratives of conspiracy on British television: a review of *Hunted, Secret State, Complicit* and *Utopia*', *Journal of Intelligence History*, 13(1), pp. 94-103.

— (2015), 'Conspiracy and the British Spy Hero', https://www.iggy.net/knowledge/creativewriting/content/conspiracy-and-the-british-spy-hero#.VqyhBfmLS71, accessed 8 August 2016.

— (2017), *Paranoid Visions. Spies, conspiracies and the secret state in British television drama*, Manchester: Manchester University Press.

O'Sullivan, Tim (2000), '*Suspect*: In search of the "superior support"', in Burton, Alan et al (eds.), *The Family Way: The Boulting Brothers and British Film Culture*, Trowbridge, Wilts: Flicks Books, pp. 200-14.

Packer, Jeremy (ed.) (2009a), *Secret Agents: Popular Icons Beyond James Bond*, Bern: Peter Lang.

— (2009b), 'The Many Beyonds: An Introduction', in Packer, Jeremy (ed.) *Secret Agents: Popular Icons Beyond James Bond*, Bern: Peter Lang., pp. 1-19.

Page, Bruce, David Leitch, and Phillip Knightley, (1968), *The Philby Conspiracy*, London: André Deutsch.

Palmer, Jerry (1978), *Thrillers: Genesis and Structure of a Popular Genre*, London: Edward Arnold.

— (2005), 'Parody and Decorum: Permission to Mock', in Lockyer, Sharon, and Michael Pickering (eds.), *Beyond a Joke: The Limits of Humour*, Houndmills, Basingstoke: Palgrave Macmillan, pp. 79-97.

Panek, LeRoy L. (1981), *The Special Branch: The British Spy Novel, 1890-1980*, Bowling Green, Ohio: Bowling Green University Popular Press.

Pearson, John (1966), *The Life of Ian Fleming*, McGraw-Hill, New York.

Penrose, Barrie and Roger Courtiour (1978), *The Pencourt File*, London: Secker & Warburg.

Petley, Julian (1988), 'A Very British Coup', *Monthly Film Bulletin*, 57 (2), pp. 95-97.

Philby, Kim (1979), *My Silent War*, London: Granada.

Phillips, Gene D. (1999), 'To Sup on Horrors: Christopher Hampton's Film Version of Joseph Conrad's *Secret Agent*', *Literature/Film Quarterly*, 27(3), pp. 173-77.

Pincher, Chapman (1978), *Inside Story*, London: Sidgwick & Jackson.

— (1981), *Their Trade is Treachery*, London: Sidgwick & Jackson.

— (1985), *The Secret Offensive*, London: Sidgwick & Jackson.

— (1987a), *A Web of Deception: The Spycatcher Affair*, London: Sidgwick & Jackson.

— (1987b), *Traitors: The Labyrinths of Treason*, London: Sidgwick & Jackson.

— (1991), *The Truth about Dirty Tricks: From Harold Wilson to Margaret Thatcher*, London: Sidgwick & Jackson.

Pixley, Andrew (1987), '*Callan*: A Blueprint for Quality', *Primetime*, 12, pp. 27-29.

— (2003a), 'Part One: Get it While It's Hot', *TV Zone*, 163, pp. 52-57.

— (2003b), 'Part Two: Into the Shadows', *TV Zone*, 164, pp. 48-53.

Plimpton, George (1997), 'John le Carré: The Art of Fiction', in Bruccoli, Matthew J., and Judith S. Baughman (eds.) (2004), *Conversations with John le Carré*, Jackson, Mississippi: University Press of Mississippi, pp. 145-61.

Porter, Bernard (1989), *Plots and Paranoia: A History of Political Espionage in Britain1790-1988*, London: Unwin Hyman.

Powell, Michael (1993), *Million-Dollar Movie*, London: Mandarin.

Pratt, Vic (2009), 'International Intrigue in a London Bedroom: *The Spy's Wife*', in *All The Right Noises*, booklet issued with the DVD *All The Right Noises* (BFIVD852).

Price, Thomas J. (1994), 'Popular Perceptions of an Ally: "The Special Relationship" in the British Spy Novel', *Journal of Popular Culture*, 28 (2), pp. 49-66.

— (1996), 'Spy Stories, Espionage and the Public in the Twentieth Century', *Journal of Popular Culture*, 30(3), pp. 81-89.

Rausch, G. Jay and Diane K. Rausch (1993), ' Developments in Espionage Fiction ', reprinted in Mauro, Laurie D. (ed.), *Twentieth-Century Literary Criticism*, 50, Detroit: Gale Research, pp 96-102.

Ray, Robert B. (1985), *A Certain Tendency of the Hollywood Cinema, 1930-1980*, Princeton, NJ: Princeton University Press.

Read, Piers Paul (2004), *Alec Guinness. The Authorised Biography*, London: Pocket Books.

Rees, Jenny (1994), *Looking for Mr Nobody. The Secret Life of Goronwy Rees*, London: Weidenfeld & Nicolson.

Reynolds, Sidney (October 1979), 'The Importance of Being Otto', *Film Making*, 17(10), pp. 32-33.

Richards, Jeffrey (1984), *Age of the Dream Palace: Cinema and Society in 1930s Britain*, London: Routledge and Kegan Paul.

— (1986a), '"Careless Talk Costs Lives": *The Next of Kin*', in Aldgate, Anthony and Jeffrey Richards, *Britain Can Take It: The British Cinema and the Second World War*, Oxford: Blackwell, pp. 96-114.

— (1986b), 'The Englishman's Englishman: *Pimpernel Smith*', in Aldgate, Anthony and Jeffrey Richards, *Britain Can Take It: The British Cinema and the Second World War*, Oxford: Blackwell, pp. 44-75.

— (1997), *Films and British National Identity*, Manchester: MUP.

Richards, Julian (2012), 'Intelligence Dilemma? Contemporary Counterterrorism in a Liberal Democracy', *Intelligence and National Security*, 27(5), pp. 761-80.

Richardson, Maurice (16 August 1964), 'Requiem for Bond', *Observer*, p. 18.

Richelson, Jeffrey T. (2003), 'The IPCRESS File: The Great Game in Film and Fiction, 1953-2002', *International Journal of Intelligence and Counter Intelligence*, 16, pp. 462-98.

Richler, Mordecai (1971), 'James Bond Unmasked', in Rosenberg, Bernard, and David Manning White (eds.), *Mass Culture Revisited*, New York: Van Nostrand Reinhold, pp. 341-55.

Rimington, Stella (2002), *Open Secret: The Autobiography of the Former Director-General of MI5*, London: Arrow Books.

Riols, Noreen (2013), *The Secret Ministry of Ag. & Fish: My Life in Churchill's School for Spies*, London: Macmillan.

Robertson, James C. (1984), '*Dawn* (1928): Edith Cavell and Anglo-German Relations', *Historical Journal of Film, Radio and Television*, 4(1), pp. 15-28.

Rosenberg, Bruce A., and Ann Harleman Stewart (1989), *Ian Fleming*, Boston: Twayne.

Royden, Barry (Summer 2009), '*The Spy Who Came in from the Cold*', *Studies in Intelligence*, pp. 11-12.

Royle, Trevor (1983), *James & Jim: A Biography of James Kennaway*, Edinburgh: Mainstream Publishing.

Rubin, Martin (1999), *Thrillers*, Cambridge: Cambridge University Press.

Russell, Ken (1991), *Altered States. The Autobiography of Ken Russell*, New York: Bantam.

Ryall, Tom (1986), *Alfred Hitchcock and the British Cinema*, Urbana and Chicago: University of Illinois Press.

— (2011), 'Gaumont Hitchcock', in Leitch, Thomas, and Leland Poague (eds.), *A Companion to Alfred Hitchcock*, Southern Gate, Chichester: Wiley-Blackwell, pp. 270-88.

Sandbrook, Dominic (2006), *Never Had It So Good: A History of Britain from Suez to The Beatles*, London: Abacus.

Sanoff, Alvin P. (1989), 'The Thawing of the Old Spymaster', in Bruccoli, Matthew J., and Judith S. Baughman (eds.) (2004), *Conversations with John le Carré*, Jackson, Mississippi: University Press of Mississippi, pp. 107-11.

Sarris, Andrew (11 February 1980), 'Paradoxical Reputations', *Village Voice*.

Sauerberg, Lars Olé (1983), 'Literature in Figures: An Essay on the Popularity of Thrillers', *Orbis Litterarum*, 38, pp. 93-107.

— (1984), *Secret Agents in Fiction: Ian Fleming, John le Carré and Len Deighton*, New York: St. Martin's Press.

— (1985), 'Reading Formula Fiction: On Absorption and Identification', *Orbis Litterarum*, 40, pp. 357-71.

Schiff, Stephen (1989), 'The Secret Life of John le Carré', in Bruccoli, Matthew J., and Judith S. Baughman (eds.) (2004), *Conversations with John le Carré*, Jackson, Mississippi: University Press of Mississippi, pp. 93-106.

Scott, Len (1999), 'Espionage and the cold war: Oleg Penkovsky and the Cuban missile crisis', *Intelligence and National Security*, 14(3), pp. 23-47.

Scott, L. V., and P. D. Jackson (2004), 'Journeys in Shadows', in Scott, L. V., and P. D. Jackson (eds.), *Understanding Intelligence in the Twenty-First Century: Journeys in Shadows*, London: Routledge, pp. 1-28.

Seaton, Jean (2015), *'Pinkoes and Traitors'. The BBC and the nation, 1974-1987*, London: Profile Books.

Sebag-Montefiore, Hugh (4 October 2001), 'Now the Truth about Enigma', *Evening Standard.*

Security Services: MI5, The (1993), London: The Stationary Office.

Seed, David (1992), 'Erskine Childers and the German Peril', *German Life and Letters*, 45(1), pp. 66-73.

— (2004), *Brainwashing. The Fictions of Mind Control*, Kent Ohio: Kent State University Press.

Sellers, Robert (2006), *Cult TV. The Golden Age of ITC*, London: Plexus.

Sewell, Brian (12 January 1987), 'This was the Blunt I knew', *Evening Standard.*

— (6 May 2003), 'Where is the Blunt I knew?', *Evening Standard.*

Sexton, Max (2014), 'The Origins of Gritty Realism on British Television: Euston Films and *Special Branch*', *Journal of British Cinema and Television*, 11(1), pp. 23-40.

Shaw, Tony (2001), *British Cinema and the Cold War: The State, Propaganda and Consensus*, London: I.B. Tauris.

Siegel, Don (1993), *A Siegel Film*, London: Faber and Faber.

Siegel, Jennifer (1995), 'British intelligence on the Russian revolution and civil war – A breach at the source', *Intelligence and National Security*, 10(3), pp. 468-85.

Simon, Reeva Spector (2010), *Spies and Holy Wars: The Middle East in 20th-century Crime Fiction*, Austin: University of Texas Press.

Sisman, Adam (2015), *John le Carré. The Biography*, London: Bloomsbury.

Smith, Michael (1996), *New Cloak, Old Dagger. How Britain's Spies Came in from the Cold*, London: Gollancz.

Smith, Jr., Myron J. and Terry White (1995), *Cloak and Dagger Fiction: An Annotated Guide to Spy Thrillers*, Westport, Connecticut: Greenwood Press.

Snyder, John R. (Summer 1977), 'The Spy as Modern Tragedy', *Literature/Film Quarterly*, pp. 216-34.

Snyder, Robert Lance (2011), *The Art of Indirection in British Espionage Fiction: A Critical Study of Six Novelists*, Jefferson, North Carolina: McFarland.

Solomon, Philip and Susan T. Kleeman (1971), 'Sensory Deprivation', *American Journal of Psychiatry*, 127, pp. 122-23.

Spooks. Behind the Scenes (2006), London: Orion.

Staniforth, Andrew (2013), *The Routledge Companion to UK Counter-Terrorism*, Abingdon, Oxon: Routledge.

Stafford, David (1981), 'Spies and Gentlemen: The Birth of the British Spy Novel, 1893-1914', *Victorian Studies*, 24(4), pp. 489-509.

— (1988), *The Silent Game: The Real World of Imaginary Spies*, London: Viking.

— (2002), *Spies Beneath Berlin*, London: John Murray.

Stempel, John D., Robert W. Pringle Jr. and Tom Stempel (2002), 'Intelligence and the Cinema', *International Journal of Intelligence and Counter Intelligence*, 15(1), pp. 115-24.

Stewart, Victoria (2011), *The Second World War in Contemporary British Fiction. Secret Histories*, Edinburgh: Edinburgh University Press.

Stone, Nancy-Stephanie (1997), *A Reader's Guide to The Spy and Thriller Novel*, New York: G. K. Hall & Co.

Stonebridge, Lyndsey (2007), *The Writing of Anxiety: Imagining Wartime in Mid-Century British Culture*, Houndmills, Basingstoke: Palgrave Macmillan.

Street, Sarah (2008), 'Heritage Crime: The Case of Agatha Christie', in Shail, Robert (ed.), *Seventies British Cinema*, London: Palgrave Macmillan, pp.105-16.

Suedfeld, Peter (1969), 'Introduction and Historical Background', in Zubek, John P. (ed.), *Sensory deprivation: Fifteen years of research*, New York: Appleton-Century-Crofts, pp. 3-15.

Summers, Anthony, and Stephen Dorril (1987), *Honeytrap. The Secret Worlds of Stephen Ward*, London: Weidenfeld & Nicolson.

Sutherland, John (1981), *Bestsellers: Popular Fiction of the 1970s*, London: Routledge & Kegan Paul.

Svendsen, Adam D. M. (2009), 'Painting rather than photography: exploring spy fiction as a legitimate source concerning UK-US intelligence co-operation', *Journal of Transatlantic Studies*, 7(1), pp. 1-22.

Symons, Julian (1972), *Mortal Consequences: A History – From the Detective Story to the Crime Novel*, New York: Harper & Row.

Tarratt, Margaret (1969), 'James Cellan Jones and the classic serial, interviewed by Margaret Tarratt', *Screen*, 10(6), pp. 33-44.

'The World of James Bond' (June 1965), *Contacts*, n.p.

Thompson, E. P. (1978), 'Introduction', in *Review of Security and the State 1978*, London: Julian Friedmann.

Thompson, Felix (2010), '*Coast* and *Spooks*: On the permeable national boundaries of British television', *Continuum: Journal of Media & Cultural Studies*, 24(3), pp. 429-38.

Thurlow, Richard C. (2000), 'The charm offensive: The "coming out" of MI5', *Intelligence and National Security*, 15(1), pp. 183-90.

Trotter, David (1990), 'The Politics of Adventure in the Early British Spy Novel', *Intelligence and National Security*, 5 (4), pp. 30–54.

Walker, Alexander (16 October 1980), 'Potter's Kiss of Life', *Evening Standard*.

— (1986), *Hollywood, England. The British Film Industry in the Sixties*, London: Harrap.

— (1986a), *National Heroes. British Cinema in the Seventies and Eighties*, London: Harrap.

— (3 September 1987), 'Mole', *Evening Standard*.

— (23 June 1988), *Evening Standard*.

— (17 May 1990), 'Plots and Paranoia', *Evening Standard*.

Wark, Wesley K. (1990), 'Introduction: Fictions of History', *Intelligence and National Security*, 5(4), pp. 1-16.

— (ed.) (1991), *Spy Fiction, Spy Films and Real Intelligence*, Abingdon, Oxon: Routledge.

West, Nigel, (2004), 'Fiction, Faction and Intelligence', in Scott, L. V., and P. D. Jackson (eds.), *Understanding Intelligence in the Twenty-First Century: Journeys in Shadows*, London: Routledge, pp. 122-34.

— (2005), 'The UK's Not Quite So Secret Services', *International Journal of Intelligence and CounterIntelligence*, 18(1), pp. 23-30.

West, Nigel, and Oleg and Tsarev (1998), *The Crown Jewels. The British Secrets at the Heart of the KGB Archives*, London: HarperCollins.

West, Rebecca (1964), *The New Meaning of Treason*, New York: Viking Press.

Wheen, Francis (2009), *Strange Days Indeed: The Golden Age of Paranoia*, London: Fourth Estate.

White, Jerry (1993), '*Hidden Agenda* and *JFK*. Conspiracy Thrillers', *Jump Cut*, 38, pp. 14-18.

White, Rosie (2007), *Violent Femmes. Women as spies in popular culture*, Abingdon, Oxon: Routledge.

Williams, Raymond (4 May 1972), 'Where does Rozanov come in? ', *The Listener*, p. 599.

Willmetts, Simon and Christopher Moran (2013), 'Filming Treachery: British Cinema and Television's Fascination with the Cambridge Five', *Journal of British Cinema and Television*, 10(1), pp. 49-70.

Winks, Robin W. (1993), 'Spy Fiction—Spy Reality: From Conrad to Le Carré', *Soundings*, 76(2-3), pp. 221-36.

Wolfe, Peter (1999), *Understanding Alan Bennett*, Columbia, South Carolina: University of South Carolina Press.

Wollen, Tana (1985), 'Memory: The Flame Trees of Thika', in Alvarado, Manuel and John Stewart, *Made for Television. Euston Films Limited*, London: BFI Publishing.

— (1991), 'Over our shoulders: nostalgic screen fictions for the 1980s', in Corner, John, and Sylvia Harvey (eds.), *Enterprise and Heritage: Crosscurrents of national culture*, London: Routledge, pp.178-93.

Woods, Brett F. (2008), *Neutral Ground: A Political History of Espionage Fiction*, New York: Algora.

Wright, Peter, with Paul Greengrass (1987), *Spycatcher*, Richmond, Victoria: Heinemann.

Wynne, Greville (1983), *The Man from Odessa. The Secret Career of a British Agent*, London: Granada.

Notes

[1] Following the partial opening up of the archives, historians have now been able to offer a more objective judgment on the myth, concluding that the *"image of a super effective British counter-intelligence agency owed as much to the failure of the German secret service than to British efficiency"* (Thurlow 2000: 187).

[2] For discussions of the more modest achievements of the American spy story, see Katy Fletcher (1987) and Christine Bold (1990).

[3] The 'conspiracy text' was another related product of the early twentieth century, Michael Newton has written of its *"coming into being in a cultural moment that united cosmopolitan anarchist terrorism, revolutionary communist hopes, the triumph of a Kafkaesque bureaucratic system, and the birth of the espionage novel"* (*Guardian*, 2 August 2014).

[4] General overviews of the British spy novel include Panek (1981), Atkins (1984), Cawelti and Rosenberg (1987), Stafford (1988), Bloom (1990), Woods (2008), Snyder (2011) and Buckton (2015). An exhaustive listing of mainly British and American spy novels is presented in Smith, Jr. and White (1995), while more selective lists are available in McCormick (1979), McCormick and Fletcher (1990) and Stone (1997).

[5] Luc Boltanski, while noting the common link to the parent genre of mystery, sees the distinction between crime and espionage fiction in terms of the former's development of the *"thematics of inquiry"*, and the latter's reliance on the *"thematics of conspiracy"* and its suspicions about the exercise of power (2014: xiv-xv).

[6] Rausch and Rausch, in a consideration of the spy as a sympathetic protagonist, have suggested that the *"lying, cheating and deception which are inseparable from espionage could be considered acceptable only after nationalism had grown strong enough to provide an acceptable motive for any action done in the name of one's country"*, and that this historical point was reached late in the 19th century (1993: 97).

[7] 'Sapper' was the pen-name of Herman Cyril McNeile. For examples of the work of these authors, see Williams, *The Secret Hand: Some Further Adventures by Desmond Okewood of the British Secret Service* (1919), 'Sapper', *Bulldog Drummond: The Adventures of a Demobilised Officer Who Found Peace Dull* (1920), Beeding, *The Seven Sleepers* (1925) and Horler, *The Secret Agent* (1934).

[8] For a discussion of a 'fiendish Oriental' myth and other aversions to foreigners in popular literature of the 1920s and 1930s, see the chapters 'The Orientation of Villainy' and 'Amid the alien corn' in Watson (1971: 109-136).

[9] To this trio of 'spy-terrorism' novels could be added John Buchan's *The Power-House* (1913), in which the hero thwarts the plans of a master criminal to loose anarchy on the world. An early thriller by its author, the book patently lacks the literary quality apparent in Conrad and Chesterton's works.

[10] See Jenkins (1990) and Trotter (1990: 33-37).

[11] See, for example, the discussion of the latest screen adaptation of *The Secret Agent* as a timely tale of espionage and terror in the *Guardian* (16 July 2016).

[12] Three novels by Compton Mackenzie are sometimes grouped in with the *Ashenden* stories, as *Extremes Meet* (1928), *The Three Couriers* (1929) and the better-known *Water on the Brain* (1933), similarly contain cynical or satirical treatments of espionage. Mackenzie like Maugham served in intelligence during the First World War.

[13] Homberger is in a minority in his view that the spy novel of the late 1930s did little more than take the urgency of the times as a useful pretext or background and bemoans the "*failure of the espionage thriller in the age of appeasement*" (1991: 89).

[14] James Bond novels have continued under the pen of various authors, including Kingsley Amis (writing as Robert Markham), John Gardner, Sebastian Faulks, William Boyd and Anthony Horowitz.

[15] For typical pieces critical of Fleming, see Paul Johnson's notorious review of *Dr No* in 1958 entitled 'Sex, Snobbery and Sadism' and Richler (1971, first published in 1968).

[16] Of course, Rohmer's most famous creation was the arch-villain Dr Fu-Manchu who first appeared in 1913, and who found a distant echo in Fleming's Dr No.

[17] McCormick and Fletcher claim that Dennis Wheatley was one of the "*first spy story writers to introduce uninhibited sex as an underlying theme*" in his Gregory Sallust stories of the 1940s (1990: 258): although it should be acknowledged that this was of an entirely different order to James Bond's conquests in the 1950s and 1960s.

[18] *Casino Royale* is sometimes seen as self-doubting and cynical.

[19] Mayo also published more traditional novels of intrigue under his real name of Stephen Coulter.

[20] Munro later published spy novels featuring the disillusioned agent David Callan under his real name of James Mitchell.

[21] Literary reviewer Laura Miller has proposed the distinction in spy fiction between the "*preposterous*" and the "*disillusioned*" (*The New York Times Book Review*, 6 June 2004).

[22] Callan first appeared in a single play television drama in 1967, and became a series character in such novels as *A Magnum for Schneider* (1969) and *Russian Roulette* (1973); while Charlie Muffin first appeared in an eponymously titled novel of 1977 and regularly thereafter.

[23] The term is used by Adam Sisman in connection with John le Carré (2015: 342).

[24] Le Carré had first visited the theme of terrorism in *The Little Drummer Girl* (1983).

[25] The authors and stories discussed in this section receive more extended treatment in Burton (2016).

[26] Story from BBC News: http://news.bbc.co.uk/go/pr/fr/-/1/hi/magazine/8166 163.stm, published 24/07/2009 (accessed 11/01/2017).

[27] On the '*Spycatcher* Affair', see Pincher (1987a).

[28] In a notorious case, Compton Mackenzie was successfully prosecuted under the Official Secrets Act in 1932 for revelations he made in his memoir *Greek Memories*, in which he gave an account of his experience in the Secret Intelligence Service in 1917. Thankfully for lovers of spy fiction this prompted the author to write his glorious satire of the Service *Water on the Brain* (1933). It has been alleged that Somerset Maugham was obliged to destroy a second volume of *Ashenden* stories before publication (West 2004: 124).

[29] In yet another instance of testing spy fiction against spy reality, a recent television documentary *The World's Greatest Spy Movies* (2016) invited a panel of intelligence insiders to rank spy films according to their authenticity.

[30] Stempel, Pringle Jnr. and Stempel quote an unnamed senior intelligence officer who makes the comment, "*Spy movies are to real world intelligence work what Donald Duck movies are to understanding the Environment*" (2002: 115). See also Richelson (2003), a scholar based at the National Security Archive, Washington, D.C. Such commentators make much of the fact that spy fiction centres on the activities of field agents rather than the prosaic but more widespread task of intelligence gathering and analysis.

[31] Quoted in http://news.bbc.co.uk/1/hi/magazine/8166163.stm (accessed 31 October 2016). It was *Kim* that the future Head of MI5 Stella Rimington read in the late 1960s, "*romantically dreaming of the Great Game*", whilst stationed in northern India working for the government propaganda outfit the Information Research Department (2002: 75, 91).

[32] Recounted at BBC News: http://news.bbc.co.uk/go/pr/fr/-/1/hi/magazine/8166163. stm (accessed 20 July 2015).

[33] Judd, actually Alan Petty, was formerly Personal Assistant to the Chief of the Secret Service Sir Colin McColl, and was able to use his connections to gain access to restricted documents.

[34] A partial list of spy authors who also had some Secret Service connection would include Valentine Williams, A. E. W. Mason, Sydney Horler, Compton Mackenzie, Bernard Newman, J.C. Masterman, John Bingham, William Haggard and Ted Allbeury.

[35] The latter picture had some distinction as one of the earliest sound features produced in Britain. A sound version of *The Four Just Men* was produced at Ealing in 1939.

[36] Tom Ryall has calculated that the thriller was a major genre of the mid-1930s with over 200 such pictures in the period, of which around 50 were espionage films, and 11 of these dealing with the First World War (2011: 282-83).

[37] As Marthe Cnockaert McKenna she turned to spy fiction in the 1930s -1950s, publishing such titles as *A Spy was Born* (1935), *Arms and the Spy* (1942) and *Three Spies for Glory* (1950).

[38] While *Journey into Fear* and *Background to Danger* (both US, 1943) and *The Mask of Dimitrios* (US, 1944) were filmed in Hollywood, the only Eric Ambler adapted for the cinema in Britain in this period was *Epitaph of a Spy* (as *Hotel Reserve* 1944).

[39] The topic is more fully discussed in Murphy (2000: 81-123).

[40] A historical overview of British cinema and the Cold War is provided in Shaw (2001) and various articles can be found in Burton and Shaw (2013).

[41] Details of the series and its episodes can be found at http://www.startrader. co.uk/Action%20TV/guide50s/spycatcher.htm (accessed 4 February 2013).

[42] Details of the series and its episodes can be found at http://www.startrader.co.uk/ Action%20TV/guide60s/fourjustmen.htm (accessed 4 February 2013).

[43] For a fuller listing, see the bibliography in Burton (2016).

[44] The Routledge series 'British Popular Cinema' has showcased recent work on British cinema genres, including *British Crime Cinema* (1999), *British Science-Fiction Cinema* (1999), *British Horror Cinema* (2001), *British Historical Cinema* (2002) and *British Comedy Cinema* (2012).

[45] See, for example, Chapman (2000 and 2002), Ryall (1986) and Miller (2003).

[46] The present economy of book publishing also tends to favour shorter works of scholarship. As it has been let slip to the author, the ideal length for academic publishers is 80.000-100,000 words. Additionally, chapters should be no longer than 8,000 words as allegedly current students are unwilling to read anything longer than this! Such imperatives obviously suit and encourage the case-study approach.

[47] Suggested formulas for the spy story, of varying complexity, are offered in Merry (1976 and 1977), Sauerberg (1984), Cawelti and Rosenberg (1987), and Woods (2008).

[48] The composer on *Dr No* was, of course, Monty Norman. However, Barry made a substantial contribution as arranger, especially with the important James Bond theme, and would be promoted to composer on the next six 007 movies.

[49] The final production cost in sterling was £392,022 (Chapman 2014: 62).

[50] Details taken from the interviews and documentaries featured on the DVD *Dr No*, MGM 16160DVD.

[51] On *Dr No* production designer Ken Adam worked miracles with a final budget of only £20,000. The sets so impressed Stanley Kubrick that Adam was hired to design the Cold War satire *Dr Strangelove* (1964).

[52] The short sequence which introduces each movie in which James Bond appears as seen down the barrel of a gun and fires at his seeming antagonist is also seen as significant, "*This opening is a distinctive trade-mark, telling us that this is a Bond film and no other*" ('The World of James Bond').

[53] *You Only Live Twice* was the first picture in the series to make less money than its predecessor, and critics have commented on Connery's apparent boredom with the role.

[54] For a summary and discussion of the critical treatment of James Bond, see Chapman (2007: 1-18).

[55] Eon allegedly stood for "*Everything or Nothing*".

[56] Key personnel who contributed to the Bond films had worked with Broccoli at Warwick, and included director Terence Young, writer Richard Maibaum, cinematographer Ted Moore and designer Ken Adam.

[57] Some of the deals Fleming entered into at this time led to future complications over rights to the character and the stories.

[58] Balio reports the following above-the-line costs: $140,000 for the property and screenplay, $40,000 for the director, $80,000 for the producer's fee, and $140,000 for the cast, including the star (1987: 257). For a recent examination of the production of *Dr No* examining new sources, see Chapman (2014: 57-63).

[59] Details relating to the production and release of *Dr No* are taken from Walker (1986) and Balio (1987).

[60] *Thunderball* was the most successful picture in the initial series, achieving a worldwide gross of $50 million (Balio 1987: 267).

[61] The initial instances of this transference of James Bond beyond the pages of the novels were the serialisation of the stories and the appearance of a strip cartoon in the *Daily Express* in 1957.

[62] The 'Bond phenomenon' and the "*broader functioning of Bond as a populasr hero*" is the preoccupation of Bennett and Woollacott (1987).

[63] The phrase was possibly first used in reference to the Basil Dearden and Michael Relph spy thriller *Masquerade* (1965) and appeared in the review published in the *Daily Mail* (14 April 1965).

[64] The film was slightly re-edited for the American release and it is this version that I have been able to view.

[65] Shonteff was provided with introductions to the British film industry by his fellow Canadian Sidney J. Furie, and both would make a significant contribution to the spy film in Britain. For Furie, see chapter 2.

[66] This of course bears resemblance to the youthful experience of Ian Fleming who spent time at school in the Tyrol.

[67] The production was a little pressed for time, with Brynner only available for a limited period and with the urgent need to commence the scenes in the Alps while the snow lasted. The production unusually required a six-week shutdown between location and studio work to manage the complex logistics and to complete rewrites of the script (Erwin 1985: 212-15).

[68] Shooting had commenced before Ekland was cast to the female lead and her exterior scenes in Austria had to be mocked up using process shots on a soundstage (Erwin 1985: 216-17).

[69] Three spy pictures were released that week, *The Double Man, Casino Royale* and *The Spy with a Cold Nose*, and an element of reviewer fatigue was creeping in.

[70] James Bond, of course, found himself in the Swiss Alps the following year in *On Her Majesty's Secret Service* (1969).

[71] See Guest's account of filming with a male star who was terrified of skiing (2001: 157-58).

[72] Compare this to the cameo Redgrave played two years later in Joseph Losey's *The Go-Between* (1970), in which the actor plumbed great depths and found considerable poignancy in a role which also required the character to confront tragic personal failure.

[73] Green, Jonathon (2004), 'McNeile, (Herman) Cyril (1888–1937)', *Oxford Dictionary of National Biography*, Oxford: Oxford University Press.

[74] Koscina was a last minute replacement for Raquel Welch, the statuesque American actress appearing in the following year's British spy thriller *Fathom* (Box 2000: 257). The fifth 'Bulldog' Drummond novel had been *The Female of the Species* (1928), but this bears no resemblance to *Deadlier than the Male* other than the famous source poem by Kipling.

[75] Box and Thomas had planned a 'Bulldog' Drummond film as early as 1963, but waited until they found the right actor in Richard Johnson (*Deadlier than the Male* press sheet, 1966).

[76] Fairlie, who made himself available to the producers, had been the original inspiration for the character of Drummond and continued writing the stories after 'Sapper's' death in 1937.

[77] The female androids of *Some Girls Do* were reincarnated as the 'fembots' in the Austin Powers' spy spoofs *International Man of Mystery* (US, 1997), *The Spy Who Shagged Me* (US, 1999) and *Goldmember* (US, 2002).

[78] The later spoof *Bullshot* (1983) was a British film comedy adapted from the American stage play *Bullshot Crummond* (1974).

[79] *Deadlier than the Male* had been shot in expansive Techniscope, while *Some Girls Do* was filmed in the more restricted and old-fashioned academy ratio.

[80] Andrew York published a further eight thrillers featuring 'The Eliminator', a series which ended with *The Fascinator* in 1975.

[81] Allen had partnered Broccoli at Warwick Films where Allen had remained unconvinced by the commercial potential of the James Bond stories (Chapman 2014: 58; Field and Chowdhury 2015: 26, 47-48).

[82] The characterisation was similar to that of the former intelligence agent turned private detective in the TV adventure series *Man in a Suitcase* (1967-68).

[83] *Espionage* is discussed in chapter 5.

[84] See Powell's version of events (1993: 497-504). Director David Greene later made the fanciful *Madame Sin* (1972) with the legendary Bette Davis as the Fu Manchu-like supervillainess who plots to steal a Polaris submarine.

[85] The practice of recruiting scholars buoyed up by numerous women for cryptography went back to the First World War, when a "*large number of academics were drafted in to help and, by the Armistice, there were forty-five code breakers, supported by forty ancillary 'ladies'*" (Smith 1996: 168). The wartime memoirs of Leo Marks were published as *Between Silk and Cyanide: The Story of SOE's Code War* (1998).

[86] The code-breaking room designed by Wilfred Shingleton was the largest set yet constructed at Twickenham Studios (*Kine Weekly*, 25 March 1967).

[87] Sebastian and Becky observe the same contrasting relationship as that between John Steed and Emma Peel in *The Avengers* (TV 1961-69), something Steve Chibnall in reference to the television series has termed a "*modern Britain with two distinct faces*": "*We see with one eye the country mansions and churchyards, fox hunts, city gents and butlers of the tourist brochures, and with the other scientists in laboratories, robots and satellite observatories*" (*New Society*, 28 March 1985).

[88] The American edition of the novel ends with Eberlin exposed in Berlin, the publishers having demanded something less overtly downbeat (*Guardian*, 23 January 1976).

[89] Marlowe wrote some further non-espionage thrillers, and these, *Echoes of Celandine* (1970), *Somebody's Sister* (1974), *Nightshade* (1975), similarly dealt with isolation and loners.

[90] http://dangerousminds.net/comments/a_dandy_in_aspic_letter_from_derek_marlowe (accessed 20 November 2016).

[91] Mann had recently directed the wartime secret mission adventure *The Heroes of Telemark* (1965).

[92] It has been claimed that Harvey was responsible for filming the final climax at the airport (Hardy, Phil 1978, *National Film Theatre Programme Notes*, 1978: n.p.).

[93] Wanamaker had recently directed *The File of the Golden Goose* (1969), a crime thriller set in London in which Yul Brynner played an American secret serviceman working with Scotland Yard on the trail of counterfeit hundred dollar bills.

[94] Location scenes were also filmed at Southampton and Malta.

[95] MacLean had been commissioned to provide two sequels (*When Eight Bells Toll* press sheet).

[96] Under his real name of James Mitchell, the author wrote the scripts and stories featuring the working-class agent Callan (see Chapter 4).

[97] Collinson had earlier been hired for *Horse Under Water*, Harry Saltzman's proposed fourth instalment of the Harry Palmer series of spy pictures, which had been aborted after the critical and commercial failure of *Billion Dollar Brain* (1967) (*Kine Weekly*, 1 February 1969). See chapter 2.

[98] The British Board of Film Censors was being assaulted by a wave of controversial films in this period, which included *The Devils* (1970), *Straw Dogs* (1971) and *A Clockwork Orange* (1972).

[99] The scenes in question involved the physical and electrical torture of Craig's genitals.

[100] This aspect of the story was clearly influenced by the notorious breakout from Wormwood Scrubs of the spy George Blake in 1966.

[101] Despite the fact, as David Robinson reported, that the production seemed to have commenced before the script by Walter Hill was finished (*Monthly Film Bulletin*, Winter 1973: 20).

[102] Casting is telling here, as Mason essentially reprises his suave villain from Alfred Hitchcock's *North by Northwest* (US, 1959).

[103] Siegel's experiences are recounted in his autobiography (1993: 407-418).

[104] *The Black Windmill* could not forgo the obligatory reference to 007, having Tarrant make a mischievous reference to Sean Connery, before correcting himself: "*Sean Kelly, I mean*".

[105] I have been unable to view either *Assassin* or *Yellow Dog* and it could be that the films are considerably more interesting than I have been led to believe.

[106] Screenwriter John Gould died shortly after the production, but had previously made several contributions to the spy drama on British television and such series as *The Mask of Janus* (1965), *The Spies* (1966) and *Spy Trap* (1972-73).

[107] The tidal wave led United Artists on occasion to threaten Continental producers with a copyright suit (Bennett and Woollacott 1987: 32).

[108] For background on the Eurospy cycle see, Blake, Matt and David Deal (2008). A typical example of the commercial exploitation of these films in the US was Four Star's distribution of eleven European spy pictures marketed as the '0011 Package'. Under the banner of "*Spy Pics are 'IN'* ... *And We've Got 'Em!*", the bundle included among their number Lindsay Shonteff's British *Licensed to Kill* (*Variety* 27 January and 16 June 1965). A more serious espionage story was tackled in the Franco-German co-production *The Defector* (1967) starring Montgomery Clift, see, *Films and Filming* (May 1967: 46-47).

[109] The picture briefly sported the title *Keep Your Fingers Crossed* while in production (*Films and Filming*, June 1971: 12).

[110] *Otley* is discussed later in the chapter.

[111] Sometime earlier in the 1970s, it came to the attention of Kim Philby in Moscow that Michael Caine was slated to play him in a movie (which was never made). The famous spy supposedly quipped: *"chap's a cockney, how could he possibly play a person of that class?"* (*Daily Express*, 1 May 1982).

[112] The picture was budgeted at a reasonable £8 million, with executive co-producers Forsyth and Caine taking deferred payments.

[113] Allegedly, Prime Minister Margaret Thatcher was an avid reader of Forsyth, an admirer of *The Fourth Protocol*, and was guest of honour at the film's premier in London (*Daily Mail*, 23 February and 20 March 1987; Hollingsworth and Fielding 1999: 247). Forsyth and Mackenzie held politically divergent views, and the two had to reach a compromise to make the picture. The director required the removal of all material dealing with the *"loony left"*, and this was acceptable to Forsyth as the story needed shortening for the screen (*Western Mail*, 4 April 1987).

[114] The story claims a secret Fourth Protocol of the Nuclear Non-Proliferation Treaty of 1968 signed by East and West and which forbade the smuggling of nuclear weapons into enemy territory. To satisfy Forsyth's mania for accuracy, technical advice for the tactical nuclear device was provided by Professor M. M. R. Williams, Head of the Department of Nuclear Engineering at Queen Mary College, University of London. For the would-be terrorist, the technical outlines of building and assembling a small nuclear bomb (with diagram), and smuggling the components into a country, are helpfully provided in the film's press sheet.

[115] *Octopussy* also centred on a rogue Russian general who tries to smuggle a tactical nuclear device into the West.

[116] Preston's disillusionment here differs from the original novel which ends with the chief of MI6 convincing the spycatcher of the *real politik* of the situation and how it serves Western interests. Reviewers, in a reference to a defining role in an earlier espionage film, saw in Preston the anti-Establishment *"Ipcress man in middle-age"* (*Hampstead & Highgate Express*, 3 April 1987).

[117] 'Hot enough for June!' is the password the reluctant spy must use to establish his credentials with the standing agent in Prague.

[118] The film was known in some territories as *Agent 8¾*.

[119] The producers later claimed to have been refused permission to shoot in Prague, rejected Vienna as unsuitable, and settled on Padua as parts of the city had been designed by an architect responsible for buildings in the Czech capital. Box agreed that Bogarde was not ideal casting for the part, the actor was initially reluctant to play another light role, but both parties went ahead with the producers needing a star and Bogarde needing the money (Box 2000: 227-230; Coldstream 2005: 382-383).

[120] The colourful tale of the businessman-spy Greville Wynne is discussed in chapter 6.

[121] The original intention had been to cast Rex Harrison as the reluctant spy.

[122] United Artists had released the film version of *Goldfinger* in September 1964.

[123] A weak linguistic joke, Schlecht means 'bad' in German.

[124] MGM had objected to the title *Passport to Oblivion* as it claimed audiences would think this referred to a sleeping pill (Guest 2001: 148).

[125] The producers had been advised by the Foreign Office against setting the picture in Iran as the situation there was so volatile (Guest 2001: 148).

[126] The story was likely inspired by the real-life Operation Boot, in which the British Secret Intelligence Service engineered the removal of the Iranian prime minister who had nationalised the oil industry and in so doing, ensured the rule of the Anglophile Shah.

[127] The producers couldn't resist a nod at James Bond, the film's tagline announcing "*From Russia, Beirut, London, Rome and Byblos with LOVE!*".

[128] It was reported that some critics in France were incensed by the film's negative portrayal of the Russians, seeing this as unhelpful at a time of growing detente (*The Guardian*, 4 March 1966).

[129] Castle Howard, Yorkshire stands in for the Kremlin.

[130] In 1963, Galton and Simpson had scripted the Cold War comedy 'Our Man in Moscow', about the British ambassador in Moscow who has to deal with a Russian musician attempting to defect and broadcast in the *Comedy Playhouse* strand on the BBC.

[131] The 'Boysie Oakes' furniture designed by UNIFLEX received its own screen credit.

[132] The proposed merchandise of 'Boysie Oakes suits, Boysie Oakes cuff links, ties and shoes' were presumably not required (*Sunday Times*, 25 April 1965).

[133] Another film to involve an American academic in intrigue in Britain was *The Internecine Project* (1974). In this story, though, the emphasis is on a murder plot, in which the professor (James Coburn) is killing off associates who know of his espionage past.

[134] The film's press release reported how the "*unusual visual effects*" were achieved through "*the use of hand-held and hidden cameras, unconventionally long lenses, zoom lenses and camera mountings that vary from a specially-built version of a bosun's chair to a unique multiple unilever extension device which turns the existing camera crane into a more flexible and mobile unit*".

[135] Binder was a regular designer for Donen, providing the titles for *Charade*, *Two for the Road* (1966) and *Bedazzled* (1967).

[136] Very late in the day the story was renamed for the British market as it was felt the title *The Chairman* suggested a film about business and the boardroom (Chibnall 2000: 315, 317).

[137] This was the time of the Sino-Soviet split which saw the deterioration of political and ideological relations between the neighbouring states of the People's Republic of China and the Union of Soviet Socialist Republics during the Cold War.

[138] The *Guardian* was referring to Frankenheimer's classic Cold War thriller *The Manchurian Candidate* (US, 1962).

[139] *Monthly Film Bulletin* called Fathom an "*amateur Modesty Blaise*" (September 1967: 140).

[140] The film was released with a 'Universal'-certificate, the moral guardians seemingly content that the phallic imagery would be beyond younger viewers.

[141] The picture was produced by Chrislaw Productions, a company co-founded by Lawson with his business partner Milt Ebbins.

[142] A similar contemporary fictional character described as the "*world's most reluctant spy*" was Eddie Brown who featured in four novels by Joyce Porter between 1966 and 1971.

[143] Waddell published three further stories with his character, *Otley Pursued* (1967), *Otley Forever* (1968) and *Otley Victorious* (1969).

[144] To bolster the film's 'swinging' credentials a small role was given to Chrissie Shrimpton, the younger sister of iconic 1960s model Jean Shrimpton, and former girl-friend of Mick Jagger (*Daily Express*, 3 April 1968).

[145] In the general confusion, reviewers sometimes accepted the imitators as parodies, as was the case at the *Sunday Times* and the film *Where the Bullets Fly*, in which "*everything is done with the idea of taking the mickey*"; to which was added the revealing proviso: "*but since the Bond films are increasingly self-parodying the idea is decreasingly feasible*" (6 November 1966).

[146] See Penelope Gilliat's untypical defence of the *Carry On* brand in her review of *Carry On Spying* in the *Observer*, where she claims "*the badness is part of the funniness*" (9 August 1964).

[147] Quoted at http://blog.ink-stainedamazon.com/?tag=british-comics (accessed 20 November 2016).

[148] O'Donnell published a total of 11 novels and two collections of short stories featuring Modesty Blaise, culminating in *Cobra Trap* in 1996. In a case of reverse influence, Modesty Blaise was the model for Halle Berry's character Jinx Johnson in the James Bond picture *Die Another Day* (2002).

[149] A contemporary press report suggested that it was the established team of Frank Launder and Sidney Gilliatt who were slated to make the picture (*New Society*, 5 May 1966: 26).

[150] The picture billed itself as a "*Fantasy Comedy Thriller*" (*Modesty Blaise* press sheet), and much later the American queer magazine *The Advocate* rated Bogarde's Gabriel, "*the gayest performance in the history of cinema up to that point*" (quoted in Miller 2003: 164).

[151] It was also widely felt that Monica Vitti, "*the playmate of the intellectuals*", was miscast as the heroine, several reviews carrying the story that the actress was unhelpfully, given the genre, scared of flying, guns and loud bangs (*New Society*, 5 May 1966: 26). See also the comments on the strained relations in Coldstream (2005: 398-401).

[152] An elaborate, improvised sequence shot in the Excelsior Hotel, Naples in which the actors played other characters, such as Bogarde paying his notorious butler from Losey's *The Servant* (1963), was left on the cutting room floor at the insistence of the producers (Ciment 1985: 255).

[153] In the 1990s, cult director Quentin Tarrantino optioned several of the Modesty Blaise novels. In 1997, it was announced that a major new film would be directed by Luc Besson starring Natasha Hentstridge, with Tarrantino set to direct one of the sequels. In the event, only the straight to video *My Name is Modesty*, starring Alexandra Staden and executive produced by Tarrantino, has appeared in 2004 (*Evening Standard*, 8 August 1997; *Independent*, 9 August 1997).

[154] In response, Eon Productions, with the forthcoming *You Only Live Twice* to sell, pasted huge cryptic posters all over London showing Sean Connery with a massive caption reading "*THIS MAN IS JAMES BOND*" (*Evening Standard*, 23 March 1967).

[155] This gave Andress the unusual distinction of playing a principal Bond girl in two pictures.

[156] Costs rose to 11 million dollars, shooting lasted 300 days, and the production required the facilities of all of Britain's major studios, Pinewood, Shepperton, Borehamwood and Elstree, and even Ardmore Studio in Ireland (*Evening News*, 10 November 1966; Duncan 2012: 134).

[157] Sellers allegedly became obsessed with reporting traffic violations to the police and time was seemingly lost while the star was in court giving evidence (*Daily Mail* 28 October 2006; Duncan 2012: 137).

[158] Actual cameos included Charles Boyer, William Holden, Jean-Paul Belmondo and George Raft, while reported cameos by Frank Sinatra, Barbara Streisand, Shirley MacLaine, Peter Ustinov, Sarah Miles, Sophia Loren, Trevor Howard, Brigitte Bardot and ballet dancer Rudolf Nureyev never came to being.

[159] Various background details taken from the documentary *The Making of* Casino Royale included on the Collector's Edition *Casino Royale* DVD (2008).

[160] Newspapers had been annoyed when reviewers were denied a press screening before the official premiere (*The Times*, 14 April 1967).

[161] Hoffman suggests his study of le Carré is less a literary and more an "*operational*" critique; concluding that, "*The mentality of le Carré's spies and counter-spies is as honest a representation of espionage as is to be found in fiction*" (2001: 8).

[162] It has been claimed that Philby's defection effectively blew le Carré's cover in SIS and prompted the part-time author to become a professional novelist (Goodman 2016: 4); although le Carré's biographer sees a problem in the chronology, Philby having left SIS and access to new information well before the author settled there in the early 1960s (Sisman 2015: 246).

[163] The shocking assassination of President Kennedy in November 1963 created a wider feeling of a loss of innocence and an emerging sense of paranoia that pervaded beyond the world of intelligence.

[164] The curious events involving Crabb, who went missing during a "*shoddy operational blunder*" while surveying a Soviet ship carrying the Russian premier (Sandbrook 2006: 603), has been investigated in a number of fictions. The novels *The Khrushchev Objective* (1987) by Noel Hynd and Christopher Creighton, *Old Flames* (1996) by John Lawton, and *Man Overboard* (2005) by Tim Binding all have views on the event. The motion picture *The Silent Enemy* (1958) treats the wartime exploits of Crabb which earned him a George Medal and was released to cash in on public interest in the submariner.

[165] These included the Romer Committee Report (1961), and the Radcliffe and Denning Reports (both 1963).

[166] A further cultural manifestation of the disquiet felt at the social and political atrophy in Britain was the satire boom of the early 1960s, and stage shows such as *Beyond the Fringe* (1960) and television series such as *That Was The Week That Was* (1962-63).

[167] Recently, in a more mellow mood, le Carré has acknowledged that, "*without Ian Fleming there could be no le Carré*", the creator of James Bond having produced a necessary appetite for spy stories (*John le Carré: The return of master spy George Smiley*, BBC Radio 4 (7 September 2017).

[168] There have been various speculations as to possible actual espionage cases which might have influenced le Carré. The story bears some resemblance to 'Operation Splinter Factor', in which the possible double-agent Noel Field, an American, was used as a witness in a series of show trials by the Communists; as does the case of the double agent Heinz Felfe who headed West Germany's counter-Soviet section while in the service of the Soviets.

[169] Reviewing the available evidence, biographer Adam Sisman suspects that the writing of the novel took considerably longer (2015: 238).

[170] As was custom, le Carré had to present the novel for clearance by MI6, and he always maintained that the story was allowed for publication as it was far from authentic – the opposite of what the critics and public would come to believe.

[171] The comments appear on the Pan paperback edition of the novel (1965).

[172] The comments of the three eminent authors were prominently featured on the dust jacket of the novel.

[173] The character's name was altered from Liz to Nan in consequence of Burton's celebrated relationship with the jealous Liz Taylor. In the transition from Liz Gold to Nan Perry, the character also lost any overt sense of her Jewishness and this reduced her empathetic link to Fiedler.

[174] See *The Times* (13 January 1966), the *Guardian* (14 January 1966) and *Films and Filming* (March 1966: 10, 12).

[175] See, for example, the *Daily Express* (7 January 1966).

[176] Hollywood stars Paul Newman and Burt Lancaster had been considered for the role before Burton was signed, while le Carré envisaged Trevor Howard or Peter Finch as ideal casting.

[177] It had been noted during production that Ritt had brought a "*new dimension*" to the western with *Hud* (US, 1963) and that he was planning something comparable with *The Spy Who Came in from the Cold* (*Daily Express*, 5 February 1965).

[178] *The Spy Who Came in from the Cold*, novel and film, was a cultural high-point for the spy story in the 1960s and unsurprisingly came in for some spoofing, as with *MAD* magazine's mock storyboard 'The Spy Who Came in With a Cold' and 'The Spy Who Came in from the Cool' episode of *The Monkees* TV show (Miller 2003: 115).

[179] Smiley appears ' retrospectively ' in le Carré's latest novel *A Legacy of Spies* (2017).

[180] Lumet generally preferred black and white, only previously having worked in colour on *Stage Struck* (US, 1958) and *The Group* (US, 1966).

[181] In a pre-production report Candice Bergen, who had just worked with Lumet on *The Group* (US, 1966), was announced for the role of Ann, but was seemingly replaced at the last minute (*Kine Weekly*, 24 February 1966).

[182] The odd reviewer was less impressed by such improvements, the *Sunday Telegraph* confessing that it "*could have done with less of the marital soul-and-sex searching*" (5 February 1967); while in contrast literary scholar Frank Cunningham argues that Lumet's deepening of Dobb's emotional life marks the filmmaker's "*most notable contribution to creating* The Deadly Affair *as an independent work of art*" (1991: 38). An executive at Columbia insisted on the name change, believing that *Call for the Dead* suggested a horror movie (Sisman 2015: 308).

[183] There were five weeks of location-shooting on the picture (*Variety*, 2 February 1966).

[184] Recent attention to the deglamorisation of spying in *The Deadly Affair* has been given by Sara Thomas, 'The Banal Staging of George Smiley's Cold War conflict in *A Deadly Affair* (1966)', unpublished paper, *Spies on British Screens* conference (June 2016).

[185] The amateurish operation mounted in the story bore some resemblance to the aggressive operations mounted against the Soviets in the Baltic countries after the war when former nationals were infiltrated back into the East, usually to be met by the KGB (see Cavendish 1990: 54-59).

[186] See, for example, Maurice Richardson's review in the *Observer* (20 June 1965).

[187] In 1993, former Home Secretary Roy Jenkins gave the same analogy of the intelligence services to the House of Lords, speaking of "*those who live in the distorting and Alice-through-the-looking-glass world in which falsehood becomes truth, fact becomes fiction and fantasy becomes reality*" (quoted in Hollingsworth and Fielding 1999: 88).

[188] A decade later le Carré admitted that, "*I have gradually come to accept, with the more rational side of my head, that I am really no good at adapting my own work*" (*Sunday Telegraph Magazine*, 21 October 1979).

[189] Critic Gavin Millar judged Jones's performance as a "*sort of smug James Dean, or a thoughtless Zbigniew Cybulski*" (*The Listener*, 8 January 1970).

[190] As early as in his script discussions with Karel Reisz, le Carré had sensed a need to make Leiser a younger man to establish greater audience identification (Sisman 2015: 270).

[191] This was done for economic reasons and producer John Box was familiar with the region having filmed there on *Dr Zhivago* (1965) (*Films and Filming*, September 1969: 30-31).

[192] The film's fashionable existential qualities are apparent in the anonymity of the heroine who is simply referred to as 'The Girl'. However, the insensitivity of the filmmakers to female subjectivity extends to the other principal women in the picture who are simply billed as 'The Girl in London' (Susan George) and 'Avery's Wife' (Anna Massey).

[193] George Smiley, a fringe character in the novel, does not appear in the film adaptation of the story.

[194] Such a comparison is made in the film's press sheet where it is stated: "*In East Germany, Leiser meets The Girl and comes to realize they can make a life together if they can escape the espionage experts of Britain, Russia and East Germany, old men who regard their activities as an enormous game in which stakes are human lives – rarely, if ever, their own!*"

[195] The American Brodkin had recently produced the television series *Espionage* (1964, discussed in chapter 5) and the feature film *Sebastian* (1968, discussed in chapter 1) in Britain.

[196] Le Carré's second novel *A Murder of Quality* (1962), although it featured George Smiley, is better considered as a detective novel, in the classic tradition of the English whodunit. The book was adapted for television in 1991. The female-centred spy novel *The Little Drummer Girl* (1983) was turned into an unsuccessful American film in 1984.

[197] Deighton combined his talents in *The Action Cook Book* (1965), a blending of thriller and gastronomy in which "*cooking is renegotiated as a masculine, heterosexual activity*" (Baker 2012: 41), and which collected together the breezy 'cook strips' he had previously provided for the *Observer*.

[198] All the comments appear on the Panther paperback edition of the novel (1966).

[199] Deighton first met Saltzman around the time of the opening of *Dr No*. The producer was apparently immediately struck by the potential of the author's revisionist novel and pursued the rights. Meantime, he set the young writer onto the screenplay of *From Russia, With Love*, although his material was not used and the scripting was passed onto other hands (Field and Chowdhury 2015: 81-82). Deighton's recollections of Saltzman can be found in (Deighton 1994).

[200] The electronic version of Kremer's book does not sport page numbers.

[201] The role had originally been offered to Christopher Plummer, who turned it down in preference for *The Sound of Music* (US, 1965), and to Richard Harris, who turned it down in favour of *Major Dundee* (US, 1965). It is interesting that Ian Fleming also sought out an ordinary and undistinguished name for his secret agent and found it on the cover of his copy of *Birds of the West Indies* by the so-named ornithologist.

[202] At the time of the film's release, the *Daily Express* referred to the character as the "*utility-model James Bond*" (18 March 1965). Pamela Church-Gibson has recently referred to him as the "*Everyman Bond*", 'Spies, Style, Class and Myths of Mobility: Novels and Cinematic Adaptations of the Early Sixties', unpublished paper, *Spies on British Screens* conference (June 2016).

[203] The long-established firm of Curry & Paxton provided the frames for both Michael Caine's Harry Palmer and Alec Guinness's George Smiley, the two most iconic sets of spectacles in spy fiction.

[204] Palmer is not seen cooking in the sequels.

[205] Deighton had one significant dispute with the characterisation of Palmer in the movie. In the film version, the agent is coerced into military intelligence after some unsavoury business in the Army on the Rhine. The author believed this "*implausible*", stating: "*This is the old boy network. These are people with tailored shirts and lace-up shoes. Despite the disrepute it suffered from harbouring traitors such as Philby – Westminster, Cambridge and the Athenaeum – the SIS retained this policy. Blackmailing a Harry Palmer into the service would have been unthinkable*" (http://deightondossier. blogspot.co.uk/p/len-deighton-q-interview-2011.html, accessed 21 November 2016).

[206] Techniscope was an inferior widescreen process to either Cinemascope or Panavision, but may have worked in the favour of the downbeat *Ipcress* in that it served-up "*depressed, washed-out images*" (Kremer 2015).

[207] As had the funding studio Universal, which similarly worried about the hero cooking (Kremer 2015).

[208] For recent examinations of the eccentric visual style of *The Ipcress File*, see Crossley (2016) and McMahon (2012). Cinematographer Phil Méheux has stressed the influence of the visual style of *Ipcress* on his shooting of the James Bond movie *Casino Royale* (2006) (Field and Chowdury 2015: 545).

[209] Jones also scripted that year's pop spy parody *Modesty Blaise* (1966).

[210] In this version of the story, Palmer idealistically leaves the papers to Samantha.

[211] Caine recalls a moment of Cold War pettiness, when East German border guards deliberately shone lights into the camera lens while the crew was filming near the Wall (1992: 225).

[212] The previous year, Penguin Books had flown journalists and booksellers to Berlin to watch the shooting of *Funeral in Berlin* on the eve of the launch of the paperback edition of the novel (*Sunday Telegraph*, 5 June 1966).

[213] Russell was tempted by a promise from Saltzman that he would subsequently bankroll a picture on the dancer Nijinsky or composer Tchaikovsky, which the producer later reneged on (Russell 1991: 55). Russell's recollections of the production are recounted in Baxter (1973: 152-160); see also the *Guardian* (26 October 1967).

[214] These were *Dr No* (1962), *Thunderball* (1965) and *You Only Live Twice* (1967), as well as the recent spy pictures *Arabesque* (1966) and *Fathom* (1967), and the television series *Espionage* (1964).

[215] At the start of the film a down on his luck Palmer is seemingly surviving on corn flakes and living in a shabby office-cum-bedsit.

[216] For a more positive appraisal of Russell, see *The Listener* (7 December 1967).

[217] Harry Palmer returned to the screen three decades later in two stories originally written for the screen, *Bullet to Beijing* (1995) and *Midnight in St. Petersburg* (1996), and these are discussed in chapter 8.

[218] Murphy (1992: 223) and Lanza (2008: 64).

[219] It is a shame that a proposed film version of *The Dolly, Dolly Spy* starring David Hemmings never materialised (*New Society*, December 1968).

[220] Callan is discussed in chapter 4 and Charlie Muffin in chapter 3.

[221] For a discussion of Deighton's agent as an archetypal detective figure, see Erisman (1977).

[222] http://www.deightondossier.net/Books/Other%20novels/spystory.html (accessed 13 November 2016).

[223] See chapter 1.

[224] Shonteff explained that he and his secretary went through the novel, crossed out what they didn't intend to use and filmed what was left (*Guardian*, 7 June 1975). The producers, with a keen awareness of the commercial advnatage, boldly asserted that the agent was Harry Palmer, but provided with a "*new name and a new look*" (*Spy Story*, press sheet).

[225] The phrase was used in the press sheet for *Ring of Spies* (1964), the film treating the Portland Spies.

[226] The official *Captured* (1959) was a military training film produced in consequence of events in the Korean War and intended to help selected soldiers face up to brainwashing and interrogation.

[227] Kennaway became a close friend of John le Carré. *The Looking-Glass War* is dedicated to Kennaway, who helped le Carré on his abortive script, and the complicated relationship between the two authors and Kennaway's wife Susan is the basis for le Carré's novel *The Naive and Sentimental Lover* (1971).

[228] In total, Adam Hall published 19 Quiller novels between 1965 and 1996.

[229] The endorsement appears on the front cover of the Fontana paperback edition of the novel (1967).

[230] *The Berlin Memorandum* won the coveted Edgar Allan Poe Award of the Mystery Writers of America and the French Grand Prix de Littérature Policière.

[231] The picture had been originally announced with the scriptwriter William Fairchild (*Films and Filming,* June 1965: 55).

[232] Pinter scholars have not generally been too impressed by the dramatist's flirtation with a popular genre. Exhibiting some cultural snobbery, William Baker and Stephen Tabachnick, for example, claim that Pinter's work on *The Quiller Memorandum* was simply that of "*translation*" rather than "*transmutation*", the outcome offering "*little more than the watered-down James Bondism*" of the original novel (1973: 91); while Joanne Klein has judged the outcome a "*relatively simplistic spy movie*" (1985: 49). Pinter was paid more handsomely for his screenplay than was Adam Hall for the rights (information helpfully supplied by James Chapman).

[233] Both *The Quiller Memorandum* and *Funeral in Berlin* filmed in the city at the same time and publicists took the opportunity of photographing Segal and Caine together (see, for example, *Kine Weekly*, 30 June 1966).

[234] The Secret Intelligence Service station in Berlin was actually located in a compound beside the stadium.

[235] The murder of his two predecessors effectively makes Quiller 'the third man' on the assignment.

[236] And unusually for a spy story from this period and with this setting, the Berlin Wall plays no part in the story.

[237] Vague plans to film the second Quiller novel *The Ninth Directive* (1966) never materialised. The later BBC television series *Quiller*, based on the Adam Hall character, is discussed in chapter 3.

[238] The title of the story is taken from a line of the poem *In the Wood of Finvara* (1899) by Arthur Symons, which reads, "*A naked runner lost in a storm of spears*".

[239] http://www.ostarapublishing.co.uk/article-53.html (accessed 13 November 2016).

[240] The comment appears on the jacket of the Hodder and Stoughton paperback edition of the novel (1967).

[241] The reviewer at the *Financial Times* criticises the picture on this point (14 July 1967).

[242] The star was in America filming *The Detective* (US, 1968).

[243] *The Naked Runner* is seemingly guarded within the Sinatra estate and is now only readily viewable in the form of a panned and scanned release on video tape from the early 1980s which does grievous violence to the striking compositions of Furie and Heller.

[244] Preminger claimed to have been offered the novel at the manuscript stage and to have been very good friends with Greene (*The New York Times*, 19 August 1979), although Greene recounted that he thought Preminger wrong for the story and would have preferred Losey (Falk 1990: 179).

[245] Greene reported that he formally approved Stoppard for the script (Falk 1990: 179), and Stoppard later admitted that, "*I was much more nervous of displeasing Greene than I was of displeasing Otto*" (quoted in Fujiwara 2008: 411). Stoppard later adapted le Carré's *The Russia House* (US, 1990).

[246] The electronic version of Foster Hirsch's biography of Otto Preminger is unpaginated.

[247] Equity had been aggrieved when it had to accept the casting of the non-professional Iman as Sarah, lest Preminger relocate the production to Ireland (Falk 1990: 183).

[248] The press referred to three European bankers (*The Telegraph*, 20 October 1979), while Hirsch reports that the recalcitrant backers were a group of Saudi Arabian financiers (2007).

[249] Fujiwara claims that Preminger had unsuccessfully approached both Richard Burton and Michael Caine to play the role of Castle, the two actors most associated with the quality spy film (2008: 411). It was elsewhere reported that Burton was offered the role of Daintry, but wanted the role of Castle (Reynolds 1979: 32).

[250] Preminger insisted on these against the advice of Stoppard and Greene (Falk 1990: 181).

[251] The debt of course was to E. M. Forster.

[252] Occasionally, an acclaimed or promising continental actress would appear in a British spy thriller, as was the case with Romy Schneider in *Otley* (1969) and Nathalie Delon in *When Eight Bells Toll* (1971). Joseph Losey's *Modesty Blaise* is a special case. An art film by dent of its filmmaker and the casting of Monica Vitti, the picture was not received as such by the critics.

[253] The term "*spyscape*" is taken from Snyder (1977: 220).

[254] The "*anti-fascist protection barrier*" was how the Communists viewed it.

[255] The more general presentation of Berlin in the movies during the Cold War is considered in Maulucci Jr. (2008).

[256] Chapman identifies *Danger Man, The Avengers, The Champions* and *Department S* as secret agent narratives.

[257] The term is Felix Thompson's, 'Locating the Cosmopolitan: the British TV Spy Drama in the 1960s and 1970s', unpublished paper, *Spies on British Screens* conference, University of Plymouth (June 2016).

[258] The term "*cloak and dagger realism*" was levelled at *Special Branch* (*Sun*, 16 September 1970).

[259] McGoohan was considered for the role of James Bond in *Dr No*, but the actor's attitude towards sex and violence hardly kept him in the running.

[260] A handful of episodes were directed by McGoohan.

[261] Similar traits were given to the agent Quiller in the popular novels of Adam Hall and who appeared on-screen in the film *The Quiller Memorandum* (1966) and the television series *Quiller* (1975).

[262] Details presented in the *TV Times* (6-13 August 1961) and digested at http://www.startrader.co.uk/Action%20TV/guide60s/topsecret.htm (accessed 5 August 2016).

[263] Wesley Britton has claimed *The Avengers* as the "*most successful of all the televised spy shows, at least in terms of being seen and appreciated by successive generations of viewers*" (2004: 58).

[264] Steve Chibnall has alighted on the same type of formula for Steed, marking him as that "*characteristically sixties figure, a* modernised *hero who can demonstrate the adaptability of the old hereditary elite to a new high-tech age*" (*New Society*, 28 March 1985, emphasis in the original).

[265] The publicity described Emma Peel as a "*new kind of swinging girl*" (*The Avengers* press sheet 1965).

[266] 'A complete Avengers Collection adapted from the TV wardrobe' was marketed by Jean Varon based on costumes worn by Diana Rigg in the series and much emphasis was placed on Emma Peel's highly desirable Lotus Elan car (*The Avengers* press sheet 1965). Peel/Rigg became a considerable object of male desire in the period and presumably for more than just the reviewer at the *Daily Mail* rekindled the "*glow of long-dead fantasies*" (26 September 1968).

[267] The Gale seasons had been sold to 14 countries including Canada, Australia and Italy (*The Avengers* press sheet 1965), and in what was billed as a coup, towards the end of the decade a "*fair number*" of episodes were sold behind the Iron Curtain to Poland, Hungary, Romania and Czechoslovakia (*Evening Standard*, 15 March 1968).

[268] The character was initially equipped with a highly desirable Jensen 428 and later with a red Lotus Europa car.

[269] Don Macpherson has intriguingly suggested a cross-fertilisation of 1950s de Sade and 1960s Mary Quant in the Mrs Peel period of *The Avengers*, tracing an influence from the late-1950s 'Sadian' horror pictures such as *Corridors of Blood* (1957) and *Circus of Horrors* (1960) apparent through the overlap of production personnel like producer Juilan Wintle and directors Robert Day and Sidney Hayers (*View* magazine, *Sunday Times*, 13 March 1983).

[270] In future, obsessives of the show would be labelled 'Avengies'.

[271] Markstein can be seen in the series as the man behind the desk in the opening sequence of each episode.

[272] An updated American-British mini-series of six episodes was aired as *The Prisoner* in 2009, but the adaptation lacked an espionage angle and attracted mixed reviews. *Magic Number Six* by Paul Gosling, a one-act play portraying the behind-the-scenes relationship between Patrick McGoohan and Lew Grade during the making of *The Prisoner*, débuted in Leicester, UK in 2012. There have been rumours that *The Prisoner* could be made into a movie, following on from other Hollywood make-over's of 1960s British adventure series such as *The Saint* (US, 1997) and *The Avengers* (US, 1998).

[273] The series is examined in chapter 5.

[274] Most of these shows are missing and believed lost. In 1969, director James Cellan Jones commented on the ruthlessness of the junking policy of the time, pointing out that when *An Enemy of the State* was repeated in the late 1960s, the BBC had to use a "*grotty 16mm copy*" (Tarratt 1969: 42). So far, even this has not shown up.

[275] Sangster also authored two spy novels featuring British Intelligence agent Katy Touchfeather (1968 and 1970).

[276] The earlier *Subterfuge* (1968) had been produced in London with financing from American television; however, in its case, the picture was released theatrically in Britain, albeit briefly. See chapter 1.

[277] I have so far only been able to view *The Spy Killer*.

[278] The production was adapted from the novel *The Gaunt Woman* by John Blackburn. I have been unable to view the movie.

[279] See chapter 2.

[280] Echoes of John Drake.

[281] American *Variety* enjoyed the opening credits, but was then "*let down*" by the show (17 September 1975).

[282] http://www.imdb.com/title/tt0163484/ (accessed 15 November 2016).

[283] Two *Quiller* episodes were purchased by ABC-TV in America for screening in its late night 'Wide World of Entertainment' strand (*Variety*, 10 December 1975).

[284] See the editions of *The Stage and Television Today* for May and June 1975.

[285] The presentation of actually unworkable high-tech kit to an adversary is known in espionage circles as a "*blind alley dangle*", and this adds another layer of meaning to the story's title. It has been speculated that false information had been fed to the Soviets regarding the Anglo-French supersonic airliner Concord, and that the problems encountered by the Russian Konkordski, which experienced two crashes and achieved only 55 commercial passenger flights, could be attributed to this deception (Pincher 1991: 252). Businessman-spy Greville Wynne claims he had a hand in this deception (1983: 276-88).

[286] See chapter 1.

[287] http://www.brianfreemantle.co.uk/charliemuffin.php (accessed 13 November 2016).

[288] Freemantle published a further 16 Charlie Muffin stories.

[289] In some overseas territories the drama was released with the title *A Deadly Game*.

[290] http://www.brianfreemantle.co.uk/charliemuffin.php (accessed 11 October 2016).

[291] The fact that *Charlie Muffin* was sold to 20 countries including South Africa would have been some consolation.

[292] Stamp was possibly encouraged by the recent success of Sir Alec Guinness in the television adaptations of John le Carré 's *Tinker Tailor Soldier Spy* (1979) and *Smiley's People* (1982). For these serials, see chapter 4.

[293] For *Reilly*, see chapter 5.

[294] Smith also wrote episodes of *Cold Warrior* (1984) discussed later in the chapter. I have been unable to view *Closing Ranks*.

[295] Clemens had previously worked on such popular and influential television series as *The Avengers*, *Thriller* (1973-76), *The New Avengers* and *The Professionals* (1977-83). Producer Bob McIntosh, BBC Scotland's 'Mr Thriller', had recently been responsible for the spy dramas *Running Blind*, *The Assassination Run* and *The Treachery Game*.

[296] Major Maxim appeared in three further novels, *The Conduct of Major Maxim* (1982), *The Crocus List* (1985) and *Uncle Target* (1988).

[297] Such a scene was part of the celebrated presentation of Daniel Craig as 007 in *Casino Royale* (2006).

[298] General Povin, the gentle traitor within the KGB, featured in two further novels by John Trenhaile, *A View from the Square* (1984) and *Nocturne for a General* (1985).

[299] *Harry's Game* and *The Glory Boys* are discussed in chapter 8.

[300] Glanville, a sometime art collector and homosexual, was clearly based on Anthony Blunt.

[301] During the 1970s, Forbes had produced some of the Conservative Party's political broadcasts (Seaton 2015: 19).

[302] Hillsden appeared in two sequel novels to *The Endless Game*, *A Song at Twilight* (1989) and *Quicksand* (1996), which bring to a conclusion his struggle with treachery within the British body politic.

[303] Forbes had recently discussed a film about Sir Maurice Oldfield, a former head of the Secret Intelligence Service, to be written by Anthony Cavendish, a former spy and writer on intelligence, but nothing came of the project (*Sunday Times*, 9 October 1988).

[304] See chapter 8.

[305] See chapter 7.

[306] The head offices of Thames Television were on Euston Road, London.

[307] Michael Fish was the fashion designer who pioneered the 'Peacock Revolution' in male fashion in the 1960s, dressing Terence Stamp in the design-conscious spy parody *Modesty Blaise* (1966).

[308] For the final series of *Special Branch* production was consolidated at Colet Court.

[309] Mower's character of Cross observed a similar relationship of hostility with his superior Callan in the eponymous espionage drama.

[310] For a history of Special Branch see, Rupert Allason (1983), *The Branch. A History of the Metropolitan Police Special Branch 1883-1983*, London: Secker & Warburg.

[311] Haggerty, we are informed, was seconded to Special Branch from the Flying Squad (*Special Branch* press sheet).

[312] While a recording of the pilot survives in the BBC archive, the series is believed lost.

[313] 'Checkpoint' consisted of long interrogations with the action confined to duologues in a single room, a dramatic device adopted by the excellent 'The Traitor', the pilot episode of the later *Mr Palfrey of Westminster* (1983).

[314] Some of the storylines in the first season were edited together as single dramas and re-broadcast as 'specials' in 1973.

[315] Out of an original total of 61 episodes, 46 are missing from the series, while many others are incomplete or survive only in an inferior format.

[316] The second and third seasons were broadcast in the spring and summer of 1980.

[317] The idea for a tough, highly-trained specialist team was probably inspired by the wartime Special Operations Executive (SOE) and the extant Special Air Service (SAS).

[318] The traditional arrogance within the actual Service has it that the CIA provides the funds and SIS the brains (Dorill 1993: 431).

[319] Ian Mackintosh wrote a handful of thriller novels, but *A Slaying in September* (1967), *Count Not the Cost* (1967), *A Drug Called Power* (1968), *The Man from Destiny* (1969) and *The Brave Cannot Yield* (1970) are now with some justification forgotten. More detail on Mackintosh and *The Sandbaggers* can be found in Robert G Folsom, *The Life and Mysterious Death of Ian MacKintosh: The Inside Story of The Sandbaggers and TV's Top Spy* (Washington D.C.: Potomac Books, 2012).

[320] Some reviewers had their faith in the authenticity of *The Sandbaggers* shaken following the revelations of appalling slackness and corruption at the Hong Kong station of GCHQ in 1980, wondering if the series was showing too shining an example of the intelligence service (*Daily Mail*, 10 June 1980; *Morning Star*, 11 June 1980).

[321] Winch had also contributed to the first series of the spy procedural *Spy Trap* (1972).

[322] The Metropolitan Anti-Terrorist Branch had been formed in the 1970s in response to the outrages of the Irish Republican Army.

[323] For two poor reviews of *Blood Money* see the *Sun* (10 September 1981) and the *New Statesman* (25 September 1981).

[324] It had been originally intended that Hepton's Chief Superintendent Meadows would again appear alongside Denison's Captain Percival, but it could have been that he was unavailable through filming John le Carré's *Smiley's People* (1982) (*Sun*, 3 July 1982).

[325] Danny had appeared as a supporting if interesting character in *Blood Money*.

[326] There were the inevitable comparisons between Percival and John Steed from *The Avengers*, both bowler-hatted, umbrella-wielding agents (*Evening Standard*, 13 September 1984).

[327] I have so far been unable to view *Cold Warrior*.

[328] The final episode of the first series, *Klansman*, controversially dealt with racism in the inner city and was not transmitted.

[329] Although it only sold to regional cable stations in America (*Evening Standard*, 23 June 1980).

[330] The clipping accessed in the British Film Institute library is undated.

[331] In November 1984, the comedy drama showcase *The Comic Strip Presents ...* included the parody 'The Bullshitters', featuring the tough crime-fighters Bonehead and Foyle; and in the 1990s Nissan ran a series of popular 'All Action' Almera advertisements spoofing the show.

[332] Even so, repeats did not seem to make it back to terrestrial television for some years.

[333] The resurrection was similar to that performed by Clemens with *The Avengers* and *The New Avengers*.

[334] The budget was variously reported as being £8.5 million and £12 million (*The Telegraph*, 10 June 1997 and 8 August 1998).

[335] Jill Gascoine had starred as Maggie Forbes in the popular police series *The Gentle Touch* (1980-84).

[336] Other female-centred shows that were singled out were *Widows* (1983), *Connie* (1985), *Roll Over Beethoven* (1985) and *Cagney and Lacey* (US, 1981-88).

[337] The EEC was the European Economic Community which Great Britain had joined in 1973.

[338] Willis had, though, previously written 'The Scent of Fear', an hour-long spy drama broadcast in ABC's *Armchair Theatre* series in 1959.

[339] For a discussion of these historical spoofs, see Nicholas J., Cull (2002), 'Camping on the borders: history, identity and Britishness in the *Carry On* costume parodies, 1963-74', in Monk, Claire and Amy Sargeant (eds.), *British Historical Cinema*, Abingdon, Oxon: Routledge, pp. 92-109.

[340] For an interesting contextual discussion of these shows, see Nicholas J. Cull (2006). 'Was Captain Black Really Red? The TV Science Fiction of Gerry Anderson in its Cold War Context', *Media History*, 12(2), August, pp. 193-207. In 1969, John William Jennison wrote two original novels based on *The Secret Service* series, *The Destroyer* and *The VIP*, under the pseudonym John Theydon.

[341] ITV had been losing viewers to the BBC's *The Brothers* (1972-76) in the Sunday evening schedule and the Corporation had recently filled the top 17 places in the ratings (*Stage and Television Today*, 17 and 24 October 1974).

[342] It was long rumoured that Jason refused permission for any repeats or release of the series as he feared his performance had been "*too raw*". However, *Briggs* had been sold to Public Broadcast stations on the east coast of America in the early 1980s (*Screen International*, 26 November 1983).

[343] Mitchell had written the play as 'The War Game' for inclusion in the BBC anthology series *Detective* (1964-69), but it was not used and offered to *Armchair Theatre* (detail taken from the documentary Callan: *This Man Alone*, Network DVD 2015).

[344] Like the *Armchair Theatre* plays, *Callan* was shot in the multi-camera television studio with a realistic 'as-if-live' aesthetic which promoted a claustrophobic environment suitable for an existential thriller. The adventure series were shot with single-camera continuity on film and accordingly borrowed a cinema aesthetic and Hollywood-style gloss. Also unlike the adventure series, *Callan* attempted some narrative continuity across episodes and running storylines. See Joseph Oldham for a developed discussion on these characteristics and distinctions (2017: 16-44).

[345] Season Two of *Callan* was scheduled for Wednesday evenings at 9.00pm where it out-performed the BBC's showcase single drama strand *The Wednesday Play*.

[346] Cockney Willie Garvin of the Modesty Blaise stories commencing in the 1960s was a harbinger in this tradition, but as a sidekick he was once removed from the main thrust of the narrative.

[347] Callan was not sadistic and such a trait would have undermined the appeal of a character who won much sympathy from viewers.

[348] Liz was centre-stage in the single episode 'A Village Called "G"', when she tackled a Section suspect whom she recognised as a ghost from her past.

[349] As we saw in chapter 4, Valentine left to head up his own espionage series *Codename* (1970), and the fiction was maintained in *Callan* that Meres was on secondment in Washington (where apparently the Americans were impressed by his particular type of 'polished villainy'). Allegedly, Mower soon developed a strong female following for his sadistic character of Cross (*Sun*, 8 March 1972).

[350] This was a particularly controversial episode and was delayed for transmission while an actual political election played out.

[351] Actor T. P. McKenna based his characterisation of the Soviet agent on the real-life Gordon Lonsdale (*Sun*, 10 May 1972).

[352] See the prime minister's article 'Callan lives ' in the *Evening News* (14 May 1970).

[353] Some placed *Callan* in the tradition of the old Hollywood pictures about investigative reporters, cynical and tough, and apt to declare themselves through with the whole rotten business (*Sun*, 20 January 1969).

[354] 10 episodes are missing believed lost, four from series one and six from series two.

[355] A number of reviewers questioned the certification of the film as 'A', allowing children accompanied by adults (*The Times* and *Morning Star*, 24 May 1974).

[356] Mitchell also published five novels featuring the Callan character, *A Red File for Callan* (1969, a novelisation of 'A Magnum for Schneider'), *Russian Roulette* (1973), *Death and Bright Water* (1974), *Smear Job* (1975) and *Bonfire Night* (2002), as well as some short stories which appeared in the *TV Times* (1967) and the *Sunday Express* (1973 and 1976). Detailed background on the production of *Callan* can be found in Andrew Pixley, *Callan: Under the Red File* (London: Network, 2014).

[357] The term was coined in a review of *Smiley's People* (*The Telegraph*, 28 September 1982).

[358] For an extended discussion of le Carré's literature and its commentary on modern Britain, see Monaghan (1983).

[359] The play had been surprisingly rejected by the BBC for inclusion in its *The Wednesday Play* strand. Oldham explains the rejection in terms of the strand's investment in indigenous authors and a tradition of realism, the producers perceiving "*no particular value in producing the work of an acclaimed bestselling author*" (2017: 80; Sisman 2015: 289).

[360] A German television dramatisation of the play was broadcast as 'Endstation' in 1973. This had shot scenes at Edinburgh's Waverley Station while studio interiors were recorded in Stuttgart (*Stage and Television Today*, 22 December 1971). I would like to thank Tom May for enabling me to view a copy of 'The End of the Line'.

[361] Le Carré's American lawyer had to "*liberate*" the character of Smiley as the author had unwittingly signed him away to Paramount Pictures as part of *The Spy Who Came in from the Cold* deal (Sisman 2015: 355).

[362] See le Carré's introduction to *Philby: The Spy Who Betrayed a Generation* (Page, Leitch and Knightly 1968). See also the material in Sisman (2015: 245-46,313-315). It should also be noted that le Carré has acknowledged striking similarities in background between himself and the famous traitor, peculiar relationships with their father, retreat into the institution of British Intelligence to fulfil the lack they felt from their father, and both ultimately taking revenge on that institution. He once, in fact, referred to Philby as his "*secret sharer*" (quoted in Plimpton 1997: 154-55; *Der Speigel*, 7 August 1989). Le Carré's view of the defector was the polar opposite of fellow spy writer Graham Greene and it is instructive to read the latter's review of *Philby* and his criticisms of le Carré's introduction (*Observer*, 18 February 1968), and bring these to bear on Greene's story *The Human Factor* (novel 1978, film 1979). Le Carré declined to meet Philby in Moscow,

where, the novelist has speculated, Philby intended to invite him to collaborate on further memoirs (2014: 298).

363 This was the script that le Carré later claimed he didn't like, reorganising as it did the complex, non-chronological narrative structure of the novel into a more linear progression, and on which he exercised his right to decline (*The Listener*, 13 September 1979; Oldham 2017: 81).

364 The co-production with Paramount was also helpful in smoothing the path to production as the company had held certain screen rights to the character of George Smiley from the time of the motion picture *The Spy Who Came in from the Cold* (1966).

365 In a brief dramatic interlude during a televised interview with le Carré, the popular comic actor Arthur Lowe had played Smiley in a scene from *Call for the Dead*, and it seems that he was considered for the part in the full dramatisations (*Guardian*, 18 October 1982; Sisman 2015: 397).

366 A narrative centred on intrigue amongst aristocratic Tsarist exiles in the 1900s, *The Birds Fall Down*, according to Joseph Oldham, *set a precedent whereby a certain kind of literary thriller might be eligible for adaptation into a classic serial"* (2017: 78).

367 The BBC had been chasing *Brideshead Revisited* and when it lost out to Granada Television it turned to *Tinker* (Seaton 2015: 300).

368 Hopcraft had written an unproduced screenplay on Kim Philby (*Tinker Tailor Soldier Spy* press sheet).

369 Douglas McNaughton, 'Cold War Spaces: *Tinker Tailor Soldier Spy* in television and cinema', *Journal of British Cinema and Television* (forthcoming).

370 This was reported in the *Sun*, but the date is indecipherable on the clipping held in the British Film Institute library.

371 See Oldham's fuller discussion of these points in (2017: 86-93).

372 Alec Guinness noted in his diary a "*long snide notice by Clive James in the* Observer. *And a dishonest one at that"* (quoted in Read 2004: 518).

373 In a sideswipe at Clive James, le Carré praised him for his attempted warnings about Smiley "*making a damn fool of himself"*.

374 Through some mix-up, both le Carré and Trevor-Roper had been invited to write on Philby for the *Sunday Times* and in the event le Carré's was used (Sisman 2015: 313). Trevor-Roper's was hastily re-directed to *Encounter* magazine and he later published *The Philby Affair* in 1968.

375 Quoted in Douglas McNaughton, 'Cold War Spaces: *Tinker Tailor Soldier Spy* in television and cinema', *Journal of British Cinema and Television* (forthcoming).

376 It was, in fact, murmured at the time of the BBC *Tinker* that Guinness could be being lined up for an adaptation of the new le Carré novel *Smiley's People* (*Guardian*, 8 September 1979).

[377] In deference to the star casting, the serial was billed as *Alec Guinness in Smiley's People.*

[378] Arthur Hopcraft was not available as he was writing a novel.

[379] It has been reported elsewhere that Mackenzie's departure was due to differences with Powell and le Carré (Read 2004: 520), or being unacceptable to Guinness (Sisman 2015: 423), and that it was this that led to production delays of six months.

[380] Langton would later direct the 'secret state' thriller *The Whistle Blower* (1986), which is dealt with in chapter 7. John Irvin was now involved with feature films.

[381] Interestingly, Hepton was married to actress Hilary Liddell, neice of the wartime deputy-director of MI5 Guy Liddell.

[382] The veteran German actor insisted his name be spelt Curd for the production rather than Curt which had been usual for his English language films. Simone Signoret had been offered, and Judi Dench cast in the small but important part of Madame Ostrakova, but it was finally fulfilled by Eileen Atkins when Dench injured her Achilles tendon (*Evening Standard,* 19 June 1981).

[383] Langton and MacMillan comment on the production in *American Cinematographer* (November 1983: 69-73).

[384] The reclusive le Carré's memoirs were published in 2016 as *The Pigeon Tunnel: Stories From My Life,* the most anticipated literary biography in years.

[385] Le Carré has only recently visited the old territory with *A Legacy of Spies* (2017).

[386] The historical novel *Winter* (1987) gives the back story for some of the characters in *Game, Set & Match.*

[387] Deighton had previously contributed five short war stories read by John Mills in the BBC's *Late Night Story* series in 1979.

[388] A mock-up of Checkpoint Charlie was also required and built in the precincts of the Manchester Television Centre (*Stage and Television Today,* 26 March 1987).

[389] An example of the insistent publicity for the colossal serial, it was calculated and stated that each of the one million frames of *Game, Set & Match* cost £5, and that the production shot 50 miles of film and was fuelled by two and a half tons of bacon butties (*Stage and Television Today,* 22 December 1988).

[390] Some sources suggest 709 out of a total of 711 scenes (*Daily Mail,* 30 January 1987), others 652 out of 656 scenes (*Stage and Television Today,* 26 March 1987).

[391] See Brian Armstrong's response to these anxieties in *Stage and Television Today* (22 December 1988). See also the *Guardian,* which had reported earlier that expensive dramas such as *Game, Set & Match* were under threat due to falling advertising revenues (4 January 1985).

[392] The role of Samson had originally been offered to Anthony Hopkins, but he had felt unable to commit to the enormous amount of time involved (*You Magazine, Mail on Sunday,* 18 September 1988).

[393] http://deightondossier.blogspot.co.uk/2011/05/q-with-len-deighton-part-two.html (accessed 13 November 2016).

[394] *Uncommonly Dangerous: Eric Ambler on TV*, http://mysteryfile.com/blog/?p=1162 (2009, accessed 12 March 2016). The two Ambler dramas have been largely forgotten and I have been unable to view them.

[395] Bennett wrote celebrated plays on Guy Burgess and Anthony Blunt and these are dealt with alongside other Cambridge Spies dramas in chapter 6.

[396] Broadcast as part of BBC's *The Wednesday Play* strand.

[397] http://www.britishtelevisiondrama.org.uk/?p=952 (accessed 8 November 2016).

[398] The two other completed plays were *Cream in My Coffee* and *Rain on the Roof*.

[399] "*A Daniel come to judgment! yea, a Daniel! O wise young judge, how I do honour thee!*", William Shakespeare, *The Merchant of Venice* (1596).

[400] While he is dosing we see a copy of General Frank Kitson's *Low Intensity Operations: Subversion, Insurgency and Peacekeeping* (1971) lying on the professor's lap, a bible for reactionaries in the 1970s.

[401] The curious master-servant relationship here recalls *The Servant* (1963), while disquiet, destruction and donnishness in a country house setting recalls *Accident* (1967), and such aspects might have been part of what interested Joseph Losey in the play.

[402] *Blade on the Feather* is "*littered with images from earlier Potter plays*" such as *Message for Posterity* (TV 1967) and *Joe's Ark* (TV 1974) (Carpenter 1998: 389).

[403] Although the writing of *Blade on the Feather* was largely completed before Blunt was exposed (Gilbert 1998: 247). Hints of homosexuality past in the relationship between Cavendish and Hill further nod a wink at Blunt.

[404] 'Soft Targets' received its first public screenings on 15 and 16 October 1982 at Riverside Studios, an arts and cultural centre in west London, as a benefit event to help save the venue (Riverside Studios press release, 7 October 1982).

[405] Poliakoff later wrote and directed the unconventional 'secret state' thriller *Hidden City* (1987), which is discussed in chapter 7; and his disappointing serial *Close to the Enemy*, about a military intelligence officer's efforts to convince a German scientist to work for the British after World War II, was broadcast towards the end of 2016.

[406] Fleming has also been the subject of the docudrama *Ian Fleming: Bondmaker* (2005) and the American drama *The Secret Life of Ian Fleming* (US TV, 1990).

[407] Charles Dance had reputedly turned down the role of James Bond before it was accepted by Pierce Brosnan (*Stage and Screen Today*, 20 August 1989); while Dominic Cooper was allegedly using *Fleming* as a calling card for the role on the expectation that Daniel Craig was about to step down (*Daily Mail*, 25 January 2014).

[408] As Bennett and Woollacott have noted, Pearson was both Ian Fleming's and James Bond's biographer. In these works, they observe, Pearson "*construes Bond as essentially an emanation of Fleming*" (1987: 47).

[409] Dominic Cooper even let slip that the serial had taken "*huge liberties*" with Pearson's biography (*The Telegraph*, 11 February 2014).

[410] Original press sheet for *Espionage*. 'The Gentle Spies' deals with Whitehall and the anti-nuclear demonstrators, and 'To the Very End' treats France's attempt to independently develop an atomic bomb.

[411] The episode 'The Whistling Shrimp' was produced in New York.

[412] It had been hoped that British new wave directors such as Lindsay Anderson and John Schlesinger would work on the series (*Kine Weekly*, 12 September 1963). Any critical interest in *Espionage* has been due to Michael Powell's participation and his two episodes 'Never Turn Your Back on a Friend' and 'A Free Agent'. See, Ian Christie, *Powell, Pressburger and Others* (London: BFI Publishing 1978). Powell's reminiscences of the series are presented in his memoirs (1993: 457-8).

[413] Original press sheet for *Espionage*.

[414] See chapter 1.

[415] The famous chase in the London Underground was filmed at Aldwych Station on a quiet Sunday, which required a vintage train and a platform dressed for 1939.

[416] See the letter from Geoffrey Household praising Frederic Raphael's adaptation of his novel for television (*Time Out*, October 1976).

[417] The BBC had first broadcast a six-part serialisation of *The Three Hostages* in 1952 starring Patrick Barr as Hannay and this is believed lost.

[418] The BBC had first broadcast a six-part serialisation of *Huntingtower* in 1957 starring James Hayter and this is believed lost.

[419] Unidentified press cutting in the library of the British Film Institute.

[420] In the original story, the foreign agents are after British naval secrets. Writer Mark Robson and executive-producer James Kenelm-Clark had wanted to do a faithful version of the book since working at Anglia Television together in 1963 (*Film Review*, October 2006).

[421] The first series of *Hannay* was broadcast during the damaging tussle of the '*Spycatcher* Affair'.

[422] More than one reviewer saw the influence of the comic strip yarn *Indiana Jones* on *Hannay*.

[423] Producer Michael Carreras had nursed the project since the mid-1970s, always planning to cast American leads, the initial ambition being Henry Winkler and Linda Wagner (the Fonz and the Bionic Woman!) (*Films Illustrated*, January 1979: 181).

[424] A continuation of the story of *The Riddle of the Sands* is provided in Sam Llewellyn's *The Shadow in the Sands* (1998), subtitled: "*Being an account of the cruise of the yacht Gloria in the Frisian Islands in April 1903 and the conclusion of the events described by Erskine Childers*".

[425] The production commenced with three days shooting in England, with two of the days spent at Frensham Ponds in Surrey where the suspenseful "*sequences of the two Englishmen groping their way between sandbanks in the Dulcibella — perhaps the most fascinating part of the book — were shot with the aid of nine large fog machines*" (*Guardian*, 6 May 1978).

[426] Other Rank pictures aimed at the family audience included *Wombling Free* (1977) and *Tarka the Otter* (1979).

[427] *Memoirs Of A British Agent* (1932) by Robert Bruce Lockhart is a classic account of secret agentry.

[428] The producers of *Reilly – Ace of Spies* made much of Ian Fleming's comment that, "*James Bond is just a piece of nonsense I dreamed up. He's not a Sidney Reilly, you know*" (press sheet).

[429] The term 'episodic serial' has been used for this type of loose sequential form.

[430] The Maltese film authority gave the producers the use of 'Sweethaven', the crazy-angled fishing village built as a giant outdoor set for the Hollywood movie *Popeye* (US, 1980). In their study of Euston Films, Manuel Alvarado and John Stewart had hoped to offer a case-study of *Reilly – Ace of Spies*; however, a "*complex*" and "*acrimonious*" production meant that Thames felt that the history was too "*confidential*" and "*sensitive*" to be discussed in print (1985: 114).

[431] Euston also produced seasons 3 and 4 of *Special Branch* (1973 and 1974) and the television movie *Charlie Muffin* (1979), both discussed in chapter 3. It was reported in the *Evening Standard* of 20 October 1967 that the Soviets had planned a screen production of Reilly's story in Russia on the 50th anniversary of the Russian Revolution and had even surprisingly negotiated on the rights to *Ace of Spies*.

[432] Recent studies of Reilly include Richard Spence's *Trust No One: The Secret World of Sidney Reilly* (2002) and Andrew Cook's *Ace of Spies: The True Story of Sidney Reilly* (2004).

[433] The execution and its method were only seemingly confirmed by Western sources following the release of official British documents in 2002 (*The Telegraph*, 9 May 2002).

[434] Master spy Reilly has continued to grip the imagination of spy writers of both fiction and fact, and has recently been the subject of the imaginative stories *The Spy Who Had No Faith in the World: A Semi-documentary Account of the Exploits 1900-1904 of Sidney Reilly AKA "the Ace of Spies" and Ian Fleming's Role Model for James Bond* (2011) by Ronald Fairfax, and *The Private War of Sidney Reilly: A Tale of Revolutionary Russia* (2014) by the American Allan Torrey. Of historical interest is *Adventures of a British Master Spy: the Memoirs of Sidney Reilly* published in 1932 (and reissued in 1986 and 2014) which claim to be the actual written memoirs of Reilly with additional material from his last wife Pepita. The historian John Long, in reviewing these memoirs, has concluded that they "*cast serious doubt on the credibility, if not the rationality, of the flamboyant British agent*" (1995, 'Plot and counter-plot in revolutionary Russia: Chroni-

cling the Bruce Lockhart conspiracy, 1918', *Intelligence and National Security*, 10(1), 128).

[435] The *Daily Star* published an "*exclusive dossier*" in the run-up to the broadcast, extracted from Robin Bruce Lockhart's *Ace of Spies*, which had been reprinted to accompany series (29 August-1 September 1983). See also, 'The Life of Super-Spy Reilly' (*Mail on Sunday Magazine*, 4 September 1983).

[436] The serial was sold to 18 countries.

[437] The idea of an upper-class masculine hero leading a band of brothers in virtuous action was later emulated in the characterisations of 'Bulldog' Drummond and the Brotherhood by 'Sapper' in the inter-war period.

[438] A recent historical account of imperial intelligence in central Asia is Peter Hopkirk's *The Great Game. On Secret Service in High Asia* (1990).

[439] Sheth was an American-Indian schoolboy in India who later became an astrophysicist.

[440] For background on the production, see John Davies's account in *The Veteran* (Winter 2008: 18-20).

[441] This was scripted by Troy Kennedy Martin who later wrote the historical spy series *Reilly – Ace of Spies* (1983) and the 'secret state' thriller *Edge of Darkness* (1985).

[442] In this story Ashenden, is required to dictate love letters on behalf of an exotic dancer to an Indian terrorist in order to lure him from neutral Switzerland. Informed viewers would have relished this as a "*classic fantasy of the homosexual writer*", "*Ashenden's words, and his insight into the human heart*", seducing "*the man where mere female flesh failed*" (*Sunday Telegraph*, 24 November 1991).

[443] Julian Hope who co-produced the series was the grandson of Somerset Maugham and used the family connection to re-acquire the rights to the stories which had languished for decades with Universal Studios in Hollywood (*Daily Mail*, 16 November 1991). David Pirie writes of his experience with *Ashenden* in 'Maugham's Secret Past' (*The Telegraph*, 14 November 1991).

[444] Boyd has authored the espionage novels *Restless* (2006), *Waiting for Sunrise* (2012), and the continuation James Bond story *Solo* (2013).

[445] The phrase belongs to screenwriter David Pirie (*The Telegraph*, 14 November 1991).

[446] In 1923, Conrad adapted the novel as a three-act stage drama of the same title.

[447] The moody evocation of Edwardian London is a prominent characteristic of the novel and has been seen as evocative of the modern age, as symbolised by the teeming, seething foggy streets of London, a 'heart of darkness'.

[448] Hampton was a specialist in literary adaptation having scripted *Dangerous Liaisons* (1988) and *Mary Reilly* (1996), and written and directed *Carrington* (1995). He had been involved as writer on David Lean's abortive attempt to film Conrad's *Nostromo* in the 1980s. *The Secret Agent* was one of four Conrad adaptations that year, which also in-

cluded the television mini-series *Nostromo* (1996), and the movies *Victory* (1996) and *Amy Foster* (1997).

[449] The remarkable cast was rounded out by Gèrard Depardieu, Robin Williams, Eddie Izzard and Christian Bale.

[450] One of the few unqualified positive reviews came from Alexander Walker at the *Evening Standard* (12 February 1998).

[451] The recent spate of historical spy stories since the end of the Cold War is dealt with in chapter 6. The war film genre in British cinema in the period is examined in Chapman (1998).

[452] The title 'The Imitation Game' derives from Turing's famous paper on artificial intelligence.

[453] Ian McEwan also wrote the historical espionage-themed novels *The Innocent* (1990) and *Sweet Tooth* (2012), and the first of these dramatised in 1993 is dealt with in chapter 8.

[454] While some secret war dramas did not always display the reverence towards the war conferred on it by later generations, after all *"The cryptanalysts did not win the war"*; but as Max Hastings has rightly asserted *"they stopped Britain losing it"* (2015: 548).

[455] http://www.filmcomment.com/article/review-the-imitation-game-benedic-cumber batch/ (accessed 17 December 2016).

[456] Many wartime code-breakers suffered temporary mental and physical collapses brought on by strain and overwork (Hastings 2015: 77).

[457] See the summary 'The Breaking of the U-boat Enigma (Shark)' in the official history of wartime intelligence (Hinsley, Thomas, Ransom and Knight 1981: 747-752).

[458] Harris lists Peter Calvocoressi's *Top Secret Ultra* (1980), F. H. Hinsley and Alan Stripp's *Codebreakers* (1993), David Kahn's *Seizing the Enigma* (1991) and Hugh Skillen's *The Enigma Symposium* (1992 and 1994) as key factual sources for the story.

[459] Director Michael Apted ironically quipped: *"Here's a film about England beating Germany in the war - and Germany paid for it"* (quoted in the *Independent*, 25 September 2001).

[460] The producers had hoped to film at Bletchley, however, as it was reported, *"Bletchley Park is now being preserved and opened to the public as a museum, there are many modern buildings around it which would encroach on the frame of a film, and the huts themselves are rather dilapidated"* ('Enigma Production Information', press release 2001). Interestingly, Chicheley Hall had been used by the Special Operations Executive as its Special Training School No. 46 from 1942 until 1943, and later for training Czech and Polish agents.

[461] Frederick Winterbotham had been the Chief of the Air Section of the Secret Intelligence Service 1930-45 and stationed at Bletchley Park. *The Ultra Secret* understandably led to a radical reappraisal of the Allied prosecution of the war.

[462] On the vital early Polish contribution to breaking ENIGMA, see, Gilbert Bloch (2001), 'Polish Reconstitution of the German Military Enigma and the First Decryptments of its Messages', *Journal of Intelligence History*, 1(1), pp. 36-44.

[463] Tony Sale, a former MI5 officer and Bletchley Park campaigner was credited as 'Historical and Technical Advisor'.

[464] Mavis Batey provides insights into wartime Bletchley in her biography of the eminent code-breaker Dilly Knox (2010).

[465] The yet unmarried Mavis Lever broke the Italian naval code in 1940 and the 'GGG' Enigma in 1942.

[466] American co-producer Lorne Michaels kept his eye on the important teen market when he pitched *Enigma* as 'Hacker wins World War 2'; while director Michael Apted hedged his bet when asserting: "*It's a smart, sexy movie, about young people who are being heroic. I hope it will challenge an audience who want to see an intriguing and romantic thriller, which takes you to places you might not normally go and teaches you something fresh about people and history, and is not predictable in the first ninety seconds*" (both 'Enigma Production Information', press release 2001) .

[467] Writer Tom Stoppard claimed that the early draft of the screenplay "*didn't have a third act with submarines, airplanes and big exteriors. It was a much more modest film*" (quoted in the *Guardian*, 29 September 2001). Actress Kate Winslet compared her character of Hester "*to George in Enid Blyton's The Famous Five - she enjoys adventure and won't stop till she gets a result and, in the end, she helps save the day*" ('Enigma Production Information', press release 2001). Novelist Robert Harris revealed that, "*I had* The 39 Steps *in the back of my mind when I wrote* Enigma. *What a pity Alfred Hitchcock is dead*" (quoted in the *Guardian*, 21 November 1995).

[468] See the letter from Tom Weir to the *Guardian*, where he complains of Turing being "*obliterated*" from history, and that, "*The 'showbusiness family values of the 21st century really are not too far from the cold shoulder of Britain towards homosexuals in the first half of the 20th century*" (2 October 2001).

[469] In addition to the popular stories of Odette and Violette Szabo already mentioned, these included Russell Braddon's *Nancy Wake* (1956), Maurice Buckmaster's *Specially Employed* (1952) and *They Fought Alone* (1958), Mathilde-Lily Carré's *I was the Cat* (1961), Peter Churchill's *Of Their Own Choice* (1952), *The Spirit in the Cage* (1954), and *Duel of Wits* (1957), Benjamin Cowburn's *No Cloak, No Dagger* (1960), Madelaine Duke's *No Passport* (1957), Roman Garby-Czerniawski's *The Big Network* (1961), Roy Farran's *Winged Dagger* (1948), Knut Haukelid's *Skis Against the Atom* (1954), George Langelaan's *Knight of the Floating Silk* (1959), George Martell's *Agent Extraordinary* (1960), George Millar's *Maquis* (1945) and *Horned Pigeon* (1946), W. Stanley Moss's *Ill Met By Moonlight: The Abduction of General Kreipe* (1950, filmed in 1957), Elizabeth Nicholas's *Death be Not Proud* (1958), Jean Overton Fuller's *Madeleine* (1952), *The Starr Affair* (1954), *Double Webs* (1958) and *Double Agent* (1961), Eric Piquet-Wicks's *Four in the Shadows* (1957), Anthony Quayle's *Eight Hours from England* (1945), Gilbert Renault-Roulier's *The Silent Company* (1948), *Courage and Fear* (1950), *Portrait of a Spy* (1955) and *Ten Steps to Hope* (1960), Paul Reynaud's *In the Thick of the Fight* (1955),

Ronald Seth's *A Spy Has No Friends* (1952), Bickham Sweet-Escott's *Baker Street Irregular* (1965), Jack Thomas 's *No Banners* (1955), Philippe de Vomécourt's *Who Lived to See the Day* (1961), Anne-Marie Walters's *Moondrop to Gascony* (1946), Charles Wighton's *Pin-Stripe Saboteur* (1959), Barry Wynne's *Count Five and Die* (1959) and *No Drums ... No Trumpets* (1961), and Gordon Young's *Cat With Two Faces* (1957) and *In Trust and Treason* (1959).

[470] Although BBC 2 was launched as the first channel in Britain to broadcast in colour, *The White Rabbit* was produced in black and white as it was to be transmitted before colour broadcasting was due to start. More does not recount Deeley's previous involvement.

[471] More reports that Attenborough said, "*We'll do The White Rabbit and show it once, and then we'll have to destroy the tapes*". Indeed, the serial is believed to have been wiped after its solitary broadcast.

[472] Glaister had also been involved with a number of secret intelligence drama serials such as *Codename* (1970), *Blood Money* (1981), *Skorpion* (1983) and *Cold Warrior* (1984).

[473] I have not been able to view the serial.

[474] Popular accounts had been published of the agents Odette Sansom (1949) and Violette Szabo (1956). The official history of SOE in France was published in 1966. In 2000, many of the surviving official papers of SOE were declassified, and there have since appeared detailed accounts of many of its female agents such as Vera Atkins, Nancy Wake and Noor Inayat Khan. An overview is provided in *The Heroines of SOE: Britain's Secret Women in France* (2010).

[475] The story is based on the notorious incident of the 'Maquis du Vercors', who responded to General de Gaulle's call for an uprising on 5 June 1944 and who, unaided, were brutally suppressed by the Germans.

[476] There was much made in the press coverage of the serial of actress Jane Asher's recent brush with death at the hands of the IRA when she had been snatched and held at gunpoint by terrorists. "*Now, as much as anyone*", it was claimed, "*she understands the dreadful fear*" the female agents "*must have felt*" (*Today*, 4 January 1988).

[477] SOE agent Lise Marie Jeanette de Baissac, a British subject of French ancestry, was the inspiration for the fanciful French film *Les Femmes de l'ombre* (*Female Agents*, 2008). The mystery television series *The Bletchley Circle* (2012 -) set in the early 1950s has former women code-breakers reunite to deal with murderous crimes.

[478] Curiously, the Special Operations Executive is unmentioned in both the novel and the film, but it is obvious Charlotte has been recruited into what would have been F-section of SOE.

[479] Author Sebastian Faulks had suggested to the producers that Cate Blanchett would be perfect casting as the heroine; at that time the actress was coincidently playing the lead role in the Almeida Theatre's revival of David Hare's play *Plenty*, a stage drama which dealt with a former wartime female agent readjusting with difficulty to the peace (Film 4 press release, February 2002).

[480] As part of her research, Blanchett met with a unamed former SOE operative, presumably either D'Artois or Wake (Film 4 press release, February 2002).

[481] *'Allo 'Allo* was a riotous television sitcom (1982-92) which spoofed the German occupation of wartime France.

[482] Gillian Armstrong feared that she wouldn't hear the essential nuances in the language if the character spoke in French; that flawless French accents for the actors would be problematic; and that subtitles for over half its length would be a problem for a popular movie (*Guardian*, 20 February 2002).

[483] It was claimed that *Charlotte Gray* at £15 million was the most expensive independent British film to date. Producer Douglas Rae was reported as excitedly saying, "*We're going to hit the 2002 Oscars*" (*Daily Telegraph*, 31 January 2001).

[484] Producer Douglas Rae had optimistically bought the film rights to Faulks's recent novel *On Green Dolphin Street* (2001), but following the failure of *Charlotte Gray*, the picture was never made (*The Telegraph*, 29 September 2001).

[485] Boyd based this episode on the actual British Security Co-ordination; as he saw it, a "*massive, organised, covert attempt to sway American public opinion into joining the war in Europe.*" (*Guardian*, 22 December 2012).

[486] http://www.bbc.co.uk/mediacentre/mediapacks/restless/william-boyd.html (accessed 13 November 2016).

[487] Ibid.

[488] On Norwood, see Burke (2008).

[489] Anthony Horowitz, the creator of the series, has recently authored *Trigger Mortis* (2015), the latest official James Bond novel.

[490] Unsworth visited the set during location-shooting and writes about it at length in the *Sunday Telegraph Magazine* (7 January 1989).

[491] Critics tired of the heavy-handed symbolism of setting suns in the film.

[492] Granada had recently adapted the Bowen stories *The Demon Lover* (TV 1986) and *The Death of a Heart* (TV 1987).

[493] With star Michael Gambon and its 1940s setting, critics made the obvious allusion to the *noir*-inspired BBC drama serial *The Singing Detective* (TV 1986).

[494] Plentiful factual material was also available in the journalistic accounts *Soviet Spy Ring* by Arthur Tietjen and *Spy Ring. The Full Story of the Naval Secret Case* by John Bulloch and Henry Miller (both 1961).

[495] In the US the film was released with the title *Ring of Treason*.

[496] See Rebecca West's contemporary listing of failures in the case (1964: 292-3).

[497] Whitemore turned his script into the successful stage play *Pack of Lies* (1983), which was adapted back for American television in 1987 starring Alan Bates and Ellen Burstyn.

[498] The authorities were occupied with managing the memoirs of politicians and soldiers who expected a certain privilege from being close to actual events, with official policy determining the release of documents through the National Archive, and with specific histories treating such secretive issues as the 'Double-Cross' system during World War Two in which German agents were 'doubled' and fed disinformation back to Nazi Germany, and the 'ENIGMA' and 'ULTRA' activities whereby the Allies broke the enemy's most elaborate codes and discerned its most secret plans.

[499] The official histories are Andrew (2009) on MI5, Jeffrey (2010) on MI6, and Michael Goodman (2014) on the Joint Intelligence Committee. Richard Aldrich's *GCHQ* (2010), although not authorised, accomplishes something similar for the Government Communications Headquarters. These institutional histories followed in the wake of F. H. Hinley's groundbreaking multi-volume *British Intelligence in the Second World War* (1979-1990), one in the series 'Official History of the Second World War'.

[500] Moran has commented on the conspicuous lack of attention paid by intelligence historians to the important literary and cinematic genre of spy fiction: "*specifically the important question of how its products relate to and reflect the real world of intelligence*" (2011: 48).

[501] *Their Trade is Treachery* was the title of a MI5 pamphlet issued in 1964 for restricted circulation to Whitehall officials warning of the ruthless Soviet methods used to trap unsuspecting civil servants and diplomats. It was part of a wider official campaign of security training for staff having access to classified information and included *Persona Non Grata* (1962), a government film charting the progress of a Soviet Bloc spy-master seeking to recruit a journalist, a Civil Servant and a RAF Sergeant.

[502] The authorities first became aware of Norwood's treachery in 1992 following the defection of the Soviet archivist Vasili Mitrokhin and who has since contributed significantly to the historiography of intelligence. For more on Norwood, see Burke (2008).

[503] Burgess and Maclean were kept out of view by the Soviet authorities until a sensational press conference in 1956. Of course, there had been wild speculation in the press regarding what had happened to the 'missing diplomats' (Mather 1955).

[504] There is now a vast literature on the Cambridge Spies and the following are a representative sample: Boyle (1980), Cecil (1984 and 1988), Costello (1988), Carter (2001), Modin (1994), Knightley (1988), Hamrick (2004), Newton (1991), Brown (1997), Philby (1979), and Holzman (2012). Other agents who served Soviet Russia and studied at Cambridge University include atom spy Allan Nunn May (codename: PRIMROSE), the British Communist Party luminary James Klugmann (codename: MAYOR), the American Michael Straight (codename: NIGEL), the film-maker and intellectual Ivor Montagu (codename: INTELLIGENTSIA), and Leo Long (codename: RALPH) a former student of Blunt. Much less is known about the network of spies recruited at the rival Oxford University. It was suspected at the Security Service in the early 1960s that the MP Bernard Floud, formerly of the Ministry of Information and the Board of Trade, had acted as a talent spotter for the Soviets at Oxford. Goronwy Rees (codenames: FLIT, GROSS) and Arthur Wynn (codename SCOTT) have been positively identified, and the code-

name of an unidentified agent BUNNY tantalisingly exists in the Soviet archives (*The Times*, 5 December 2009).

[505] Philby was kept more before the public than his fellow traitors, the Soviets having realised that the "*high level of public interest in his activities could be harnessed as a continuing, nagging embarrassment to the West*" (Smith 1996: 145). Correspondingly, a fictional afterlife has been created in a number of stories for the glamorous traitor who has most attracted the attention of writers and the public. In Alan William's thriller *Gentleman Traitor* (1975) Philby makes a break from Moscow and is pursued by the KGB and MI6. In Joseph Hone's *The Sixth Directorate* (1975) Philby is called on by the KGB to advise on tracking down traitors in the organisation. In Ted Allbeury's *The Other Side of Silence* (1981) an investigator must assess the complex reasons behind Philby's request to return to Britain; while in Frederick Forsyth's *The Fourth Protocol* (1984) Philby is the British expert in the planning of Aurora, a Soviet operation to explode a nuclear device on an American airbase and tumble Britain into revolution. Eva Horn has speculated that the lack of real insight in Philby's "*tight-lipped*" biography *My Silent War* (1968) had left a void and that subsequently "*innumerable texts ... inscribe themselves into this empty figure ... trying to explain the structure that enabled his treason*" (2013: 266).

[506] The first the subtitle given to John Costello's *Mask of Treachery* (1988), a best-selling spy biography of Anthony Blunt, and the latter the title of a recent television documentary on Guy Burgess.

[507] An early manifestation of the revisionist biopic was the film *10 Rillington Place* (1971), about the mid-century serial killer John Christie. The screen in Britain has continued to explore the criminal, seedier and more controversial side of the national experience in the recent past in such dramas as *In Praise of Hardcore* (TV 2005), *Lucan* (TV 2013), *The Look of Love* (2013), *The Great Train Robbery* (TV 2013) and *Against the Law* (TV 2017).

[508] The period of the 1950s and early 1960s was one of intense concern and debate regarding homosexuality in British society. In such a climate the revelations regarding Burgess and Maclean developed into an atmosphere of moral panic regarding the degeneration of manhood, political subversion and national decline (Sandbrook 2006: 598-601).

[509] David Markham who played MI5 interrogator William Skardon was active on behalf of Soviet dissidents and once underwent an 11-hour interrogation by the KGB in Moscow (*TV Times*, 26 May 1977: 5).

[510] Oliver Wake, 'Ian Curteis', posted at http://www.britishtelevisiondrama.org.uk/?p=2600 (accessed 19 March 2017).

[511] Herbert Morrison was the Labour Home Secretary who had to field the flak following the disappearance of Burgess and Maclean.

[512] Broadcast on the eve of the summer celebrations of the Queen's Silver Jubilee, the drama chose a controversial period of history to exhume.

[513] I have so far been unable to view the drama.

[514] A further stage drama which drew on the life of Burgess was *A Morning with Guy Burgess* (2011); while *The Turning Point*, broadcast live on television in 2009, was a dramatisation of an actual meeting between Burgess and Winston Churchill in 1938.

[515] It was claimed the character of Judd was based on *"Esmond Homilly and John Cornford, two 'Thirties Communists who died young"* (Goldcrest press sheet).

[516] Peter Moffat screenwriter of the later *Cambridge Spies* aptly referred to Burgess as the *"loudest spy in the history of espionage"* (*Cambridge Spies* press sheet).

[517] For influential discussions of the heritage film, see Higson (2003). The main locations of the school scenes in the film were Apethorpe Hall, Northamptonshire and Brasenose College, Oxford University, the latter an ironic choice as the wider story was so strongly associated with Cambridge University.

[518] The production made headlines once reporters realised that Viscount Althorp, the younger brother of Princess Diana, was serving as an extra on *Another Country*, something the popular press dubbed *"Di's kid brother in gay spy film"* (*Sun*, 7 September 1983).

[519] Mitchell replied that he had written the scenes for the original stage play, but had not used them (*Sunday Express*, 10 June 1984).

[520] Biographers of the Cambridge Spies have readily delved into the public school experience of their subjects to discern a framework of personality formation. For example, Andrew Boyle has acknowledged *"a number of useful clues to their developing characters in boyhood and youth"* in the written records of the schools attended by Burgess, Maclean and Philby (1980: 514). Miranda Carter similarly gave weight to the schoolboy experience of Blunt (2001: 18-44).

[521] Kim Basinger was originally announced for the role.

[522] The text of the parliamentary admission is given in Boyle (1980: 489-492). Prime Minister Thatcher somewhat symbolically made the disclosures on the 5 November, a date traditionally celebrated for the thwarting of the Elizabethan traitor Guy Fawkes. It was reported that Euston Films planned to film Andrew Boyle's *Climate of Treason* about the Cambridge Spies, but this never materialised (*Stage and Television Today*, 17 January 1980).

[523] In 1994, Yuri Modin the former KGB controller of the Cambridge Spies published his memoirs *My Five Cambridge Friends* and claimed a role for Blunt similar to the one presented in the drama.

[524] As intelligence historian Christopher Andrew observed, *"Rather oddly, 'Blunt' is about neither of the two really dramatic episodes in his career with the KGB – his recruitment at Cambridge and his work for MI5"* (*The Telegraph*, 12 January 1987).

[525] In the words of the *Daily Mail*: *"A behind-the-scenes drama is brewing which threatens to discredit what is undoubtedly a majestic performance by Richardson and a play with award-winning potential"* (6 January 1987). In the outcome the play won no major awards.

[526] On the public exposure of Blunt in 1979, Sewell acted as a kind of self-appointed representative for the humiliated former spy and, to the increasing annoyance of his mentor, was ever available for a press comment (Carter 2001: 478-80, 494-96).

[527] Rees's wife's maiden name was Hardy, and this could have been her brother. The BBC's historical drama serial *The Monocled Mutineer* (1986) had recently caused great controversy for its interpretation of the Percy Topliss story and was referred to in a number of reviews of 'Blunt'.

[528] Hughes claimed that she worked on an 18-month contract which, unlike for other key-personnel, was not renewed. She confirmed that work started before Blunt died in 1983, and that the original intention had been for a longer 6-part serial, then a 3-part serial, and finally a 90-minute play. She was previously part of the original *Sunday Times* Insight team which had investigated Kim Philby after his flight to Moscow in 1963.

[529] Chapman and Thompson confronted accusations of "*bias and distortion*" on the BBC television programme *Open Air* (*Observer*, 18 January 1987).

[530] Hughes and Sewell strongly contested an ongoing sexual relationship between the men.

[531] Christopher Andrew suggested that some of the errors in the play might be attributed to "*confused and contradictory evidence*" derived from Rees.

[532] For a subsequent reassessment of Goronwy Rees, see Rees (1994). This source quotes from *Influence*, an unpublished screenplay co-written by Goronwy Rees with the critic Paul Mayersberg which dramatically dealt with some aspects of the friendship and scandal.

[533] A prestige television production, it premiered at the London Film Festival a week before its broadcast.

[534] Bennett felt himself unsuitable to play Blunt on screen as the physical differences would be too great, explaining "*it would be all wig*". He believed James Fox "*extraordinarily like Blunt*" (quoted in *The Sunday Telegraph*, 11 August 1991).

[535] *A Question of Attribution* was Lloyd's final production after a distinguished career at BBC Drama.

[536] Browne recounts the experience of meeting Burgess in 'The Spy and I', *Glasgow Herald* (28 November 1983), and of telling the story to Bennett and playing in *An Englishman Abroad* in 'Coral Browne as herself', *Radio Times*, (26 November-2 December 1983: 92-94). Interestingly, the actors Edward Woodward and Ian Holm were junior members of the company and both would later feature in leading spy dramas such as *Callan* (1967-72) and *Game, Set & Match* (1988). See Holm's brief comments on meeting Guy Burgess in the *Daily Mail* (3 October 1988).

[537] Bennett gives details in (1988: 221-2). It was sardonically commented at the *Glasgow Herald*, "*How fitting, too, that the production should turn to Scotland's local authority housing to find a domestic environment suitably bleak for the spy*" (3 December 1983). It has been reported that on arrival in the Soviet Union at the town of Kuibyshev, Burgess

described it as like "*Glasgow on a Saturday night in the nineteenth century*" (quoted in Carter 2001: 356). The Czech sequences in *Tinker Tailor Soldier Spy* (1979 had been shot in Glasgow and possibly set a precedence.

[538] 'Traitor' is discussed in chapter 4.

[539] As with Dennis Potter, Bennett's interest in exile might have stemmed from his own 'defection' from his native and class environment in the north of England to Oxford University.

[540] An authentic part of the meeting, the additional irony was that Browne had been jilted by Buchanan ('The Spy and I', *Glasgow Herald*, 28 November 1983).

[541] This final scene particularly delighted critics.

[542] In a filmed introduction to the recent release of *An Englishman Abroad* on DVD, Bennett speculates that had Burgess lived until he was 80, he would have been venerated, welcomed back to England with open arms and done the rounds of chat shows and *Desert Island Discs* (*Bennett at the BBC* 2009).

[543] Of course, it was Peter Wright who assumed the long task of questioning Blunt following his confession in April 1964 (1987: 213-264; Carter 2001: 451-454). In the drama *A Question of Attribution*, Chubb shows an amateur interest in art and this material was probably derived from an informal interrogation of Blunt, following the flight of Burgess and Maclean in 1951, by ace interrogator William Skardon when the pair discussed a small Degas pastel (Boyle 1980: 471; Carter 2001: 353).

[544] The issue of denying anonymity caused some soul-searching in the higher echelons of government as it was felt that traitors would less likely volunteer their secrets if the threat of public exposure hung over them (Boyle 1980: 496-500).

[545] In actuality, Blunt remained Surveyor until 1972, and then took on the role of Adviser to the Royal Collection until 1978, while it was known officially that he had served the Soviets. McKechnie finds this final scene "*affecting*" and suggests it makes evident Bennett's sympathy for the character of Blunt (2007: 102).

[546] It was the first dramatic British TV portrayal of The Queen, and the depiction on stage had greatly worried the Board of the National Theatre (McKechnie 2007: 100). Both *Englishman* and *Question* centre on a dramatic confrontation between the traitor and a female protagonist.

[547] The screen production was able to shoot at the Courtauld which had in fact been empty for three years, but had to recreate in the studio the picture gallery at Buckingham Palace.

[548] In actual fact, the Queen had been informed of Blunt's treachery at the time he was given immunity from prosecution (Carter 2001: 448).

[549] The "*metaphoric bond between the restoration work on the fake Titian and the process of unmasking Blunt the human fake*" was, of course, fakes aside, more explicitly rendered on screen than it could have been on stage (*Sight and Sound*, January 1992: 58).

[550] 'Philby, Burgess & Maclean' had been made at Granada in Manchester.

[551] See Miranda Carter's comments on the process by which the elusive Blunt became viewed as an older version of Sewell, which culminated in Fox's performance in *A Question of Attribution* (2001: 495).

[552] Simon suggested that the "*strangulated vowels we could hear were those of none other than the ubiquitous Mr Brian Sewell*".

[553] In a similar fashion, a number of former students had spoken out in defence of Blunt at the time of his exposure (Boyle 1980: 494).

[554] *Sight and Sound*'s observation regarding Bennett's revelation that he found it "*hard to get worked up about Blunt's treachery*" being a potential pitfall for the drama, there being a "*real danger of passing on such impassivity to the audience*", was not seemingly widely felt (January 1992: 58).

[555] *Televisual* (April 2003: 22).

[556] Shivas had previously produced the costume spy dramas *Rogue Male* (1976) and *The Three Hostages* (1977). See chapter 5.

[557] The production of *Sylvia Plath* (2003) starring Gwyneth Paltrow was welcomed to Trinity a few weeks later.

[558] A budget of £4.5 million was claimed, and this, despite the late loss of a reported £1.3 million (£800,000 in some reports) following a change in the regulations governing film subsidies, necessitated a restrictive 13-week shoot (*Variety*, 20 April 2003; *Televisual*, April 2003: 22-24). Moffatt had originally scripted an eight-hour drama, but this was reduced to four-hours.

[559] Several viewers made reference to the classic costume serial, Thomas Sutcliffe in the *Independent* describing *Cambridge Spies* as an "*undercover version of* Brideshead Revisited" (12 May 2003).

[560] There was, of course, a considerable irony in the Russian's accusations. As the journalist and biographer Francis Beckett coldly observed, "*Gordievsky was a traitor. We call him a defector, but that's just politeness*" (*Guardian*, 8 May 2003).

[561] Actor Rupert Penry-Jones had said: "*I admire the spies for their courage and bravery. They were heroic*" (quoted in *The Times*, 23 April 2003).

[562] Anthony Gardner speculated that the current controversial handling of the Iraqi crisis would help shape a sympathetic response from part of the audience, but the connection was not seemingly picked up elsewhere (*Telegraph Magazine*, 25 April 2003).

563 Conscientious actor Samuel West claimed to have consulted Miranda Carter's *Anthony Blunt: His Lives* (2001), Simon Freeman and Barrie Penrose's *Conspiracy of Silence: The Secret Life of Anthony Blunt* (1986) and watched Corin Redgrave's *Blunt Speaking*, a stage monologue judged sympathetic to the man. Critic James M. Murphy set his industrious readers to consult "*Christopher Andrews and Vasili Mitrokhin's* The Sword and the Shield: The Mitrokhin Archive *(2000) and a dozen other books found in good libraries*" (*Times Literary Supplement*, 23 May 2003).

564 The noun was used by Thomas Sutcliffe in his account in the *Independent* (12 May 2003).

565 In this regard, critic Mark Lawson complained of "*rather too many shots of Philby on top of women*" (*Guardian*, 28 April 2003).

566 This is the reverse of the case with conventional heritage dramas, which through their recourse to the picturesque potentially deny any radical-critical intent that they might have. Here, we have a drama dealing with revolutionary subjects which cannot break the sway of traditional nationalistic values.

567 In a similar concern with class and privilege, Peter Ackroyd, in his review of *Another Country*, had noted the priority afforded the privileged classes, and suggested it would be "*hard to imagine the life of Michael Bettaney being filmed*", "*although it might actually be more interesting*" (*Spectator*, 16 June 1984).

568 Burgess and Blunt had been members of the select Apostles club at Cambridge University, which placed belief on freedom of thought and expression, a denial of moral restraint, and prioritised loyalty to one's friends (Smith 1996: 129). However, Philby and MacLean had not been members.

569 The depth of friendship and intimacy varies across accounts. KGB controller Yuri Modin argues a more closely bonded picture of the spies in his revealingly titled biography *My Five Cambridge Friends* (1994).

570 Several reviewers suggested 'Blunt' was best appreciated as a "*male love story; a story of desertion rather than a study of espionage and treachery*" (*Western Mail*, 17 January 1987).

571 Forster made the famous comments in his essay 'Credo', first published in the *London Mercury* in September 1938. It has been claimed that Burgess was immediately taken with the sentiment and would recite it *ad nauseam* to anyone who would listen (Boyle 1980: 194, 304).

572 Wynne had initially sold the outline of his story to the *Sunday Telegraph* and the *Chicago Tribune* in 1964.

573 It has been claimed that Penkovsky's intelligence enabled the President to ignore the hawks in the military who were arguing for a pre-emptive nuclear strike against Russia at the time of the Cuban Missile Crisis (Smith 1996: 150). For a more critical view on Penkovsky's role, see Scott (1999).

574 *An Enemy of the State* is thought lost, *The Naked Runner* is dealt with in chapter 2 and *The Russia House* is dealt with in chapter 8.

[575] It has been alleged that both of Wynne's accounts were ghost written (Duns 2013: 253).

[576] In *The Man from Odessa*, Wynne claims he and Penkovsky were flown to Washington to meet with President Kennedy during one of the briefings in London, an absence of 18 hours the Soviet minders would likely to have noticed, and that Penkovsky was introduced to Earl Mountbatten as a substitute for the Queen (1983: 220-35). The intelligence historian M. R. D. Foot has judged *The Man from Odessa* as "*fanciful*" and Wynne had evidently blown-up his own importance ('Wynne, Greville Maynard (1919–1990)', rev. *Oxford Dictionary of National Biography*, Oxford University Press, 2004). It is now widely believed that Penkovsky was summarily shot shortly after the trial (https://www.cia.gov/news-information/featured-story-archive/2010-featured-story-archive/colonel-penkovsky.html (accessed 10 December 2016).

[577] Excerpts were published in the *Observer*.

[578] The Oleg Penkovsky story has also been treated in the BBC television documentary *Inside Story: Fatal Encounter* (1991), and in the BBC docudrama *Nuclear Secrets. The Spy from Moscow* (2007). The latest account of Oleg Penkovsky is given in *Dead Drop* (2013) by Jeremy Duns, which draws on a mass of documents declassified by the US authorities and paints a less flattering picture of Wynne.

[579] *The Keeler Affair* had been programmed by Derek Hill in the cinema's 'Forbidden Film Festival', and even he was forced to admit that it was "*undoubtedly the worst film they had ever shown*" (quoted in the *Evening Standard*, 4 February 1971).

[580] *A Thoroughly Filthy Fellow*, in development at Euston Films, was vetoed by the board when it was revealed it dealt with Stephen Ward, and *High Places*, another screenplay about Ward and Christine Keeler, was in development at Zenith Productions (Central Television), but was eventually dropped when "*The Independent Broadcasting Authority promptly condemned the proposed film and said it would never be shown on ITV*" (*Sunday Times*, 19 February 1989; *Daily Mail*, 29 July 1988).

[581] Donald Pleasance and David Suchet were mentioned in connection with the role of Profumo, but it is not clear if they turned down the part (*Daily Mail*, 17 October 1987). It has been suggested that senior established male actors declined the part, fearful of their later chances of a knighthood (Finney 1996: 156).

[582] The final film featured an unnamed former matinee idol played by Trevor Eve who seduces Keeler and Rice-Davies.

[583] Keeler took the opportunity to release yet another version of her story with a movie tie-in of her biography called *Scandal!* (1989).

[584] Accepting the role of John Profumo did no harm to McKellen who received his knighthood in 1991.

[585] The political and moral corruption of the early 1960s is the setting for the crime-espionage novel *A Little White Death* (1998) by John Lawton, and aspects of the 'Profumo Affair' have featured in the stage drama *A Letter of Resignation* (1997) by Hugh Whitemore, and the musical *Stephen Ward* (2013) by Andrew Lloyd Webber.

[586] Miramax seemingly pressured Palace for a more explicit picture, but eventually had to stand down or face an uncommercial X-rating (Finney 1996: 160; *7 Days Magazine*, *Sunday Telegraph*, 20 August 1989). *Scandal* made number eight in *Variety* magazine's box office league table for the period.

[587] Since the scandal, Profumo had dedicated himself to good work in the poor districts of the East End of London.

[588] In a less charitable attitude, the Bishop was alleged to have encouraged local residents to make as much noise as possible so as to disrupt location shooting taking place in his parish (Finney 1996: 158).

[589] A World Charity Premiere in aid of the Terrence Higgins Trust demonstrated an attempt by the producers to claim a measure of the moral high ground in the controversy. As well as cast members from the film, the event was attended by Christine Keeler and 'Madam Cyn', Cynthia Payne.

[590] Another source suggested the image was of John Hurt as Stephen Ward (*Independent*, 3 March 1989).

[591] In an act of seeming obstruction, Kennedy was denied access to the official transcripts of the trial.

[592] The book faced some publication difficulties and was held up in Britain, a television documentary based on the book, which was in production for the BBC *Rough Justice* series, was abandoned shortly after Michael Checkland became director general in February 1987, and Caroline Kennedy was convinced that her telephone was tapped during her research into the Ward case (*Sunday Times*, 19 February 1989).

[593] Summers and Dorril have written that the "*police pursuit of Ward began within days of a meeting between the Home Secretary, the Commissioner of Police and the Head of MI5*" (1987: 3).

[594] Mervyn Griffith-Jones, the QC who prosecuted Ward, had prosecuted at the notorious *Lady Chatterley's Lover* trial in 1960, another landmark legal case marking the new sexual morality of the decade.

[595] Parkinson was a Conservative Cabinet Minister, Halpern a prominent businessman, Fergusson the father of the Duchess of York, and Bough a popular television presenter.

[596] O'Brien was one of the last people to speak with Ward and received one of his suicide notes.

[597] The *Daily Mail* judged that *Scandal* was the "*most vivid and controversial of all of the recent series of films that mix fact with fiction*" (27 January 1989), and Bruce Babington has sensed *Scandal*'s "*self-conscious placing of itself in a line of 1980s films which replay the 1950s*" (2005: 198).

[598] With an admirable sense of mischief, Channel 4 Television screened *Scandal*, "*Michael Caton-Jones's 1989 film of the Profumo scandal which led directly to the fall of Macmillan's Tory administration in 1963*", at the end of polling for the 1992 election (*Time Out*, 8 April 1992).

[599] For many critics, the best-selling Denning Report was a whitewash, vilifying Ward, *"while being hugely polite to the Minister whose folly triggered the trouble"* (Summers and Dorril 1987: 3). From the perspective of the Security Service, former Head Stella Rimington has recorded that, *"The Denning Report is to this day the guide for Director-Generals if they are ever in any doubt as to whether they should tell the Prime Minister anything they might know about the behaviour of his colleagues"* (2002: 192).

[600] MI5 was likely to have been briefed on Ivanov by Oleg Penkovsky, a fellow GRU officer. Keeler has latterly claimed: *"Ward was a Russian spy and that he entrusted her, a teenager with no education and a lot of shady friends, to deliver three letters to the Soviet Embassy"* (quoted in the *Village Voice*, 2 May 1989). A critical observer of events, Rebecca West wrote that Ward *"mucked about with security in the shadow of the Soviet Union"* (1964: 341).

[601] In contradiction to the conclusions of Denning, the authors suggested that the *"evidence bears, rather, the fingerprints of British Intelligence, manoeuvring against Soviet Intelligence, groping to please its counterparts at the CIA"* (1987: 73).

[602] Shortly after the release of the film (and the end of the Cold War) in June 1990, the Soviet authorities announced that Ivanov was alive and well and living in Moscow, and as a seeming act of disinformation, that the naval attaché had participated in the Portland spy ring (Pincher 1991: 317). Ivanov's ghost-written memoirs *The Naked Spy* appeared in 1992, with a foreword by Keeler, and here it was claimed that he had been able to obtain significant military intelligence by accessing British political circles.

[603] It is in this sense of nostalgia that the title of Bennett's *The Old Country* resonates.

[604] See chapter 4.

[605] It has been estimated that the cost of the intelligence services increased by 100 per cent during the 13 years of Conservative rule (Dorril 1993: 183).

[606] Cass is in every scene of the drama except an expository flashback. *A Season in Hell* was a poem published by Arthur Rimbaud in 1873.

[607] Rob Walker was the artistic director at the Half Moon, a small political theatre in East London, and the pair decided to work together on a television thriller.

[608] *Spooks* is discussed in chapter 8.

[609] The phrase, of course, belongs to Richard Hofstadter (1964) and coined in regard of American political culture.

[610] Christopher Moran has argued the significance of the 'Buster' Crabb affair as a *"climacteric for the intelligence community and its relationship with Fleet Street, rupturing long-standing taboos about secret service work and bringing to the fore a brand of investigative journalist determined to make front-page news of intelligence shortcomings and failure"* (2011b: 676).

[611] The first five years of Margaret Thatcher's premiership saw the sweeping powers of Section 2 of the Official Secrets Act invoked once every eighteen weeks (Moran 2013: 5) and the prime minister order MI5 to undertake 10 leak enquiries (Dorril 1993: 18). The

intelligence historian Richard Aldrich has referred to the Thatcher regimes as a "*legend-ary period of Whitehall secrecy*" (2004: 950). In a wider discussion of "*political espio-nage*" in Britain, the democratically-inclined historian Bernard Porter has noted the following of Margaret Thatcher: "*She clearly had no feeling for 'civil liberties' as they were generally understood; no instinctive objection to people's being watched, recorded, filed or indexed, by the proper authorities. She had no great esteem for democracy, or even for freedom, except of the individualistic kind*". In his view, "*it was far easier to imagine a government like this misusing its security services than any other British government of any political complexion for the past 150 years*" (1989: 220, 221).

[612] For a wide-ranging and lively discussion of the climate of paranoia in the 1970s, see Wheen (2009).

[613] Suspicion of extremism in MI5 had surfaced from time to time, and even Lord Alan-brooke, the Chief of the Imperial General Staff, recorded concerns in his diary at the end of the Second World War that there was a "*grave danger of it falling into the clutches of unscrupulous political hands of which there are too many at present*" (quoted in Smith 1996: 58).

[614] Stephen Dorril has claimed as many as a million public and private posts are subject to some form of security vetting (1993: 159).

[615] In the 'Year of Intelligence,' the notable investigations were 'The 1975 United States President's Commission on CIA Activities within the United States', headed by Nelson Rockefeller, the 'Select Committee on Intelligence' of 1975, headed by Otis G. Pike, and the 'United States Senate Select Committee to Study Governmental Operations with Respect to Intelligence Activities' of 1975, headed by senator Frank Church. In addition, a burglary of a small FBI office in March 1971 had led to the anonymous sending of files to leading newspapers which published the revelations regarding a domestic counter-intelligence programme against American citizens thought to be radical and subver-sive.

[616] In 1983, the Labour Party published its proposals for reform of MI5, *Freedom and the Security Services*, but it had no opportunity of acting in the decade. Many on the left of the Party were continually disappointed in Labour's lack of engagement with security when in power and with the minister's seeming thrall with the Security Service.

[617] Investigative journalists who were at the forefront of exposing the activities of the secret world were Richard Norton Taylor (*Guardian*), Richard Donkin (*Financial Times*), Nick Davies (*Observer* and *Guardian*), David Leigh and Paul Lashmar (*Observer*), Barrie Penrose (*Sunday Times*) and Duncan Campbell (*New Statesman*).

[618] Despite much support and campaigning for freedom of expression the two men were eventually deported in May 1977.

[619] It has been claimed that the accused were targeted for special long term surveil-lance by a vindictive Security Service (Murray 1993: 261). Duncan Campbell was in hot water again in 1986 when his BBC television documentary *Secret Society* was sup-pressed by the government.

[620] Despite its humiliating failure in this regard, the government immediately set about gagging former MI6 officer Anthony Cavendish, who attempted to publish his memoirs which claimed a smear campaign against Maurice Oldfield, former Chief of MI6 (1990); and was concurrently involved in trying to halt publication of Joan Miller's *One Girl's War* (1986), a memoir of the wartime MI5, which held for a while in Britain, but failed in Ireland.

[621] Some younger members of staff became disenchanted with the political bias within the Security Service. Michael Bettaney (convicted of attempting to pass secrets to the Soviets) alleged that MI5 "*cynically manipulates the definition of subversion and thus abuses the provisions of its charter so as to investigate and interfere in the activities of legitimate political parties, the Trade Union Movement and other progressive organisations*". While Miranda Ingram was discomfited by "*monitoring one's fellow citizens*", by the "*prevailing right-wing atmosphere*", and actively discouraged from voicing dissent for fear of harming one's career (both quoted in Smith 1996: 66-67). Former Head of MI5 Stella Rimington rather nonchalantly passed over the claims of burglary and bugging as "*what has to be done to carry out eavesdropping and search operations*" (2002: 194).

[622] For a long, contextual discussion of the book, its importance and possible merits, see Gelber (1989).

[623] For security purposes it carried the name 'Henry Worthington' (note the initials).

[624] The CIA was always concerned that it was primarily American secrets that the British traitors were betraying.

[625] David Leigh lists 11 political figures and eight prominent Labour supporters who were defamed by MI5 (1988: 91-92). When Stonehouse 'disappeared' to Australia to avoid his creditors, the conspiratorial-minded immediately jumped to the conclusion that he had defected to Moscow.

[626] Wilson's resignation followed the 'unusual' departure from office of two other left-of-centre leaders, Willi Brandt of West Germany and Gough Whitlam of Australia, both of whom it would later be revealed having fallen foul of western intelligence agencies which considered them 'security risks' (Gill 1994: 198). It has been speculated that the fall of Secretary of State for War John Profumo in 1963 might have been instigated by MI5 which saw him as sexually compromised (Summers and Dorril 1987: 171). Anthony Cavendish, a confident of MI6 chief Maurice Oldfield, has speculated on secret knowledge that Oldfield held over Wilson, that this could be linked to the premier's unexpected resignation, and further might explain Oldfield's unprecedented advancement to the Grand Cross of the Most Distinguished Order of St Michael and St George by a grateful Tory Party (1990: 164). Conservative writer Chapman Pincher has pooh-poohed this idea, claiming that Oldfield's conspiracy was against him! (1991: 147-151).

[627] The Conservative Prime Minister Edward Heath officially declared four 'states of emergency' during his premiership of 1970-74, the most of any modern leader.

[628] The armed services and some in the Ministry of Defence saw the hand of the Soviet master in Labour's military cutbacks and retreat from defence 'East of Suez' at the end of the 1960s.

[629] Pincher claims that when a field officer in the 1950s, Young had been deeply involved in the successful plot to overthrow the Iranian Prime Minister Mossadeq, and in the abortive plots to assassinate President Nasser of Egypt, making him an experienced hand at destabilising and toppling regimes (1991: 102).

[630] As well as 'evidence' from MI5 dossiers, *Private Eye* also received a Christmas card sent to Wilson by the Soviet trade minister filched from 10 Downing Street, and private papers burgled from Wilson's archive (Leigh 1988: 247).

[631] It should be borne in mind that on occasion the 'secret state' wished to discredit and silence establishment figures further to the right, as was the case with the countering of former intelligence officers Peter Wright and Anthony Cavendish who sought to publish their professional memoirs.

[632] The reporters were dubbed 'Pencourt' in *Private Eye* in a mocking reference to the 'Woodstein' shorthand applied to Bob Woodward and Carl Bernstein, the journalists from the *Washington Post* who broke the Watergate story in America. A drama-documentary *The Plot Against Harold Wilson* detailing 'Pencourt's' secret meetings with Wilson and other informants was broadcast on the BBC in 2006.

[633] On the *Lobster* website, "*parapolitics*" is defined as the "*impact of the intelligence and security services on history and politics*".

[634] In an ironic turn of events, the right-wing Pincher's earlier *Inside Story* (1978) "*offered an unprecedented insight into the British State's operations against the domestic left-wing, especially the Labour Party*", and alerted many on the Left to the political operations of the 'secret state' (*Lobster* 11, 1986: n.p.). In a subsequent book, Pincher retracted on some of the assertions about a plot to undermine Wilson, claiming himself a victim of a disinformation exercise by Maurice Oldfield, then head of MI6 (1991: 151).

[635] Unsurprisingly, *Spycatcher* came in for much criticism, both from politicians and those connected with the security services, and from intelligence historians who decried its sensationalism. However, there have been writers and interested parties on the left who have welcomed its revelations. Journalist Stephen Dorril for example has written of it in the following terms: "Spycatcher *is probably one of the most important books to be published about Britain since the Second World War. It provided a unique glimpse into Britain's secret state and the way factions and bureaucracies of the permanent government operate in denying citizens the rights and liberties associated with a mature democracy*" (1993: 66). Wright's accusations received some support in another intelligence memoir, Desmond Bristow's *A Game of Moles: The Deceptions of an MI6 Officer* (London: Little, Brown and Co., 1993).

[636] In 1970, crime author Colin Watson made what at the time might have seemed an odd observation: that Britain's popular spy literature amounted, in fact, to a secret police literature; concluding that, "*It is curious that something of which the English have always loudly declared their abhorrence is now an established element of their entertainment*" (*Guardian*, 10 September).

[637] Such a scheme maps effectively onto the major developments of the spy story in the history British popular fiction, James Bond excepted.

[638] Left-wing espionage novels of the period include *A Spy at Evening* (1977) by Donald James in which a right-wing patriotic organisation known as Action England is manipulated by a rogue intelligence officer to bring about a political coup, and *Days Like These* (1985) by Nigel Fountain in which a left-wing journalist thwarts a right-wing take-over.

[639] Cramer (2016) prioritises the "*supernatural*" identity of *The Ωmega Factor*. Conspiracy narratives centred on paranormal phenomena would reach their zenith in *The X-Files* (US, 1993–2002).

[640] The two Englishmen Douglas Hurd and Andrew Osmond had met at the Foreign Office in the 1960s. Hurd went onto a distinguished service in the Conservative Party, serving as both Home and Foreign Secretaries. Osmond was associated in a variety of ways with the satirical magazine *Private Eye*, and pursued a career as a journalist and novelist. Hurd and Osmond collaborated again on the political novel *War Without Frontiers* (1982).

[641] The Scots diplomat Michael Shea, writing as Michael Sinclair, also published two thrillers in the early 1970s which dealt with Scottish nationalism, *Folio Forty One* (1972) and *The Dollar Covenant* (1973).

[642] The BBC also pointed out that the novel had been serialised in a Scottish newspaper without attracting comment (*Guardian*, 4 May 1973).

[643] It was believed for a long period that the serial had been wiped, but it was revealed in 2012 that episodes 1, 4 and 5 survive in the archives of BBC Scotland (http://www.625.org.uk/progfile/sotrocks.htm (accessed 21 November 2016).

[644] Controversy over Scottish nationalism and the security services erupted again briefly in 1985 with the mysterious death of the vice-chairman of the SNP Willie McRae. There were suspicions that he had been murdered in a 'deniable operation' due to his involvement in extreme politics and groups such as the Scottish Civilian Army (Dorril 1993: 255-258).

[645] The television production had been preceded by a BBC radio version in 1982.

[646] The first series had a small role for Mandy Rice-Davies, one of the principals of the Profumo Affair of the 1960s.

[647] Scriptwriter Ron Hutchinson had previously served in the Civil Service working as an investigator with the Department of Social Security and this furnished him with valuable insights for the story (*Bird of Prey* press sheet).

[648] It seems that *Bird of Prey* was also successful in overseas territories and this helped convince the BBC for a follow up serial (*The Telegraph*, 8 September 1984).

[649] At the time of the publication, Worsthorne was associate editor of *The Telegraph*, a paper he would edit between 1986 and 1991.

[650] Mullin was singled out in the ultra-right-wing news sheet *Background Briefing on Subversion* for his "*perpetual vendetta against British security arrangements*" (quoted in Dorril 1993: 31).

[651] An interesting comparison can be made between *A Very British Coup* and the spy thriller *The Fourth Protocol* (1984) by the more right-wing novelist Frederick Forsyth, as both treat the prospect of an extremist socialist government and the American siting of nuclear missiles in Britain, but from opposing political perspectives.

[652] David Leigh reports that the CIA was placing agents within British trade unions in the early 1970s as part of its "*defence of the West*" (1988: 213).

[653] *A Very British Coup* was more overtly leftist in its politics than the recent 'secret state' thrillers broadcast on the BBC. Chris Mullin claimed at the time that, "*In the current climate the BBC would not be permitted to show a series like this*" (quoted in *The Telegraph*, 9 May 1988).

[654] Research for the drama was undertaken by investigative journalist Duncan Campbell, described in the *Sunday Telegraph* as "*everyone's favourite subversive*", and former co-defendant in the 'ABC Trial' (26 June 1988).

[655] Channel 4 covered its back at the press screening with a brief warning that the drama did not propose a "*What is*" scenario, but rather a "*What if ...?*" (Quoted in the *New Statesman*, 17 June 1988).

[656] Livingstone was then Labour Member of Parliament for the London constituency of Brent East.

[657] A letter to the *Guardian* from a Dennis Outwin surprisingly interpreted the drama as "*effective right-wing propaganda*", rather alarmingly claiming: "*We learn from the play that if we are reckless enough to dismiss the Thatcher government from office, we shall be faced with chaos, a financial crisis, American enmity, sabotage and possibly a Russian takeover*" (25 June 1988).

[658] See Benn's later review of David Leigh's *The Wilson Plot* (1988), 'The Case for Dismantling the Secret State', *New Left Review*, 190, pp. 127–30.

[659] See also the *Sunday Times* (3 July 1988) and the *Scotsman* (30 June 1988) for prominent references to dream analogy.

[660] Chris Mullin distributed a paper to accompany the show, in which he reminded journalists/reviewers of events supportive of the fiction: the US pressure on New Zealand's anti-nuclear stance; Cathy Massiter's revelation of the phone-tapping of CND; covert US intervention in the 1987 election; and the Peter Wright disclosures (*Guardian*, 21 June 1988).

[661] Several reviewers were either offended or intrigued by the opening scene of Harry Perkins peeing into a urinal, apparently a television first (*The Telegraph, Guardian, Independent*, all 20 June 1988).

[662] Joseph Oldham has downplayed the political controversy generated by *A Very British Coup*, believing that the serial's "*satirical element*" defused any right-wing backlash (2017: 142). The recent rise to popularity of Left Labour leader Jeremy Corbyn brings renewed interest to the plots and schemes dramatised in *A Very British Coup*.

[663] 'The Russian Soldier' (1986), a BBC drama in the *Screen Two* strand, dealt with the contamination of cattle on a remote farm and a sinister man for the 'Ministry' who tries to cover things up, but the play had no discernible 'intelligence' dimension.

[664] Campbell later directed the James Bond movies *Goldeneye* (1995) and *Casino Royale* (2006).

[665] The working title for the serial was Magnox, the name of a brand of nuclear reactor; however, fear of trouble from British Nuclear Fuels and the Central Electricity Generating Board prompted the BBC to insist that Troy Kennedy Martin find a different title (*Guardian*, 13 December 1985). *Dark Forces* was briefly considered before the serial was broadcast with the more teetering title *Edge of Darkness* (Pixley 2003b: 50).

[666] Emma remained in the drama as a spectral presence, an "*Earth Goddess*" guiding Ron in his search for the truth and instructing him on the ability of the planet to look after itself, and some found this supernatural element "*irritating*" (*Sunday Times*, 7 November 1985; Cooke 2007: 157).

[667] The American CIA agent likely derived his name after 'Operation Jedburgh', in which British and American servicemen (as with Ron and Darius) combined on clandestine operations supporting D-Day in World War II.

[668] Several reviews commented on the extraordinary grief depicted in the drama following Ron's loss of Emma. The *Daily Mail*, for example, believed that the writer had broken "*new ground with a sustained exploration of private agony*" (5 November 1985).

[669] *Edge of Darkness* publicity release (26 September 1985); Cornerhouse news release (17 October 1985). It was felt that the BBC had recently lost some ground to the ITV companies in the production of drama serials after the popular and critical successes of *Brideshead Revisited* (1981) and *Jewel in the Crown* (1984) both made at Granada Television (*Glasgow Herald*, 9 November 1985).

[670] Wearing was also struck by the story's traditional aspects, noting in the press release that, "*Like 'The Thirty Nine Steps', it is a thriller set in the world of political power play – a man alone against an unfathomable system, buffetted by forces beyond his control, but who remains undespairingly resourceful. It is the story of a journey – with key moments set against some well-known British landmarks, the House of Commons, the hotels and restaurants of London, the Barbican Centre, the BBC itself and a climax in Scotland at Gleneagles*". A handful of newspapers made the same connection (*The Telegraph*, 26 November 1985).

[671] As three double episodes on consecutive evenings. A respectable four and a half million viewers tuned in for the weekly serial on the minority channel BBC 2 and this figure doubled for the repeats.

[672] The final question posed by the serial as to "*what happens when the planet decides that mankind itself has become the expendable threat to its survival as a life force?*" was an invention of the drama (*Edge of Darkness* press release).

[673] Other 'mystical' elements were woven into the story, although some were so obscure as to likely pass the typical viewer by. These included Craven's embodiment of the 'Green Man' figure of Nature, Grogan's linking with the Knights Templar and Jedburgh with the Knight of the Marches (Pixley 2003a: 54).

[674] Kennedy Martin received a "*lot of help*" in his scripts from serial consultant Walter Patterson, the principal energy specialist with the Friends of the Earth and unofficial historian of nuclear power in Britain (*Daily Mail*, 2 November 1985; *Guardian*, 13 December 1985).

[675] The same Willie McRae mentioned previously in connection with *Scotch on the Rocks* and Scottish nationalism (Murray 1993: 209-216).

[676] Powell had previously produced the acclaimed John le Carré thrillers *Tinker Tailor Soldier Spy* (1979 and *Smiley's People* (1982) at the BBC.

[677] In America, the serial was not acquired by such major sponsors of television drama as Mobil and Exxon and was instead picked up by the local WNYC-TV for broadcast on Channel 31 (*The New York Times*, 8 October 1986).

[678] An Anglo-American motion picture *Edge of Darkness* starring Mel Gibson and directed by Martin Campbell was released in 2010 to mixed reviews. The film's approach was essentially that of a revenge thriller and the production singularly lacks the quality and intelligence of the original television drama.

[679] http://www.channel4.com/info/press/news/gabriel-byrne-interview (accessed 19 July 2105).

[680] As described by Chapman Pincher, electronic warfare involves the sending out of "*ferreting*" vessels so that "*adversaries turn on their counter-measures which can then be recorded and analysed*" (1991: 238).

[681] The use of Royal Navy vessels for signals intelligence went back as far as 1924. The early 1980s witnessed an expansion of the Royal Navy's SIGINT capability and according to one expert now provided a "*major contribution to NATO's tactical planning*" (quoted in Smith 1996: 183).

[682] The mystery of the *Gaul* was gone over in 'Riddle of the "spy-ship" and the killer sub', *Daily Mail* (11 November 1983), published at the time of the broadcast of the serial.

[683] The name may have derived from the notorious maverick investigator Barry Quartermain who was in the news throughout the late 1960s and early 1970s, eventually being jailed in 1974.

[684] Judith Williamson more broadly argued that with the archetype of the "*cynical-tough-guy-gone good*", the film conformed to the classic Hollywood thriller (*New Socialist*, February 1986: 41).

[685] The elimination of Mullen puts the picture in line with *The Parallax View* (US, 1974), a more pessimistic New Hollywood conspiracy thriller in which a troublesome journalist is removed.

[686] The system had been set up in 1971, but only came to prominence with the Agee and Hosenball case. Stephen Dorril has pointed out that, "*Panel members were also known as the 'three blind mice' because its pretence at any kind of justice was a disgrace*" (1993: 120).

[687] In the story, the Americans send over an expert to test Dodgson with a Polygraph. In fact, there was discussion to introduce Polygraph tests at GCHQ in the eighties, and, to the great disappointment of the Americans, the plans were withdrawn for political reasons (Pincher 1991: 232).

[688] See scriptwriter Julian Bond's discussion of adapting the novel (*Films and Filming*, December 1986: 20).

[689] In contrast, a stinker of a review appeared in the left *New Socialist*, which found the film "*politically naïve*" and a "*pale imitation of* Edge of Darkness" (Summer 1987: 50).

[690] American critic Amy Taubin rejoiced in a story which "*tells you at every opportunity that the CIA is the evilest, most paranoid institution in human history*" (*Village Voice*, 21 July 1987); while in contrast David Denby at the *New Yorker* bristled at the picture's "*righteous tone*" and "*standard villains of left-wing sentimentality, America and the upper classes*" (3 August 1987).

[691] Frances Stonor Saunders reports of an unfortunate incident in 1950 involving documents prepared by MI5, when, before the introduction of shredders, "*fragments of secret waste that had been placed in a malfunctioning incinerator floated up the chimney and out into the streets of Mayfair*" ('Stuck on the Flypaper, MI5 and the Hobsbawm File', *London Review of Books*, 37 (7), 9 April 2015, posted at https://www.lrb.co.uk/v37/n07/frances-stonorsaunders/stuck-on-the-flypaper, accessed (23 March 2017).

[692] The inspiration for this was the Freemasons' temple underneath Regent Street (*What's On*, 22 June 1988).

[693] Poliakoff claimed to have been influenced by Otto Preminger's untypical presentation of London in *Bunny Lake is Missing* (1965), where the Hollywood filmmaker made the city look "*very weird*" (*What's On*, 22 June 1988).

[694] A number of writers suggested that the British screen observed a comparable relationship to 'The Troubles' in Northern Ireland as Hollywood had to the Vietnam War in the 1970s (see Gilbert Adair in the *Sunday Telegraph Review*, 10 November 1996).

[695] Dourif and McDormand had recently featured together in *Mississippi Burning* (US, 1988), another political film, this time about the American Civil Rights Movement.

[696] Two earlier projects Loach and Allen had nursed for television, first with the BBC and then later with Channel 4, had foundered (*Time Out*, 2 January 1991).

[697] The Ministry of Defence defined 'psy-ops' as "*planned psychological activities in peace and war directed towards enemy, friendly and neutral audiences, in order to create behaviour favourable to the achievement of political and military objectives*" (quoted in Dorrill 1993: 68).

[698] While acknowledging the place of IRA propaganda and conspiracy theory, one writer on intelligence has concluded: "*there is no doubt that in the early days a number of killings did take place – at least one in the Irish Republic*"; adding, that in addition, "*a number of wanted IRA men were lifted from across the border and brought into Northern Ireland where they could be arrested by the security forces*" (Smith 1996: 228). Following a perceived "*feerer hand*" for the security forces in 1981, 40 IRA terrorists were claimed to have been shot by undercover agents (Dorril 1993: 90).

[699] Historian of political espionage Bernard Porter has written of a "*blatant cover-up*", the "*smearing*" and then "*removal*" of the senior British policeman appointed to inquire into it, "*when it looked as though he might be nosing out the truth*" (1989: 223). The Stalker Affair was dramatised on television as *Shoot to Kill* (Yorkshire Television, 1990). See the senior policeman's account in *Stalker* (London: Harrap, 1988).

[700] See the thesis presented in the special issue, 'Wilson, MI5 and the Rise of Thatcher. Covert Operations in British Politics 1974-78'. There, the editorial claimed: "*Mrs Thatcher (and 'Thatcherism') grew out of a right-wing network in this country with extensive links to the military-intelligence establishment. Her rise to power was the climax of a long campaign by this network which included a protracted destabilisation campaign against the Liberal and Labour Parties - chiefly the Labour Party - during 1974-6*". "*We are not offering a conspiracy theory about the rise of Mrs Thatcher*", it professed, "*but we do think that the outlines of a concerted campaign to discredit the other parties, to engineer a right-wing leader of the Tory Party, and then a right-wing government, is visible*" (*Lobster*, number 11 1986).

[701] Intelligence insider Anthony Cavendish sees the hand of MI5 in smear campaigns targeting "*Edward Heath, Harold Wilson, Edward Short, roughly twenty other MPs and the first Catholic Chief Constable of the RUC (from 1973-1976), James Flanaghan*". He doesn't rule out an unsuccessful plot by MI5 to assassinate Maurice Oldfield, former Chief of rival Service MI6 who took over the lead in intelligence matters in Northern Ireland in 1979 (1990: 171, 173).

[702] Both advised on the production, although only Holroyd received a screen credit. For a sympathetic treatment of Wallace, see Paul Foot (1990).

[703] The previous year's Cannes Film Festival had been marked by British tabloid outrage at American star Mickey Rourke and his support of the IRA (*Independent*, 19 April 1990; *Guardian*, 28 May 1990).

[704] For a French view of *Hidden Agenda* at the time of the Festival, see 'IRA, *ira pas?* Kenneth Loach dans la tourmente irlandaise', *Le Nouvel Observateur* (10 May 1990).

[705] Loach wrote in response to the review in *The Times*, refuting the accusation that the film had "*no real evidence*" to offer, citing testimony presented to the European Court of Human Rights and to a parliamentary select committee, and material contained in an official police report (22 January 1991).

[706] Loach summarises his views on the commercial and political censorship of his film in *Index on Censorship*, 6 (1995: 158-59)

[707] In an unusual variant, policeman Ron Craven in *Edge of Darkness* is 'guided' by his dead daughter Emma, who has already paid the ultimate sacrifice.

[708] It was Pincher's contention that Wilson's paranoia about a 'mythical' MI5 plot stemmed from a 'real' but legitimate media plot to harm the standing of the Labour leader; and in a further inversion of thinking on the situation, claimed that in all likelihood "*Wilson did far more to undermine MI5 than MI5 ever did to undermine him*" (1991: 125, 147).

[709] For Chapman Pincher, the "*plot*" recounted by Wright was little more than delusion and at best a "*'cowboy' operation*" (1991: 182). The academic historian Bernard Porter believes a 'Wilson Plot' to be "*definite, albeit somewhat vague*", suspiciously noting that with the ruin of the Liberal Party leader Jeremy Thorpe, the unexpected resignation of Wilson, the ousting of the 'soft' Tory Edward Heath and his replacement as leader of the Conservative Party by the right-wing Margaret Thatcher, "*This was what the 'plotters' had been after*" all along (1989: 210-212).

[710] For a sympathetic treatment of the 'secret state', see Peter Hennessy's *The Secret State: Whitehall and the Cold War* (2002), from a constitutional historian who was ennobled as Baron Hennessy of Nympsfield in 2010. Moran praises this work as an "*excellent study*", which makes an "*impressive case for the view that the UK intelligence community, far from being a rogue elephant, comprised a noble band of skilled patriots, and was instrumental in defending the realm and keeping Britain out of a nuclear war*" (2011: 47).

[711] See the reviews by David Leigh (*Guardian*, 10 October 2009) and Bernard Porter (*London Review of Books*, 31(2), 2009).

[712] With the assassination of the journalist Nick Mullen and his helper Nina Beckman at the end of the picture, the original film story of *Defence of the Realm* with its fatalism and denial of the narratively expected romantic coupling could be added to this trio; as could *Edge of Darkness* with the death of the two hero-protagonists and an unchecked military-industrial-complex and its toadying Security Service. The film version of *The Whistle Blower* bucks the trend with its increased agency for the protagonist and its offering of a potentially optimistic ending where justice might be done.

[713] See the arguments laid out in Norton-Taylor (1990).

[714] For a critique of the Official Secrets and Security Service Acts, which were "*far from the liberalising measures lauded by the government*", see Birkinshaw (1990). For an overview of recent changes on the intelligence framework, see Gill (1996).

[715] A new attitude to the retention and preservation of files prevailed in 1998 following discussions between the Public Records Office and selected historians. In future, protection would be accorded to files relating to: major investigations; important subversive figures, terrorists or spies; individuals involved in historical events; *causes célèbre* in a security context; major changes in the Service's policy, organisation or procedures, and milestones in the Service's history; and cases in which the Service had a public profile (Hennessey and Thomas 2011: 215).

[716] It was significant that Rimington was allowed to publish a (vetted) autobiography *Open Secret* in 2001, which, however, was not the first of its kind, the authorities having surprisingly allowed Sir Percy Sillitoe's *Cloak Without Dagger* to publication in 1955. Critics have seen the appointment of Rimington as a "*symbolic gesture of openness, rather than any genuine willingness to make the service accountable – a typical Whitehall tactic which lets as little light into the secret world as possible, while brushing aside the need for accountability and oversight*" (Dorril 1993: 125).

[717] At the time of the end of the Cold War, one writer commented on the lack of allure of the intelligence services, the outdated image and morality of James Bond, and the "*mediocre world*" conjured up in the novels of John le Carré which all served as a bar to recruitment (Dorril 1993: 129). In contrast, Stella Rimington has more recently written that a "*large percentage*" of candidates for the Civil Service now "*put MI5 first*" (2002: 183).

[718] This public relations aspect to the new intelligence services was evident in the spy series *Spooks* (2002-11), the first episode including a public relations woman taking a group of journalists round MI5 HQ in London. It has been suggested that Stephen Lander, who replaced the modernising Rimington in 1996, reverted once again to a damaging traditional, secretive, cautious, bureaucratic approach (Hollingsworth and Fielding 1999: 236).

[719] Stella Rimington in the lecture 'National Security and International Understanding', 1995 (quoted in Smith 1996: 267).

[720] The 'foreign' intelligence services of GCHQ and MI6 were first tasked with contributing to the fight against 'serious crime' in the 1993 Intelligence Services Bill.

[721] At a low point of morale for the Service, Michael Bettaney was the first traitor within MI5 to be caught and the first officer to appear in the dock since the end of the Second World War. Shayler wrote out a detailed submission to a Cabinet Review; however, this was refused as evidence and has been printed in Hollingsworth and Fielding (1999: 271-288).

[722] The irony has not been lost on some that following the collapse of the Berlin Wall greater freedom of access and information existed among the secret files of the former Eastern Bloc countries than in the UK, the KGB for example having allowed access to western historians and even opening up a public relations centre (Pincher 1991: 316).

[723] Stella Rimington's autobiography of 2001 clearly served to quieten some of the criticisms of British Intelligence. In it she wrote of MI5's "*strict adherence to the law and to the operational rules*", dismissed whistleblowers as "*partial*" and invariably "*motivated by a grudge*", and complained of "*ill-informed and often hostile comments on our affairs*" (2002: 179, 187, 253).

[724] This long-running series also starred David Jason who had featured in *The Top Secret Life of Edgar Briggs*.

[725] Producer Verity Lambert was associated with both *Adam Adamant* (1966-67) and *Sleepers*.

[726] *Sleepers* was specially written for Warren Clarke by John Flanagan and Andrew McCulloch.

[727] Seymour's previous thrillers *Harry's Game* (1982), *The Glory Boys* (1984) and *The Contract* (1988) had been adapted at Yorkshire Television.

[728] Details taken from the Carlton Television press release dated 13 October 1999. Burt had previously been producer on *Reilly – Ace of Spies* (1983), see chapter 5.

[729] See chapter 6.

[730] http://www.deightondossier.net/Author/Interviews/november2011.html (accessed 30 October 2016).

[731] A few years earlier, Caine had featured in *Blue Ice* (US, 1992) in which he played another superannuated intelligence officer who now ran a jazz club in London and who is drawn into a puzzling intrigue involving a prematurely pensioned-off British spymaster (Ian Holm) now attempting to sell illegal weapons to an Arab state. It was a routine action movie featuring a protagonist created by the British spy writer Ted Allbeury; although, in deference to Caine and his association with the spy film, the character was renamed from Tad to 'Harry' Anders, an agent who has a talent for cooking, is betrayed by a superior officer, undergoes an interrogation with obvious allusions to *The Ipcress File* ("*My name is Harry Anders*"), and in retrospect could seem like a rehearsal for bringing Palmer back to the screen.

[732] There is a large and growing literature examining intelligence and ethics and for an introduction the reader might look at Michael Herman (2004), 'Ethics and Intelligence after September 2001', *Intelligence and National Security*, 19(2), pp. 342-58; Julian Richards (2012), 'Intelligence Dilemma? Contemporary Counterterrorism in a Liberal Democracy', *Intelligence and National Security*, 27(5), pp. 761-80; and Ross Bellaby (2012), 'What's the Harm? The Ethics of Intelligence Collection', *Intelligence and National Security*, 27(1), pp. 93-117.

[733] *Page Eight* was playwright Hare's first original screenplay in 20 years.

[734] Toolis had previously produced the documentaries *The Cult of the Suicide Bomber* (2005) and *The History of the Car Bomb* (2008).

[735] http://www.channel4.com/info/press/news/complicit-production-notes (accessed 14 December 2016). Oyelowo had previously been a regular cast member on *Spooks*.

[736] Yorkshire TV also produced Seymour's spy thriller *The Contract* (1988) which is discussed in chapter 3.

[737] 'Cleanskin' is a term used for an infiltrator with no previous convictions, so therefore unknown to national security services. The alternative term of 'invisible' is used in Stella Rimington's novel *At Risk* (2004), also about a suicide bomber.

[738] Terror unleashed on London was the subject of the American action picture *London Has Fallen* (US, 2016), a sequel to *Olympus Has Fallen* (US, 2013), about a terror assault on the White House. The former film was poorly reviewed and criticised as being a "*terrorsploitation*" fantasy spreading unnecessary fear (*Independent*, 3 March 2016).

[739] Le Carré's espionage novel *The Tailor of Panama* (1996) was filmed as an American–Irish co-production in 2001.

[740] The epithet was formed by actor Peter Firth (quoted in the *Radio Times*, 22 September 2006: 21).

[741] http://www2.warwick.ac.uk/knowledge/arts/screen-spies/ (accessed 14 November 2016).

[742] *Spooks* was broadcast with the title of *MI-5* in North America where it was a hit, and also sold, perhaps surprisingly, to Russia and Iran (Spooks. *Behind the Scenes*, 2006: 6).

[743] *Spooks* was claimed to have been inspired in-part by the recent autobiography of Stella Rimington, the former head of MI5. However, when the idea for *Spooks* had been presented to Channel 4 before 9/11, it was turned down as "*it thought nobody was interested in spies and the stories they had to tell*" (Executive producer Jane Featherstone, quoted in *Time Out*, 28 May-4 June 2003).

[744] Nick Day ran Diligence, a "*corporate intelligence company staffed with ex-MI5, CIA and KGB officers*".

[745] Playwright Howard Brenton contributed scripts to the first four seasons of *Spooks*. He was the controversial author of the stage plays *The Churchill Play* (1974) and *Romans in Britain* (1980), and scripted the stylish television conspiracy thriller *Dead Head* (1986) which is discussed in chapter 7.

[746] Writer Howard Brenton later recalled that the few MI5 officers he met during the making of the series were indeed young and wore Armani suits (commentary, *Dead Head*, Eureka DVD 2012). Felix Thompson has briefly discussed the implications of social and ethnic diversity in the series (2010).

[747] Shayler reports that he jokingly supplied the title of *Spooks*.

[748] It was claimed that the popularity of the series was helped by the media interest in the off-screen romance which developed between Keeley Hawes and Matthew McFadyen. Later seasons settled down to a respectable five-six million viewers and celebrity fans included Conservative Party leader David Cameron and Prince William (*The Telegraph*, 5 December 2008).

[749] Female recruits were often put to the 'safer' roles of surveillance work and monitoring terrorists.

[750] According to *The Times*, the shock killing was a "*rare moment of bravery and originality in a dire series*" (7 June 2002).

[751] The terrorist attacks on the London transport system in July 2005 –reality now being "*so much worse*" – also had an effect in softening attitudes towards the show (*Time Out*, 14 September 2005).

[752] Barbara Korte, "'I do not like moral horror'": *Spooks* and the Ethical Challenge of the Secret Services in 21st Century Britain', *Journal of British Cinema and Television* (forthcoming).

[753] http://www2.warwick.ac.uk/knowledge/arts/screen-spies/ (accessed 14 November 2014).

[754] At the time there was a vogue for spin-off series from popular established shows. *Dr Who* spawned *Torchwood* (TV 2006-11), while *Casualty* and *Holby City* fused into *Holby Blue* (TV 2007-08).

[755] We are told that Code 9 is the MI5 code name for a nuclear attack on London.

[756] *This Life* (TV 1996-97) was a popular drama series about a group of young professionals.

[757] This was a continuation of the saga begun in *Game, Set & Match* (see chapter 4).

[758] See chapter 6.

[759] Nick Barnett, 'Cold War Nostalgia in the 21st Century', unpublished paper, *Spies on British Screens* conference (June 2016).

[760] McEwan had previously written the secret war screen drama 'The Imitation Game' (1980), which is discussed in chapter 6.

[761] On 'Black Friday' 29 October 1948, the Soviets executed a massive switch in their cryptographic systems, effectively blinding allied code-breakers. The Russian shift from wireless to landlines meant allied intelligence was tempted to target the telegraphic and phone systems.

[762] A detailed account of the extraordinary operation has now been published as *Spies Beneath Berlin* (2002) by David Stafford.

[763] Sanford Sternlicht (1996), 'And the Walls Came Tumbling Down: *The Innocent* and *Black Dogs*', in Jack Slay, Jr. (ed.), *Ian McEwan*, New York: Twayne Publishers, *Literature Resource Center* (accessed 19 January 2013).

[764] Ian McEwan has recently published the historical spy novel *Sweet Tooth* (2012), about a young female graduate groomed by MI5 and sent on an undercover operation in Great Britain in 1972.

[765] *An Englishman Abroad* and *A Question of Attribution* are discussed in chapter 6.

[766] As has become increasingly the case in the screen adaptations, le Carré was supportive of the project, was credited as an executive producer, was available for consultation and played an extra in the film. To use the character of Smiley, Working Title had to negotiate with Paramount Pictures which retained the screen rights from the time of *The Spy Who Came in from the Cold* in the1960s.

[767] There were also popular BBC radio versions in 1988 and 2009.

[768] Without developing the point, Eric J. Morgan has claimed a critique of nostalgia in the film, although this seems farfetched, and a likely fascination or interest in the 1970s was the more probable motivation for its intended audience (2016: 97).

[769] Douglas McNaughton, 'Cold War Spaces: *Tinker Tailor Soldier Spy* in television and cinema', *Journal of British Cinema and Television* (forthcoming).

[770] http://www.davidbordwell.net/blog/2012/01/23/tinker-tailor-a-guide-for-the-per plexed/ (accessed 20 November 2016). *Tinker Tailor Soldier Spy*'s main intertextual connection with an earlier cinema is the use of 'The Second- Best Secret Agent in the World' as background music at the office Christmas party, the title song from the American release of the low-budget spy picture *Licensed to Kill* (1965).

[771] http://collider.com/tinker-tailor-soldier-spy-2-sequel-eric-fellner/ (accessed 22 November 2016). In the recent television documentary *The World's Greatest Spy Movies* (TV, 2016), a panel of intelligence insiders chose the film version of *Tinker Tailor Soldier Spy* as the best representation of espionage in the cinema.

[772] Douglas McNaughton, 'Cold War Spaces: *Tinker Tailor Soldier Spy* in television and cinema', *Journal of British Cinema and Television* (forthcoming).

[773] The defence journalist and writer on espionage Chapman Pincher persistently warned about *Spetsnaz* activities, buried caches of arms, and *"local freelance saboteurs ... assigned to assist with the 'reduction' of certain prime targets"* (1991: 27-28).

[774] *Radio Times* (28 November 2013), accessed 16 December 2016.

[775] Judd has also written the historical spy novel *The Kaiser's Last Kiss* (2003).

[776] At the time of broadcast *Tinker Tailor Soldier Spy* was being repeated on BBC 4, and some critics felt the new drama was not being helped by the comparison.

[777] For example, Ted Allbeury's *The Special Collection* (1975) and *All Our Tomorrows* (1982).

[778] Nicholas Barnett, 'Cold War Nostalgia in *The Game* (2014)', *Journal of British Cinema and Television* (forthcoming).

[779] Review reproduced at http://www.startrader.co.uk/Action%20TV/guide2000/stateof play.htm (accessed 16 December 2016).

[780] Joseph Oldham, 'From "Pop" to Surveillance Culture: *Bugs* as the "Avengers for the 90s"', unpublished paper, *Spies on British Screens* conference (June 2016).

[781] Of course, concerns about technology and enhanced surveillance had been around for some time, and already by the late 1980s the terms 'total surveillance system' and the 'maximum security society' had come into usage (Gill 1994: 135).

[782] This part of the plot was no doubt inspired by the real-life 'spy in the bag' case in which MI6 insider and mathematician Gareth Williams was found dead, padlocked inside a bag at his home in 2010.

[783] In between these two comedies, Working Title produced the 'serious' *Tinker Tailor Soldier Spy* (2011).

[784] The character of the inept secret agent had originally been devised for a series of television commercials in the 1990s advertising a leading credit card. The agent of MI7, then named Richard Latham and played by Atkinson, was similarly supported by his sidekick Bough.

[785] Mr Bean was another bumbling Rowan Atkinson character from film and television.

[786] Stephanie Jones, '"Get your clothes on and I'll buy you an ice cream": The Unlikely History of James Bond and the New Man', unpublished paper, *Spies on British Screens* conference (June 2016).

[787] Christopher Holiday, 'Blow Up: James Bond, London and Post-7/7 Visions of a Cinematic City', unpublished paper, *Spies on British Screens* conference (June 2016).

[788] The copyright to the story passed from Columbia, the studio behind the 1967 film, to Sony in 1989 when the latter acquired the former.

[789] Bond and Le Chiffre now compete at poker, the original card game of baccarat being considered old fashioned, elitist and unknown to a modern audience.

[790] The films were directed by Sam Mendes, the first Oscar winner to helm an official Bond picture.

[791] Q, in the guise of Ben Whishaw, is modernised in the form of a "*young 'tec geek*" and a gay persona. This characterisation is reinforced by Whishaw's starring in *London Spy* (2015) and its prominent gay love affair. Claire Hines, '"Now Pay Attention 007": The New Q, Contemporary Masculinity and the Bond Franchise', unpublished paper, *Spies on British Screens* conference (June 2016).

[792] The three elements of the monarch, the Olympics and James Bond were brilliantly fused in a short film in which 007 accompanies the Queen from Buckingham Palace to the Games and both (seemingly) parachute into the stadium, and screened as part of the celebrated opening ceremony.

[793] A broader study would show that genre transformation was evident in British cinema in the 1960s and 1970s, apparent in such genres as the horror film, the historical film, the youth film and the war film.

Index

D

www.ingramcontent.com/pod-product-compliance
Lightning Source LLC
Chambersburg PA
CBHW071352170526
45165CB00001B/9